NICHO

THE O
SURVE
THE WATERWAYS

2 CENTRAL

Series editor: David Perrott

Robert Nicholson Publications

Also available in this series:

Nicholson/Ordnance Survey Guide to the Waterways 1. South
Nicholson/Ordnance Survey Guide to the Waterways 3. North
Nicholson/Ordnance Survey Guide to the River Thames (and Wey)

The indication of a towpath in this book does not necessarily imply a public right of way. If you are in any doubt, check before you proceed with the latest published Ordnance Survey map.
Pathfinder Series (1:25 000 scale or 2½ in to 1 mile). These OS walker and rambler maps show the countryside in great detail, including rights of way in England and Wales.
Landranger Series (1:50000 scale or about 1¼ in to 1 mile). This OS series covers the country in 204 sheets and is ideal for detailed exploring by car or on foot.

First published 1983 by **Robert Nicholson Publications Limited**, 17 Conway Street, London W1P 6JD and **Ordnance Survey**, Romsey Road, Maybush, Southampton SO9 4DH.

2nd edition 1985

Original research: Paul Atterbury, Andrew Darwin and David Perrott

Thanks are extended to the Electric Boat Association who supplied information on recharging points.

Cover photograph: Derek Pratt

Typeset by Rowland Phototypesetting Ltd, Bury St Edmunds, Suffolk
Printed in Great Britain by
Blantyre Printing and Binding Co Ltd
Blantyre, Glasgow

ISBN 0 905522 74 5

INTRODUCTION

The canals and navigable rivers of Britain were built as a system of new trade routes at a time when roads were virtually non-existent. After their boom period in the late 18th and early 19th centuries, they gradually declined in the face of fierce competition from the new railway companies, and large-scale commercial carrying ended by the time of the Second World War, when many of the routes had slipped into decay and ruin. It is true that in a few areas goods continue to be carried profitably to this day, but for the majority of canals it was the new traffic of pleasure boats that provided the impetus for rescue and restoration.

The founding of the Inland Waterways Association by L.T.C. Rolt and Robert Aickman in 1946 brought together enthusiasts from all over the country who were to campaign to save and restore these 2000 miles of navigable waterways that are so much a part of our history. More and more people are now realising that what had been abandoned as little more than a muddy ditch and a convenient place to dump rubbish can be transformed into a linear park, full of interest and a place of recreation for all.

There is something for everyone in the canals: engineering feats like aqueducts, tunnels and flights of locks (all of which amazed a world that had seen nothing like it since Roman times); the brightly decorated narrow boats which used to throng the waterways; the wealth of birds, animals and plants on canal banks; the mellow, unpretentious architecture of canalside buildings like pubs, stables, lock cottages and warehouses; and the sheer beauty and quiet isolation that is a feature of so many canals.

Use this book to discover the waterways for yourself; it is one of four volumes covering the South, Centre and North of England and the rivers Thames and Wey, published jointly by Nicholson and the Ordnance Survey, in response to public demand.

CONTENTS

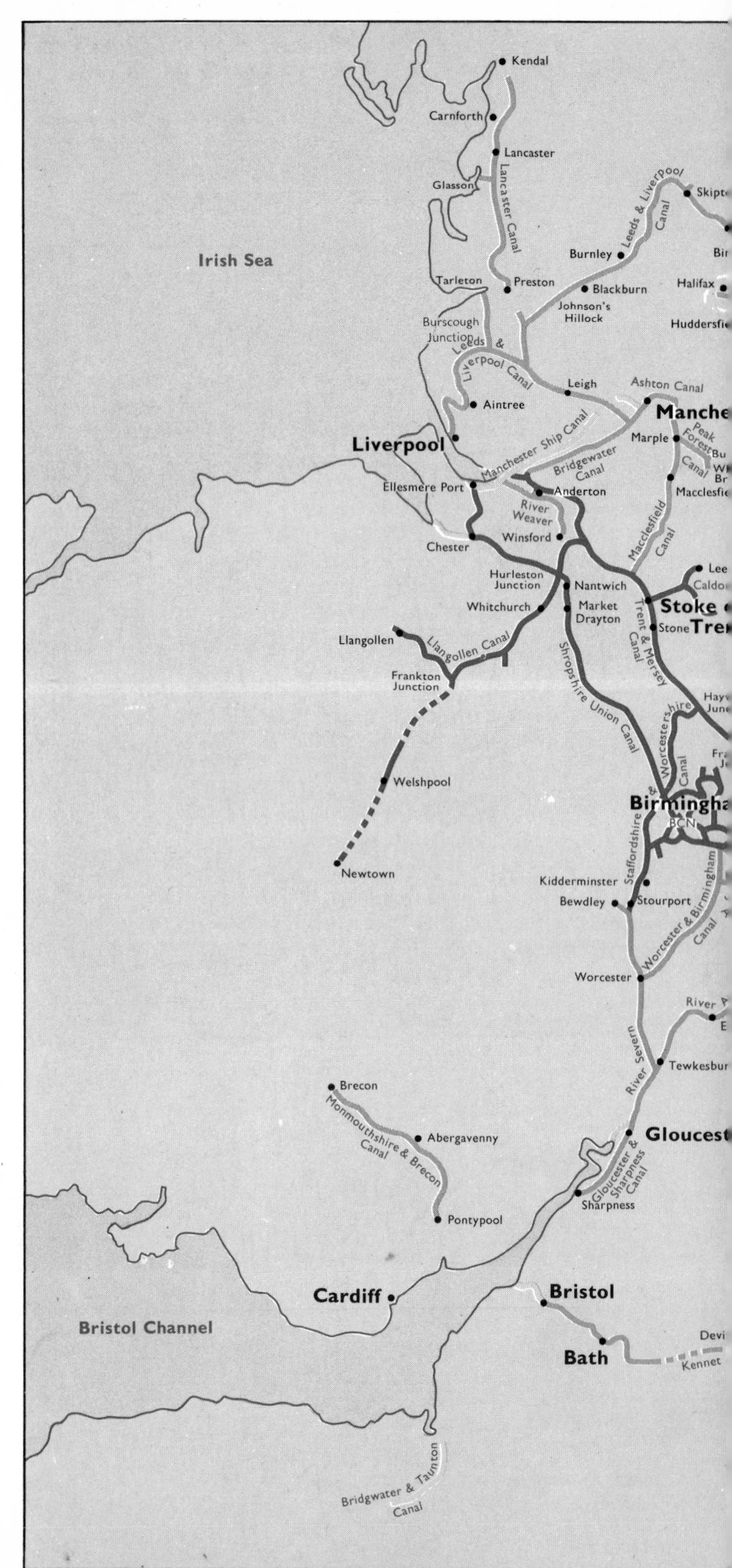
Irish Sea
Kendal
Carnforth
Lancaster
Lancaster Canal
Glasson
Leeds & Liverpool Canal
Burnley
Preston
Tarleton
Blackburn
Johnson's Hillock
Burscough Junction
Leeds & Liverpool Canal
Leigh
Ashton Canal
Aintree
Liverpool
Manchester Ship Canal
Bridgewater Canal
Marple
Peak Forest Canal
Ellesmere Port
Anderton
River Weaver
Winsford
Chester
Macclesfield Canal
Hurleston Junction
Nantwich
Whitchurch
Market Drayton
Stone
Trent & Mersey Canal
Llangollen
Llangollen Canal
Frankton Junction
Shropshire Union Canal
Staffordshire & Worcestershire Canal
Welshpool
BCN
Newtown
Kidderminster
Bewdley
Stourport
Worcester & Birmingham Canal
Worcester
River Severn
Brecon
Abergavenny
Monmouthshire & Brecon Canal
Gloucester & Sharpness Canal
Sharpness
Pontypool
Cardiff
Bristol
Bristol Channel
Bath
Kennet
Bridgwater & Taunton Canal

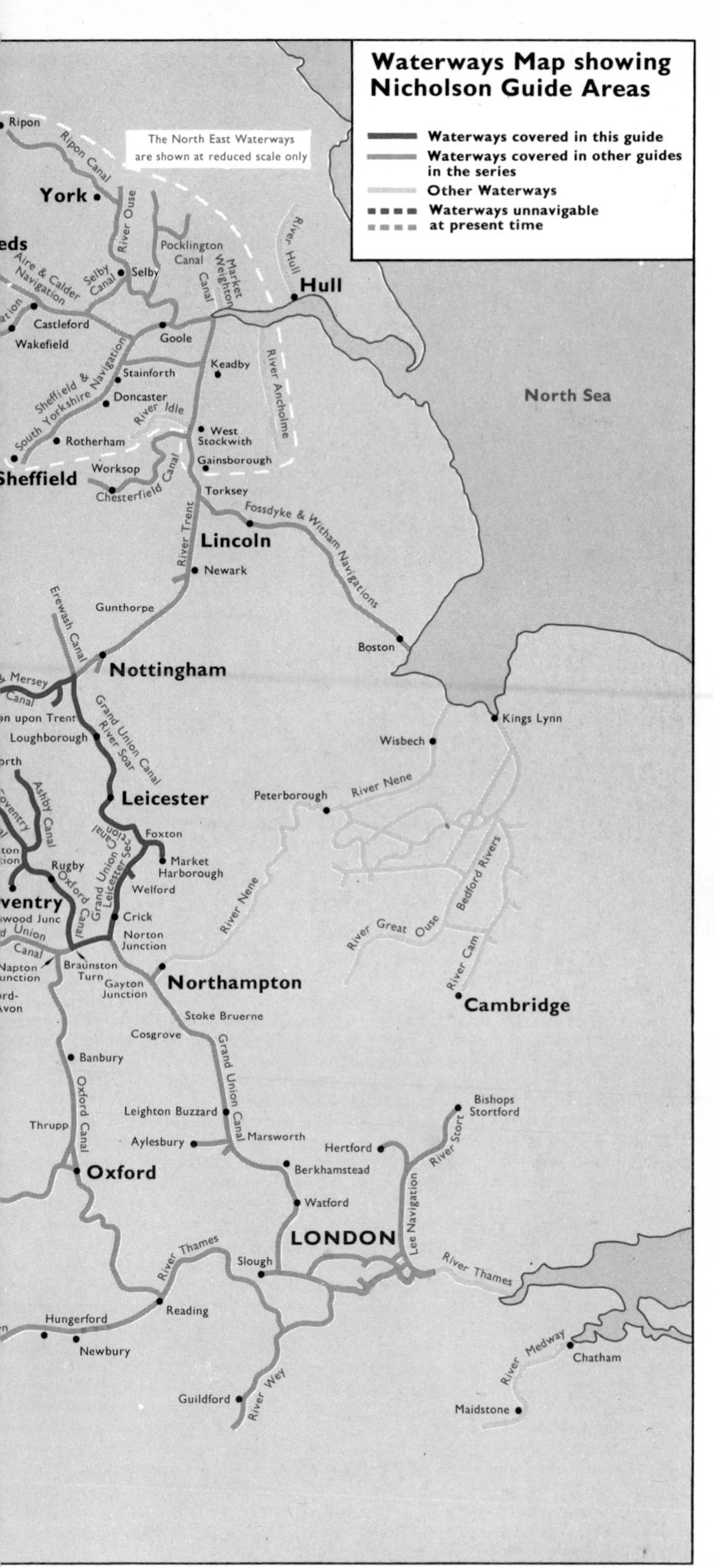
Waterways Map showing Nicholson Guide Areas
Waterways covered in this guide
Waterways covered in other guides in the series
Other Waterways
Waterways unnavigable at present time
The North East Waterways are shown at reduced scale only
Ripon
Ripon Canal
York
River Ouse
Pocklington Canal
Market Weighton Canal
River Hull
Hull
Selby Canal
Selby
Aire & Calder Navigation
Castleford
Wakefield
Goole
Keadby
River Ancholme
Stainforth
Sheffield & South Yorkshire Navigation
Doncaster
River Idle
Rotherham
West Stockwith
Gainsborough
Worksop
Chesterfield Canal
Torksey
Fossdyke & Witham Navigations
Lincoln
River Trent
Newark
North Sea
Gunthorpe
Erewash Canal
Boston
Nottingham
Kings Lynn
Loughborough
Grand Union Canal River Soar
Wisbech
River Nene
Peterborough
Leicester
Ashby Canal
Foxton
Market Harborough
Grand Union Canal Leicester Section
Rugby
Oxford Canal
Welford
Bedford Rivers
River Nene
Crick
Norton Junction
River Great Ouse
River Cam
Braunston Turn
Gayton Junction
Northampton
Cambridge
Stoke Bruerne
Cosgrove
Banbury
Grand Union Canal
Oxford Canal
Leighton Buzzard
Bishops Stortford
Thrupp
Aylesbury
Marsworth
Hertford
River Stort
Oxford
Berkhamstead
Watford
Lee Navigation
LONDON
River Thames
Slough
River Thames
Reading
Hungerford
Newbury
River Medway
Chatham
River Wey
Guildford
Maidstone

HOW TO USE THIS GUIDE

The maps are drawn at a scale of two inches to one mile. Adjacent to each map section is a description of the countryside and places of interest together with a commentary on the course of the canal or river. Details of boatyards correspond to the symbol Ⓑ on the map, and pubs near the waterway are also named and in some cases described. Those with a restaurant are indicated by the symbol ✕ and wine bars and licensed premises by ▾. Other symbols used on the maps are:

Locks, with number and 'rise'. The symbol points uphill.

Staircase locks.

Bridge and its number. Many are named.

Tunnel—often described in the text.

Aqueduct—often described in the text.

Winding hole—turning point for boats longer than the ordinary width of the canal (it's pronounced as in the wind that blows). Canal junctions are also good places to 'wind'.

Weir.

R is refuse disposal, **S** is sewage or 'Elsan' disposal, **W** is a water point, **P** is petrol, **D** is diesel and **E** is electric boat recharge. Many of these facilities are often available at boatyards; 'pump-out' toilet emptying machines may also be available—see the text entry for each boatyard.

A feature of these guides is the 'milestone' which appears on every map thus:

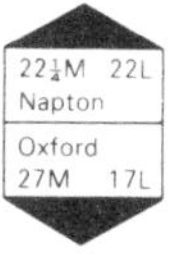

This performs many useful functions. It reminds you of your direction of travel—in this example **up** the page is towards Napton, **down** the page is towards Oxford; it denotes distances and indicates the number of locks between the milestone and strategic points (usually junctions) along the waterway—in this example, Napton is 22¼ miles (M) with 22 locks (L) from the 'milestone', and Oxford is 27 miles and 17 locks from the milestone. By deducting the miles and locks on one milestone from those on the next, distances from page to page can be accurately estimated. Using the 'lock-miles' system (see **Planning a cruise**, page 12) the time your journey will take can be calculated, and with a little experience based on your speed of travel and lock operation, your own time formula can be arrived at.

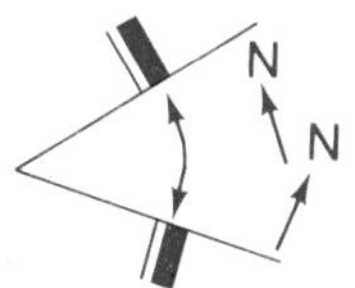

Where this device occurs on a map it simply means that the actual route of the waterway would not fit neatly onto the page, so the cartographer has 'bent' the map, using two north points. The navigator on the water, or the walker on the bank, will notice nothing amiss. Distances in this book should be measured along the thick blue line only, not including these gaps.

LOCKS AND THEIR USE

The different locks and their attendant machinery are a source of endless fascination for all waterway users. Understanding why they are there and the principle upon which they work will help you in their use.

A lock is a device for transporting craft from a higher water level to a lower level, or vice versa, for example when a canal crosses a range of hills. It consists of a box with gates at each end, and a separate means of letting water in at the top (higher level) and out at the bottom (lower level). This is controlled by paddles. These paddles may simply open and shut holes in the gates (gate paddles), or they may open and shut underground culverts (ground paddles). A windlass (carried on the boat) is used to wind the paddles open and shut. Whilst locks differ in detail, the following instructions will apply in the case of the vast majority of *narrow* canal locks. Some extra points regarding wide locks are covered later.

A typical narrow lock

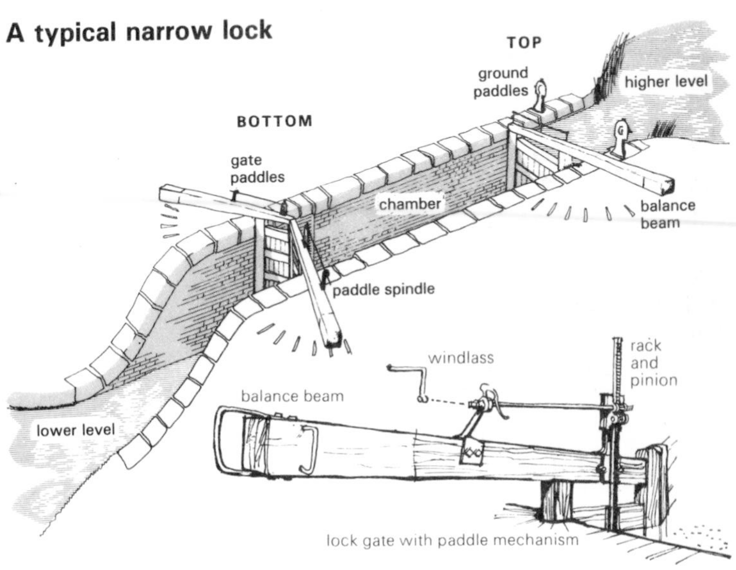

How to go through a lock

PRELIMINARIES

Stop the boat well outside the lock and secure it. If members of your crew can get off the boat before the lock (at the narrow point under a bridge for example) and run ahead to prepare the lock, this will save time.

GOING UP IN A LOCK (LOCKING UP)

Lock empty—ie water at lower level

Open bottom gate(s)
Drive boat in
Close bottom gate(s)
Check bottom paddles closed
Keep boat near to the bottom of lock
Open top paddles to fill lock
Open top gate(s) when lock is full
Drive boat out
Close top gate(s)
Close top paddles

Lock full—ie water at higher level

Check top gate(s) and paddles closed
Open bottom paddles to drain lock
Open bottom gate(s)
Drive boat in
Close bottom gate(s) and paddles
Keep boat near to the bottom of lock
Open top paddles to fill lock
Open top gate(s) when lock is full
Drive boat out
Close top gate(s)
Close top paddles

GOING DOWN IN A LOCK (LOCKING DOWN)

Lock full—ie water at higher level

Open top gate(s)
Drive boat in
Close top gate(s)
Check top paddles closed
Keep boat near to the bottom of the lock
Open bottom paddles to empty lock
Open bottom gate(s)
Drive boat out
Close bottom gates and paddles

Lock empty—ie water at lower level

Check bottom gate(s) and paddles closed
Open top paddles to fill lock
Open gate(s)
Drive boat in
Close top gate(s) and paddles
Keep boat near to the bottom of the lock
Open bottom paddles to empty lock
Open bottom gate(s)
Drive boat out
Close bottom gate(s) and paddles

If you have to drain or fill a lock in order to enter it, make sure there is no boat approaching that could usefully use the lock before you. Always try to conserve water, which is being continually passed down the canal from its summit and thus requires constant replenishment at a higher level.

SOME GENERAL DO'S AND DONT'S AT LOCKS

Do not leave your windlass slotted onto the paddle spindle—if something slips it could be thrown off and cause injury.

Always leave all gates and paddles closed when you leave, but look out for notices which may give other instructions for the proper operation of a particular lock.

Always wind the paddles down—letting them drop is bad practice, and causes damage.

Beware of protrusions in the side walls of the lock chamber that may damage the boat, and don't use fenders in narrow locks—they may jam.

When opening and closing lock gates, keep to the landward side of the balance beam.

Don't rush around at locks, especially in wet weather, when the sides are slippery. Never jump across partly opened gates.

Always make the safety of the crew and boat your prime concern and remember that if things do start to go wrong, you can stop everything by closing the paddles.

There is no reason why your children, wearing buoyancy aids and properly supervised, should not help at locks—it is all part of the fun, after all—but impress upon them the potential dangers, and establish some commonsense rules. You have no authority over other people's children, and their participation should be discouraged. Great difficulties could ensue should they be injured in any way.

Beware of fierce top gate paddles, especially in wide locks.

Don't leave your windlass behind; hundreds are lost this way each year.

WIDE LOCKS

Taking a narrow boat (7ft beam) through a wide lock (14ft) can present special difficulties, especially when locking up. If all the top paddles were to be opened fully at the same time, the boat would be buffeted considerably. The diagram below illustrates one method of ensuring a smooth passage. The stern line held ashore will provide added security.

Locking up in a wide lock

(a suggested technique)

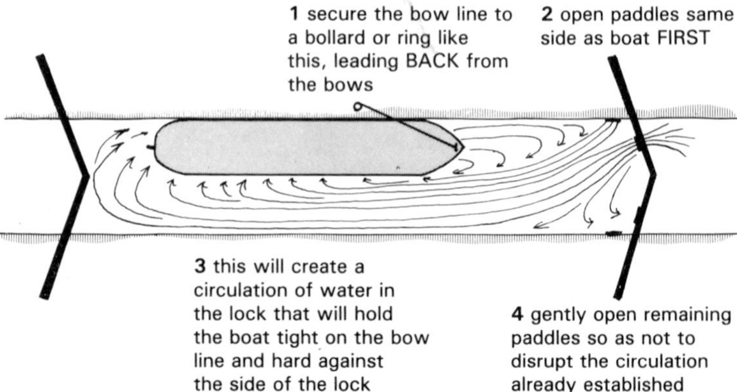

STAIRCASE LOCKS

Where the top gates of one lock are the bottom gates of the next. Usually there is a board nearby giving operating instructions—read it carefully and make sure you understand it before you start. And remember: in a narrow staircase you can't pass a boat coming the other way.

GENERAL CRUISING INFORMATION

The vast majority of the waterways covered in this series are controlled by the British Waterways Board. All craft using BWB canals must be licensed and those using BWB rivers must be registered. Charges are based on the length of the boat and a canal craft licence covers all the navigable waterways under the Board's control. Permits for permanent mooring on the canals are also issued by the Board. Apply in each case to:

Craft Licensing Office,
Willow Grange,
Church Road,
Watford WD1 3QA.
(Watford 26422).

The Licensing Office will also supply a list of all BWB rivers and canals. Other river navigation authorities relevant to this book are mentioned where appropriate.

Getting afloat

There is no better way of discovering the joys of canals than by getting afloat. The best thing is to hire a boat for a week or a fortnight from one of the boatyards on the canals. (Each boatyard has an entry in the text, and most of them offer craft for hire; brochures may be easily obtained from such boatyards.)

General cruising

Most canals are saucer-shaped in section and so are deepest in the middle. Very few have more than 3–4ft of water and many have much less. Try to keep to the middle of the channel except on bends, where the deepest water is on the *outside* of the bend. When you meet another boat, the rule is to keep to the right, slow down, and aim to miss the approaching boat by a couple of yards: do not steer right over to the bank or you will most likely run aground. The deeper the draught of the boat, the more important it is to keep in the middle of the deep water, and so this must be considered when passing other boats. If you meet a loaded working boat, keep right out of the way. Working boats should always be given precedence, for their time is money. If you meet a boat being towed from the bank, pass it on the outside rather than intercept the towing line. When overtaking, keep the other boat on your starboard, or right, side.

Speed

There is a general speed limit of 4mph on most British Waterways Board canals. This is not just an arbitrary limit: there is no need to go any faster, and in many cases it is impossible to cruise even at this speed. Canals were not built for motor boats, and so the banks are easily damaged by excessive wash and turbulence. Erosion of the banks makes the canal more shallow, which in turn makes running aground a more frequent occurrence. So keep to the limits and try not to aggravate the situation. It is easy to see when a boat is creating excessive turbulence by looking at the wash—if it is 'breaking' or causing large waves, you are going too fast and should slow down.

Slow down also when passing moored craft, engineering works and anglers.

Slow down when there is a lot of floating rubbish on the water: old planks and plastic bags may mean underwater obstacles that can damage a boat or its propeller if hit hard. Try to drift over obvious obstructions in neutral.

Slow down when approaching blind corners, narrow bridges and junctions.

Running aground

The effective end of commercial traffic on the narrow canals has resulted in canals being shallower than ever. Running aground is a fairly common event, but is rarely serious, as the canal bed is usually soft. If you run aground, try first of all to pull the boat off by gently reversing the engine. If this fails, use the pole as a lever against the bank or some solid object, in combination with a tow rope being pulled from the bank. Do not keep revving the engine in reverse if it is obviously having no effect. Another way is to get your crew to rock the boat from side to side while using the pole or mooring lines. If all else fails, lighten your load; make all the crew leave the boat except the helmsman, and then it will often float off quite easily.

Remember that if you run aground once, it is likely to happen again as it indicates a particularly shallow stretch—or that you are out of the channel. If you are continually bumping the bottom in a shallow stretch, it may be that you are going too fast, causing the boat to 'dig in' at the back. Going less fast may make things more comfortable.

In a town it is common to run aground on sunken rubbish; this is most likely to occur near bridges and housing estates. Use the same methods, but be very careful as hard objects can very easily damage your boat or propeller.

Remember that winding holes are often silted up—do not go further in than you have to.

Mooring

All boats carry metal stakes and a mallet. These are used for mooring when there are no rings or bollards in sight, which is usually the case. Generally speaking you may moor anywhere to

BWB property but there are certain basic rules. Avoid mooring anywhere that could cause an obstruction to other boats; do not moor on a bend or a narrow stretch, do not moor abreast boats already moored. Never moor in a lock, and do not be tempted to tie up in a tunnel or under a bridge if it is raining. Pick a stretch where there is a reasonable depth of water at the bank, otherwise the boat may bump and scrape the canal bed—an unpleasant sensation if you are trying to sleep. For reasons of peace and quiet and privacy it is best to moor away from main roads and railway lines.

Never stretch your mooring lines across the towpath; you may trip someone up and face a claim for damages.

There is no need to show a riding light at night, except on major rivers and busy commercial canals.

Beware of mooring at unrecognised sites in cities—you may attract the unwelcome attention of vandals.

So long as you are sensible and keep to the rules, mooring can be a pleasant gesture of individuality.

Knots

A simple and easy way of securing a rope to a bollard or mooring stake is to use a couple of round turns and a half hitch made with a loop and pulled tight. This can be released quickly by pulling the loose end, which will have been left tidily coiled.

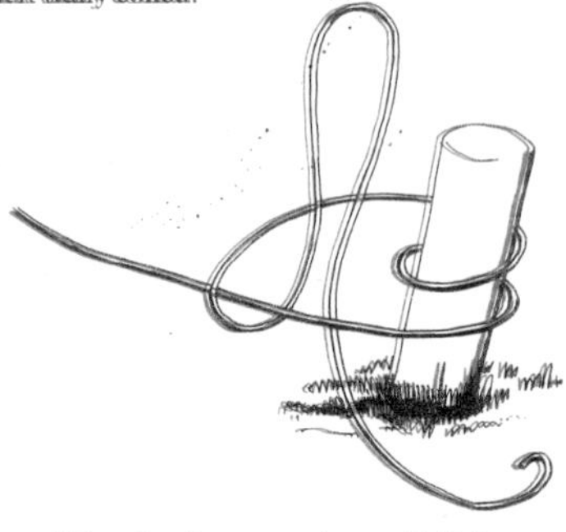

When leaving a mooring, coil all the ropes up again. They will then be out of the way, but ready if needed in a hurry. Many a sailor has fallen overboard after tripping on an uncoiled rope.

Fixed bridges

At most bridges the canal becomes very narrow, a means of saving building costs developed by the engineers. As a result, careful navigation is called for if you are to avoid hitting either the bridge sides with the hull or the arch with the cabin top. As when entering a lock, the best way to tackle 'bridgeholes' is to slow down well in advance and aim to go straight through, keeping a steady course. Adjustments should be kept to a minimum for it is easy to start the boat zig-zagging, which will inevitably end in a collision. One technique is to gauge the width of the approaching bridgehole relative to the width of the boat, and then watch one side only, aiming to miss that side by a small margin—say 6in; the smaller you can make the margin, the less chance you have of hitting the other side of the bridge. If you do hit the bridge sides when going slowly it is not likely to do much damage; it will merely strengthen your resolve to do better next time.

Moveable bridges

Swing and lift bridges are an attractive feature of some canals and cannot be ignored as they often rest only 2 or 3ft above the water. They are moved by being swivelled horizontally, or raised vertically. Operation is usually manual, although some have gearing to ease the movement. There are one or two mechanised versions; these have clear instructions at control points. Before operating any bridge make sure that approaching road traffic is aware of your intention to open the bridge. Use protective barriers if there are any and remember to close the bridge again after you.

Some *lift bridges are very unstable*, and could close while your boat is passing underneath, with disastrous consequences. For this reason it is prudent to have your strongest (or heaviest) crew member hold it open until the boat is clear. Many swing bridges are very heavy to operate, and require two strong people to move them.

Tunnels

Many people consider a canal incomplete without one or two tunnels, and certainly they are an exciting feature of any trip. Nearly all are easy to navigate, although there are a few basic rules:

Make sure your boat has a good headlight in working order and *always* use it.

If it is a narrow tunnel (ie 7ft) make sure there is no boat coming the other way *before* you enter. Craft of 7ft beam can pass in some wide tunnels—slow right down when you meet to lessen the almost inevitable bump.

In most tunnels the roof drips constantly, especially under ventilation shafts. Put on a raincoat and some form of hat before going in.

A notice on the tunnel portal will give its length, in yards, and will say whether unpowered craft are permitted to use it.

Where there are restrictions on time of entry, and one-way systems, these must be adhered to. To meet head on half way through a long narrow tunnel would create great difficulties.

Care of the engine

Canal boats are generally powered by either diesel, petrol or two-stoke engines. If you have a hire craft, the boatyard will give you instructions for your daily maintenance, which will no doubt include some or all of the following:

Every day before starting off, you should:

Check the oil level in the engine.
Check the fuel level in the tank.

If your engine is water-cooled, check that the filter near the intake is clean and weedfree. Otherwise the engine will over-heat, which could cause serious damage.

Check the level of distilled water in the battery, and ensure that it is charging correctly.

Lubricate any parts of the engine, gearbox or steering that need daily attention.

Check that the propeller is free of weeds, wire, plastic bags and any other rubbish. The propeller and the water filter should be checked whenever there is any suspicion of obstruction or overheating—which may mean several times a day.

Pump the bilges everyday

When navigating in shallow water, keep in mind the exposed position of the propeller. If you hit any underwater obstruction put the engine into neutral immediately. When running over any large floating object put the engine into neutral and wait for the object to appear astern before re-engaging the drive.

Fuel

Petrol engines and petrol/oil outboards are catered for by some boatyards and all road-side fuel stations. Fuel stations on roads near the canal are shown in the guide, and these should be considered when planning your day's cruise. Running out is inconvenient; remember you may have to walk several miles carrying a heavy can.

Diesel-powered craft, and narrowboats in particular, can usually cruise for over two weeks before needing to be refilled. Those using diesel-powered hire craft rarely need to be concerned about fuel. Those with their own boats, however, should bear in mind that boatyards are few and far between on some parts of the network, and should a diesel-powered boat run out of fuel, the system will need to be bled before the engine can run again. Most boatyards sell marine diesel (indicated D in the text), which is cheaper than the road fuel.

Electrically powered boats

These are becoming very popular on the inland waterways, in view of their quietness and lack of environmental pollution. Indicated E under the **BOATYARD** heading are those establishments known to offer recharging facilities—polite enquiry by electric boat users will certainly reveal more. If you are lucky enough to be using this form of power, please note the following:

All boats using this information are assumed to have a battery charger on board and 50 metres of cable fitted with standard 13 amp terminals. You are advised to offer a £2 fee (1984) for an overnight re-charge if not equipped to measure what you take.

It is essential for the safety of the boater, the owner of the supply and the general public that a proper residual current circuit breaker (RCD) be carried by the boat and fitted between the boat's cable and the supply unless the supply is already so protected. The RCD must be tested for correct operation before battery charging starts.

Water

Fresh water taps occur irregularly along the canals, usually at boatyards, BWB depots, or by lock cottages. These are marked on the maps in the guide. Ensure that there is a long water hose on the boat (BWB taps have a ½-inch slip-on hose connection). Fill up every day.

Lavatories

Some canal boats are fitted with chemical lavatories which have to be emptied from time to time. Never empty them over the side or tip them into the bushes. Use the sewage disposal points marked on the map S, for which you will need a BWB key, or at boatyards. Many boats now have pump-out toilets, which must be emptied with a special machine—usually at boatyards and indicated in the text. This symbol at the canalside indicates just such a 'pump-out station' (although not all boatyards with the facility display it). Expect to have to pay.

Some BWB depots and boatyards have lavatories for the use of boat crews; again, you may need your BWB key.

Litter

Some canals are in a poor state today because they have long been misused as unofficial dumps for rubbish, especially in towns. Out of sight is only out of mind until some object is tangled round your propeller. So keep all rubbish until you can dispose of it at a refuse disposal point, indicated R on the map, or at a boatyard equipped to deal with it.

Byelaws

Although no-one needs a 'driving licence' to navigate a boat, boat users should remember that they have certain responsibilities to others on the waterways. Prospective navigators are advised to obtain a copy of the byelaws relevant to the waterways on which they are to travel.

Stoppages

Although the BWB and other navigation authorities plan their maintenance for the winter months, it often becomes necessary to carry out repairs during the cruising season. Many of the structures on the canal system are beginning to show their age (especially the tunnels) and repairs are a lengthy and costly affair, sometimes resulting in stoppages lasting many years. A long dry spell can lower water levels and restrict lock operation, and of course a canal bank can breach at any time.

To avoid disappointment it is wise to check that your planned route is clear before you set off, and that there are no time restrictions on locks that may upset your schedule. Those using hire craft may be able to get this information from their boatyard, although some are surprisingly lax. It is best to check for yourself by ringing the BWB Area Amenity Assistants (listed on page 173) or the relevant navigation authority. News of any last minute stoppages is available on 'Canalphone', as a recorded message. Ring (01)-723 8486 for the North and Midlands, or (01)-723 8487 for the South and Midlands.

PLANNING A CRUISE

It is wise when planning a cruise to establish a means of calculating the time it takes to travel any given length of canal. This ensures that you can reliably work out whether you will reach a shop or pub before closing time. And of course for those who have hired their boat for a week, it is vital to return on time to the starting point.

The time taken to navigate any canal depends, of course, on the average cruising speed of your boat and the amount of time it takes to negotiate the locks along the way. Remember that there is in any case an overall legal speed limit of 4 mph on all canals. In practice, 3 mph is a realistic canal cruising speed for most boats and 2 mph is the maximum which can be achieved on shallow canals, such as the Peak Forest.

To the uninitiated, 3 mph may sound an unbearably slow rate of progress through the countryside; but a few hours of gentle cruising on a fine day is usually enough to convert most people to this pace. For only by proceeding at walking pace can you appreciate the peace and beauty of the countryside, watch the bird life, and see the scurry of voles, rats and other creatures as they suddenly notice the slowly approaching boat.

The length of time taken to work through a lock depends on several things: whether the lock is full or empty, wide or narrow, deep or shallow. It depends on the number and size of the paddles that control the sluices, on the presence or otherwise of other boats near the lock, and of course on the number and competence of the boat crew. Most people take around 10 minutes on average to work through a typical lock—or, to put it another way, they take as long to get through a lock as they would have taken to travel another ½ mile at 3 mph. Herein lies the basis for a simple method of estimating time required to travel along a given length of canal: take the number of miles to be travelled and add half the number of locks to be negotiated on the way. This gives the number of 'lock-miles'. Divide this by your average cruising speed, and the result is the approximate length of time it will take, in hours. Thus if you intend to travel 30 miles, and there are 42 locks along the way, the calculation is as follows: 30 + (42 divided by 2) = 30 + 21 = 51 lock-miles. 51 divided by 3 (mph) = 17 hours. So this particular journey will take you around 17 hours, assuming your average cruising speed to be 3 mph and assuming you take about 10 minutes to get through the average lock. (If you're a beginner, it might take a little longer than this to start with.) The length of your journey and the number of locks can easily be calculated using the 'milestones' that appear on every map in this series of guides. To refine the system, simply tailor it more closely to the actual cruising speed of your boat and the efficiency of your lock-operating technique.

An excellent fortnight's trip, for example, would be the circuit formed by the River Soar and Trent and Mersey, Coventry, Oxford and Grand Union (Leicester Section) canals. This is 170 miles and 74 locks long (about 70 hours cruising time), and takes you through some of the very best parts of Leicestershire. You will see the Foxton staircase locks, Braunston Tunnel and the delightful canal village of Shardlow, and if you have time to spare you can explore the lock-free Ashby Canal (22 miles long—2 days there and back) or the meandering course of the unspoilt Market Harborough arm, 5 miles long.

A good round trip in terms of contrasts would be the Grand Union main line, north Oxford, Coventry and Birmingham & Fazeley canals, which at 106 miles and 88 locks (about 50 hours cruising time) would be an energetic week's cruising. On this route you could see Braunston and Hillmorton, the long level of the north Oxford and Coventry Canals broken by the 11 locks at Atherstone, and then the industrial outpost of Fazeley. Once out in Warwickshire, you encounter the 5 wide but modern locks at Knowle and the 21 locks of the Hatton Flight. Then you are in the valley of the Warwickshire Avon, and after passing Warwick and Leamington Spa you start locking up out of the valley again to rejoin the Oxford Canal at Napton.

These are just two examples of the many circular cruising routes available—a glance at the planning map on pages 4 and 5 will reveal many more. Of course, there is also much to be said for a straight out and back cruise—it will all look different when you are coming the other way, and you can arrange to re-visit that favourite pub again. The whole secret is to allow plenty of time, for shopping, for exploring and for gentle cruising. Many a holiday has been spoilt by becoming a race against time.

See also 'Stoppages' in the ***General Cruising Information*** *section.*

ASHBY

Maximum dimensions

Length: 72′
Beam: 7′
Headroom: 6′ 6″

Mileage

MARSTON JUNCTION (Coventry Canal) to
Burton Hastings: 3
Hinckley Wharf: 6
Stoke Golding Wharf: 8¾
Dadlington: 10
Shenton Aqueduct: 13
Market Bosworth Wharf: 15
Congerstone: 17¼
Shackerstone: 18¼
Snarestone Tunnel: 21
CANAL TERMINUS: 21¾

No locks

Looking at this canal on a map it appears to be very much out on a limb. In fact the Ashby Canal—often referred to as the Ashby de la Zouch Canal—was originally intended to be a through route from the River Trent at Burton to the Coventry Canal near Bedworth, but this plan was repeatedly shelved. In 1792 however an Ashby Canal Company was formed and a Bill promoted, mostly by the owners of Leicestershire limeworks and the new coalfields near Ashby de la Zouch, who decided that an outlet southwards was required from their various works. The problem that soon arose was that while the proposed canal could be built level for 30 miles from the junction with the Coventry Canal at Marston Jabbett, near Bedworth, to Moira, the section north of Moira would require expensive and complicated works including locks, reservoirs, pumping engines and possibly a tunnel. Part of this cost was in fact avoided by building an extensive system of tramroads to and around the various coalmines and limeworks. However while the canal was still being built (by a succession of engineers—Jessop, Outram, Whitworth senior and junior, and Thomas Newbold), the new coalmines near Ashby Woulds were found to be less productive than had been hoped. This, combined with the fact that the canal was never extended north to the Trent, was instrumental in preventing the Ashby Canal from making a profit for 20 years. However a new coal mine sunk at Moira in 1804 (2 years after the completion of the canal) eventually produced coal of such excellent quality that it became widely demanded in London and southern England. The canal flourished at last.

In 1845 the Midland Railway bought up the Ashby Canal—with the approval of all concerned except the Coventry and Oxford Canal companies, who stood to lose a lot in tolls if the coal traffic from Moira switched to rail carriage. These 2 companies managed to hamstring the Midland Railway so effectively over its management of the canal that instead of switching to carriage by rail, the coal traffic from Moira continued along the canal at a substantial level right through to the turn of the century. It is therefore hard to see what real benefit the railway company gained by buying the canal.

Subsidence from the coal mines near Measham has caused great damage in this century to the canal that served them. This subsidence has brought about the abandonment of over 9 miles of the canal, so that the canal now terminates just north of Snarestone, outside the coalfield. There is no regular trade left on the canal, the last load of coal being carried to Croxley (Herts) from Gopsall Wharf in 1970.

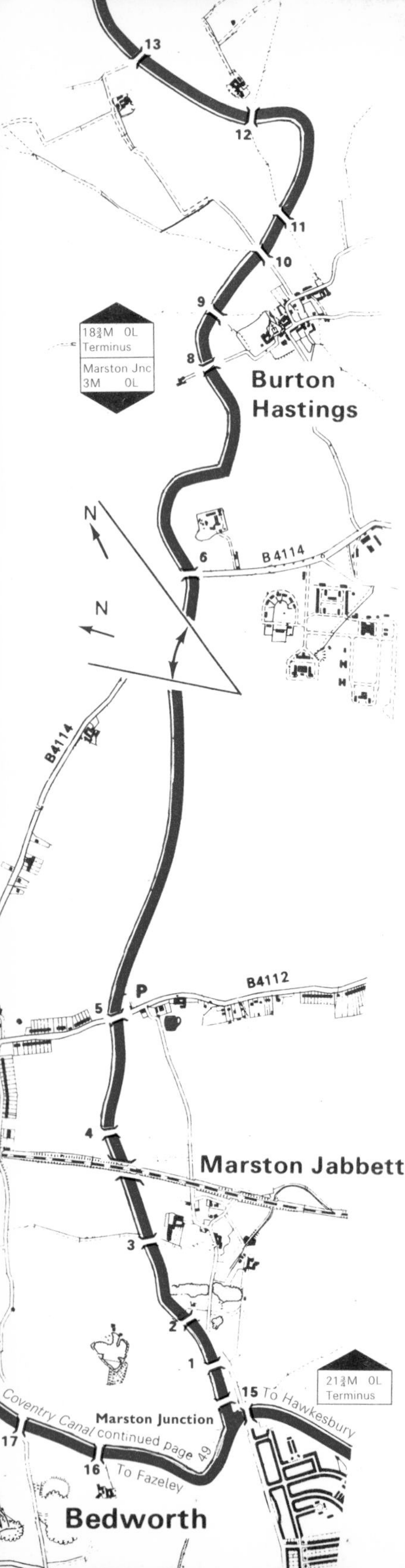

Burton Hastings

At Marston Junction the Ashby Canal branches east off the Coventry. Free guides to the canal are kept in a box at the junction (BWB key required). As soon as it leaves Marston, the canal changes completely and dramatically. The industry and housing estates that had accompanied the Coventry Canal through the Nuneaton–Bedworth conurbation suddenly vanish to be replaced by green fields, farms and trees. In this way the character of the Ashby Canal is established at once: also the first of the typical stone arched bridges occurs which, together with the shallow and clear water, suggests a rurality far from the industrial Midlands. Only the power lines that criss-cross this stretch are a memory of the other world to the west. A long wooded cutting leads the canal towards Burton Hastings, a typical farming village. Then the canal turns north, setting a course for Hinckley passing, to the east of bridge 13, Stretton Baskerville, a 'lost' village. In many places along the canal the towpath disappears, making walking very difficult. The B4114 and the B4112 cross the canal.

Burton Hastings
Warwicks. PO tel, stores. Quiet village set on a hill in open farmland. The pretty, well-placed church has a decorated font of 1300.

PUBS

Navigation Marston Jabbett, near bridge 5. Food. (Tel and garage nearby.)

Corner House Hotel Bulkington Lane, Marston Jabbett. Very large friendly pub with a public bar and a vast wood panelled lounge. Marstons real ale, good bar meals, garden.

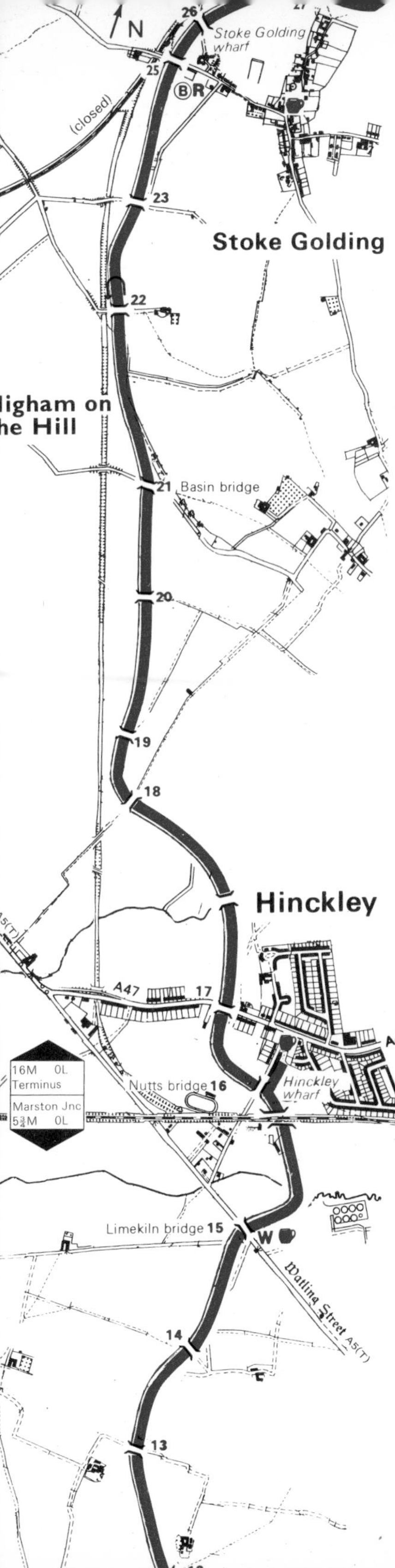

Hinckley

Keeping west of Hinckley, the canal continues through the fine rolling farmland that typifies the Ashby Canal; a short arm runs east to the town wharf. The canal then runs fairly straight to Stoke Golding where there is one of the finest churches in Leicestershire. There are no locks, but the typical Ashby accommodation bridges occur regularly. Throughout its length the Ashby Canal is remote and rural, a haven from the industry that surrounds it, and an ironic contrast to its *raison d'être*, the Ashby coalfields. The A5 (Watling Street) and the A47 cross near Hinckley. There is no navigation on the Hinckley Wharf Arm, which is used as a boat club mooring. The towpath is non-existent between bridges 17 and 18.

Stoke Golding
Leics. EC Wed. PO, tel, stores, garage. The church is very beautiful, full of original 13th and 14thC work. It is large, on a hill, and the spire dominates the landscape. The carving of the windows and the column capitals is especially fine. Crown Hill, near the wharf, marks the place where Henry Tudor was crowned king after the battle of Bosworth Field in 1485. There are good moorings between bridges 27 and 28.

Higham on the Hill
Leics. PO, tel, stores. 1 mile west of bridges 21 and 23. Quiet village on a hill overlooking the canal. To the west is the huge proving ground used by the Motor Industry Research Association for testing new vehicles. The end of the banking can be seen from the canal.

Hinckley
Leics. EC Thur. MD Mon. PO, tel, stores, garage, station, cinema. A hosiery manufacturing town that can boast of having installed the first stocking machine in Leicestershire, in 1640. There are few buildings of interest, and only the mound of the castle remains. A row of timber-framed thatched cottages survives in Bond Street, a memento of a pre-industrial era.

BOATYARDS

Ⓑ **Ashby Narrow Boat Company** The Canal Wharf, Stoke Golding, Nuneaton, Warwicks. (Hinckley 212671). R S WD Pump-out, narrow boat hire, gas, moorings, chandlery, toilets. Boat and engine repairs and paintings. *Open daily.*

PUBS

George & Dragon Stoke Golding. Food.
White Swan Stoke Golding. Food.
Wharf Inn Hinckley. Marstons real ale, food. Snacks, garden. Good general store and butchers shop nearby.
Lime Kilns Inn Watling Street, Hinckley. Canalside. Marstons real ales in an unself-consciously preserved pub, with a tap room and a large basic public bar; traditional pub games and lively conversation are the entertainment. Moorings for patrons, garden. W Warning: beware of 'Merrie Monk' mild.
Three Horse Shoes Stoke Golding. Food. Children welcome.

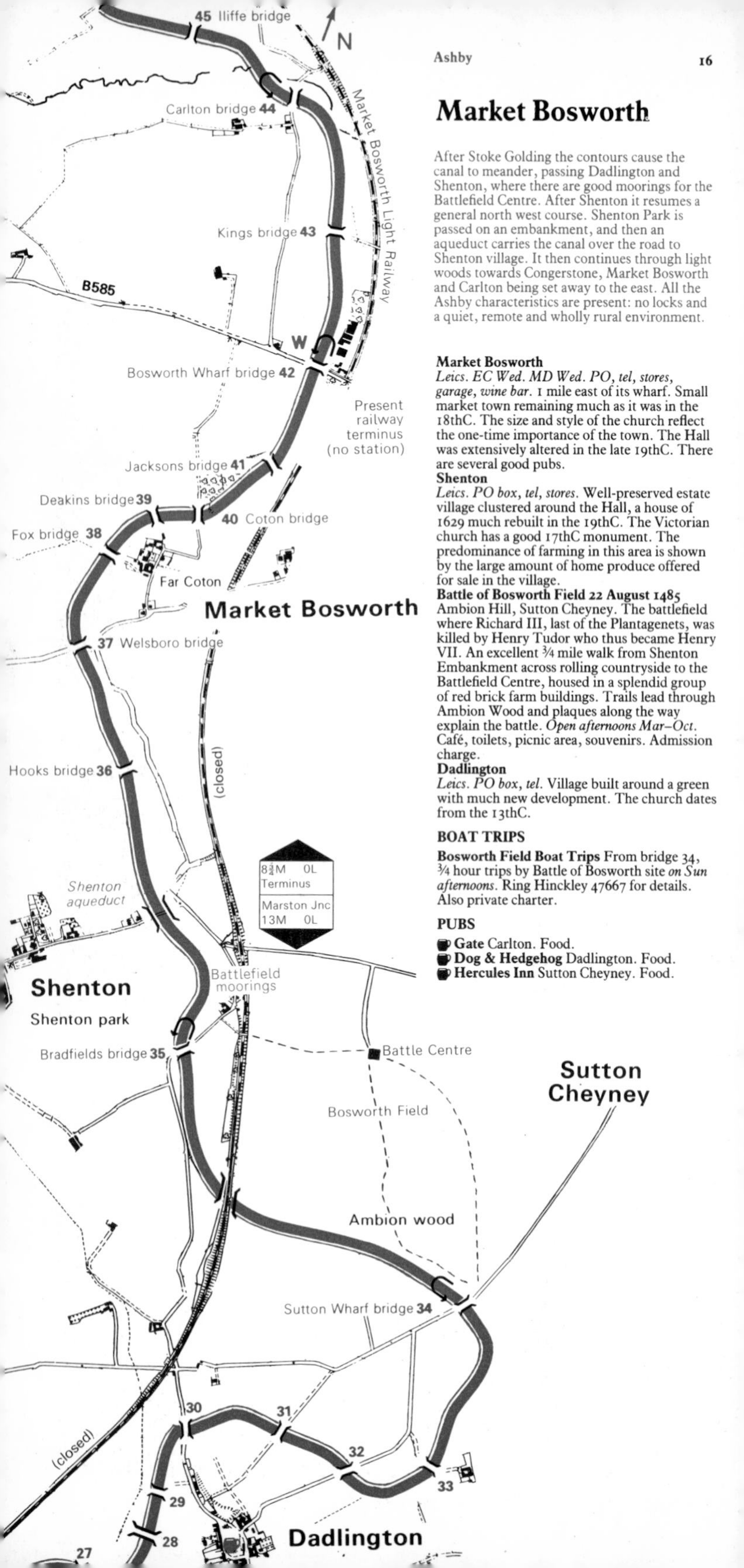

Market Bosworth

After Stoke Golding the contours cause the canal to meander, passing Dadlington and Shenton, where there are good moorings for the Battlefield Centre. After Shenton it resumes a general north west course. Shenton Park is passed on an embankment, and then an aqueduct carries the canal over the road to Shenton village. It then continues through light woods towards Congerstone, Market Bosworth and Carlton being set away to the east. All the Ashby characteristics are present: no locks and a quiet, remote and wholly rural environment.

Market Bosworth
Leics. EC Wed. MD Wed. PO, tel, stores, garage, wine bar. 1 mile east of its wharf. Small market town remaining much as it was in the 18thC. The size and style of the church reflect the one-time importance of the town. The Hall was extensively altered in the late 19thC. There are several good pubs.

Shenton
Leics. PO box, tel, stores. Well-preserved estate village clustered around the Hall, a house of 1629 much rebuilt in the 19thC. The Victorian church has a good 17thC monument. The predominance of farming in this area is shown by the large amount of home produce offered for sale in the village.

Battle of Bosworth Field 22 August 1485
Ambion Hill, Sutton Cheyney. The battlefield where Richard III, last of the Plantagenets, was killed by Henry Tudor who thus became Henry VII. An excellent ¾ mile walk from Shenton Embankment across rolling countryside to the Battlefield Centre, housed in a splendid group of red brick farm buildings. Trails lead through Ambion Wood and plaques along the way explain the battle. *Open afternoons Mar–Oct.* Café, toilets, picnic area, souvenirs. Admission charge.

Dadlington
Leics. PO box, tel. Village built around a green with much new development. The church dates from the 13thC.

BOAT TRIPS

Bosworth Field Boat Trips From bridge 34, ¾ hour trips by Battle of Bosworth site *on Sun afternoons*. Ring Hinckley 47667 for details. Also private charter.

PUBS

- **Gate** Carlton. Food.
- **Dog & Hedgehog** Dadlington. Food.
- **Hercules Inn** Sutton Cheyney. Food.

N
45 Iliffe bridge
Carlton bridge 44
Market Bosworth Light Railway
Kings bridge 43
B585
W
Bosworth Wharf bridge 42
Present railway terminus (no station)
Jacksons bridge 41
Deakins bridge 39
40 Coton bridge
Fox bridge 38
Far Coton
Market Bosworth
37 Welsboro bridge
Hooks bridge 36
(closed)
8¾M 0L Terminus
Marston Jnc 13M 0L
Shenton aqueduct
Shenton
Shenton park
Battlefield moorings
Bradfields bridge 35
Battle Centre
Sutton Cheyney
Bosworth Field
Ambion wood
Sutton Wharf bridge 34
(closed)
30
31
32
33
29
28
27
Dadlington

Bosworth Wharf on the lock-free Ashby Canal. *Derek Pratt*

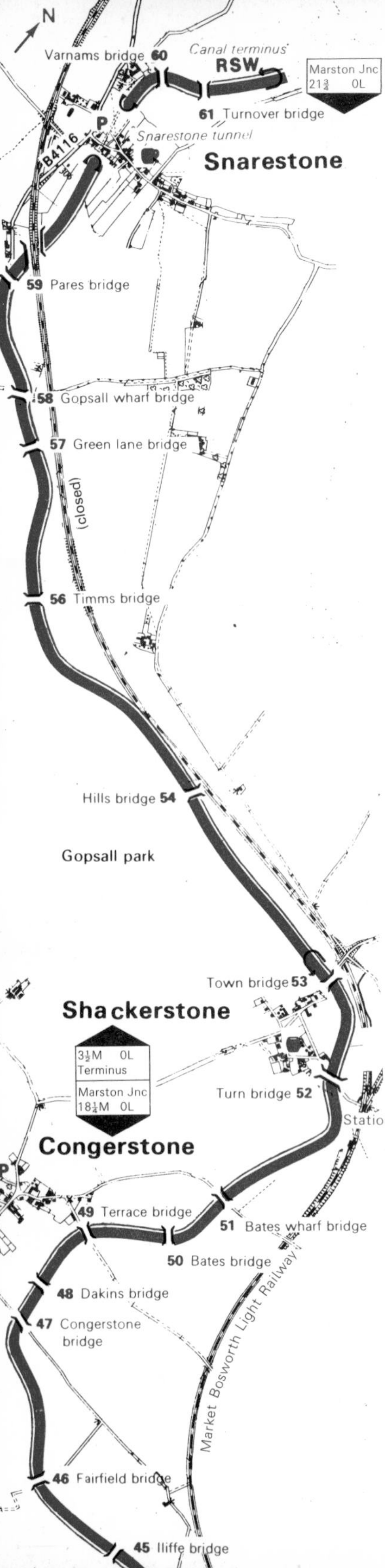

Snarestone

Continuing north west, the canal passes Congerstone and Shackerstone, crossing the River Sence. After Gopsall Park the hills become more prominent, although the quality of the landscape does not change. Snarestone sits on a ridge at right-angles to the canal, which passes beneath the village through the tunnel, the only one on the canal. After the tunnel there are two more stone arched bridges, and then the present terminus is reached. There is a winding hole, sanitary station and picnic area. The canal once continued for another nine miles to Moira, passing through Measham on the way; constant trouble from subsidence made it impossible to retain this last section. The same subsidence may account for the rather poor state of the towpath in places. The present terminus means that the Ashby Canal is idyllic and rural throughout its length. There is no hint of the coal mines and heavy industry that prompted its creation.

Snarestone
Leics. PO, tel, stores, garage. An 18thC farming village built over the top of the canal, which passes underneath through the crooked tunnel (250 yds). The Victorian Gothic waterworks, ½ mile north, mark the end of the canal.
Shackerstone
Leics. PO, tel, stores. Undeveloped and unchanged. Shackerstone is a farming village that reflects the pre-industrial feeling of the whole of the Ashby Canal. West of the village the canal flanks Gopsall Park; the house where Handel is reputed to have composed the 'Messiah' was pulled down in 1951, and the park has since lost its original dignity and quality.
Market Bosworth Light Railway
Although the railway line that follows the Ashby Canal is now closed, the former Shackerstone Junction station (near canal bridge 82), has come to life again as a small railway museum and a depot for preserved steam locomotives which run trips on *Sun afternoons and B. Hols Easter to Oct.* Café.
Congerstone
Leics. PO, tel, stores, garage. Scattered village of small interest. 1 mile west of the village is a gibbet put up in 1800 to hang a local murderer.

PUBS

Globe Inn Snarestone. Food.
Rising Sun Shackerstone. Food, garden.
Horse & Jockey Congerstone. Food. Day tickets for fishing.

BIRMINGHAM CANAL NAVIGATIONS (BCN)

Maximum dimensions

Length: 71′ 6″
Beam: 7′
Headroom: 6′ 6″

Mileages

Birmingham Canal new main line
BIRMINGHAM Gas Street to
SMETHWICK JUNCTION (old main line): 2⅞
BROMFORD JUNCTION: 4⅞
PUDDING GREEN JUNCTION (Wednesbury Old Canal): 5⅝
TIPTON FACTORY JUNCTION (old main line): 8¾
DEEPFIELDS JUNCTION (Wednesbury Oak loop): 10
Bradley Workshops: 2¼
HORSELEY FIELDS JUNCTION (Wyrley & Essington Canal): 13
Wolverhampton Top Lock: 13½
ALDERSLEY JUNCTION (Staffordshire & Worcestershire Canal): 15⅛

Locks: 24 (3 up, 21 down)

Birmingham Canal old main line
SMETHWICK JUNCTION to
Junction with Engine Branch: ½
SPON LANE JUNCTION: 1½
OLDBURY JUNCTION (Titford Canal): 2½
BRADESHALL JUNCTION (Gower Branch): 3½
Aqueduct over Netherton Tunnel Branch: 4⅜
TIPTON JUNCTION (Dudley Canal): 5½
FACTORY JUNCTION (new main line): 6

Locks: 3

Dudley Canal line no. 1
TIPTON JUNCTION to
Dudley Tunnel (north end): ⅜
PARK HEAD JUNCTION: 2⅜
Black Delph Bottom Lock (Stourbridge Canal): 4½

Locks: 12

Dudley Canal line no. 2
PARK HEAD JUNCTION to
WINDMILL END JUNCTION: 2⅝
HAWNE BASIN: 5½

No locks

Netherton Tunnel Branch
WINDMILL END JUNCTION to
DUDLEY PORT JUNCTION: 2⅞

No locks

Wednesbury Old Canal
PUDDING GREEN JUNCTION to
RYDER'S GREEN JUNCTION: ⅝

No locks

Walsall Canal
RYDER'S GREEN JUNCTION to
Ryder's Green Bottom Lock: ¾
TAME VALLEY JUNCTION: 1⅜
Junction with Anson Branch (for Bentley Canal): 5⅛
WALSALL JUNCTION: 6⅞

Locks: 8

Walsall Branch Canal
WALSALL JUNCTION to
BIRCHILLS JUNCTION (Wyrley & Essington Canal): ⅞

Locks: 8

Wyrley & Essington Canal
HORSELEY FIELDS JUNCTION to
WEDNESFIELD JUNCTION (Bentley Canal): 1¼
SNEYD JUNCTION: 6¼
BIRCHILLS JUNCTION (Walsall Branch Canal): 8
PELSALL JUNCTION (Cannock Extension): 12⅞
Norton Canes Docks: 2
CATSHILL JUNCTION: 15⅜
OGLEY JUNCTION (Anglesey Branch): 16⅜
Anglesey Basin and Chasewater: 1½

No locks

Daw End Branch
CATSHILL JUNCTION to
LONGWOOD JUNCTION (Rushall Top Lock): 5¼

No locks

Rushall Canal
LONGWOOD JUNCTION to
RUSHALL JUNCTION: 2¾

Locks: 9

Tame Valley Canal
TAME VALLEY JUNCTION to
RUSHALL JUNCTION: 3½
Perry Barr Top Lock: 5½
SALFORD JUNCTION: 8½

Locks: 13

The BCN network

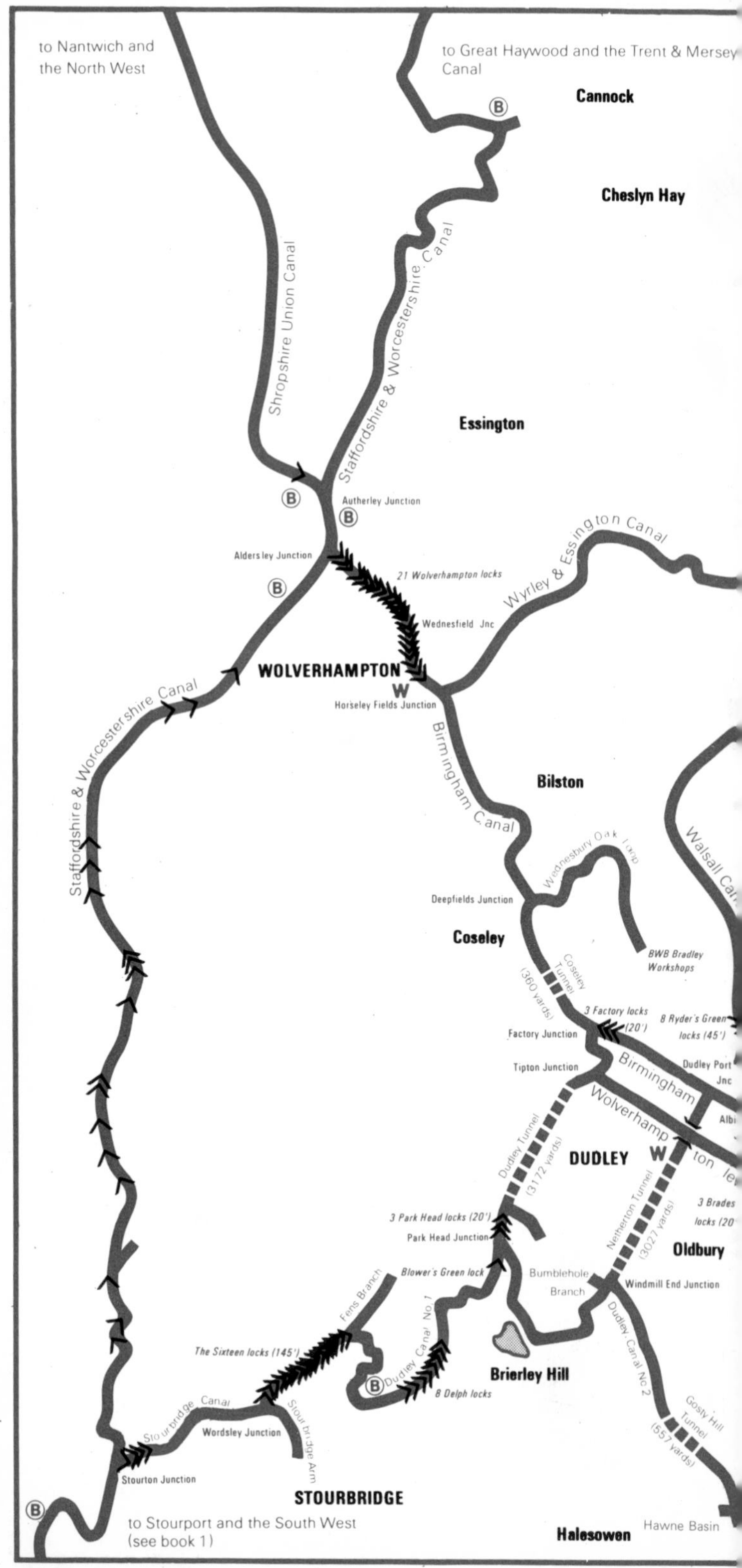

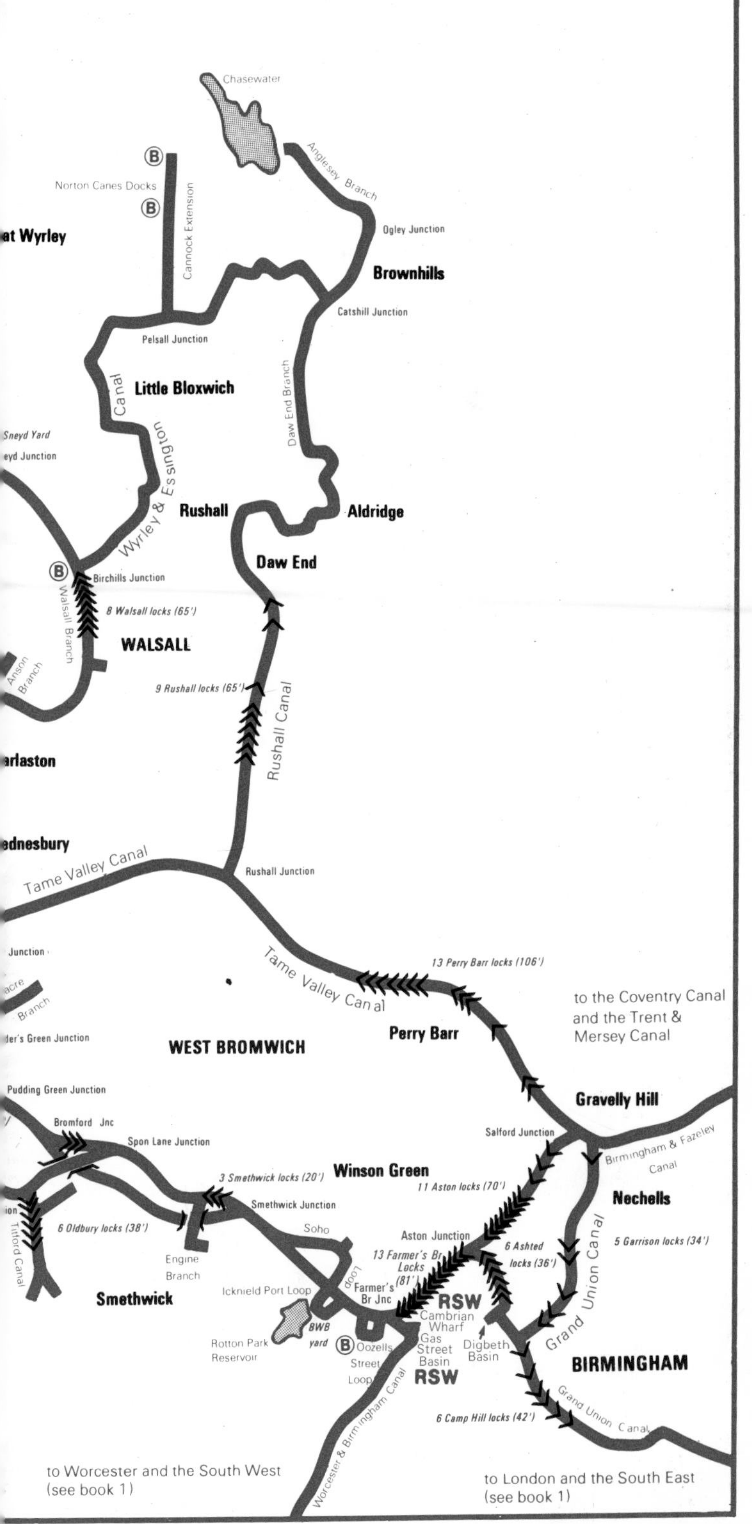

Chasewater
Anglesey Branch
Norton Canes Docks
Cannock Extension
at Wyrley
Ogley Junction
Brownhills
Catshill Junction
Pelsall Junction
Little Bloxwich
Canal
Daw End Branch
Sneyd Yard
eyd Junction
Wyrley & Essington
Rushall
Aldridge
Daw End
Birchills Junction
Walsall Branch
8 Walsall locks (65')
WALSALL
Anson Branch
9 Rushall locks (65')
Rushall Canal
arlaston
ednesbury
Tame Valley Canal
Rushall Junction
Junction
acre Branch
13 Perry Barr locks (106')
Tame Valley Canal
to the Coventry Canal and the Trent & Mersey Canal
der's Green Junction
WEST BROMWICH
Perry Barr
Pudding Green Junction
Gravelly Hill
Bromford Jnc
Spon Lane Junction
Salford Junction
Birmingham & Fazeley Canal
Winson Green
3 Smethwick locks (20')
11 Aston locks (70')
Nechells
Smethwick Junction
Tiftord Canal
6 Oldbury locks (38')
Soho
Aston Junction
Engine Branch
6 Ashted locks (36')
5 Garrison locks (34')
13 Farmer's Br Locks (81')
Loop
Grand Union Canal
Smethwick
Icknield Port Loop
Farmer's Br Jnc
RSW
Cambrian Wharf
Rotton Park Reservoir
BWB yard
Oozells Street Loop
Gas Street Basin
Digbeth Basin
RSW
BIRMINGHAM
Worcester & Birmingham Canal
6 Camp Hill locks (42')
Grand Union Canal
to Worcester and the South West (see book 1)
to London and the South East (see book 1)

BIRMINGHAM CANAL NAVIGATIONS

The Birmingham Canal Company was authorised in 1768 to build a canal from Aldersley on the Staffordshire & Worcestershire Canal to Birmingham. With James Brindley as engineer the work proceeded quickly. The first section, from Birmingham to the Wednesbury collieries, was opened in November 1769, and the whole 22½-mile route was completed in 1772. It was a winding, contour canal, with 12 locks taking it over Smethwick, and another 20 (later 21) taking it down through Wolverhampton to Aldersley Junction. As the route of the canal was through an area of mineral wealth and developing industry, its success was immediate. Pressure of traffic caused the summit level at Smethwick to be lowered in the 1790s (thus cutting out 6 locks—3 on either side of the summit), and during the same period branches began to reach out towards Walsall via the Ryder's Green Locks, and towards Fazeley. Out of this very profitable and ambitious first main line, there grew the Birmingham Canal Navigations, more commonly abbreviated to BCN. After a long dispute about the building of the canal from Birmingham to Fazeley, the Birmingham Company bought up the embryonic Birmingham & Fazeley Canal Company; in 1794 the cumbersome title created by this merger, 'The Birmingham and Birmingham & Fazeley Canal Company', was changed to the simpler BCN. The battle for the right to build the Fazeley line was long and hard, and was fought with considerable intrigue and bitterness, a pattern of behaviour that tended to surround all the activities of the Birmingham Company. Being first in the field, it generally behaved in a high-handed manner, holding the whip hand over rivals when extensions and developments were proposed. Generally it exacted high compensatory tolls, and exercised strict controls over water rights—habits that pleased the shareholders but infuriated competitors.

The BCN network that exists today developed from 3 rival companies each seeking to capture traffic from the others. This intense competition resulted in a very intricate network, which was thus able to cater for all the material and distribution needs of the developing industries in the area. The web of lines forming the BCN became the veins of the Black Country, carrying the life blood of its commerce and wealth.

Apart from the Birmingham Company, there were 2 other companies instrumental in the creation of the BCN network. Over the other side of the Rowley Hills, the Dudley and Stourbridge Companies had set up a rival route to the Staffs & Worcs, to the annoyance of the Birmingham Company. Thomas Dadford, who had worked with Brindley earlier, was appointed engineer, and in 3 years (1776–79) it was completed as planned to a point just below the present Blower's Green Lock. Immediately there were plans to extend it underground to link with Lord Ward's private canal, and with the Birmingham at Tipton. After several setbacks this extension was completed between 1785 and 1792, including the long Dudley Tunnel. Then once again the directness of the Dudley Company prompted it to undertake a further extension to link with the recently authorised Worcester & Birmingham Canal at Selly Oak, a means of avoiding the severe compensation tolls exacted by the Birmingham Company for the junction at Tipton. This new line, 11 miles long, was opened in 1798. It included 2 tunnels, that at Lappal being the fifth longest in Britain. Cut through rock strata with great difficulty, this tunnel suffered continuously from subsidence and roof falls, and had to undergo frequent closure for repairs. The financial strain of this last extension nearly crippled the Dudley Company, and it only just managed to survive until 1846, when it was absorbed by the BCN. Lappal Tunnel was finally closed in 1917.

Up in the north, the Wyrley & Essington Company joined the fray, completing a line from Wolverhampton to Wyrley in 1795 under the direction of William Pitt. This company also grew quickly, extending initially to Brownhills, and then to join the Coventry Canal at Huddlesford via the Ogley flight of 30 locks. Several branches were added to serve the rich coalfields around Cannock and Brownhills, which were destined to serve the BCN and West Midlands well when the Black Country pits began to decline. Indeed the meandering line of the Wyrley & Essington saw some of the last commercial traffic on the whole BCN network. The Birmingham Company had spread northwards to Walsall, but because of ill-feeling and rivalry, the logical link with the Wyrley & Essington line was not made until 1840, when the Walsall Branch Canal was built.

Traffic continued to increase, and with it the wealth of the BCN. The pressures of trade made the main line at Smethwick very congested, and brought grave problems of water supply. Steam pumping engines were installed in several places to recirculate the water, and the company appointed Thomas Telford to shorten Brindley's old main line. Between 1825 and 1838 he engineered a new main line between Deepfields and Birmingham, using massive cuttings and embankments to maintain a continuous level. These improvements not only increased the amount of available waterway (the old line remaining in use), but also shortened the route from Birmingham to Wolverhampton by 7 miles.

Serious congestion had also arisen at Farmer's Bridge Locks, which could not keep up with the traffic although they operated 24 hours a day and 7 days a week. Land was not available for a duplicate flight in the immediate area, and so an earlier plan to build a canal following the valley of the River Tame was revived. However, it was not until railway control and amalgamation with the Wyrley & Essington came in 1840 that the necessary impetus was found to promote the Tame Valley Canal, and the whole series of extensions and improvements to the network that accompanied it. These developments led to the building of a relief for the narrow Dudley Tunnel: the Netherton Tunnel, cut on a parallel course, included a towpath on each side and gas lighting throughout. The last addition to the network was the Cannock Extension Canal to Hednesford Basin, with its link to the Staffs & Worcs Canal via Churchbridge Locks.

Railway control of the BCN meant an expansion of the use of the system, and a large number of interchange basins were built to promote outside trade by means of rail traffic. This was of course quite contrary to the usual effect of railway competition upon canals. Trade continued to grow in relation to industrial development, and by the end of the 19thC it was topping 8½ million tons per annum. A large proportion of this trade was local, being dependent upon the needs and output of Black Country industry. After the turn of the century this reliance on local trade started the gradual decline of the system as deposits of raw materials became exhausted. Factories bought from further afield, and developed along the railways and roads away from the canals. Yet as late as 1950 there was over a million tons of trade, and the system continued in operation until the abrupt end of the coal trade in 1966, a pattern quite different from canals as a whole. Nowadays there is no significant commercial traffic—a dramatic contrast to the roaring traffic on the new Birmingham motorways.

As trade declined, so parts of the system fell out of use and were abandoned. In its heyday in 1865, the BCN comprised over 160 miles of canal. Today just over 100 miles remain. However, all the surviving canals of the BCN are of great interest; although not every one is ideal for leisure cruising, they represent a most vivid example of living history and will reward exploration—one of the most important monuments to the Industrial Revolution.

Much has been done in recent years in landscaping waste land (as at the south end of Dudley Tunnel), dredging old basins (such as at the top of the Wolverhampton '21'), and restoring disused buildings (such as the Pump House at Smethwick). The Birmingham Inner City Partnership is implementing a programme of improvements, having recognised the unique recreational potential of the canal system and its value as an area of retreat for the harassed city dweller and as a tourist attraction.

Natural history

Birmingham's canals are in places derelict and dirty but nearly all bring a vein of the countryside right into the heart of England's second largest city. The hub of the network is Gas Street Basin and here many varieties of fern grow on walls, posts, etc. Two of the commonest are polypody and hartstongue. From July until September, the beautiful pink flowers of the rosebay willow herb can be seen wherever there is a piece of waste ground. Fireweed, as it is called, was once very rare in England but since bomb-damage and demolition created many open spaces, it has become one of our most common and beautiful wild flowers. It is called 'fireweed' because it is a 'first coloniser', often appearing very soon after a fire has cleared an area, especially in woodland. This flower is much enjoyed by the caterpillars of the elephant hawk moth.

Also common is the yellow flowered ragwort which can be seen growing by the canal on walls and even in neglected gutters. Ragwort contains a poison which destroys the liver of any animal that eats it and has to be eradicated on all land on which livestock is kept. But it lends a touch of sunshine gold to many urban canals.

The bird life of Birmingham is surprisingly rich. If you are lucky you may see, beside blackbirds, thrushes, tits and wagtails, the black redstart with its grey head and back, black chest and bright rusty red tail feathers. Black redstarts are nowhere common in Britain but they have actually nested in the centre of Birmingham only a few hundred yards from Gas Street Basin itself. Kestrels are quite common in the city; they nest on the larger buildings and feed on small mammals and birds. Most evenings, as dusk begins to fall, flocks of starlings arrive in the city, commuting to their favourite roosting sites in the warmth from their feeding grounds in the surrounding countryside. Before finally settling down for the night, they perform one of the most spectacular flying displays ever seen, yet most human commuters scurry past oblivious of this beautiful aerial ballet over their heads. Up to 50,000 starlings roost in the city centre.

Moorhens nest quite close to the city and in the spring their untidy nests can be seen along the canal banks, always in imminent danger of being flooded by the wash from passing boats. Moorhens are very shy and often hide underwater with only their bills showing when danger threatens. Kingfishers are not uncommon on Birmingham canals—a pair has nested in the Edgbaston area and they have been seen in Gas Street Basin. They feed on sticklebacks, which abound in the BCN. Although parts of the BCN suffer from industrial pollution, the fishing is very good in places. This is useful in an area of poor fishing facilities.

Sticklebacks themselves feed on the great variety of invertebrate life which lives in the seemingly dead waters of the canal. Wherever there is a patch of weed or reeds you can find dragonfly nymphs, water beetles, freshwater shrimps, leeches, frogs, newts and tadpoles.

Many small rodents make their homes along the banks. The most common are water voles, vegetarians feeding on reeds and grass; you can often see their tracks in the mud, and look out for their latrines since they are tidy animals and leave their droppings in one place. Their burrow systems are quite large, with at least 2 entrances—1 being underwater for a quick exit in case of danger. The brown rat is also common and the water vole is often mistaken for it. Rats swim readily but they are not so skilful as water voles and always come out looking bedraggled since their fur is not waterproof. Voles and rats cause major problems through burrowing into the canal banks.

Few people realise that Birmingham has a large fox population, at night in early springtime you may hear the eerie wailing call of the vixen and the sharp yapping bark of the dog fox as they advertise their willingness to mate. Foxes are useful scavengers and help to keep down the rat population. The best place to see and hear them is on the Worcester & Birmingham Canal as it runs through Edgbaston, and a good time is early in the morning as they return to their earths after the night's hunting. While you are listening for foxes, you will almost certainly hear the call of the tawny owl proclaiming his territorial rights. Tawny owls are common in Birmingham, nesting in trees and old buildings.

Willows are interesting trees; apart from providing wood for cricket bats and osiers for basketmaking, their bark also contains salicin, a salt of salicilic acid. This is the major constituent of aspirin. On the canal, willows provide a refuge for many small birds, and food for many tiny animals, for example the larvae of the pussmoth. This beautiful bright green caterpillar with its velvety-brown back is well camouflaged. When disturbed, however, it extends two large bright red tails which it lashes about fiercely, rearing the front part of its body into the air and presenting its bright pink face to a potential enemy. If you are not deterred by this display, the caterpillar may as a last resort squirt formic acid at you.

These are just a few of the many fascinating plants and animals which can be found on the Birmingham Canal Navigations.

Smethwick

The Worcester & Birmingham Canal terminates in Worcester Bar Basin (Gas Street), at the famous Worcester Bar. The main line of the Birmingham Canal Navigations (BCN) leaves the basin, passing immediately under Broad Street Bridge, which has been extended so many times that it is now virtually a tunnel; the towpath continues beside the canal. North of Broad Street is Farmer's Bridge Junction, a canal crossroads. Here the Birmingham & Fazeley Canal swings away to the east, passing immediately Cambrian Wharf and the Longboat pub, and then starting the descent through 13 very tidy locks to Aston Junction (see page 36). The main line turns west at Farmer's Bridge, while the short Oozells Street loop goes to the south, quickly disappearing behind old warehouses. This loop, and the others further along, are surviving parts of Brindley's original contour canal, now known as the Birmingham Canal Old Main Line, which pursued a rather meandering course. The delays caused by this prompted the Birmingham Canal Company to commission Telford to build a straighter line, the Birmingham Canal New Main Line. This was constructed between 1823 and 1838, and when completed reduced Brindley's old 22½-mile canal to 15 miles. The Oozells Street loop reappears from the south, and then, after 2 bridges, the Icknield Port loop leaves to the south. This loop acts as a feeder from Rotton Park reservoir; adjoining it are the BWB maintenance yard and area offices. Originally built to supply water to the Birmingham Canal, the reservoir is now used for water sports and recreation as well. The loop rejoins after ¼ mile at another canal crossroads—the Winson Green or Soho loop, which leaves the main line opposite the Icknield Port loop. This last loop is the longest of the 3, running in a gentle arc for over a mile before rejoining the main line again. It is also the only loop to have a towpath throughout its length. At its eastern end are Hockley Basins, formerly railway-owned but now a recreational area for the young people of Birmingham. There are house boats, a community hall, toilets, showers, dry dock and workshops. At the point where the loop rejoins, there is an island in the middle of the canal, the site of one of the many toll offices that existed throughout the system. The main line continues towards Smethwick, still flanked on both banks by factories and warehouses, none of which pays any attention to the canal. A railway crosses to the west, the busy electrified main line that accompanies the canal all the way to Wolverhampton, and then a gentle curve leads to Smethwick Junction. Here there is a choice of routes; Brindley's old main line swings to the right, while Telford's new main line continues straight ahead. The 2 routes run side by side, but the old line climbs to a higher level via the 3 Smethwick Locks. Here there are 2 flights of locks side by side, the extra flight built by Smeaton to overcome the traffic hold-up. Brindley's original flight is now disused and so boats should use the southern or left-hand locks—Smeaton's flight. Beyond the junction, Telford's new line enters a steep-sided cutting. This 40ft-deep cutting enabled Telford to avoid the changes in level of the old line, and thus speed the flow of traffic. The 2 routes continue their parallel courses, the one overlooking the other, until the lower line passes under the Telford Aqueduct. This elegant single span cast-iron structure carries the Engine Branch, a short feeder canal that leaves the old line, crosses the new line, and then turns back to the south for a short distance. This arm is named after the first Boulton & Watt steam pumping engine to be bought by the Birmingham Canal Company. This continued to feed the old summit level for 120 years. It was then moved to Ocker Hill to pump water from disused mine workings until the 1950s when it was finally retired. (It is now in the Birmingham Museum of Science & Industry.) It is easy to walk from the new line up to the old at this point, although there is no access to the surrounding area from the canals. This isolation has meant that the canals are an oasis among the drab industrial surroundings. The sides of the cutting are richly covered with

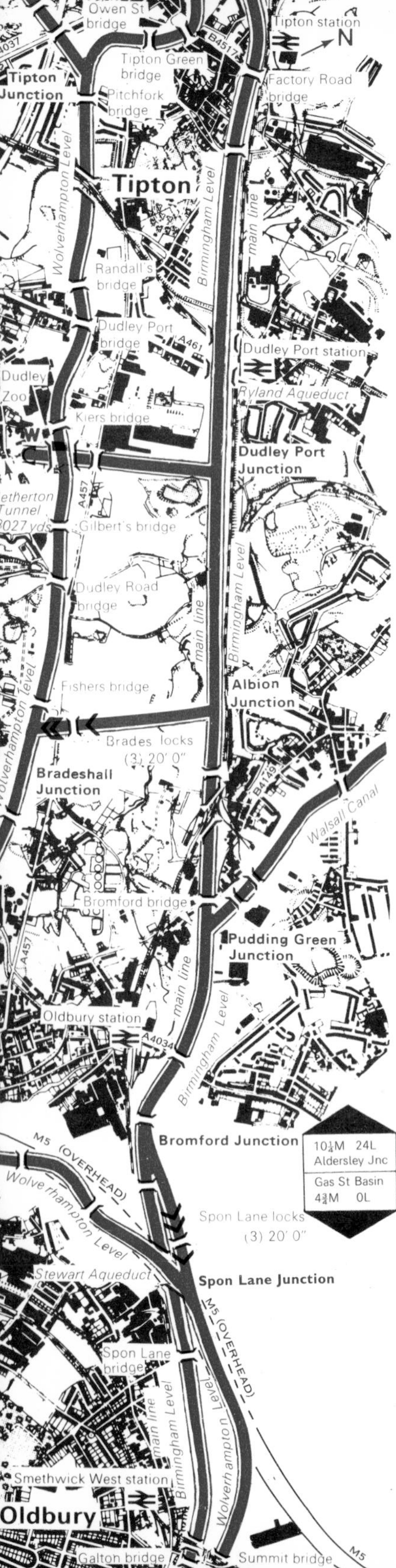

wild flowers and blackberry bushes, and the seclusion of the whole area has turned it into an unofficial nature reserve. The old pumping station at Brasshouse Lane is to be restored after years of disuse as part of the new Galton Valley Canal Park development. The 2 canals continue through this natural wilderness to Telford's Galton Bridge, which carries Roebuck Lane across the cutting in one magnificent 150ft cast-iron span. This famous bridge is preserved as an ancient monument.

PUBS

Long Boat Cambrian Wharf. Canalside pub with strong Waterways theme—one of the bars is a floating narrow boat. Ansells real ale, food usually available.

Dudley

The old and the new Birmingham canal lines continue their parallel course, and soon the pleasant semi-rural isolation of the cutting ends, to be replaced by a complex meeting of 3 types of transport system. The M5 motorway swings in from the east, carried high above the canal on the slender concrete pillars; the railway stays close beside Telford's new line; and the canals enter a series of junctions that seem to anticipate modern motorway practice. The new line leaves the cutting, and continues in a straight line through industrial surroundings. It passes under Stewart Aqueduct, and then reaches Bromford Junction. Here a canal 'sliproad' links the old and the new lines via the 3 Spon Lane Locks, joining the new at an angle from the east. The old line swings south west following the 473ft contour parallel to the M5, crossing the new line on Stewart Aqueduct. Thus canal crosses canal on a flyover. Spon Lane Locks, the linking 'sliproad', survive unchanged from Brindley's day, and are among the oldest in the country. The old and the new lines now follow separate courses. The old line continues below the motorway to Oldbury Locks Junction. Here the short Titford Canal, not shown on this map, climbs away to the south via the 6 Oldbury Locks; this canal serves as a feeder from Rotton Park reservoir. After the junction the old line swings round to the north west, and continues on a parallel course to the new line once again, but a mile to the south. At Bradeshall Junction the Gower Branch links the 2 lines, descending to the lower level of the new line through 3 locks, 2 of which are a staircase, unique on the BCN. At Tividale the old line crosses the Netherton Tunnel Branch on an aqueduct, another canal flyover, and then continues to Tipton Junction. To the south west is the branch leading to Dudley Tunnel, reopened in 1973 after joint restoration by volunteers, BWB and Dudley Corporation. This branch connects with the Dudley Canal, the Stourbridge Canal, and thus with the Staffs & Worcs. The old line turns north at the junction, turning towards the new line which it rejoins at Factory Junction. After Bromford the new line continues its straight course towards Wolverhampton. At Pudding Green Junction the main line goes straight on; the right fork leads to Wednesbury, the Walsall Canal route to the Wyrley & Essington Canal, and the Tame Valley Canal to Rushall, and Salford Junction. Beyond Pudding Green the railway crosses to the north bank, staying close beside the canal. At Albion Junction the Gower Branch turns south to join the old link at Bradeshall. At Dudley Port Junction the Netherton Tunnel Branch joins the main line, having passed under the old line at Tividale. The tunnel mouth can be seen from the junction. The Netherton Branch goes through the tunnel to Windmill End Junction; from here boats can either turn south down the old Dudley Canal to Hawne Basin, or west towards the Stourbridge Canal, and thus to the Staffs & Worcs. North of Dudley Port the new line crosses a main road on the Ryland Aqueduct; this structure was completely rebuilt in 1968, because the narrowness of the old aqueduct was hindering a road rebuilding scheme. One of the cast-iron name plates from the original aqueduct is preserved at the Waterways Museum, Stoke Bruerne. There is a convenient

access point for walkers at the aqueduct, and all services for boats are close at hand. Continuing its elevated course the new line reaches Tipton, where there are attractive landscaped moorings with all services close by. Tipton station is right by the canal, and it is possible to walk from platform to towpath. Leaving the station, Factory Bottom Lock comes into view, the first of 3 which carry the new main line up to join the old Wolverhampton level.

Bilston

The new line climbs the 3 Factory Locks, flanked by the old boatmen's mission and weigh-house, now industrial premises, and then immediately reaches Factory Junction, where the old line comes in from the south. The long parallel course of the 2 canals is over. Uninviting and drab surroundings flank the canal as it approaches Coseley. Here there is a short tunnel, another sign of Telford's new route, for the old canal used to wind round Coseley Hill. The tunnel is of wide bore, with a towpath on each side; the style is the same as the much longer Netherton Tunnel, opened in 1858, and indeed Coseley was cut to the same specification, as a trial run. Beyond the tunnel, the canal continues straight to Deepfields Junction. Here the old canal swings away to the east in what was once a long, meandering loop (the Wednesbury Oak loop) passing through the heart of the Black Country. The southern half of the loop has been filled in, leaving 2 miles of twisting canal which end at Bradley repair yard, a BWB maintenance depot where among other things, lock gates are made. Just before Deepfields there is a boatyard, with groups of narrow boats belonging to Alfred Matty. There is easy access here, and from here to Wolverhampton access to and from the towpath at locks and bridges is much simpler. North of the junction the canal swings in a curve round the site of Bilston Steel Works, where the blast furnace was the last example working in the country. The canal now continues its wandering course towards Horseley Fields Junction, its twisting and turning revealing that Brindley's original line was not altered by Telford north of Deepfields.

Navigational note

Between Bromford Junction and Factory Junction the new main line is crossed by a series of 2-arched bridges. Boats going towards Wolverhampton should pass through the northern, or *right-hand* arches. The other ones are shallow, and sometimes impassable. Likewise, boats passing in the same direction should keep to the *right* of toll office islands.

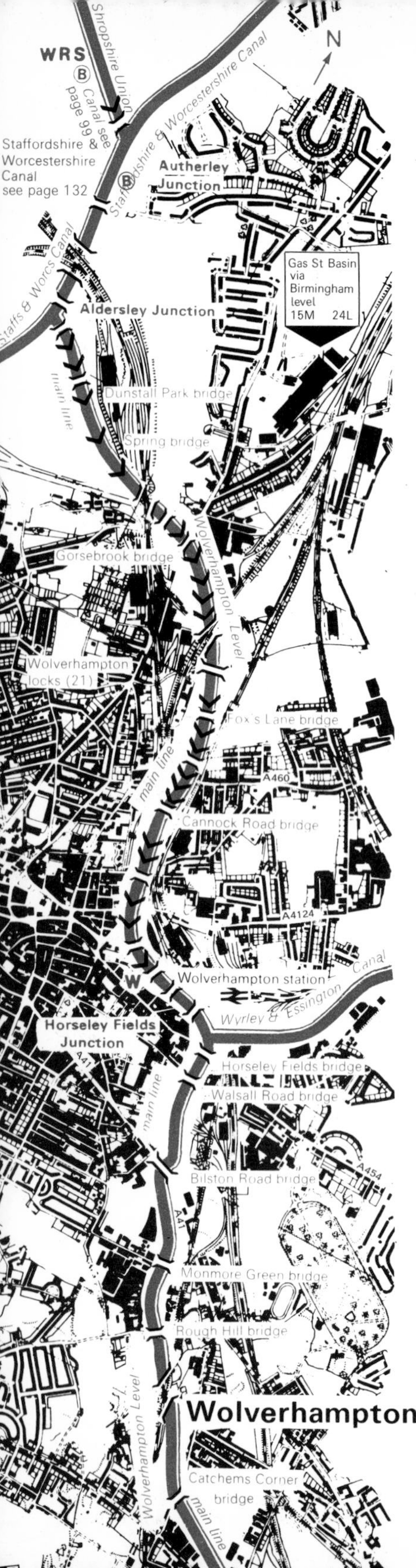

Wolverhampton

The canal continues its winding course through the heart of industrial Wolverhampton. Factories surround the canal, shutting it off from the rest of the town, but access is not difficult. Just north of Bilston Road Bridge there is a railway-canal interchange basin (Chillington Wharf), still intact, the sidings running beside the covered wharf. It is a reminder of the busy traffic that once filled the BCN. At Horseley Fields Junction, set in the middle of Wolverhampton, the main line goes straight on. To the east, the Wyrley & Essington Canal starts its meandering contour course towards Brownhills. Originally this canal continued through Lichfield to join the Coventry Canal at Huddlesford, but now it has largely vanished east of Ogley Junction. However it is still possible to complete a wide circle via the Rushall and Tame Valley Canals. Soon after the junction the canal reaches the top lock of the Wolverhampton flight. From here 21 locks carry the canal down to join the Staffordshire & Worcestershire Canal at Aldersley Junction. The locks take the canal from the heaviest industry to quiet open countryside, a sharp contrast with the miles of industrial canal that lie to the south. Half the locks are flanked by industry, and railways criss-cross over and around the canal, but gradually this background yields until the last 3 locks are virtually rural. Access is possible at several places in the flight, but the most convenient services are near the Cannock Road Bridge and the Stafford Road Bridge. Beyond the bottom lock there is a welcome old-fashioned brick arched bridge, and then the Birmingham Canal main line ends at Aldersley Junction, inconspicuous when approached from the Staffs & Worcs. (For the Staffordshire & Worcestershire Canal, see page 133.)

Waterways of the BCN

Cruising the BCN is an unusual, and often dramatic, experience; the canals provide a continuous panorama of the history of the Black Country, and of the Industrial Revolution. There are frequent reminders of the importance of the canals in the development of the area, the toll islands isolated in the middle of the canal, the railway interchange basins, the factory arms and basins, often revealed today only by the arch of the towpath bridge buried in the brickwork, the loading bays of the factories which at one time were totally dependent upon the canals, the engine houses (the best example near the south portal of Netherton Tunnel), and the disused and abandoned arms and branches, some closed so long ago that their course is now difficult to trace. Although industry has turned its back on the BCN, the canals are far from derelict or depressing. Scattered among the older buildings are new developments, many of which accept the canal as a natural part of the landscape. Cambrian Wharf is the obvious example, but in a different way the motorway interchange (commonly known as 'Spaghetti Junction'), built in the air above Salford Junction and the Tame Valley Canal, and the Post Office Tower that dominates Farmer's Bridge Locks are equally impressive. Not all the BCN is built up and industrial. For most of its length the Wyrley & Essington is a rural canal, following a winding contour line. The Rushall Canal and the Daw End Branch are also largely undeveloped, offering a quiet alternative to the busy Birmingham main line. Even the industrial stretches are often quiet and remote, enjoying the isolation imposed on them by the end of commercial traffic. Kestrels now hover above the waters of the Walsall Canal.

The guide does not cover all the BCN in the usual scale, and so details of many of the features that make up the BCN network are given alphabetically below.

Anglesey Branch
The branch leaves the Wyrley & Essington Canal at Ogley Junction, and runs north west to Chasewater. It is predominantly a rural canal, passing through heathland before ending in the wide basin, overshadowed by the dam that contains the reservoir. Despite its rural nature, this canal saw the last regular coal traffic on the BCN, carrying coal from the Cannock mines until 1967. Landscaping and tree planting has been carried out along the route, and Anglesey Wharf can still be seen. The branch is the ideal approach to the pleasure park that now surrounds the reservoir.

Cannock Extension Canal
Opened in 1858, the Cannock Extension was built to serve the coalmines of Cannock Chase. It was the last BCN canal to be built, and it was also one of the last to carry regular commercial traffic. As built it ran in a straight line to Churchbridge Locks which linked it with the Staffs & Worcs Canal, but the northern half has vanished completely beneath the A5 and the neighbouring coalfields. It now serves Norton Canes Docks, a centre for narrow boat building and maintenance. Despite its recent industrial past, the Cannock Extension is totally rural; heath and woodland surround it, and there are few buildings to be seen. The water is clear, the towpath rich in wild flowers. The late building of the canal is revealed by its straightness, and by the distinctive blue brick bridges.

Dudley Canal
The Dudley Canal, whose history is intimately involved with that of the Stourbridge Canal, was built in several stages. Today it survives only in truncated form, but still serves as the vital link between the BCN and the west of England via the Staffs & Worcs Canal. The canal starts at the 8 Black Delph Locks, which were rebuilt in 1858. The 9 old locks can be seen to the west of the present flight. Park Head Locks, reopened in 1973, lead to Dudley Tunnel. From Park Head Junction the canal continues eastwards along a meandering contour line which takes it round Netherton Hill, dominated by the tower of Netherton Church. Much of the land around the canal is open land, so there are good views to the south. After the short Bumblehole Branch, the canal divides at Windmill End Junction. The northern line leads to Netherton Tunnel, the southern to Hawne or Coombeswood Basin. Originally this line continued in a wide circle to join the Worcester & Birmingham Canal via the notorious Lappal Tunnel, which was closed in 1917 because of subsidence. 3795yds long, this rocky tunnel was the longest in the BCN network and one of the narrowest in the country. The short Gosty Hill Tunnel (577yds) precedes Hawne Basin, the present end of the Dudley Canal.

Dudley Tunnel
Reopened to boats in 1973 with the rebuilding of Park Head Locks, Dudley Tunnel is one of the wonders of the BCN. This narrow tunnel, 3172yds long, was opened in 1792, after the usual delays and problems, to connect with the Birmingham Canal at Tipton. Inside the tunnel there is a vast network of natural caverns, basins and branches serving old quarries and mines. In all there are over 5000yds of underground waterway, some cut off and abandoned, others still accessible. Internal combustion engines must not be used in this tunnel.

Netherton Tunnel
Opened in 1858, Netherton was the last canal tunnel to be built in Britain, and the most luxurious, 3027yds long, it was built with a bore sufficient to allow a towpath on both sides, and when opened it was equipped with gas lighting, later converted to electricity. The Netherton line joins the Birmingham main line at Dudley Port. The tunnel was built to relieve congestion in the Dudley Tunnel, and runs on a parallel course.

Tame Valley Canal
Opened in 1844, the canal was built to overcome the long delays caused by the Farmer's Bridge

Birmingham and the Black Country

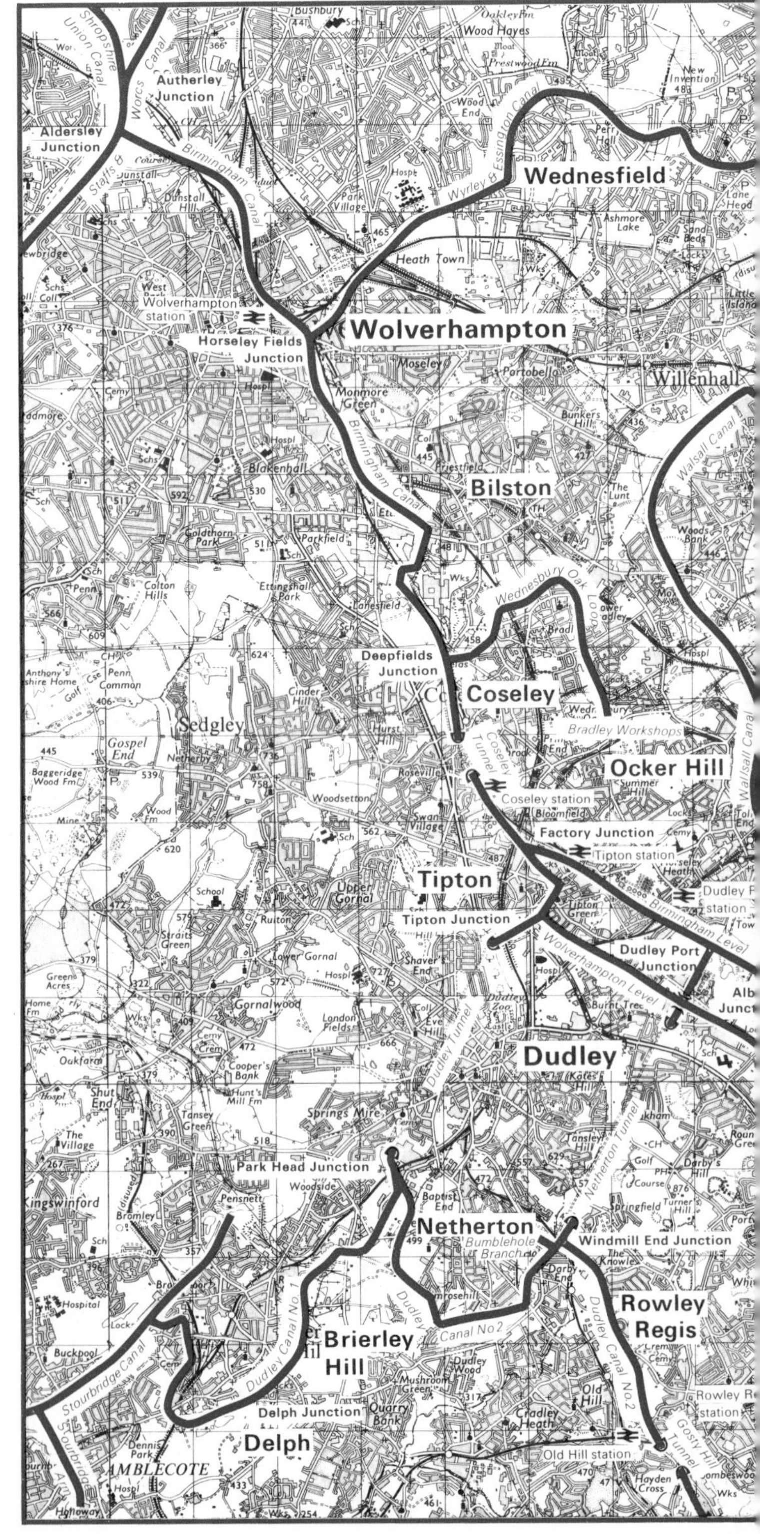

Daw End
Birchills Junction
Walsall station
Walsall
Wyrley & Essington Canal
Walsall Branch
Daw End Branch
Rushall Canal
Bescot station
Wednesbury
Tame Valley Canal
Rushall Junction
Tame Valley Junction
Ridgacre Branch
Great Barr station
Perry Barr
Ryder's Green Junction
West Bromwich
Perry Barr station
Pudding Green Junction
Spon Lane Junction
Bromford Junction
Oldbury Junction
Smethwick Rolfe Street station
Smethwick Junction
Winson Green
Oldbury
Titford Canal
Smethwick West station
Engine Branch
Soho Loop
Smethwick
Langley station
Farmers Bridge Junction
Icknield Port Loop
Birmingham & Fazeley Canal
Rotton Park Reservoir
Warley
Oozells Street Loop
New Street station
Worcester & Birmingham Canal
Birmingham

Locks. With towpaths on both banks, this straight canal leaves the Birmingham & Fazeley at Salford Junction, its north-westerly course overshadowed at first by the motorway. As it climbs Perry Barr Locks it comes into more open country, passing through the gradual stages of suburbia. There is a fine view of Birmingham from the top of the locks. At Rushall Junction the canal swings to the west, crossing the M5 motorway, the railway and the River Tame on one great embankment. Its elevated course continues as the surroundings become more industrial, and finally it joins the Walsall Canal at Tame Valley Junction, dwarfed by the cooling towers of Ocker Hill power station. The Rushall Canal was built in 1847 to connect the Tame Valley with the Daw End Branch of the Wyrley & Essington, and thus to capture some of the coal trade from the Cannock mines. It continues the northern line of the Tame Valley Canal to Longwood Junction, the 9 locks raising the canal through open country.

Titford Canal

Opened in 1837, the canal climbed originally to Causeway Green via the 6 Oldbury Locks. Today it survives in shortened form, serving as a feeder from Rotton Park reservoir and terminating at Titford Pools, the site of two IWA National Rallies.

Walsall Canal

The Walsall Canal runs from Ryder's Green Junction to Birchills Junction, making an alternative link between the Birmingham Canal main line and the Wyrley & Essington. It connects with the Tame Valley Canal. It was started in 1786 as a branch from the Birmingham line to serve Walsall, but did not reach Walsall until 1799. The link with the Wyrley & Essington was not made until 1841 because of company rivalry, but in that year the short Walsall Branch Canal was built to connect the 2 via 8 locks. The course of the Walsall Canal is largely industrial, with a large number of basins, wharves and old arms. Despite the industry the canal is now quiet and remote, for much of its surroundings are now derelict.

Wednesbury Old Canal

The specification for the original Birmingham Canal included a branch to Wednesbury, to leave the main line at Pudding Green Junction. It was opened in 1769. Today it serves as a vital link between the Birmingham main line and the Walsall Canal, while its original course survives as the Ridgeacre Branch, continuing eastwards towards West Bromwich.

Wyrley & Essington Canal

Opened throughout in 1797, the canal connected the Birmingham Canal with the Birmingham & Fazeley, running in a meandering contour line from Horseley Fields Junction to Huddlesford, via Lichfield. From Huddlesford it was able to connect with the Coventry, Oxford and Trent & Mersey Canals. The Wyrley & Essington was prompted by the coal trade, and there were several branches to serve the various coalfields. However its trade did not really develop until the Cannock fields were exploited in the 19thC. The most important was the Hay Head (or Daw End) Branch, running southwards from Catshill Junction, for this was later linked with the Tame Valley Canal via Rushall. The Wyrley & Essington was built as a rural canal, and today this is still largely the case. Most of its wandering course takes it through heath and woodland, although there are continual reminders of the industrial heritage of the area. The water is clear, and a great variety of plants grow on the towpath. In 1954 the main line between Ogley Junction and Huddlesford was abandoned, and much of this has now completely vanished, although its course through Lichfield and west of Huddlesford can still be traced. Today the canal ends abruptly at Ogley, but its connections with the Tame Valley and Walsall Canals, and with the Birmingham main line, make it an important part of the BCN network, a part that is emphasised by the rural nature of the canal.

The old main line of the BCN at Smethwick. *Derek Pratt*

Birmingham and the Black Country

Geographically the Black Country is a large area of the Midlands stretching north west from Birmingham. Birmingham is not part of the Black Country, but could be called the root from which the whole area developed. The Black Country is a vast industrial conurbation, filling a square roughly bounded by Stourbridge, Wolverhampton, Brownhills and Birmingham. Many of the towns and villages swallowed by this square are old enough to have individual histories dating back to the medieval period and beyond. Although these are often very hard to trace today, the traditions die hard, and each town tries to preserve some vestige of individuality. The large-scale industrial development is comparatively recent, for prior to the 18thC the area was still predominantly agricultural; since medieval times there had been some exploitation of mineral resources, iron, coal, limestone and clay, and the area was known for its lock, nail and buckle making, a localised and limited industrial development. The great change came in the 18thC when, following Abraham Darby's example at Coalbrookdale, the Midlands iron founders turned to smelting with coke instead of charcoal. All the necessary ingredients were available in the area in huge quantities, and so industrial growth was inevitably very rapid. Iron works and coal mines soon filled the landscape, and at the same time existing industries, for example the glass making at Stourbridge, underwent rapid expansion. The land and sky, darkened by smoke and industrial debris, gradually assumed the familiar character of the Black Country, and the foundations of 19thC prosperity were laid.

A vital part of the industrial development of the Black Country was the network of canals, well established by the end of the 18thC. These were built to ease communication within the area, and to connect it with markets throughout England and Europe. They provided the essential transport links which were the foundation of the prosperity of the Black Country.

Birmingham
West Midlands. Birmingham is not well known as one of the great tourist centres of Britain. Although the city has a medieval past—Smithfield Market stands on the site of a moated manor, and the Bull Ring shopping centre is named after the habit of bull baiting—Birmingham is a memorial to the Industrial Revolution of the 18th and 19thC. Industrial and commercial development occurred so rapidly throughout the 19thC that the city soon became the trade centre of the Midlands, and of England generally. It still holds this position today, and extensive rebuilding programmes have made it one of the most modern cities in Britain, with an elaborate system of urban motorways that inevitably pay scant heed to anyone wanting to walk round the city. The growth of Birmingham during the late 18thC was aided by many famous industrialists and scientists who lived in the area, for example John Baskerville, William Murdock, Joseph Priestley, Matthew Boulton, James Watt.

The development of the Black Country conurbation has inevitably merged many of the original towns and villages, and it is difficult to be aware of town boundaries while navigating the canals.

The centre of Birmingham is easily accessible from Gas Street Basin. There are pubs, restaurants, theatres, cinemas and museums to suit all tastes, but of particular interest to those on the canals will be the:

Black Country Museum
Tipton Road, Dudley. (021-557 9643). An open air museum of original buildings re-erected on the site. Workers' homes, shops, the Bottle and Glass pub (where you can buy a pint) and tram rides. There is a restored colliery, a replica Newcomen engine, and a chain-makers' workshop. Down by the canal there are lime kilns, a boat dock, and trips through Dudley Tunnel. The steam narrow boat 'President' is based here, although it may be away at rallies etc during the summer months. *Open 10.00–17.00 Apr to Dec. Admission charge.*

BOATYARDS

Ⓑ **Canal Transport Services** Norton Canes Docks, Lime Lane, Pelsall, Staffs. (Brownhills 4370). On the Cannock Extension Canal. R S W P D Gas, chandlery, drydock and slipway, moorings, winter storage, boat-building, sales and repairs, inboard engine sales and repairs.
Ⓑ **M. E. Braine** Norton Canes Docks, Lime Lane, Pelsall, Staffs. (Brownhills 4888). On the Cannock Extension Canal. R S W D Gas, slipway, moorings and winter storage, toilets, boat-building and conversions, inboard engine sales and repairs. *Closed Sat afternoon and Sun.*
Alfred Matty Biddings Lane, Deepfields, Coseley, Staffs. (Bilston 42725). On the BCN main line. Dredging and piling contractors, waterways maintenance and construction work. Boats built in their yard.
Ⓑ **Brummagem Boats** Sherborne Street Wharf (Oozell's Street loop). (021-643 8397). R S W D E Pump-out, boat hire, gas, boat building and repairs, chandlery, books and souvenirs, brokerage, toilets, safe mooring close to the city centre. *Winter Sun by appointment only.*
British Waterways Board
Area Office, Icknield Port Road, Birmingham. (021-454 7091).

BOAT TRIPS

Dudley Tunnel
Trips through the 3172yd tunnel in an electric narrow boat based at the Black Country Museum. For information contact the Black Country Museum, (021-557 9643).

The Dog & Doublet, Bodymoor Heath, on the Birmingham & Fazeley Canal. *David Perrott*

BIRMINGHAM & FAZELEY

Maximum dimensions

Length: 72′
Beam: 7′
Headroom: 7′ 6″

Mileage

FARMER'S BRIDGE JUNCTION (Birmingham Canal) to ASTON JUNCTION (Digbeth Branch): 1½
SALFORD JUNCTION (Tame Valley Canal): 3¼
Minworth Top Lock: 6¼
Curdworth Tunnel: 8½
Bodymoor Heath Bridge: 11½
FAZELEY JUNCTION (Coventry Canal): 15 miles
Hopwas: 17¾
Whittington Brook: 20½

Locks: 38

Digbeth Branch

ASTON JUNCTION (main line) to DIGBETH Basin: 1 mile, 6 locks

The Birmingham & Fazeley has never been more than a useful junction canal. It was authorised in 1784, after a great deal of opposition from the well established Birmingham Canal Company (who very soon merged with it), as a link between Birmingham and the south east. Until then, London-bound goods from Birmingham had to go right round by the River Severn. Naturally the canal was useless until the Coventry Canal had at least reached Fazeley, but the new B & F company ensured—even before its enabling Act was passed—that the other canals important to its success were completed. Thus at Coleshill in 1782 the Oxford Canal Company agreed to finish its line to Oxford and the Thames; the Coventry Canal Company agreed to extend its line from Atherstone to Fazeley; the new B & F company agreed to build its proposed line and continue it along the defaulting Coventry route from Fazeley to Whittington Brook; and the Trent & Mersey Company pledged to finish the Coventry's line from Whittington Brook to Fradley Junction on the T & M.

This rare example of co-operation among canal companies paid off; when in 1790 the great joint programme was finished, traffic immediately began to flow along the system. The Birmingham & Fazeley employed John Smeaton to build their canal: he completed it in 1789. The flights of narrow locks at Farmer's Bridge and Aston became very congested, especially after the Warwick canals had joined up with the B & F at Digbeth; 2 new canals were built to bypass this permanent obstacle, one on each side. The Tame Valley Canal and the Birmingham & Warwick Junction Canal were opened in 1844, and traffic flowed more smoothly. After this the Birmingham & Fazeley Canal became more attractive to carriers and it continued to be an important link route—which it remains.

Birmingham

Turning north east off the main line of the Birmingham Canal, one arrives shortly at Cambrian Wharf—a startlingly attractive canal basin with a modern canal pub, BWB moorings and a generally smart and tidy appearance, all overlooked by 4 big blocks of flats. There are some well-painted locks too, for from this point the Farmers Bridge flight of 13 locks descends steeply into the heart of Birmingham. Many of the locks were built very close together and so the intervening pounds were expanded as much as possible in every direction. This results in one side of each lock becoming like a peninsula, flanked by water. Restoration work has made the passage through the locks a more attractive prospect than it once was. There is now a public viewing area at Newhall Bridge, by the Science Museum, an indication of how the forgotten world of the Birmingham canals is being opened up to the residents. After passing the base of Birmingham's Post Office Tower the canal levels out as the locks come to an end. But soon comes Aston Junction, marked by the old iron turnover bridge, on which is cast 'Horseley Iron Works Staffordshire 1828'. To the north east is the main line of the Birmingham & Fazeley, falling through the 11 Aston locks to Salford Junction. The area of the junction by Ashted Top Lock has been landscaped and tidied up, another sign of the steady regeneration taking place on the Birmingham canals. One of the bridges along here has girders that restrict the headroom to 7ft 9in; nearby is a canalside petrol station. At the second lock from the bottom is a lock keeper's cottage; its gate onto the road gives access to a small grocery, a petrol station and a pub. The towpath is in excellent condition. Towards Salford Junction itself, the buildings become fewer and lower. A half-sunken narrow boat along here provides a wonderful natural water-garden for many flowering weeds. Up above, motorways fill the sky.

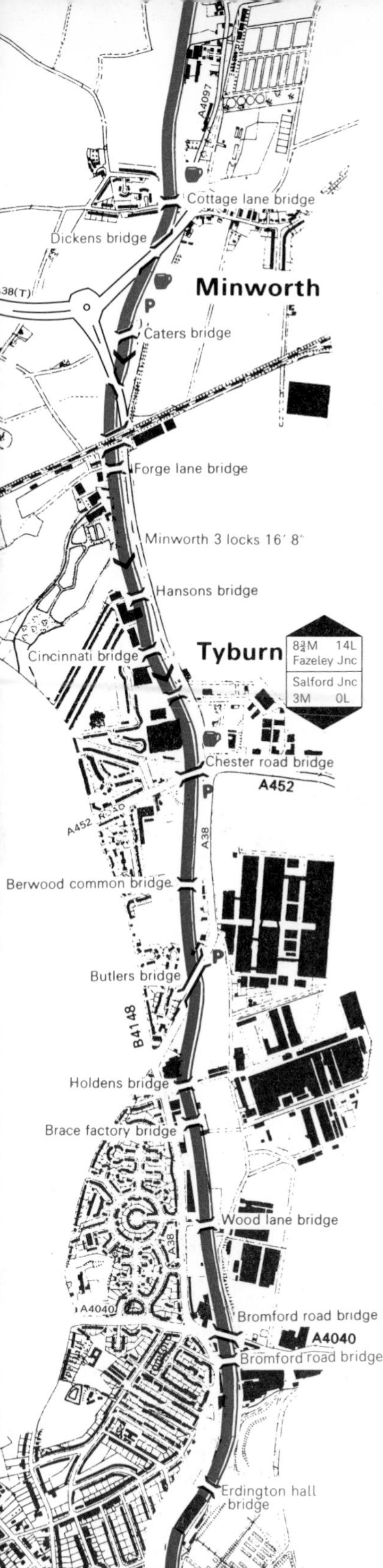

Tyburn

Leaving behind the motorway interchange at Salford Junction, the Birmingham and Fazeley Canal runs eastwards out of Birmingham. Power stations give way to industry, which in turn is slowly replaced by the spreading Birmingham suburbs. Named bridges are a feature of this stretch, a useful means of orientation, while at one point (near Erdington Hall Bridge) the canal is actually roofed over for 150yds by an enormous industrial building. As the canal progresses, the water becomes clearer. All facilities are readily available along the canal, although the factories limit the access; the bridge carrying the A452 across the canal at Tyburn is a convenient access point. Most of the factories ignore the canal, although the Cincinnati works are a laudable exception: landscaped lawns and gardens run down from the buildings to the water's edge. Minworth Locks start the descent.

PUBS

Hare & Hound Minworth. Canalside, by Cottage Lane Bridge. Food.

Boat Minworth. Canalside, by Caters Bridge. Ansells real ale, snacks.

Tyburn House Chester Road Bridge (just above top lock). Canalside.

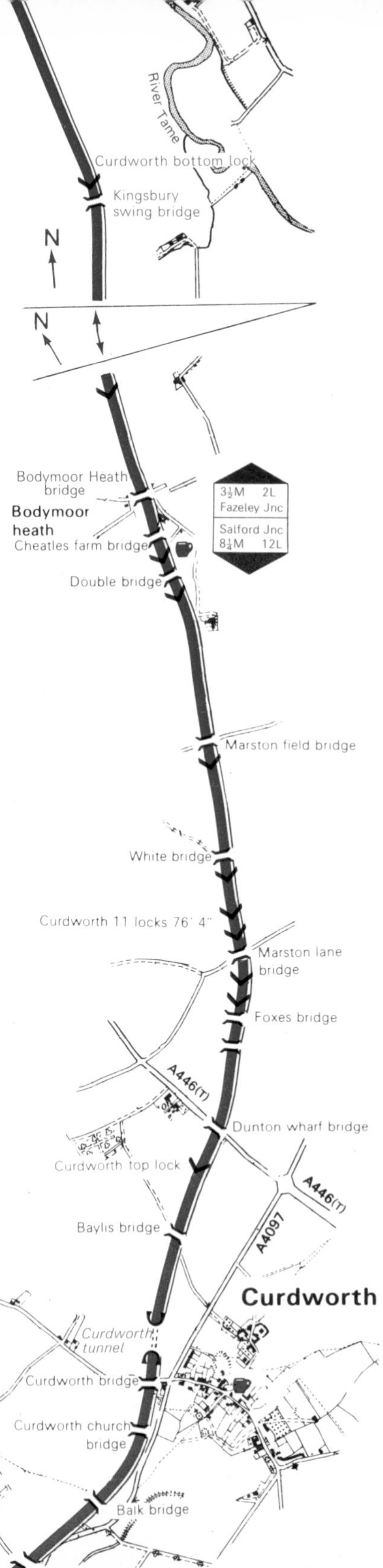

Curdworth

Continuing north east the canal leaves the industry that has followed it from Birmingham. A short cutting leads to Curdworth, whose church tower has been visible for some time. The cutting continues past the village, light woods screening it from view, and then the canal enters a short tunnel (57yds). The towing path passes through the tunnel, but it is very slippery. From now on until Fazeley the canal flows in complete isolation through the empty fields, only the 11 locks falling down to the junction breaking its journey. The lack of hedges is very noticeable, and partly explains the bleakness of this area; only the towing path hedge seems to have survived. As the canal swings to the north, hedges and trees reappear, and after Bodymoor Heath the trees line the canal on both sides for 2 miles. By the bottom lock there is a swing bridge, the first of 2 on this canal. The A4097 leaves the canal at Curdworth, where the A446 crosses.

Bodymoor Heath
Warwicks. PO, tel. A scattered village beyond which gravel pits, many flooded and overgrown, break up the fields. Yet amidst the dereliction are occasional 18thC buildings, surviving as a memory of the pre-industrial Midlands. The pub, the 'Dog & Doublet' is a fine example.

Curdworth
Warwicks. PO, tel, stores, garage. Set between 2 main roads in a predominantly industrial area. The squat church is partly Norman; note the finely carved font.

PUBS

Dog & Doublet Bodymoor Heath. Canalside. M & B real ale, snacks.

Beehive Curdworth. Ansells real ale. Food.

White Horse Curdworth. M & B real ale. Food.

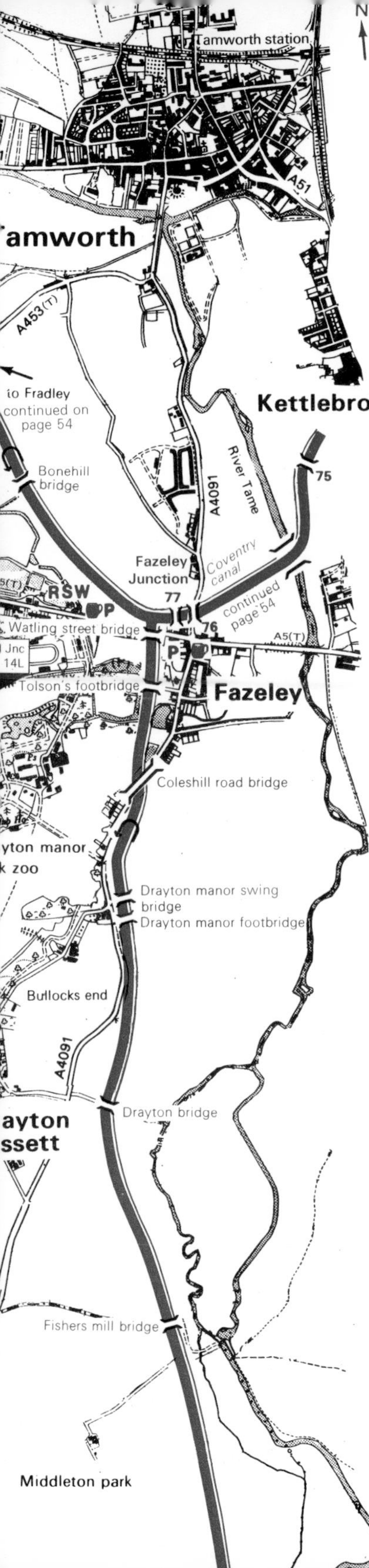

Fazeley

Continuing north, the canal runs through open farmland, flanked on both sides by oak trees, their roots projecting into the water. The isolation of the canal ends at Drayton Bassett where the A4091 swings into run parallel to the canal as far as Fazeley. By Drayton Bassett is a curious footbridge, a marvellous folly, and immediately after it the second swing bridge. These features make the Birmingham and Fazeley Canal pleasantly eccentric, despite its unexciting course. The country gives way to the outskirts of Fazeley, which are quickly followed by the junction with the Coventry Canal. There are no locks. Fazeley is bisected by the A5 and A4091.

Fazeley
Staffs. EC Wed. PO, tel, stores, garage. Its importance as a road and canal junction determines the character of Fazeley; it is a small, industrial centre that has grown up around the communication network. From the canal the town appears more attractive than it really is. Useful as a supply centre, with a large number of garages and fish and chip shops.
Fazeley Junction
Staffs. The Birmingham and Fazeley Canal joins the Coventry which comes in from the east. Originally the Coventry was to continue westwards to meet the Trent and Mersey at Fradley; however the Coventry company ran out of money at Fazeley, and so the Birmingham and Fazeley continued on to Whittington. The Trent & Mersey company then built a linking arm from Fradley to Whittington, which was later bought by the Coventry company, thus becoming a detached section of their canal. The architecture of the buildings at the junction is in the best tradition of the canals and its recent restoration has made it a very pleasant place to moor.
Drayton Bassett
Staffs. EC Mon. PO, tel, stores, fish & chips. The village is set ½ mile to the west of the canal. The best feature is the charming and totally unexpected Gothic style footbridge over the canal. Its twin battlemented towers would look quite commanding but for their ridiculously small size. This bridge is unique, and there seems to be no explanation for its eccentricity, thus greatly increasing its attraction.
Drayton Manor Park & Zoo Alongside the canal, off the A4091 at Drayton Manor Bridge. Formerly the house of Sir Robert Peel. 15 acres of wood and parkland with monkeys, birds, lions, pumas, llamas, sea lions and bears. Daily milking demonstration. *Open daily, Sun only in winter.*

BOATYARDS

BWB Fazeley Wharf 200yds west of the junction. R S W

PUBS

Plough & Hare Watling Street, Fazeley. Food.
Three Tuns Fazeley. Manns real ale, bar food, garden. Overnight mooring for customers. W

The Black Lion at Consall Forge, Caldon Canal. A very remote pub. *Derek Pratt*

CALDON

Maximum dimensions

Length: 72′
Beam: 7′
Headroom: 6′ 6″

Mileage

ETRURIA TOP LOCK (Trent & Mersey Canal) to
Hanley: 2
Foxley: 4½
Stockton Brook Summit: 7
Hazelhurst Junction (Leek Branch): 9½
LEEK TERMINUS: 12¼
Cheddleton flint mills: 11½
FROGHALL TERMINUS: 17

Locks: 17

The Caldon Canal—or, more correctly, the Caldon Branch of the Trent & Mersey Canal—was designed as an outlet for the Caldon limestone quarries near Froghall on to the canal system. It was opened as a single branch to Froghall in 1779, tramways being constructed to bring the vast quantities of limestone down from Caldon Low quarries a couple of miles to the east. Froghall became a very busy terminus. 18 years later the Caldon's owners, the Trent & Mersey Canal Company, decided to build a secondary branch from the Caldon Canal to Leek, the main purpose of the extension being to use the line as a feeder from their new reservoir at Rudyard. The fact that the feeders from Rudyard had to enter the summit level of the canal, and the later advent of the railway, brought about significant changes in the layout of the canal between Endon and Hazelhurst, resulting in the exciting 'cross-over' junction that exists at Denford today.

In 1811 yet another branch was completed from Froghall down the Churnet Valley for 13 miles to Uttoxeter. This branch was shortlived, however. In 1845 a railway line was built, much of the track using the canal bed. One can still trace the remaining sections of the Uttoxeter branch near the railway.

The limestone from Froghall remained the chief commodity carried on the Caldon Canal for years. With its 17 locks and roundabout route the Caldon must have been an obvious target for railway competitors. However, the canal, with the rest of the Trent & Mersey, was owned by a railway company (the North Staffordshire Railway) from the 1840s onward, so presumably the NSR saw no point in competing against itself.

But at the beginning of the 20thC a new railway line was eventually opened and inevitably canal traffic slumped badly. After that time the canal gradually deterioriated until it became more or less unnavigable in the early 1960s.

The Caldon Canal Society led the struggle to reopen the canal; public interest grew and local authorities recognised the great recreational potential of this beautiful canal for the thousands of people living in the nearby Potteries. Much was achieved in the way of essential works by BWB and volunteer efforts and the canal was finally fully reopened to navigation in 1974, representing a splendid addition to the cruising network, and a much-needed 'linear park' for the Potteries.

Hanley

The Caldon Branch of the Trent & Mersey Canal leaves the main line at Etruria Top Lock, negotiating a series of amazing loops and turns that leave one wondering where the canal will go to next. The first 2 locks up are 'staircase' locks—the only ones in north Staffordshire; they are set in an urban wasteland. All around, the little hills and valleys are crowded with terraced houses and factory chimneys. Planet Lock is soon reached; shops and pubs are close by. Now one passes through Hanley Park with its meticulously kept flower beds, lawns and bowling greens; east of the park, the canal twists round the built-up hillside that is topped by Hanley. As industrial stretches go, this is an interesting one, for several 'bottle' kilns still stand near the navigation, and the 'Milton Maid', 'Queen', or 'Princess' may be moored along here. These narrow boats were specially built to carry pottery along the canal to Milton: the firm that operates them finds it substantially cheaper and safer than shifting the fragile goods by road. It is ironic to reflect that Josiah Wedgwood used precisely the same argument when supporting the proposed construction of the Trent & Mersey Canal over 200 years ago. Always give way to these craft. Note that bridge 11, Ivy House, is a particularly heavy lift bridge. It may be necessary to use a mooring line to pull it open, and HOLD IT OPEN while the boat passes; however it is due to be replaced by a hydraulically operated metal bridge in 1985, which should simplify matters.

Hanley
Staffs. All services. Hanley is one of the 6 towns that were amalgamated in 1910 to form the present Stoke-on-Trent. It has been modernised and redeveloped as the shopping and business centre of the district. There is a rather unusual circular building housing Lewis's store, with a striking statue 'Fire' by David Wynne. Arnold Bennett was born here in 1867. Stoke City Museum and Art Gallery is in Broad Street, Hanley. (See page 155.)

BOATYARDS

BWB Etruria Yard at junction with Trent & Mersey Canal. (Stoke-on-Trent 25597). R S W Toilet.

PUBS

Plenty in Hanley city centre.

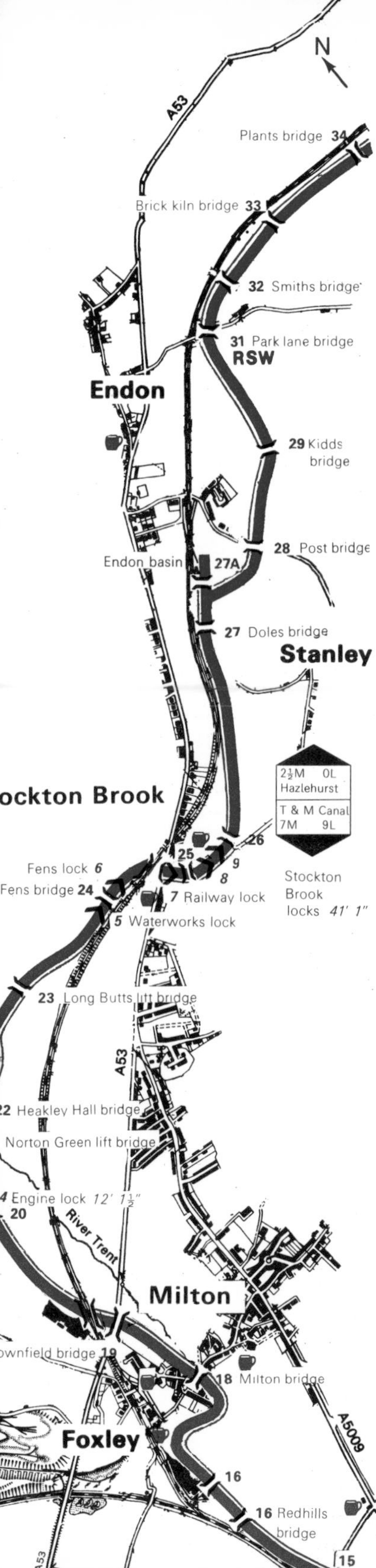

Stockton Brook

At Foxley the navigation turns sharp right: there is a pub on the corner, which is where the ½ mile-long Foxley Arm used to branch off: it is now filled in and difficult to trace. Engine Lock is not far off; it is so called because a huge beam engine used to be housed just up the hill, employed to pump water from mine workings. At the next pretty lift bridge the (unnavigable) feeder from Knypersley reservoir joins the canal. By now the countryside is thoroughly attractive, and the Potteries are safely distant. 5 locks at Stockton Brook raise the canal up to the summit level 484ft above the sea. Soon the canal begins to hug once more the side of a hill.

Endon
Staffs. PO, tel, stores, garage, bank. The real village is up the hill just north of the main road and is attractive, especially during its traditional 'well-dressing' ceremony. Good views may be had from the Victorian church. Endon Basin (built in 1917, and once a canal/railway interchange basin) is the local wharf used as the Stoke-on-Trent Boat Club's base. Near the basin are the remains of a former light railway swing bridge over the canal, where it used to join the then busy main line.

Stanley
Staffs. PO, tel, stores. A stiff climb southwards from bridge 28 leads to a brown stone hill village, still looking much as it did when farming predominated. There is, happily, little new development. There are fine views across the valley to Endon.

Stockton Brook
Staffs. PO, tel, stores. From the canal, a pleasant and useful place. The 5 locks have a charming position, with views back down the headwaters of the River Trent. There is a splendid Victorian waterworks at the bottom of the flight, and pubs and shops near the middle.

Knypersley reservoir
3½ miles north of Milton. This feeds water to the Trent & Mersey summit level via the Caldon Canal. The head of the River Trent is within its catchment area. Surrounded by woodland, the reservoir is a delightful setting for picnicking and rambling. The upper dam is covered with rhododendrons. Fishing rights are exercised by an angling club.

Milton
Staffs. PO, tel, stores, fish& chips. A little village on the side of a hill, forming an agreeable background to the canal.

PUBS

Plough Endon. Food.
Travellers Rest Stanley.
Sportsman Stockton Brook, close to Railway Lock.
Foaming Quart, Norton Green. North of bridge 21. Shops nearby.
Miners Arms Milton.
Millrace Milton.
Both the above by bridge 18.
Foxley Canalside, at the junction with the former Foxley Arm. Food, children's room.

Leek Branch

At Hazelhurst the canal divides: the main line falls through 3 locks before turning east and south to join the River Churnet, while the Leek Branch bears right along the hillside, then crosses the main line on a large aqueduct. The railway and the Endon Brook are also traversed by aqueducts: thus the Leek Branch reaches the north side of the narrow valley. After this very interesting section, the canal clings to the hillside, flanked by beautiful mature trees, as it follows the tortuous course of the River Churnet. The railway runs along the valley floor, but only the occasional goods train uses it. There is a large 'lagoon' just before the 130-yd Leek Tunnel. Beyond the tunnel, only a short stretch of canal remains, ending on a fine stone aqueduct over the River Churnet. The last ½ mile beyond the Churnet and straight along to Leek Basin has been filled in and covered with a new industrial estate. However, one can take a pleasant walk across the fields westwards by following the feeder that brings water down from Rudyard Lake into the navigation at its present terminus. An altogether delightful stretch of canal.

Leek
Staffs. EC Thur. MD Wed. All services. Essentially a textile town situated on the slope of a hill, and often referred to as the 'capital of the moors'. It was here that Thomas Parker, the first Earl of Macclesfield, was born in 1666, and his house can still be seen in the market place. James Brindley, the canal engineer, started in business as a millwright in Leek (the now restored mill is *open summer weekends*). The parish church of St Edward is 14thC, but was restored in 1856, and the chancel rebuilt in 1867.

Coombes Valley
3 miles south east of Leek. An attractive valley through which a trout stream runs. It is a reserve of the Royal Society for the Protection of Birds and it is possible to see kestrels, sparrowhawks, kingfishers, green and great spotted woodpeckers, dippers and redstarts. There are also a number of badger setts. *Open Apr–Aug Sat, Sun, Tue, Thur.* A nature trail has been laid out and guides may be obtained from the warden at Six Oaks Farm, Bradnop, near Leek, Staffs.

Rudyard Lake
3 miles north west of the canal terminus near Leek. A very long, thin reservoir in a pleasant wooded setting used for feeding water into the Trent & Mersey Canal summit level via the Caldon Canal. The Rudyard Hotel adjoins the reservoir headbank.

PUBS

Wheel ½ mile north of Horse Bridge 6.
New Inn ½ mile north west of Horse Bridge 6.
Hollybush Canalside, near bridge 38. Small traditional canal pub serving Ind Coope Burton real ale and snacks. Children's room, telephone outside.

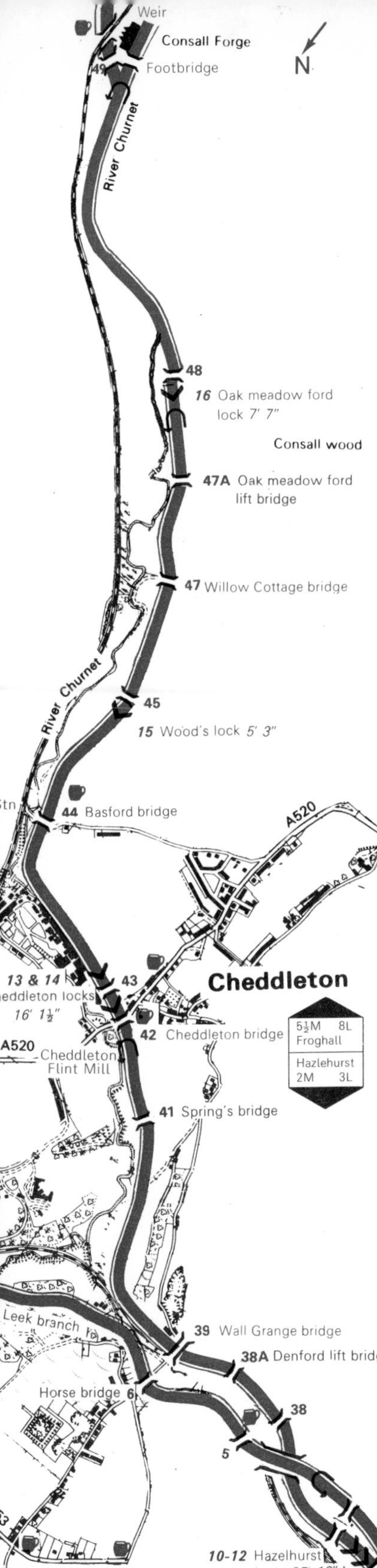

Cheddleton

Here the main line to Froghall drops down 3 locks and passes under the Leek Branch, soon taking up a position at the foot of the hills. At the former canalside Wall Grange station, the railway veers off towards Leek: it is soon replaced by the River Churnet, and the 2 waterways flow side by side for the next 7 miles. This must be one of the most beautiful valleys in Staffordshire, and the canal makes its own special contribution to the scenery. At Oakmeadow Ford Lock the canal enters the River Churnet and the 2 waterways share the same course for 1 mile to Consall Forge. See Navigational note 2. For most of the way, the Churnet valley is enclosed by very steep and thickly wooded hills whose sides reach right down to the river and adjacent canal. It is a superlative landscape, almost untouched and unspoilt by man's incursions. Yet it has been busy in the past, when boats and trains laden with limestone from Caldon competed for trade. Now the canal carries only a few pleasurecraft and the railway a few trains a day, so there is little to break the peace of this splendidly secluded place.

Navigational note 1
If your boat does not fit the Froghall Tunnel profile displayed at Cheddleton, you are reminded the last full length winding hole before the tunnel is at Consall Forge.
Navigational note 2
The canal and river share a common course between Oak Meadow Ford Lock and Consall Forge, and care should be exercised along here. If the river level is over 6in up on the gauge at Oak Meadow Ford Lock **do not enter this section.**

Cheddleton
Staffs. PO, tel, stores, garage, restaurant. A large main road rumbles through the village, but away from this are the 2 fine water mills, hard by the canal as it enters the village. These flint-grinding mills were restored to their former glory and opened to the public in 1969: the big wooden water wheels now turn at the touch of a lever. (Ground flint has always been a vital raw material for the pottery industry.) The village proper is up the steep hill, grouped about the ancient stone church of St Edward the Confessor. Little of the original building remains but the 14thC work is worth examining.
Cheddleton Flint Mill Watch two waterwheels driving the flint grinding machinery in this charming and picturesque setting. A beautifully restored narrow boat is moored at the wharf. *Open weekend afternoons.*
North Staffordshire Railway Company Cheddleton Station (Churnet Side 360522). Near bridge 44. Railway trips to Oakmoor, following the canal as far as Froghall. *Summer Sun.*

PUBS

Boat Cheddleton, Canalside, at bridge 44. There is an old bridge across the Churnet nearby, also Cheddleton station, the museum of the Churnet Valley Steam Railway.
Red Lion Cheddleton, on the main road.
Black Lion Cheddleton, near the church.
Hollybush Canalside, near bridge 38. Small traditional canal pub serving Ind Coope Burton real ale and snacks. Children's room, telephone outside.

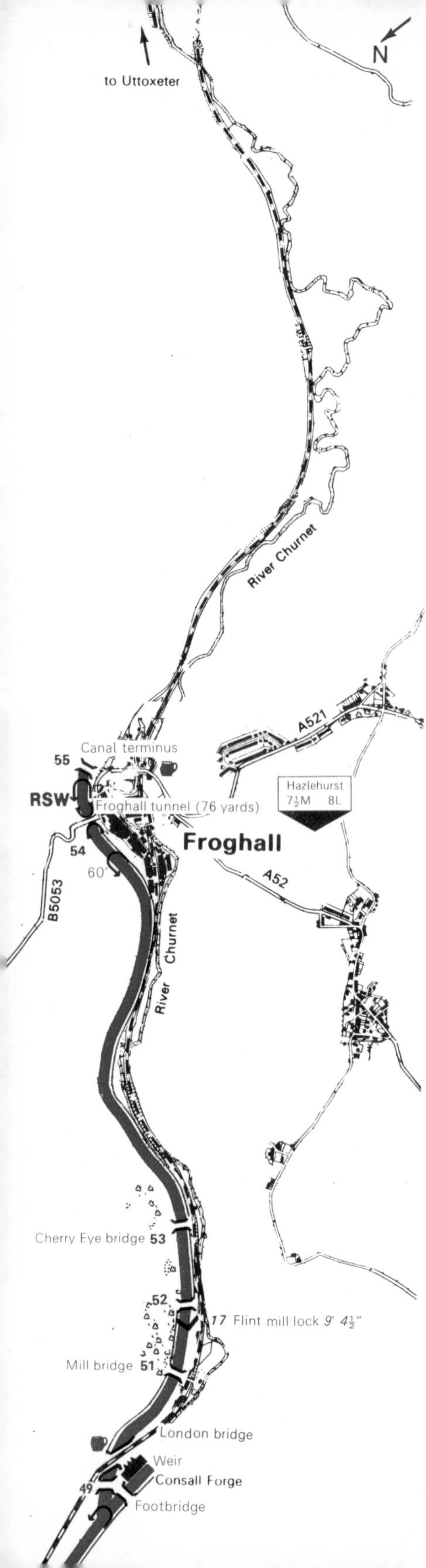

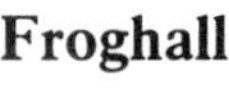

Froghall

This is another very beautiful and secluded length of canal. Passing along the wooded valley that contains the River Churnet, one arrives at Consall Forge. This, once bustling with various mineral works, is now a quiet backwater, ruffled occasionally by passing goods trains. In this unlikely situation the visitor will find a pub with no access by public road. The canal and the river split at Consall Forge, the canal proceeding along the north east side of the steep valley to Flint Mill Lock and the adjacent flint mill. This is, in a way, another piece of living industrial archaeology, where Australian sand is ground to dust for use in glazing pottery. The machinery is still run entirely by water power: water from the canal drops 15ft to drive an underground turbine. The remains of the huge old water wheel can still be seen. Beyond the mill, the navigation creeps along the side of a wooded hill as the valley floor drops away. Beyond here, one finds the large scale industrial works that dominate Froghall. There are moorings before the tunnel for those whose boat cannot pass through (your hire base will inform) and a 60ft winding hole. The terminus is just beyond the tunnel, where there is a full length winding hole.

Froghall
Staffs. PO, tel. Tucked away in the heart of unspoilt Staffordshire, Froghall has been an outpost of industry ever since the advent of the canal fostered the growth of the Caldon lime quarries a few miles east. The limestone was carted down the hills by a plate tramway, being transhipped into waiting canal boats at Froghall Basin. Much of the trade was later lost to the railways. Just west of the final bridge by the basin, one can still see the junction with the old canal arm to Uttoxeter: this locked down to the Churnet valley. The branch was closed in 1847 and the present railway from Froghall to Uttoxeter now occupies most of the canal's course, although much of the canal bed can still be traced. Froghall nowadays comprises almost entirely the factories and dwellings associated with Thomas Bolton's big copper works.

BOAT TRIPS

Froghall Wharf Passenger Service Canal Basin, Foxt Road, Froghall, Cheadle, Stoke-on-Trent (Ipstones 486). 50 seater horse drawn narrow boat. *Public service summer Thur and Sun at 14.00.* Also available for private charter. Craft shop and eating place in the old wharf house.

PUBS

Railway Froghall, near the old station.
Black Lion Consall Forge. A canalside pub of outstanding isolation serving Bass Worthington real ale. Meals, sandwiches, teas, etc usually available.

COVENTRY

Maximum dimensions

Length: 72′
Beam: 7′
Headroom: 6′ 6″

Mileage

COVENTRY Basin to
HAWKESBURY JUNCTION (Oxford Canal): 5½
MARSTON JUNCTION (Ashby Canal): 8¼
Boot Wharf, Nuneaton: 10½
Hartshill: 14
Atherstone Top Lock: 16½
Polesworth: 21½
Alvecote Priory: 23¼
Glascote Bottom Lock: 25½
FAZELEY JUNCTION (Birmingham & Fazeley Canal): 27
Hopwas: 29¾
Whittington Brook: 32½
Huddlesford Junction: 34
FRADLEY JUNCTION (Trent & Mersey Canal): 38

Locks: 13

The Coventry Canal, whose enabling Act of Parliament was passed in 1768, was promoted with 2 main objectives: to connect the fast growing town of Coventry with the great new trade route called the Grand Trunk, now known as the Trent & Mersey Canal; and to provide Coventry with cheap coal from Bedworth coalfield 10 miles to the north.

The first, long-term objective was not achieved for some years until the company had overcome some financial difficulties, but—wisely—the stretch between Coventry and Bedworth was completed early on, so that the profitable carriage of local coal was quickly established along the canal, in 1769. It is interesting to note that several of the collieries in the Bedworth area had already used their own independent canal system for years: these were of course all connected to the main line of the new canal.

By the time the canal reached Atherstone in 1771, all the authorised capital had been spent and James Brindley, the original engineer of the canal, had been sacked. For these reasons, and because of an interminable wrangle with the Oxford Canal Company whose scheme to link Coventry with southern England had followed hard upon the original Coventry scheme—the Coventry Canal did not reach Fazeley (nearly 12 miles short of its intended terminus at Fradley) until 1790.

By this time, the Birmingham & Fazeley Canal had been built and was extending along the Coventry Canal's original proposed line to Whittington Brook, whence the Grand Trunk Canal Company carried it north to Fradley, thus completing the line. (The Coventry company later bought this section back, which explains the fact that there is now a detached portion of the Coventry Canal from Whittington Brook to Fradley Junction.

In 1790 also, the Oxford Canal was completed through to Oxford and thus to London by the Thames. The profits of the Coventry Canal rose quickly, and rose even higher when the Grand Junction Canal was completed in 1799, shortening the route to London by 60 miles. Other adjoining canals contributed to the Coventry's prosperity: the Ashby, the Wyrley & Essington and the Trent & Mersey Canals. The extension of the Grand Junction via Warwick to Birmingham naturally dismayed the Coventry, but the numerous locks—and high tolls on the stretch of the Oxford Canal between Braunston and Napton Junctions—ensured that a lot of traffic to and from Birmingham still used the slightly longer route via the Coventry and Birmingham & Fazeley Canals, especially after the Oxford Canal was shortened by 14 miles between Braunston and Longford.

One could attribute the continuous financial success of the Coventry Canal first to its being part of so many long distance routes and secondly to the continued prosperity of the coal mines along its route. It was certainly one of the most persistently profitable canals ever built in Britain, paying a dividend up to 1947.

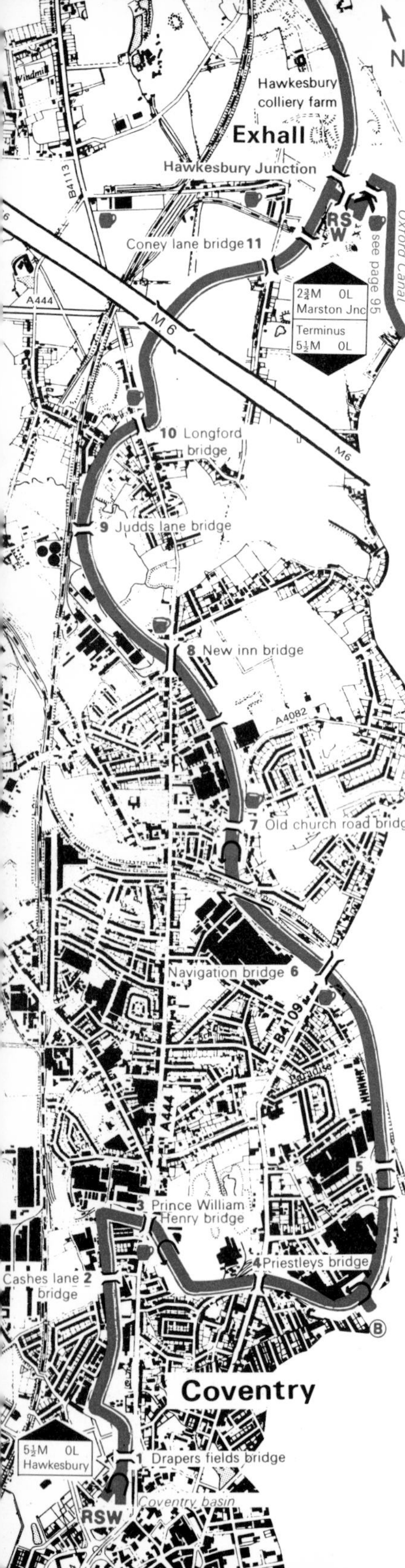

Coventry

The Coventry Canal begins at a large basin near the town centre. It is an interesting situation on the side of a hill: overlooked by tall new buildings and attractive old wooden canal warehouses, this large stretch of amazingly clean water is ideal for an imaginative development scheme; unfortunately at present it is not recommended for overnight mooring, suffering the same problems as most city centre sites. The old toll house is now a shop and information centre. Leaving the basin, the canal winds through industrial areas almost to Hawkesbury. The navigation is often narrow, and mostly flanked by buildings. Observant travellers will notice the course of another canal alongside the Coventry Canal between Longford Bridge and Hawkesbury Junction. This used to be the Oxford Canal running right beside the Coventry before actually joining it at Longford. In 1836 this was replaced by the present junction at Hawkesbury.

Hawkesbury Junction
Hawkesbury Junction is also known as Sutton Stop, after the name of the first lock keeper. It was always a busy canal centre, and remains so today, with plenty of narrow boats permanently moored at the junction. There are other things to see here: a canal pub, a stop lock and disused pumping house. The latter used to pump water up into the canal from a well. Its engine was installed in 1821, having been previously employed for nearly 100 years at Griff Colliery (a few miles up the canal towards Nuneaton). This Newcomen-type atmospheric steam engine, called 'Lady Godiva' is now in Dartmouth Museum. It ceased work in 1913. Hawkesbury Junction is now a conservation area, and an excellent leaflet giving more details of the buildings can be had for 5p at the shop next to the Greyhound pub.

Longford Bridge
PO, tel, stores, off-licence, chandlery. Near bridge 10. Useful for supplies.

Coventry
West Midlands. EC Thur, MD Wed/Fri/Sat. PO, tel, stores, garage, station, cinema, theatre. The town was largely destroyed during the Second World War and consequently today is a modern and well-planned city.

Herbert Art Gallery & Museum Jordan Well. Collections of local art including natural history, archaeology, industry. Frequent loan exhibitions. Collection of Sutherland sketches for the Coventry Cathedral tapestry. *Open Mon to Sat and Sun afternoons.*

Coventry Cathedral Designed by Sir Basil Spence and completed in 1962. The modern stained-glass windows all reflect their light towards the altar, behind which is a tapestry by Graham Sutherland. The font, a boulder from a hillside near Bethlehem, stands in front of the Baptistry window by John Piper.

Cathedral Church of St Michael Only the ruins of the old cathedral destroyed by the Luftwaffe in 1940 still remain. The earliest portion is the door leading into Bayley Lane belonging to an earlier church built about 1300. Splendid view from the tower.

St John's Church Built in the 14thC and used as a prison when the Scots were defeated by Oliver Cromwell. From the incident comes the phrase 'sent to Coventry'.

BOATYARDS

Ⓑ **Club Line Cruisers** Swan Lane Wharf, Coventry. (58864) R S W D Pump-out, hire craft, slipway, gas, boat building and repair, toilets, showers, winter storage. Safe moorings near the city centre.

PUBS

- **Black Horse** Longford Road, Exhall. Garden, snacks.
- **Boat** Black Horse Road, Exhall. Unusual pub and sweet shop. Approach both the above from bridge 11.
- **Greyhound** Hawkesbury Junction. Canalside. Groceries next door.
- **The Engine** by bridge 12.
- **Fiesta** Canalside at bridge 8.
- **Royal Hotel** near bridge 7.
- **Navigation** Canalside, at bridge 6.
- **Prince William Henry** by bridge 3.

Nuneaton

Leaving Hawkesbury Junction, the canal runs through an open industrial wasteland, the only focal point being Hawkesbury Colliery Farm—a strange looking survivor in this kind of landscape. The canal passes Bedworth via a long cutting: the town seems to be composed entirely of vast housing estates, but it is convenient as a supply centre. At Marston Junction the Ashby Canal branches to the east—a free guide to the canal is available from the dispenser (BWB key required). The Coventry Canal continues north towards Nuneaton, passing a disused colliery arm to the west. There is a short stretch of open fields followed immediately by the suburbs of Nuneaton. There are good moorings and easy access to the town by Boot Bridge (20). The canal runs round the town and so its route is marked by a succession of housing estates and allotments. A railway and the A444 follow the canal to the west, and the B4113 crosses at Bedworth.

Nuneaton
Warwicks. EC Thur. MD Sat. PO, tel, stores, garage, station, cinema. A rather typical Midlands town with much industrial development. On the derelict Griff colliery canal arm are the hollows said to be the origin of the Red Deeps of the 'Mill on the Floss' by George Eliot, who was born here in 1819. *By bridge 21 there are stores, fish and chips and Chinese take-away.*
Nuneaton Museum & Art Gallery
Riversley Park. Archaeological specimens of Nuneaton from prehistoric to medieval times, and also items from the local earthenware industry. Geological and mining relics, ethnography from Africa, Asia, America and Oceania. Paintings, prints and water colours. Personalia collection of the novelist George Eliot. *Open Mon–Fri afternoons, all day weekends.*
Arbury Hall 2 miles south west of canal off B4102. Originally an Elizabethan house, gothicized by Sir Roger Newdigate in 1750–1800 under the direction of Sanderson Miller, Henry Keene and Couchman of Warwick. Fine pictures, furniture, and china and glass. The Hall is in a beautiful park setting. *Open from Easter Sun–Oct on Sun, B. Hol Mon & Tue following B. Hol.*
Chivers Coton
Warwicks. Suburb of Nuneaton. Its church dates from 1946 and was designed by H. N. Jepson and built by German prisoners of war.
Bedworth
Warwicks. EC Wed. MD Tue/Fri/Sat. The most impressive parts of this mining town are its church by Bodley and Garner, 1888–90, and the almshouses built in 1840. Good shopping centre.

BOATYARDS

Ⓑ **Magpie Line Cruisers** by Boot Bridge. (Nuneaton 327107). S W D Pump-out, hire craft, boat repairs, mooring, chandlery, souvenirs, maps and guides.
Ⓑ **Gilbert Bros.** Charity Dock. Furnace Road, Bedworth. (313122). D Moorings, dry dock to accommodate 2 full length narrow boats, chandlery. Build and repair wooden narrow boats.

PUBS

Board Inn Near bridge 22.
Boot Boot wharf, Nuneaton. Canalside. Food, garden, games room.
Wharf Inn Wharf Inn bridge, Nuneaton. Canalside. M & B beer, food, children's room, garden.
Cut Along Bedworth. Canalside, at bridge 14
Engine Inn & Royal Scott Grill Kings Street, Bedworth. Food, reductions for children. West of bridge 14.
Prince of Wales West of bridge 14.
Travellers Rest West of bridge 14.

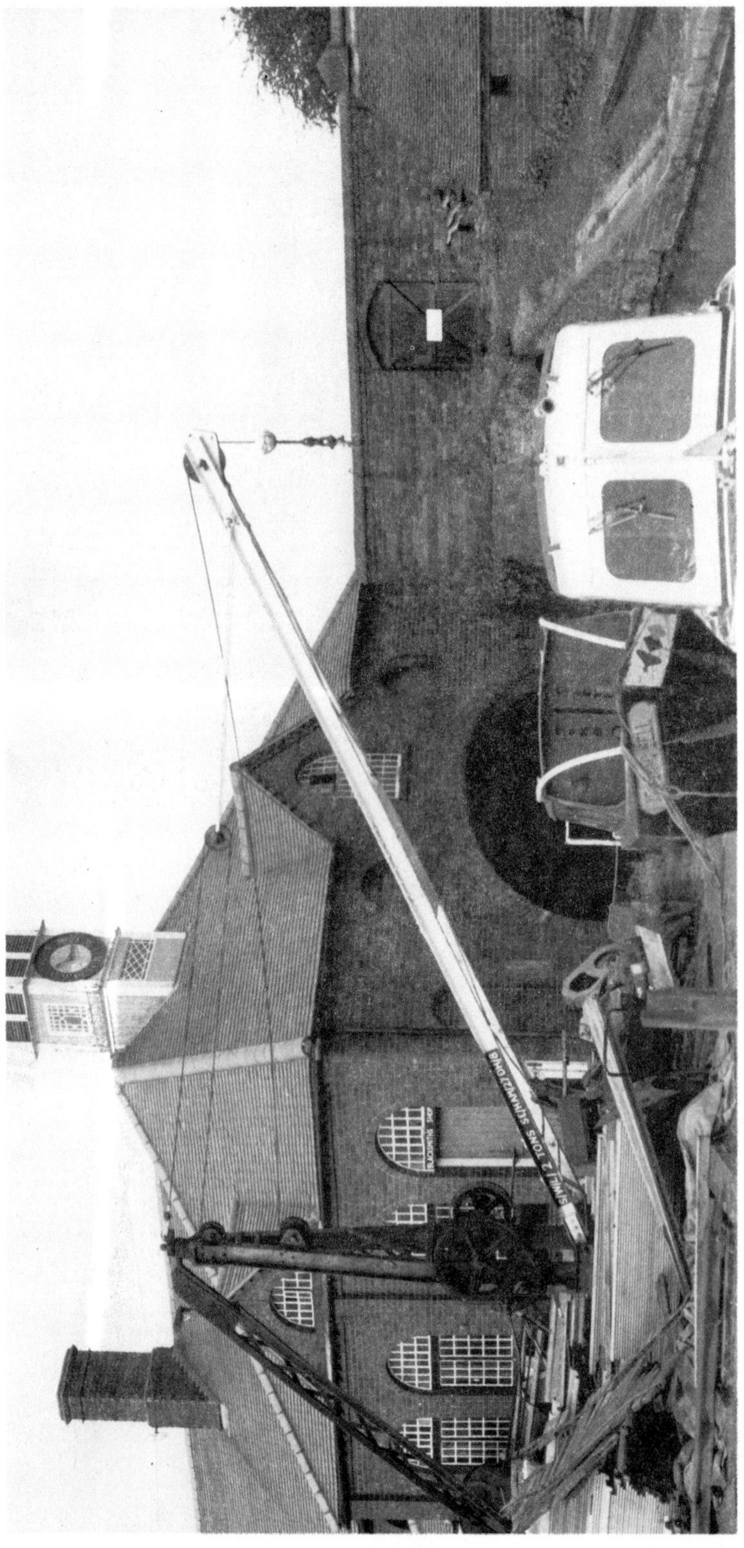

The traditional buildings of BWB Hartshall Yard. *David Perrott*

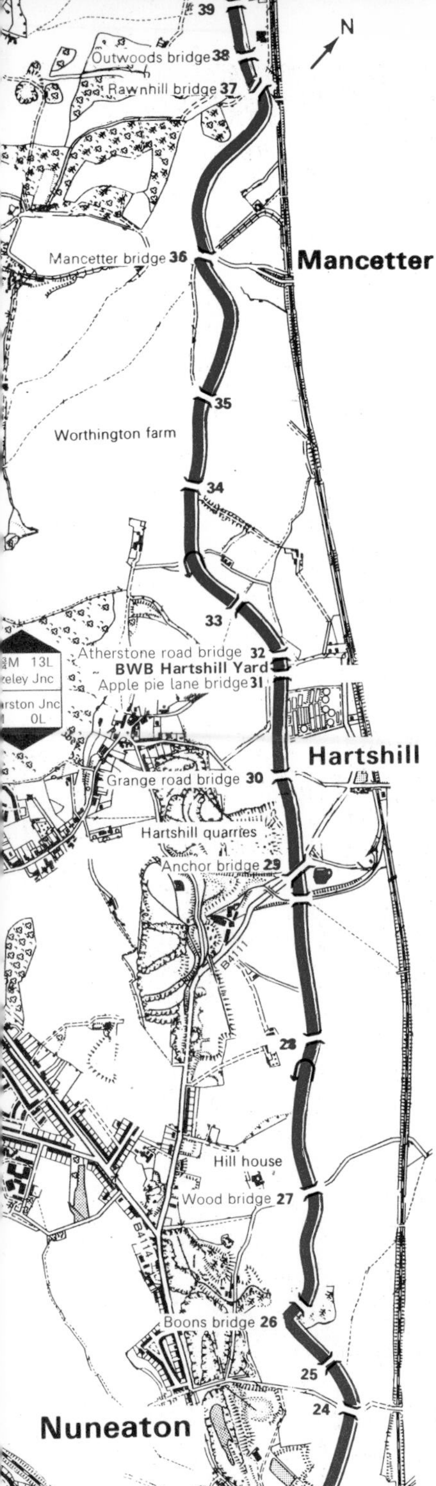

Hartshill

Continuing north west out of Nuneaton, the canal winds along the side of a hill into a landscape which is curiously exciting. Quarries and spoil heaps, now landscaped in part, are broken up by unexpected stretches of open countryside with fine views away to the north across the Anker valley. The earth has given the water a distinct rust colour. The canal passes below Hartshill; the attractive buildings in the BWB yard are crowned by a splendid clock tower. The canal continues towards Mancetter leaving the quarry belt and moves temporarily into open rolling country backed by thick woods to the west. A railway follows the canal to the east, and the A4131 crosses at Hartshill.

Mancetter
Warwicks. PO, tel, stores, garage. ½ mile east of bridge 36. The church dates from the 13thC, but its best feature is the large collection of 18thC slate tombstones displaying all the elegance of Georgian incised lettering. There are some almshouses of 1728 in the churchyard, and across the road another row with pretty Victorian Gothic details. The manor, south of the church, is rather over restored.
Hartshill
Warwicks. PO, tel, stores, garage. A Nuneaton suburb and as such is hardly of interest. The canal passes through a man-made landscape now being landscaped and reclaimed. Granite quarrying once devastated the country, but the results are spectacular. It is hard to imagine that there was once a castle at Hartshill.

BOATYARDS

BWB Hartshill Yard Clock Hill, Hartshill. (Chapel End 392250). WD emergency only *in normal working hours*).

PUBS

Plough Mancetter. Food.
Stag and Pheasant 300 yards behind Hartshill BWB Yard. Food (*Mon–Sat*).
Anchor Hartshill. By bridge 29. Canalside. Food.
White Horse Nuneaton, near bridge 23. Food (*Mon–Fri*).

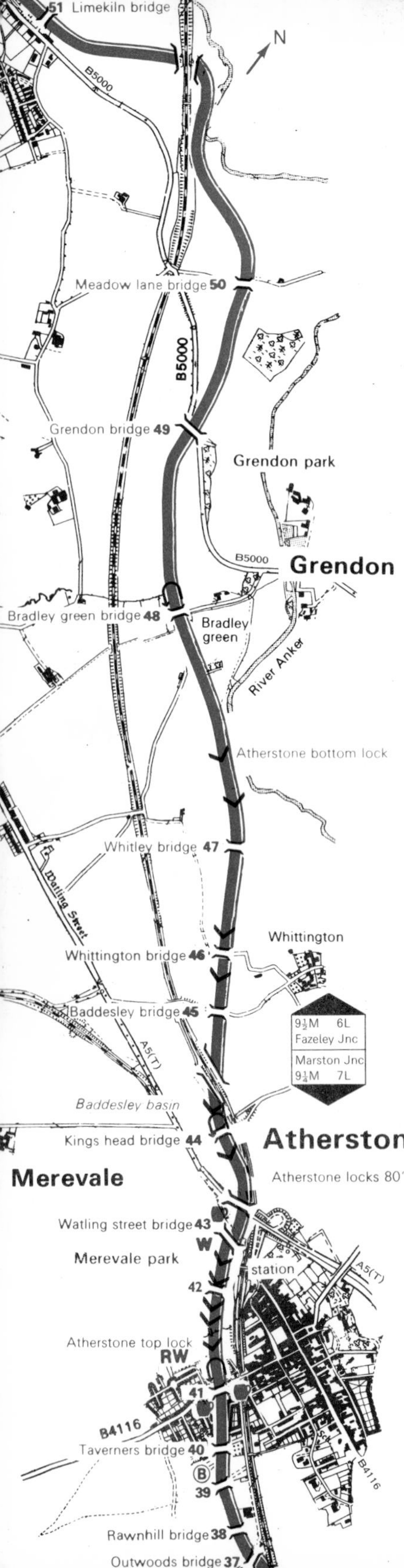

Atherstone

Continuing north west, the canal skirts to the south of Atherstone and begins to descend the locks. Wooded hills to the west reveal Merevale Hall overlooking a remote rural landscape. The 11 narrow locks empty at a remarkable speed, due to their outsize paddles. The flight is extremely attractive and varied, falling through housing, allotments and open countryside. The small basin at the top has been lovingly restored and is cared for by the lock keeper. When Rothens boat and butty (Buckden and Dipper) are moored there the scene is charming and complete. It is a pity that all except one of the side ponds on the flight are now sealed off. At the bottom, the River Anker converges with the canal from the east. A farm by bridge 48 is useful for supplies. Arable land accompanies the canal, lined with oak-trees as it passes Grendon. Only the skyline to the west reveals the industrial belt that is approaching. At this distance the skyline looks romantic, an 18thC vision of industry. As the canal turns towards Polesworth, it passes the remains of an iron swing bridge, a curiosity on this canal. The railway accompanies the canal, crossing from west to east after Grendon. The A5 runs through Atherstone and the B5000 crosses at Grendon.

Grendon
Warwicks. ½ mile north east of bridge 48. Grendon is just a small church set in very beautiful parkland. The woods and rolling fields are a last refuge before the industrial landscape that precedes Tamworth.
Atherstone
Warwicks. EC Thur. MD Tue, Fri. PO, tel, stores, garage, station, cinema. A pleasant town, with a strong 18thC feeling, especially in the open market place in front of the church, a large early Victorian building. There are interesting houses from the 16thC. On Shrove Tuesday medieval football is played in the town to commemorate the game originally played in Warwickshire and Leicestershire in the 12thC. Hundreds of people take part and there are no obvious rules or boundaries to the area of play. Shop windows are boarded up and all traffic is stopped in the town. The game is started by a famous sporting personality who throws the ball out of the window of the 'Three Tuns' pub.
Merevale A large battlemented house set among trees high to the west is Merevale Hall, an early 19thC mock Tudor mansion. To the west are the remains of the 12thC abbey and the very pretty 13thC church which contains fine stained glass, monuments and brasses.

BOATYARDS

Ⓑ **Valley Cruisers** Atherstone. (2602). R W D Pump-out, narrow boat hire and boat-building, slipway, gas, repairs, mooring, toilets.

PUBS

Red Lion Long Street, Atherstone. Bass real ale, snacks.
Kings Head Atherstone. By A5 bridge. Canalside. Davenports real ale, food.
Westwood House Atherstone. North of bridge 41. M & B real ale. Garden.
Maid of the Mill Atherstone. South of bridge 41. Friendly plain and homely pub with large games and children's room, and a cheerful public bar. The 'mill' is a felt hat factory next door. Davenports real ale and garden. Coleshill Road Stores opposite is useful for supplies.

Polesworth

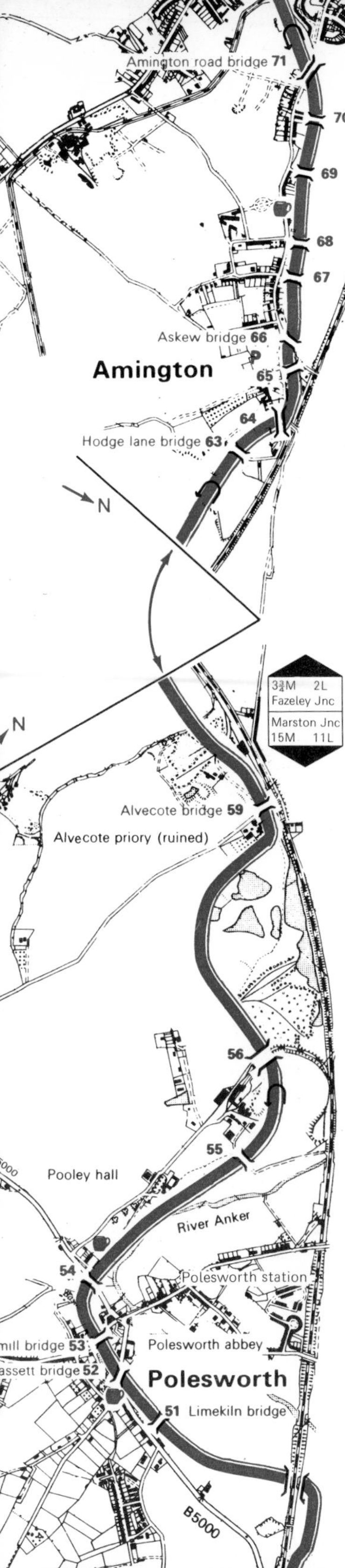

Now the canal runs along the side of a hill overlooking the Anker valley. Turning south of Polesworth it passes Pooley Hall, and an area of reclaimed spoil heaps, now a pleasant area of scrubland, with a golf course. Cows graze near Pooley Hall, and wildlife is filling the vacuum left by industry. Subsidence has affected the towpath which becomes difficult to follow at times. This landscape continues past Alvecote where the tree-surrounded ruins of the priory provide a sudden glimpse of history; and then at Amington it gives way to the suburbs of Tamworth. Throughout this stretch the views are striking across the valley to the hills beyond. The railway follows the canal; the B5000 crosses at Polesworth.

Amington
Staffs. PO, tel, stores, garage. A residential suburb of Tamworth notable for the church built by Street in 1864 which has a Burne-Jones stained glass window. To the south of bridges 68 and 69 is the Canal Craft Shop, where you can have 'Buckby' canal ware painted to order.

Alvecote
Warwicks. PO, tel, stores. A mining village surrounded by the landscaped remains of industrialisation. The church has a weatherboarded bellcote and surviving Norman work inside.

Polesworth
Warwicks. EC Wed. PO, tel, stores, garage, fish and chips, station. The splendid gatehouse and the clerestory are all that remain of the 10thC abbey; most of the fragments are incorporated in the church. ½ mile to the north Pooley Hall, a Tudor brick mansion of 1509, overhangs the canal which is cut into the side of the hill.

PUBS

Gate Inn Amington. Canalside. Marstons real ale, large garden, snacks. PO box, tel.
Royal Oak Polesworth. Food.
Bulls Head Tamworth Road, Polesworth. M & B and Bass real ale.

Tamworth

The canal runs through suburban housing, turning in a wide sweep south west past Tamworth towards Fazeley Junction. Houses and factories flank the canal as it passes Kettlebrook Wharf, and then it moves briefly into more open country, crossing the River Tame on an impressive aqueduct. At Fazeley Junction the Coventry meets the Birmingham and Fazeley Canal which then continues north west towards Fradley or south to Birmingham. Then follow lightly wooded open fields towards Hopwas Hill. The 2 Glascote Locks are the only ones on this stretch—the side ponds may be used if the paddle gear is intact. The A51, A4091 and the A453 cross the canal, while the A5 runs through Fazeley.

Fazeley Junction
Now tastefully restored with good moorings and a canalside seat made from a balance beam. Access to the pub is easy, and Carly's Stores, by the crossroads, is recommended.

Tamworth
Staffs. EC Wed. MD Sat. PO, tel, stores, garage, station, cinema. Tamworth was originally a Saxon town, and although only earthworks survive from this period, the town has much more quality and style than the industry that surrounds it. It is built predominantly of grey-black stone which is seen very effectively in the long railway viaduct to the east of the town centre. The castle is of Norman origin, but dates mostly from the time of Henry VIII; the town hall was built by Sir Thomas Guy, founder of Guy's Hospital, London. St Editha's Church contains monuments and stained glass by William Morris.

Castle Museum Coins from the Tamworth mint of the Saxon and Norman periods. Also Roman antiquities and items of local interest.

BOATYARDS

BWB Fazeley Yard 200yds west of the junction, R S W Slipway, moorings at the junction.

Ⓑ **Central Line Cruisers** Basin Lane, Glascote, Tamworth. (68733). R S W Pump-out, hire craft, boat building and repair, mooring, slipway, dry dock.

PUBS

Chequers Inn Hopwas. Canalside. Courage real ale; food, reductions for children. Garden.

Red Lion Hopwas. Canalside. Food.

Three Tuns Fazeley Junction. Manns real ale, bar food, garden. W

Peel Arms Market Street, Tamworth. Food, reductions for children.

Anchor Anchor Bridge. Glascote. Canalside. M & B real ale, garden, snacks.

Park Inn Bridge 74. Ind Coope beer, food.

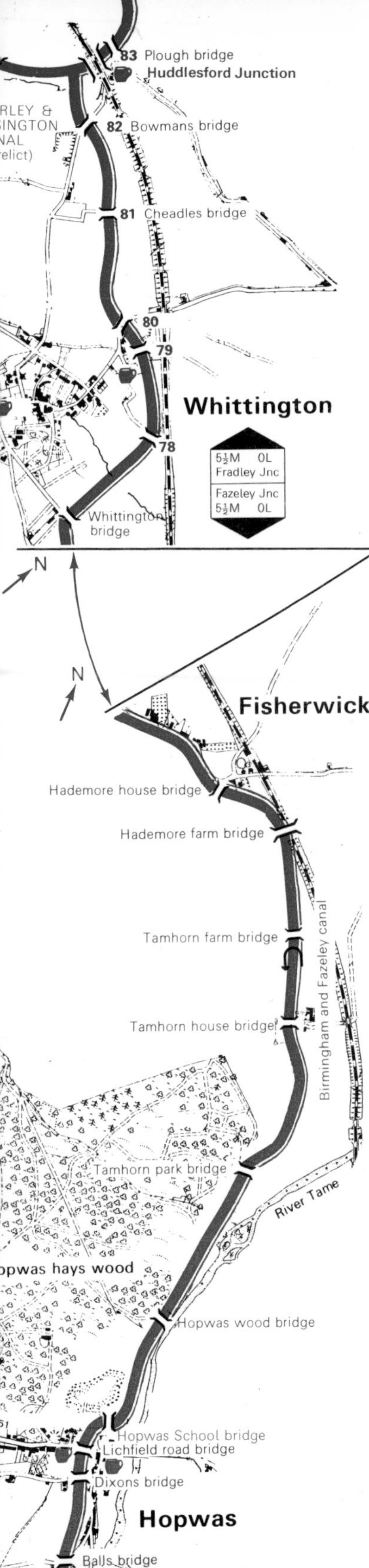

Whittington

Through open fields the canal follows the course of the River Tame very closely, passing below Hopwas. Beyond the village is a delightful wooded stretch that covers the side of the hill. Landing is forbidden because of the Whittington firing ranges. After the wood the canal continues in a side cut embankment with a view of Tamworth away to the east. It then wanders round Whittington, its course directed by the low hills on both sides. As it crosses Whittington Brook, the canal changes back from being the Birmingham & Fazeley to the Coventry; a note in the introduction to the Coventry Canal explains the reason. This also explains why the bridges are numbered again from here onwards. (Bridge 77 is at Fazeley Junction.) At Huddlesford the remains of the eastern end of the Wyrley and Essington Canal branches to the west. The railway joins the canal after Hopwas and follows it closely to Huddlesford: the A51 crosses at Hopwas.

Huddlesford
Staffs. PO box. A well-named hamlet cut in half by the railway line. At Huddlesford Junction the Wyrley & Essington Canal used to join the Coventry, but this end has long been abandoned: the first ¼ mile is used for moorings. The Wyrley & Essington was opened in 1792 to link Birmingham with Cannock Chase coalfield. It was extended to Huddlesford in 1797 to provide a more direct link with the Trent and the north east via Fradley Junction.
Whittington
Staffs. PO, tel, stores, garage. The only part of Whittington on the canal is a large housing estate. The village centre is further to the south, and is more attractive, held together by the large 19thC church with a conspicuous spire.
Fisherwick
Staffs. Tel. A small hamlet overlooking the canal.
Hopwas
Staffs. EC Wed. PO, tel, stores. Village built on the side of a hill at whose foot the canal and the River Tame run side by side. Set among trees above the village is the very unusual church, an early 20thC Arts and Crafts design. There is a wharf by Hopwas School Bridge. To the north is Hopwas Wood, a large area of planted and natural forest. Anyone walking should look out for the danger flags for Whittington firing ranges.

PUBS

Plough Plough Bridge (83). Ansells real ale, food, garden, mooring.
Bell Main Street, Whittington. Food.
Dog Inn Whittington. Food.
Swan Whittington. Food.

Fradley

The canal runs northwards through flat, open country towards Fradley Junction. Lichfield lies away to the west. After being crossed by the busy roar of the A38, a Roman road, the canal turns west, passing the perimeter of the disused airfield. There are no locks, but a swing bridge near the junction provides interest. At the junction the Coventry Canal meets the Trent and Mersey. There is a mooring at Bell Bridge, from which you can visit the garage and shop (*closed Sun afternoon*).

Fradley
Staffs. PO, tel, stores. A small village set to the east of the canal. It owed its prosperity to the airfield which is not used as such any more.
Fradley Junction
Staffs. PO box, tel, garage. The junction, a well-established canal centre, marks the northern end of the Coventry Canal. The Trent and Mersey runs west to Staffordshire, Shropshire and the North West, and east to Nottingham and the North East.
Lichfield
Staffs. PO, tel, stores, garage, cinema, station. 2 miles south west along the A38. Although not on the canal, Lichfield is well worth a visit. The town has a long history, its earliest charter being granted in 1387. The huge brown stone cathedral, built in 1195–1325, is unique in that it has retained its 3 spires known as the 'Ladies of the Vale'. The west front has over 100 carved figures, many restored in the 19thC. The streets close by the cathedral and leading to the market square are the oldest, dating from the Tudor period. A fine 17thC house in the market square is the birthplace of Dr Johnson, now a museum. David Garrick and Joseph Addison came from Lichfield: so did Erasmus Darwin, the founder of the famous Lunar Society. Most of the 'Lunatics' (so called because they used to meet every full moon) were eminent men like Wedgwood, Boulton, Watt and Priestley. They met in Darwin's Lichfield house to discuss current scientific, philosophical and political affairs of mutual interest.
Art Gallery & Museum Bird Street. Local history and temporary art exhibitions displayed in the Norman castle. There is also the Staffordshire Regimental Museum.

BOATYARDS

BWB Fradley Maintenance Yard Fradley Junction. (Burton on Trent 790236). R S W Toilets.
Ⓑ **Swan Line Cruisers** Fradley Junction. (Burton on Trent 790332). W D Pump-out (not weekends), moorings, chandlery, boat hire, gas, dry dock, boat building & repairs, provisions. 42-seater trip boat. *Closed Sat afternoon and Sun in winter.*
Ⓑ **Lichfield Marina** Streethay Basin. Burton Road, Streethay, Lichfield, Staffs. (Lichfield 51981). R S W Moorings, slipway. Boat sales and repairs, outboard engine sales and service. Chandlery. *Closed Tue.*

PUBS

Swan Fradley Junction. Canalside. The focal point of the junction and justly famous. A fine public bar with a coal fire and pub games, a comfortable lounge for families, and a lively cellar bar. Ind Coope beers and bar meals (*not Sun*).
Plough Plough Bridge (83). Ansells real ale, food, garden, mooring.

GRAND UNION

LEICESTER SECTION AND THE SOAR NAVIGATION

Maximum dimensions

Norton Junction to Foxton Junction
Length: 72′
Beam: 7′
Headroom: 7′ 6″

Market Harborough to Leicester
Length: 72′
Beam: 10′
Headroom: 7′

Leicester West Bridge to River Trent
Length: 72′
Beam: 14′ 4″
Headroom: 7′ 6″

Mileage

NORTON JUNCTION to
Crick: 5
Welford arm: 15½
Market Harborough arm: 23¼
Blaby: 36
Leicester West Bridge: 41¼
Cossington Lock: 49
Barrow upon Soar: 53¼
Loughborough Basin: 57¼
Zouch Lock: 60½
RIVER TRENT: 66¼

Locks: 59

The River Soar is a tributary of the River Trent and is approximately 40 miles long. It runs mainly through Leicestershire, rising at Smockington Hollow on the Warwickshire border. For most of the way from Aylestone (just south of Leicester) to the Trent, the Soar forms the Leicester section of the Grand Union Canal.

In 1634 Thomas Skipworth of Cotes attempted to make the River Soar 'portable for barges and boats up to the town of Leicester' by means of a grant from King Charles I in return for 10% of the profits. This scheme was a failure. But after several other attempts, prominent citizens of Loughborough secured an Act of Parliament in 1776, and the River Soar Navigation (Loughborough Canal) was opened 2 years later, bringing great prosperity to the town. The continuation of the navigation up to Leicester (the Leicester Canal) was built under an Act passed in 1791. Its opening was marked by the arrival in Leicester of 2 boats loaded with provisions from Gainsborough on the 21st of February 1794. The engineers concerned with construction of the Soar Navigation were John Smith and John May (Loughborough Canal) and William Jessop (Leicester Canal). With the completion of the Grand Junction Canal between Brentford and Braunston, a connection was soon established between this and the Soar Navigation, built to the narrow gauge, thwarting the Grand Junction's scheme for a system of wide canals.

The Loughborough Navigation was one of the most prosperous canals in England, by virtue of its position in relation to the Nottinghamshire-Derbyshire coalfield and the Erewash Canal. However, railway competition took its usual toll, and although trade revived when the Grand Union Canal purchased the Loughborough and Leicester Navigations in 1931, the improvement proved temporary. However, it is a pretty, rural river and is much enjoyed by the owners of pleasure craft.

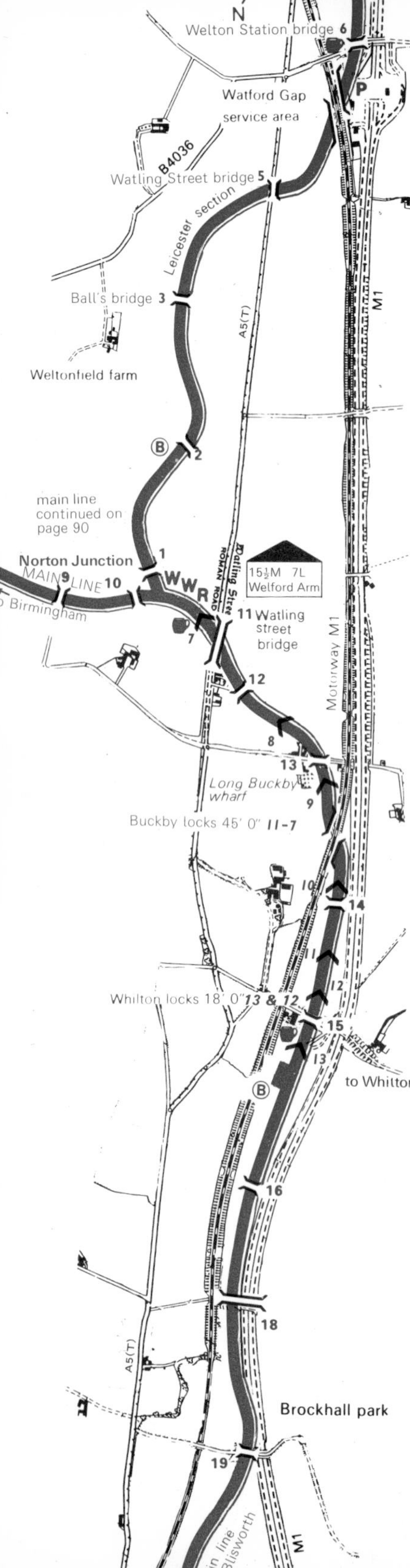

Norton Junction

Leaving Norton Junction there is a quiet, meandering mile through light woods and rolling fields before the motorway and railway take over; the canal passes the backdoor of the Watford Gap service area. The noise and bustle of the motorway and main railway line intrude, accentuating the sedate pace of those using the original of the three transport systems.

Buckby Wharf
Northants. PO box, tel, stores. A scattering of houses accompanies the canal through Buckby Locks. By the top lock, where the A5 crosses, there is a general store.

Whilton
Northants. PO, tel, stores. 1 mile east of the canal at the end of a road that goes nowhere. Whilton is quiet and unchanged, especially at the east end. There are several fine stone houses, including a pretty Georgian rectory. To the west is the site of Banaventa, a Roman settlement.

BOATYARDS

Ⓑ **Weltonfield Narrowboats** Weltonfield Farm, by bridge 2 (Long Buckby 842282). S W D Pump-out (telephone in advance), narrow boat hire, gas, boat building and repairs, toilet, shop, boat lift.

Ⓑ **Whilton Marine** Whilton Locks, on the main line (Long Buckby 842577). R S W P D Moorings, repairs, chandlery, slipway, restaurant & bar, toilets, showers, boat sales.

PUBS

Stag's Head Watford Gap. Canalside. Free house with lovely canalside rose garden.

New Inn Canalside, at Buckby Top Lock. Cosy alcoved free house, serving Marstons real ale and food. Next door is Gingers Canal Stores, for provisions and souvenirs.

The Locks By bridge 15. Large modern pub serving Charles Wells beers and food. Telephone kiosk close by.

Crick

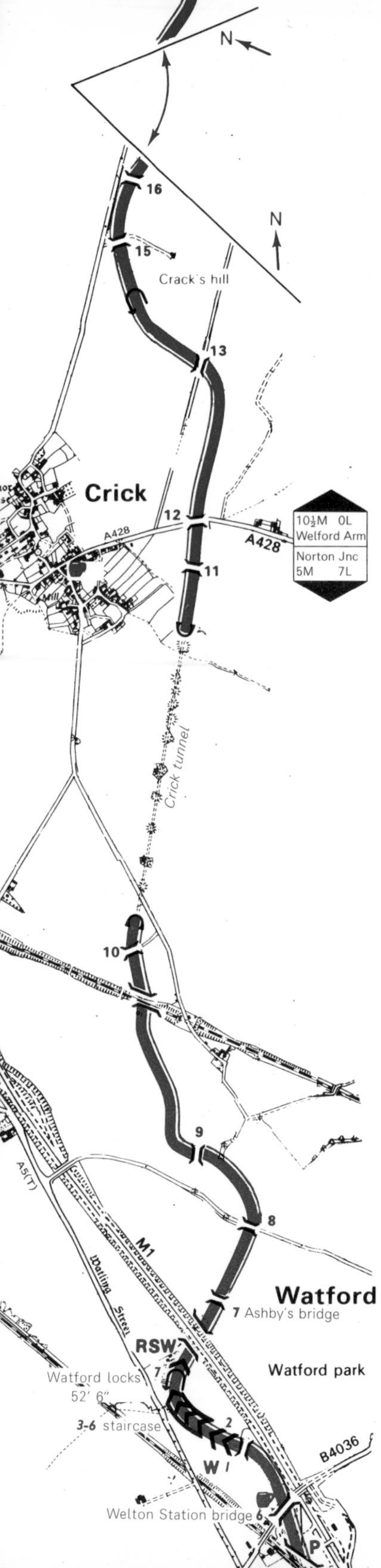

The Leicester line of the Grand Union is very attractive, quiet and in no hurry to reach Foxton. It wanders through rolling, hilly country, riverlike with constant changes of direction that guide it gently north eastwards. It avoids villages and civilisation generally; only the old wharves serve as a reminder of the canal's function. The slow course of the canal, its relative emptiness and its original plan combine to make it very narrow in places; reeds, overhanging trees and shallow banks quite often do not allow 2 boats to pass. After negotiating Watford Locks and reaching the summit level of 412ft there is nothing strenuous to look forward to, as this level continues for the next 22 miles. 4 of these locks form a staircase—adopt a 'one up, one down' procedure, and use both ground and side paddles when going either up or down. Progress is slow and delays are likely if a queue builds up. At Watford the canal swings east away from the M1 for good. The locks and Crick Tunnel with its wooded approaches offer canal excitement to contrast with the quiet of the landscape. The A428 crosses east of Crick.

Crick
Northants. PO, tel, stores. Large village built round the junction of 2 roads. There are several attractive stone houses, and the large church has managed to escape restoration. It contains much decorative stonework and a circular Norman font.
Crick Tunnel 1528yds long, the tunnel was opened in 1814. All tunnels built in this area suffered great problems in construction. Quicksands caused the route of the tunnel to be changed and greatly affected work. Stephenson found similar difficulties when building in nearby Kilsby Tunnel for the London to Birmingham railway.
Watford
Northants. EC Sat. PO, tel, stores. Set in the middle of wooded parkland, Watford gives the impression of being a private village. The Church and Watford Court dominate, and luckily the M1 has made no impact. The 13thC church contains some interesting monuments. The Court is partly 17thC although there are Victorian additions. The rich brown stone used throughout the village adds to the feeling of unity.

PUBS

Red Lion Inn Main Street. Crick. Food, skittles.
Wheatsheaf 15 Main Street, Crick.

Yelvertoft

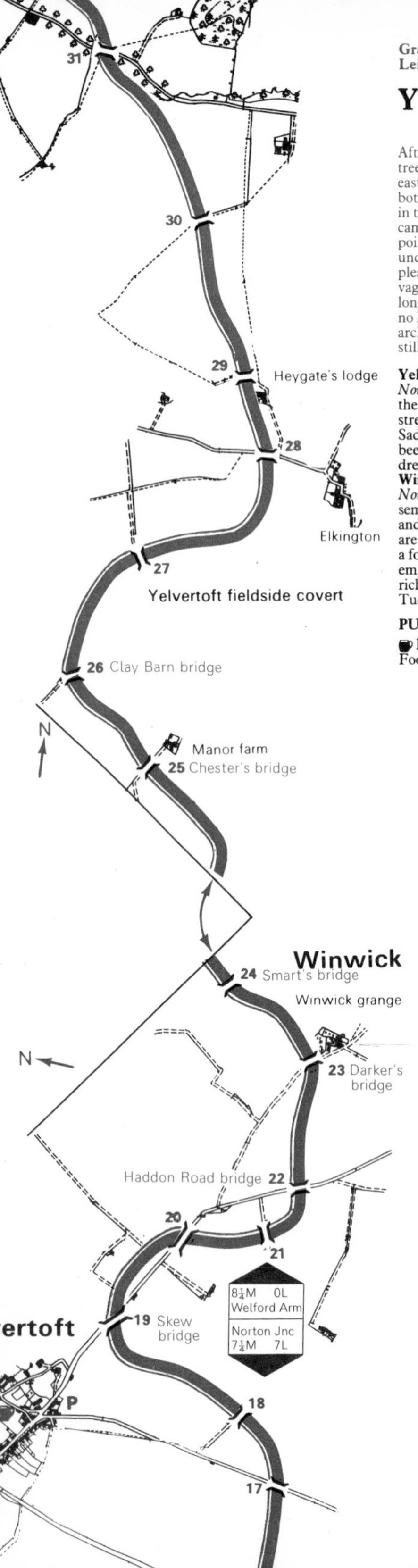

After skirting Crack's Hill, a curious tree-topped mound, the canal wanders to the east in a series of loops which cause it to miss both Yelvertoft and Winwick, the only villages in the section. Hills surround the course of the canal, encouraging its meandering. At one point it passes under the same road 3 times in under a mile. Occasional woods add to the pleasure of the isolation. After Winwick, a vague north east course is resumed, passing the long abandoned village of Elkington. There are no locks, but a regular procession of brick arched bridges serves as a reminder that it is still a canal.

Yelvertoft
Northants. PO, tel, stores, garage. Set back from the canal, the village is built round a wide main street, terminated in the east by the church. Sadly, many of the original thatched roofs have been replaced by corrugated iron painted dreary colours.

Winwick
Northants. 1 mile south east bridge 23. A semi-deserted village, with many empty houses and a closed church. Many villages in this area are in a similar state, showing that this is really a forgotten part of England. Yet amidst the emptiness is the Manor House, built 16thC of richly decorated brick, with an ornamental Tudor gateway.

PUBS

Knightly Arms High Street, Yelvertoft. Food.

Welford

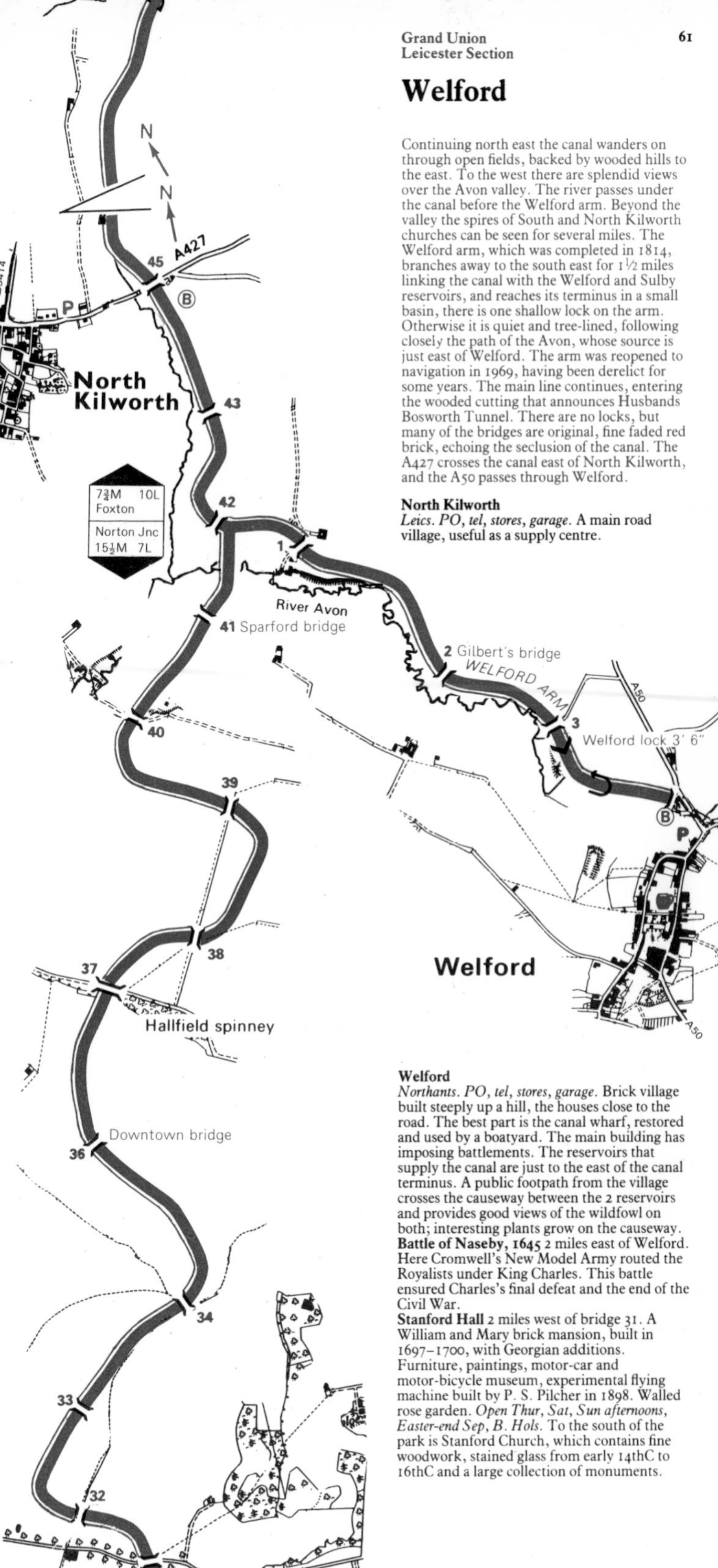

Continuing north east the canal wanders on through open fields, backed by wooded hills to the east. To the west there are splendid views over the Avon valley. The river passes under the canal before the Welford arm. Beyond the valley the spires of South and North Kilworth churches can be seen for several miles. The Welford arm, which was completed in 1814, branches away to the south east for 1½ miles linking the canal with the Welford and Sulby reservoirs, and reaches its terminus in a small basin, there is one shallow lock on the arm. Otherwise it is quiet and tree-lined, following closely the path of the Avon, whose source is just east of Welford. The arm was reopened to navigation in 1969, having been derelict for some years. The main line continues, entering the wooded cutting that announces Husbands Bosworth Tunnel. There are no locks, but many of the bridges are original, fine faded red brick, echoing the seclusion of the canal. The A427 crosses the canal east of North Kilworth, and the A50 passes through Welford.

North Kilworth
Leics. PO, tel, stores, garage. A main road village, useful as a supply centre.

Welford
Northants. PO, tel, stores, garage. Brick village built steeply up a hill, the houses close to the road. The best part is the canal wharf, restored and used by a boatyard. The main building has imposing battlements. The reservoirs that supply the canal are just to the east of the canal terminus. A public footpath from the village crosses the causeway between the 2 reservoirs and provides good views of the wildfowl on both; interesting plants grow on the causeway.
Battle of Naseby, 1645 2 miles east of Welford. Here Cromwell's New Model Army routed the Royalists under King Charles. This battle ensured Charles's final defeat and the end of the Civil War.
Stanford Hall 2 miles west of bridge 31. A William and Mary brick mansion, built in 1697–1700, with Georgian additions. Furniture, paintings, motor-car and motor-bicycle museum, experimental flying machine built by P. S. Pilcher in 1898. Walled rose garden. *Open Thur, Sat, Sun afternoons, Easter-end Sep, B. Hols.* To the south of the park is Stanford Church, which contains fine woodwork, stained glass from early 14thC to 16thC and a large collection of monuments.

BOATYARDS

Ⓑ **Black Prince Narrowboats** Canal Wharf, Welford. (519). R S W D Pump-out, narrow boat hire, gas, boat building & repair, mooring, toilets.

Ⓑ **North Kilworth Narrowboats** (Hucker Marine) Kilworth Marina, North Kilworth, Lutterworth. (Market Harborough 880484). By bridge 45. R S W D Pump-out, gas, narrow boat hire, long term mooring (cruisers only), overnight mooring, slipway, provisions, books and maps, toilets.

PUBS & RESTAURANTS

Swan North Kilworth.

Shoulder of Mutton High Street, Welford.

Wharf House Hotel Welford. At the end of the Welford Arm.

The end of the Welford Arm, soon after its restoration. *David Perrott*

Husbands Bosworth

Continuing north east, the canal enters a remote, but attractive stretch. It wanders along a wooded cutting to the tunnel, then passes empty fields. Hills make a backdrop to the west, while to the east there are long views over fertile agricultural land. The wooded Laughton Hills come right down to the west bank for over a mile, the canal clinging to the hillside. There are no villages on the canal here, Husbands Bosworth being hidden by the tunnel. The A50 crosses over the tunnel and meets the A427 in Husbands Bosworth.

Husbands Bosworth
Leics. PO, tel, stores, garage. A pleasant village to the east of the canal tunnel. (Access from canal: walk up the lane from bridge 46). There is a good church with a stumpy spire. Gliders glide from the little airfield just outside the village; and Husbands Bosworth is also the home of an annual steam engine rally, so on summer weekends strange vehicles can often be seen rattling along the main street.
Husbands Bosworth Tunnel 1166yds long, the tunnel was opened in 1813.

PUBS & RESTAURANTS

Bell High Street, Husbands Bosworth. Food.
Fernie Lodge Berridges Lane, Husbands Bosworth (Market Harborough 880551). Large pleasantly old fashioned English restaurant. *Closed Sat lunch, Sun & Mon.* Not too expensive. Children's portions.

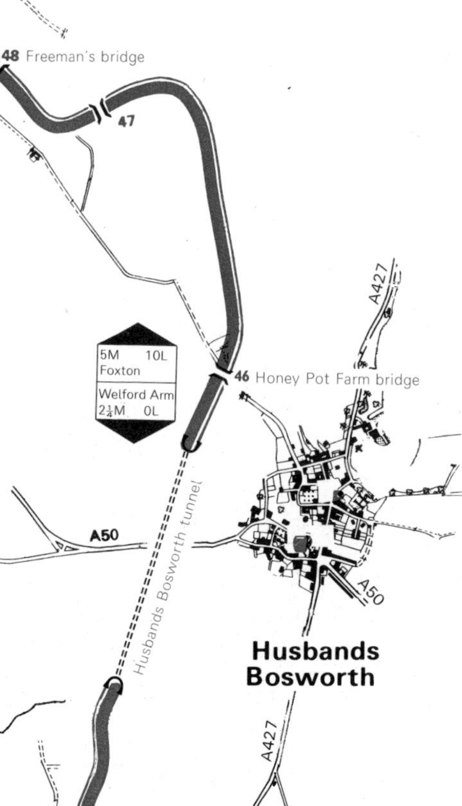

Foxton

The canal runs north east through fields to the top of Foxton Locks. It then falls 75ft to join the 'Old Union' line to Leicester. At the bottom of the locks the 5¾ mile Market Harborough Arm branches off to the east and runs along the side of the hills which dominate the landscape to the south and cause the canal to meander extensively before reaching Market Harborough. To the north the fields fall away from the canal. It is a quiet, rural arm, with no

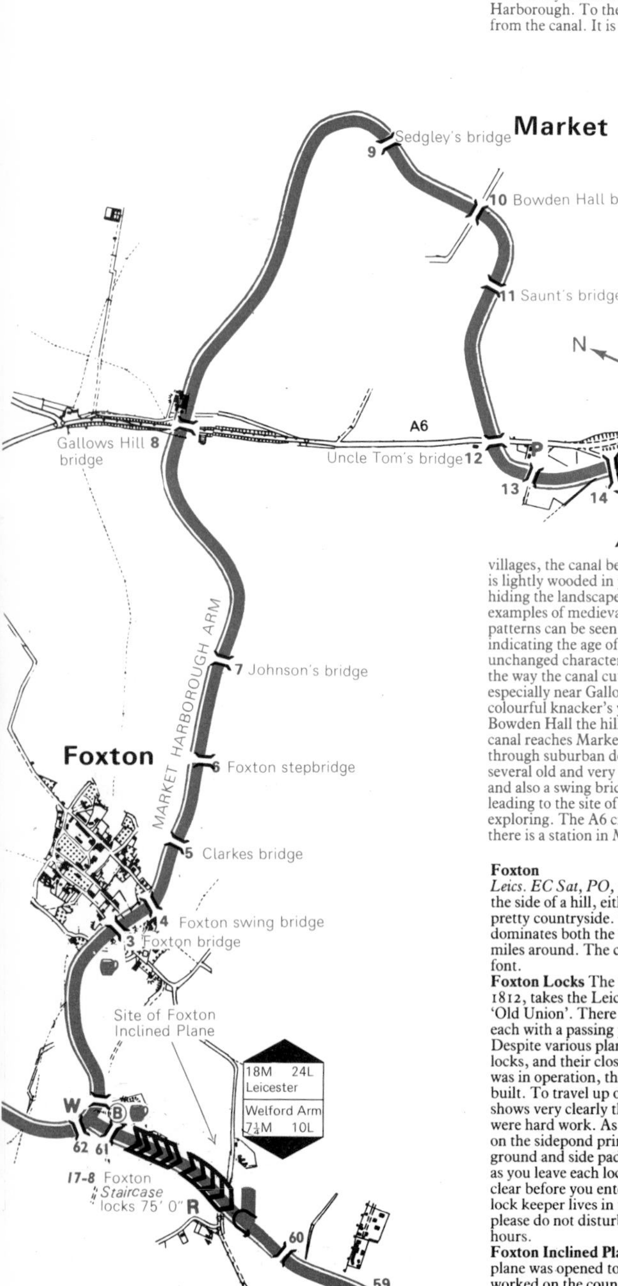

villages, the canal becoming very river-like. It is lightly wooded in parts, with short cuttings hiding the landscape from view. Several examples of medieval ridge and furrow field patterns can be seen along the south bank, indicating the age of the countryside and its unchanged character. It is interesting to note the way the canal cuts across these ridges, especially near Gallow Hill—where there is a colourful knacker's yard. After passing Great Bowden Hall the hills rise to the south and the canal reaches Market Harborough Basin through suburban development. There are several old and very decayed brick arch bridges and also a swing bridge near Foxton. The cut leading to the site of the inclined plane is worth exploring. The A6 crosses the arm twice, and there is a station in Market Harborough.

Foxton
Leics. EC Sat, PO, tel, stores. A village built on the side of a hill, either side of the canal, in pretty countryside. The church tower dominates both the village and the valley for miles around. The church contains a Norman font.

Foxton Locks The Foxton staircase, opened in 1812, takes the Leicester line down to join the 'Old Union'. There are 2 staircases of 5 locks each with a passing pound in the middle. Despite various plans to widen or duplicate the locks, and their closure while the inclined plane was in operation, they remain today as first built. To travel up or down is exciting, and shows very clearly that canals in their heyday were hard work. As at Watford the locks work on the sidepond principle, so use both the ground and side paddles, and close them both as you leave each lock. Check each flight of 5 is clear before you enter. The friendly and helpful lock keeper lives in the cottage at the top; please do not disturb him outside working hours.

Foxton Inclined Plane. In 1900 an inclined plane was opened to bypass Foxton Locks. It worked on the counter balance system. 2 caissons carrying either 2 narrow boats or 1 barge moving sideways on rails up and down the plane. A steam driven winch pulling an endless cable was used to start the caissons moving. The journey time was reduced from 70 to 12 minutes. Mechanical problems and high running costs, plus the fact that the planned widening of the Watford flight never took place, soon made the plane a white elephant. In 1908 the Foxton Locks were reopened to traffic, and in 1911 the plane was closed to traffic. It was finally broken up in 1928, and the machinery sold for scrap. Today little remains; the foundations of the engine house are still visible, the cut leading to the bottom of the plane is still navigable, and among the trees and undergrowth the plane itself can still be traced, running at right angles to the east of the locks. It must have been a magnificent sight. The buildings are now being restored and an exploratory trail can be followed.

Market Harborough
Leics. EC Wed. MD Tue/Sat. PO, tel, stores, garage, banks, station. Established as a market town by 1203, Market Harborough still retains much of its rural elegance and local importance. The centre of the town is built round the church of St Dionysius which contains fine window tracery; however the most important and spectacular element is the spire, one of the finest in England. Visually it sets the scale for the whole town and holds it all together. The pleasure of the town centre is weakened by the presence of the A6, but the approach by canal is superb.

Archaeological & Historical Society Museum County Library, The Square. Contains the society's own collection and illustrates local life from the earliest times. Relics of the Battle of Naseby.

Parish Church of St Dionysius High Street. Built in the 14thC by Scropes and enlarged a century later. The broach spire and west tower are notable.

Old Grammar School High Street. Founded by Robert Smyth who was born here. It stands on wooden carved pillars, and behind the arches was held the ancient butter market. The building was used as the grammar school until 1892 and is now a meeting hall.

BOATYARDS

Ⓑ **Anglo-Welsh Narrow Boats; Harborough Marine Ltd** The Canal Basin, Leicester Road, Market Harborough. (66910). R S W P D E Pump-out (*Mon–Fri*). Narrow boat hire, slipway, gas, dry dock, boat building & repair, mooring, chandlery, toilets.

Ⓑ **Foxton Boat Services** Bottom Lock, Foxton. (Kibworth 2285). R S W P D Pump-out. Boat hire, slipway, gas, boat building, repairs (24 hrs), mooring, chandlery, toilets, showers, provisions, winter storage, cafe, restaurant, bar.

BOAT TRIPS

Trip boat Vagabond Canal trips for casual visitors on summer *Sundays and B. Hols.* from Foxton bottom lock; available for charter by parties any other day (minimum 20 passengers, maximum 51). Telephone Kibworth 2285 for information.

PUBS

Angel Hotel High Street, Market Harborough. Food.

Red Cow High Street, Market Harborough.

Six Packs Leicester Road, Market Harborough. Food.

✕ **Three Swans Hotel** High Street, Market Harborough. Food.

Bridge 61 In the midst of Foxton Boat Services, a wonderful environment in which to enjoy Everards real ale and other guest beers.

Black Horse Foxton. Canalside. Food.

Shoulder of Mutton Main Street, Foxton.

Descending Foxton Locks. *David Perrott*

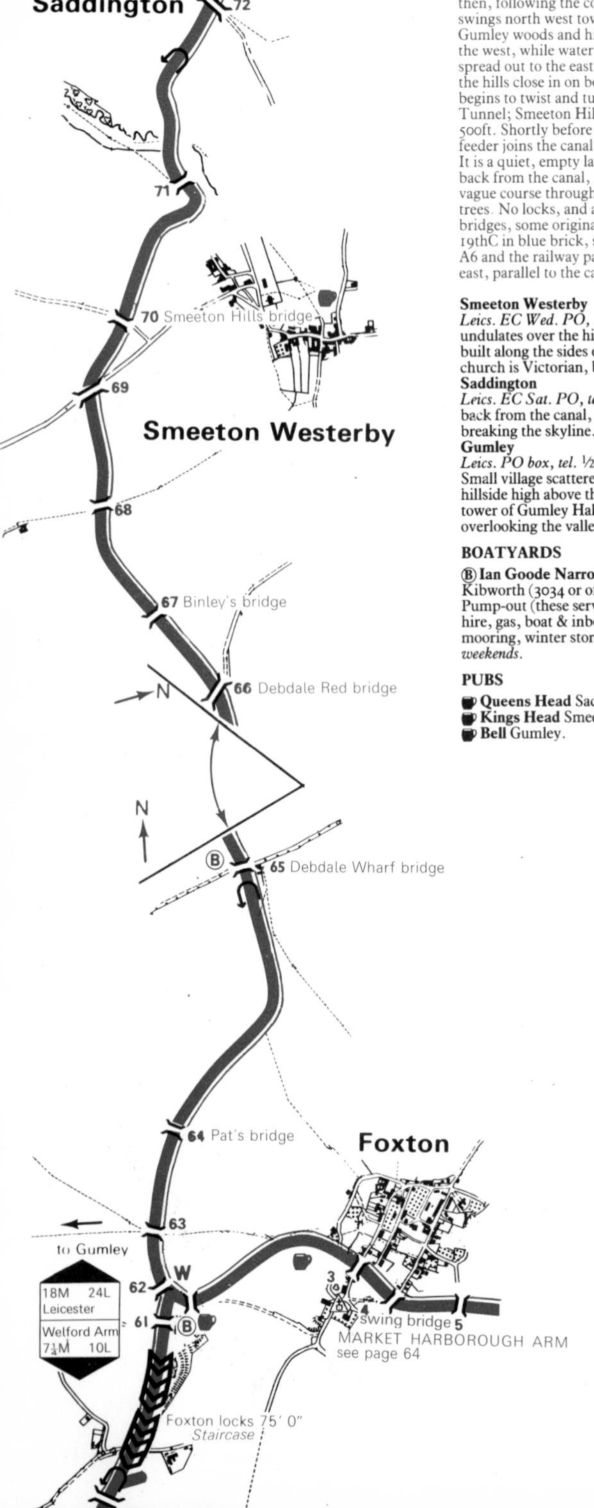

Smeeton Westerby

From Foxton the canal continues north, and then, following the contours of the valley, it swings north west towards Leicester. At first Gumley woods and hills dominate the canal to the west, while water meadows and pasture spread out to the east towards Foxton. Later, the hills close in on both sides, and the canal begins to twist and turn prior to Saddington Tunnel; Smeeton Hill, to the west, rises to over 500ft. Shortly before the tunnel an unnavigable feeder joins the canal to Saddington reservoir. It is a quiet, empty landscape, all villages set back from the canal, leaving it to pursue a vague course through open fields and occasional trees. No locks, and a curious mixture of bridges, some original, some rebuilt in the 19thC in blue brick, some more modern. The A6 and the railway pass beyond the hills to the east, parallel to the canal.

Smeeton Westerby
Leics. EC Wed. PO, tel, stores. The village undulates over the hills to the east of the canal, built along the sides of the main street. The church is Victorian, by Woodyer.
Saddington
Leics. EC Sat. PO, tel, stores. Small village set back from the canal, only the church tower breaking the skyline.
Gumley
Leics. PO box, tel. ½ mile west bridge 63. Small village scattered among trees, set on a hillside high above the canal. The Italianate tower of Gumley Hall rises above the trees, overlooking the valley.

BOATYARDS

Ⓑ **Ian Goode Narrow Boats** Debdale Wharf, Kibworth (3034 or office 0536 771336). R W D Pump-out (these services *Mar–Oct only*). Boat hire, gas, boat & inboard engine repairs, mooring, winter storage. *Closed winter weekends.*

PUBS

- **Queens Head** Saddington.
- **Kings Head** Smeeton Westerby.
- **Bell** Gumley.

Fleckney

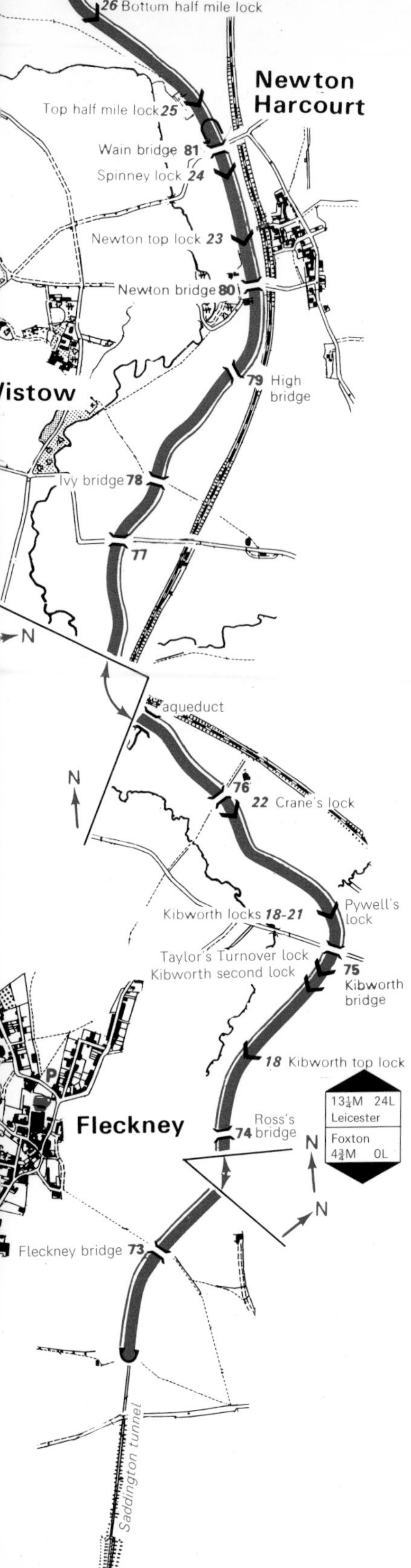

The canal passes through Saddington Tunnel and turns briefly north east before returning to its original course. It remains quiet and remote, although the peace is periodically shattered by the presence of the railway to the east which at times runs almost along the towpath. The hills give way after the tunnel to open fields and woods which give fine views to the west, especially across Wistow Park. The canal is often river-like and very shallow in places. Newton Harcourt breaks the rule of this canal by being beside it, the other villages keep their distance, which, in the case of Fleckney is just as well. The tunnel, the bridges, and the locks which begin the descent to Leicester provide plenty of canal interest although the amount of rubbish in the cut begins to increase. The A6 and the main railway slowly encroach on the canal to the east.

Newton Harcourt
Leics. EC Sat. PO, stores. Scattered village bisected by the railway in a cutting. This hides most of it from the canal, which sees only the church and manor, set pleasantly among trees. The church tower is 13thC, the rest Victorian. The canalside position is its best feature. The Hall is 17thC, with later rebuilding; it has a fine gateway. Newton Harcourt is a well-known Leicester beauty spot, popular on Sunday afternoons.

Wistow
Leics. For a while the canal runs through woods and parkland to the west adjoining Wistow Park. Wistow itself has a church and a Hall, the church with Norman work but mostly 18thC, including fine monuments. The Hall is Jacobean in principle but was largely rebuilt in the 19thC.

Fleckney
Leics. EC Wed. PO, tel, stores, garage. A grim industrial village, curiously placed in the middle of open fields, with no obvious reason for its existence. Useful for supplies and fish and chips.

Saddington Tunnel 880 yds long, the tunnel was completed in 1797, after great difficulties owing to its being built crooked. Naturalists enthuse about the bats that nowadays live in the tunnel.

PUBS

Several pubs in Fleckney: unfortunately none in Newton Harcourt.

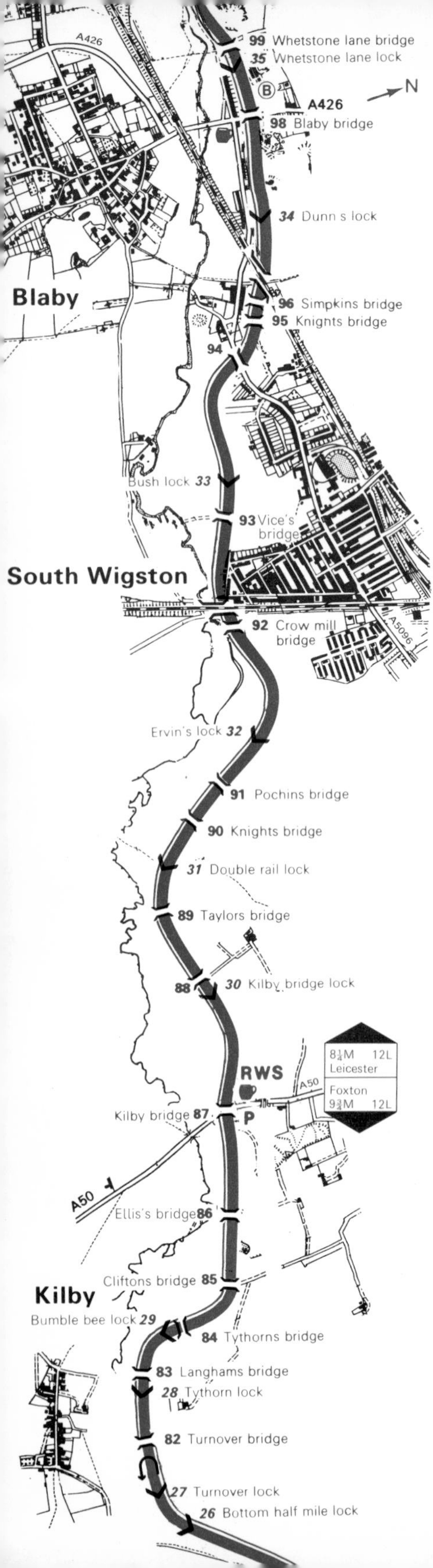

Wigston

The canal follows the north westerly course of the River Sence, bounded by low hills to east and west. Still remote, until Kilby Bridge where indications of the town of Leicester begin with distant views of housing estates and factories. By the disused rail bridge at South Wigston the town seems to take over. There is no shortage of facilities. The locks continuing the steady fall, give the stretch its individuality. The A50 crosses at Kilby Bridge, the A426 at Blaby, and the railway keeps the canal company to the east.

Blaby
Leics. PO, tel, stores, garage. The church is partly 14thC, with a fine 18thC gallery unsuited to the Blaby of today. The County Arms, a monumental 1930s roadhouse by the A426 bridge, is more in keeping.
Wigston
Leics. PO, tel, stores, garage. Wigston is now a part of Leicester but traces of its earlier independence can still be found. Much of the handsome church dates from the 14thC, especially the interior, while the cottages in Spa Lane with their long strips of upper window indicate an old Leicester industry, stocking making. At Wigston Parva there is a tiny Norman church and a monument to the Roman town of Veronae. Unfortunately only housing estates and a school can be seen from the canal, but exploration is worth while.
Kilby Bridge
Leics. PO, tel, garage.

BOATYARDS

BWB Kilby Bridge Yard Kilby Bridge. (Leicester 882795). R S W
Ⓑ **Blaby Marine Centre** Wharf Way, Glen Parva, Leicester. (Leicester 778899). R S W Slipway, boat building & repair, mooring, chandlery, toilets, winter storage. *Closed Tue.*

PUBS

County Arms Blaby. Enormous Beefeater Steak House.
Black Horse Blaby
George Blaby
Navigation Kilby Bridge. Lively saloon and tiny public bar with inglenook, coal fire and brasses. Ind Coope real ale.

Aylestone

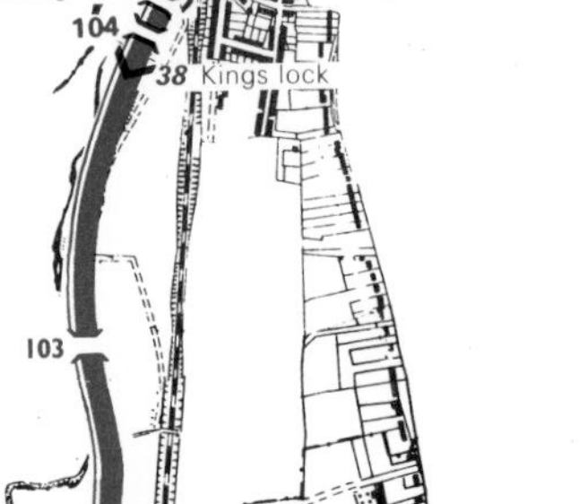

Following the River Sence to its junction with the Soar, the canal swings wide round Glen Parva and then flows north into Leicester along the Soar valley. After Glen Parva the buildings suddenly cease, and there follows a mile of very pleasant rural canal, lightly wooded to the east, and the extensive water meadows of the Soar to the west. The river and canal flow side by side separated only by the towpath, inevitably in winter this causes flooding, and so anyone intending to navigate this stretch out of season should check the state of the water before proceeding. Only the pylons and the distant views of Braunstone and Aylestone reveal the closeness of Leicester. The canal and the Soar meet by the gasworks where there is a huge weir; care is needed during times of flood. The canal enters Leicester along a pleasant cutting. A variety of buildings line the banks and there is a fine canalside walk under the ornamental bridges that lead straight into the town centre by West Bridge. These factors combine to make the canal entry to Leicester outstanding among large towns. The A46 and A426 run parallel to the canal, but the railway which follows it, the old Great Central line, is now closed.

Navigational note
Canal and River Soar meet just above Freeman's Meadow Lock, where there is an enormous unprotected weir. Care is needed, especially in time of flood. KEEP WELL OVER TO THE TOWPATH SIDE.

Aylestone
Leics. PO, tel, stores, garage. A Leicester suburb coming down to the east bank of the canal. The church contains an interesting stained glass window of 1930. To the west of the canal the Soar is crossed by an old stone packhorse bridge of 8 low arches, perhaps dating from the 15thC.

Glen Parva
Leics. PO, tel, stores, garage. Suburb of Leicester inseparable now from the main town. Curiously enough there was a Saxon cemetery in the town from which 6thC grave ornaments have been excavated.

Leicester

For almost all of its journey through the city of Leicester, the navigation pursues a course quite separate from the river, the navigation having been rebuilt towards the end of the 19thC as part of Leicester's flood prevention scheme. The City Council still has to maintain all the works, including 3 locks. For ½ a mile south of West Bridge, the navigation, a section known locally as 'The Straight', is like a formal avenue, tree-lined and crossed by several ornamental iron bridges, but where it curves under the old Great Central railway the navigation begins to follow a less public course through the nether regions of Leicester. A combination of locks, derelict canal basins, tall factory buildings and a substantial stretch of parkland adds up to a stretch of urban canal that offers a greater variety of interest than exists in most other cities. At Belgrave Lock the canal joins the Soar, which proceeds to meander carelessly through the city's outskirts. Fortunately the broad margin of water-meadows succeeds in keeping these at arm's length for most of the way. As is the case with all large towns, if you moor at an unprotected site ma' · sure your boat is well locked if you leave it unattended.

Navigational note
It is worth remembering that the River Soar floods frequently in winter, so boaters travelling out of season should enquire about the navigational conditions in advance in order to avert the risk of running aground in the middle of a water meadow.

Thurmaston
Leics. PO, tel, stores, garage. This unexciting suburb stretches along the old Fosse Way, now bypassed by a dual carriageway. However the opportunity thus afforded to Thurmaston has not been exploited. Evidence of Roman habitation was discovered in 1955, when excavation of an Anglo Saxon cemetery brought to light 95 urns dating from 50 years after Julius Caesar's invasion.

Leicester
EC Mon. MD Wed, Fri, Sat. All services. A prosperous city with a thriving university. Fortunes were founded on the hosiery and boot & shoe trades, but now a variety of light industries flourish in Leicester. There is a great deal of things to see, for this was the Roman town of Ratae, and there is plenty of evidence of the Roman buildings, plus a castle that dates from 1088, with the delightful church of St Mary de Castro next to it. The travel agent Thomas Cook started business in Leicester; in 1841 he organised the first publicly advertised excursion by train. It was a great success, and Cook made the organising of such trips a regular occupation. Leicester has a particularly good selection of museums, and it is fortunate that most of these are near the Grand Union Canal that flows through the centre of the city. The large shopping centre is to the east of West Bridge.

Leicester Abbey Abbey Park. All that remains of the abbey is a mansion built from the ruins and the old stone wall surrounding the grounds. Cardinal Wolsey was buried here in 1530. *Open daily.*

Railway Museum London Road, Stoneygate. East Midlands locomotives and items relating to local railway history. *Open Thur & Fri afternoons, Sat & Sun all day.*

The following Leicester museums are all open daily from Mon to Sat and Sun afternoons.
Leicester Museum & Art Gallery New Walk. Italian, Spanish and Flemish old masters. 18th-20thC English paintings. Also French Impressionists and German Expressionists. Also ceramics, silver, archives and geology.
Newarke Houses Museum. The Newarke social history of the area from 1500 to the present day. Locally made clocks and a clockmaker's workshop. Also shows the history of the hosiery, costume and lace industries.
Belgrave Hall Thurcaston Road. Small Queen Anne house and garden. Good collection of early 18th and 19thC furniture. Also stables, coaches and agricultural exhibits.
Jewry Wall & Museum of Archaeology Great Central Street. Leicester was once a Roman capital named Ratae Coritanorum. The Jewry Wall, a small portion of which remains, may have been part of a basilica or baths. Two Roman mosaic pavements can be seen in situ.
Guildhall Guildhall Lane. Contains fine oak panelling and an elaborately carved chimney-piece dated 1637.
Magazine The Newarke. The museum of the Leicester Regiment, honoured in the old stone gateway to the Newarke.

Museum of Technology in the Abbey Lane Pumping Station, Corporation Road. A new museum of mechanical exhibits, including 4 19thC beam engines (which operate on certain weekends), hosiery machinery, a transport collection and an 84 ton steam shovel.

Tourist Information Bishop Street. (Leicester 556699).

BOATYARDS

Ⓑ **Leicester Marina** Old Bridge, Thurcaston Road, (Leicester 62194). WDS Pump-out. Gas, mooring, slipway, chandlery, boat building & repairs, toilets, winter storage. Trip boat for charter.

PUBS

Joiners Arms Sanrey Gate, Leicester. South east of North Bridge.
Richmond Arms King Richards Road, Leicester. West of West Bridge.
Princess Charlotte Oxford Street. East of bridge 1.
Sir Robert Peel Jarrow Street. East of bridge 1, behind the Infirmary.

Paired working boats in Thurmaston Lock. *David Perrott*

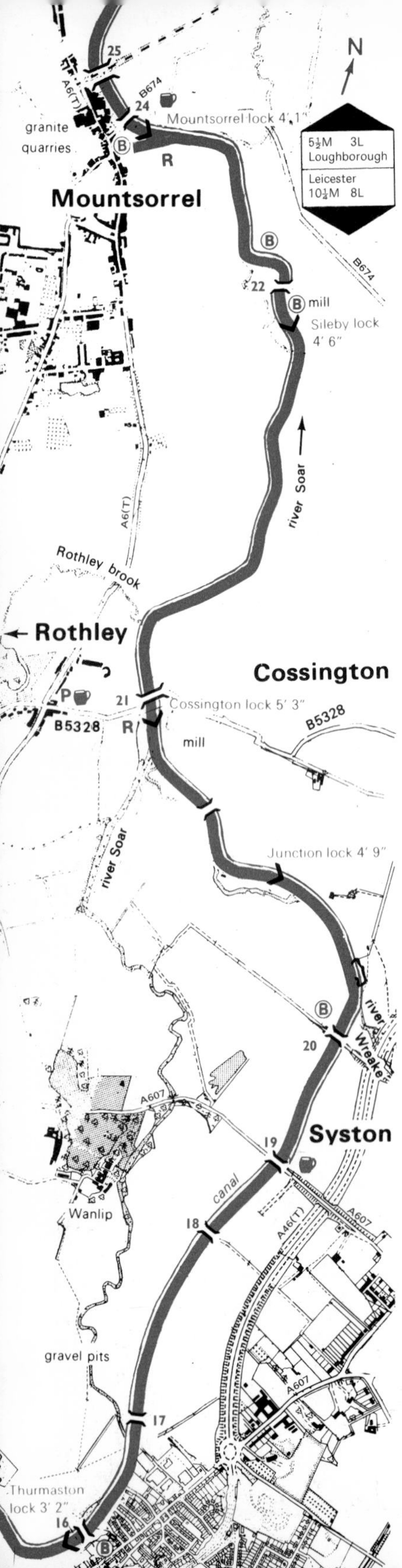

Mountsorrel

North of Thurmaston the canal leaves the river and heads north through an area scarred by busy gravel workings where, quite astonishingly, loads are carried to the ready mix concrete plant at Syston by *paired narrow boats*. Keep a look out for them, and give them priority. North of the Hope & Anchor pub more natural surroundings reappear, unspoilt by the nearby dual carriageway. Just beyond the boatyard, the River Wreake flows in from the north-east; the name of the nearby boatyard and the next lock hints at the significance of this little river. The River Soar rejoins the canal by Cossington Lock. The mill here is many centuries old and is now a restaurant. The villages of Cossington and Rothley are one mile away from Cossington Lock, on opposite sides of the Soar. The Rothley Brook joins the canal north of the lock. The river continues northwards, flanked by low green hills on the west side and pleasant water-meadows on the other. At Sileby Lock is another water mill but this one is of little interest compared to the one at Cossington. From here it is a short distance to Mountsorrel. The lock here is very much a waterways showplace and the boatyards and the lockside pub make it a busy one.

Mountsorrel
Leics. PO, tel, stores, garage, bank. It is but a few yards from the lock here to the centre of the village where the facilities in the long main street include a cheese shop, a saddler and a launderette. The A6 thunders through the village, but fails to destroy the dignity of the old buildings lining the road. The old covered market cross still survives. The church and the vicarage face each other over this village street; the generous dimensions of the vicarage and its elegant façade have more appeal than the rather plain church. In the hills that rise steeply behind the village are the extensive quarries that supply the well-known Mountsorrel granite, distinguished by its pinkish tinge. The stone is crushed there and used for road chippings.

Cossington
Leics. PO, tel. A mile east of Cossington Lock, this is a pretty village with wide, well-kept grass verges and plenty of trees. Although there is much new building, it mixes well with the old. The church is set apart among trees. Much rebuilt in Mountsorrel granite, it contains excellent Victorian stained glass.

Rothley
Leics. PO, tel, stores, garage. Lies in the valley of the Rothley Brook which runs to the south of the village and through the grounds of Rothley Temple, once a preceptory for the Knights Templar. The 13thC chapel with a figure of a Knight Templar still remains beside the Elizabethan house, once the home of the Babington family, and the birthplace of the poet, historian and dramatist Lord Macaulay. It is now an hotel. The Norman church in Rothley village is built mainly of granite, the massive tower, nave and aisles being subsequent additions. In the churchyard is a tall Anglo-Saxon cross, thought to be over 1000 years old.

The Wreake Navigation & the Oakham Canal
This waterway was opened in 1795 as a broadlocked river navigation from the canal north of Syston to Melton Mowbray, 15 miles away to the east. Beyond Melton the Oakham Canal extended the navigation as far as Oakham, in Rutland. When the railways were built the 2 waterways could not compete and the Oakham Canal was closed as early as 1846. More than a century later, some lengths still hold water; in other places the former canal bed is only a faint depression. The general course of the canal, which follows the contours of the land, can be traced on a 1in O.S. map. It is interesting to note how the railway follows a similar, but more direct, course. The Wreake Navigation was closed to traffic in 1877. The

old navigation works are easily recognisable and the remains of the first lock can be found under ½ mile from its junction with the canal.

BOATYARDS

Ⓑ **Sileby Boatyard** Mountsorrel Lane, Sileby. (3404). R S W D Pump-out, slipway, moorings, gas, chandlery, café, toilets, winter storage.

Ⓑ **Soar Valley Boatyard** Sileby Road, Mountsorrel, Leics. (Leicester 302642). Chandlery (also clothing), slipway, moorings. Boat sales & repairs. *Open daily.*

Ⓑ **L. R. Harris & Son** Old Junction Boatyard, Meadow Lane, Syston, near Leicester. (Leicester 692135). R W D Gas, chandlery, slipway, winter storage. Boat sales & repairs, inboard and outboard engines sales & repairs. Welding specialists. *Open daily.*

Ⓑ **Charnwood Marine** (Mill Lane Boatyard), Thurmaston, Leics. (693069). R S W D Pump-out, narrow boat hire, slipway, gas, boat sales, mooring, chandlery, toilets, showers, winter storage.

PUBS

Waterside Inn Mountsorrel Lock. Comfortable pub serving Everards real ale, bar snacks, restaurant meals, *daily except Sat lunch and Sun dinner.*

Dog & Gun Mountsorrel.

✕ **Red Lion** Rothley, at crossroads up the hill west of Cossington Lock. Ind Coope real ale, restaurant meals, *daily except Sun dinner.*

Royal Oak Cossington.

Hope & Anchor Syston. Canalside: good moorings.

Bakers Arms Syston.

The River Soar near Loughborough. *Derek Pratt*

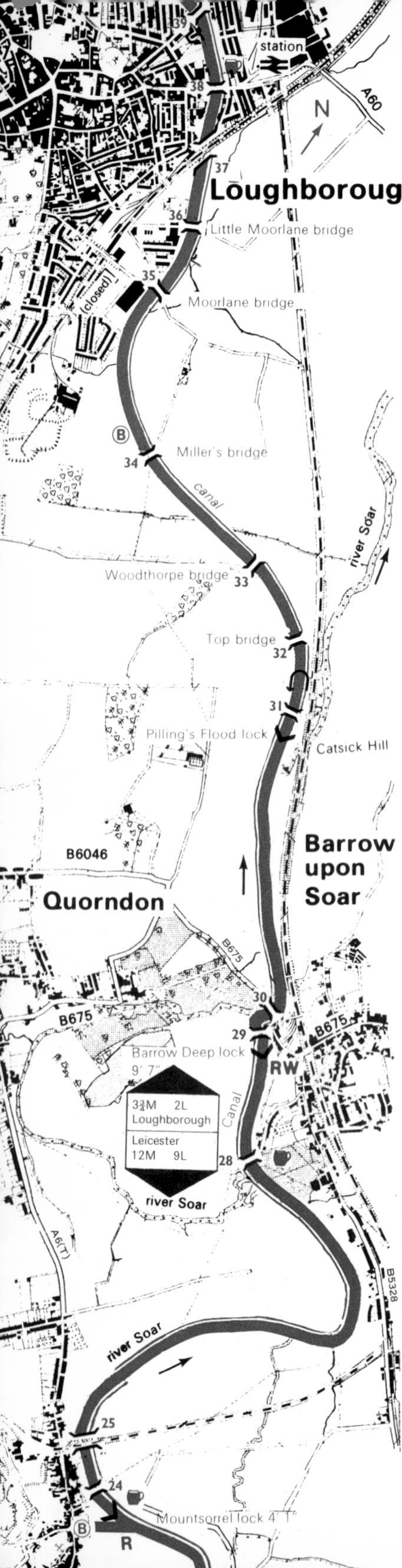

Loughborough

Leaving Mountsorrel Lock the navigation passes under first a red brick railway bridge, dated 1860 in bold figures; trucks containing Mountsorrel granite pass over this bridge on their way from the quarry to the main line. 300yds north of it are the remains of another, much smaller, bridge; this used to carry the towpath across the river. The canal crosses the valley, reaching the pretty village of Barrow upon Soar. A bridge and a canalside pub introduce a short section of canal that bypasses a wide meander of the River Soar. Before the canal rejoins the river its level is changed by a very deep lock; beyond it, the river reappears at the old 5-arched bridge. Beyond, there follows a superb wooded stretch for nearly a mile, terminated by Pillings Flood Lock: boats heading downstream should keep left to avoid the weir. Since this is a flood lock, all the gates are usually open and one may pass straight through into the long canal section which enters the northern outskirts of Loughborough. The pleasant landscape is soon replaced by the lengthy back wall of an engineering works. The canal then passes under the old Great Central Railway and circles Loughborough to a T-junction. This marks the end of the Leicester Navigation and the start of the Loughborough Navigation, which completes the remaining 9 miles to the River Trent.

Navigational note
There are flood warning lights at Barrow Deep, Bishop Meadow and Redhill Locks—do not pass if red light shows.

Loughborough
Leics. EC Wed, MD Thur, Sat. A busy industrial town famed for church bells which have been cast by John Taylor & Co for over a century. More important to the town's prosperity are the Brush companies, part of the Hawker Siddeley Group, who in the last 70 years have produced mechanical equipment like horse-buses, fuse links, rolling stock and a vast number of diesel locomotives for British Railways. But it is the bells by which Loughborough is known and remembered, for Taylor's bells ring in churches throughout England and abroad. (One of their largest bells is Great Paul, in St Paul's Cathedral, London). The town's War Memorial is a Carillon Tower, the only municipal grand carillon in the country.

Barrow upon Soar
Leics. PO, tel, stores, garage, bank. Most of the village is on the hill on the far side of the railway cutting, but the prettiest part is down by the river, where the old stone bridge, the canal lock, the overhanging trees and the mêlée of small boats draw many visitors on a summer Sunday afternoon.

BOATYARDS

Ⓑ **Sablecraft** Beeches Road, Loughborough (262719). R S W Pump-out, day hire narrow boats, long term mooring, slipway, books, maps, souvenirs.

PUBS

Albion Loughborough. Canalside, on towpath just north of the junction.

Boat Loughborough. Canalside, at bridge east of junction. Unspoilt pub serving Marstons real ale.

Duke of York Loughborough. Canalside, at the bridge near the station. Grocer and fish & chips nearby.

Navigation Barrow upon Soar. Shipstones real ale in a fine canalside pub. Garden.

Riverside Inn Barrow upon Soar. Near the river bridge. Everards real ale in a wood panelled pub. Food. Petrol nearby.

Normanton on Soar

The Loughborough Navigation has the same physical characteristics as the Leicester Navigation. It continues the fall towards the Trent with the same pattern of meandering river reaches and the occasional canal cut, with locks bypassing the weirs. In spite of the entrance of streams along the way, the River Soar does not seem to get any wider. Leaving Loughborough Wharf, the navigation follows a fairly straight and open course out into the country. Two locks bring it eventually back into the river, and from this point to its junction with the Trent, the Soar forms the county boundary between Leicestershire on the west side and Nottinghamshire on the east. Normanton on Soar is visible some way away because of its prominent church steeple; on approaching, one finds the church is only a matter of yards from the river bank. However the inhabitants of Normanton guard their waterfront jealously, making it extremely difficult to get ashore. Even the formal garden of the riverside pub displays a selection of notices strictly prohibiting the mooring of boats out of licensing hours. Below Normanton is the settlement of Zouch which, although tattier than Normanton, has a certain weary and less conventional charm, easier access and more facilities. Below Zouch Lock the A6 reappears and follows the side of the hill; the river is well shielded from this road by trees, but these are powerless against the multiple tracks of vast pylons which stalk along the valley here. At Devil's Elbow boats heading downstream should keep right to stay in the main navigation channel. The village of Sutton Bonington to the east is identified by its church spire.

Navigational note
Boaters are reminded that this is basically a river navigation, liable to flood in wet weather. Keep well clear of the weirs. If the warning light at Bishop Meadow Lock shows red—do not pass.

Whatton House
Visible from the river near the Devil's Elbow, this mansion was built about 1802, damaged by fire and restored in 1876. Its fine 25-acre gardens are *open summer Sun afternoons*.

Normanton on Soar
Notts. PO, tel. A quiet and carefully preserved village with wide grass verges and some discreetly pretty buildings, notably the post office, which is a black and white timbered building with a thatched roof and steep gable ends, unusual in this part of the country. The cruciform church has a central tower and spire, rare in so small a church. On the east wall of the nave there are some excellent stone carvings; the centre one is an elaborate coat of arms with a quizzical lion in the middle. The plain glass windows make the church enjoyably light. A ferry here once again links Nottinghamshire to Leicestershire. A ramshackle array of small chalets line the riverbank.

BOATYARDS

Ⓑ **BWB Loughborough Yard** (Loughborough 212729). W.

PUBS

Anchor Sutton Bonington.

Rose and Crown Zouch. Canalside. Manns real ale, good food, a friendly atmosphere and convivial host. Patrons may moor at the attractive garden.

Plough Normanton. Large old riverside pub with a garden where Ansells and Ind Coope real ale can be enjoyed.

Albion Inn Unlikely looking canalside pub north of Loughborough serving Shipstones beers.

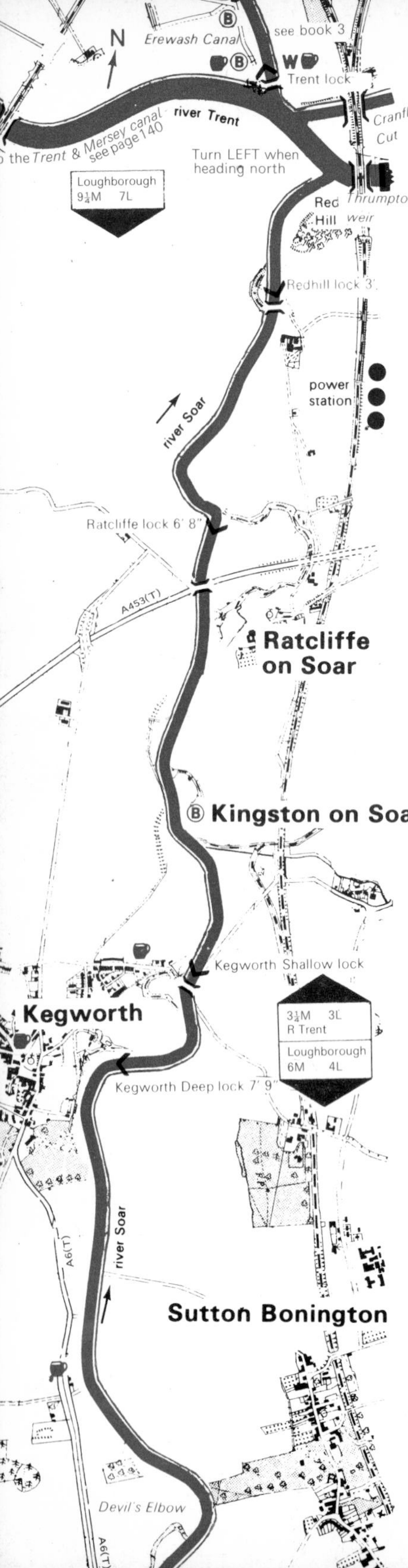

Kegworth

This is yet another stretch of pleasant meandering river. At the point where the A6 and the Soar almost touch there is a riverside pub and the headquarters of the Soar Boating Club. North of the pub a willow-lined reach leads to a stone mansion with spreading lawns where the channel divides. To the left (nearer Kegworth) is a maze of shallow and weedy backwaters, weirs and a water mill; boats should keep to the right for Kegworth Deep Lock. After another sharp swing to the north the channel divides again, and northbound boats should once more bear right for Kegworth Shallow Lock—this is a flood lock and so all 4 gates are usually open. There is a pub near here and a home bakery up the road. From this lock to the Trent the navigation is somewhat more isolated, but two notable landmarks are the spire of Ratcliffe on Soar church and the 8 cooling towers and vast chimney of the Ratcliffe Power Station that totally dominates the landscape for miles around. The adjacent railway (the main line from Derby, Nottingham and Sheffield to London) passes close to the works, feeding it constantly with trainloads of coal on the 'merry-go-round' principle. The navigation skirts round the west side of Red Hill. The last lock here has beautifully kept lawns and a well-painted bridge—on which are shown the flood levels for 1955 and 1960. Milk, eggs and bread are available here. A few hundred yards below Red Hill Lock the Soar flows into the River Trent and loses its identity in this much bigger waterway.

Navigational note
Boats negotiating the junction of the rivers Soar and Trent should keep well away from Thrumpton Weir, which is just east (downstream) of the big iron railway bridge. Navigators are reminded that the main line of the Trent Navigation is the Cranfleet Cut. This begins 200yds upstream of the mouth of the Soar, hard by the large, wooden building which houses one of the many sailing clubs on the Trent. The entrance to the Erewash Canal is also here, marked by a lock and a cluster of buildings. If the warning light at Redhill Lock shows red—do not pass.

Ratcliffe on Soar
Notts. PO, tel, stores. A tiny village with a spired church dating from the 13thC. The interior of the nave is pleasantly uncluttered and rather spartan. There is no stained glass to darken it, and the white-washed walls accentuate the bold and ancient arches. In the chancel, on the other hand, there is a profusion of stone effigies and wall memorials, many of them to the Sacheverell family.

Kingston on Soar
Notts. PO, tel, stores. Situated east of the railway embankment, this is a small quiet estate village which looks much as it must have done 50 years ago. The church, still very much the focus of the village, is a pretty building of 1900, incorporating earlier fragments; there are some fine tombs.

Kegworth
Leics. PO, tel, stores, bank. Kegworth has an attractive situation up on a wooded hill that is crowned by the church spire, but although it is close to the river, access is easy only from Kegworth Shallow Lock; anyway the walk into the village is not really rewarding, although the late Decorated church has a fine angel roof. Perhaps Kegworth has been traversed for too long by the A6. The M1 motorway runs just west of the village.

BOATYARDS

Ⓑ **Kegworth Marine** Kingston Lane, Kegworth, Leics. (Kegworth 2300). Moorings, gas, repairs, winter storage.

PUBS

Anchor Kegworth, near Shallow Lock. Bass real ale and food.

White House Riverside, south of Kegworth. Bar meals most days.

Cap & Stocking Borough Street, Kegworth. M & B real ales dispensed from jugs in a family run pub.

LLANGOLLEN CANAL

Maximum dimensions

Length: 72′
Beam: 6′ 10″
Headroom: 7′

Mileage

Hurleston Junction (S.U. main line) to
Frankton Junction: 29
Pontcysyllte Aqueduct: 40
Llangollen: 44½
Llantisilio: 46

Locks: 21

In 1791 a plan was published for a canal from the Mersey to the Severn, to pass through Chester, the iron and coal fields around Ruabon, Ellesmere and Shrewsbury. There were to be branches to the limestone quarries at Llanymynech, and to the Chester Canal via Whitchurch. The new terminus on the Mersey was to be at the little fishing village of Netherpool, known after 1796 as Ellesmere Port. After extensive arguments about routes, the company received its Act in 1793. William Jessop was appointed engineer, and work began. By 1796 the Wirral line from Chester to Ellesmere Port was open, and was immediately successful, carrying goods and passengers (in express 'fly-boats') to Liverpool. The same year, the Llanymynech Branch was completed. The company continued to expand and build inwards, but failed to make the vital connections with the Dee and the Severn; the line south to Shrewsbury never got further than Weston, and the line northwards to Chester stopped at Pontcysyllte. By 1806 the Ellesmere company had opened 68 miles of canal, which included lines from Hurleston on the Chester Canal to Plas Kynaston via Frankton, and from Chester to Ellesmere Port; there were branches to Llanymynech, Whitchurch, Prees and Ellesmere, and a navigable feeder to Llangollen; the two great aqueducts at Chirk and Pontcysyllte were complete. However it was a totally self-contained system, its only outlet being via the old Chester Canal at Hurleston. Despite this, the Ellesmere Canal was profitable; it serviced a widespread local network, and gave an outlet to Liverpool (via the River Mersey) for the ironworks and the coalfields that were grouped at the centre of the system. This profitability was dependent upon good relations with the Chester Company. An attempted take-over in 1804 failed, but in 1813 the inevitable merger took place, and the Ellesmere & Chester Canal Company was formed. Today the Llangollen Canal is perhaps the most popular cruising canal in the country and as a result can be very crowded during the summer months. Those who cruise out of the peak season, or avoid the mid-week rush to Llangollen, will enjoy it more.

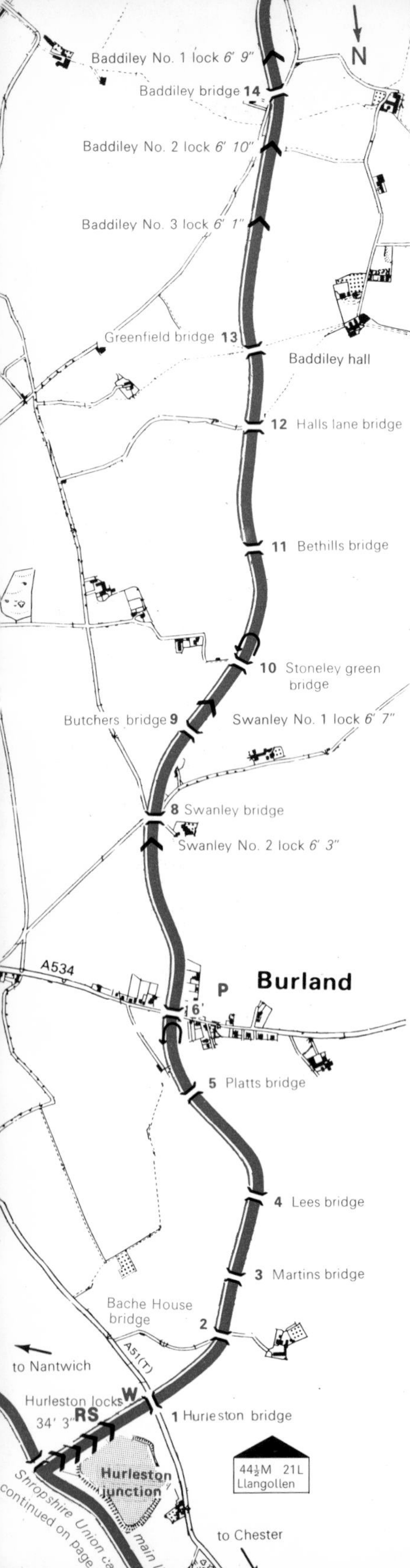

Hurleston

The Llangollen rapidly establishes its character as a quiet and pretty canal. Considering the spectacular scenery further west, it is hardly surprising that this is the most popular cruising waterway in the country—so much so, in fact, that in the height of the summer up to 400 boats a week use the canal. Leaving Hurleston, the canal runs through a very shallow valley past the hamlet of Burland to Swanley Locks. There is an old canalside house at Swanley Bridge (8) with a beautiful garden and weeping willows overhanging the water. The next 3 locks encountered are Baddiley Locks (note the unusual paddle gear at lock no 2); the tall Georgian house surrounded by trees to the west of the bottom lock is Baddiley Hall.

Navigational note
The Llangollen Canal is fed directly by the River Dee at Llantisilo, and there is a noticeable flow of water from west to east. Navigators should allow more time for journeys to Llangollen—*against the flow*.

Burland
Ches. Tel, stores, garage. A straggling settlement by the canal, useful as a supply centre; the general store here is open every day. And the petrol station is almost beside the canal.

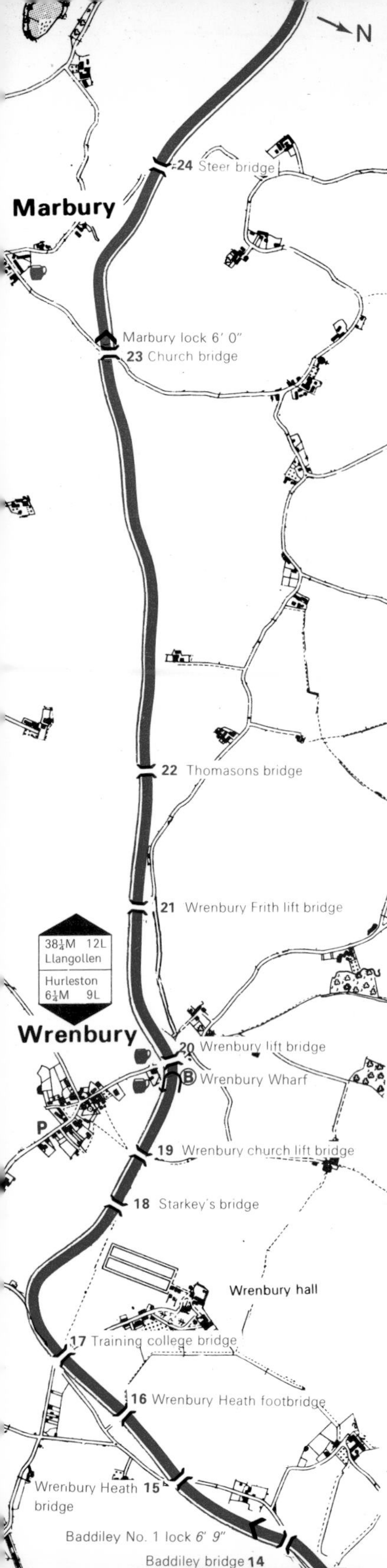

Wrenbury

The canal moves past Wrenbury Hall, formerly the home of Sir John Stapleton Cotton (one of Wellington's generals) and now a college. towards Wrenbury. The old farmhouse west of bridges 14 and 15 sells local honey, cheese, eggs, milk, etc. Wrenbury Wharf is a delightful spot. The bridge is an old-fashioned lift bridge, of a type often seen in Holland and Van Gogh's paintings—it is operated with your windlass. There are some fine warehouses and a former mill here, and a nearby pub. Beyond the wharf, the soft green Cheshire countryside leads to Marbury Lock. The tall obelisk visible to the south is at distant Combermere Park.

Navigational note
The passage through most of the lift bridges is restricted—beware of injuring the crew or damaging the cabin. Go very slowly, and if in doubt, 'walk' the boat through. Make sure everyone is inboard, especially the children.

Marbury
Ches., tel. An enchanting village ½ mile south of Marbury Lock. Centred on an old farm, the village boasts several other old and timbered buildings. The church is a gem, and its setting is unrivalled: it stands on top of a little hill that overlooks a beautiful mere. The church grounds contain not just a graveyard but a garden, and the interior is correspondingly attractive and interesting. The sympathetically restored rectory stands next door.
Wrenbury
Ches. PO, tel, stores, garage, station. A quiet village ¼ mile from the wharf. There are some thatched cottages and a large church. It is refreshing to find a railway station still operating today in a village as small as this. The line goes from Crewe to Shrewsbury.
St Margaret's Church Overlooking the village green, this is a large, battlemented church with an early 16thC west tower and 18thC chancel and pulpit. The interior is very light and airy and contains a number of fine monuments of the last century, as well as several brasses.

BOATYARDS

Ⓑ **English County Cruises** Wrenbury, in the old mill by bridge 20. (Crewe 780544, office 061-941 1816). R S W D Pump-out, gas, narrow boat hire, mooring, dry dock with hydraulic boat lift, repairs, souvenirs.

PUBS

Swan Marbury. Greenall Whitley beers in a handsome black and white pub with colourful window boxes and comfortable bars, facing a green. Small garden. Snacks.
Cotton Arms near Wrenbury Bridge. Greenall Whitley beers. Snacks, children's room.
Dusty Miller Wrenbury. Large pub in a handsome converted 19thC mill. Robinsons real ale, meals and snacks. Canalside garden and rose garden.

Grindley Brook

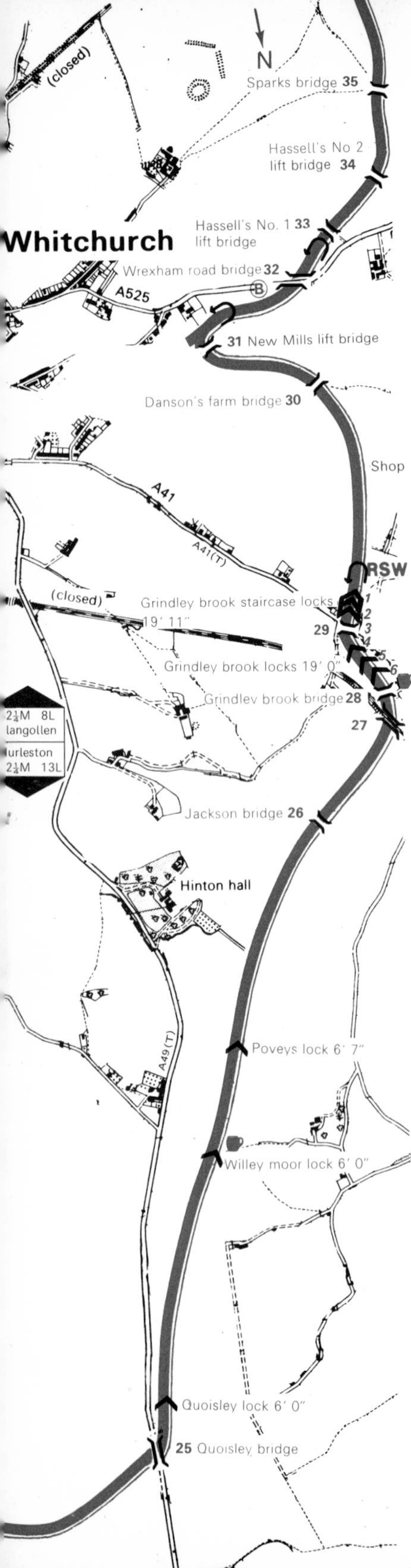

The canal continues to rise through a series of isolated locks as the sides of the valley begin to encroach on either side. One of them, Willey Moor, has a restaurant beside it. Hinton Hall, a large Victorian building, is shrouded in trees on the side of a hill. At the end of a straight stretch a massive railway embankment precedes a sharp bend to the bottom of the 6 locks at Grindley Brook; care should be exercised on the approach to the locks, and any boats stopping to visit the garage, shop or pub nearby should remain below the railway embankment. The first 3 locks are followed at the A41 bridge by 3 'staircase' locks. Anyone requiring assistance or advice should look for the lock keeper, whose unusual house is at the top lock. There is a convenient store selling fresh vegetables, meat, provisions and souvenirs beside the staircase locks, and a cottage at the top lock where home made pies can be bought. Another cottage to the south also offers home cooked food. The canal now swerves round the side of a hill near Whitchurch: the first of a spattering of lift bridges marks the entrance to the long-abandoned Whitchurch Arm, now the subject of detailed restoration schemes.

Whitchurch
Shropshire. EC Wed. MD Fri. PO, tel, stores, garage, bank, station. A very fine town with some beautiful old houses of all periods in the centre. The streets are narrow and there is much to discover by wandering around. The striking church of St Alkmund on the hill was built in 1713, after the old church, called the Norman White Church—hence the name of the town—'fell ye 31 of July 1711'. Oxford Canal connoisseurs will recognise its similarity to the magnificent church of the same vintage at Banbury. It has very big windows: indeed the whole church is on a grand scale. There are plenty of splendid pubs in the town, but unfortunately none near the canal.

BOATYARDS

Ⓑ **Bridge Canal Cruisers** Wrexham Road, Whitchurch, Shropshire. (2012). Near bridge 32 (Wrexham Road Bridge). R S W P D Pump-out, boat hire, slipway, gas, boat & engine repairs, mooring, chandlery, toilets, provisions, winter storage.

PUBS

Black Bear Whitchurch. Greenall Whitley beers. Booked meals in pub; pies etc.
Red Cow Whitchurch. Sandwiches and pies.
White Bear Whitchurch. Food. B&B.
Horse and Jockey Grindley Brook, near bottom lock. Greenall Whitley beers, garden, bar meals and snacks.
The Willeymoor Lock Bar and restaurant for grills. Children welcome.

Whixall Moss

The canal now winds round the side of a succession of low hills as it begins to traverse a very remote and underpopulated area, passing no villages for miles but many farms and hundreds of healthy-looking cows. At Platt Lane the navigation straightens out and is carried on an embankment across the strange area of Whixall Moss, where peat cutting is still carried on. A solitary lift bridge interrupts the long straight, then there is a junction with the Prees Branch, which leads, past 2 lift bridges, to a marina. The main line veers off to the north west along another straight embankment, this time accompanied by woodlands, passing the border between England and Wales.

Prees Branch
Sometimes known as the Edstaston Branch, this arm curves round to Quina Brook. (It never did reach Prees.) The arm's principal value in recent years lay in the clay pits just over a mile from the junction: the clay from here was used until a few years ago for repairing the 'puddle' in local canals. The arm has been disused for some years, but the first ½ mile has been dredged and reopened to give access to a new marina constructed in the old clay pit. It is a very pleasant canal arm with 2 splendid old lift bridges—one of which is a rare skewed bridge. Naturalists find interesting plant communities along the unrestored section of the branch: enquiries may be made to the Nature Conservancy at the address given below.

Whixall Moss
A raised bog rich in flora and insect fauna—including mosquitoes! Like other meres and bogs in the area, Whixhall Moss came into existence at the end of the Ice Age, as huge blocks of ice were left behind when the remainder of the ice cap melted and drained off into what is now the Severn valley. The peat surface remains, in spite of constant cutting of the peat for garden use. Naturalists can obtain information regarding access, etc, from the Regional Officer (Midlands), Nature Conservancy, Attingham Park, Shrewsbury, Shropshire.

Platt Lane
Shropshire. Tel, store. A tiny settlement on the edge of the Moss with an equally tiny village store.

BOATYARDS

Ⓑ **Black Prince Marina** at the end of the Prees Branch. (Whixall 420). R S W D E Pump-out, gas, narrow boat hire, chandlery, showers, repairs. Souvenirs, groceries and off-licence.

PUBS

Waggoners Platt Lane, Whixhall. Basic Greenall Whitley pub, with a garden.

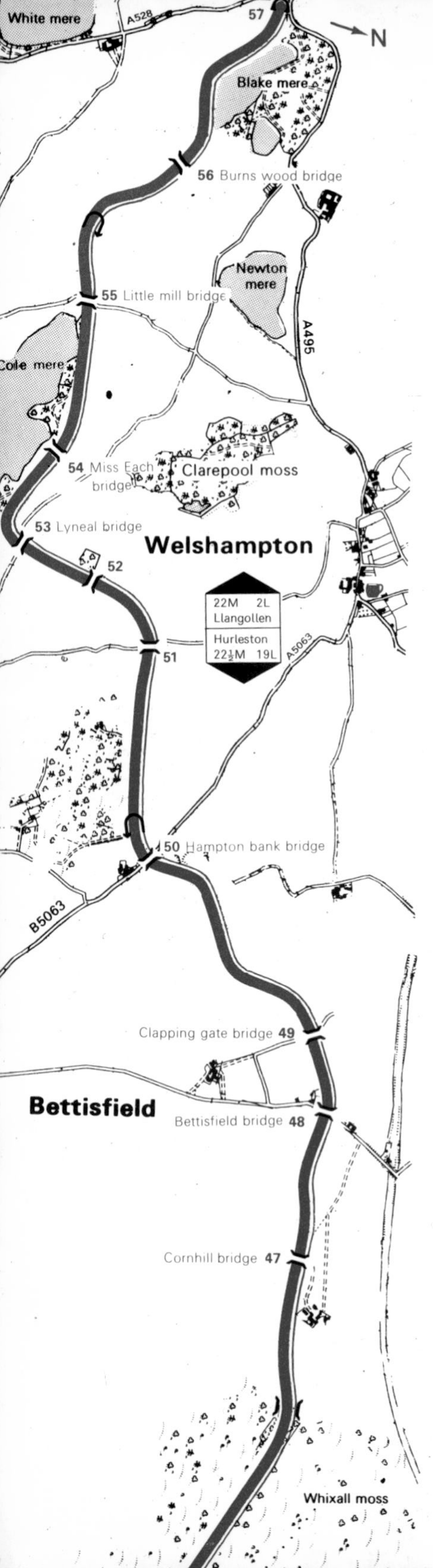

Bettisfield

Leaving Whixhall Moss, the canal passes Bettisfield and begins to wind this way and that, passing into Wales and out again. Soon the open countryside gives way to the hilly wooded landscape that precedes Ellesmere and contains several beautiful meres. The canal skirts first Cole Mere, which is below and mostly hidden from it by tall trees; there is a delightful timbered cottage at the west end. Then the navigation runs right beside Blake Mere: this is a charming little lake, surrounded by steep and thickly wooded hills. It is inhabited by many fish, and also ducks and other wild birds. One plunges immediately afterwards into the 87yd Ellesmere Tunnel and out into the open parkland beyond.

Welshampton
Shropshire. PO, tel, stores, garage. 1 mile west of bridge 50, the village contains the only pub since Platt Lane.

Bettisfield
Clwyd. PO, tel, stores (off-licence). There is little life in Bettisfield now: the pub and railway have closed and the station has become a private house. The church occupies a good position on the hill—it is a pretty Victorian building.

PUBS

Sun Welshampton. Greenall Whitley pub with a garden.

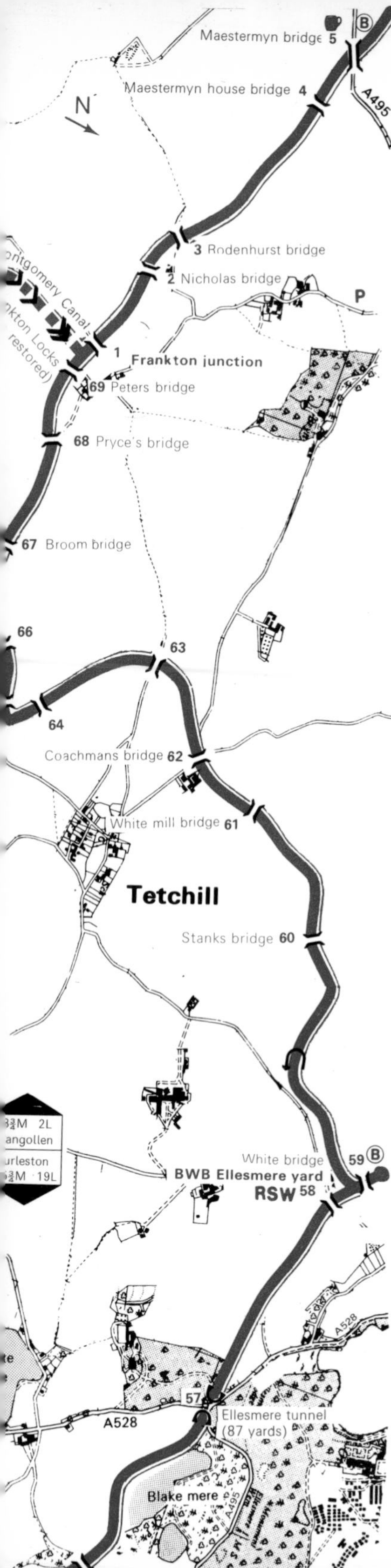

Ellesmere

Leaving Blake Mere and the tunnel, one soon arrives at Ellesmere. The town itself is reached via a short arm: at the end of the arm is a large dairy and a boat hire company close to the centre of town. Old warehouses and a small canalside crane testify to the canal trading that used to be carried on from here. The main line of the canal to Llangollen bears round sharply to the south west at the junction: the fine old buildings here house the BWB maintenance yard with facilities for pleasure boats. Within the yard is 'Beech House', once the canal company's office. Beyond the yard, the country once again becomes quiet and entirely rural, while the canal's course becomes very winding. Frankton Junction is where boats used to branch off down the old Montgomery Canal south to Newtown: the canal is unnavigable, although the staircase locks by the junction, disused since 1936, have been restored (see below). West of this junction, the bridge numbering on the Llangollen Canal starts again, because originally the Llangollen was only a branch of the Montgomery line.

The Montgomery Canal
When the Ellesmere Canal plans were published, they inspired a separate company to plan a canal from Newtown northwards to join the Llanymynech Branch of the Ellesmere Canal at Carreghofa. The canal was authorised in 1793, and by 1797 the line was open from Carreghofa to Garthmyl. The Montgomery Canal was mainly agricultural; apart from the limestone, it existed to serve the farms and villages through which it passed, and so was never really able to make a profit. The lack of capital and income greatly delayed the completion of the western extension to Newtown, which was not finally opened until 1821, having been financed by a separate company. The canal was never reopened after a breach about two miles beyond Frankton Junction in 1936. Although parts of the canal have been restored, notably 6 miles at Welshpool, where a trip boat plies, there are still serious obstacles to complete restoration. It is, however, an excellent cross country walk.

Tetchill
Shropshire. PO, tel, stores, garage. A small farming village, quiet and unpretentious. There is no sign of a church.

Ellesmere
Shropshire. EC Thur. PO, tel, stores, garage, bank. This handsome 18thC market town with its narrow winding streets is an attractive place to visit. There are many tall red brick houses and several terraces of old cottages. It takes its name from the large and beautiful mere beside it. The castle that once defended the people of Shropshire from their barbarous Celtic neighbours was destroyed long ago, and its ancient site is now used as a bowling green with a fine view of the surrounding countryside.
St Mary's Church Standing on a hill overlooking the mere, the general appearance of this large red stone church is Victorian, belying its medieval origins. It contains a medieval chest hewn out of a solid block of oak, many fine effigies and a beautiful 15thC octagonal font.

BOATYARDS

BWB Ellesmere Yard at junction with Ellesmere arm R S W. Dry dock for hire.
Ⓑ **Ellesmere Boats** on the Ellesmere arm. (Ellesmere 2610). Pump-out, hire cruisers.
Ⓑ **Maestermyn Marine** see next page.

PUBS

Bridgewater Arms Hotel Ellesmere. Real ale. Restaurant: lunches and dinners daily.
Swan Ellesmere. Greenall Whitley beers.
White Hart Ellesmere. A very old timbered building where Border real ale is available. Food, garden.

Henlle Park

The navigation continues to run west and north through quiet, green countryside. At Hindford Bridge there is a pub and restaurant. Beyond, the canal climbs through the 2 New Marton Locks—the last to be encountered on the way to Llangollen. There is a shop, run by the lock keeper, at the top lock; and by bridge 13 is a useful shop selling provisions, souvenirs, beer and wine. Next door you can watch pots being made, and buy them if you wish. Gradually the land becomes hillier as one passes Wat's Dyke and Henlle Park. The A5 joins the navigation near Chirk Bank.

Rhoswiel
Shropshire. PO, tel, stores. A tiny mining village on the Welsh border; the canal runs through it in a slight cutting.

BOATYARDS

Ⓑ **Maestermyn Marine** Ellesmere Road, Whittington, Shropshire. (Oswestry 62424). R S W D Pump-out, gas, narrow boat hire, slipway, chandlery, boat sales and repairs, provisions, off licence, overnight mooring.

PUBS AND RESTAURANTS

Lion by bridge 17. Snacks.
Mad Jacks by bridge 11. Meals, snacks, provisions, craft shop. Children welcome. W Gas, overnight mooring. *Closed Mon.*
New Inn Gledrid, Chirk. Canalside, at bridge 19 and on A5 road. Banks's real ale. Restaurant: lunches and dinners daily. Children welcome, showers.
Narrowboat Inn by bridge 5. Real ale, snacks and canalside garden.

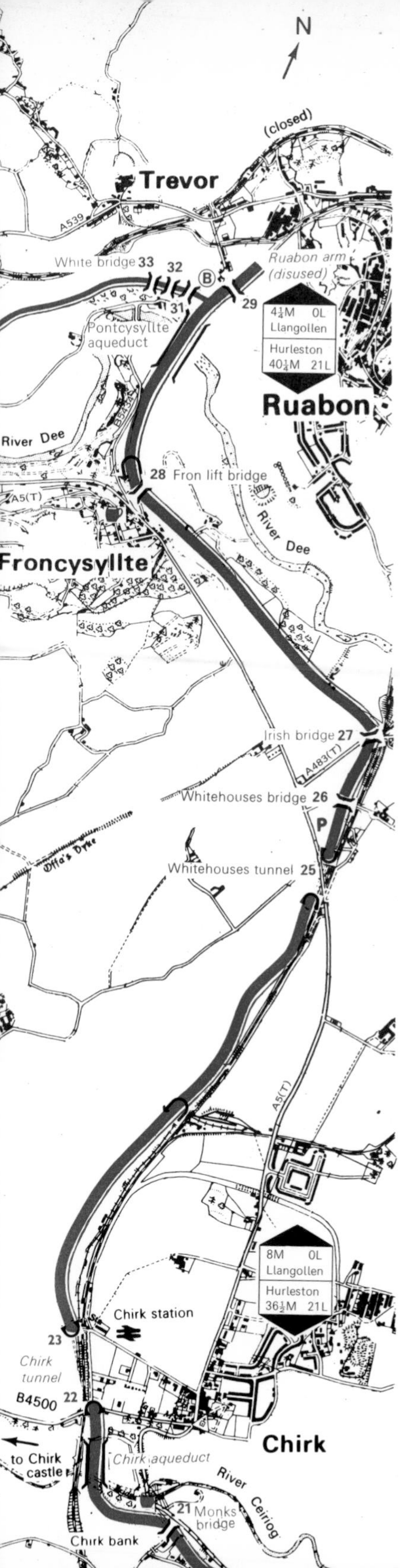

Chirk and Pontcysyllte

One soon begins to realise why this canal is so famous. The approach of the Welsh mountains drives the navigation into a side cutting half way up the side of a hill. Passing Chirk Bank, one rounds a corner and suddenly finds oneself on Chirk Aqueduct—an impressive structure by any canal enthusiast's standards, but slightly overshadowed by the railway viaduct alongside. At the end of the aqueduct the canal enters a tunnel immediately. At the north end of the tunnel a strong smell of chocolate betrays a canalside cocoa factory; Chirk station is conveniently nearby. A long wooded cutting follows, then the railway reappears alongside. Another, shorter tunnel at Whitehouses is negotiated before the canal meets the valley of the River Dee. Here the railway charges off to the north on a magnificent viaduct, while the canal clings to the hillside. By now the scenery is superb and the views excellent. But more is yet to come! Passing the village of Froncysyllte (*PO, tel, stores*), the canal launches out into this deep valley on a massive embankment, then crosses the River Dee on the breathtaking Pontcysyllte Aqueduct. At the north end of the aqueduct there is a boatyard and a tricky 90-degree turn. From this point to Llangollen the canal is very narrow and is not recommended to boats drawing more than 21in. The short arm towards Ruabon was originally projected as the canal's main line towards Chester and the Mersey. (The dry dock at the Trevor Junction dates from this time.) The line from Trevor to Llantisilio was envisaged purely as a navigable feeder. However the idea of a direct line to Chester was soon dropped and a connection made instead with the Chester Canal at Hurleston Junction.

Navigational note
The canal now becomes very shallow, accentuating the flow 'downstream'. Just go slowly and revel in the Welsh scenery.

Pontcysyllte Aqueduct
Easily the most famous and most spectacular feature on the whole canal system, this aqueduct cannot fail to astonish the visitor. Apart from its great height of 120ft above the River Dee and its length of over 1000ft, the excitement to be derived from crossing this structure by boat is partly due to the fact that, while the towpath side is safely fenced off with iron railings, the offside is completely unprotected from about 12in above the water level. The safest way for children to enjoy the great aqueduct is inside the boat. Boats cannot pass each other on the aqueduct, so do not enter it if another boat is coming in the opposite direction. The aqueduct was built by Thomas Telford, and is generally reckoned to be one of his most brilliant and most successful works. The concept of laying a cast iron trough along the top of a row of stone piers was entirely new, and entirely Telford's: he realised that such a high crossing of the Dee valley was inevitable if time- and water-wasting locks were to be avoided, and it was obvious to the canal company that a conventional brick or stone aqueduct would be quite unsuitable. His plan for the aqueduct was greeted at first with derision; but the work went ahead, was completed in 10 years and opened in 1805. One can hardly imagine the utter amazement felt by people of that time as they witnessed boats moving easily across this tall, beautiful and unique structure. Today, the aqueduct remains as built, apart from recent renewals of balustrading and the towpath structure. The masonry is apparently in prime condition (note the very thin masonry joints), and the dovetailed joints in the iron trough hardly leak at all. The cast iron side plates of the trough are all wedged-shaped, like the stones in a masonry arch. It is, without doubt, a masterpiece.

Chirk
Clwyd. EC Thur. PO, tel, stores, garage, bank, station. An unassuming place whose 18thC village centre is full of A5 traffic. Most of Chirk is in Wales but a few houses on the south side are in England, including the Bridge Inn.
Chirk Castle 1 mile west of Chirk Tunnel.

Built in 1295 as a Marcher Fortress, it has been the home of the Myddelton family since 1595. The dungeon under the west range remains as built, the interior rooms are richly decorated and the entrance gates are a remarkable example of wrought-iron work, made in 1721. There are traces of Offa's Dyke within the park. *Open Tue, Wed, Thur and Sun afternoons in summer, also B. Hol Mon.* Light lunches and teas.

Chirk and Whitehouses Tunnels
Neither of these tunnels is wide enough for 2 boats to pass—although each tunnel has a towing path running through it. Chirk Tunnel is 459yds long. Whitehouses Tunnel is 191yds.

Chirk Aqueduct
Opened in 1801, this is a splendidly massive brick and stone aqueduct carrying the canal in a narrow cast iron trough from England into Wales. The River Ceiriog flows 70ft below, and the great railway viaduct is beside and a little higher than the aqueduct.

BOATYARDS

Ⓑ **Anglo-Welsh Narrow Boats** Canal Wharf, Trevor, Llangollen, Clwyd. (821749). In the Ruabon Arm. R S WD E Pump-out, gas. Hire narrow boats. Dry dock. Sale & repair of diesel engines. Local shops, tel, toilet. *Services available Mon–Fri.*

PUBS

Mill Inn Trevor, near Anglo-Welsh.
Aqueduct Froncysyllte. Border beers and snacks.
Britannia Froncysyllte. Border beers.
Hand Hotel Church Street, Chirk. Border beers. Restaurant: lunches and dinners (*except Sun evening*).
Bridge Chirk Bank. 'Last pub in England', on the A5 downhill from bridge 21. Banks's real ale. Sandwiches etc.

The Pontcysllte aqueduct. *David Perrott*

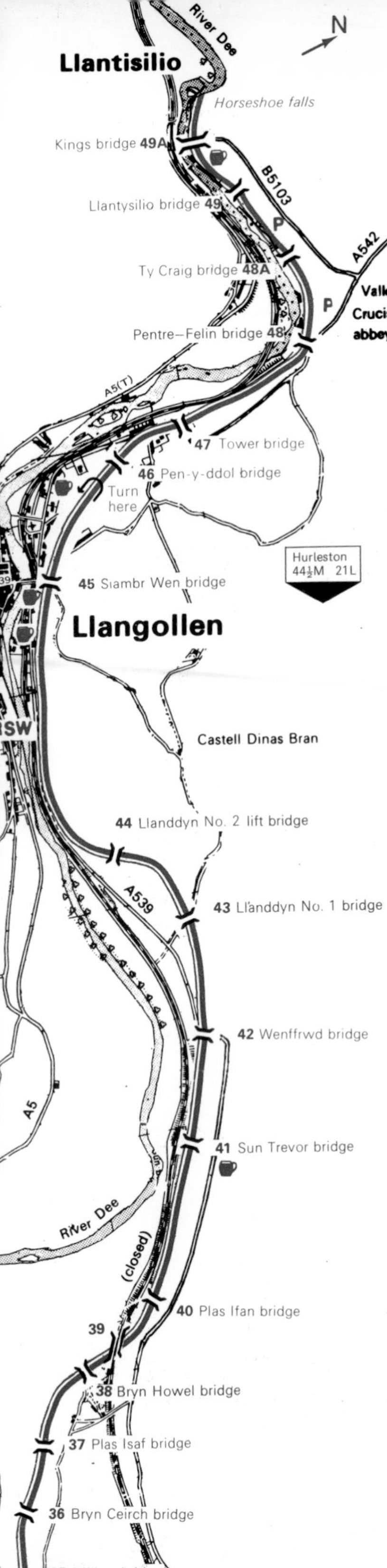

Vale of Llangollen

This is another stretch of very great beauty. All the way to Llangollen the navigation sidles along the tree-covered mountains, with views down into the Vale of Llangollen. In places the mountainside is very steep, making the canal so narrow that only one boat can negotiate the channel at a time. This incredible canal passes high above Llangollen, but it doesn't stop there: the tiny channel continues as a feeder to weave up the valley to Llantisilio. At this delightful spot the Horseshoe Falls (in fact a large semi-circular weir built by Telford across the River Dee) provide the water which is constantly passed from the river through a sluice and meter into the canal. Then it flows past Llangollen and the aqueducts, right back down to Hurleston reservoir—to the tune of 6 million gallons a day.

Navigational note
There is **no** turning point west of the winding hole at Llangollen, so boats longer than about 10ft should not venture up the feeder. However the towpath is in excellent shape and it makes a very enjoyable walk. There are good temporary moorings and other facilities at Llangollen.

Llantisilio
The village is set on a steep hillside among trees that overlook the Horseshoe Falls. The Victorian church is of interest: parts of the interior are taken from the nearby Valle Crucis Abbey, and the south window still contains 16thC glass.
Valle Crucis Abbey 1½ miles north west of the town. Picturesque ruins of the Cistercian abbey founded in 1201 by Madoc, Lord of Powys. The abbey fell into neglect after the Dissolution of the Monasteries in 1539.
Eliseg's Pillar ¼ mile north of the abbey. Erected in 18thC to commemorate Eliseg, who built the fortress on the top of Dinas Bran.
Llangollen
Clwyd. EC Thur, MD Tue. PO, tel, stores, garage, bank. Renowned for its International Musical Eisteddfod every July, it is in one of the finest stretches of the Dee valley. The canal runs along the hillside overlooking the town, which is built steeply along the fast flowing river. The centre of the town is on the south side of the 14thC bridge across the Dee, and contains many stone-built Victorian buildings. Great centre for pony trekking and other outdoor pursuits, especially climbing and walking. The parish church of St Collen in Church Street is a fine 13thC building, enlarged in 1865 and containing a superb carved oak ceiling. One place well worth a visit is the Llangollen Pottery in Regent Street, where the pottery is all hand-made and hand-decorated—a fascinating sight. The railway line is closed, although a railway society has some steam locomotives which run along a ¾ mile restored section on *summer Suns*. The Tourist Information office is in Parade Street.
Plas Newydd On southern outskirts of town. An attractive black and white timbered house which, from 1779–1831, was the home of the eccentric Lady Eleanor Butler and Miss Sarah Ponsonby, known as the 'Ladies of Llangollen'. Their visitors, who included Browning, Tennyson, Walter Scott and Wordsworth, presented them with antique curios, which are now on display in the elaborately panelled rooms. Part of the 12-acre grounds is a public park. *Open daily May–Sep.*
Castell Dinas Bran ½ mile north of canal. The ruins of the castle built for Eliseg, Prince of Powys, are conspicuous from boats approaching the town, and stand on a 1100ft mountain accessible to energetic walkers from various points along the canal, including bridge 45. It was once an important fortress, defending Wales from the English. From the summit there is a glorious view of the district.

BOAT TRIPS AND EXHIBITION

The Wharf, Llangollen. (860702). Fine museum of canal history. *Open daily in summer*. Horse-drawn boat trips to Pentrefelin, public trips and private charter—ring for details.

PUBS AND RESTAURANTS

Chain Bridge Hotel near Horseshoe Falls. Meals and residential.
Royal Hotel Llangollen. Meals and residential.
Royal Oak Llangollen. Pub in a very old barn.
Jenny Jones On A 593, 300 yds west of bridge 45. Spacious beamy pub serving real ale and bar food. Garden.
Bridge End Below bridge 45. Large and comfortable pub serving Robinsons real ale, bar snacks and meals in the Tudor Grill. Wonderful taxidermist shop next door.
Ceasars (Llangollen 860133). Tiny restaurant on south side of the bridge over the river. Limited menu based on fresh produce. Only 8 tables so booking is essential. *Dinner only*.
Gales 18 Bridge Street, Llangollen (860089). Tasteful wine bar with simple but excellent food. *Closed Sun & Mon in winter. No children allowed in after 20.00*.
Ponsonby Arms On A 539 east of bridge 45. Border ales and large garden.
Sun Trevor Above bridge 41. Beautifully situated pub with exceptional views. Brasses, beams and fine inglenook with a cosy curved settle. Castle Eden real ale, excellent food. Garden, telephone outside.

A beautifully wooded stretch of the Llangollen Canal near Ellesmere Tunnel. *Derek Pratt*

NORTH OXFORD
AND GRAND UNION (NORTON JUNCTION TO BRAUNSTON TURN)

Maximum dimensions

Length: 70′
Beam: 7′
Headroom: 7′

Mileage

BRAUNSTON TURN to:
Hillmorton Bottom Lock: 7½
Rugby Wharf Arm: 10¼
Stretton Stop: 15¾
HAWKESBURY JUNCTION (Coventry Canal): 22¾

Locks: 4

The Oxford was one of the earliest and for many years one of the most important canals in southern England. It was authorised in 1769, when the Coventry Canal was in the offing, and was intended to fetch coal southwards from the Warwickshire coalfield to Banbury and Oxford, at the same time giving access to the River Thames. James Brindley was appointed engineer; he built a winding contour canal 91 miles long that soon began to look thoroughly out-dated and inefficient for the carriage of goods. Brindley died in 1772, and was replaced by Samuel Simcock; he completed the line from Longford, where a junction was made with the Coventry Canal, to Banbury in 1778. After a long pause, the canal was finally brought into Oxford in 1790, and thereafter through traffic flowed constantly along this important new trade route.

In 1800, however, the Grand Junction Canal opened (excepting the tunnel at Blisworth) from London to Braunston, and the Warwick & Napton and Warwick & Birmingham Canals completed the new short route from London to Birmingham. This had the natural—and intended—effect of drawing traffic off the Oxford Canal, especially south of Napton Junction; but the Oxford company protected itself very effectively against this powerful opposition by charging outrageously high rates for their 5½-mile stretch between Braunston and Napton that had become part of the new London-Birmingham through route. Thus the Oxford maintained its revenue and very high dividends for many years to come.

By the late 1820s, however, the Oxford Canal had become conspicuously out of date with its extravagant winding course; and under the threat of various schemes for big new canals which, if built, would render the Oxford Canal almost redundant, the company decided to modernise the northern part of their navigation. Tremendous engineering works were therefore carried out which completely changed the face of the canal north of Braunston. Aqueducts, massive embankments and deep cuttings were built, carrying the canal in great sweeps through the countryside and cutting almost 14 miles off the original 36 miles between Braunston Junction and the Coventry Canal. Much of the old main line suddenly became a series of loops and branches leading nowhere and crossed by elegant new towpath bridges inscribed 'Horseley Ironworks 1828'.

This very expensive programme was well worth while. Although toll rates, and thus revenue, began to fall because of keen competition from the railways, dividends were kept at a high level for years; indeed a respectable profit was still shown right through to the 20thC.

This part of the Oxford Canal, along with the Grand Union between Norton Junction and Braunston Turn, is included to complete the popular Grand Union (Leicester section), River Soar, Trent and Mersey, Coventry, and North Oxford cruising circuit.

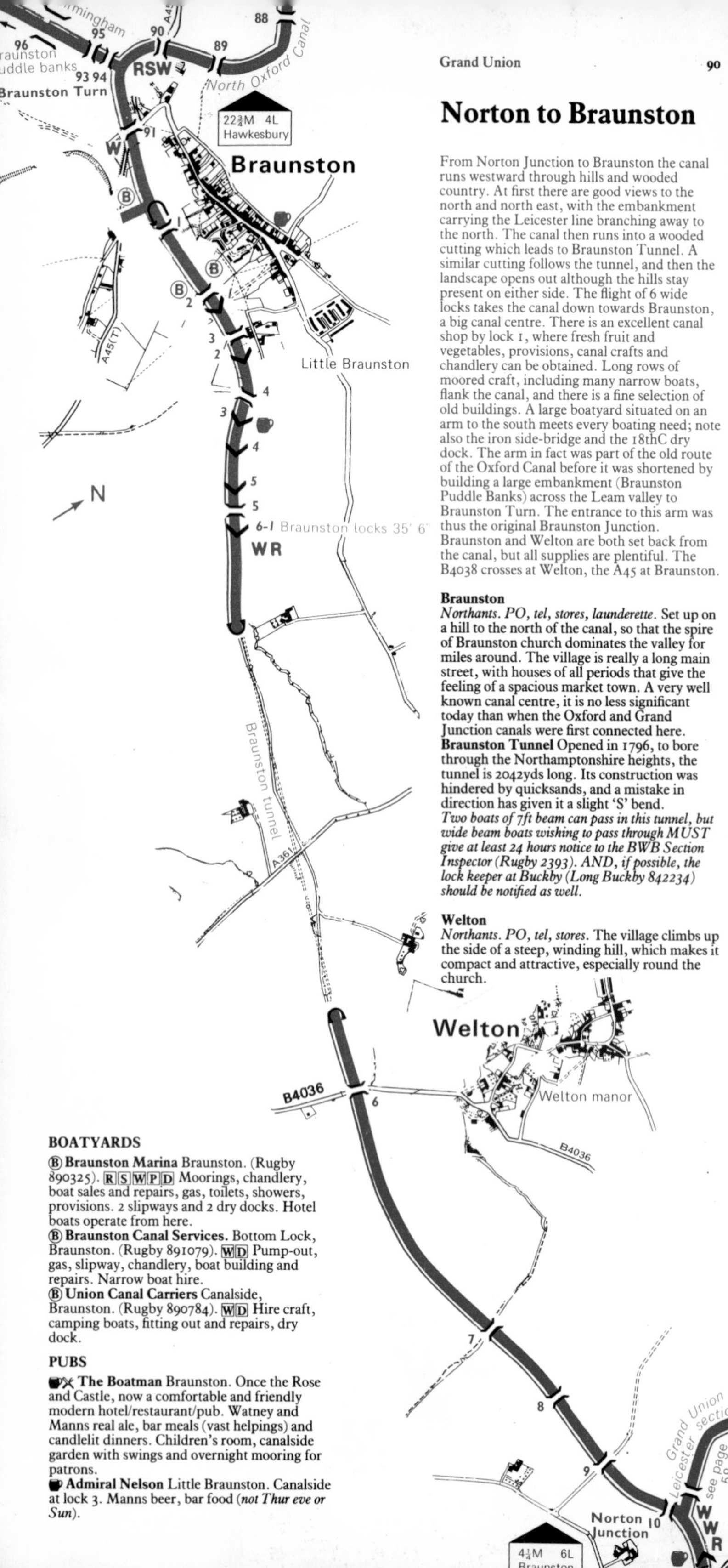

Norton to Braunston

From Norton Junction to Braunston the canal runs westward through hills and wooded country. At first there are good views to the north and north east, with the embankment carrying the Leicester line branching away to the north. The canal then runs into a wooded cutting which leads to Braunston Tunnel. A similar cutting follows the tunnel, and then the landscape opens out although the hills stay present on either side. The flight of 6 wide locks takes the canal down towards Braunston, a big canal centre. There is an excellent canal shop by lock 1, where fresh fruit and vegetables, provisions, canal crafts and chandlery can be obtained. Long rows of moored craft, including many narrow boats, flank the canal, and there is a fine selection of old buildings. A large boatyard situated on an arm to the south meets every boating need; note also the iron side-bridge and the 18thC dry dock. The arm in fact was part of the old route of the Oxford Canal before it was shortened by building a large embankment (Braunston Puddle Banks) across the Leam valley to Braunston Turn. The entrance to this arm was thus the original Braunston Junction. Braunston and Welton are both set back from the canal, but all supplies are plentiful. The B4038 crosses at Welton, the A45 at Braunston.

Braunston
Northants. PO, tel, stores, launderette. Set up on a hill to the north of the canal, so that the spire of Braunston church dominates the valley for miles around. The village is really a long main street, with houses of all periods that give the feeling of a spacious market town. A very well known canal centre, it is no less significant today than when the Oxford and Grand Junction canals were first connected here.
Braunston Tunnel Opened in 1796, to bore through the Northamptonshire heights, the tunnel is 2042yds long. Its construction was hindered by quicksands, and a mistake in direction has given it a slight 'S' bend.
Two boats of 7ft beam can pass in this tunnel, but wide beam boats wishing to pass through MUST give at least 24 hours notice to the BWB Section Inspector (Rugby 2393). AND, if possible, the lock keeper at Buckby (Long Buckby 842234) should be notified as well.

Welton
Northants. PO, tel, stores. The village climbs up the side of a steep, winding hill, which makes it compact and attractive, especially round the church.

BOATYARDS

Ⓑ **Braunston Marina** Braunston. (Rugby 890325). R S W P D Moorings, chandlery, boat sales and repairs, gas, toilets, showers, provisions. 2 slipways and 2 dry docks. Hotel boats operate from here.
Ⓑ **Braunston Canal Services.** Bottom Lock, Braunston. (Rugby 891079). W D Pump-out, gas, slipway, chandlery, boat building and repairs. Narrow boat hire.
Ⓑ **Union Canal Carriers** Canalside, Braunston. (Rugby 890784). W D Hire craft, camping boats, fitting out and repairs, dry dock.

PUBS

The Boatman Braunston. Once the Rose and Castle, now a comfortable and friendly modern hotel/restaurant/pub. Watney and Manns real ale, bar meals (vast helpings) and candlelit dinners. Children's room, canalside garden with swings and overnight mooring for patrons.
Admiral Nelson Little Braunston. Canalside at lock 3. Manns beer, bar food (*not Thur eve or Sun*).

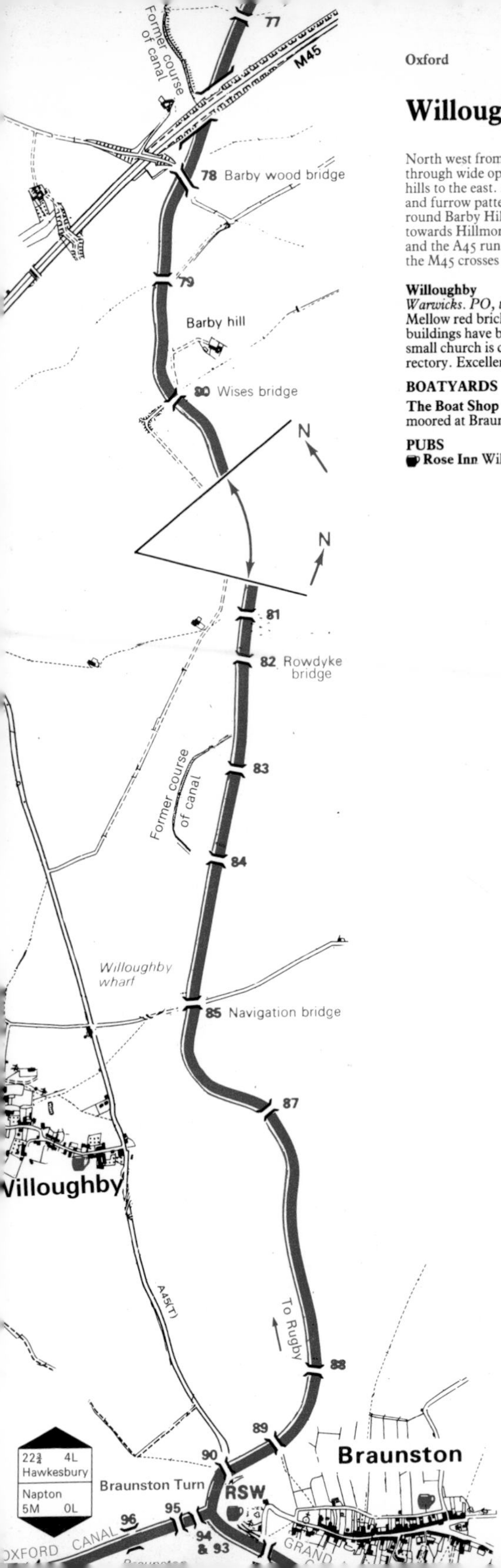

Willoughby

North west from Braunston the canal runs through wide open country, backed by bare hills to the east. At bridge 87 the medieval ridge and furrow patterns are in evidence. Skirting round Barby Hill, the canal swings north east towards Hillmorton and Rugby. The railway and the A45 run to the west of the canal, and the M45 crosses after Barby Hill.

Willoughby
Warwicks. PO, tel, stores, garage, transport café. Mellow red brick village to which new buildings have been unobtrusively added. The small church is dominated by a fine 18thC rectory. Excellent home bakery.

BOATYARDS

The Boat Shop Crafts and gifts on board a boat moored at Braunston Turn.

PUBS

Rose Inn Willoughby.

Hillmorton

After running north east for 2 miles, the canal swings in a wide arc round Rugby. To the east the radio masts dominate the landscape. The canal descends Hillmorton Locks, 3 paired narrow locks, (not often found), which fill and empty very quickly, are well maintained and a pleasure to use, and passes the attractively sited BWB maintenance yard and hire craft base. There is an excellent all-purpose grocer's shop at bridge 71. The railway accompanies the canal through Hillmorton and the A428 crosses south of the town. The little brick footbridge at the bottom locks is a delight to the eye.

Hillmorton
Warwicks. PO, tel, stores, garage. Its church dates from c1300, but there have been additions as late as the 18thC. There is an interesting medieval cross in the centre of the village, but the independence this implies has long since been swallowed up by Rugby.

BOATYARDS

BWB Section Inspector, Rugby. (2393).
Ⓑ **Clifton Cruisers** Clifton Wharf, Vicarage Hill, Rugby. (3570). R S WD Pump-out, boat hire, gas, repairs, toilets. *Phone first in winter.*
Ⓑ **Rugby Boatbuilders** (Inland Marine Leisure) Hillmorton Wharf, Crick Road, Rugby. (4438). S WD Steel narrow boats built, repaired or fitted out. Engines overhauled. Narrow boat hire, pump-out, gas, dry dock, mooring, chandlers, toilets, gift shop. *Closed winter weekends.*

PUBS

Stag & Pheasant Hillmorton. Food.
Old Royal Oak Canalside at bridge 73. Substantial brick pub with a very tidy garden.
Arnold Arms Barby. 1¼ miles south of bridge 76. Food.

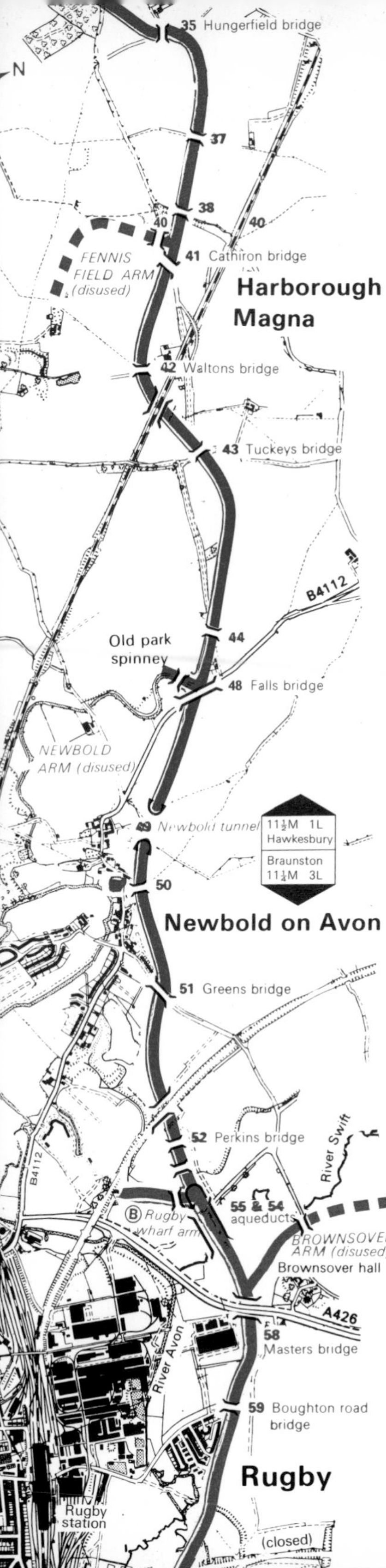

Rugby

Continuing the swing round Rugby, the canal enters a side cut embankment whose tall towpath hedge hides the town from view. There are shops to the south of bridge 59 and a picnic area below bridge 58. The River Avon is crossed by an aqueduct, and the Rugby arm branches to the west; there is a boatyard on the arm. A short open stretch and then another deep cutting take the canal to Newbold, where the short tunnel and thickly-wooded cutting lead the canal into open countryside. The iron bridges over the various arms reveal the course of the old canal. The B4112 accompanies it through Newbold.

Harborough Magna
Warwicks. PO, tel, stores. Quiet red brick village 1 mile to the north of the canal from bridges 43 or 48. The 14thC church has many Victorian additions, including an interesting stained glass window.

Newbold on Avon
Warwicks. PO, tel, stores, garage, fish & chips, launderette. A pleasant village with an interesting 15thC church and attractive cottages. At the wharf near the tunnel mouth are 2 pubs right next door to each other: why not try both?

Newbold Tunnel This 250yd long tunnel was built during the shortening of the Oxford Canal in the 1820s. The old route was at right angles to the new, and the old tunnel mouth can be seen from the south by Newbold church. The new tunnel was cut wide enough to allow for a towpath on both sides, a luxury at that date.

Rugby
Warwicks. EC Wed, MD Mon/Sat. PO, tel, stores, garage, station, cinema, theatre. Famous for the Rugby School where Rugby football was first played. St Andrew's parish church dates from the 13thC, but was almost completely rebuilt by Butterfield in 1877–79. The town was important for its agriculture for over 600 years and then grew as a railway town, but today heavy electrical industries flourish and determine the character of the area.

Library Exhibition Gallery & Museum St Matthew Street. Regular loan exhibitions by local societies and occasional exhibitions of the borough's collections of modern art which include Paul Nash and Graham Sutherland. The museum contains agricultural by-gones. *Open daily.*

BOATYARDS

Ⓑ **Willow Wren Hire Cruisers** Rugby Wharf, off Consul Road, Leicester Road, Rugby. (62183). R S W P D Pump-out, narrow boat hire, gas, boat building and repairs, toilets. Hotel boats. *Closed Sun.*

PUBS

Golden Lion Harborough Magna. Food.

Boat Newbold Wharf. Canalside. Food, skittles.

Barley Mow Newbold Wharf. Canalside. Food, skittles, children's room.

Three Horseshoes Hotel Sheep Street, Rugby. Food.

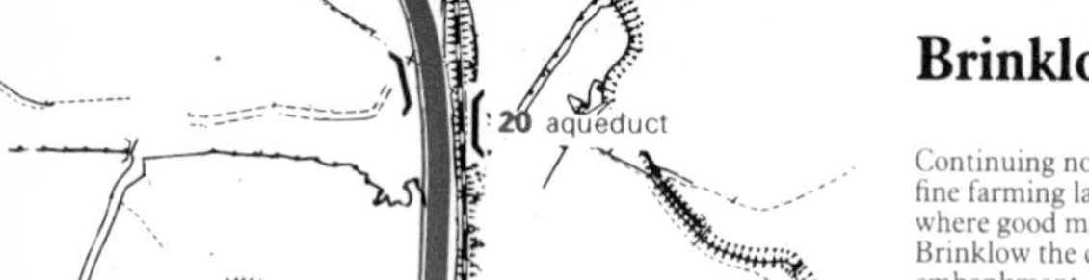

Brinklow

Continuing north west, the canal runs through fine farming land, and passes All Oaks Wood, where good moorings have been provided. By Brinklow the canal passes over an embankment, which was originally an aqueduct; the arches have long been filled in. Brinklow arm to the west is unnavigable. The long embankment continues through Stretton Stop and past Stretton Arm, used for mooring. Open, rolling fields follow, and then the canal enters a deep cutting, spanned by the new motorway. The M6 cuts through this stretch, and has greatly altered the landscape. The elegant iron bridges that occur periodically mark the course of the old Oxford Canal, prior to the 1829 shortening. The railway follows the canal to the east. The A4114 crosses through Brinklow.

Brinklow
Warwicks. PO, tel, stores, garage. A spacious pre-industrial village built along a wide main street, the A4114. The church is alongside the earthworks that mark the site of the castle built to defend the Fosse Way, and is unusual in having a distinctly sloping floor.

BOATYARDS

Ⓑ **Rose Narrowboats** Brinklow Marina, Stretton Stop. (Rugby 832449). R W P D Pump-out, moorings, repairs, narrow boat hire, gas, gift shop, chandlery, provisions. Pottery made adjacent to the boatyard.

PUBS

- **Railway Inn** Stretton Stop. Canalside. Food.
- **White Lion** Brinklow. Food.
- **Bull's Head** Brinklow. Food.
- **Raven** Brinklow. Food.

Shilton

Continuing north west, the canal leaves the cutting and crosses a long embankment, which is shared by the railway. The open landscape continues to Ansty, although the motorway is never far away. After the village the first signs of Coventry appear, with views of pylons and housing estates. The new Wyken colliery arm leaves to the west: it was built to replace the old one eaten up by the motorway which comes alongside the canal at this point. Sharp bends then lead to the stop lock before Hawkesbury Junction, the end of the Oxford Canal where it joins the Coventry. The last stretch of the Oxford is characterised by the 1820s shortenings, the straight cuttings and embankments obviously date from this period, while the cast iron bridges mark the old route. The railway turns away before Ansty.

Ansty
Warwicks. PO, tel, stores, garage. Tiny village that grew up along the canal, now disturbed by the A46. To the north are the church and Hall together; the Hall is mostly 18thC. This area has been much altered by motorway construction. Ansty Stores is extremely useful, and also runs a taxi service.
Shilton
Warwicks. PO, tel, stores, garage. ½ mile north of bridge 17. Main road village left bewildered by the railway and the A46.

PUBS

Greyhound Hawkesbury Junction. Canalside. M & B real ale in a listed canalside building. Food.
Elephant and Castle Canalside, by bridge 4. M & B beers, food. Fishing tackle opposite.
Crown Ansty. Food.
Crown Shilton. Food.

Wardle Lock. The Middlewich Branch of the Shropshire Union Canal. *David Perrott*

SHROPSHIRE UNION

Maximum dimensions

Autherley to Nantwich, and Middlewich Branch
Length: 72′
Beam: 7′
Headroom: 8′
Nantwich to Ellesmere Port
Length: 72′
Beam: 13′ 3″
Headroom: 8′

Mileage

AUTHERLEY JUNCTION (Staffs & Worcs Canal) to Norbury: 15½
Market Drayton: 27
HURLESTON JUNCTION (Llangollen Canal): 40¾
Barbridge Junction (Middlewich Branch): 42
Chester Junction with Dee Branch: 58
ELLESMERE PORT JUNCTION with Manchester Ship Canal: 66½

Locks: 47

Middlewich Branch
Middlewich (Trent & Mersey Canal) to Barbridge Junction: 10

Locks: 4

The Chester Canal

In 1772 an enabling Act was passed for a canal from the River Dee in Chester to join the Trent & Mersey Canal at Middlewich, with a spur to Nantwich. The building of the Trent & Mersey was the cause of this new venture, for it was seen as a threat to the future of the River Dee Navigation and the port of Chester. The new canal was designed to bolster Chester as an alternative port to Liverpool, and so was planned as a barge canal, with locks 80ft by 14ft 9in. Work started in Chester in the middle of 1772 and progressed very slowly. There were engineering and financial problems, and the main line of the new canal was altered to terminate at a basin and warehouses just outside Nantwich: the proposed line to Middlewich was now to be a branch. The Nantwich–Chester link was completed in 1779, but the spur to Middlewich was not built until 54 years later. When the Nantwich–Chester Canal was finished, arguments with the Dee River Company delayed the building of the river lock. By this time competition with the Trent & Mersey was out of the question. Although regular freight and fast passenger services were run, the canal was wholly uneconomic and in 1787 the company collapsed. In 1790 it was revived and the canal repaired, for the directors saw the publication of the plans of the Ellesmere Canal as their last chance to complete the line to Middlewich.

The Birmingham & Liverpool Junction Canal

The future prosperity of the Ellesmere & Chester was limited by the lack of an outlet to the south, without which its trade could never be more than local. So the company was much cheered by the plans for the Birmingham & Liverpool Junction Canal which received its Act in 1825. The line from Nantwich to Autherley, on the Staffordshire & Worcestershire Canal, would give a direct link between Liverpool and the Midlands, and thus with the canal network as a whole. After serious engineering difficulties the canal was opened in 1835, shortly after the opening of the long-planned branch from the Chester Canal to the Trent & Mersey at Middlewich, providing access to Manchester and the Potteries. Railway competition was close at hand by this date, and so the Birmingham & Liverpool Junction and Ellesmere & Chester companies worked closely together to preserve their profits. Ellesmere Port was greatly enlarged, and by 1840 steam haulage was in use on the Wirral line and on the Mersey itself. In 1845 the two companies merged, and then shortly after were reformed as the Shropshire Union Railways and Canal Company.

The Shropshire Union

The Shropshire Union Railways & Canal Company was formed under the shadow of railway expansion. Its initial plans were to build railways instead of canals, on the principle that it would halve the construction costs to lay a railway along the bed of an existing canal. By 1849 this plan had been abandoned, for the slow development of railways in Wales had shown the company that canals could still be profitable. Throughout the mid 19thC the Shropshire

Union network remained profitable, and did not experience the steady decline of other major canal systems. The London and North Western Railway Company was a major shareholder in the Shropshire Union, and they were very happy to let the canals remain as they provided the company with a significant tentacle into Great Western Railway territory. As a result the Shropshire Union was allowed to expand steadily; in 1870 the company owned 213 narrow boats, and in 1889 there were 395. By 1902 this fleet had increased to 450 boats. A few branches were threatened with closure on the grounds of unprofitability, but none were carried out.

The flourishing trade continued until the 1914–18 war, which started a pattern of regular heavy losses from which the company was never able to recover. In 1921 the company gave up canal carrying, and sold most of its fleet of boats to private operators. Locks were closed at weekends, and standards of maintenance began to slip. In 1922 the Shropshire Union Company was bought out by the London and North Western Railway, which then was swallowed in turn by the newly-formed London Midland and Scottish Railway. Despite these changes the network remained open, although trade declined rapidly. Many traders were driven away by the lack of maintenance, which meant that most boats could only operate half empty. In 1936 a breach occurred on the Montgomery Canal 1 mile south of Frankton Junction; the company set out to repair the damage and then changed their minds. (The Weston line had been similarly abandoned after a breach in 1917.) With trade at a standstill there were no complaints, and in 1944 an Act was passed making closure official. This Act also officially abandoned 175 miles of the old Shropshire Union network. Out of this mass closure only the main line and the Middlewich Branch remained, although the Llangollen Branch (see page 77) luckily also escaped closure, being originally retained as a water supply channel.

The Shropshire Union Canal. *Derek Pratt*

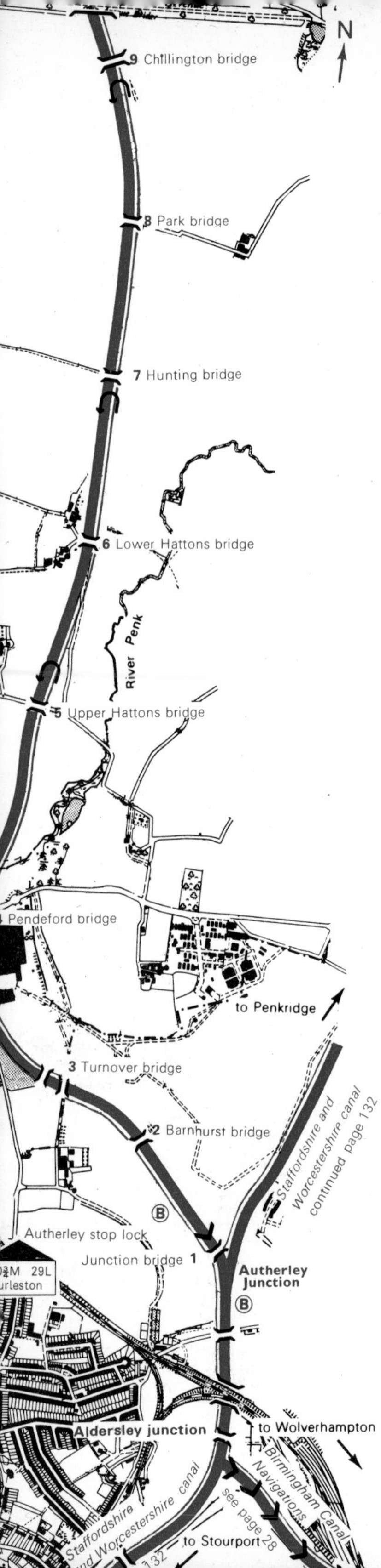

Autherley Junction

The Shropshire Union Canal leaves the Staffordshire & Worcester Canal at Autherley Junction, and runs straight along the side of the former Wolverhampton Aerodrome at Pendeford (now being developed). Passing the Wolverhampton Boat Club, the canal soon enters a short cutting, which is through rock, and narrow in places. Emerging briefly into the green and quiet countryside that is found along the whole length of this navigation, the canal plunges into a deep, long cutting that is typical of this particular stretch.

Autherley Junction
An important and busy canal junction, where in 1830 Thomas Telford brought his Birmingham & Liverpool Junction Canal (now part of the Shropshire Union system) to join the much older Staffordshire & Worcestershire Canal (built by James Brindley and opened in 1772). There is a former canal toll office here, also a boatyard and a boatclub. The stop lock has a fall of only about 6in: it was insisted upon by the Staffs & Worcs Company to prevent the newer canal 'stealing' water from them. Autherley Junction is sometimes confused with Aldersley Junction, ½ mile to the south, where the Birmingham Canal Navigations join the Staffs & Worcs Canal from the east after falling through the Wolverhampton flight of 21 locks.

BOATYARDS

Ⓑ **Water Travel** Autherley Junction, Oxley Moore Road, Wolverhampton, West Midlands. (Wolverhampton 782371). R S W P D E Pump-out, gas. Hire craft, chandlery, slipway, moorings, groceries, toilets, telephone, gift shop, build & fit out steel boats.
Ⓑ **Gregory's Canal Cruisers** Oxley Moor Road, Autherley Junction, Wolverhampton. (783070). On the Staffs & Worcs. R W Pump-out, boat hire, gas, boat and engine repairs, toilets, provisions.

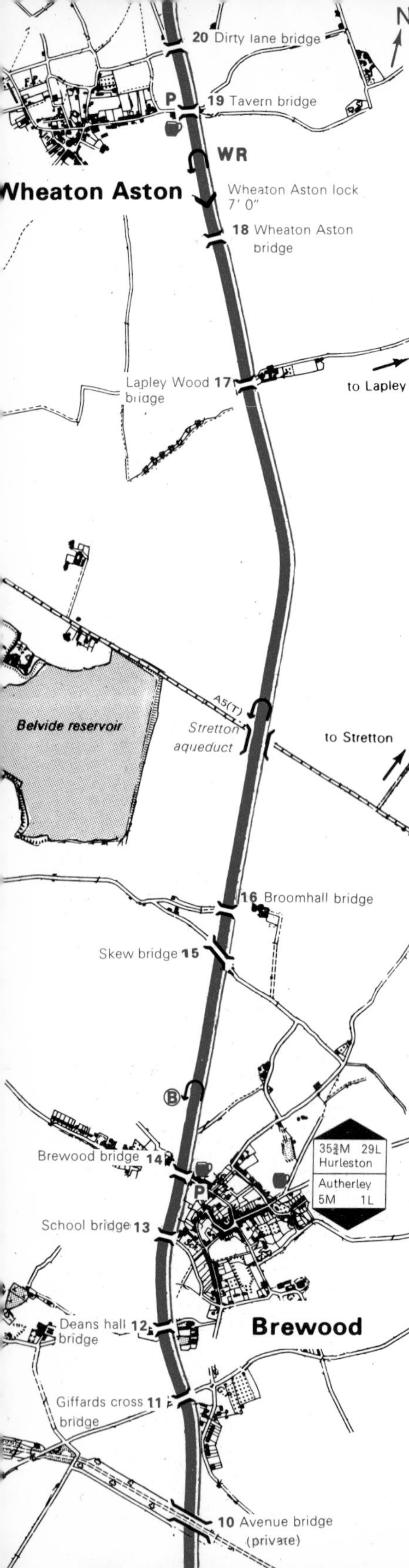

Brewood

Leaving the balustraded Avenue Bridge (10), which leads westward to Chillington Hall, the canal curves in a bold cutting past the village of Brewood and its attractive wharf—and moves north west along a very straight embankment. The head bank of the big Belvide reservoir can be seen on the west side; its feeder stream enters the canal just south of Stretton Aqueduct. This solid but elegant cast iron structure carries the canal over the A5. Crossing the aqueduct by boat tends to give the canal traveller an air of great superiority over the teeming motorists below. After another long wooded cutting the canal reaches Wheaton Aston Lock. This lock marks the end of the long 'pound' from Autherley and the beginning of the 17-mile level that lasts almost to Market Drayton.

Wheaton Aston
Staffs. PO, tel, stores, garage. Overrun by new housing. The village green around the church (rebuilt in 1857) is a memento of a more pleasant past. The garage beside the canal repairs boats' engines and sells chandlery; while at the lock cottage local hand-painted canal ware may be bought.
Lapley
Staffs. ¾ mile north east of bridge 17. The central tower of the church dominates the village. It is an interesting building with fine Norman windows, an old Dutch font and traces of medieval paintings on the nave wall. The church as we see it now was completed in the 15thC.
Stretton
1 mile north east of Stretton Aqueduct off the A5. The church was rebuilt in the 19thC but retains its original chancel and fragments of medieval glass in the east window.
Stretton Hall Built in 1620 to designs by Inigo Jones. Most interesting features are the vast fireplace with steps up to it for chimneysweep boys, and the remarkable staircase suspended by chains from the roof. The house is private.
Belvide reservoir
A large nature reserve open to naturalists. The Royal Society for the Protection of Birds is developing the reserve to include displays and hides, enabling enthusiasts to have a greater opportunity to observe the many species of birds. There is only private club fishing and no sailing on the reservoir, so as to preserve the bird sanctuary.
Brewood
Staffs. EC Wed. PO, tel, stores, bank, garage. The name (pronounced 'Brood') derives from Celtic 'Bre' meaning 'hill', thus giving 'wood on the hill'. It originally consisted of a Roman fort on Beacon Hill to defend Watling Street but is now a beautiful, quiet village with some extremely attractive Georgian houses in groups. The village church is a tall, elegant building which has been greatly restored but still contains a 16thC font and several 16thC effigies and 17thC monuments commemorating the Giffard family of Chillington Hall.
Chillington Hall
1½ miles west of canal, south west of Brewood, this has been the home of the Giffard family since the 12thC. The existing hall was built in the 18thC, and the wooded park in which it stands was designed by 'Capability Brown'. The hall is approached by an avenue of trees, at the eastern end of which is Giffard's Cross. This is said to mark the spot where Sir John Giffard in 1513 shot a wild panther with his crossbow, thus saving the lives of a woman and her child. The panther, a gift from a friendly Oriental, had escaped from its cage. *Open Thur afternoons, May–Aug.*

BOATYARDS

Ⓑ **Countrywide Cruisers** The Wharf, Brewood, Staffs. (850166). Just north of bridge 14. R S WD Pump-out, narrow boat hire, slipway, gas, boat fitting & repairs, mooring, toilets, provisions, winter storage.

PUBS

Hartley Arms Canalside, at Tavern Bridge. Wheaton Aston. Food.
Coach & Horses Wheaton Aston.
Swan Brewood.
Lion Brewood.
Admiral Rodney near Brewood church.
Bridge Inn Canalside, at Brewood Bridge. Snacks.
Three Stirrups Brewood. Food, garden, children's room.

The elegant balustraded Avenue Bridge near Brewood. Shropshire Union Canal. *Derek Pratt*

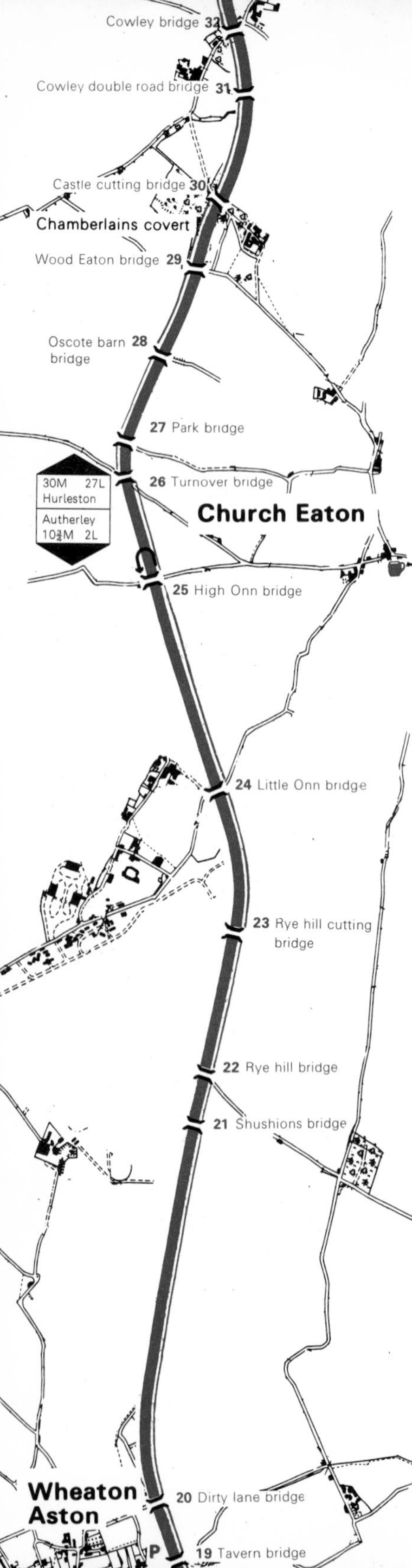

Church Eaton

The canal now proceeds along the very long pound, alternately in cuttings and on embankments. Both offer interest; the cuttings for their rich vegetation, and the embankments for the excellent views over quiet, unspoilt grazing land.

Church Eaton
Staffs. EC Wed. PO, tel, stores. 1 mile north east of bridge 25. Parts of the old village remain, especially at the end of the village street in the vicinity of the fine church: St Editha's, a Norman structure with the spire added to the tower in the 15thC. The east window dates from about 1400 and almost fills the wall.

PUBS

- **Royal Oak** Church Eaton.
- **Swan** Church Eaton.

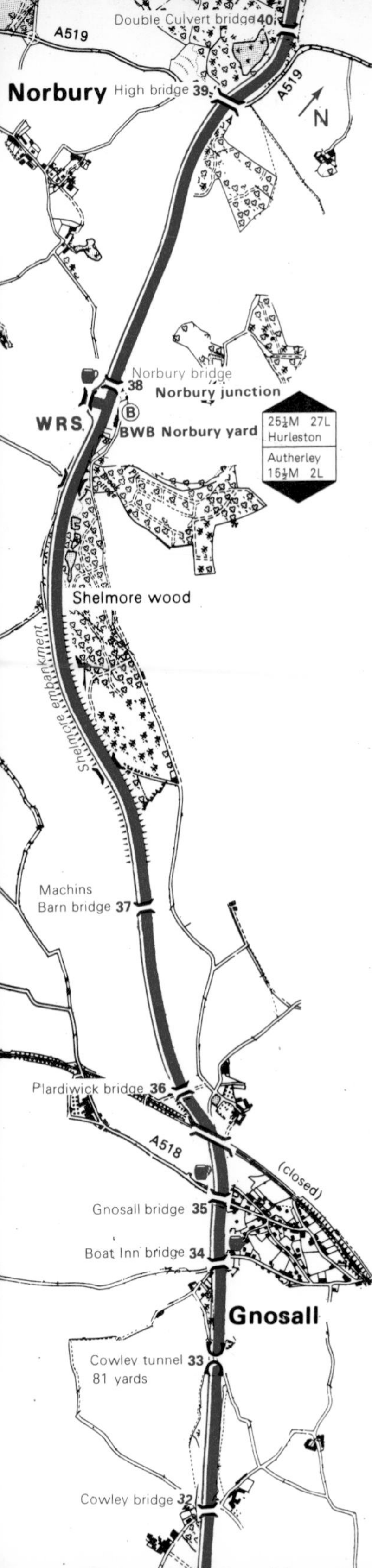

Norbury Junction

The canal now enters the very deep and almost vertical cutting that terminates in Cowley Tunnel. North of the tunnel is Gnosall; shortly after this, the canal moves round the side of Shelmore Wood and crosses the mighty Shelmore Embankment before reaching Norbury Junction, where the Newport Branch used to lock down from the main line. North of here is the long Grub Street cutting which features the well known High Bridge with a masonry strut, carrying a short telegraph pole, built across its tall arch.

Norbury Junction
This was once the outlet for the Shrewsbury, Newport and Trench branches on to the rest of the Shropshire Union Canal system. There was a long flight of locks from the junction down to Newport, but these are now closed and the Shropshire canals are disused and forgotten. Norbury Junction is still full of interest, however: there is a boatyard, a canal maintenance yard and a popular canalside pub.

Shelmore Embankment
The construction of this great embankment 1 mile long, just south of Norbury Junction, was the source of endless grief and expense to the Birmingham & Liverpool Junction Canal Company in general and to Thomas Telford, their engineer, in particular. It was an enormous task anyway to shift the millions of cubic feet of earth to build the bank; but while the contractors struggled to complete it, the bank slipped and collapsed time and again. By early 1834, Shelmore Embankment was the only unfinished section of the whole canal. It was not until 1835, after 5½ years solid work on it and well after Telford's death, that the embankment was completed by William Cubitt and the B&LJ Canal was opened as a through route.

Gnosall
Staffs. PO, tel, garage, stores. The main feature of interest in the village is the Church of St Laurence, a mile east of the canal. It is a 15thC building with original Norman tower arches. The east window has fine decorated tracery, framing modern stained glass. There is a canal shop by bridge 35.

Cowley Tunnel
This short tunnel was originally intended to be much longer—700yds—but most of it was opened out at an early stage in construction (during the early 1830s) because of dangerous faults in the rock, and now only 81yds remain. The tunnel is unlined, and to the south of it a very steep narrow cutting through solid rock stretches a considerable distance—an awe-inspiring sight.

BOATYARDS

BWB Norbury Yard Norbury Junction. (Woodseaves 253). R S W Toilets.
Ⓑ **Shropshire Union Cruisers (Dartline)** Norbury Junction, Staffs. (Woodseaves 292). R W P D Pump-out, narrow boat hire, slipway, dry dock, mooring, chandlery, toilets, provisions, gift shop, winter storage.

PUBS

- **Junction Inn** Canalside, at Norbury Junction.
- **Navigation** Canalside, at bridge 35.
- **Royal Oak** Gnosall.
- **Boat** Canalside, at Boat Inn Bridge.

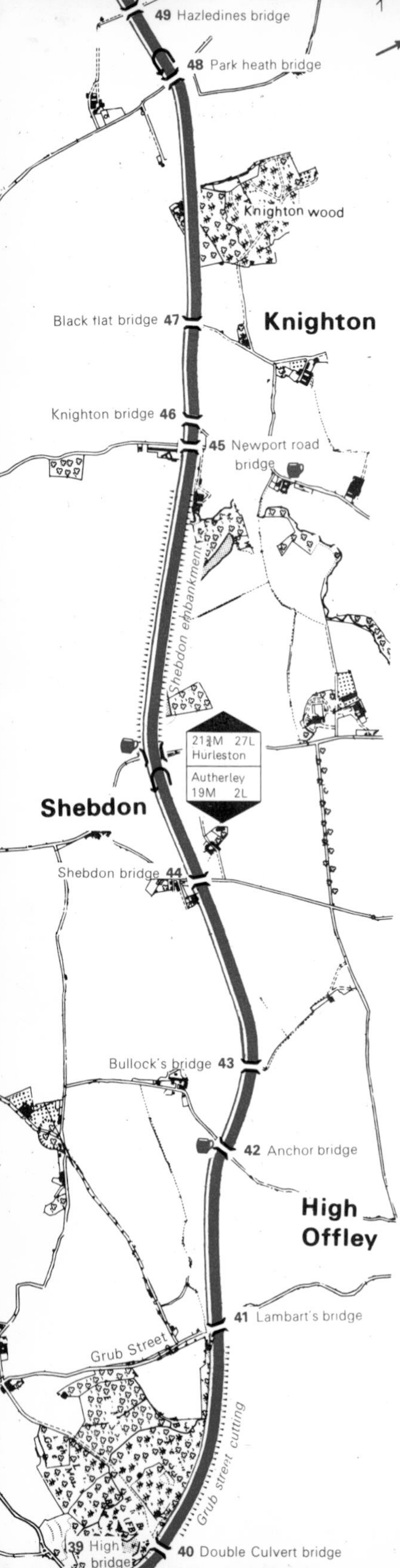

Shebdon

The canal moves out of Grub Street cutting through the unusual double arched bridge, containing a small telegraph pole and, passing the village of High Offley on a hill to the north, continues in a north-westerly direction through the quiet open farmland that always accompanies this canal. Along this stretch are 2 canalside pubs--both amaze the traveller by their very survival, situated as they are on quiet roads and an even quieter canal. The great Shebdon embankment is heralded by an aqueduct; at the far end is a large ex-chocolate factory (now producing only dried milk), whose goods used to be carried to and from Bournville (on the Worcester & Birmingham Canal) by canal boat. Knighton post office, stores and telephone are by bridge 45.

High Offley
Staffs. Tel. Hill-top farming village, scattered round a large 15thC church. Good views in all directions.

PUBS

Haberdashers Arms Knighton, ½ mile north east of bridge 45.
Wharf Inn Canalside, below Shebdon Aqueduct. Snacks, garden.
Anchor Inn Canalside, at Offley Bridge (42). Unspoilt hostelry with an open fire, Ansells and Marstons real ale, and draught cider. *Closed weekday lunchtimes, and Mon & Tue in winter.*
Royal Oak High Offley.

Cheswardine

The canal continues north west through the quiet, empty landscape. Hills rise to the right, while the massive bulk of the Wrekin is clearly visible to the south west, 15 miles away. After passing Goldstone Wharf, with its thriving pub, the canal plunges into the very deep rock cutting near Woodseaves. One can hardly fail to be impressed by the magnitude of a work like this, cut as it was entirely by men without powered machines. At the north end of this wooded cutting is the delightful group of buildings (dated 1840) comprising Tyrley Wharf, now a canal craft shop; here the 5 Tyrley Locks begin the fall towards Market Drayton.

Cheswardine
Shropshire. PO, tel, stores, garage. Situated 1 mile up a long hill east of bridge 55, the village has a traditional, well-knit feeling about it. The church is sited on a rise overlooking the village street. It contains some good 19thC glass.

PUBS

Wharf Tavern Canalside, at bridge 55. Dinners, light lunch, garden.
Fox & Hounds Cheswardine.
Red Lion Cheswardine.

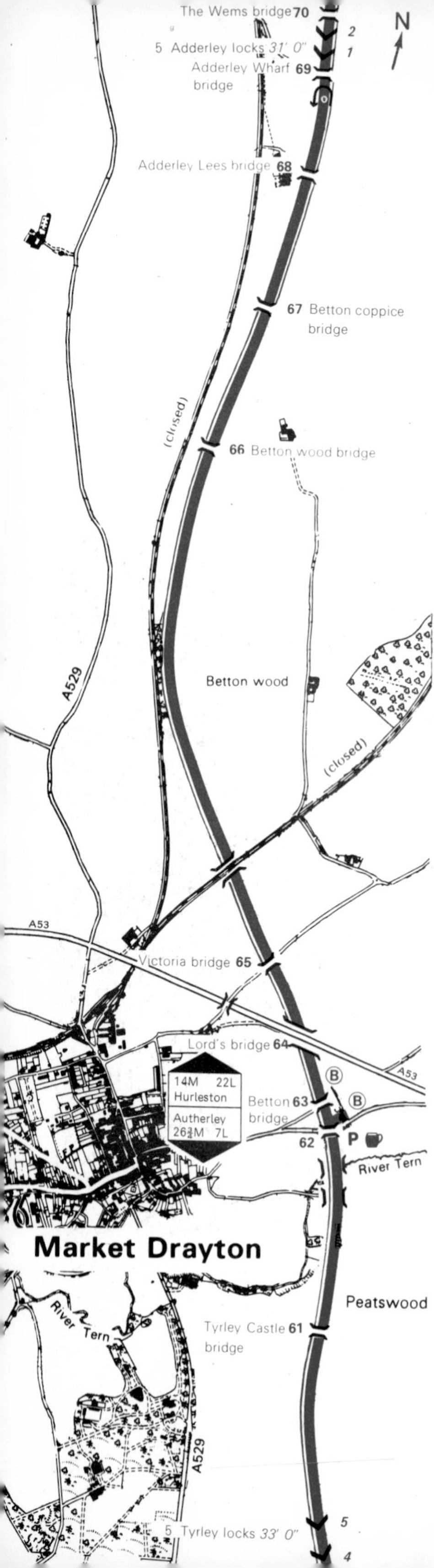

Market Drayton

The canal continues to fall through Tyrley Locks, which in places are almost roofed over by trees, then crosses a minor road and the River Tern via aqueducts, and arrives at Market Drayton. There are 2 large boatyards here, so there are always many boats about and great care is needed in navigation. North of Market Drayton the canal regains its peaceful isolation, passing through a pleasant wooded cutting (which is alleged by the superstitious to shelter a vociferous ghost) before arriving at the 5 Adderley Locks, winners in 1980 of the 'best kept lock' competition.

Market Drayton
Shropshire. EC Thur. MD Wed. PO, tel, stores, garage, bank, launderette. On the west bank of the canal, it is the market centre for the surrounding district, and is a very attractive town with some splendid old buildings. It was destroyed by fire in 1651, but fortunately picturesque black and white timberframing was again used for the rebuilding, the best of which is the National Westminster Bank in the market square and the adjacent Sandbrook Vaults (1653) in Shropshire Street. The parish Church of St Mary is large and well-sited overlooking the Tern valley and dates from the 12thC. The Corbet Arms Hotel is a fine centre-piece to the main square.

BOATYARDS

Ⓑ**Drayton Marina**. Betton Road, Market Drayton, Shropshire. (3101). North of bridge 63. [R][S][W] Boat and motor sales and repairs. Gas, chandlery. Slipway, moorings, winter storage, toilets.

Ⓑ **Holidays Afloat** The Boatyard, Market Drayton, Shropshire. (2641). At bridge 62. Hire cruisers, gas, chandlery, slipway, moorings, winter storage. *Closed winter Suns.*

PUBS AND RESTAURANTS

Corbet Arms Hotel High Street, Market Drayton. Restaurant: lunches and dinners.

Sandbrook Vaults Market Drayton.

Talbot Canalside, at bridge 62.

Crown Near the market place, Market Drayton.

Audlem Wharf. *David Perrott*

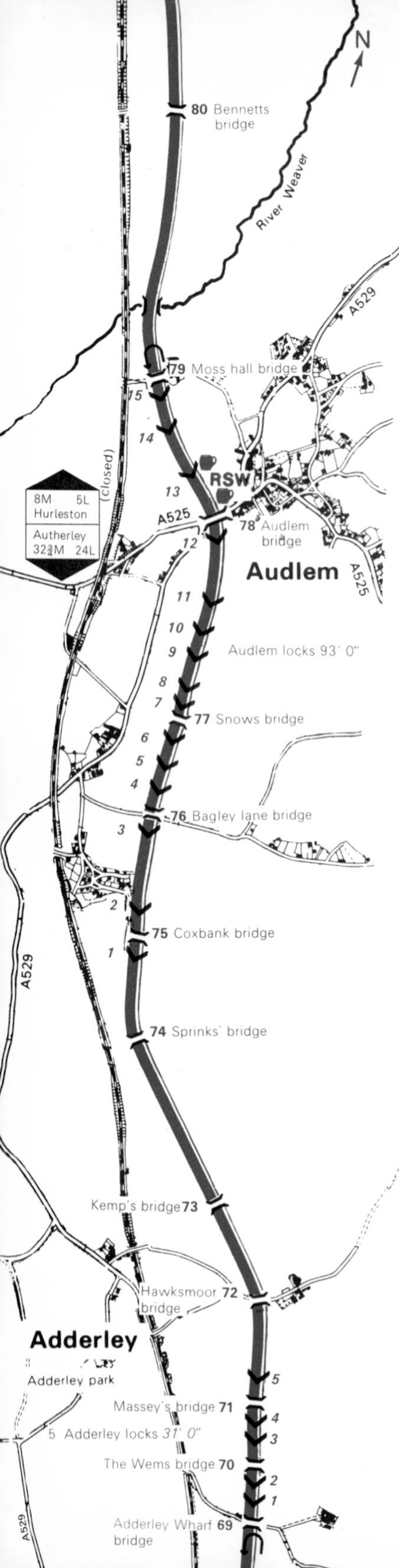

Audlem

Adderley Locks, the middle of the 3 main groups of locks between Autherley & Nantwich, are shortly followed by the 15 locks in the Audlem flight, lowering the canal by over 90ft to the dairylands of southern Cheshire. The locks are close together and provide over 2 hours' energetic navigating; there is an attractive cottage at the top lock, the wharf has a craft shop and a café, and there are two pubs near bridge 78, along with a general store. The bottom of the locks is marked by a well restored canal stable and just to the north a minor aqueduct over the tiny River Weaver.

Audlem
Ches. PO, tel, stores, garage, bank. Some pleasant houses are grouped around the church in this expanding and well-kept canalside village. The massive shape of the 15thC church seems to spill down from its hillock in battlemented layers. The colonnaded structure at its foot was once a butter market. The mellow old buildings on the canal wharf have been well renovated and there are good moorings by the old wharf crane.

Adderley
Shropshire. PO, tel, stores, garage. A rather under-populated village, bisected by the now closed railway and flanked by the large Shavington and Adderley Parks. The unusual church, set by itself, was rebuilt of red sandstone in 1801 in neo-classical style. In 1958 a large portion of the church was closed to reduce maintenance costs, including the tower dated 1712, the transepts and the chancel. As a result the much smaller interior is better suited to contemporary needs and feels more like a large formal drawing room than a cold decaying church.

Shavington Hall Adderley. An impressive red brick house dating from 1685 with 19thC additions and alterations. A fine park surrounds the house, which is not open to the public.

PUBS

Bridge Canalside, at Audlem Bridge. Marstons real ale, snacks and garden.

The Shroppie Fly Audlem. Canalside. This nicely converted warehouse serves Bass from a bar built like a narrow boat (complete with cratch). Food, garden.

Crown Audlem.

Lamb Hotel Audlem. Food.

Lord Combermere Audlem.

Hack Green

The canal flows northwards through an undisturbed stretch of pastoral land. Cows graze either side, clearly intent on maintaining Cheshire's reputation as a prime dairy county. It is chilling to reflect that in 1968 hardly a single beast was left alive for miles around here after the ravages of foot and mouth disease. Hack Green Locks briefly interrupt the navigation. The railway which once accompanied the canal has long since closed, although the line crossing from Shrewsbury to Nantwich and Crewe is still open. At the end of this section the tower of Nantwich church is clearly visible to the east, while Dorfold Park appears on the left.

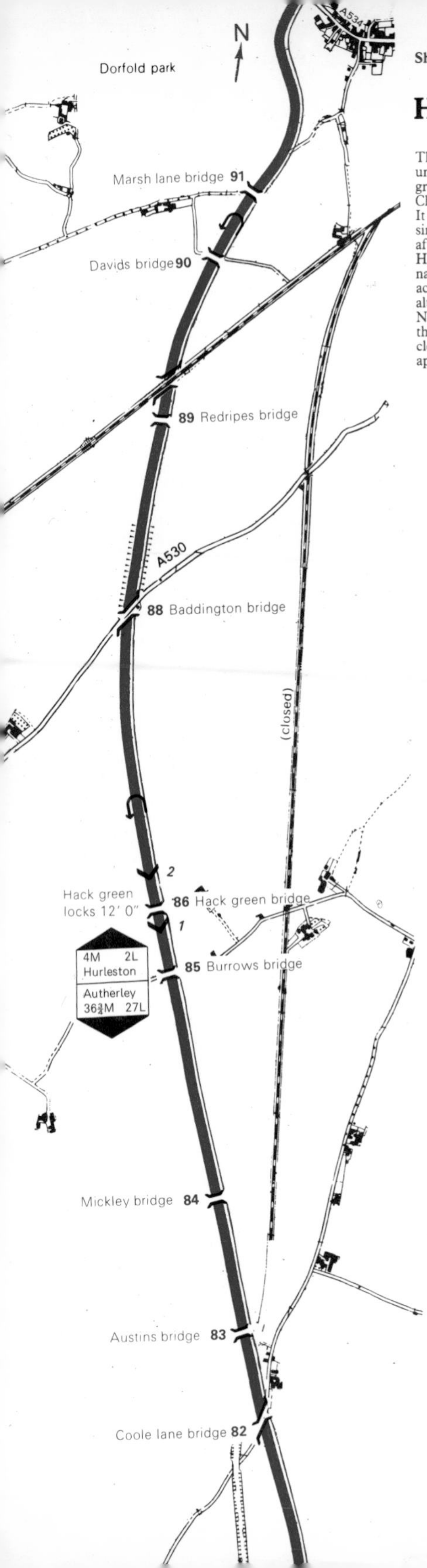

N
A534
Dorfold park
Marsh lane bridge 91
Davids bridge 90
89 Redripes bridge
A530
88 Baddington bridge
(closed)
2
Hack green locks 12' 0"
86 Hack green bridge
1
4M 2L Hurleston
Autherley 36¾M 27L
85 Burrows bridge
Mickley bridge 84
Austins bridge 83
Coole lane bridge 82

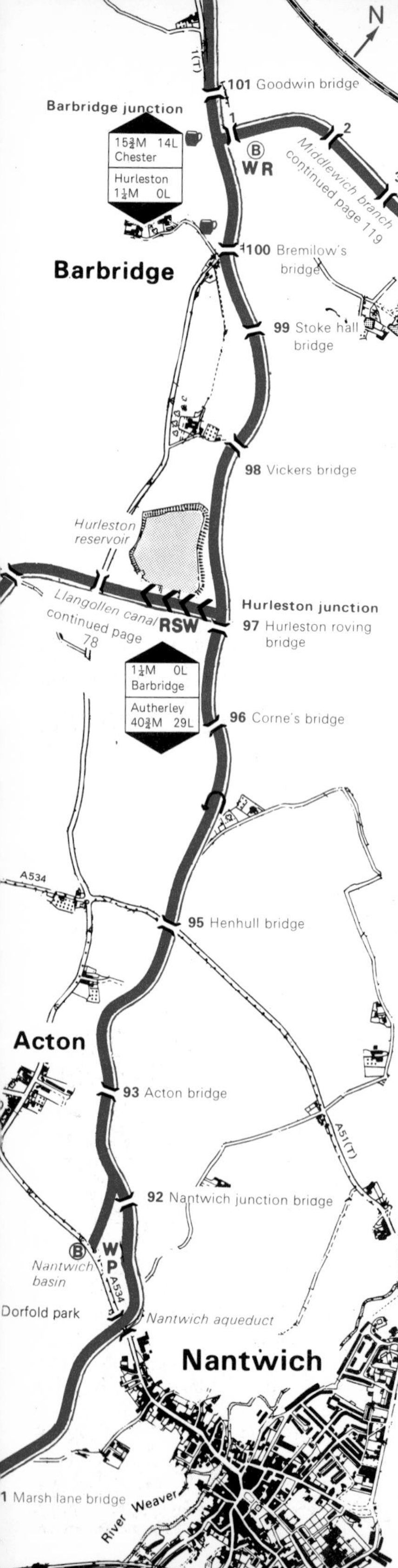

Nantwich

Swinging round Dorfold Park on a long embankment, the canal crosses the Nantwich–Chester road on a fine cast iron aqueduct and soon reaches an oblique canal junction at Nantwich Basin: this is where Telford's narrow Birmingham & Liverpool Junction Canal joins the older Chester Canal. The stop-gates to be seen at each end of the embankment are a precaution against flooding in the event of a breach or damage to the aqueduct. The wide bridgehole at the next and all subsequent bridges reveals the difference in gauge of the 2 canals. The Chester Canal's width is complemented by its sweeping course, as it curves gracefully round the hillside to Hurleston Junction. Here the Llangollen Canal branches off up 4 narrow locks on its way to North Wales (see page 78). Meanwhile the main line of the Shropshire Union soon reaches Barbridge (*PO, tel, stores, garage*) where there is a junction with the Middlewich Branch. This branch (see page 119) connects the Shropshire Union system to the Trent & Mersey Canal.

Acton
Ches. PO, tel, stores. A small village with a large church of red stone and an old pub with a mounting block outside.

Dorfold Hall
¼ mile south west of Nantwich Basin. Built by Ralph Wilbraham in 1616, this beautiful Jacobean house is approached along an avenue of trees. The panelled rooms contain fine furnishings and family portraits. *Open Mon afternoons May–Sep.*

Nantwich Basin
A busy, canal basin, once the terminus of the isolated Chester Canal from Nantwich to Ellesmere Port. When the B & LJ Canal was first authorised in 1826, Telford intended to bring it from Hack Green across Dorfold Park and straight into Nantwich Basin; but the owner of the park refused to allow it and forced the company to build the long embankment right round the park and the iron aqueduct over the main road. This proved a difficult and costly diversion since, as at Shelmore, the embankment repeatedly collapsed. Today the old canalside cheese warehouses have been skilfully restored by the BWB and there are 2 boatyards and a boat club based here.

Nantwich
Cheshire. EC Wed. MD Thur, Sat. All services. A very fine old town, prosperous since Roman times because of its salt springs, which made it the country's main salt mining centre until the 19thC. The town was devastated by fire in 1583 but rebuilt in fine Tudor style. Many of the half-timbered houses still remain: 2 especially interesting buildings on the road into town from the basin are the Cheshire Cat Inn and a tiny cottage built in 1502 and restored in 1971. In London Road are the Tollemache Almshouses built in 1638 by Sir Edmund Wright, who became Lord Mayor of London in 1641.

Church of St Mary Church Lane. Focal point of the town centre, it is a large and magnificent red sandstone church which stands behind its former graveyard, now an open green. It dates from the 14thC though it was greatly restored in 1885. It has an unusual octagonal tower and the vaulted chancel contains 20 ornate 14thC choir stalls with canopies.

✕♥ **Churche's Mansion** Hospital Street, Nantwich. In the centre of the town is this fine example of an Elizabethan merchant's half-timbered house built in 1577, with oak-panelling interior. *It is open during the summer*, and has a fine timbered restaurant.

BOATYARDS

Ⓑ **Mike's Marine** Barbridge Marina, Warale, Nantwich, Ches. (Wettenhall 682). R W Slipway, gas, boat & engine repairs, mooring, chandlery, boat sales, provisions, winter storage.

Ⓑ **British Waterways Hire Cruiser Base** Basin End, Chester Road, Nantwich, Ches. (625122). At Nantwich Basin. R S W Pump-out, narrow boat hire, gas, dry dock, mooring, toilets, canal shop. *Closed Sun.*

Ⓑ **Simolda** Basin End, Nantwich. (624075). Narrow boat hire, pump-out, boat repairs and gantry.

PUBS

Jolly Tar Barbridge Junction.

Barbridge Inn by bridge 100. Food, garden.

Star Acton.

✕ **Crown Hotel** Nantwich. Restaurant: lunches and dinners daily. An interesting old coaching house, built in the late 16thC.

Tyrley Top Lock.

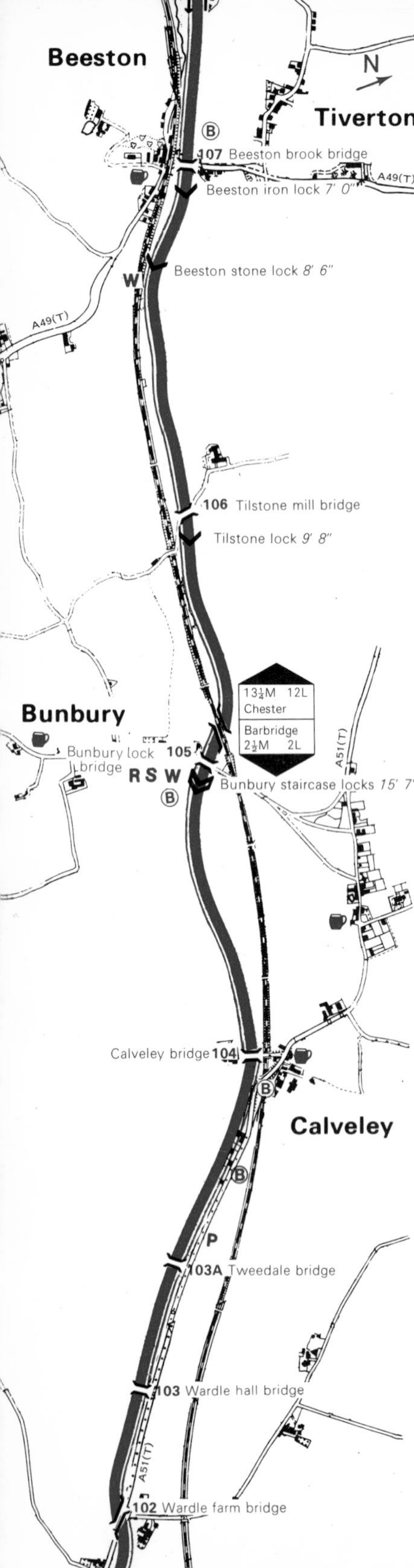

Bunbury

The canal moves almost westwards now alongside a busy main road, passing an enormous radar scanner. At Calveley, large modern cheese warehouses remind the traveller that Cheshire cheese is not merely local produce but a major export. Here the towpath changes sides and the Crewe–Holyhead railway joins the canal. At Bunbury Wharf 2 staircase locks require thought before action: they are also 14ft wide, like all subsequent locks between here and Chester. There is a fine range of stables beside Bunbury Locks, now used as a boat yard, and a former warehouse beside the bridge which still displays the Shropshire Union Railways & Canal Company's name on its gable wall. Beyond the wharf, wooded hills crowd in on the canal, which flows like a river through a narrow valley. There are occasional views to the west of the ruined Beeston Castle on its isolated hill. An old water mill beside Tilstone Lock is now used as an outdoor activities base by the local Scout group. At Beeston 2 contrasting lock-chambers are encountered: one is made of stone, the other of cast iron flanged plates to overcome running sand below it (do not attempt to pass 2 narrow boats through together—the sides have bowed). The water point at the stone lock is in the lockside lobby. There were once similar lobbies at all locks on the SU main line: only 3 now survive. Up the hill to the north of the 2 locks is Tiverton. (*PO, tel, stores, garage*). There is a convenient café to the south of bridge 7, open 7 *days a week (also groceries*).

Bunbury
Ches. EC Wed. Sat. PO, tel, stores, garage, bank. A mile south west of Bunbury Locks, the village is bigger than it looks at first, being virtually split into 3 sections. The attractive part is nearest, around the church. This is an outstanding building: supremely light, airy and spacious, it stands as a fine monument to workmanship of the 14th and 15thC, and represents a powerful contrast to the unimaginative architecture that characterises so many modern buildings. The ornamental tomb in the sanctuary contains the body of Sir George Beeston: he is said to have commanded one of the British ships against the Spanish Armada, at the remarkable age of 88.

Calveley
Ches. Tel, stores, garage. This rather insignificant village has been practically overwhelmed by the canal, road & railway that carve their respective ways through it. Old wharf buildings now house a canal shop.

BOATYARDS

Ⓑ **Chas. Hardern** Beeston Castle Wharf, near Tarporley. Ches. (Tarporley 2595). R W D Pump-out. Gas, nire craft, moorings, boat and engine repairs. Toilets, gift shop.
Ⓑ **Dartline Cruisers** The Canal Wharf, Bunbury, near Tarporley, Ches. (Bunbury 260638). R S W D Pump-out, narrow boat hire, slipway, gas, boat building & repairs, mooring, chandlery, toilets, provisions.
Ⓑ **Wandra Boats** Calverley, Tarporley, Ches. (Bunbury 260186). W D Pump-out, gas, provisions, gifts, slipway, moorings.

PUBS AND RESTAURANTS

Wild Boar Motor Lodge Inn Beeston. Restaurant in a large mock Tudor building.
Beeston Castle Hotel. Beeston.
Nags Head Bunbury.
Dysart Arms Bunbury, by the church.
Tollemache Arms ½ mile north east of Bunbury Wharf. Food.
Davenport Arms Calveley, near the wharf. Lunchtime snacks.

Bate's Mill

Leaving Beeston, the canal moves out of the narrow valley into more open countryside. From Wharton Lock an excellent view is obtained of the massive bulk of Beeston Castle, a landmark which can be seen from places up to 30 miles away. As one moves westward, the romantic-looking turrets of neighbouring Peckforton Castle come into view, revealing the long ridge of hills of which Beeston Castle forms the eastern end. The countryside here is flat and quiet, and packed with cows and buttercups. The railway accompanies the canal for some of the way: so does the tiny River Gowy, which fed the old Bate's Mill. There is a pipe works near Crow's Nest Bridge.

Beeston Castle
The impressive ruins of a 13thC castle built by the Earl of Chester. Situated on top of a steep hill dominating the surrounding countryside, it was in an ideal, almost unassailable position. From the castle, one may have a remarkable view of the Cheshire Plain, and one can see the well in the courtyard. It is 360ft deep. *Open Mon to Sat and Sun afternoons.*

PUBS

Aldersey Arms Hotel 200yds south west of Crow's Nest Bridge. Food.

Shady Oak Canalside, at Bate's Mill Bridge. Food.

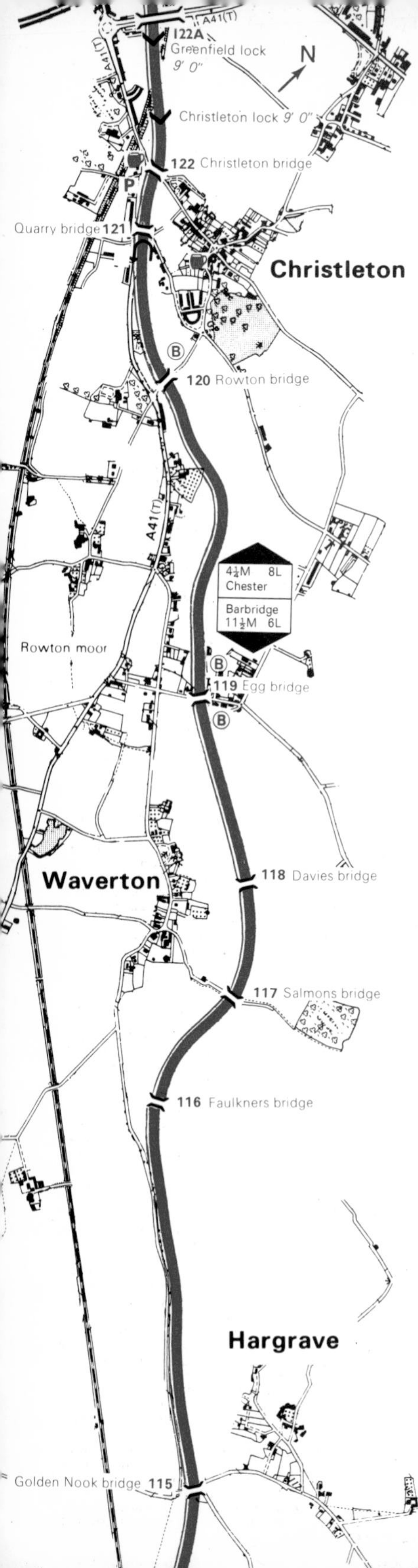

Christleton

The canal continues through the flat but very green landscape of the Cheshire Plain past Waverton with its conspicuous church tower and, past a fine brick mill by Egg Bridge, along through the unprepossessing Rowton Moor to the delightful village of Christleton. Here the towers and chimneys of Chester come into view and the railway dives under the canal in a short tunnel. Nearly all motorists sound their horn before crossing Christleton Bridge, so this is a bad place for an overnight mooring.

Christleton
Ches. PO, tel, stores. A very pleasant village near the canal, well worth visiting. The village green is still very much the centre of the village: church and pub are beside it, as are several well-kept elegant houses. It is refreshing to find a village so near to a big town that has so defiantly retained its identity.
Battle of Rowton Moor. It was here, three miles from Chester, that one of the last major battles of the Civil War took place in 1645. The Parliamentarians completely routed the Royalists who, still under fierce attack, retreated to Chester. It is said that King Charles I watched the defeat from the walls of Chester, but it is more probable that he only saw the final stages under the walls of the city. Charles fled, leaving 800 prisoners and 600 dead and wounded.
Waverton
Ches. PO, tel, stores. The sturdy church tower carries a pleasing, modest spire. Inside the church, which was greatly restored by the Victorians, the low aisle arches lend a certain cosiness to the building.

BOATYARDS

Ⓑ **Deans Marina** Rowton Bridge, Christleton, near Chester. (Chester 35523). R W Gas, chandlery, slipway, moorings, boat & motor sales, toilets.
Ⓑ **Eggbridge Marina** 1a Fox Lane, Eggbridge, Waverton, Chester. (Chester 36604). Just north of bridge 119. R S W D Pump-out, boat hire, slipway, gas, boat building & repairs, mooring, chandlery, toilets, winter storage.
Ⓑ **Holidaymakers** (Cheshire) Waverton Mill, Eggbridge Lane, Waverton, Chester. (Chester 36456). Just south of bridge 119. R S W Pump-out, gas, toilets.

PUBS

Ye Old Trooper Canalside, at Christleton Bridge. Snacks.
Ring O' Bells Christleton.

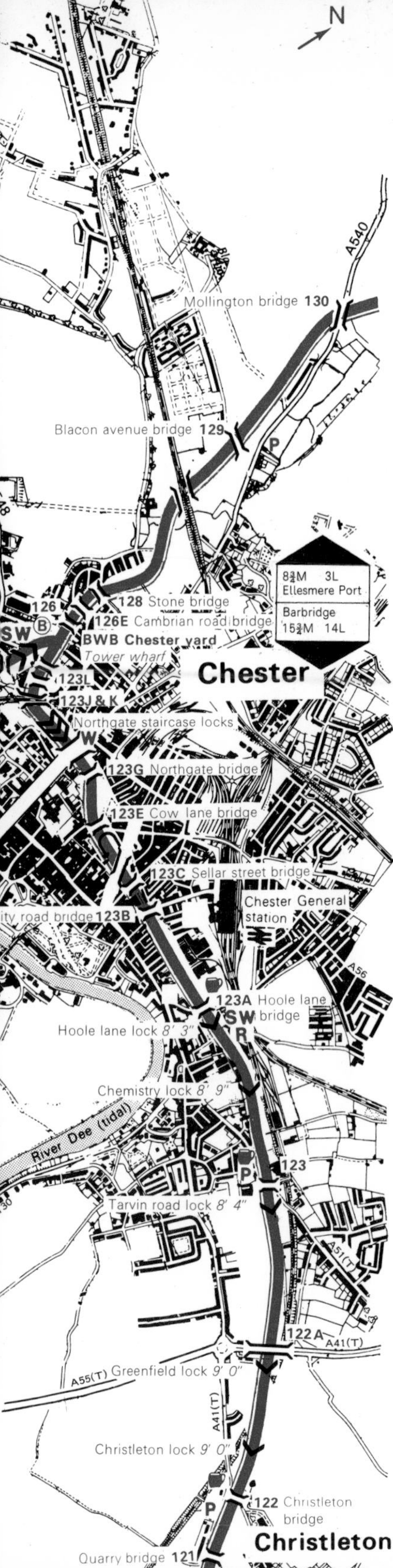

Chester

This is a most interesting and unusual stretch of canal. Leaving Christleton, the canal drops down into the ancient city of Chester through 5 locks: none of these have top gate paddles, and they all take rather long to fill. The canal goes straight through the middle of the town and is very much open to view. Passing a large lead works—with its tall chimney and 'shot tower'—and a great variety of bridges, the navigation approaches the old city and suddenly curves round into a very steep rock cutting: the city wall is high up on one side. King Charles' Tower stands on the wall. Soon the Northgate Locks (a staircase) are reached: at the bottom is a sharp right turn to Tower Wharf, a good place to tie up for the night. There is a boatyard at the head of the arm leading down into the River Dee.

Chester
Ches. EC Wed. MD Tue, Thur. All services. There is a wealth of things to see in this Roman city, which is the sort of place that is enjoyable to walk round even in the rain. It is in fact an excellent town to see on foot, partly because a costly new inner ring road has obviously generated more traffic congestion than it has alleviated, but more especially because of the amazing survival of almost all the old city wall. This provides Chester with its best and rarest feature—one can walk right round the city on this superb footpath, over the old city gates and past the defensive turrets, including King Charles' Tower above the canal, which contains an exhibition depicting the Civil War. Chester is in fact the only city in England with its walls still complete in their 2 mile circuit. Portions of the original Roman work still remain, but in the Middle Ages several gates and towers were added, one of which—the Eastgate—has, since 1897, carried an elaborate clock to commemorate Queen Victoria's Diamond Jubilee. Other splendid features are the race course—the Roodee—(just outside the city wall and therefore well inside the modern town) where Chester Races are held each year in May, Jul and Sep—it can easily be overlooked for free from the road that runs above and beside it; the superb old cathedral; the bold new theatre; the 'Rows'—unique double-tier medieval shopping streets; and the immense number of old and fascinating buildings throughout the town, such as Leche House, God's Providence House and Bishop Lloyd's Palace in Watergate Street.

Chester Cathedral Northgate Street. A magnificent building of dark red stone on the site of a 10thC minster. In 1092 the Earl of Chester and St Anselm founded a Benedictine abbey, which was dissolved in 1540, but in the following year it was made a cathedral and the seat of a bishop. The monastery buildings still remain: in the cathedral the 14thC choir stalls with their intricate carvings depict the Tree of Jesse showing the genealogy of Christ.

Abbey Square Outside the cathedral, opposite the Victorian town hall, the square is entered through a massive gateway built in 1377, where the 'Chester Mystery Plays' were performed.

Church of St John the Baptist St John's Street. Impressive 12thC church that was built on the site of an earlier Saxon church. The nave contains fine examples of austere Norman pillars and arcades. The ruins of the choir at the east end still remain, as well as those of the tower which collapsed in 1573.

Chester Castle Grosvenor Road. The original timber structure c1069 was replaced by stone walls and towers by Henry III. Unfortunately in 1789 the defensive walls were removed to make way for the incongruous Thomas Harrison group of buildings, which include the Grand Entrance and Assize Courts. The main part of the castle is occupied by troops of the Cheshire Regiment, but the 13thC Agricola Tower is open to the public. The county archives, which include numerous documents relating to the canal, are kept here.

Museum of the Cheshire Regiment Situated inside the tower of the Castle, it contains relics of many wars, including maps, plans, photographs and standards.

Grosvenor Museum Grosvenor Street. Exhibits the archaeology and natural history of

Chester. Fine collection of Anglo-Saxon coins. *Open May–Sep, closed Sun morning.*

Stanley Palace Watergate Street. Beautifully timbered house built in 1591 as the town house of the Stanleys, Earls of Derby. It was restored in 1935 and is now used as the headquarters of the English-Speaking Union. *Open Mon–Fri.*

Northgate Locks
Hewn out of solid rock, these 3 staircase locks lower the canal by 33ft, an impressive feat of engineering and a suitable complement to the deep rock cutting nearby. The locks are now sandwiched between a large new flyover and a low railway bridge.

The Dee Branch
This branch into the tidal River Dee runs through 3 wide locks from the boatyard near Tower Wharf. There used to be a large basin below the second lock, but this has now been filled in. The bottom lock and bridge are new, having been built to replace an old single-tracked swing bridge on a main road. There is a very sharp bend into the branch from Tower Wharf. Anyone wishing to take a boat into the River Dee *must* give at least 2 days notice to the BWB section inspector (Chester 372620) during working hours. (The bottom lock has to be kept padlocked to prevent silting up at high water.) It is practicable to enter or leave the River Dee at this point only for 1 hour either side of high water, since there is insufficient water at the entrance for the rest of the time.

BOATYARDS

Ⓑ **David Jones Boatbuilders** Upper Cambrian View, Chester. (376363). At junction with Dee Branch. Shipwrights, wood & steel boats built, all repairs and specialise in antique boats. *Open Mon–Fri, weekends by appt.*

Ⓑ **BWB Chester Yard** Tower Wharf. (Chester 372620). Dry dock and slipway.

BOAT TRIPS

The Chester Packet Horse drawn trips from Tower Wharf, Chester. Public trips and private charter. Also a summer waterbus service to Chester Zoo and The Boat Museum, Ellesmere Port. Ring Chester 373950 for details.

PUBS

There are many fine pubs in Chester.

- **Pied Bull** Northgate
- **Ye Olde Custom House** Watergate.
- **Lock Vaults** by Hoole Lane Lock. Snacks.
- **Bridge** Near Tarvin Road Lock.

The Boat Museum at Ellesmere Port: a good reason to venture north of Chester. *Derek Pratt*

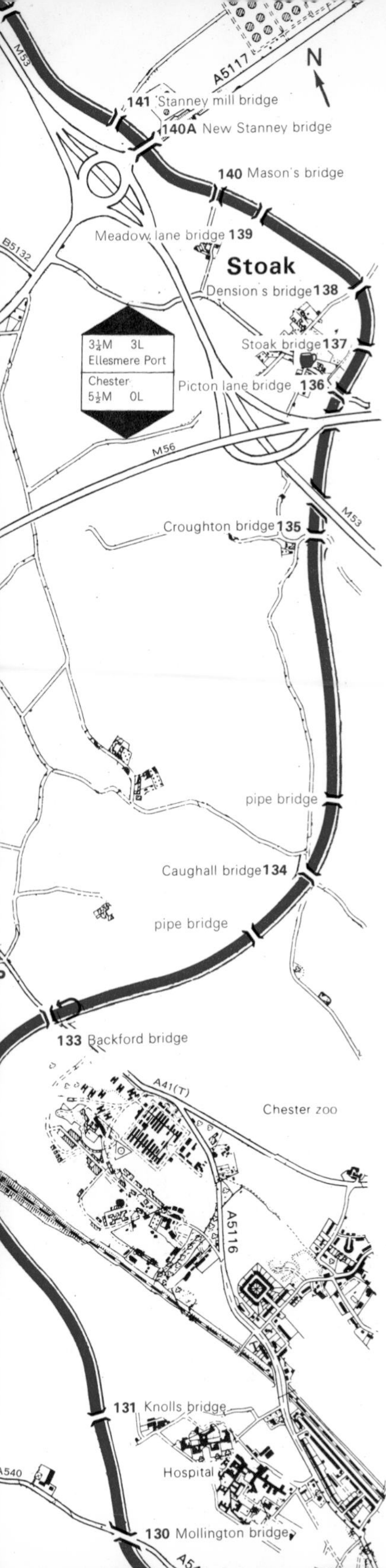

The Wirral

Sweeping northwards along the lockfree pound from Chester to the Mersey, the canal enters for the last time open country as it crosses the Wirral. The handsome stone railway viaduct over the navigation carries the Chester–Birkenhead line; here one turns briefly eastwards, passing along a shallow, green and peaceful valley. Chester Zoo is only ½ mile south of the cast iron Caughall Bridge. Stoak (or Stoke—alternative spellings) is now surrounded by canal and motorway. The church is conspicuous from the navigation; north of the village, the distant oil refineries and chimneys herald the industrial activity along Merseyside.

Stoak
Ches. Tel. There is little of interest in this scattered village except a pleasant country pub and a small, pretty church.

Chester Zoo
½ mile south of Caughall Bridge (134). Wide variety of animals, shown as much as possible without bars and fences, enhanced by attractive flower gardens and its own miniature canal. Largest elephant house in the world. *Open daily 9.00–dusk.*

PUBS

Bunbury Arms Stoak. Food, garden.

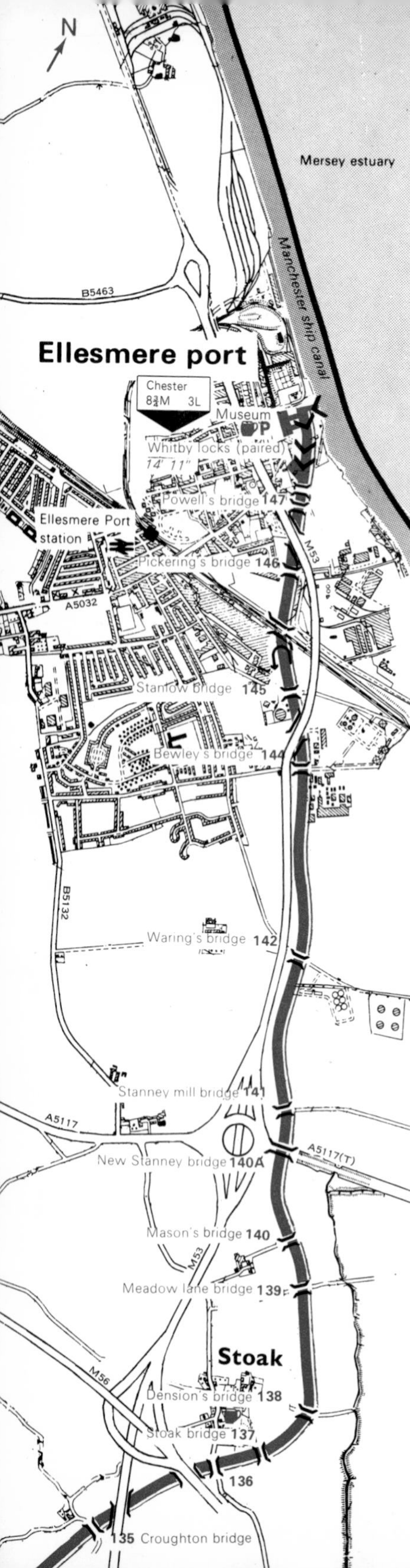

Ellesmere Port

The canal now rapidly enters an area of large scale industries, crossed and re-crossed by the new Wirral motorway. Oil refineries and chemical works seem to predominate in a gaunt, manmade landscape in which the canal is completely forgotten and shunned by industry which it fostered long ago. The docks and basins of the port itself, where the Shropshire Union Canal meets the Manchester Ship Canal, are—or were—very extensive. Telford's famous warehouses in which the narrow boats and barges were loaded and discharged under cover were regrettably set alight by local hooligans and had to be demolished in the interests of safety. But now part of the old dock complex is the home of the Boat Museum, making the journey beyond Chester well worthwhile. There is still access for boats from the Shropshire Union through several wide locks down into the Manchester Ship Canal. But no pleasure boat may enter the Ship Canal without previously seeking permission from the Manchester Ship Canal Company. Boat owners should remember that amongst other conditions the company insists on before considering granting entry to pleasure boats is that every boat should carry conventional navigation lights; an anchor and cable, at least 50 fathoms of rope, and third party insurance cover worth at least £50,000.

Ellesmere Port
Ches. EC Wed. MD Fri. All services. An industrial town of little interest apart from the fine Victorian railway station.
The Boat Museum (051-355 1876). Established in the old Ellesmere Port basins. Exhibits, models and photos trace the development of the canal system from early times to its heyday in the 19thC. Vessels on display in the basin include narrow boats, a tunnel tug and a weedcutter. An exciting and expanding venture, not to be missed. *Open 10.00–17.00. Closed Xmas day and Boxing day.*
Stanlow Abbey
Beside the Mersey, 1½ miles east of the canal on Stanlow Point. Remains of the Cistercian abbey founded in 1178 by John, Baron of Halton. Now isolated by the Ship Canal.

PUBS

Bulls Head Ellesmere Port.
Horse and Jockey Ellesmere Port.

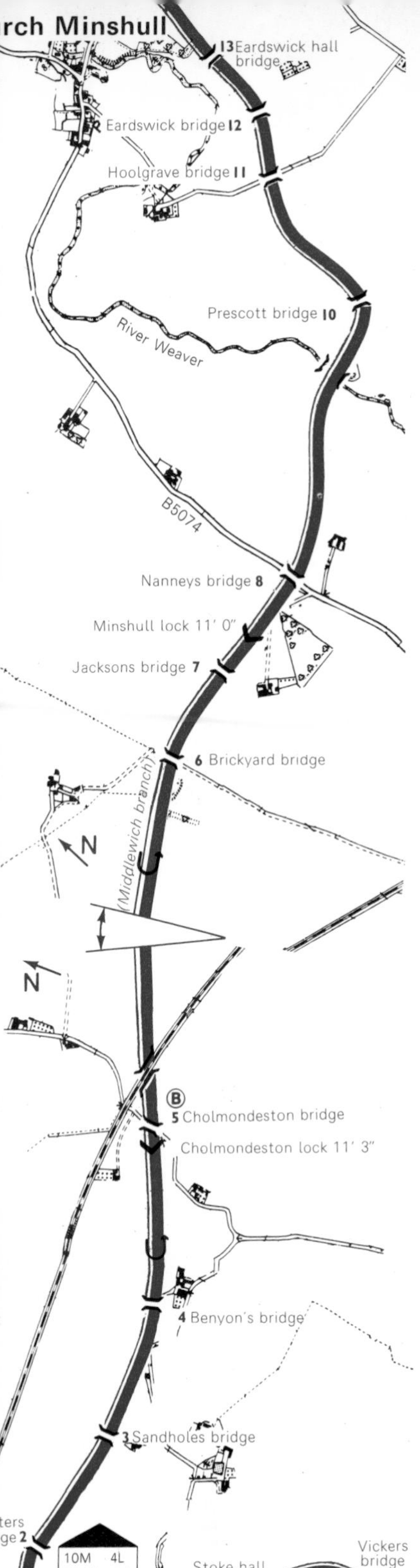

Barbridge

This attractive and under-rated link canal leaves the main line at Barbridge Junction, passing a boatyard and heading east through quiet and remote countryside. By Cholmondeston Lock there is a huge marina. After passing another lock, the canal crosses the River Weaver on an aqueduct as it approaches the village of Church Minshull.

Church Minshull
Ches. PO, tel, stores, garage. An old and mellow village beside the River Weaver. The notable 18thC church in the centre of the village is the subject of a Preservation Order. It is certainly the core of this most attractive place—and next to it is an old country pub.

BOATYARDS

Ⓑ **Venetian Marine** Cholmondeston Lock, Nantwich, Ches. (Wettenhall 251). R S W Gas, chandlery, lagoon moorings, slipway, provisions.

Ⓑ **Mike's Marina** Barbridge Marina, Wardle, Nantwich. Ches. (Wettenhall 682). R W Slipway, gas, boat & engine repairs, mooring, chandlery, boat sales, provisions, winter storage.

PUBS

- **Kings Arms** Barbridge. Canalside, at Bremilow's Bridge.
- **Jolly Tar** Barbridge Junction.
- **Badgers Arms** Church Minshull. Food.

Middlewich

This is a quiet stretch of canal passing through rich farmland interspersed with woods. There are superb views to the west over the River Weaver and Winsford Top Flash. At bridge 22A the main London–Glasgow electric railway line makes a noisy crossing. The canal then descends through 2 locks to Middlewich, where it joins the Trent and Mersey. This last 20yds of the Middlewich Branch used to belong to the Trent and Mersey, and the bridge over the entrance to the branch is grandiosely inscribed 'Wardle Canal 1829'. There are good moorings at the boatyard to the left of the junction.

For details of Middlwich—town, boatyards and pubs, see page 160.

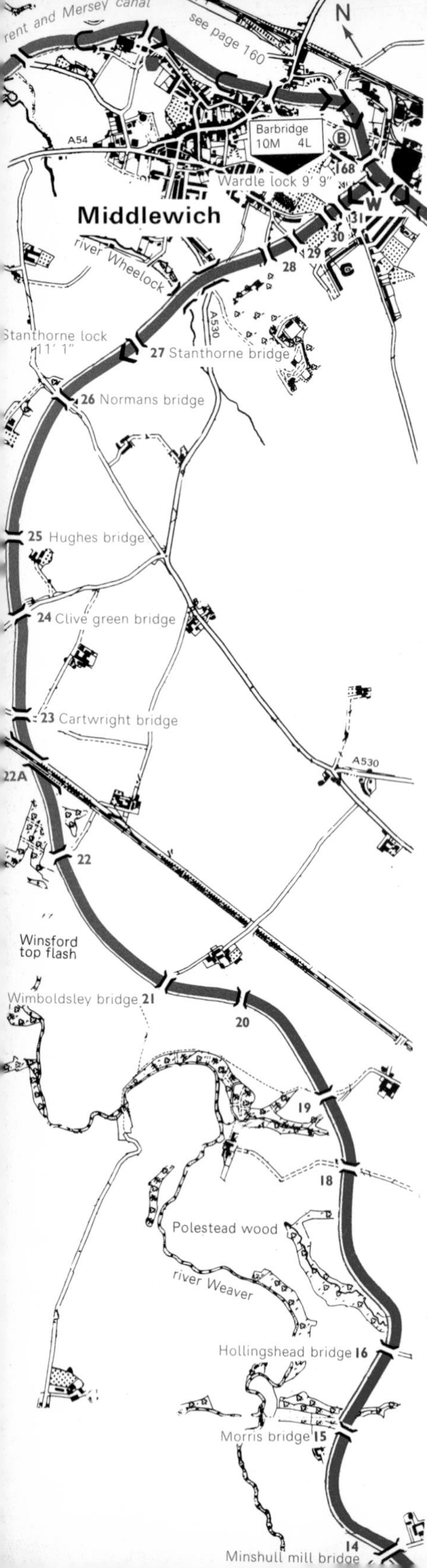

STOURBRIDGE

Maximum dimensions

Length: 70′
Beam: 7′
Headroom: 6′

Mileage

STOURTON JUNCTION to
Wordsley Junction: 2
Stourbridge: 3¼
BLACK DELPH bottom lock: 5¼

Locks: 16

The Stourbridge and Dudley Canals are to some extent inseparable, being part of the same grand scheme to link the Dudley coal mines with the Stourbridge glass works, and with the Severn Navigation by means of the Staffs & Worcs Canal. The Acts for the 2 canals were passed on the same day in 1776. Well supported by local glass masters, the Stourbridge Canal was soon under way, with Thomas Dadford as engineer. From a junction with the Staffs & Worcs at Stourton, the canal ran to Stourbridge. There was a 2 mile branch to the feeder reservoirs on Pensnett Chase, with 16 rising locks, and another level branch ran to Black Delph, where it met the Dudley Canal.

Combined with the Dudley Canal, the Stourbridge was soon profitable, and it was not long before the 2 companies were seeking to increase their revenue. They decided to try to capture some of the rich traffic on the Birmingham Canal. A joint proposal for a junction with the Birmingham Canal line via the Dudley Tunnel was authorised in 1785, and the through route was opened in 1792. Although the 2 companies worked so closely together, they resisted the temptation to amalgamate, relying on their mutual dependence to sort out any problems. Although the Dudley Canal became part of the BCN system the central position of the Stourbridge made it a very profitable undertaking, and throughout the early years of the 19thC the trade steadily increased. Even the opening of the rival Worcester & Birmingham Canal in 1815 did not affect the profits. Revenues were further increased in 1840 when the Stourbridge Extension Canal, later GWR owned, was opened to capture the coal trade from the Shut End collieries.

In the middle of the 19thC, railway competition began to affect the canal, first from the Oxford Worcester & Wolverhampton Railway, and later from the Great Western Railway. Revenues began their inevitable decline, but the Stourbridge was able to maintain its profits, and thus its independence until nationalisation in 1948, although by then it was in the same run down state as most canals in Britain. Commercial traffic died away, and by the 1950s the canal was no longer usable.

In 1964 the Staffs & Worcs Canal Society and the BWB decided to restore the 16 locks, and reopen the line between Birmingham and the Severn. Using volunteer labour provided by the Society and money and know-how provided by BWB, work slowly progressed, and in 1967 the Stourbridge Canal was reopened to traffic. Recently the town arm has been dredged, and plans have been made to develop the terminus.

Stourbridge

The Stourbridge Canal leaves the Staffs & Worcs at Stourton Junction. From the junction the canal runs east and starts at once the climb towards Birmingham. Two locks are followed by the A449 bridge, where the towpath turns over to the north bank on a separate iron split bridge. The waterside gardens of Stewponey village accompany the canal through two more locks and then pretty wooded countryside surrounds it all the way to Wordsley Junction. Only the occasional bridge breaks the rural seclusion, and these carry little traffic. As the canal approaches Wordsley Junction, where the Stourbridge Arm (now a conservation area) joins the main line, houses appear over the crest of the hill, and soon industrial and domestic development surrounds it. West of the junction, where the Stourbridge town arm leaves the main line, there is a small aqueduct, carrying the canal over the River Stour. The main line goes straight on, starting immediately the climb up 16 locks. Wordsley lies to the north and Amblecote to the south of the flight, but the 2 places are barely distinguishable. There is easy access to the towns from the bridges that interrupt the flight. The surroundings become steadily more industrial and there are many traces of the role played by the canal in the Stourbridge glass industry. Beyond lock 13 the canal passes the Stuart Crystal factory, where one of the old bottle-shaped glass kilns, now restored, can be seen, and by lock 12 there is a large covered wharf, now disused. When the canal reaches the top of the flight, the main line swings to the south-east. Straight ahead is the Fens Branch, which leads to Pensnett reservoir (or Fens Pools). This is a feeder for the canal. The towpath stays on the north for the branch, but turns over to the south bank on the main line. It swings south round Brierley Hill, and then a more open landscape flanks the canal in the last stage of its journey. After passing under the last bridge Delph bottom lock comes into sight, and here the Stourbridge Canal ends. The Dudley Canal continues the journey into Birmingham, joining the Birmingham Canal via the Netherton Tunnel.

Brierley Hill Glass Museum
Branch Library, Moor Street, Brierley Hill, Staffs. Access from Delph top lock. Stourbridge has been a centre of the glass industry since the 17thC, reaching its greatest development during the 19thC. The museum includes examples of local glass, and has a pictorial display of the history and techniques of glass making. *Open Mon–Fri afternoons and all day Sat.*

Stourbridge
Worcs. EC Thur, MD Fri/Sat. All services. Although the origins of Stourbridge go back to the Middle Ages, there is little trace of this today. It is almost entirely a 19thC town, reflecting the great expansion of the glass industry during that period. There is one 18thC church, St Thomas's, and a great variety of Victorian ones, none of which is remarkable.

BOATYARDS

Ⓑ **Delph Lock Boats** Unit 3, Canalside Works, Brierley Hill. (72411). WD Pump-out, gas, chandlery, overnight mooring, boat building, slipway, crane.

STAFFORDSHIRE & WORCESTERSHIRE

Maximum dimensions

Length: 72′
Beam: 7′
Headroom: 6′ 6″

Mileage

STOURPORT to:
Kidderminster Lock: 4½
Wolverley Lock: 6
STOURTON JUNCTION: 12¼
Swindon: 16¾
Bratch Locks: 19
ALDERSLEY JUNCTION: 25
AUTHERLEY JUNCTION: 25½
GREAT HAYWOOD JUNCTION: 46

Locks: 31

Construction of this navigation was begun immediately after that of the Trent & Mersey, to effect the joining of the Rivers Trent, Mersey and Severn. After this, only the line down to the Thames was necessary to complete the skeleton outline of England's narrow canal network.

Engineered by James Brindley, the Staffs & Worcs was opened throughout in 1772, at a cost of rather over £100,000. It stretched 46 miles from Great Haywood on the Trent & Mersey to the River Severn, which it joined at what became the bustling canal town of Stourport. The canal was an immediate success. It was well placed to bring goods from the Potteries down to Gloucester, Bristol and the West Country; while the Birmingham Canal, which joined it halfway along at Aldersley Junction, fed manufactured goods northwards from the Black Country to the Potteries via Great Haywood. Stourport has always been the focal point of the canal, for the town owed its birth and rapid growth during the late 18thC to the advent of the canal. It was here that the cargoes were transferred from narrow boats into Severn Trows for shipment down the estuary to Bristol and the south west.

The Staffordshire & Worcestershire Canal soon found itself facing strong competition. In 1815 the Worcester & Birmingham Canal opened, offering a more direct but heavily locked canal link between Birmingham and the Severn. The Staffs & Worcs answered this threat by gradually extending the opening times of the locks, until by 1830 they were open 24 hours a day. When the Birmingham & Liverpool Junction Canal was opened from Autherley to Nantwich in 1835, traffic bound for Merseyside from Birmingham naturally began to use this more direct, modern canal, and the Staffs & Worcs lost a great deal of traffic over its length from Autherley to Great Haywood. Most of the traffic now passed along only the ½-mile stretch of the Staffs & Worcs Canal between Autherley and Aldersley Junctions. This was, however, enough for the company, who levied absurdly high tolls for this tiny length. The B & LJ company therefore cooperated with the Birmingham Canal company in 1836 to promote in Parliament a Bill for the 'Tettenhall & Autherley Canal and Aqueduct'. This remarkable project was to be a canal 'flyover', going from the Birmingham Canal right over the profiteering Staff & Worcs and locking down into the Birmingham & Liverpool Junction Canal. In the face of this serious threat to bypass its canal altogether, the Staffs & Worcs company gave way and reduced its tolls to a level acceptable to the other 2 companies. In later years the device was used twice more to force concessions out of the Staffs & Worcs.

In spite of this setback, the Staffs & Worcs maintained a good profit, and high dividends were paid throughout the rest of the 19thC. When the new railway companies appeared in the West Midlands, the canal company would have nothing to do with them; but from the 1860s onwards, railway competition began to bite, and the company's profits began to slip. Several modernisation schemes came to nothing, and the canal's trade declined. Like the other narrow canals, the Staffordshire & Worcestershire faded into obscurity as a significant transport route by the middle of this century, although the old canal company proudly retained total independence until it was nationalised in 1947. Now the canal is used almost exclusively by pleasure craft—and it is certainly a most delightful canal for cruising (or walking), especially in the southern reaches in the sandstone area.

Wild flowers

The Staffordshire & Worcestershire Canal provides a very attractive long-distance walk, and one of particular interest to nature lovers. Most of the towpath is in excellent condition and provides a lovely walk, especially along the sandstone cuttings near Wolverley. Here the walker is often preceded for miles by low-flying herons.

Probably the most conspicuous plant along this canal is the Himalayan balsam. It was introduced in about 1840 and the valley of the Smestow Brook was one of the first places to be colonised. Although this is an annual plant, it grows up to 10ft high and has beautiful flowers ranging from pinkish-purple to white. The seeds are dispersed by an explosive mechanism—try to gather some ripe seeds and you will realise this! Although primroses are not found, in spring the towpath is a blaze of colour with the yellow lesser celandine and the white cow parsley with its fern-like leaves. Bluebells are uncommon but if you look across west from below Swindon Lock you will see the woods covered with a mass of blue. Generally the earliest flower to appear is coltsfoot—the purplish stems with many scales bearing dandelion-like flowers and appearing before the leaves. This is an old-fashioned remedy against sore throats and many countryfolk consider 'coltsfoot rock' a pleasant and efficacious cure. Another early flower is stitchwort, of rather grass-like appearance and with beautiful white flowers.

The canal is accompanied by hawthorn hedges in which grow wild roses and sometimes the wild cherry. Often the bushes are covered with the climbing white bryony and its red berries in the autumn. The large convolvulus has lovely flowers, generally white but occasionally various shades of pink. Sometimes everything is smothered with wild clematis or traveller's joy, the seeds of which are covered with white plumes; these give the plant the alternative name of 'old man's beard'. Nestling at the bottom of the hedge grows 'lords and ladies'; this sends up arrow-shaped leaves in the spring, then a pale green hood and finally a short spike of orange-red berries. You will often find scrambling up the hedge the woody nightshade, sometimes mistakenly called deadly nightshade—a plant which does not grow here. The flowers are an attractive mixture of purple lobes and yellow anthers. This plant is slightly poisonous.

Everyone who walks the canal will be fascinated by the narrow locks, and it is surprising how many plants grow on the lock walls. Perhaps the most beautiful is the small skullcap with its pairs of bright-blue flowers. A beautiful flower that is spreading quickly is rose-bay, with its tapering spikes of pinkish-purple flowers and with long silky hairs attached to the seeds. In wet places grows an allied plant, 'codlins and cream', with larger flowers. Nettles, of course, unfortunately abound but they do support the caterpillars of the lovely peacock butterfly—which, together with the small tortoiseshell and orange-tip, is the butterfly most commonly found on this canal. An interesting flower in early spring is butterbur, which sends up short heads of lilac-pink flowers. Later come the very large leaves, on stout stalks; these give the plant the common name of 'wild rhubarb'. In the waterway itself the commonest plant is water plantain with branched spikes of lilac-white flowers with three petals. Close to the water grows common valerian—very different from the red-flowered variety that flourishes on walls. This has small, very pale pink flowers. Near this you will often find bur-marigold with nodding heads of a deep yellow. Another water loving plant is water figwort, a tall plant with square stems and small reddish-brown flowers. Of the scented flowers perhaps the most attractive is meadowsweet with clusters of tiny cream-coloured flowers.

In some places grows the hemlock, a tall plant with spotted stems, beautiful and finely cut leaves and clusters of small white flowers. It was the poison from this plant that the Athenians used to execute the philosopher Socrates in 399 BC. A plant that flourishes almost anywhere is mugwort (a plant once used to give a pleasant flavour to mugs of ale). This is tall and branched with small oval yellow flowers. Allied to this is wormwood, with greyer leaves, more aromatic and slightly larger flowers. From this family is made the French liqueur absinthe.

Some plants will be found in flower throughout the year whenever conditions are suitable. These include the white deadnettle, groundsel (so well known to gardeners!) and Oxford ragwort, a bushy perennial with glossy, lobed leaves and bright yellow flowers. This originally grew on old walls at Oxford but started to spread last century. It was probably helped by the Great Western Railway—the ballast formed an ideal site for the plant and the rushing trains helped to spread the seeds. It is still found growing on some college walls. 'Common' ragwort is taller and stiffer; it flowers only during the late summer. If you are interested in uncommon flowers then in the southern section of the canal you may find shepherd's rod, with small round heads of white flowers and with purple anthers.

Growing almost everywhere on the towpath are members of the geranium family, their flowers generally pink and the fruit ending in a long pointed beak, giving rise to the common name of cranesbill. Varieties include herb robert with fern-like leaves, dovesfoot with round leaves and small-flowered cranesbill with the leaves divided. A tall-growing plant is mallow, with crinkly leaves and pinkish-purple petals with darker veins. The fruits—the so-called cheeses—are arranged in a ring. Another common flower is St John's wort, about 2ft high with golden yellow flowers. The leaves have minute perforations. Formerly the plant was looked upon as holy and a protection against the Devil. This so enraged the Devil that he stabbed the leaves through and through with a needle!

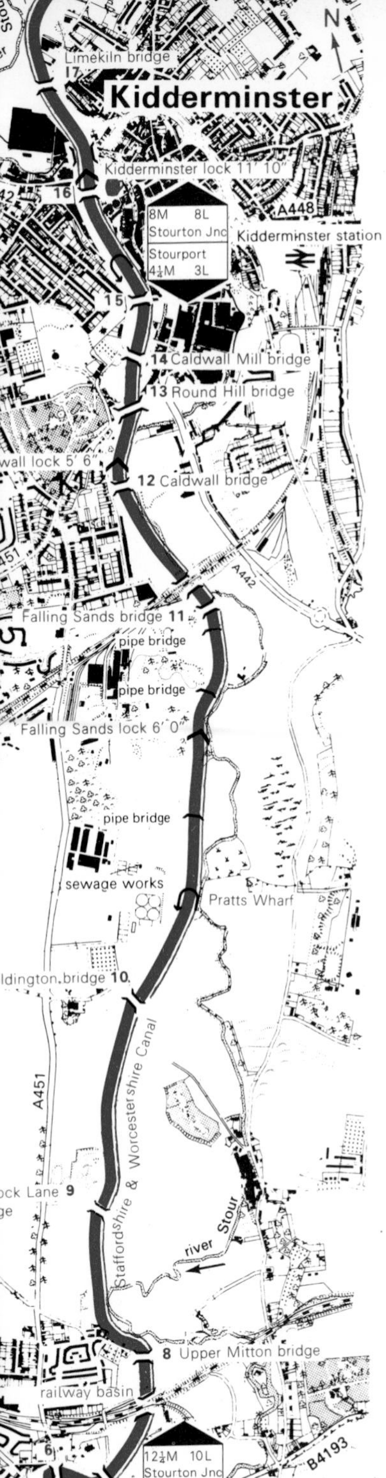

Stourport and Kidderminster

Few who quit the River Severn to navigate the Staffs & Worcs Canal will regret their decision. The lazy, monotonous and sweeping course of the river is replaced by the fascination and ever-changing scenery of a narrow canal, threading its intimate way through pleasantly irregular countryside. This canal is, without doubt, one of the prettiest waterways in England. First one must negotiate the locks and basins at Stourport—a pleasant task, for the combination of all kinds of engineering features, fine buildings and pleasure boats makes this a lively, colourful scene. The famous clock tower looks out over all. There are 2 sets of locks here, narrow and broad—*they are open from 08.00 to 20.00 during the summer, in the winter they are closed at 16.00*. The narrow locks are those most commonly in use, and they are in a staircase—the lock keeper is usually around to help if you have difficulties. *For an enlarged map of the Stourport Basin area see page 126*. To reach the Staffs & Worcs Canal itself, boats should proceed to the eastern corner of the upper basins, pass under the bridge and climb the deep lock at York Street. There is a useful shop and off-licence by the lock. Above the lock are good temporary moorings, opposite a boatyard which has carefully preserved and utilised the old canal buildings. Although it is still in the middle of Stourport, the canal has already acquired a secluded, unspoilt character, flanked by discreet, gently decaying houses and walls and accompanied by a rural towpath. The navigation seems to creep through the town, twisting along past the big disused Milton Railway Basin at a railway bridge and emerging quickly into the country. It follows the west side of a little valley, the steep slopes rising sharply from the water. The River Stour approaches and at Pratt's Wharf the towpath rises over an almost unrecognisably overgrown lock that once joined the canal to the Stour. This river used to be navigable from here for 1¼ miles down to the Wilden Ironworks. The sweet smell from an adjacent sewage works spurs the traveller on towards Kidderminster and suddenly the canal's surroundings change, for the hillside on the west bank becomes a dramatic cliff of crumbling red rock rising sheer from the canal. This is the southern end of a geological feature that stretches almost to Wombourn, 15 miles away. Falling Sands and Caldwall Locks both enjoy delightful situations at the foot of the sandstone, and both have split iron bridges of a type usually associated with the Stratford-on-Avon Canal. Kidderminster is now reached, and the canal's course through the centre of it is truly private, passing along a corridor of high walls, factories and warehouses that clearly date from the arrival of the canal in Kidderminster. As the buildings mount up, the navigation narrows until it escapes by diving into a short tunnel, at the end of which is a deep lock. One surfaces to find a very different scene: this is open townscape, with traffic all around, shopping streets close by and a church just ahead, on a rise. Nearby is a statue of Richard Baxter, the 17thC thinker who 'advocated unity and comprehension' in religion. Just above Kidderminster Lock, the River Stour appears from nowhere: the canal crosses it on an aqueduct. Continuing northwards, the canal curves away to leave the town centre behind, passing now more modern and less picturesque industrial works.

Kidderminster

Worcs. EC Wed. MD Thur, Sat. Kidderminster exists above all for carpet weaving. The industry was first introduced here in 1735, when the town was already a prosperous cloth manufacturing centre, and today there are many factories in Kidderminster involved in the production of carpets. Born here in 1793 was Rowland Hill, who founded the Penny Post in 1840: his statue in front of the head post office commemorates his 'creative mind and patient energy'. From the canal, one sees little but the older industrial side of Kidderminster, which is not without interest. The best place for access to the town is from Kidderminster Lock;

the public baths are conveniently beside bridge 15. There is not much to see in the town, which has few buildings of real interest—there is, however, a fine selection of pubs. The centre itself is better now than it was, enjoying the benefit of quiet streets uncluttered by vehicles; but this has been achieved at the expense of widespread demolition to clear the way for a modern dual carriageway—an inner ring road. This road unfortunately passes the door of the impressive, dark church of St Mary, cutting it off completely from Church Street, in which Kidderminster's few Georgian houses are situated.

Kidderminster Museum & Art Gallery Market Street. Collection of archaeological finds and exhibits of local interest. Small permanent art collection, including some Brangwyn etchings. (There is much more to see at the Worcestershire County Museum in Hartlebury Castle. *See below*). *Closed Sun.*

Stourport-on-Severn
Worcs. EC Wed. PO, tel, stores, garage, bank. When the engineer James Brindley surveyed the line for the Staffordshire & Worcestershire Canal in the early 1760s, he chose to meet the River Severn at the hamlet of Lower Mitton, 4 miles downstream of Bewdley where the little River Stour flowed into the Severn. Basins and locks were built for the boats, warehouses for the cargoes and cottages for the workmen. The canal company even built in 1788 the great Tontine Hotel beside the locks. The hamlet soon earned the name of Stourport, becoming a busy and wealthy town. The 2 basins were expanded to 5 (1 has since been filled in) and the locks were duplicated. Nowadays, plenty remains of Stourport's former glory, for the basins are always full of boats (there is a boat club and boatyards). The delightful clock tower still functions, a canal maintenance yard carries on in the old workshops by the locks, and the Tontine Hotel still has a licence. Mart Lane (on the north-east side of the basins) is worth a look--the original 18thC terrace of workmen's cottages still stands. Numbers 2, 3 and 4 are listed as ancient monuments. In contrast with the basin area, the town of Stourport is not interesting, and although it was built on account of the canal, the town has no relationship at all with the basins now. It seems to have grown up away from the canal.

Hartlebury Castle 2 miles east of Stourport on the B4193. The home of the Bishops of Worcester, this castle was built in the 15thC, virtually destroyed in 1646 and rebuilt in the 18thC. *Open Sun and B. Hol. afternoons.*

The Worcestershire Company Museum is housed in part of the Castle. It shows the story of the archaeology, geology, crafts and industries of the county. *Closed Fri, Sat and Sun mornings, and Dec and Jan.*

BOATYARDS

Ⓑ **BWB Stourport Yard** Stourport Basin. (2838). R S W close by.

Ⓑ **Dartline** Parkes Passage, off York Street, Stourport on Severn (2970). R S W D Pump-out (*Mon–Fri*), narrow boat hire, mooring, gift shop, toilets, winter storage.

Ⓑ **Heads Boatshop** Stourport Basin. (2044). R S W Slipway, gas, dry dock, mooring, chandlery, toilets, provisions.

Severn Valley Cruisers York Street, Boatyard, Stourport. (71165). R D W Pump-out (*not Sat*), boat hire, slipway, gas, boat building & repair, mooring, chandlery, toilets, winter storage.

PUBS AND RESTAURANTS

Bridge Inn Kidderminster. East of bridge 16. Snacks.

Bay Horse Market Street, Kidderminster. Snacks.

Boars Head Worcester Street, Kidderminster. Food.

Green Man and Still Oxford Street, Kidderminster.

Bird in Hand Stourport. Canalside, south of the railway bridge.

Black Star Stourport. Canalside, by bridge 5.

Lock, Stock & Barrel by bridge 5. Intimate restaurant. *Closed Sun.*

Bell Hotel Stourport, opposite York Street Lock.

White Lion Near the Bell.

Tontine Hotel Stourport Basin. Banks's real ale in a large pub built in 1788 by the canal company.

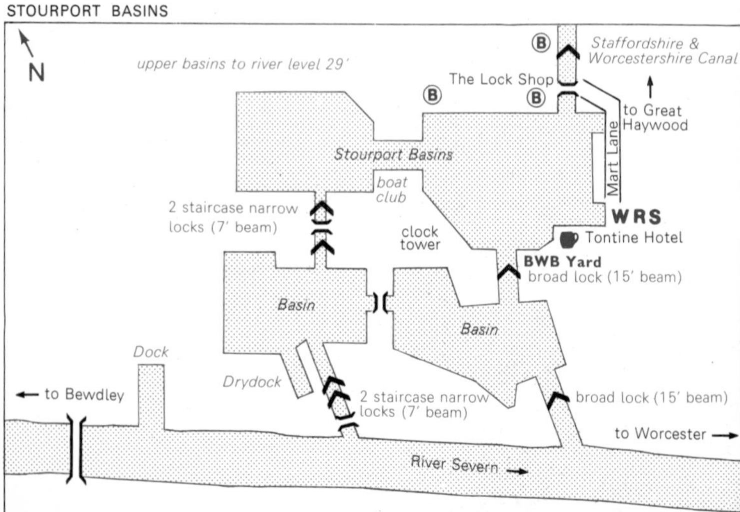

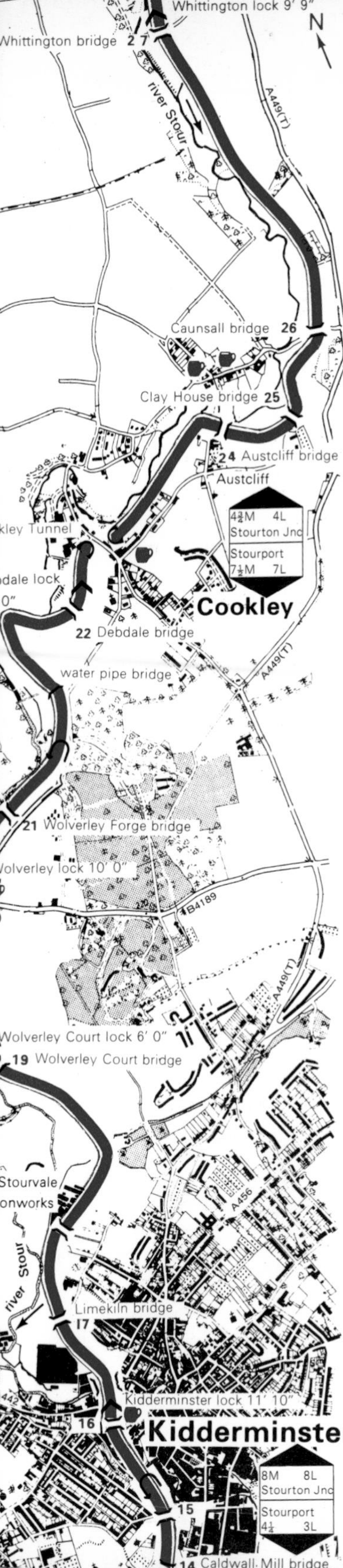

Wolverley

This is another delightful stretch of waterway. Leaving Kidderminster, the navigation moves into an area of quiet watermeadows created by the little River Stour, which is now on the west side. Past an isolated lock, the village of Wolverley on the other side of the valley is given away by its unusual Italianate church standing on a large outcrop of rock. The approach to the deep Wolverley Lock is lined by trees. There is a pub beside the lock, and good moorings above and below it. Beyond here, the course of the canal becomes really tortuous and narrow as it proceeds up the narrow, thickly wooded valley, forced into endless diversions by the steep cliffs of friable red sandstone. Vegetation of all kinds clings to these cliffs, giving the impression of jungle foliage. At one point the navigation opens out, becoming momentarily like a normal canal; but soon the rocks and trees encroach again, returning the waterway to its previous constricted width. An impressive promontory of rock compels the canal to double back on itself in a great horse-shoe sweep that takes it round to the pretty Debdale Lock. A doorway reveals a cavern cut into the solid rock here; this was used as an overnight stable for towing horses. Beyond Cookley Tunnel, the steep rocks along the right bank culminate in a remarkable geological feature where, unnervingly, the Austcliff Rock actually leans out, trees, bushes and all, right over the canal. Then the rocks recede for a short distance. Thick woods here keep the nearby A449 road at bay. Across the River Stour, ¼ of a mile west of bridge 26, is the small settlement of Caunsall. There are farms here, and 2 pubs, but little else.

Cookley
Worcs. PO, tel, stores, garage, fish& chips. The village is set well above the canal, which passes underneath it in a tunnel. Although it has an attractive situation, Cookley is not a particularly pretty village, and there is little to visit. There is a big steel works near the canal, where the biggest bulldozer wheel in the world was made. Down in the valley, near the River Stour, there are the older, more attractive cottages of the village. And clearly visible are the entrances to caves in the cliff face. To reach Cookley from the canal, it is best to moor west of the tunnel, then walk up the path to the village.

Wolverley
Worcs. PO, tel, stores. 400yds north west of bridge 20. A very unusual and pretty village on the west side of the Stour valley. The church is predominant, a dark red structure built in 1772 in a precise Italianate style. It stands on a sandstone rock so steep that the building has to be approached by a zigzag path cut through the constantly eroded sandstone. Most of the village is clustered just to the north of the church, near the little-used but dignified stone buildings of the old grammar school. The school was endowed in 1629, but most of the buildings date from 1820. Around it is the bulk of this small village, where gardens make the most of the brook that flows through. There is an attractive pub in the centre, and another, with spacious gardens, up the hill. Wolverley is a village certainly worth visiting—it is easily accessible from Wolverley Lock.

PUBS

- **Rock** Caunsall, ¼ mile west of bridge 26.
- **Anchor** Caunsall, ¼ mile west of bridge 26. Snacks.
- **Queens Head** Caunsall, near the Rock.
- **Bulls Head** Cookley. Up the hill from the tunnel, near the shops.
- **Lock** Canalside, at Wolverley Lock. Terrace fronting the canal. Food usually available.
- **Queens Head** Wolverley, near the old school. Terrace.

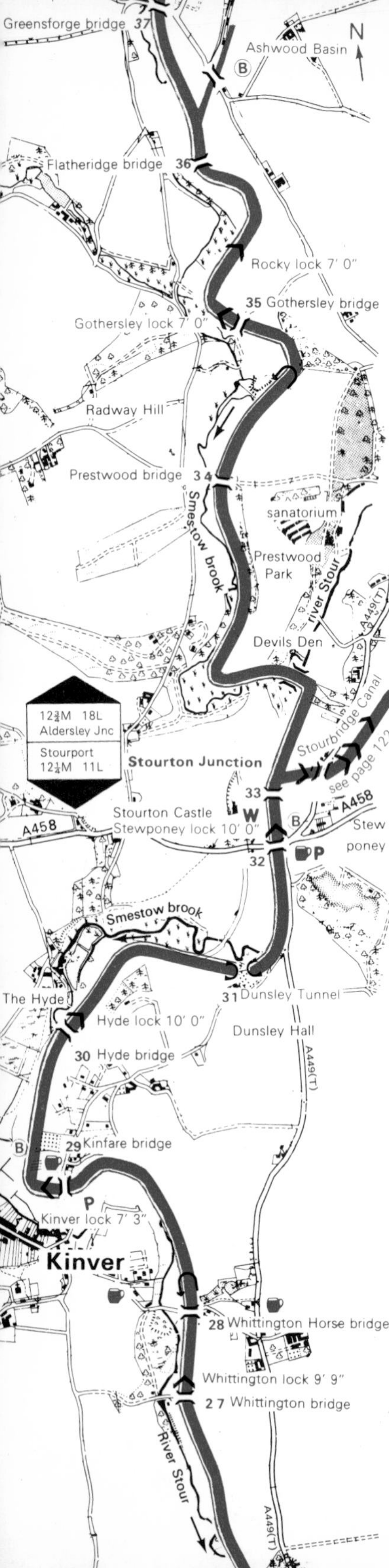

Kinver

Between bridges 26 and 27 the canal passes from Worcestershire into Staffordshire, but the surroundings of this remarkable waterway do not change: it continues through secluded woodlands, the rocky hillside on the east bank steepening as the valley narrows again. The nearby main road remains unnoticed, while the canal reaches Whittington Lock, a pretty lock cottage beside it. The bridge at the lock tail is typical of this navigation, its parapet curving fluently round and down to the lower water level. A couple of hundred yards north is another delightful scene, where on either side of the canal a few cottages, pretty gardens and moored boats face the waterway and the (very low) iron bridge. Then really tall, steep hills appear on the east bank, rising to over 250ft. 3 isolated cottages cling to the hill in a clearing among the trees. The canal leaves this damp, mossy area and bends round to Kinver Lock. There is a pub here, and a road, leading round to the village, which is behind the bold modern (1939) waterworks. This pumps from the vast underground lake that lies deep below the great sandstone ridge stretching from Kidderminster to Wombourn. Upstream of Kinver Lock are the Kinver Cruiser Club moorings and the Kinver Lock Marina. At the next lock (Hyde Lock) is another fine cottage: some canal wares may be bought here, as well as excellent home made provisions—cakes, scones and bramble jelly. Beyond the lock, the canal wanders along the edge of woods on the east side of the valley, passing through the charmingly diminutive (25yds long) Dunsley Tunnel, a rough-hewn bore with overhanging foliage at each end. The next lock is at Stewponey, where Stourton Castle stands just over the river. The Stourbridge Canal leaves at Stourton Junction, north of the wharf; the first of the many locks that carry the canal up towards Dudley and the Birmingham Canal Navigations is just a few yards away. (*See page 122*). Beyond Stourton Junction, a 90-degree bend to the left takes the canal to an aqueduct over the River Stour: this river now disappears to the north east and is not seen again. Its place near the canal is taken by the little Smestow Brook as far as Swindon. At the far end of the aqueduct is a curious narrow boathouse (known as the Devil's Den) cut into the rock. Prestwood Park is concealed in the woods above the east bank. The hall is now a hospital: it used to be the home of the Foleys, a family of Black Country ironmasters. Meanwhile the canal continues through Gothersley and Rocky Locks, reaching eventually a fork: the narrow entrance on the right leads into the very long Ashwood Basin, where there is a boatyard.

Ashwood Basin
This used to be a railway-connected basin owned by the National Coal Board. After the line was closed, the basin was disused for some years; but now it provides a pleasant mooring site for a large number of pleasure boats. There is a boatyard and a boatclub here. A road is carried over the basin by a small viaduct.

Stewponey Wharf
An interesting wharf at the head of Stewponey Lock with a restored octagonal toll office. Near the wharf can be seen the long-abandoned track of the Kinver Valley Light Railway, which used to run from Stourbridge to Kinver. From Stewponey to Kinver it followed a route close to the canal. Just across the river from the wharf is the impressive bulk of Stourton Castle, while in the opposite direction—but shielded by trees—is a fast main road, a built up area and a large roadhouse serving food. There is a telephone box and a small grocery hard by. A petrol station is not far away.

Stourton Castle Just a few yards west of Stewponey Wharf, this building is a curious mixture of building styles and materials. The castle is notable as the birthplace of Cardinal Pole in 1500. A friend of Mary Tudor, Pole became Archbishop of Canterbury in her reign after Cranmer had been burned at the stake. The Castle is private.

Kinver
Staffs. PO, tel, stores, garage, bank, launderette. Kinver clearly has a reputation as a Very Pretty Village. It is surrounded by tall hills and

consists of a long main street of reasonably attractive houses, but its chief glory is its situation—it nestles among tall wooded hills, a position that must strike the visitor as remarkable for a village so close to the industries and unexciting geographical features of the West Midlands. Kinver Edge (National Trust property), west of the village, is a tremendous ridge covered in gorse and heather, and for anyone prepared to toil up to the top from the valley it provides a splendid view of the Cotswold and Malvern Hills. Kinver church is near the Edge, and is reached by a steep zigzag road. The church overlooks the village and contains several things of interest, including plaques recording the Charter granted by Charles I in 1629 and the Charter granted by Ethelbad in 736, giving '10 cessapis of land to my general Cyniberte for a religious house'.

BOAT YARDS

Ⓑ **Ashwood Marina** (Kingswinford 295535). [S][W][D] Gas, chandlery, slipway, trimming shop, showers, licensed club, overnight moorings. Boat building and repairs, breakdown service.

Ⓑ **Kinver Lock Marina** The Paddock, Kinver, Staffs. (2363). [R][S][W][D] Pump-out, slipway, mooring, chandlery, toilets, provisions, winter storage, licensed club & restaurant. *Closed during the winter.*

PUBS AND RESTAURANTS

The Stewponey Hotel 50yds east of Stewponey Lock. Meals and snacks.

Vine By Kinver Lock.

Ye Old White Hart Kinver.

Whittington 300yds east of bridge 28, along a footpath. Dating from 1300, this building has an impressive history. It was the home of Dick Whittington's grandfather, and much later of Lady Jane Grey, whose ghost is sometimes encountered. There are also priest holes and a tunnel to the nearby Whittington Hall. Restaurant and wine bar.

The picturesque Bratch Locks.

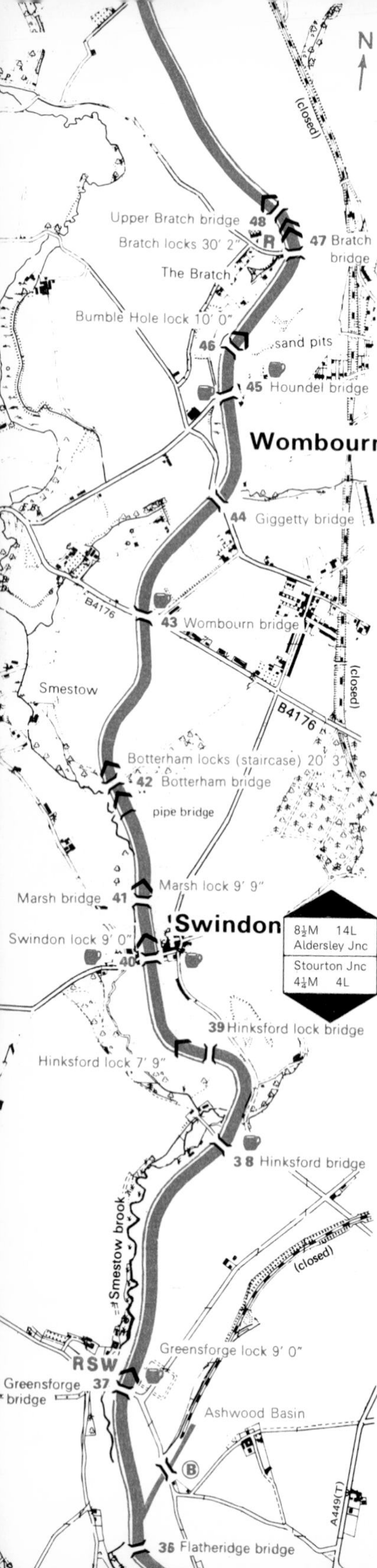

The Bratch

North of Rocky Lock, the outcrops of sandstone are seen less frequently, the countryside becoming flatter and more regular. However the locks do not disappear, for the canal continues the steady rise up the small valley of the Smestow Brook through southern Staffordshire towards Wolverhampton. At Greensforge Lock there is an attractive pub, and another of the pretty, circular weirs that are found, often hidden behind a wall or a hedge, at many of the locks along this delightful canal. Another wooded, rocky section leads again to more open country. At Hinksford there is a residential caravan site down in the valley, and another pub near bridge 38, with a public telephone outside. On through the isolated Hinksford Lock, the navigation bends round to Swindon. Strengthening girders under bridge 40 have reduced its headroom to 6ft 6in. There are 4 locks hereabouts, Botterham being a 2-step staircase with a bridge crossing in the middle. North of here, the canal begins to lose its rural character as it encounters the modern outskirts of Wombourn, passing under a new bridge that, happily, retains the original cast-iron name plates. There is a pub by this bridge (43) and a few shops not far to the north east of the next one (44). Yet another pub is at the next bridge (45); beyond it is Bumble Hole Lock, near the old gravel quarries. The 3 Bratch Locks are next, raising the canal level by over 30ft. Navigators may at first be completely foxed by these unique locks, but in fact they are much less complicated than they look (*see below*). From the top of the locks, one may enjoy a good view back down the valley, with the spire of Wombourn Church backed by the great ridge of the Orton Hills to the east. At the foot of the locks is the great florid Bilston Waterworks, built in 1895. Leaving the Bratch, the canal wanders through open farmland parallel to a long-closed railway, arriving at the pleasantly situated Awbridge Lock, with its circular weir and farm beside it.

Bratch Locks
With their octagonal toll office, attractive situation and very unusual layout, these 3 locks are well known among students of canal engineering and architecture. At first sight they appear curiously illogical, with an impossibly short pound between the bottom of one lock and the top gate of the next; but the secret of their operation is the side ponds hidden behind the towpath hedge and the culverts that connect these to the intermediate pounds. In fact, to work through these locks, boaters should simply treat each one as a separate lock like any other on the canal. *However, it is especially important when locking through to close the gates and paddles of each lock before operating the paddles of the next.* The big mistake is to consider the locks as a staircase—this will inevitably lead to things going wrong. Busy in summer.

Wombourn
Staffs. PO, tel, stores. This town used to be an attractive village, before an expansion scheme flooded the town with acres of council houses.

Swindon
Staffs. PO, tel, store, fish& chips. A small village, once a mixture of farming and industry. The 19thC ironworks has been demolished, replaced by a housing estate.

PUBS

- **Mount Pleasant** at bridge 45. Food, garden.
- **Royal Oak** Canalside, at bridge 45.
- **Waggon & Horses** Near the canal at bridge 43, on B4176. Food.
- **Green Man** Swindon Ironworks, 100yds west of bridge 40.
- **Old Bush Inn** Swindon village, 150yds east of bridge 40.
- **The Bush** Hinksford, 100yds north east of bridge 38. Garden.
- **Navigation** Greensforge. Canalside, at the lock. Snacks and local draught beer.

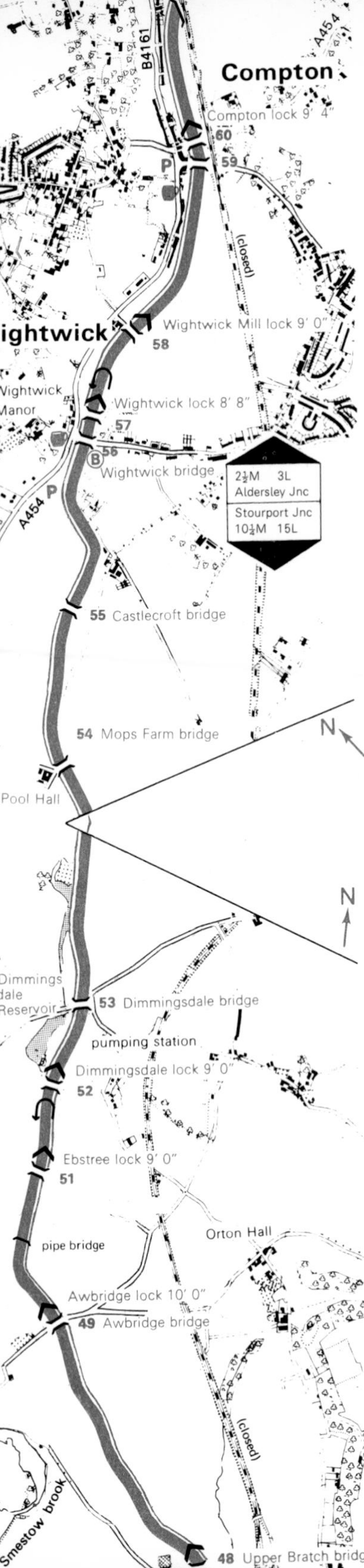

Dimmingsdale

North of Wombourn, the countryside becomes less interesting. Although it is still quiet, and remote from roads and railways, the canal is pestered by overhead power lines for a mile as it rises through Awbridge, Ebstree and Dimmingsdale Locks. The modest, pretty lakes alongside here are in fact canal-feeding reservoirs, of considerable interest to fishermen. Ahead, the hills of Wightwick overlook the navigation as it approaches a shallow valley and a busy main road. This valley—in places an artificial cutting—contains the canal right through to the flatter land at Autherley. Houses, mostly modern, are never far away, although the canal manages to preserve intact its rural character all the way through what are in effect the western outskirts of Wolverhampton. Compton Lock marks the end of the 31-lock climb from the River Severn at Stourport, a rise of 294ft. From here northwards, a 10-mile level pound takes the Staffs & Worcs on to Gailey, where the first of 12 locks begins the fall towards the Trent & Mersey Canal.

Compton
Staffs. PO, tel, stores, launderette. A busy but uninteresting village with a modern shopping centre and pubs that are less than picturesque. The canal lock was the first that James Brindley built on the Staffs & Worcs in the late 1760s, but unfortunately the cottage here has been demolished. However the nearby coal wharf still handles coal, although of course the waterway is no longer used for this trade—nor for any other.

Wightwick
Staffs. (pronounced 'Wittick'). Once a village, now a suburb. But there is a hill and plenty of trees, and in spite of the busy A454 it is a pleasant scene around the canal bridge and the old country pub.

Wightwick Manor 300yds north west of bridge 56, across the A454 and up the hill. Built between 1887 and 1893, the manor has an exterior that embodies many of the idiosyncrasies of the time. Inside, it is furnished with original wallpapers and fabrics by Morris and various contributions by the Pre-Raphaelites. This certainly makes a change from the usual venerable stone or timbered buildings that are open to the public. National Trust property. *Open afternoons on Thur, Sat and B. Hol weekends, also Wed from May to Sep. Closed Feb.*

BOATYARDS

Ⓑ **Mermaid Hire Cruisers** Wightwick Wharf, Castlecroft, Wolverhampton (763818). By bridge 56. Hire cruisers, engine and boat repairs. Groceries and fuel nearby. Mooring.

PUBS

Oddfellows Hall Compton, 50yds west of bridge 59.
Swan Compton, near the Oddfellows.
Mermaid Wightwick. 50yds north west of bridge 56. Buffet lunches.

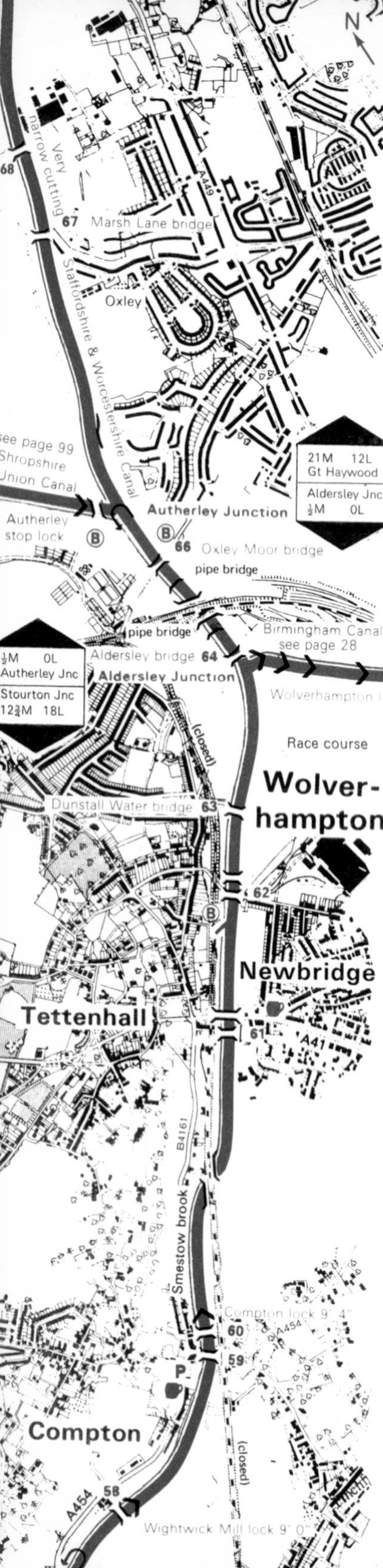

Aldersley & Autherley Junctions

The canal continues along the pleasant cutting through the Wolverhampton outskirts, passing under the big iron bridge that carries a closed railway. Trees on either side shield the navigation from the houses of Tettenhall. A large concrete road bridge that dwarfs the nearby original brick-arched bridge reminds the traveller of the hurly-burly world on either side of this quiet corridor of green. Several boating centres are passed, then the trees of Dunstall Park appear on the right, followed by Aldersley Junction. At this secluded place the bottom of the 21 Wolverhampton locks brings the main line of the Birmingham Canal into the Staffordshire & Worcestershire Canal. There is a towpath 'roving' bridge at the junction; past it is a criss-cross of railway and pipe bridges, then the cutting eases away and the canal goes under a road bridge, emerging at last in a rather flat, open landscape, with council housing estates to the east. The big white bridge on the towpath side marks Autherley Junction: the stop lock here is at the entrance to the Shropshire Union main line. There is a large boatyard north of the stop lock, and extensive BWB moorings. Straight ahead at Autherley is the continuation of the Staffs & Worcs to the Trent & Mersey Canal at Great Haywood Junction.

Tettenhall
Staffs. PO, tel, stores, garage, pub and other facilities are conveniently placed by bridge 61. A comfortable residential suburb of Wolverhampton (the city centre is a mere 2 miles to the south east). There is little to see, but the battlemented tower of the Norman church is worth a look—it is 300yds north of bridge 61. The church was burnt down in 1950, only the tower surviving the conflagration. The new church, built in 1955, contains some interesting stained glass.

BOATYARDS

Ⓑ **Water Travel** Autherley Junction, Oxley Moore Road, Wolverhampton, West Midlands. (782371). On the Shropshire Union. RSWPDE Pump-out, hire craft, slipway, gas, mooring, chandlery, toilets, provisions, cranage.
Ⓑ **Gregory's Canal Cruisers** Oxley Moor Road Bridge, Autherley Junction, Wolverhampton. (783070), RW Pump-out, boat hire. Gas, boat and engine repairs, toilets, provisions.
Ⓑ **Double Pennant Boatyard** Hordern Road, Wolverhampton. (752771) RWD Boat hire, slipway, gas, engine repairs, mooring, chandlery, toilets.

BOAT TRIPS

Narrow boat 'Stafford' is available for parties of up to 42. All enquiries to Wolverhampton 757494.

PUBS

Newbridge Tettenhall, 50yds east of bridge 61. Meals here *on weekdays.* The inn sign is a picture of Thomas Telford.

Coven

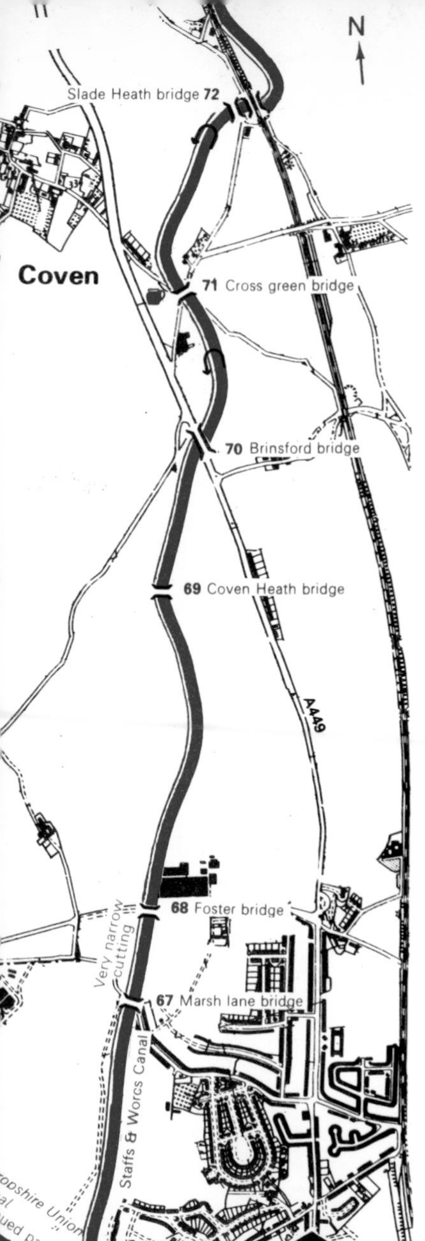

Leaving Autherley and the junction with the Shropshire Union Canal (see page 99), the Staffs & Worcs runs through a very narrow cutting through rock: there is room for only 1 boat here, so a good lookout should be kept for oncoming craft. Soon the navigation leaves behind the suburbs of Wolverhampton and enters pleasant farmland. The bridges need care: although the bridgeholes are reasonably wide, the actual arches are rather low. The age of this canal shows itself in its extremely twisting course after passing the railway bridge. There are few real centres of population along this stretch, which comprises largely former heathland.

Coven
Staffs. PO, tel, stores, garage. The only true village on this section, Coven lies beyond a dual carriageway north west of Cross Green Bridge. There is a large number of shops, including a launderette.
Autherley Junction
A busy canal junction with a full range of boating facilities.

BOATYARDS

See previous page.

PUBS

Anchor Canalside, by Cross Green Bridge. Steak bar.
The Aldersley Part of Wolverhampton Stadium. Bar snacks. Sport in the stadium.

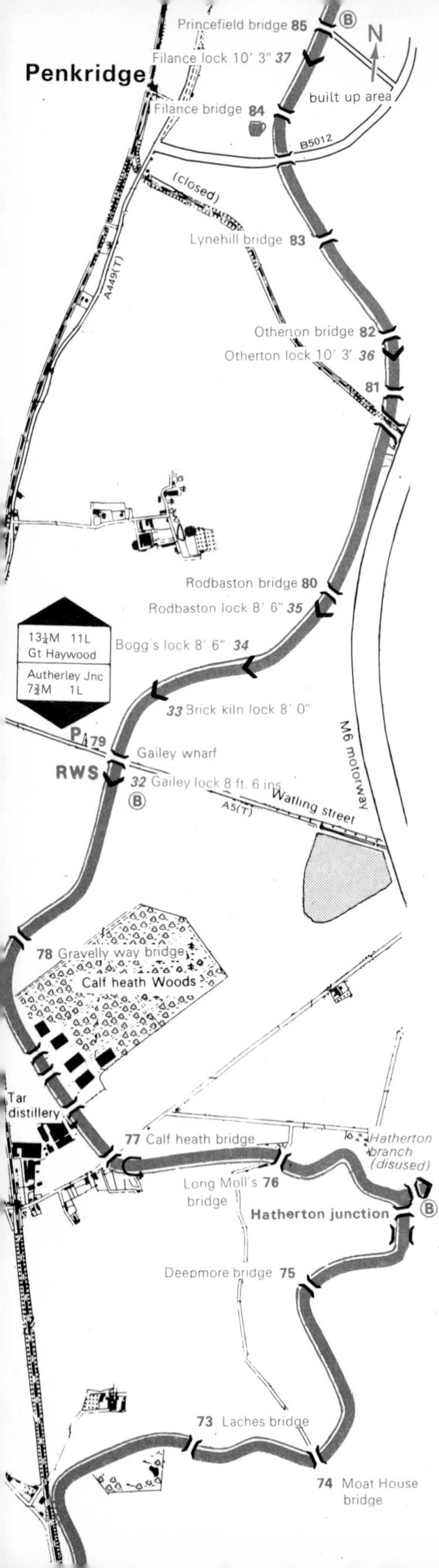

Gailey Wharf

Hatherton Junction marks the entrance of the former Hatherton Branch of the Staffs & Worcs Canal into the main line. This branch used to connect with the Birmingham Canal Navigations. The branch is closed now, but water is still fed down the locks into the Staffs & Worcs Canal, which explains the unusual clearness of the water hereabouts. There is a very handy all-purpose shop at the junction, surrounded by delightful rose gardens. Not far away, a big tar distillery is encountered astride the canal in what used to be woodlands. Gailey Wharf is about a mile further north: it is a small canal settlement that includes a post office and a large, round toll keeper's watchtower. The canal itself disappears under Watling Street and falls rapidly through another 5 locks towards Penkridge. The M6 motorway comes alongside for ½ mile, screening the reservoirs which feed the canal. These are very attractive locks: many of them are accompanied by little brick bridges.

Gailey and Calf Heath reservoirs ½ mile east of Gailey Wharf, either side of the M6. The 3 are feeder reservoirs for the canal though rarely drawn on. The public has access to them as nature reserves to study the wide variety of natural life, especially the long established heronry which is thriving on an island in Gailey Lower reservoir. In the Gailey Upper, fishing is available to the public from the riparian owner and in Gailey Lower a limited number of angling tickets are available on a season ticket basis each year from the BWB, Nantwich Basin, Chester Road, Nantwich, Cheshire. There is a club sailing on 2 of the reservoirs.

BOATYARDS

(B) **Gailey Marine** The Wharf, Watling Street, Staffs. (Standeford 790612) R S W D Pump-out, boat hire, gas, boat building & repair, mooring, toilets. *Closed winter Suns.*
(B) **Calf Heath Marina** Hatherton Junction. (Standeford 790909). W D Pump-out, gas, hire craft, mooring, repairs, slipway, dry dock. Post office and shop.

PUBS

Cross Keys Canalside, at Filance Bridge 84. Once a lonely canal pub, now it is surrounded by housing estates. W

Penkridge
Princefield bridge 85
Filance lock 10' 3" *37*
N
built up area
Filance bridge 84
B5012
(closed)
Lynehill bridge 83
A449(T)
Otherton bridge 82
Otherton lock 10' 3' *36*
81
Rodbaston bridge 80
Rodbaston lock 8' 6" *35*
13¾M 11L
Gt Haywood
Autherley Jnc
7¾M 1L
Bogg's lock 8' 6" *34*
33 Brick kiln lock 8' 0"
M6 motorway
P 79
Gailey wharf
RWS
32 Gailey lock 8 ft. 6 ins.
Watling street
A5(T)
78 Gravelly way bridge
Calf heath Woods
Tar distillery
77 Calf heath bridge
Hatherton branch (disused)
Long Moll's 76 bridge
Hatherton junction
Deepmore bridge 75
73 Laches bridge
74 Moat House bridge

Penkridge

The navigation now passes through Penkridge and is soon approached by the little River Penk: the 2 water courses share the valley for the next few miles. Apart from the noise of the motorway, this is a quiet and pleasant valley: there are plenty of trees, a handful of locks and the large Teddesley Park alongside the canal. At Acton Trussell the M6 roars off to the north west and the canal moves along to the blissful isolation that surrounds Deptmore Lock. There is an inhabited lock cottage here; the residents' easiest means of access to the 'civilised' world is by boat to Radford Bridge.

Acton Trussell
Staffs. PO, tel, stores. A village overwhelmed by modern housing: much the best way to see it is from the canal. The 15thC church stands to the south, overlooking the navigation. There is a very fine old house at Acton Moat Bridge.

Teddesley Park
On the east bank of the canal. The Hall, once the family seat of the Littletons, was used during the last war as a prisoner-of-war camp, but has since been demolished. Its extensive wooded estate still remains.

Penkridge
Staffs. EC Wed, MD Mon. PO, tel, stores, coffee house, garage, bank, station. Above Penkridge Lock is a good place to tie up in this village which is relatively old. It is bisected by a trunk road, but luckily most of the village lies to the east of this road. The church is tall and sombre, and looks well kept. Early English—mostly 12thC, but restored in the 1880s. There is a fine Dutch 18thC wrought iron screen, and the tower is believed to date from about 1500.

BOATYARDS

Ⓑ **Teddesley Boat Company** Park Gate Lock, Teddesley Road, Penkridge, Staffs. (4692). D Pump-out, narrow boat hire, gas, boat building, boat & engine repairs, mooring, extensive chandlery, winter storage, cranage. *Closed Sun Dec & Jan.*

Ⓑ **Bijou Line** Penkridge Wharf, Cannock Road, Penkridge, Staffs (2732) At Penkridge Lock. W Pump-out, narrow boat hire, gas, boat building. *Closed in winter.*

PUBS

Boat Canalside, by Penkridge Lock.
Horse & Jockey Penkridge.
Littleton Arms Penkridge. Food; B & B.

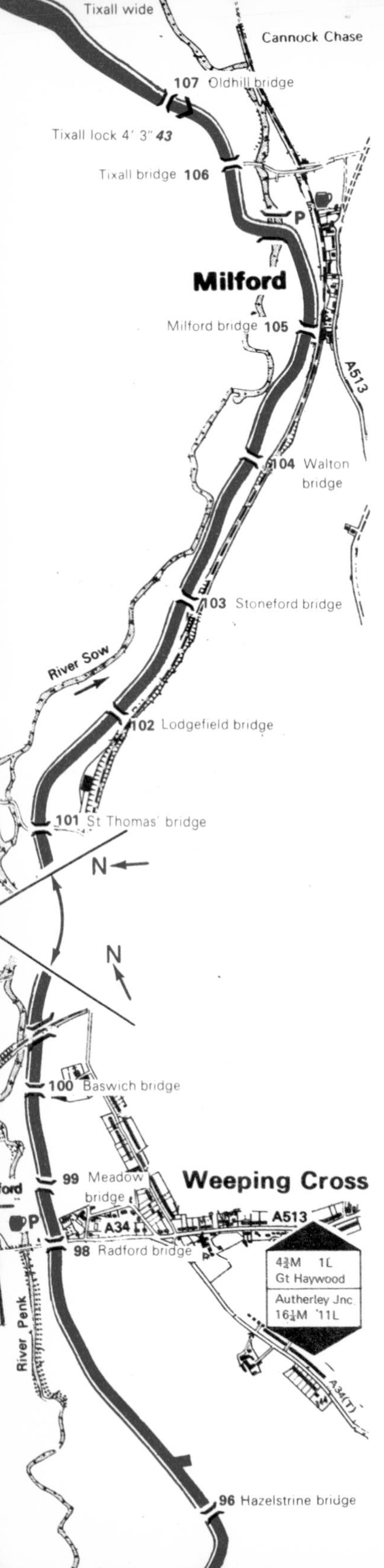

Sow Valley

Flowing north along the shallow Penk valley, the canal soon reaches the low Radford Bridge, the nearest point to Stafford (about 1½ miles to the centre of town—there is a frequent bus service). A mile north of here the canal bends around to the south east and follows the River Sow. The Sow is a pretty valley and the canal water is very clean, in spite of the occasional industrial works. At Milford the navigation crosses the Sow via an aqueduct—an early structure by James Brindley, carried heavily on low brick arches. Tixall Lock offers some interesting views in all directions: the castellated entrance to Shugborough Railway Tunnel at the foot of the thick woods of Cannock Chase and the distant outline of Tixall Gatehouse.

Milford
Staffs. PO, tel, stores, garage. The village straggles parallel and close to the canal but access is obstructed by the busy railway: it is best reached from Tixall Bridge (106). Milford is an estate village on the fringes of Cannock Chase; there is a great big green near the pub. Milford Hall is hidden by trees.
The Stafford Branch
Just west of bridge 101 one may see the remains of the lock that used to take a branch off the Staffs & Worcs to Stafford. The branch, 1 mile long, was unusual in that it was not a canal but the canalised course of the River Sow, which joins the River Penk just by the former lock (Baswich Lock). The branch has not been used for years.
Stafford
Staffs. EC Wed, MD Tue, Fri, Sat. All services. This town is well worth visting, since there is here a remarkable wealth of fine old buildings—including even the main post office. The Market Square survives, its best feature being the National Westminster Bank. There is a handsome City Hall complex of ornamental Italianate buildings, c1880. The robust-looking gaol stands nearby; and the church of St Mary's stands in very pleasing and spacious grounds. There are some pretty back alleys: Church Lane contains a splendid-looking eating house, and at the bottom of the lane a fruiterer's shop is in a thatched cottage built in 1610. All this in the middle of a town as large as Stafford is truly rewarding.
Museum & Art Gallery The Green. On first floor of Stafford Central Library. Small museum with exhibits depicting the art, history and industrial development of the locality. *Closed Sun.*

PUBS

Barley Mow Milford. Steak bar.
Trumpet Canalside, at Radford Bridge. Grills.
As you would expect, there are plenty of pubs in Stafford.

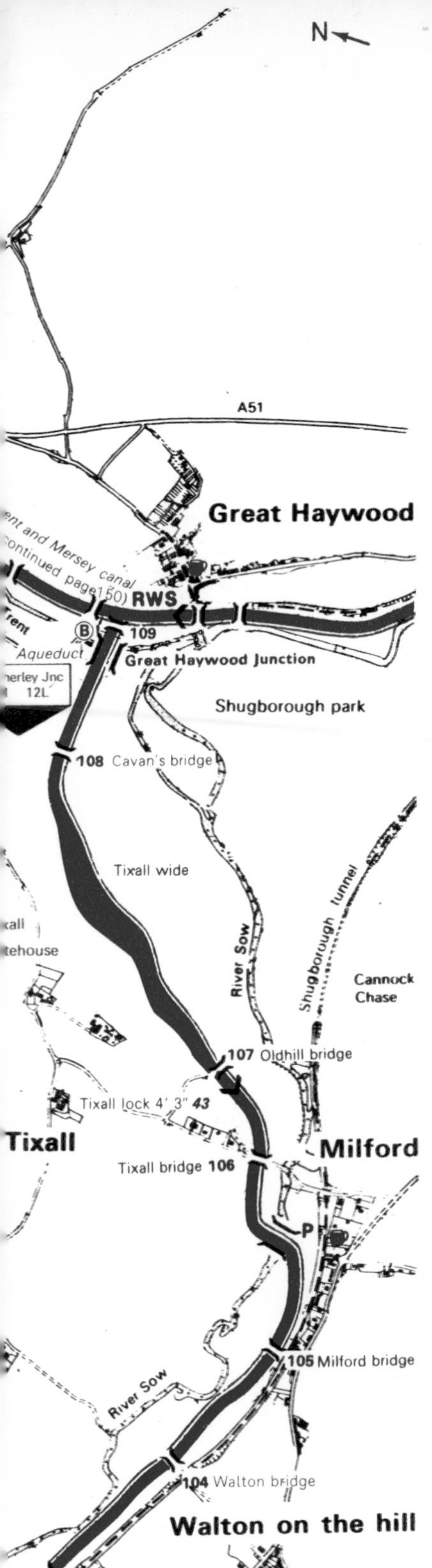

Tixall

The canal now quickly completes its journey to the Trent & Mersey Canal at Great Haywood. It is a length of waterway quite unlike any other. Proceeding along this very charming valley, the navigation enters Tixall Wide—an amazing and delightful stretch of water more resembling a lake than a canal, and navigable to the edges. The Wide is noted for its kingfisher population. Up on the hill to the north is the equally remarkable Tixall Gatehouse, while woods across the valley conceal Shugborough Hall. The River Trent is met, on its way south from Stoke-on-Trent, and crossed on an aqueduct. There is a mill, wharf and towpath bridge across Haywood Junction.

Great Haywood
For details, see page 150
Tixall
Staffs. PO, tel, stores. A quiet and unspoilt hamlet facing the wooded slopes of Cannock Chase. Just to the east are the stables and the Gatehouse of the long-vanished Tixall Hall. This massive square Elizabethan building is fully 4 storeys high and restored for holiday lets! It stands alone in a field; one can only wonder at the size of the former hall with a gatehouse as huge as this. It is clearly visible from the canal: indeed Tixall Wide may have been made to resemble a 'broad' purely because it was in full view of the Gatehouse and the Hall.

BOATYARDS

Ⓑ **Anglo Welsh Narrowboats** The Canal Wharf, Mill Lane, Great Haywood, Staffs. (Little Haywood 881711). At Great Haywood Junction. R S W D E Pump-out (*Mon–Fri*), narrow boat hire, boat & engine repairs, mooring, toilets.

BOAT TRIPS

M. E. Braine operate two 46-seater trip boats from Great Haywood. Bookings: Little Haywood 881328.

PUBS

Clifford Arms Great Haywood. Snacks.
✕ **Barley Mow** Milford. Steak bar.

A distinctive Trent & Mersey Canal milepost. *David Perrott*

TRENT & MERSEY

Maximum dimensions

Derwent Mouth to Burton upon Trent
Length: 72′
Beam: 13′ 6″
Headroom: 7′
Burton upon Trent to Great Haywood
Length: 72′
Beam: 7′
Headroom: 6′ 3″
Great Haywood to Middlewich
Length: 72′
Beam: 7′
Headroom: 5′ 9″
Middlewich to Anderton
Length: 72′
Beam: 14′ 6″
Headroom: 7′
Anderton to Preston Brook
Length: 72′
Beam: 7′
Headroom: 7′

Mileage

DERWENT MOUTH to
Swarkestone Lock: 7
Willington: 12¼
Horninglow Wharf: 16½
Barton Turn: 21¼
Fradley, junction with Coventry Canal: 26¼
Great Haywood, junction with Staffs & Worcs Canal: 39
Stone: 48½
Stoke Top Lock, junction with Caldon Canal: 58
Harding's Wood, junction with Macclesfield Canal: 63¾
King's Lock, Middlewich, junction with Middlewich Branch: 76¼
Anderton Lift, for River Weaver: 86½
PRESTON BROOK north end of tunnel and Bridgewater Canal: 93½

Locks: 76

This early canal was originally conceived partly as a roundabout link between the ports of Liverpool and Hull, while passing through the busy area of the Potteries and mid-Cheshire, and terminating either in the River Weaver or in the Mersey. One of its prime movers was the famous potter Josiah Wedgwood (1730–1795). Like the Duke of Bridgewater a few years previously, he saw the obvious enormous advantages to his—and others'—industry of cheap, safe and rapid transport which a navigation would offer compared with packhorse carriage (the only alternative then available). Wedgwood was greatly assisted in the promotion of the canal by his friends, notably Thomas Bentley and Erasmus Darwin. Pamphlets were published, influential support was marshalled; and in 1766 the Trent & Mersey Canal Act was passed by Parliament, authorising the building of a navigation from the River Trent at Shardlow to Runcorn Gap, where it would join the proposed extension of the Bridgewater Canal from Manchester.

The ageing James Brindley was appointed engineer of the new canal. Construction began at once and much public interest was excited in this remarkable project, especially in the great 2900-yd tunnel under Harecastle Hill.

Once opened in 1777 the Trent & Mersey Canal was a great success, attracting much trade in all kinds of commodities. Vast tonnages of china clay and flints for the pottery industry were brought by sea from Devon and Cornwall, then transhipped into canal boats on the Mersey and brought straight to the factories around Burslem, taking finished goods away again. Everyone near the canal benefited: much lower freight costs meant cheaper goods, healthier industries and more jobs. Agriculture gained greatly from the new supply of water, and of stable manure from the cities.

The Trent & Mersey soon earned its other name (suggested by Brindley) as the Grand Trunk Canal—in the 93 miles between Derwent Mouth and Preston Brook, the Trent & Mersey gained connection with no fewer than 9 other canals or significant branches.

By the 1820s the Trent & Mersey was so busy that the narrow and slowly-sinking tunnel at Harecastle had become a serious bottleneck for traffic. Thomas Telford was called in; he recommended building a second tunnel beside Brindley's old one. His recommendation was eventually accepted by the company, and a tremendous burst of energy saw the whole tunnel completed in under 3 years, in 1827. A much-needed towpath was included in this new tunnel.

Although the Trent & Mersey was taken over in 1845 by the new North Staffordshire Railway Company, the canal flourished until the Great War as a most important trading route. Today there is practically no trade at all along the canal, but it is assured (by statute) of a future as a pleasure cruising waterway. There used to be 4 tunnels on the Trent & Mersey apart from the pair at Harecastle. One of these was at Armitage, a 130-yd bore through solid rock. But mining subsidence began to affect the tunnel, and during 1971–2 it was opened out and a road bridge built to carry the main road (A513) that crosses at this point.

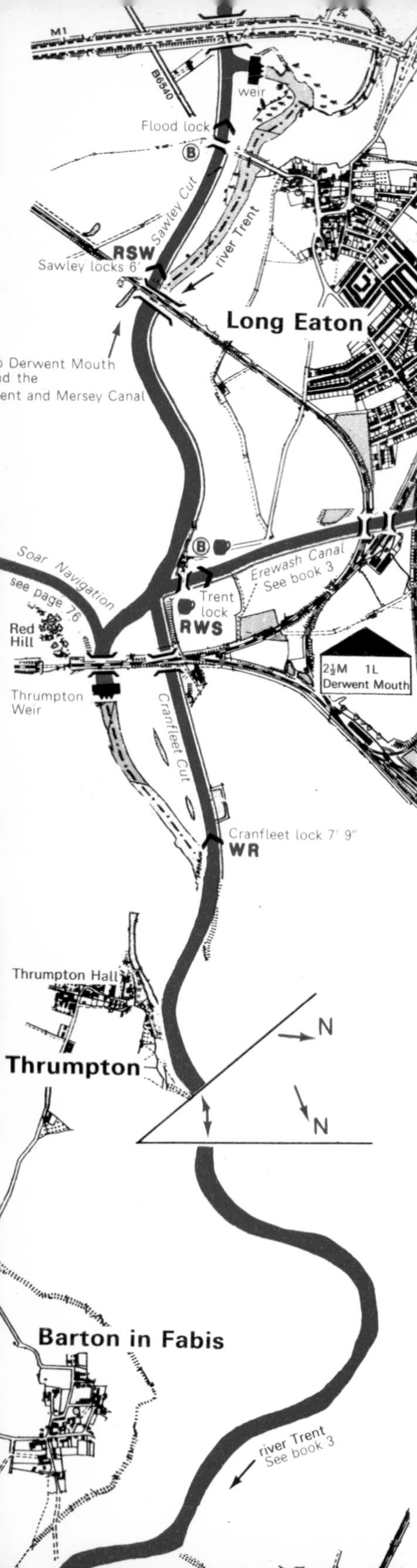

River Trent

The Trent and Mersey Canal begins at Derwent Mouth, some 2½ miles upstream of the point where the Soar Navigation enters the River Trent at a complicated waterways junction. Navigators leaving the Soar and heading towards the Trent and Mersey should turn LEFT (west) thus avoiding Thrumpton Weir, which lies beyond the large railway bridge. The entrances to the Cranfleet Cut and Erewash Canal (Trent Lock) are passed, both lying to the right, while continuing upstream to the railway bridge where the paired Sawley Locks (power operated, by the keeper) will be seen at the entrance to the Sawley Cut. The flood lock is usually open, but should it need operating, be sure to leave a paddle open at each end after you have passed through. Keep to the LEFT when travelling upstream, or to the RIGHT when travelling downstream, to avoid another large weir by the M1 motorway bridge.

Trent Lock
A busy and unusual boating centre at the southern terminus of the Erewash Canal. There is a boatyard and 2 pubs here.

Sawley
Notts. PO, tel, stores, garage, fish and chips. The tall church spire attracts one across the river to Sawley, and in this respect the promise is fulfilled, for the medieval church is very beautiful and is approached by a formal avenue of lime trees leading to the 600-year-old doorway. But otherwise Sawley is an uninteresting main road village on the outskirts of Long Eaton.

Sawley Cut
In addition to a large marina and a well-patronised BWB mooring site, the Derby Motor Boat Club have a base on the Sawley Cut where well over 100 boats are kept. All kinds of boats are represented here: canal boats, river boats and even sea-going boats. It is certainly no place to be passing through on a summer Sunday late-afternoon, for there will be scores of craft queueing up to pass through the locks after spending the weekend downstream. There are windlasses for sale at Sawley Lock, as well as the more conventional facilities.

BOATYARDS

Ⓑ **Sawley Bridge Marina** Long Eaton, Nottingham. (Long Eaton 4278, 2343). W D Gas, chandlery, slipway, moorings, canal craft sales, provisions.

Ⓑ **Davison's Boatyard** Trent Lock, Long Eaton, Nottingham. (Long Eaton 4643). W Pump-out, hire cruisers. Drydock, boat building and fitting out. On the Erewash Canal, just above the lock.

PUBS

Steamboat Inn Canalside at Trent Lock. Shipstones real ale, food, garden. A friendly and attractive place to visit.

✕ **Trent Navigation Inn** Trent Lock. Large popular riverside pub with a garden serving Homes real ale.

Harrington Arms Sawley.

White Lion Sawley. Ind Coope real ale. Children welcome.

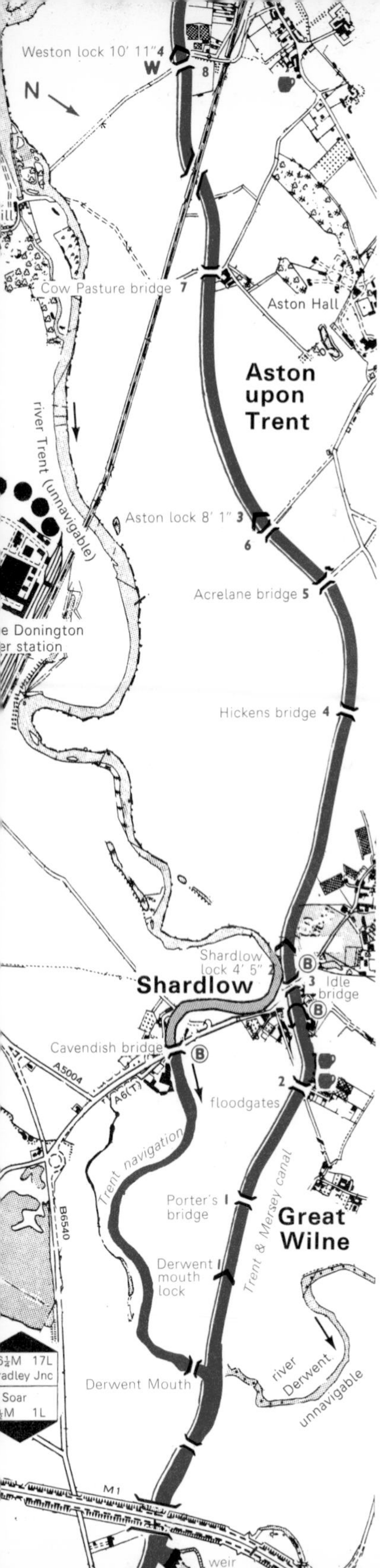

Shardlow

The Trent and Mersey Canal begins at Derwent Mouth, a 'crosswater' formed by the junction of the canal, the River Derwent and the River Trent. The Trent is navigable virtually to Shardlow (turn left under the concrete footbridge) thus making it possible to visit this remarkable village by either canal or river. The Derwent, although attractive, is not navigable. The first canal lock, Derwent Mouth Lock, is overlooked by a big shady chestnut tree, beyond which is Shardlow, one of the most interesting 'canal villages' on the whole inland waterway network. The Trent & Mersey Canal is very much the main street of Shardlow, and so one has an excellent view of the place from a boat. On the side of the little brick arch bridge at Aston Lock is a keystone inscribed 'J.C. 1770'. The letters could possibly refer to Josiah Clowes, an early canal trader and engineer, but the date establishes this canal bridge as among the oldest in the country. The canal now progresses through a wide flat valley with the unnavigable River Trent to the south, leaving behind the massive towers of Castle Donnington power station. Overhead fly aeroplanes from the East Midlands Airport.

Navigational note
Those heading towards the River Trent should not pass Shardlow floodgates if the warning light shows red.

Aston upon Trent
Derbs. PO, tel, stores, petrol. A pleasant village nearly a mile from the canal and, despite its name, over a mile from the river. (Access by a footpath from Aston Lock.) The sturdy stone church dates from the 12thC to the 15thC. Inside are fine monuments and good Victorian stained glass. The white-painted Hall, now a hospital, is visible from the canal.

Shardlow
Derbs. PO, tel, stores, garage. Few canal travellers will want to pass through Shardlow without stopping. It is a magnificent example of a small canal port in a prime state of preservation. Everywhere there are living examples of large-scale canal architecture, as well as old-established necessities like canal pubs and a boat-building yard. By the lock is the biggest and best of these buildings—the 18thC Trent Mill, which has a large central arch for boats to enter and unload. Restored in 1979 as a canal centre, it retains all its original proud elegance. Other buildings in Shardlow are built in this handsome but functional style. To the north of the village is an 18thC stone-fronted hall.

BOATYARDS

Ⓑ **Plus Pleasure Marina** London Road, Shardlow. (Derby 792844). In the restored Trent Corn Mill, just below Shardlow Lock. R S WD Pump-out, hire fleet, slipway, toilets, showers, restaurant, shop, exhibition. Trip boat for charter.

Ⓑ **Dobson's Boatyard** The Wharf, Shardlow, Derbs. (Derby 792271). On the canal R S WD Pump-out, slipway, gas, boat building & repair, mooring, chandlery, toilets, winter storage.

Ⓑ **Shardlow Marina** On the River Trent (Derby 792832). R S WD Pump-out, gas, slipway, moorings, boat sales, inboard and outboard engine sales, chandlery. Trip boat.

BOAT TRIPS

60 seater trip boat 'Aquarius' available for charter, ring Derby 792285 for details.

PUBS AND RESTAURANTS

Malt Shovel Aston.

White Hart Aston.

Navigation By bridge 3, Shardlow. Davenports real ale, food.

Malt Shovel Shardlow. Superb old (1779) canalside pub, with small beamed bars and collection of beer mugs. Marstons real ale and good bar food. Garden.

New Inn Shardlow, next to the Malt Shovel. Bass Charrington real ale.

Lady in Grey Shardlow. Elegant restaurant/hotel. The 'lady' is a ghost.

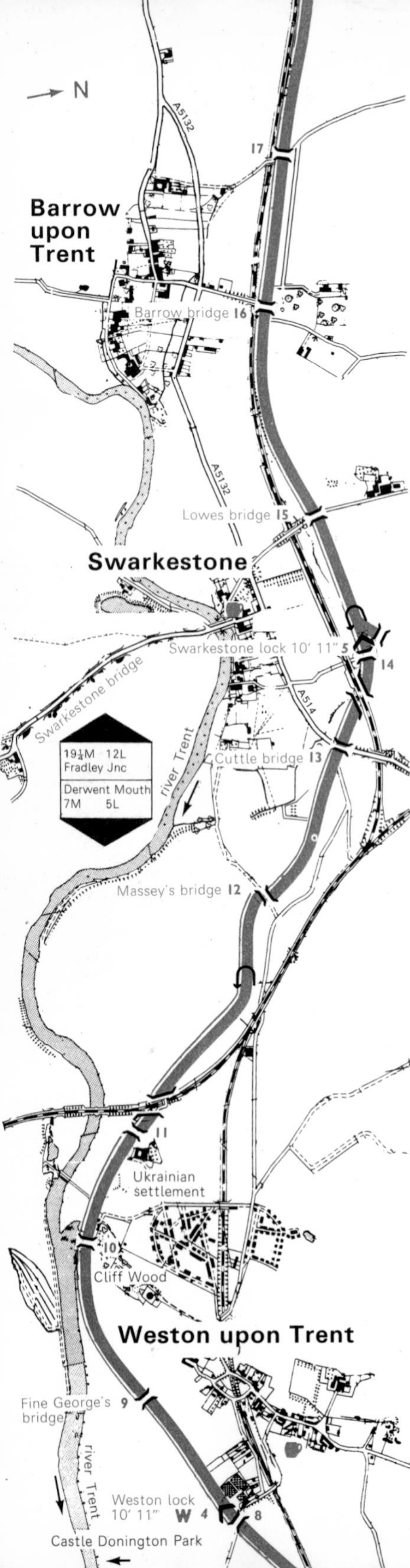

Swarkestone Junction

The village of Weston upon Trent is near Weston Lock. The wooden lock balance beams of the bottom gates, impeded by the bridge, are of necessity short; but they are massively wide—22in square at the end. One may enjoy a pleasant walk by going down the lane south east from the lock to the river opposite King's Mills. The church and the rectory stand to the north of the village, on a hill with a fine view of the Trent valley. There are two enormous copper beech trees in front of the rectory. Leaving Weston, the canal passes a thickly wooded hillside—anyone who goes ashore at bridge 10 and walks up the hill is in for a surprise, for as likely as not he will find a group of men in front of a house arguing volubly—*in Russian*. For this is a farming settlement run by and for expatriate Ukrainians. The colony has been established here since the war and is entirely self-supporting. At Swarkestone Lock there is a short arm, used for moorings, all that remains of the Derby Canal. The old toll house at the junction has however found a new role as the headquarters of the Swarkestone Boat Club. The lock here is very deep, with a fall of almost 11ft. As with the other deep locks, it has very low top gates which incorporate substantial paddles. The River Trent continues its course to the south of the canal, and can be seen at intervals through the hedges and trees. The countryside is green and pleasant, with only the occasional freight train rumbling by to disturb the peace.

Barrow upon Trent
Derbs. PO, tel, stores. A small, quiet village severed from the canal by the busy A514. A lane from the church leads down to the river. Until recently the old hall stood next to the church, very much the focus of the village. But now bright modern houses stand in its place and the surviving lodge house looks uncomfortably irrelevant. Opposite is a mellow terrace of old workmen's cottages; these would also have served the hall.

Swarkestone
Derbs. PO, tel, stores. The main feature of Swarkestone is the 18thC 5-arched stone bridge over the main channel of the River Trent. An elevated causeway then carries the road on stone arches all the way across the Trent's flood plain to the village of Stanton by Bridge. Away from the river, Swarkestone seems a rather tired village. The small church is tucked away in the back lanes; it contains interesting monuments of the Harpur family. In a field nearby are the few remains of Sir Richard Harpur's Tudor mansion, a barn, a gateway and a summer house.

Weston upon Trent
Derbs. PO, tel, stores. A scattered village that is in fact not very close to the Trent. The isolated church is splendidly situated beside woods on top of a hill, its sturdy tower crowned by a short 14thC spire. Inside are fine aisle windows of the same period. The lock gardens make the approach from the canal particularly attractive.

PUBS

Crew & Harpur Swarkestone, by the river bridge. Food.

Plough Weston upon Trent.

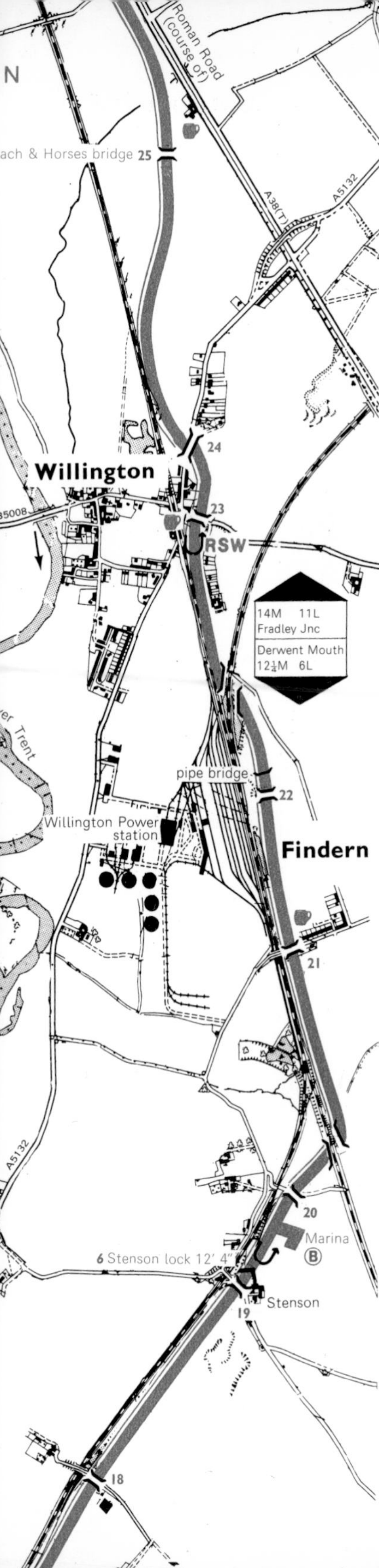

Stenson Lock

The canal passes through bridge 18, which is an unusual one—although the decking is a new concrete one, the old brick abutments have been retained and the concrete girders have been so laid that they seem to float above the abutments. The old cast iron bridge number plate has been cemented back into the concrete. Just by the bridge is Arleston House, an attractive old building with ground floor walls of stone and the upper tiers of brick. Stenson Lock is the last of the wide locks until Middlewich—it has a massive fall of 12ft 4in. Stenson is a small farming centre, always a popular mooring spot and now benefiting from the large marina to the north. After passing through a railway bridge, the canal changes course and heads off in a south easterly direction for Burton upon Trent. The village of Findern is up a hill to the north, while to the south is the large Willington Power Station. Willington village has fine moorings by landscaped gardens, a sanitary station and a choice of 3 pubs, making it an excellent overnight stop. The A38 and the busy railway line now converge on the canal and escort it almost to Alrewas.

Repton
Derbs. 1½ miles south east of Willington (over the River Trent) is Repton, one of the oldest towns in England. It was once the capital of Mercia and the crypt below St Wystan's Church was built in the 10thC. One of the finest examples of Saxon architecture in the country, this crypt was completely forgotten until the end of the 18thC when a man fell into it while digging a grave. Repton public school dates from 1551 and there is much of historical interest in the school and the town.

Willington
Derbs. PO, tel, stores, fish & chips. The railway bisects by an embankment this busy little village, which has an artistically inclined butcher and fully 3 pubs, all huddled together.

Findern
Derbs. PO, tel, stores, fish & chips. A small, quiet village where Jedekiah Strutt, the inventor of the ribbed stocking frame, served a 7-year apprenticeship with the local wheelwright. Until several years ago the village green was no more than a waste patch used by cars as a short cut and a parking place. When suggestions were made to turn it into a formal cross roads, the indignant Women's Institute galvanised the villagers into actually uprooting all traces of tarmac from the green and turfing the whole area properly. With the spired Victorian church beside it, the green is nowadays an ideal place for a summer snooze. A pub is nearby.

BOATYARDS

Ⓑ **Black Prince Narrowboats** Stenson Marina, Stenson, Derby. (Burton on Trent 703113). R W D E Pump-out, gas, toilets, narrow boat hire, mooring, marina shop and pub.

BOAT TRIPS

'Stenson Bubble' is an electric wide beam boat available for public trips and private charter—ring Burton on Trent 703113 for details.

PUBS

Every Arms On A38 west of bridge 25 (but access only from bridge 26 to avoid crossing private land). Cold snacks.
Green Man Willington.
Rising Sun Willington. Food.
Green Dragon Willington. Food, garden. All three pubs at Willington are near bridge 23.
Greyhound Findern. Canalside, at bridge 21. Large garden for children, and outside bar (sometimes). Many moored boats here.

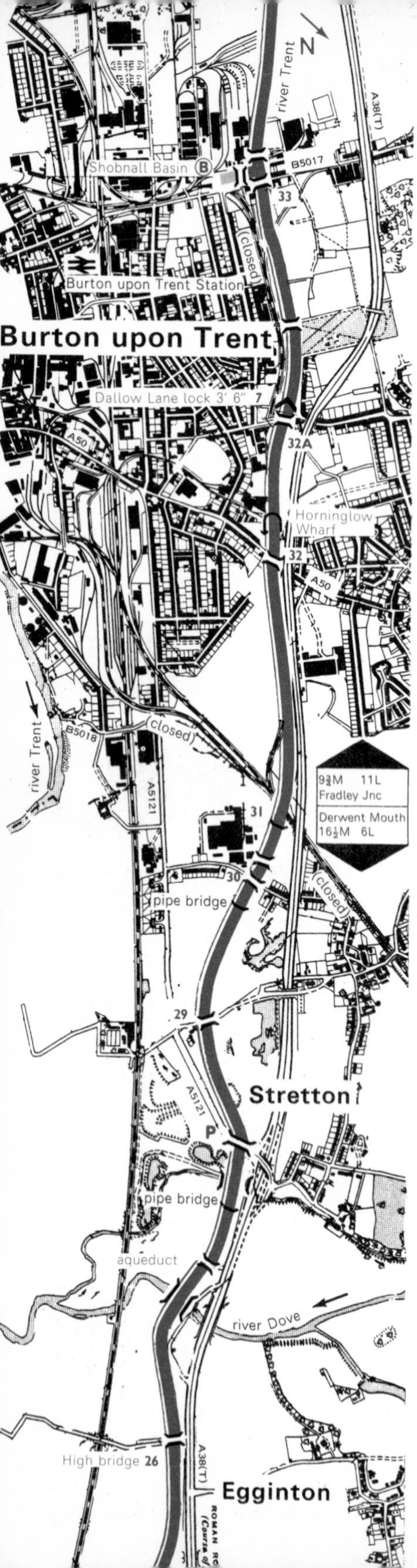

Burton upon Trent

A 9-arched stone aqueduct carries the canal over the River Dove, beside a handsome 5-arched bridge, no longer in use. Factories and car parks herald the outskirts of Burton upon Trent. The canal passes along one side of Burton, without entering the town. Much of the old canalside architecture has been demolished and there is little of interest to see by the canal. The lovely smell of malt and hops is strongest to the west of the town, where the canal passes between the Marstons and Bass breweries. Dallow Lane Lock is the first of the narrow locks, an altogether easier job of work than the wider ones to the east. Shobnall Basin is now used by a boatyard, and secure moorings may be available from which to explore the town.

Burton upon Trent
Staffs. EC Wed. MD Thur, Sat. All services. Known widely for its brewing industry, which originated here in the 13thC, when the monks at Burton Abbey discovered that an excellent beer could be brewed from the town's waters, because of their high gypsum content. In 1708 the first full-scale brewery was established, and by mid-century ale was being exported, 2 customers being Peter the Great and the Empress Catherine of Russia. At one time there were more than 20 breweries: alas now only a handful remain. Perhaps the most widely known of Burton's products is IPA, India Pale Ale. Originally intended for export, it was released on the home market by underwriters after being salvaged when a boat carrying a cargo to India sank. The advent of the railways had an enormous effect on the street geography of Burton, for gradually a great network of railways took shape, connecting with each other and with the main line. These branches were mostly constructed at street level, and until recent years it was common for road traffic to be held up by endless goods trains chugging all over the town. Little of this system remains. The east side of the town is bounded by the River Trent, on the other side of which are pleasant hills. Near the site of the old abbey is an unusual bridge; it is an iron trestle footbridge stretching for over ¼ mile across the water meadows. The main shopping centre lies to the east of the railway station.
Museum and Art Gallery Guild Street, Burton on Trent. Exhibits largely devoted to local history. Extensive collection of British and foreign birds. *Closed Sun.*
The Bass Museum Horninglow Street, ¾ mile from Horninglow Basin. All aspects of brewing during the late 19thC. Also a preserved steam engine, café and shop. Conducted tours around the new brewery. *Open daily. Admission charge.*
Shobnall Basin
This is all that remains of the former Shobnall Branch, a canal which used to give the breweries the benefit of modern transport until the coming of railways. The old branch was in fact bought by the North Staffordshire Railway Company (along with the whole of the Trent & Mersey Canal), and replaced by a railway track, leaving just a short dock. The LMS Railway Company, which succeeded the North Staffordshire Company, used to deliver canal maintenance materials to Shobnall Basin to be collected by maintenance boats from Fradley Junction. Disused until recently, it has now been dredged and brought back to life as a boatyard. The dignified entrance bridge still remains. There even used to be a canal pub at this point.
Egginton
Derbs. PO, tel, stores. A quiet village lying off the A38. The church, set apart from the village, is pleasingly irregular from the outside, with a large chancel and squat tower. Unusual Tudor windows in the south wall make the inside very light.

BOATYARDS

Ⓑ **Jannel Cruisers** Shobnall Marina, Shobnall Road, Burton on Trent. (42718). In Shobnall Basin. R W D Pump-out, hire fleet, gas, dry dock, toilets. Boat building and boat and engine repairs. Moorings.

PUBS

Pubs in Burton are not scarce and the majority sell real ale, usually Bass or Marstons. Walk east from Shobnall Basin.

Trent Mill, Shardlow, now part of a marina complex. *David Perrott*

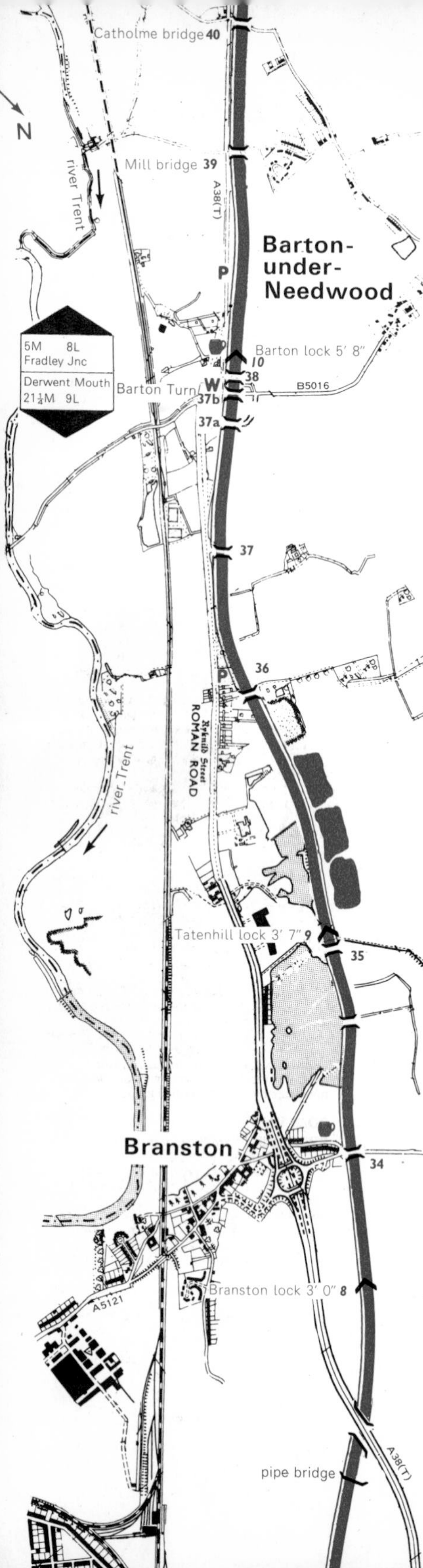

Barton Turn

The straight A38 runs beside the canal for several miles, depriving the navigator of any peace. The road is mostly a dual carriageway, and this contrasts massively with the narrow canal and its tiny old narrow bridges, many with a 2-ton weight restriction. Up on the hills to the north-west is the well-wooded Sinai Park—the moated 15thC house here, now a farm, used to be the summer home of the monks from Burton Abbey. At Branston Bridge is the only canalside pub for several miles in either direction—an excellent place to sample some of the best of Burton's produce. Beside Tatenhill Lock is an attractive cottage, and at the tail of the lock is yet another of the tiny narrow brick bridges that are such an engaging feature of this navigation. Above the lock is one of the many old cast iron distance posts still surviving on this canal; they all show the mileage to Shardlow and Preston Brook, the 2 ends of the Trent & Mersey Canal. More are now being replaced, paid for by willing sponsors. After passing flooded gravel pits and negotiating the tiny brick arch of bridge 36, the canal and the A38, the old Roman road, come close together—thankfully the settlement of Barton Turn has been passed, leaving the main street (the old Roman road of Ryknild Street) wide and empty. One can enjoy working through the lock and visiting the pub unmolested by motor traffic. There is a telephone here, and a petrol station.

Barton-under-Needwood
Staffs. PO, tel, stores. Many years ago, when there were few roads and no canals in the Midlands, the only reasonable access to this village was by turning off the old Roman road, Ryknild Street; hence, probably, the name Barton Turn. The village is indeed worth turning off for, although unfortunately it is nearly a mile from the canal (bridges 38, 39 or 40). A pleasant footpath from Barton Lock takes one a quiet back way to the village, which is set on a slight hill. Its long main street has many attractive pubs. The church is battlemented and surrounded by a very tidy churchyard. Pleasantly uniform in style, it was built in the 16thC by John Taylor (Henry VIII's private secretary) on the site of his cottage birthplace. The former Royal forest of Needwood is to the north of the village.

Branston
Staffs. PO, tel, stores, garage, fish & chips. Although this is apparently the place where the famous pickle originated, it is a small, unexciting village, severed from the canal by the improvement of the A38, virtually to motorway standard. So the village has no sense of cohesion, and the canal traveller would have little reason to suspect its existence were it not for the map. Most of those on the canal will see no more than the excellent pub.

PUBS AND RESTAURANTS

Bell Barton-under-Needwood. Restaurant (*closed Sun evenings and all day Mon*).
Three Horseshoes Barton-under-Needwood. Food.
Little Chef Canalside at Barton. *Open 07.00–22.00 daily.*
Shoulder of Mutton Barton-under-Needwood.
Vine Barton Turn, just opposite Barton Lock. Marstons beer.
Bridge Canalside, at Branston Bridge (34). Smart and cosy pub with an open fire on cold days. Marstons real ale served straight from the cask, and snacks. Large sheltered garden.

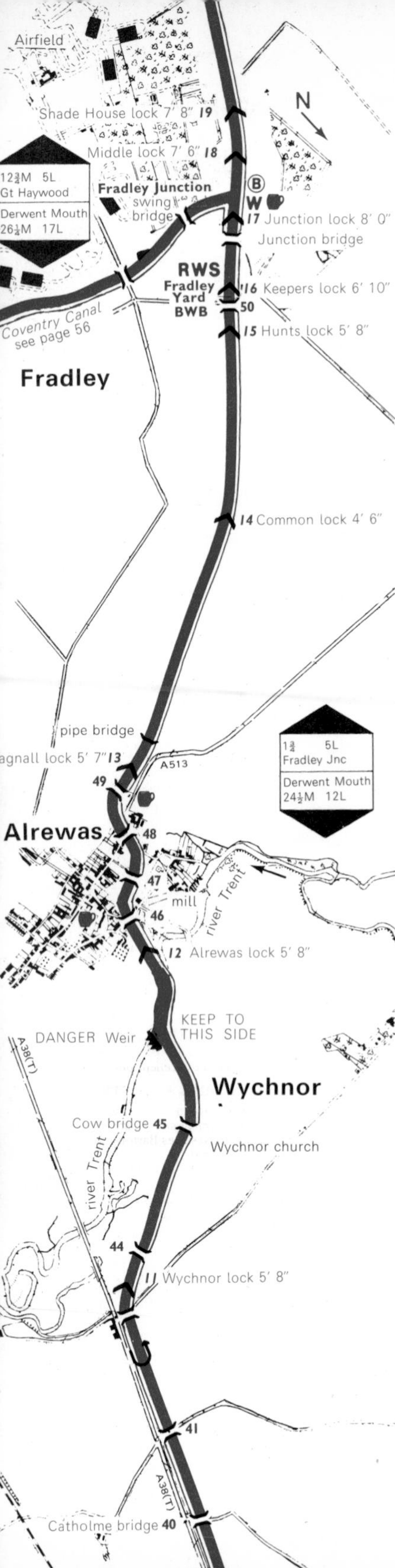

Fradley Junction

Boaters will be pleased to have reached Wychnor Lock—for here the A38 finally parts company with the canal, and some peace returns. To the west is the little 14thC Wychnor Church. It is a delightful scene, especially in the early morning or late afternoon: the cows grazing in the wide watermeadows or being herded across the wooded trestle bridge, the church with its small Elizabethan brick tower looking out over the swans, reeds and endless backwaters and side channels that run through the valley; and in the distance are the trees and church tower of Alrewas. All the way along here, little sluices and weirs carry water off the navigation down to the Trent; before Alrewas Lock the canal actually joins the River Trent—there is a large weir which should be given a wide berth. The towpath rises onto a trestle bridge, no doubt to keep the feet of boatmen leading horses dry in times of flood. **In times of flood great caution should be exercised along this stretch—keep well over to the towpath side at all times.** The canal winds through the pretty village of Alrewas, passing the old church, several thatched cottages and a brick bridge. There is a canalside pub at Bagnall Lock before the navigation enters open country at Fradley, and its junction with the Coventry Canal.

Fradley Junction
A long-established canal centre where the Coventry Canal joins the Trent & Mersey. Like all the best focal points on the canals, it is concerned solely with the life of the canals, and has no relationship with local roads or even with the village of Fradley. The junction bristles with boats, for, apart from it being an inevitable meeting place for canal boats, there is a boatyard, a British Waterways maintenance yard, BWB moorings, a boat club and a popular pub all in the middle of a 5-lock flight.

Alrewas
Staffs. PO, tel, stores, garage, restaurant. Away from the A513, this is an attractive village whose rambling back lanes harbour some excellent timbered cottages. The canal's unruffled passage through the village gives the place a restful air, and the presence of the church and its pleasant churchyard adds to this impression. The River Trent touches the village (note the old mill building) and provides it with a fine background which is much appreciated by fishermen. The somewhat unusual name 'Alrewas', pronounced 'olrewus', is a corruption of the words 'Alder Wash'—a reference to the many alder trees which once grew in the often-flooded Trent valley and gave rise to the basket weaving for which the village was once famous.

Alrewas Church A spacious building of mainly 13thC and 14thC construction, notable for the unmatching nave arches (octagonal and quatrefoil) and the old leper window, which is now filled by modern stained glass.

BOATYARDS

BWB Fradley Yard Burton upon Trent. (790236) R S W

Ⓑ **Swan Line Cruisers** Fradley Junction, Alrewas, Burton upon Trent, Staffs. (Burton upon Trent 790332). W D Pump-out (*not weekends*), hire craft, gas, chandlery, dry dock, moorings. Boat building, sales and repairs, inboard engine sales and repairs. Groceries. 42-seater trip boat. *Closed Sat afternoon and Sun in winter.*

PUBS

Swan Fradley Junction. Canalside; the focus of the junction and justly famous. A fine public bar with a coal fire and pub games, a comfortable lounge used by families, and a lively cellar bar. Ind Coope beers and bar meals (*not Sun*).

Crown Alrewas, near bridge 46. Snacks.

Navigation Alrewas, near Bagnall Lock. Food (*not Mon eve*).

✕ **George & Dragon** High Street, Alrewas. Marstons real ale, bar food and restaurant in an old village local. Garden.

William IV Alrewas. Marstons real ale, snacks.

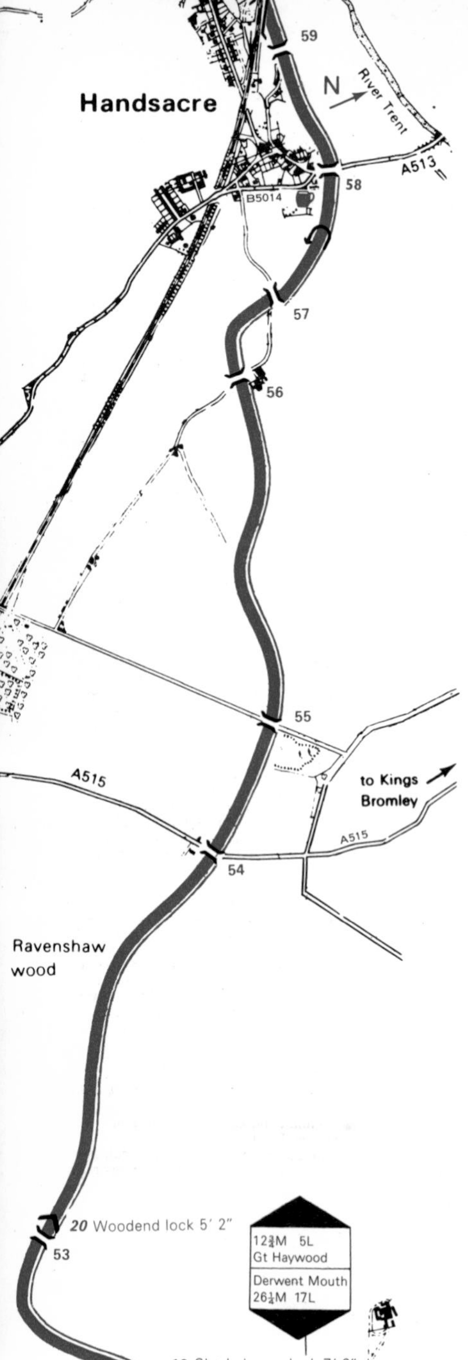

Handsacre

Leaving the Coventry Canal at Fradley Junction, the Trent & Mersey climbs past wooded heathland and abruptly changes course from southwest to northwest, a direction it generally maintains right through to its terminus at Preston Brook, over 67 miles away. The isolated Woodend Lock introduces a further stretch of woodland; beyond this the canal winds towards Armitage as the River Trent and the railway converge on either side. There is a useful general store 500yds south of bridge 59, and fish and chips near bridge 58.

Kings Bromley
Staffs. PO, tel, stores. A village 1½ miles north of bridge 54, along the A515. There are some pleasant houses and an old mill to be seen here, as well as what is reputed to have been Lady Godiva's early home. The Trent flows just beyond the church, which contains some old glass and a 17thC pulpit and font.

BOATYARDS

Ⓑ **Swan Line Cruisers** *See page 147.*

PUBS

Crown Handsacre. Canalside, at bridge 58. Children's room. Grocer and fish & chips nearby.

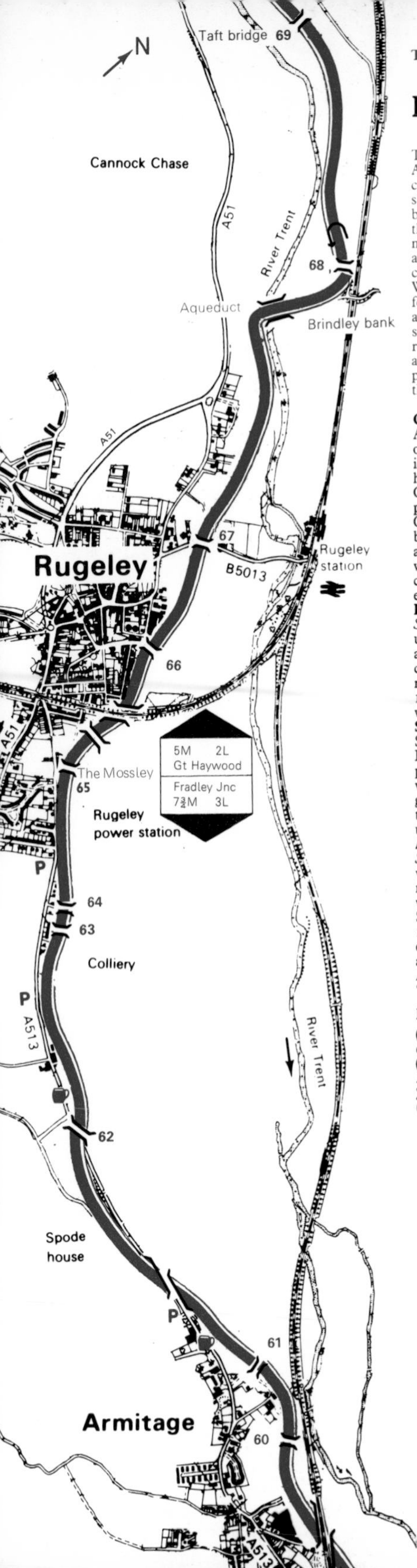

Rugeley

The canal now skirts Armitage, passing the Armitage pottery and church. Then the A513 crosses the canal on a new bridge where the short (130yds) Armitage Tunnel used to run before its roof was removed in 1971 to combat the subsidence effects of coal being mined nearby. There is a distinguished restaurant just across the road here, very much a rarity on canals in general and this area in particular. West of the tunnel stands Spode House, a former home of the pottery family. The towers and chimneys of the colliery and huge power station come into view; they take a long time to recede. The passage past Rugeley is not attractive—although improvements are planned. North of the town, the canal crosses the River Trent via a substantial aqueduct.

Cannock Chase
An area of outstanding natural beauty and officially designated as such in 1949. The Chase is all that remains of what was once a Norman hunting ground known as the King's Forest of Cannock. Much of the existing forest has been planted and tended by the Forestry Commission, about 7000 acres of land having been acquired since 1920. Flora and fauna are abundant and include a herd of fallow deer whose ancestors have grazed in this area for centuries. Shugborough Park is at the north end of the Chase.

Rugeley
Staffs. PO, tel, stores, garage, banks, station. An unexciting place with a modern town centre and a dominating power station. There are 2 churches by bridge 67: one is a heap of 14thC ruins, the other is the parish church built in 1822 as a replacement. Cannock Chase rises west of the town.

Spode House
Skirted by the canal. Spode House and Hawkesyard Priory stand side by side. The priory, which is only a small community now, was founded in 1897 by Josiah Spode's grandson and his niece Helen Gulson when they lived at Spode House. The latter is now used as a conference centre.

Armitage
Staffs. PO, tel, stores, garage. A main road village, whose church is interesting: it was rebuilt in the 19thC in a Saxon/Norman style, which makes it rather dark. The font is genuine Saxon, however, and the tower was built in 1690. The organ is 200 years old, and enormous: it came from Lichfield Cathedral and practically deafens the organist at Armitage. The town is widely known for its 'Armitage Ware' water closets.

PUBS AND RESTAURANTS

Ash Tree Canalside, at bridge 62. A boat club is based here.

Plum Pudding Canalside, west of Armitage. Food.

Old Farmhouse Restaurant Armitage (490353). A very popular English restaurant.

Great Haywood

One now enters an immensely attractive area that is full of interest. Accompanied by the River Trent, the canal moves up a narrowing valley bordered by green slopes on either side, Cannock Chase being clearly visible to the south. Wolseley Hall has gone, but Bishton Hall (now a school) still stands: its very elegant front faces the canal near Wolseley Bridge. Passing Colwich, an important railway junction, the canal reaches the perimeter of Shugborough Park: the impressive façade of the Hall can be seen across the parkland. At Great Haywood Junction the Staffs & Worcs Canal (see page 137) joins the Trent & Mersey from the west under a graceful towing path bridge—there is a useful boatyard here. Then the Trent valley becomes much broader and more open. Hoo Mill Lock (provisions available) is a busy spot: a boatyard stretches either side of it. North of the lock a busy road joins the hitherto quiet canal for a while. To the west is Ingestre Hall.

Great Haywood
Staffs. PO, tel, stores. Centre of the Great Haywood and Shugborough Conservation Area, the village is not particularly beautiful but is closely connected in many ways to Shugborough Park, to which it is physically linked by the very old Shugborough Bridge, where the crystal clear waters of the River Sow join the heavily polluted Trent on its way down from Stoke. Haywood Lock is beautifully situated between this packhorse bridge (which is an Ancient Monument) and the unusually decorative railway bridge that leads into Trent Lane. The lane consists of completely symmetrical and very handsome terraced cottages: they were built by the Ansons to house the people evicted from the former Shugborough village. There is an interesting-looking Roman Catholic church in Great Haywood: the other curious feature concerns the Anglican church. About 100yds south of Haywood Lock is an iron bridge over the canal. This bridge, which now leads nowhere, used to carry a private road from Shugborough Hall which crossed both the river and the canal on its way to the church just east of the railway. This was important to the Ansons, since the packhorse bridge just upstream is not wide enough for a horse and carriage, and so until the iron bridge was built the family had to *walk* the 300yds to church on Sunday mornings!

Shugborough Hall *National Trust property.* This splendid mansion is very close to the canal and should be visited. The present house dates from 1693, but was substantially altered by James Stuart around 1760 and by Samuel Wyatt around the turn of the 18thC. It was at this time that the old village of Shugborough was bought up and demolished by the Anson family so that they should enjoy more privacy and space in their park. Family fortunes fluctuated greatly for the Ansons, the Earl of Lichfield's family; eventually crippling death duties in the 1960s brought about the transfer of the estate to the National Trust. The Trust have leased the property to Staffordshire County Council who now manage the whole estate. The house has been restored at great expense. There are some magnificent rooms and many treasures inside.

Museum of Staffordshire Life This excellent establishment, which is effectively Staffordshire's county museum, is housed in the old stables adjacent to Shugborough Hall. Open since 1966, it is superbly laid out and contains all sorts of exhibits concerned with old country life in Staffordshire. Amongst other things it contains an old fashioned laundry, the old gun-room and the old estate brew-house, all completely equipped. Part of the stables contains harness, carts, coaches and motor cars. There is an industrial annexe up the road, containing a collection of preserved steam locomotives and some industrial machinery. *House, grounds and museum open Tue–Fri, Sat and Sun afternoons Mar–Oct. (Industrial annexe open weekends only.)*

Shugborough Park There are some remarkable sights in the large park, that encircles the Hall. Thomas Anson, who inherited the estate in 1720, enlisted in 1744 the help of his famous brother, Admiral George Anson, to beautify and improve the house and the park. And in 1762 he commissioned James Stuart, a neo-Grecian architect, to embellish the park. 'Athenian' Stuart set to with a will, and the spectacular results of his work can be seen scattered round the park. The stone monuments that he built have deservedly extravagant names like the 'Tower of the Winds' the 'Lanthorn of Demosthemes' etc.

BOATYARDS

Ⓑ **Kingfisher Line** Hoo Mill Lock, Great Haywood, Staffs. (Little Haywood 881384). S W D Pump-out, repairs, slipway, dry dock, short period moorings, shop, groceries, coffee.

Ⓑ **Anglo-Welsh Narrowboats**. The Canal Wharf, Mill Lane, Great Haywood, Staffs. (Little Haywood 881711). R S W D E Pump-out (*Mon–Fri*), narrow boat hire, boat & engine repairs, mooring, toilets.

PUBS

Coach & Horses Near bridge 77. Lunches and dinners.
Clifford Arms Great Haywood. B&B.
Fox & Hounds Great Haywood.
Lamb & Flag Little Haywood.
Red Lion Little Haywood.
Wolseley Arms Near bridge 70. Tea rooms, all home made food, opposite.

The Trent & Mersey near Great Haywood. *Derek Pratt*

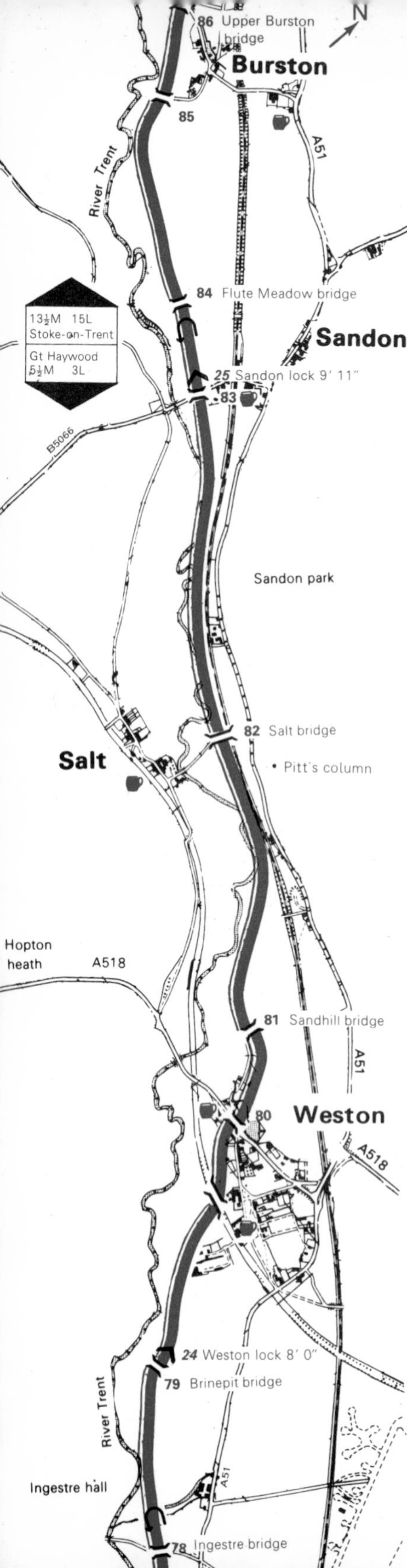

Sandon Park

Continuing up the Trent valley past Ingestre Hall and Park, the canal enjoys a length in which locks are few and far between. Weston (*PO, tel, stores*) is left behind and railway and main road converge as the valley narrows. The wooded Sandon Park rises steeply on the north bank; the canal passes now through quiet meadows to the little village of Burston.

Burston
Staffs. Tel. A hamlet apparently untouched by modern times, in spite of the proximity of 3 transport routes. Most of the village is set around the village pond. A very quiet place.
Sandon
Staffs. Tel. A small estate village clustered near the main gates to Sandon Park. The main road bisecting the place is enough to send any canal boatman scurrying back to the safety of the pretty Sandon Lock. There is a pub, however, opposite the park gates. All Saints Church, up the hill, is 13thC to 15thC with a Norman font and a 17thC wall painting.
Battle of Hopton Heath This was fought 1½ miles west of Weston. An inconclusive Civil War battle on the 19th March 1643, it reflected the strategic importance to both sides of Stafford, only 4 miles south west of the battlefield. In the engagement, 1800 Parliamentarians met 1200 Royalists (mostly cavalry). Supported by 'Roaring Meg'—a 29-pound cannon—the Royalists took the initiative, making several bold and effective cavalry charges against the enemy. However, the Roundheads' musketry fought back strongly, and after the Royalist leader (the Earl of Northampton) was killed, the Cavaliers weakened and fell back. Eventually both sides were exhausted and nightfall brought an end to the battle. Casualties—at under 200—were surprisingly light, and neither side could claim a victory. The Cavaliers returned to Stafford, but 2 months later they lost the town for good to the Roundheads.
Ingestre Hall ½ mile south west of bridge 78. Originally a Tudor building, the Hall was rebuilt in neo-Gothic style following a disastrous fire in 1820. The house is surrounded by large attractive gardens. Now a residential arts centre open to visitors only on the *first Sat in Jul*.

PUBS

Greyhound Burston. Food.
Dog & Doublet Sandon. Snacks. *Closed Sun.*
Holly Bush Salt. Access from a stile near bridge 82; then walk up the lane.
Saracen's Head Weston, by bridge 80. Garden.
Woolpack Weston. Food.

Stone

The 100-year-old tower of Aston Church is prominent as the canal continues up through the quiet water meadows of the Trent valley. Soon Stone is entered; below the bottom lock is a good place to tie up for the night—a lockside pub and shops are very close by. These locks are deeper than most on a narrow canal—their average rise is about 10ft. Just above the second lock is a boatyard and 3 dry docks: there is another boatyard a few yards further on. Lock 29 is accompanied by a little tunnel under the road for boat horses. The Stone Locks are followed by another flight of 4, climbing up the valley to Meaford. The present Meaford Locks replaced an earlier staircase of 3, the remains of which can be seen by lock 33. Here the electric railway line draws alongside.

Stone
Staffs. EC Wed, MD Tue, Thur, PO, tel, stores, garage, bank, station, cinema. A busy and pleasant town with excellent boating and shopping facilities. The old priory church began to fall down in 1749, so in 1753 an Act of Parliament was obtained to enable the parishioners to rebuild it. The new church (St Michael's in Lichfield Road) was consecrated in 1758, having cost £5000: it is a handsome building in open ground (no graves) on a slope at the east end of the town.

BOATYARDS

Ⓑ **Canal Cruising Co** Stone, Staffs. (813982). R W D Pump-out, hire craft, gas, dry dock, boat building & repairs, toilets.
Ⓑ **Stone Boatbuilding** Newcastle Road, Stone, Staffs. (812688). W P D Gas, slipway, breakdown service, souvenirs, toilets. Boat sales and repairs, outboard sales.
Ⓑ **Staffordshire Narrowboats** The Wharf, Newcastle Road, Stone. (816871). R W D E Pump-out, narrow boat hire, long term mooring, overnight mooring, slipway, books and maps, toilets.

PUBS

Rising Sun Near Stone top lock. Snacks.
Crown & Anchor Stone.
Crown Hotel High Street, Stone. Lunches and dinners in this establishment designed by Henry Holland in 1779.
Star Canalside, at Stone bottom lock. Bass Worthington and M & B real ale is served in this 13-room pub where apparently no 2 rooms are on the same level. Snacks, quiet children allowed in at lunchtime. No winking lights or bleepers in the bar.

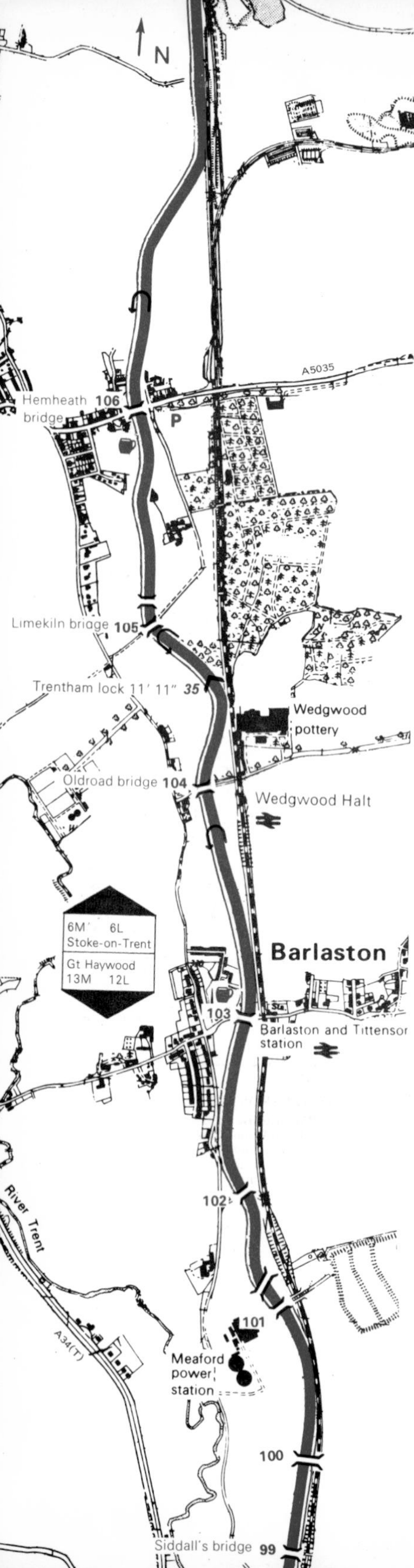

Barlaston

The valley widens out now and becomes flatter and less rural. Meaford Power Station and the railway flank the canal as it approaches straggling Barlaston. Just before Trentham Lock is the Wedgwood pottery, set back from the canal. The factory is conveniently served by Wedgwood Halt. North of Hem Heath Bridge, Stoke-on-Trent looms up with its periphery of bleak industrial wastelands.

Trentham Gardens
1 mile west of bridge 106. The Hall, which was built by Barrie and which formerly belonged to the Duke of Sutherland, was demolished in 1909 except for the ballroom and orangery. Now used as a leisure centre, the place possesses formal Italian gardens and, among other facilities, a lake for fishing and boating, an open air swimming pool, and a miniature railway. Concerts are held in the ballroom.

Wedgwood Factory
The Wedgwood Group is the largest china and earthenware manufacturer in the world. It was started in 1759 in Burslem by the famous Josiah Wedgwood, the 'Father of English Potters', who came from a small pottery family. By 1766 he was sufficiently prosperous to build a large new house and factory which he called Etruria—a name suggested by his close friend Dr Erasmus Darwin—to use the canal, of which he was a promoter, for transport. It was here that he produced his famous Jasper unglazed stoneware with white classical portraits on the surface. He revolutionised pottery making with his many innovations and after his death in 1795 the company continued to expand. In the 1930s the Wedgwoods decided to build a new factory because mining subsidence had made Etruria unsuitable. The Etruria factory has unfortunately since been demolished but the large new factory began production in 1940 in Barlaston and is still the centre of the industry, with 6 electric tunnel ovens which produce none of the industrial smoke that is commonly associated with the Potteries. The Wedgwood Museum at Barlaston has a vast range of exhibits of Wedgwood pottery. The works is only a few yards from the canal, accessible from bridge 104. The Visitor Centre is *open weekdays*, and a small charge is made. There are demonstrations, a shop, a museum and refreshments (children under 5 are restricted to certain areas). Parties of 12 people and over must book (Barlaston 3218). A stop here should be on every canal traveller's itinerary.

PUBS

Roebuck Hotel (Hunting lodge restaurant) near Hem Heath Bridge.
Plume of Feathers Barlaston. Canalside.

Stoke-on-Trent

This is an intensely industrial length of canal, passing right through Stoke-on-Trent with all its factories and warehouses. The signs of the pottery industry are everywhere. But the most remarkable manifestation of the industry is the 'bottle kilns'—the brick furnaces shaped like gigantic bottles about 30ft high that still stand, cold and disused now (but, happily, to be preserved), at the side of the canal. Near Stoke-on-Trent station can be seen the remains of the canal arm to Newcastle under Lyme; what is left of the arm is now used as a boat club mooring. Unfortunately Josiah Wedgwood's original factory in Etruria no longer exists. This entire area tends to bemuse some canal travellers by its overpowering industries and total disregard for the canal that was once its lifeblood; but industrial archaeologists are not alone in enjoying seeing what is made in this proud and prosperous town and the incongruity of scenes like pleasure boats creeping through the Shelton steelworks. The Caldon Canal (see page 42) leaves the main line just above Stoke Top Lock—the BWB sanitary station is just past the junction, on the Caldon. Note: the canal bridges in Stoke are mostly very low, with a minimum of 6ft 8in headroom.

Stoke-on-Trent
Staffs. EC Thur, MD Wed, Fri, Sat. All services. The city was formed in 1910 from a federation of 6 towns (Burslem, Fenton, Hanley, Longton, Stoke and Tunstall) but became known as 'The Five Towns' in the novels of Arnold Bennett. The thriving pottery and coal industries are the source of the city's great prosperity, but they also brought in their wake their inevitable dirt and ugliness. Many of the pottery factories have in recent years been dealing with the problem. One to visit is the famous Spode China works which is right in the centre of the town in Church Street. The Town Hall in Glebe Street, is an imposing and formal 19thC building. Opposite the Town Hall is the parish church of St Peter, a 19thC structure in Perpendicular style which contains a commemorative plaque to Josiah Wedgwood, who is also remembered in the bronze statue that welcomes visitors at the station. By lock 39 canal travellers will see the fine flint and bone mill, dated 1857, and served by a short arm. The actual city centre is Hanley.
City Museum Art Gallery Broad Street, Hanley. As one might expect, it contains one of the world's most outstanding collections of ceramics including work from Egypt, Persia, China, Greece and Rome. The historical development of pottery manufacture in Stoke-on-Trent is also traced from Roman times to the present day. *Open weekdays and Sun afternoons.*
Tourist Information Central Library, Bethesda Street, Hanley. (Stoke-on-Trent 21242).

BOATYARDS

Ⓑ **BWB Etruria Yard** At junction with Caldon Canal. (Stoke-on-Trent 25597). R S W Toilet.
Ⓑ **Dolphin Boats** Near bridge 112. (Stoke-on-Trent 49390). W Gas, boat and engine sales and repairs, chandlery, breakdown service, mooring, slipway. Fishing tackle and bait.

PUBS

Nothing canalside on this section, and not a particularly good area to leave your boat unattended. However, the centre of Stoke is only a short walk south west from bridge 113; a good selection of pubs is to be found there. More are to be found in Hanley, a mile east of bridge 117.

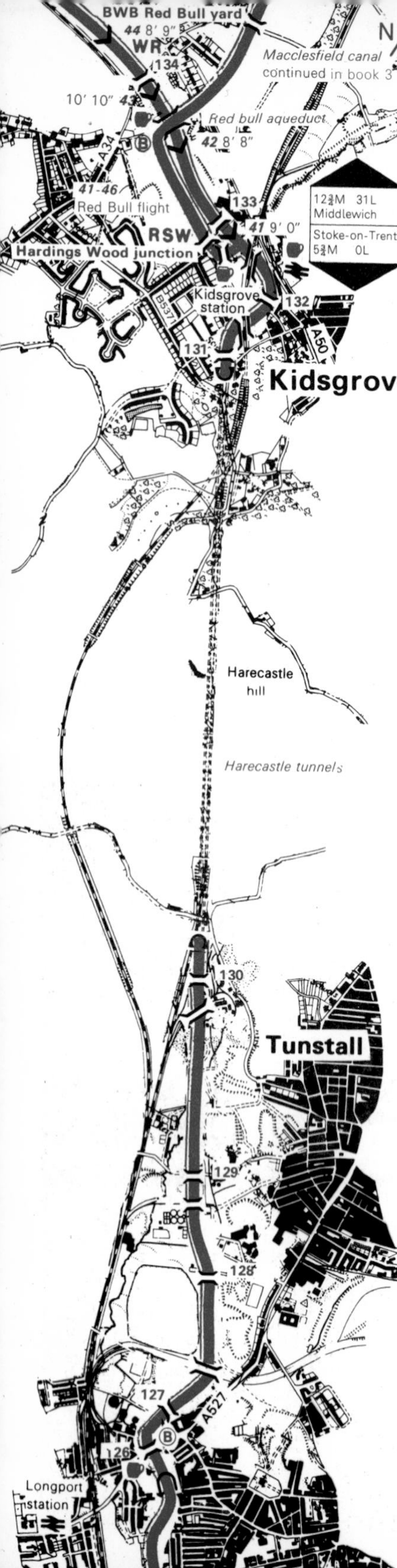

Harecastle Tunnel

The canal continues for a while through a heavily industrial area mostly connected with the pottery business and its needs. Before long the navigation abandons its very twisting course and makes a beeline for Harecastle Hill and the tunnels through it. (The odd colour of the water here is caused by local ironstone strata). Only one of the tunnels is navigable now. The tunnel is too long to see through, so no boat may proceed through it unless in accordance with the instructions given on the notice board and summarised below. At the north end of the tunnel, the navigation passes Kidsgrove station: just beyond it is Harding's Wood Junction with the Macclesfield Canal where there are 2 pubs and a grocer. The Trent & Mersey proceeds to descend from the summit level through a flight of paired narrow locks. Just below the second lock, the Macclesfield Canal crosses to T & M on Red Bull Aqueduct. By now the industrial built-up area of the Potteries is being rapidly replaced by pleasant countryside.

Kidsgrove
Staffs. All services. Originally a big iron and coal producing town. Kidsgrove was much helped in its growing size and prosperity by the completion of the Trent & Mersey Canal, which gave the town an outlet for these goods. James Brindley is buried in the town in a churchyard at Newchapel.
St Saviour's Church Butt Lane. This building is unusual in looking quite unlike a church. Built in 1878, it was designed in black and white Tudor style.
The 3 Harecastle Tunnels
There are altogether 3 parallel tunnels through Harecastle Hill. The first, built by James Brindley, was completed in 1777, after 11 years work. To build a 9ft wide tunnel 1¾ miles long represented engineering on a scale quite unknown to the world at that time, and the world was duly impressed. Since there was no towpath in the tunnel the boats—which were of course all towed from the bank by horses in those days—had to be 'legged' through by men lying on the boat's cabin roof and propelling the boat by 'walking' along the tunnel roof. (The towing horse would have to be walked in the meantime over the top of the hill.) This very slow means of propulsion, combined with the great length of the narrow tunnel and the large amount of traffic on the navigation, made Harecastle a major bottleneck for canal boats. So in 1822 the Trent & Mersey Canal Company called in Thomas Telford, who recommended that a second tunnel be constructed alongside the first one. This was done: the new tunnel was completed in 1827, with a towpath, after only 3 years work. Each tunnel then became one-way until in the 20thC Mr Brindley's bore had sunk so much from mining subsidence that it had to be abandoned. An electric tug was introduced in 1914 to speed up traffic through Telford's tunnel; this service was continued until 1954. Subsidence has necessitated the removal of much of the towpath, although some parts remain, at water level and below.
The third tunnel through Harecastle Hill was built years after the other 2, and carried the Stoke–Kidsgrove railway line. It runs 40ft above the canal tunnels and is slightly shorter. This tunnel was closed in the 1960s: the railway line now goes round the hill and through a much shorter tunnel. Thus 2 out of the 3 Harecastle tunnels are disused.

NAVIGATING THROUGH THE HARECASTLE TUNNEL

April 1 to October 31 (summer working)
NORTH END
Weekdays: craft may enter the tunnel on the instruction of the tunnel keeper between *08.00 and 16.00.*
Fridays only: craft may enter the tunnel between *19.00 and dusk.*
Weekends and B. Hols: craft may enter the tunnel between *15.00 and dusk.*

SOUTH END
Weekdays: craft may enter the tunnel on the instruction of the tunnel keeper between *08.00 and 16.00*.
Weekends and B. Hols: craft may enter the tunnel between *dawn and 13.00*.

In practice this means the last passage on a weekday in your direction of travel MIGHT BE 1½ hours before the finishing times given, with no way of knowing in advance.

Nov 1 to March 31 (winter working).

NORTH END
Craft may enter between *13.30 and dusk*.
SOUTH END
Craft may enter between *dawn and 11.30*.

Do not enter in an unpowered craft. A loading gauge at each end indicates the headroom, so you shouldn't get stuck.

BOATYARDS

Ⓑ **BWB Red Bull Yard** North of bridge 134 (Kidsgrove 5703). [R][W]
Ⓑ **David Piper** Red Bull Basin, Church Lawton, Stoke-on-Trent, Staffs. (Kidsgrove 4754). On Macclesfield Canal. [W][D] Pump-out, slipway, moorings, winter storage, boat building, sales, boat & engine repairs.
Ⓑ **Black Prince Narrowboats** Longport Wharf, Station Street, Stoke-on-Trent. (812674). [R][S][W][D] Pump-out, narrow boat hire, slipway, gas, boat & engine repairs, boat building, mooring, chandlery, toilets, winter storage. *Closed winter Sun.* Shops and pubs close by.

PUBS

Red Bull Canalside, in the Red Bull flight of locks. Garden, food.
Blue Bell At junction with Macclesfield Canal.
Canal Tavern opposite the Blue Bell.
Duke of Bridgewater Near bridge 126. The lounge is full of narrow boat parts. Bass real ale.
Pack Horse Station Street. Near bridge 126. Ansells and Ind Coope real ale.

Longport Wharf, Stoke-on-Trent: a traditional boat and butty prepare to leave. *David Perrott*

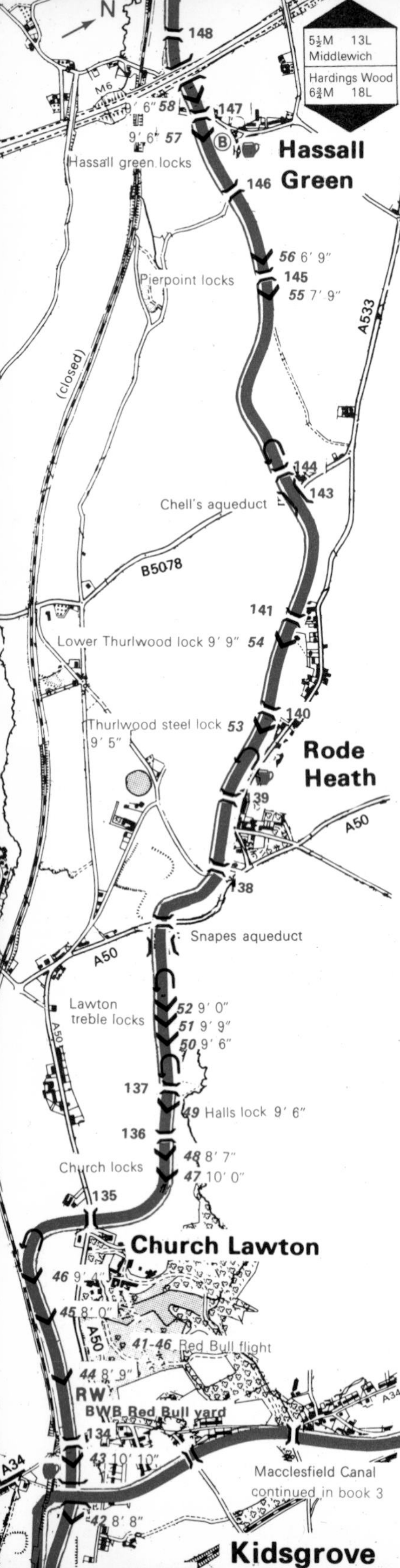

Rode Heath

Leaving behind the spire of Church Lawton, the canal continues to fall through a heavily locked stretch sometimes called, unfairly, 'heartbreak hill'. The countryside is entirely rural and pleasant, slightly hilly and wooded. 2 minor aqueducts are encountered, but the locks are more interesting: they are all pairs of narrow locks, side by side. Some of the duplicate locks are unusable or even filled in, but many of them are in good condition, so navigators can choose whichever lock is set in their favour. One of the strangest locks on the whole canal system is Thurlwood Steel Lock, a gigantic and complicated affair with a massive steel superstructure, constructed in 1957 to combat local brine-pumping subsidence. There is a conventional lock adjoining, which is the one to use. At Hassall Green a *PO, tel and stores* incorporating a canal shop and boatyard services can be found just by the new concrete bridge. The M6 motorway crosses noisily nearby.

Rode Heath
PO, tel, stores. A useful shopping area right by bridge 139.

BOATYARDS

Ⓑ **Vistra Marina** Hassall Green (Sandbach 2266). W D, Pump-out, mooring, gas, general store, canal shop, coffee and tea. Superb meat and potato pies.
BWB Red Bull Yard North of bridge 134 W R

PUBS

Romping Donkey Hassall Green. A pretty country pub. Leave your wellington boots in the boat. Snacks, garden.
Broughton Arms Rode Heath. Canalside. Snacks.

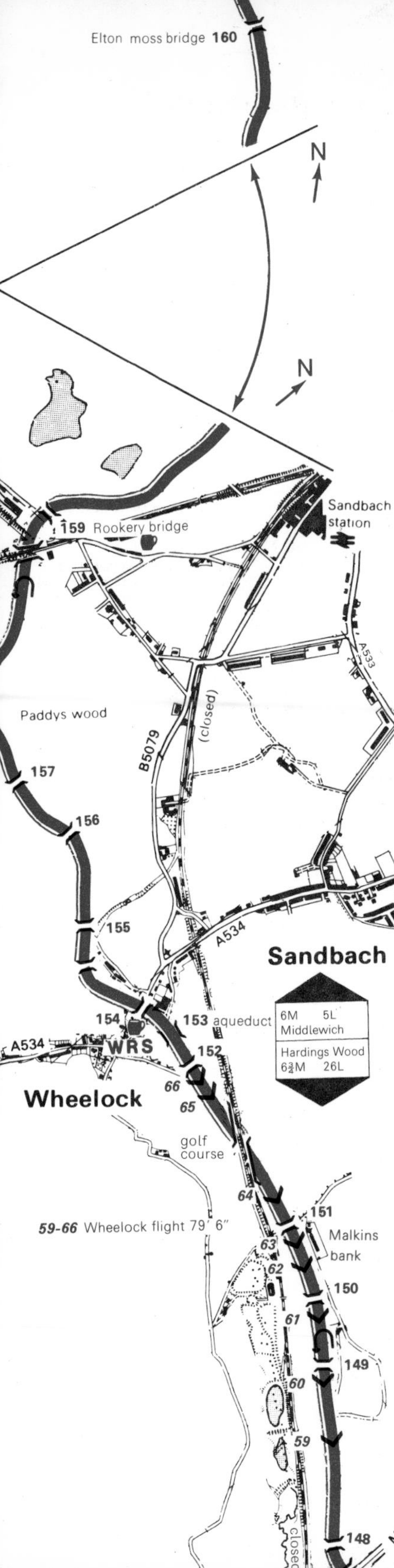

Wheelock

The canal now descends the Wheelock flight of 8 locks, which are the last paired locks one sees when travelling northwards. The countryside continues to be quiet and unspoilt but unspectacular. The pair of locks halfway down the flight has a curious situation in the little settlement of Malkin's Bank; overlooked by terraced houses, the navigator can get the distinct feeling that his lock operating routine is a very public performance. The boatman's co-op used to be here, but the small terrace of cottages which housed it is to be demolished. At the bottom of the flight is the village of Wheelock; west of here the navigation curls round the side of a hill before entering the very long-established salt-producing area that is based on Middlewich. The 'wild' brine pumping and rock-salt mining that has gone on hereabouts has resulted in severe local subsidence; the effect on the canal has been to necessitate the constant raising of the banks as lengths of the canal bed sink. This of course means that the affected lengths tend to be much deeper than ordinary canals. Non-swimmers beware of falling overboard.

Sandbach
Ches. EC Tue, MD Thur. PO, tel, stores, garage, bank, station. 1½ miles north of Wheelock. An old market town that has maintained its charm despite the steady growth of its salt and chemical industries.
Ancient Crosses In the cobbled market place on a massive base stand 2 superb Saxon crosses, believed to commemorate the conversion of the area to Christianity in the 7thC. They suffered severely in the 17thC when the Puritans broke them up and scattered the fragments for miles. After years of searching for the parts, George Ormerod succeeded in re-erecting the crosses in 1816, with new stone replacing the missing fragments.
St Mary's Church High Street. A large, 16thC church with a handsome battlemented tower. The most interesting features of the interior are the 17thC carved roof and the fine chancel screen.
The Old Hall Hotel An outstanding example of Elizabethan half-timbered architecture, which was formerly the home of the lord of the manor, but is now used as an hotel.
Wheelock
Ches. EC Tue. PO, tel, stores, garage, fish and chips. Busy little main road village on the canal.

PUBS

Cheshire Cheese Wheelock. Canalside. Food, garden.
Nag's Head Wheelock.
Market Tavern The Square, Sandbach. Opposite the crosses. Food, garden.

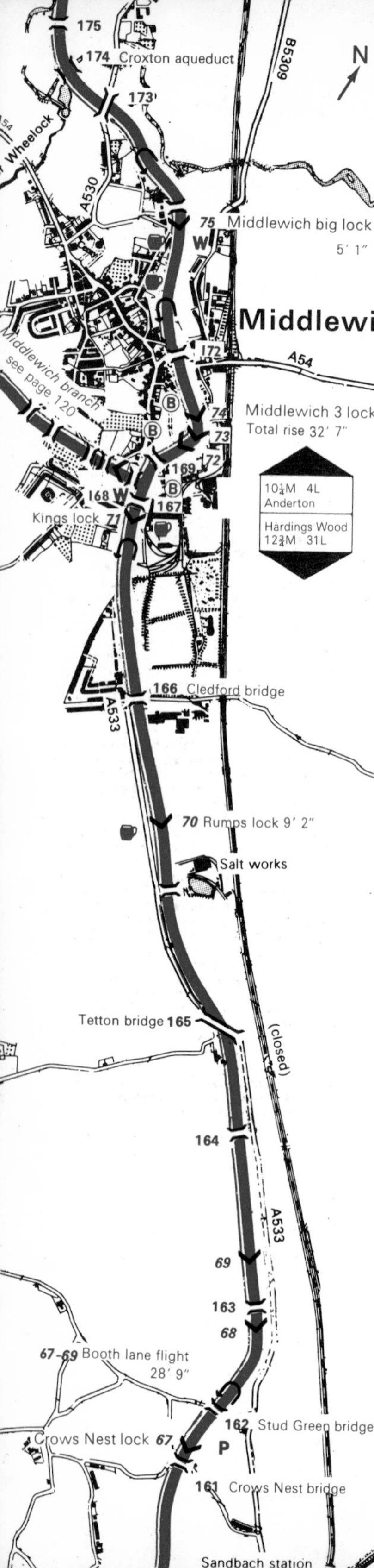

Middlewich

The navigation now begins to lose the rural character it has enjoyed since Kidsgrove. Falling through yet more locks, the canal is joined by a busy main road (useful for fish and chips and Chinese take away) which accompanies it into increasingly flat and industrialised landscape, past several salt works and into Middlewich, where a branch of the Shropshire Union leads off westwards towards that canal at Barbridge. The Trent & Mersey skirts the centre of the town, passing lots of moored narrow boats and through 3 consecutive narrow locks, arriving at a wide (14ft) lock (which has suffered from subsidence) with a pub beside it. This used to represent the beginning of a wide, almost lock-free navigation right through to Preston Brook, Manchester and Wigan (very convenient for the salt industry when it shipped most of its goods by boat), but Croxton Aqueduct had to be replaced many years ago, and is now a steel structure only 8ft 2in wide. The aqueduct crosses the River Dane, which flows alongside the navigation as both water courses leave industrial Middlewich and move out into fine open country.

Middlewich
Ches. EC Wed. PO, tel, stores, bank, garage. A town that since Roman times has been dedicated to salt extraction. Most of the salt produced here goes to various chemical industries. Subsidence from salt extraction has prevented redevelopment for many years, but a big renewal scheme is now in progress. The canalside area is a haven of peace below the busy streets. Tourist Information is by bridge 172.

St Michael's Church A handsome medieval church which was a place of refuge for the Royalists during the Civil War. It has a fine interior with richly carved woodwork.

BOATYARDS

Ⓑ **Andersen Boats** Wych House, St Anne's Road, Middlewich, Ches. (3668). R Pump-out, boat hire, gas, groceries, gifts.

Ⓑ **Middlewich Narrow Boats** Canal Terrace, Lewin Street, Middlewich. (2460). R S W P D Pump-out, boat hire, gas, dry dock, boat building & repairs, mooring, chandlery, toilets, trip boat. *Closed Nov–Feb.* Have a look at the beautifully decorated house and garden round the back.

Ⓑ **Kings Lock Boatyard** At the junction, Middlewich. (3234). Hire cruisers.

PUBS

Big Lock Middlewich. Canalside. Food.

Newton Brewery Inn Canalside above big lock. Garden.

Cheshire Cheese Lewin Street, Middlewich. Food.

Kings Lock Middlewich. Canalside. Fish and chips opposite.

Kinderton Arms Close to canal 1 mile south of Middlewich, by lock 70. Ignore its dour appearance and walk in.

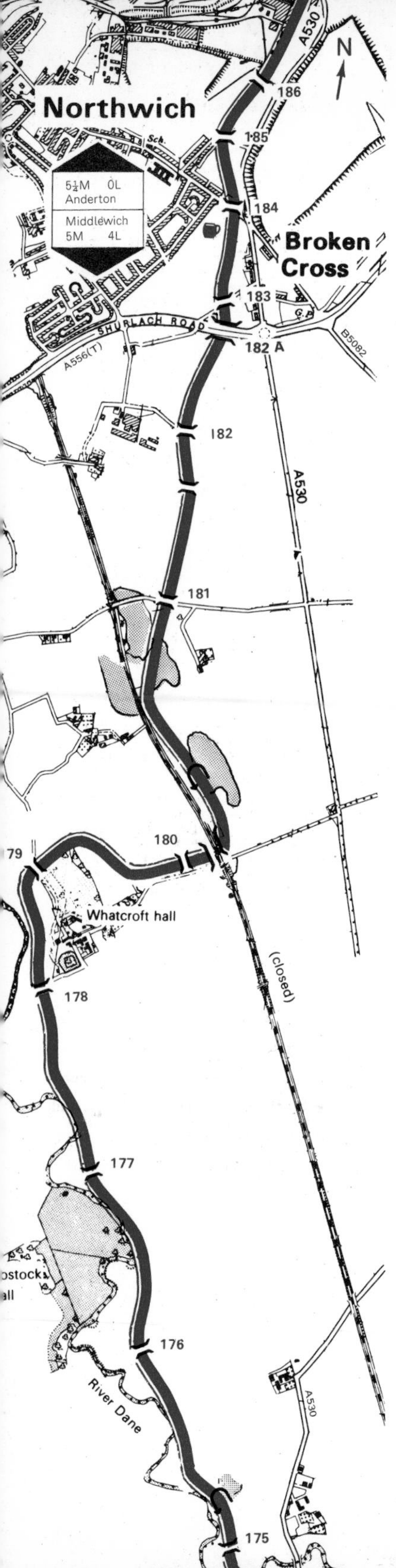

Dane Valley

Initially, this is a stretch of canal as beautiful as any in the country. Often overhung by trees, the navigation winds along the side of a hill as it follows the delightful valley of the River Dane. The parkland on the other side of the valley encompasses Bostock Hall, a school for subnormal children. At Whatcroft Hall (privately owned), the canal circles around to the east, passing under a derelict railway before heading for the industrial outskirts of Northwich and shedding its beauty and solitude once again. The outlying canal settlement of Broken Cross acts as a buffer between these 2 very different lengths of canal. **Note:** There are several privately owned wide 'lagoons' caused by subsidence along this section of the Trent & Mersey, in some of which repose the hulks of abandoned barges and narrow boats, lately being salvaged. Navigators should be wary of straying off the main line, since the offside canal bank is often submerged and invisible just below the water level.

Northwich

Ches. EC Wed, MD Fri, Sat. All services. Regular buses from Barnton. A rather attractive town at the junction of the Rivers Weaver and Dane. (The latter brings large quantities of sand down into the Weaver Navigation, necessitating a heavy expenditure on dredging.) As in every other town in this area, salt has for centuries been responsible for the continued prosperity of Northwich. (The Brine Baths in Victoria Road are still open throughout the year for the benefit of salt-water enthusiasts). The Weaver Navigation has of course been another very prominent factor in the town's history, and the building and repairing of barges, narrow boats, and small seagoing ships has been carried on here for over 200 years. Nowadays this industry has been almost forced out of business by foreign competition, and the last private shipyard on the river closed down in 1971. (This yard—Isaac Pimblott's—used to be between Hunt's Locks and Hartford Bridge. Their last contract was a tug for Aden.) However the big BWB yard in the town continues to thrive; some very large maintenance craft are built and repaired here. The wharves by Town Bridge are empty, and are an excellent temporary mooring site for anyone wishing to visit the place. The town centre is very close; much of it has been completely rebuilt very recently. There is now an extensive shopping precinct. Although the large number of pubs has been whittled down in the rebuilding process, there are still some pleasant old streets. The Weaver and the big swing bridges across it remain a dominant part of the background.

PUBS

Old Broken Cross Canalside, at bridge 184. An attractive old canal pub. Shops and launderette a short way past the pub.

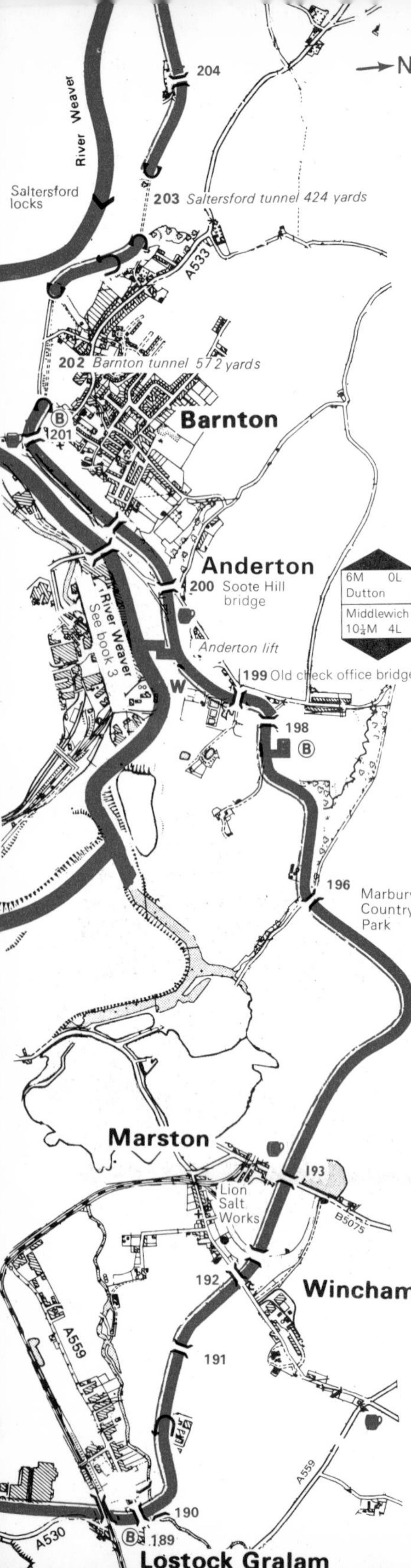

Anderton Lift

This is another length in which salt mining has determined the nature of the scenery. Part of it is heavily industrial, with enormous ICI works dominating the scene; much of it is devastated but rural (just), some of it is nondescript, and some of it is superb countryside. Donkey engines can still be seen in surrounding fields pumping brine. Leaving the vicinity of Lostock Gralam and the outskirts of Northwich, one passes Marston and Wincham (*PO, tel, stores*). Just west of the village, one travels along a ½ mile stretch of canal that was only cut in 1958, as the old route was about to collapse into—needless to say—underground salt workings. Beyond the woods of Marbury Country Park (attractive short stay moorings) is Anderton (*PO, tel, stores*)—the short entrance canal to the famous boat lift down into the Weaver Navigation is on the left. The main line continues westward, winding along what is now a steep hill and into Barnton Tunnel. At the west end one emerges onto a hillside overlooking the River Weaver, with a marvellous view straight down the huge Saltersford Locks. Now Saltersford Tunnel is entered: beyond it, one finds oneself in completely open country again. Henceforth, the salt extraction industry can be safely forgotten.

Navigational note
Both Barnton and Saltersford Tunnels are crooked, affording only a brief glimpse of the other end. 2 boats cannot pass in the tunnels, so take care they are clear before proceeding.

Anderton Lift
An amazing and enormous piece of machinery built in 1875 by Leader Williams (later engineer of the Manchester Ship Canal) to connect the Trent & Mersey to the flourishing Weaver Navigation, 50ft below. As built, the lift consisted of 2 water-filled tanks counterbalancing each other in a vertical slide, resting on massive hydraulic rams. It worked on the very straightforward principle that making the ascending tank slightly lighter—by pumping a little water out—would assist the hydraulic rams (which were operated by a steam engine and pump) in moving both tanks, with boats in them, up or down their respective slide.
In 1908 the lift had to have major repairs, so it was modernised at the same time. The troublesome hydraulic rams were done away with; from then on each tank—which contained 250 tons of water—had its own counterweights and was independent of the other tank. Electricity replaced steam as the motive power. One of the most fascinating individual features of the canal system, it draws thousands of sightseers every year. Recent mechanical and structural problems have unfortunately cast some doubt over its future—ring Northwich 74321 if you plan to use it, to check if it is operational.
Marston
Ches. Tel. A salt-producing village, suffering badly from its own industry. The numerous gaps in this village are presumably caused by the demolition or collapse of houses affected by subsidence. Waste ground abounds. The Lion Salt Works is open on *summer afternoons*, and is well worth visiting. You can buy natural brine salt 'in the lump' here.

BOATYARDS

Ⓑ **Clare Cruisers** Tunnel Road, Barnton, Northwich. (77199). R W D Pump-out, narrow boat hire, gas, repairs.
Ⓑ **Anderton Marina (Inland Marine Leisure)** Uplands Road, Anderton. (Northwich 79642). R S W D Water borne pump-out ('Two-loos Lautrec'), narrow boat hire, gas, slipway, mooring, boat and engine repairs, boat sales, gifts, toilets, coffee shop. *Closed winter weekends*. Groceries from Anderton PO and stores, 5 minutes walk away.
Ⓑ **Colliery Narrow Boat Co** Wincham Wharf (bridge 189) Lostock Gralam, Northwich. (44672). D W E Pump-out, gas. Electric trip boat, day boat hire, dry dock, repairs and servicing, boat building, chandlery. Off-licence and groceries close by.

PUBS

Red Lion Barnton, just east of bridge 201. Food, garden, children's room.
Stanley Arms Canalside, overlooking the Anderton Lift. Food, real ale, putting green.
New Inn Marston.
Black Greyhound ½ mile east of bridge 192. Good food, garden, children welcome lunchtime.

'Hotel' boat and butty visiting the Lion Salt Works, Marston. *David Perrott*

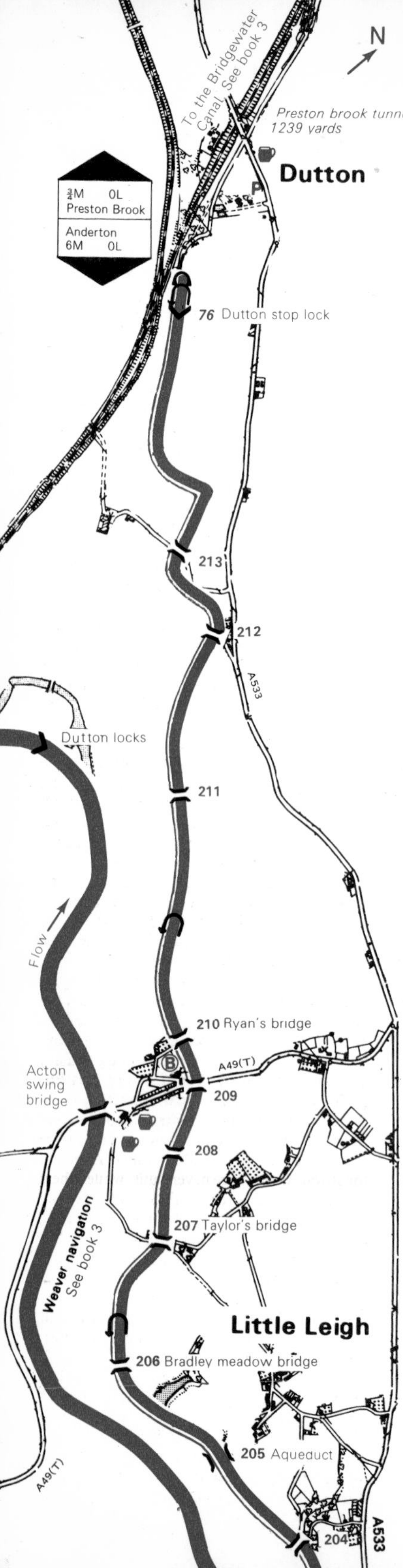

Dutton

This, the northernmost stretch of the Trent & Mersey, is a very pleasant one and delightfully rural. Most of the way the navigation follows the south side of the hills that overlook the River Weaver. From about 60ft up, one is often rewarded with excellent views of this splendid valley and the large vessels that ply up and down it. At one point one can see the elegant Dutton railway viaduct in the distance; then the 2 waterways diverge as the Trent & Mersey enters the woods preceding Preston Brook Tunnel. There is a stop lock just south of the tunnel; it has only one gate. At the north end of the tunnel a notice announces that from here onwards one is on the Bridgewater Canal, covered in detail in book 3 of this series.

Dutton
Ches. PO, tel, stores, garage. Small settlement on top of Preston Brook Tunnel, at the end of the lane uphill from the south end of the tunnel. There is a large hospital up the road, and a pub.
Preston Brook Tunnel 1239yds long and forbidden to unpowered craft. No towpath. *On summer weekends and B. Hols* entry is as posted on the notices at each end. It is crooked, like Barnton and Saltersford Tunnels, and 2 boats cannot pass, so at other times, make sure it is clear before entering.

BOATYARDS

Ⓑ **Black Prince Narrowboats** Bartington Wharf, Acton Bridge, Northwich. (Weaverham 852945). S W D Pump-out, boat hire, gas, boat & engine repairs, mooring, chandlery, toilets, provisions. Trip boat 'Lapwing'.

PUBS

Talbot Arms Dutton. Food, garden.
Horns 200yds south of bridge 209 on A49. Food lunchtime and evenings.
Leigh Arms ¼ mile south of bridge 209, beside the Weaver. Sandwiches.

A BRIEF HISTORY OF BRITISH CANALS

River navigations, that is rivers widened and deepened to take large boats, had existed in England since the Middle Ages: some can even be traced back to Roman times. In 1600 there were 700 miles of navigable river in England, and by 1760, the dawn of the canal age, this number had been increased to 1300. This extensive network had prompted many developments later used by the canal engineers, for example, the lock system. But there were severe limitations: generally the routes were determined by the rivers and the features of the landscape and so were rarely direct. Also there were no east-west, or north-south connections.

Thus the demand for a direct inland waterway system increased steadily through the first half of the 18thC with the expansion of internal trade. Road improvements could not cope with this expansion, and so engineers and merchants turned to canals, used extensively on the continent.

One of the earliest pure canals, cut independently of existing rivers, was opened in 1745, at Newry in Northern Ireland, although some authorities consider the Fossdyke, cut by the Romans to link the rivers Trent and Witham, to be the first. However, the Newry is more important because it established the cardinal rule of all canals, the maintenance of an adequate water supply, a feature too often ignored by later engineers. The Newry Canal established the principle of a long summit level, fed by a reservoir to keep the locks at either end well supplied. Ten years later, in England, the Duke of Bridgewater decided to build a canal to provide an adequate transport outlet for his coal mines at Worsley. He employed the self-taught James Brindley as his engineer, and John Gilbert as surveyor, and launched the canal age in England. The Bridgewater Canal was opened in 1761. Its route, all on one level, was independent of all rivers; its scale of operations reflected the new power of engineering and the foresight of its creators. Although there were no locks, the engineering problems were huge; an aqueduct was built at Barton over the River Irwell, preceded by an embankment 900yds long; 15 miles of canal were built underground, so that boats could approach the coal face for loading—eventually there were 42 miles underground, including an inclined plane—the puddled clay method was used by Brindley to make the canal bed watertight. Perhaps most important of all, the canal was a success financially. Bridgewater invested the equivalent of £3 million of his own money in the project, and still made a profit.

Having shown that canals were both practical and financially sound, the Bridgewater aroused great interest throughout Britain. Plans were drawn up for a trunk canal, to link the 4 major rivers of England: the Thames, Severn, Mersey and Trent. This plan was eventually brought to fruition, but many years later than its sponsors imagined. Brindley was employed as engineer for the scheme, his reputation ensuring that he would always have more work than he could handle. The Trent and Mersey, and the Staffordshire and Worcestershire Canals received the Royal Assent in 1766, and the canal age began in earnest.

Canals, like the railways later, were built entirely by hand. Gangs of itinerant workmen were gathered together, drawn by the comparatively high pay. Once formed these armies of 'navigators'—hence 'navvies'—moved through the countryside as the canal was built, in many cases living off the land. All engineering problems had to be solved by manpower alone, aided by the horse and the occasional steam pump. Embankments, tunnels, aqueducts, all were built by these labouring armies kept under control only by the power of the section engineers and contractors.

The Staffordshire and Worcestershire Canal opened in 1770. In its design Brindley determined the size of the standard Midlands canal, which of course had direct influence on the rest of the English system as it was built. He chose a narrow canal, with locks 72ft 7in by 7ft 6in, partly for reasons of economy, and partly because he realised that the problems of an adequate water supply were far greater than most canal sponsors realised. This standard, which was also adopted for the Trent and Mersey, prompted the development of a special vessel, the narrow boat with its 30-ton payload. Ironically this decision by Brindley in 1766 ensured the failure of the canals as a commercial venture 200 years later, for by the middle of this century a 30-ton payload could no longer be worked economically.

The Trent and Mersey was opened in 1777; 93 miles long, the canal included 5 tunnels, the original one at Harecastle taking 11 years to build. In 1790 Oxford was finally reached and the junction with the Thames brought the 4 great rivers together. From the very start English canal companies were characterised by their intense rivalries; water supplies were jealously guarded, and constant wars were waged over toll prices. Many canals receiving the Royal Assent were never built, while others staggered towards conclusion, hampered by doubtful engineering, inaccurate estimates, and loans that they could never hope to pay off. Yet for a period canal mania gripped British speculators, as railway mania was to grip them 50 years later. The peak of British canal development came between 1791 and 1794, a period that gave rise to the opening of the major routes, the rise of the great canal engineers, Telford, Rennie and Jessop, and the greatest prosperity of those companies already operating. At this time the canal system had an effective monopoly over inland transport: the old trunk roads could not compete, coastal traffic was uncertain and hazardous, and the railways were still a future dream. This period also saw some of the greatest feats of engineering.

A contemporary view of canal promoters. *Eric de Maré.*

The turn of the century saw the opening of the last major cross-country routes; the Pennines were crossed by the Leeds and Liverpool Canal between 1770 and 1816, while the Kennet and Avon (opened in 1810) linked London and Bristol via the Thames. These 2 canals were built as broad navigations: already the realisation was dawning on canal operators that the limits imposed by the Brindley standard were too restrictive, a suspicion that was to be brutally confirmed by the coming of the railways. The Kennet and Avon, along with its rival the Thames and Severn, also marks the introduction of fine architecture to canals. Up till now canal architecture had been functional, often impressive, but clearly conceived by engineers. As a result, the Kennet and Avon has an architectural unity lacking in earlier canals. The appearance of architectural quality was matched by another significant change: canals became straighter, their engineers choosing as direct a route as possible, arguing that greater construction costs would be outweighed by smoother, quicker operation, whereas the early canals had followed the landscape. The Oxford is the prime example of a contour canal, meandering across the Midlands as though there were all the time in the world. It looks beautiful, its close marriage with the landscape makes it ideal as a pleasure waterway, but it was commercial folly.

The shortcomings of the early canals were exploited all too easily by the new railways. At first there was sharp competition by canals. Tolls were lowered, money was poured into route improvements; 14 miles of the Oxford's windings were cut out between 1829 and 1834; schemes were prepared to widen the narrow canals; the Harecastle Tunnel was doubled in 1827, the new tunnel taking 3 years to build (as opposed to 11 years for the old). But the race was lost from the start. The 19thC marks the rise of the railways and the decline of the canals. With the exception of the Manchester Ship Canal, the last major canal was the Birmingham and Liverpool Junction, opened in 1835. The system survived until this century, but the 1914–18 war brought the first closures, and through the 1930s the canal map adopted the shape it has today. Effective commercial carrying on narrow canals ceased in the early 1960s, although a few companies managed to survive until recently. However, with the end of commercial operation, a new role was seen for the waterways as a pleasure amenity, a 'linear national park 2000 miles long'.

Water supply has always been the cardinal element in both the running and the survival of any canal system. Locks need a constant supply of water—every boat passing through a wide lock on the Grand Union uses 96,000 gallons of

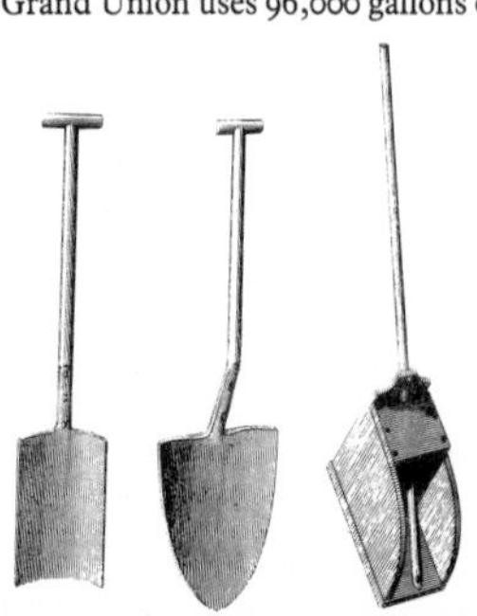

The rudimentary tools of the early 'navvies' *Hugh McKnight*

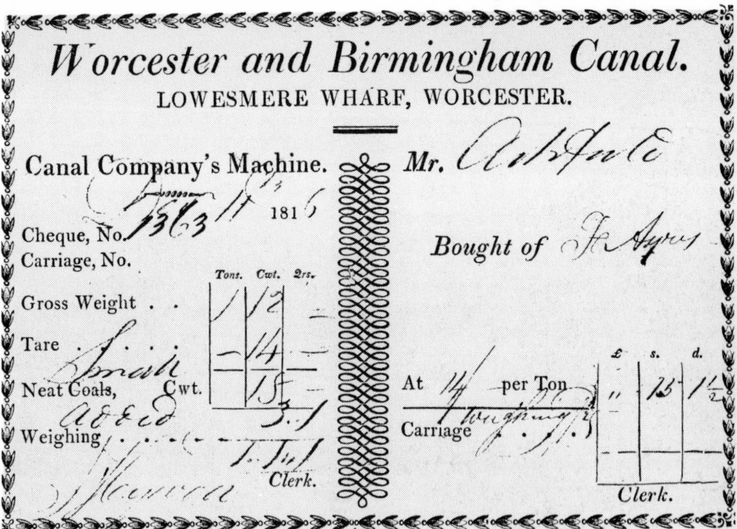

Worcester and Birmingham Canal.

LOWESMERE WHARF, WORCESTER.

Canal Company's Machine.

Mr.

181

Cheque, No.

Carriage, No.

Bought of

	Tons.	Cwt.	Qrs.
Gross Weight . .			
Tare			
Neat Coals, Cwt.			
Weighing			

Clerk.

	£	s.	d.
At per Ton			
Carriage . . .			

Clerk.

Printed by R. Jabet and Co. Herald Office, High-street, Birmingham.

Worcester and Birmingham Canal Company toll ticket dated 1816. *Hugh McKnight*

water. Generally 2 methods of supply were used: direct feed by rivers and streams, and feed by reservoirs sited along the summit level. The first suffered greatly from silting, and meant that the canal was dependent on the level of water in the river; the regular floods from the River Soar that overtake the Grand Union's Leicester line show the dangers of this. The second was more reliable, but many engineers were short-sighted in their provision of an adequate summit level. The otherwise well-planned Kennet and Avon always suffered from water shortage. Where shortages occurred, steam pumping engines were used to pump water taken down locks back up to the summit level. The Kennet and Avon was dependent upon pumped supplies, while the Birmingham Canal Navigations were fed by 6 reservoirs and 17 pumping engines. Some companies adopted side ponds alongside locks to save water, but this put the onus on the boatman and so had limited success. Likewise the stop locks still to be seen at junctions are a good example of 18thC company rivalry; an established canal would ensure that any proposed canal wishing to join it would have to lock *down* into the older canal, which thus gained a lock of water each time a boat passed through.

Where long flights or staircase locks existed there was always great wastage of water, and so throughout canal history alternative mechanical means of raising boats have been tried out. The inclined plane or the vertical lift were the favoured forms. Both worked on the counterbalance principle, the weight of the descending boat helping to raise the ascending. The first inclined plane was built at Ketley in 1788, and they were a feature of the west country Bude and Chard canals. The most famous plane was built at Foxton, and operated from 1900–10. Mechanical failure and excessive running costs ended the application of the inclined plane in England, although modern examples work very efficiently on the continent, notably in Belgium. The vertical lift was more unusual, although there were 8 on the Grand Western Canal. The most famous, built at Anderton in 1875, is still in operation, and stands as a monument to the ingenuity shown in the attempts to overcome the problems of water shortage.

Engineering features are the greatest legacy of the canal age, and of these, tunnels are the most impressive. The longest tunnel is at Standedge, on the now derelect Huddersfield Narrow Canal. The tunnel runs for 5456yds through the Pennines, at times 600ft below the surface. It is also on the highest summit level, 656ft above sea level. The longest navigable tunnel is now Dudley Tunnel, 3154yds, which was re-opened in 1973 after being closed for many years. Others of interest include the twin Harecastle Tunnels on the Trent and Mersey, the first 2897yds, and now disused, the second 2926yds; Sapperton, which carried the Thames and Severn Canal through the Cotswolds and Netherton on the Birmingham Canal Navigations. This last, built 1855–58, was the last in England, and was lit throughout by gas lights, and at a later date by electricity.

The Netherton Tunnel was built wide enough to allow for a towing path on both sides. Most tunnels have no towing path at all, and so boats had to be 'legged', or walked through.

The slowness and relative danger of legging in tunnels led to various attempts at mechanical propulsion. An endless rope pulled by a stationary steam engine at the tunnel mouth was tried out at Blisworth and Braunston between 1869 and 1871. Steam tugs were employed, an early application of mechanical power to canal boats, but their performance was greatly limited by lack of ventilation, not to mention the danger of suffocating the crew.

An electric tug was used at Harecastle from 1914 to 1954. The diesel engine made tunnel tug services much more practical, but diesel-powered narrow boats soon put the tugs out of business: by the 1930s most tunnels had to be navigated by whatever means the boatman chose to use. Legging continued at Crick, Husbands Bosworth and Saddington until 1939.

Until the coming of the diesel boats, the

Islington Tunnel during construction. *Hugh McKnight*

horse reigned supreme as a source of canal power. The first canals had used gangs of men to bow-haul the boats, a left over from the river navigations where 50–80 men, or 12 horses, would pull a 200-ton barge. By 1800 the horse had taken over, and was used throughout the heyday of the canal system. In fact horse towage survived as long as large-scale commercial operation. Generally 1 horse or mule was used per boat, a system unmatched for cheapness and simplicity. The towing path was carried from one side of the canal to the other by turnover bridges, a common feature that reveals the total dominance of the horse. Attempts to introduce self-propelled canal boats date from 1793, although most early experiments concerned tugs towing dumb barges. Development was limited by the damage caused by wash, a problem that still applies today, and the first fleets of self-propelled steam narrow boats were not in service until the last quarter of the 19thC. Fellows, Morton and Clayton, and the Leeds and Liverpool Carrying Co ran large fleets of steam boats between 1880 and 1931, by which time most had been converted to diesel operation. With the coming of mechanical power the butty boat principle was developed: a powered narrow boat would tow a dumb 'butty' boat, thereby doubling the load without doubling the running costs. This system became standard until the virtual ending by the late 1960s of carrying on the narrow canals. Before the coming of railways, passenger services were run on the canals; packet boats, specially built narrow boats with passenger accommodation, ran express services, commanding the best horses and the unquestioned right of way over all other traffic. Although the railways killed this traffic, the last scheduled passenger service survived on the Gloucester and Berkeley Canal until 1935.

The traditional narrow boat with its colourful decoration and meticulous interior has become a symbol of English canals. However this was in fact a late development. The shape of the narrow boat was determined by Brindley's original narrow canal specification, but until the late 19thC boats were unpainted, and carried all male crews. Wages were sufficient for the crews to maintain their families at home. The increase in railway competition brought a reduction in wages, and so bit by bit the crews were forced to take their families with them, becoming a kind of water gipsy. The confines of a narrow boat cabin presented the same problems as a gipsy caravan, and so the families found a similar answer. Their eternally wandering home achieved individuality by extravagant and colourful decoration, and the traditional narrow boat painting was born. The extensive symbolic vocabulary available to the painters produced a sign language that only these families could understand, and the canal world became far more enclosed, although outwardly it was more decorative. As the canals have turned from commerce to pleasure, so the traditions of the families have died out, and the families themselves have faded away. But their language survives, although its meaning has mostly vanished with them. This survival gives the canals their characteristic decorative qualities, which make them so attractive to the pleasure boater and to the casual visitor.

FISHING

Many anglers start their fishing careers on the canals and navigable rivers, mainly because our system of waterways has always offered excellent opportunities for the thousands of angling enthusiasts throughout Great Britain.

Most of these cross-country waterways have natural reed-fringed and grassy banks, and in addition to the delightful surroundings the fishing is generally good. In most areas there has been a steady improvement in canal fishing in recent years and in many places new stocks of fish have been introduced. The popular quarry are roach, perch and bream, but the canals also hold dace, tench, chub and carp in places, in addition to pike and other species in particular areas.

Canals afford good hunting grounds for those seeking specimen fish (that is, fish above average size) and these are liable to be encountered on almost any water. The canals also make good venues for competition fishing, and in most places nowadays matches are held regularly at weekends throughout the season.

The Statutory Close Season for coarse fish is March 15 to June 15 inclusive, but in some areas, notably the Yorkshire River Authority, the Close Season is from February 28 to May 31. The Close Season for pike in some areas is March 15 to September 30.

Permits and fishing rights

Most parts of the waterways system are available to anglers. The big angling associations—e.g. the London AA, Birmingham AA, Reading & District AA, Coventry & District AA, Nottingham AA plus many smaller clubs—rent fishing rights over extensive areas on the system. In most cases, day tickets are available.

On arrival at the water-side it is always advisable to make enquiries as to who holds the fishing rights, and to obtain a permit if one is required *before* starting to fish. Remember, also, that a River Authority rod licence is usually required in addition to a fishing permit. It is essential to obtain this licence from the relevant River Authority *before* starting to fish. Some fishing permits and licences are issued by bailiffs along the bank, but local enquiry will help to determine this.

A canalside pub or a local fishing tackle shop are good places to enquire if permission or day tickets are required for the local stretch of water. Canal lock keepers are usually knowledgeable about the fishing rights in the immediate locality, and often a lock keeper may be found who issues day tickets on behalf of an angling association, or owner. It is likely that he will also know some of the better fishing areas, as well as local methods and baits which may be considered most successful.

The fishing rights on most canals are owned by the British Waterways Board and many miles of good fishing are leased to clubs and angling associations. They also issue day tickets on certain lengths, so it is worth enquiring at the local British Waterways office when planning a trip. Special arrangements are made for fishing from boats; again, enquire with the BWB locally.

'Private fishing' notices should *not* be ignored. If the owner's name and address is on the board then application can be made for permission for a future occasion. Once permission has been obtained it would be advisable to find out if there are any restrictions imposed, since some clubs and associations ban certain baits, or have restrictions on live-baiting for pike: and on some fisheries pike fishing is not allowed before a specified date.

Other restrictions may concern size-limits of fish, and this certainly applies to the London AA canal fisheries. Some River Authority bye-laws prohibit the retention of under-sized fish in keep nets. A local club holding the fishing rights may have imposed their own size-limits in order to protect certain species. Such restrictions are generally printed on permits and licences.

Tackle

In the slow moving, sluggish waters of canals the float tackle needs to be light and lines fine in order to catch fish. When fishing for roach and dace lines of 1½lb to 2lb breaking strain are the maximum strength normally needed in order to get the fish to take a bait—particularly when the water is clear, or on the popular reaches that are 'hard-fished'.

Fine tackle also means small hooks, sizes 16 and 18—or even as small as 22 at times. Such light gear is also effective when fishing for the smaller species, such as gudgeon and bleak. This tackle will require a well-balanced float to show the slightest indication of a bite.

Bait

Baits should be small, and maggots, casters (maggot chrysalis), hempseed, wheat, tiny cubes of bread crust, or a small pinch of flake (the white crumb of a new loaf) may take fish. It always pays to experiment with baits; bait that is effective on one occasion will not necessarily prove to be as effective the next. With slight variations, similar fishing methods can be used effectively on the majority of waterways.

Northern anglers who regularly compete in contests on canals use bloodworms as bait. They have become extremely skilful in using this tiny bait and often take fish on bloodworms when all other baits fail. Bloodworms are the larvae of a midge, and are a perfectly natural bait. The anglers gather the bloodworms from the mud and, apart from a wash in clean water, the baits are ready for use.

A popular groundbait that has had great success is known as 'black magic'! This is a mixture of garden peat and bread crumbs mixed

Barbel
Bleak
Bullhead
Common Bream
Common Carp
Chub
Dace
Freshwater Eel
Gudgeon
River Lamprey
Perch
Minnow
Roach
Pike
Rudd
Ruffe
Stickleback
Tench
Brown Trout

dry and carried to the water. When dampened and mixed it can be thrown in in the usual way. The basis of most groundbaits is bread, and many other materials may be added, although stodgy mixtures should be avoided when canal fishing. Canals are not waters which respond to heavy groundbaiting tactics. It is far better to use a cloud-bait, and this can be purchased ready for use. Some successful Midland anglers wet their cloudbait with milk instead of water to increase the cloud effect.

Methods

Once the swim—that is the area of water to be fished—has been decided upon, and the tackle set up, use a plummet to find the depth and adjust the float, but be cautious when doing so in clear waters. At times it may be best to find the depth by trial and error. Often most fish will be caught from around mid-water level, but always be prepared to move the float further up the line in order to present the bait closer to the bottom, where the bigger fish are usually to be found. At frequent intervals toss a few samples of the hook-bait into the top of the swim to keep the fish interested.

Fish in different waters may vary in the way they take a bait and this creates a different bite registration. It may be found that fish take the hook-bait quickly, causing the float to dip sharply or dive under the surface. The strike should be made instantly, on the downward movement. On some canals the fish are even quicker—and perhaps gentler—not taking the float under at all, and in this case the strike should be made at the slightest unusual movement of the float.

Roach and dace abound in many lengths and although working the float tackle down with a flow of water takes most fish, better quality fish—including bream—are usually to be taken by fishing a laying-on style, with the bait lying on the bottom. This method can often be best when fishing areas where there is no flow at all. This is done with float tackle, adjusted to make the distance from float to hook greater than the depth of water, so that when the float is at the surface the bait and lower length of line are lying on the bottom.

The alternative method of fishing the bottom is by legering, the main difference in the methods being in the bite indication. Without a float a bite is registered at the rod-tip where, if need be, a quiver-tip or swing-tip may be fitted. These bite detectors are used extensively on Midland and Northern waters. Legering is a method often used in the south, where in some southern canals barbel and chub are quite prolific. These species grow to good sizes in canal waters—chub up to 7lb and barbel up to 14lb have been taken—but these are exceptional and the average run of fish would be well below those weights. Nevertheless, both species are big fish and big baits and hooks may be used when fishing for them.

Many bigger than average fish—of all species—have been taken by fishing the bait on the bottom. Whatever the style of leger fishing, always choose the lightest possible lead weight, and position it some 12 to 18in up from the hook. There are no hard and fast rules governing the distance between lead and hook, so it pays to experiment to find the best to suit the conditions.

Anglers who regularly fish the Northern and Midland canals invariably use tiny size 20 and 22 hooks, tied to a mere ¾lb breaking strain line, and when float-fishing use a tiny quill float—porcupine or crow quill. A piece of peacock quill is useful because it can be cut with scissors to make it suit prevailing conditions. Such small floats only need a couple of dust-shot to balance them correctly, and usually the Midland anglers position this shot on the line just under the float so that the bait is presented naturally. Once the tackle has been cast out, the bait falls slowly through the water along with hook-bait samples, which are thrown in at the same time. This is called 'fishing on the drop'. A fine cloud-bait is also used with this style.

Canals which have luxuriant weed growth harbour many small fish, which are preyed upon by perch. These move in shoals and invariably the perch in a shoal are much the same size. Usually the really big perch are solitary, so it pays to rove the canal and search for them. They are to be caught from almost any canal and although they may be caught by most angling methods, the most effective is usually float-fishing. The fishing depth can vary according to conditions, time of year, and actual depth of the canal, so it pays to try the bait at varying depths. The usual baits for perch are worms, small live-baits (minnows etc) and maggots. Close by wooden lock gates is often the haunt of large perch.

In certain places canals and rivers come together and take on the characteristics of the river (i.e. with an increased flow) and different methods are needed. These places are often noted for splendid chub (and sometimes barbel) in addition to roach and other species. Trotting the stream is a popular and effective fishing style.

Weather

Weather conditions have to be taken into consideration. Canals usually run through open country and catch the slightest breeze. Even a moderate wind will pull and bob the float, which in turn will agitate the baited hook. If bites are not forthcoming under such conditions then it may be best to remove the float and try a straightforward leger arrangement.

When legering, the effects of the wind can be avoided by keeping the rod top down to within an inch or two of the water level—or even by sinking the rod-tip below the surface. Anglers in the North and Midlands have devised a wind-shield for legering that protects the rod-tip from the wind and improves bite detection. Nevertheless, in some circumstances a slight wind can be helpful because if a moderate breeze is blowing it will put a ripple on the water, and this can be of assistance in fishing in clear waters.

Where to fish

Most canals are narrow and this makes it possible to cast the tackle towards the far bank, where fish may have moved because they had been disturbed from the near bank. Disturbance will send the fish up or downstream and often well away from the fishing area. So always approach the water quietly, and remember to move cautiously at all times. When making up the tackle to start fishing it is advisable to do so as far back from the water as possible to avoid scaring the fish. It pays to move slowly, to keep as far from the bank as possible, and to avoid clumping around in heavy rubber boots. If there is cover along the bank—shrubs, bushes, tall reeds and clumps of yellow flag iris—the wise angler will make full use of it.

There are some canals that are no longer navigable, and these are generally weedy. At certain times in the season the surface of the water disappears under a green mantle of floating duckweed, which affords cover and security for the fish. It is possible to have the best sport by fishing in the pockets of clear water that are to be found.

Some canals have prolific growths of water lilies in places, and are particularly attractive for angling. They always look ideal haunts for tench, but they can also be rather difficult places from which to land good fish. Tench are more or less evenly distributed throughout the canals and the best are found where weed growth is profuse. It may be best to fish small areas of clear water between the weeds. Groundbait can encourage tench to move out from the weed beds, and to feed once they are out. Sometimes it is an advantage to clear a swim by dragging out weeds or raking the bottom. This form of natural groundbaiting stirs the silt, which clouds the water and disturbs aquatic creatures on which the fish feed.

Bream seem to do well in canals and some fairly good fish up to 5lb may be taken. Any deep pools or winding holes (shown as ↶ on map) are good places to try, particularly when fishing a canal for the first time.

Other places worth fishing are 'cattle drinks' regularly used by farm animals. These make useful places to fish for bream, roach and dace. The frequent use of these drinking holes colours the water, as the animals stir up the mud, and disturb various water creatures. The coloured water draws fish into the area—on the downstream side of the cattle drink when there is the slightest flow.

Pike are to be found in every canal in the country—they are predators, feeding on small fish (which gives a sure indication of the most effective baits). Any small live fish presented on float tackle will take pike. The best places to fish are near weed beds and boats that have been moored in one place a long time.

Many of our canals are cut through pleasant and peaceful countryside, and this enables anglers to spend many delightful hours along the banks—and always with the chance of making a good catch. As a general rule, never fish in locks on navigable canals, or anywhere that could obstruct the free passage of boats. Remember that you will inconvenience yourself as well as the boatman if you have to move in a hurry, or risk a broken line. Never leave discarded line or lead weights on the bank, and never throw these items into the water. Waterfowl become entangled in the line, and are poisoned by the lead shot, which they swallow when grubbing for food. All responsible anglers take their spoilt tackle home with them, where it can be disposed of safely.

The BWB Fisheries Officer at Watford welcomes specific enquiries about fishing on BWB canals from individuals, associations and clubs. He will also supply the name and address of the current Secretary of each Angling Association in the country.

Charles Mackerras

Edited by

Nigel Simeone and John Tyrrell

THE BOYDELL PRESS

First published 2015
The Boydell Press, Woodbridge

ISBN 978 1 84383 966 8

The Boydell Press is an imprint of Boydell & Brewer Ltd
PO Box 9, Woodbridge, Suffolk IP12 3DF, UK
and of Boydell & Brewer Inc.
668 Mount Hope Ave, Rochester, NY 14620–2731, USA
website: www.boydellandbrewer.com

A catalogue record for this book is available from the British Library

This publication is printed on acid-free paper

Designed and typeset in Warnock Pro and Myriad Pro
by David Roberts, Pershore, Worcestershire

Printed and bound in Great Britain by
TJ International Ltd. Padstow, Cornwall

For Cathy
and
in memory of her mother
Judy Mackerras

Contents

Illustrations

Plates (between pp. 106 and 107)

Text figures

Abbreviations

AO	Australian Opera
BBC	British Broadcasting Corporation
CBSO	City of Birmingham Symphony Orchestra
CM	Charles Mackerras
CPO	Czech Philharmonic Orchestra
d.	designer
ENO	English National Opera
FOK	Symphony Orchestra of the Capital City Prague FOK
JM	Judy Mackerras
LPO	London Philharmonic Orchestra
LSO	London Symphony Orchestra
Met	Metropolitan Opera, New York City
NT	National Theatre
OA	Opera Australia
OAE	Orchestra of the Age of Enlightenment
p.	producer/stage director
perf(s)	performance(s)
PRO	Prague Radio Orchestra
QEH	Queen Elizabeth Hall
RAH	Royal Albert Hall
RAM	Royal Academy of Music
RFH	Royal Festival Hall
RLPO	Royal Liverpool Philharmonic Orchestra
ROH	Royal Opera House, Covent Garden
RPO	Royal Philharmonic Orchestra
SCO	Scottish Chamber Orchestra
SDH	St David's Hall
SO	Symphony Orchestra
SWO	Sadler's Wells Opera
WNO	Welsh National Opera

Preface and Acknowledgments

THE idea for this book came originally from members of the Mackerras family, particularly Charles's widow, Judy, who saw the text in proof before her death on 13 December 2014, his daughter Catherine (Cathy) and his sisters Joan and Elizabeth. Since both authors have been passionate admirers of Mackerras's conducting for many years, it was an opportunity we relished. At our initial meeting with Cathy, she encouraged us to develop the project as we thought best, and offered generous support. This included access to her father's private papers, which has enabled us to publish a number of letters and documents for the first time, shedding light on several significant aspects of his career and his working methods. An important consideration from the outset was how our book could usefully complement Nancy Phelan's admirable 1987 biography, *Charles Mackerras: A Musician's Musician*. One obvious way was to concentrate on the years since Phelan's book was published, which included some of the busiest and most rewarding of Charles's career. Moreover, this book was an opportunity to evaluate the whole of a remarkable life in music. To do that more effectively, we decided to include chapters on specific composers and on his relationships with particular musicians, opera companies and orchestras.

This book is neither a conventional biography, nor is it a symposium, but it aims to combine elements of both: chapters on periods in Mackerras's career are interwoven with more specialised essays and shorter contributions which aim to illuminate his approach to music-making from those who saw it at close quarters. To do this effectively, we asked a number of people who worked closely with Mackerras to write about their collaborations with him. The response from all those we asked was unfailingly positive, and their contributions are informative as well as affectionate, helping the reader to understand more fully how he worked and some of the life-long musical enthusiasms that drove him. Specialist chapters include consideration of Mackerras's crucial work on behalf of Czech composers, particularly Janáček and Martinů, and his devotion to Sullivan's music is also explored.

The list of composers in which Mackerras had a profound interest ranged far and wide: it would have been just as appropriate to have included chapters on, say, Handel, Mozart, Beethoven, Donizetti, Brahms, Strauss and Delius – but space was not limitless. The broader biographical chapters aim to include discussion of some of the composers with whom Mackerras was most closely associated but who are not the focus of individual chapters. The most obvious of these is Mozart: his *Marriage of Figaro*, in particular, was an emblematic work throughout Mackerras's career – not only because it was probably his favourite opera (along with *Hansel and Gretel*), but also because it inspired some of his most exciting and important musicological endeavours. The same could just as easily be said for Handel, starting with the famous recordings of the *Fireworks Music* in 1959 and *Messiah* in the mid-1960s. His closeness to Britten in the 1950s (as musical director of the English Opera Group, and as the first conductor of *Noye's Fludde*) is well known, and Mackerras spoke frankly after Britten's death about the circumstances of their falling out in 1958. But what came as a heartening surprise was the warmth of Britten's hitherto unpublished correspondence from the mid-1960s, carefully preserved in a file which Mackerras labelled 'Important Documents'.

The private Mackerras family archives are extensive and have been a priceless source of new and unpublished material. Mackerras's extensive correspondence with his family and friends has proved a rich seam – including some vibrant and lively letters to his mother, Catherine, as well as correspondence with composers, conductors and singers. Later in life, Mackerras was a devoted user of the fax machine, and a series of admirable secretaries saw to it that his often amazingly detailed letters and faxes were carefully filed. None was more assiduous than his last secretary, Mina Dell, who was able to tell us how everything had been arranged (as well as sharing her memories of working at Hamilton Terrace). These archives are also the source of almost all the illustrations in the book. Eventually this large collection of papers and documents will join the scores and orchestral parts that have already been given to the Royal Academy of Music, but at present they remain within the family. Unless otherwise stated, all quotations from correspondence, diaries and other unpublished papers are from material in the Mackerras family archives.

Our gratitude to all our contributors is enormous: they include singers, instrumental soloists, orchestral players, musicologists, a stage director, administrators and fellow conductors. We thank all of them: Dame Janet Baker, Alfred Brendel, Aleš Březina, Alexander Briger, Rosenna East, Dame Anne Evans, Sir Nicholas Hytner, Simon Keenlyside, David Lloyd-Jones, David Mackie, Chi-chi Nwanoku, Sir Antonio Pappano, John Stein, Heinz Stolba, Patrick Summers, Malcolm Walker, David Whelton and Jiří Zahrádka. Their contributions focus variously on Mackerras as a musician who was an inspiring presence on the podium and in rehearsal, a ceaselessly inquiring interpreter, a pioneer in historically informed performance, a pragmatist who could animate and energise, an ambassador for Czech music, a brilliant orchestrator and arranger, and a conductor who was constantly alert to how musicology could inform his work on the concert platform or in the pit of an opera house.

Warmest thanks go to the numerous members of the Mackerras family who have encouraged our work and shared their memories. Charles's sisters, Elizabeth Briger and Joan Hall, provided copies of correspondence and other documents as well as their own lively reminiscences. At the start of this project, Joan's interest in what we were doing – supplemented by packages of interesting programmes and photocopies of letters – helped us to establish some of the aspects of Charles's career that our book could explore. Like their brother, Elizabeth and Joan combine enthusiasm with scrupulous attention to detail, and they have answered our questions with patience and wit. The conductor Alex Briger spent a day talking to us about his uncle, not only with humour, frankness and affection but also with the insights of a fellow musician. Other members of the family, including Peter, Chloe and Daniel Templeton, Graeme and Bartholomew Hall and Peter Brook, all helped to fill out the portrait of Charles's personality – especially during his later years – and all gave generously of their time. Two of those closest to Charles have our heartfelt gratitude. His widow, Judy, allowed us to make numerous visits to her flat in order to consult correspondence, photographs, scores and recordings, and to reminisce about her husband. Their daughter Cathy has been a wellspring of energy and kindness throughout the genesis of this book. Nothing has been too much trouble for her, and she has been a constant source of reassurance and support.

A number of others have helped in various ways. These include John Allison, Sigrid Arnold, Mark Audus, Clive Barda, Nick Clark, Matthias Creutziger, Jonathan Crown, Sophie Dand, Michal Dejmal, Mina Dell, Don Draper, David Gideon, Fflur Huysmans, Rosie Johnson, Sarah Lenton, Rosemary Lowther, Rodney Milnes, Isabel Murphy, Michael Pedersen, Simon Rees, Peter Reynolds, Ronald Schneider, Jan Smaczny, John Snelson, Neville Sumpter, Robin Thomson, Sacha Wagner, Christopher Webb and Louise Wylie. The online archive of *Opera* magazine has been an invaluable resource, and Northamptonshire Library Service has provided free access to a number of essential newspaper archives. A special word of thanks is due to Kathy Adamson, Librarian at the Royal Academy of Music, for making us so welcome on research visits to the Mackerras Collection at the RAM. We are particularly indebted to the Dvořák Society for its generous subvention to commemorate its long-term patron, Charles Mackerras.

Grateful acknowledgment is made to the Trustees of the Britten–Pears Foundation for allowing us to publish the Britten letters to Mackerras, which are the copyright of the Britten–Pears Foundation, Aldeburgh, and to all the other correspondents and authors who have kindly granted permission to use their work. The editors are also grateful to the following publications for permission to quote from reviews: *Gramophone*, the *Herald* (Glasgow), the *Guardian*, the *Independent*, the *Musical Times*, the *Observer*, *Opera*, the *Daily Telegraph* and *Sunday Telegraph*, *The Times* and the *Sunday Times*. Every effort has been made to trace copyright holders and to obtain their permission for the use of material quoted in this book.

At Boydell & Brewer our thanks go to Michael Middeke, Megan Milan, Rohais Haughton and Rosie Pearce. Naomi Laredo was a most helpful copy-editor, and David Roberts produced the stylish design of the book.

Finally, thanks of a more personal nature go to Jasmine Simeone and Jim Friedman for their constant support.

Nigel Simeone and John Tyrrell, December 2014

About the Contributors

Dame Janet Baker was one of the finest mezzo-sopranos of her day, incomparable as a recitalist and a much-loved performer on the stages of the leading British opera houses. She had a particular rapport with Mackerras, singing on his recording of Handel's *Messiah* and in several memorable roles at ENO, including Charlotte (*Werther*) and the title roles in *Mary Stuart* and Handel's *Julius Caesar*. Her retirement from the operatic stage included two operas conducted by Mackerras: Gluck's *Alceste* at the ROH and *Mary Stuart* at ENO.

Alfred Brendel KBE has been renowned for his masterly interpretations of the piano music of Haydn, Mozart, Beethoven, Schubert, Brahms and Liszt for well over half a century. His final public appearance was in 2008, with Mackerras conducting the Vienna Philharmonic. They collaborated regularly, especially in performances of the Mozart piano concertos, several of which they recorded with the SCO. A stimulating thinker as well as musician, he has continued to develop his writing career since retiring from the concert stage.

Aleš Březina is a Czech composer and musicologist. He has been the Director of the Bohuslav Martinů Institute in Prague since 1994. He is Chairman of the Editorial Board of the Bohuslav Martinů Collected Critical Edition and has prepared many of Martinů's compositions for revised or Urtext publications. Encouraged by Mackerras, he reconstructed the first version of *The Greek Passion*, first performed at Bregenz in 1999 and subsequently conducted by Mackerras at the Royal Opera House. He has published in Czech and foreign journals and lectured in Europe and the USA.

Alexander Briger is a conductor who has worked extensively in Europe and Australia, and he is founder of the Australian World Orchestra. Born in Sydney, he studied at the city's Conservatorium and later in Munich. He worked closely with Boulez and the Ensemble InterContemporain, and on numerous projects with Mackerras, his uncle. The Australian World Orchestra was founded in Sydney in 2011, bringing together Australia's most successful musicians from around the world. Its inaugural concerts were given in memory of Mackerras.

Rosenna East is a violinist. She was a member of the SCO from 2005 until 2014, working regularly with Sir Charles Mackerras in the last years of his life. She writes for a variety of publications, including *The Herald*, *Classical Music Magazine* and *Gramophone online*. Rosenna presents and curates live arts events for a number of establishments, also broadcasting for BBC Radio Scotland. She teaches at St Mary's Music School, Edinburgh, and is Chair of the Board of Noise Opera. Her work with children in post-conflict communities has taken her to Bosnia, Croatia, Sri Lanka and Palestine.

Dame Anne Evans began her career at Sadler's Wells Opera and performed many roles under Mackerras at SWO/ENO. After four triumphant seasons as Brünnhilde in the Bayreuth Festival *Ring* conducted by Barenboim, she subsequently sang Isolde in the WNO *Tristan und Isolde* with Mackerras. She retired in 2003 with a performance of scenes from *Der Rosenkavalier* at the Proms, conducted by Mackerras, who coaxed her out of retirement for a Wagner concert to celebrate his eightieth birthday in 2005.

Sir Nicholas Hytner was Artistic Director of the National Theatre in London from 2003 to 2015. One of his first posts was as assistant to Colin Graham at English National Opera and beyond the NT some of his greatest successes have been in opera and musical theatre. He worked closely with Mackerras on three productions: *Xerxes* (ENO), *The Cunning Little Vixen* (Paris Châtelet) and *Così fan tutte* (Glyndebourne).

Simon Keenlyside CBE is one of today's most acclaimed baritones, equally successful in opera and as a lieder singer. With Mackerras he sang two of the great Mozart baritone roles at the ROH: Papageno in *The Magic Flute* (which he also sang on Mackerras's Chandos recording) and the title role in *Don Giovanni* in Francesco Zambello's production, released on DVD.

David Lloyd-Jones began his career in 1959 on the music staff of the Royal Opera House and in 1972 became Associate Conductor to Mackerras at ENO. Here he conducted an extensive repertoire, which include the British stage premieres of Prokofiev's *War and Peace* and Iain Hamilton's *The Royal Hunt of the Sun*. He was appointed founding Music Director of Opera North in 1978 and in twelve years conducted over fifty new productions. Since then he has travelled the world conducting operas and concerts and has made over sixty recordings (including *Pineapple Poll*). He is an Honorary Member of the Royal Philharmonic Society.

David Mackie joined the D'Oyly Carte Opera Company as repetiteur in 1975. He became chorus master and associate musical director in 1976, serving until the closure of the company in 1982. Since 1982 he has worked as a freelance accompanist, repetiteur and conductor. In collaboration with Charles Mackerras he reconstructed Sullivan's 'lost' Cello Concerto, and in 1989 he wrote and presented fourteen interval talks on BBC Radio 2 for the network's series of the complete Gilbert and Sullivan operas.

Chi-chi Nwanoku MBE is a double bass player and founding member of the Orchestra of the Age of Enlightenment and the chamber ensemble Endymion. As principal double bass of the OAE she played regularly for Mackerras from 1987 until his death, including his very last performance of *Così fan tutte* at Glyndebourne. During her childhood she excelled at both music (initially as a pianist) and sport (as a sprinter), before devoting herself to the double bass, which she studied at the Royal Academy of Music and with Franco Petracchi in Italy.

Sir Antonio Pappano has been Music Director of the Royal Opera House since 2002 and is also Music Director of the Orchestra dell'Accademia nazionale di Santa Cecilia. He has conducted a vast operatic repertoire at the ROH, from Mozart to the world premieres of Birtwistle's *The Minotaur* and Turnage's *Anna Nicole*. Pappano invited Mackerras to conduct numerous productions at the ROH, ranging from Handel to Janáček.

Nigel Simeone is a writer and teacher. His books include *Janáček's Works* (a previous collaboration with John Tyrrell, dedicated by the authors to Charles Mackerras) and, most recently, *The Leonard Bernstein Letters*. He has published extensively on Messiaen (co-author of an admired biography, also translated into French) and on music in Paris, and has written on conductors from the nineteenth century to the present. Since 2003 he has reviewed new and historic recordings for *International Record Review* and he has been a contributor to several broadcasts in the BBC Radio 4 series *Tales from the Stave*.

John Stein was co-founder of the Welsh National Opera Orchestra and its leader from its formation in 1970 until 2008. He led the orchestra throughout Mackerras's time as Music Director of WNO and at his subsequent performances with the company. After working closely for many years, they established the Sir Charles Mackerras Orchestral Leader Scholarship at the Royal Welsh College of Music and Drama in 2008, with Stein as its tutor.

Heinz Stolba joined the staff of the Viennese publisher Universal Edition as an editor in 1987 and is now the head of its editorial department. He devotes his working time to the music of Leoš Janáček, Gustav Mahler, Alban Berg, Béla Bartók, Alexander Zemlinsky, Arnold Schoenberg and Kurt Weill, as well as many other composers.

Patrick Summers has been Artistic and Music Director of Houston Grand Opera since 1998. He worked closely with Mackerras at San Francisco Opera in the 1990s. As well as conducting a wide operatic repertoire from Handel to Strauss, he has also advocated important new works by Philip Glass, Jake Heggie, Carlisle Floyd and others. Along with guest engagements at the Met and San Francisco (where he succeeded Mackerras as Principal Guest Conductor) he has also conducted regularly at the Bregenz Festival.

John Tyrrell is Honorary Professor of Music at Cardiff University. His books on Janáček include the two-volume biography *Janáček: Years of a Life*, currently being translated into Czech. With Charles Mackerras he edited the 'Brno 1908' version of *Jenůfa*, which restored Janáček's original intentions and which has been extensively performed throughout the world. John Tyrrell was awarded honorary doctorates for his work on Janáček and Czech music by the Masaryk University of Brno and the Janáček Academy of Performing Arts.

Malcolm Walker is a recording industry historian and discographer. He joined EMI in 1959, becoming Classical Press Officer (1963–65). He was Assistant Editor (1966–72) and later Editor (1972–80) of *Gramophone*, and Contributing Editor of *Gramophone Classical Catalogue*, later *CD Catalogue* (1980–99). He worked for EMI Classics as Discographical Consultant (1999–2012) and is currently a consultant for Warner Classics. He has compiled over 50 discographies (including the Mackerras discography in Phelan 1987) in addition to articles on the classical recording industry.

David Whelton has been Managing Director of the Philharmonia Orchestra since 1988. He trained as a pianist and organist before taking up appointments at the Yorkshire Arts Association and the Arts Council of Great Britain. He persuaded Mackerras to become the Philharmonia's Principal Guest Conductor in 2002 and worked closely with him over the next decade.

Jiří Zahrádka PhD is curator of the Janáček collections of the Moravian Museum in Brno and teaches at the Institute of Musicology of Masaryk University. His work on Janáček includes a book (in Czech and English) on Janáček and the National Theatre in Brno, specialist chapters in John Tyrrell's Janáček biography and critical editions of *Šárka, The Excursions of Mr Brouček, Fate, The Cunning Little Vixen, The Makropulos Affair* (several in collaboration with Mackerras), the *Sinfonietta* and the *Glagolitic Mass*, as well as several chamber works. He is dramaturg of the biennial International Janáček Festival in Brno.

Charles Mackerras: A Chronology

1925 born (17 November), Schenectady, New York, to Australian parents
1928 family moves to Sydney, Australia
1932 studies violin, later piano and flute
1933 takes part in annual Gilbert and Sullivan productions at his school, St Aloysius College
1933 first compositions (song settings)
1933 hears first opera (*Carmen*) and is immediately opera-struck
1937 attends Sydney Grammar School, devoting much time to musical activities
1938 conducts student performance of *Bastien und Bastienne* at the New South Wales Conservatorium of Music
1939 composes opera and a cantata, *Marsyas*, performed at the Conservatorium
1940 boards at The King's School; runs away several times and is expelled
1941 studies oboe, piano and composition at the Conservatorium; earns additional income from performing on commercial radio and writing orchestral scores from recordings
1943 joins ABC Sydney Orchestra as second oboist
1944 becomes principal oboist with ABC Sydney Orchestra
1944 music for film *The Fighting Rats of Tobruk*
1946 music for film *Namatjira the Painter*
1947 sails for England (6 February) on one of the first passenger ships to leave Sydney after the war, stopping briefly on Pitcairn Island, where he hears the islanders singing a decorated version of *God Save the King*
1947 lands at Tilbury (20 March)
1947 auditions for BBC Symphony Orchestra (2 April); not taken on, but given encouragement by Sir Adrian Boult
1947 temporary work with BBC Scottish Orchestra before joining SWO as second oboist, cor anglais player and repetiteur (12 May)
1947 marries Judy Wilkins, a clarinettist with SWO (22 August)
1947 awarded a British Council Scholarship to study conducting in Czechoslovakia at the Academy of Music in Prague
1947 CM and JM leave for Czechoslovakia (24 September)
1947 hears his first Janáček opera, *Káťa Kabanová*, at Prague NT, conducted by Václav Talich (15 October)
1948 after the Communist coup (February), Václav Talich is dismissed from his post at Prague NT and is able to give CM private conducting lessons
1948 conducting lessons at Academy with Karel Ančerl; befriends conducting student Milan Munclinger
1948 CM and JM rent flat at 12 Pembridge Crescent, Notting Hill Gate (August)
1948 rejoins SWO as repetiteur/conductor (September) (to 1954)

1948 conducting debut at SWO in *Die Fledermaus* (20 October)

1949 birth of first daughter, Fiona (8 August)

1949–50 conducts operas in London and on tour (*Bartered Bride, Fledermaus, Pagliacci, Barber of Seville, Madame Butterfly* and first Mozart opera, *Così fan tutte*)

1950 conducts several operas at WNO

1950 birth of second daughter, Catherine (17 November)

1951 conducts premiere of his ballet *Pineapple Poll*, arranged from Sullivan's music (13 March)

1951 conducts the London premiere of *Káťa Kabanová*, the first Janáček opera staged in the UK (10 April)

1951 conducts *The Marriage of Figaro* at SWO (23 October)

1952 CM and JM buy a semi-detached house in Templars Crescent, Finchley

1954 conducts premiere of his ballet *The Lady and the Fool*, arranged from music from Verdi's lesser-known operas (31 March)

1954 principal conductor of the BBC Concert Orchestra (to 1956)

1954 first experience in television opera as assistant conductor, later as chief conductor

1955 conducts Philharmonia Orchestra for the first time, for recording of *The Lady and the Fool* (9 June)

1956 principal conductor of English Opera Group (to 1958)

1956 summer holiday at Donaueschingen, where CM consults early score of *Figaro*

1957 BBC broadcast of 'Vocal Embellishments in Mozart' (including decorated arias from *Figaro*), with CM conducting Jennifer Vyvyan (22 March)

1957 conducts English Opera Group in *Turn of the Screw* on tour in Stratford, Ontario

1957 CM and JM buy Essex House, Southgate

1958 conducts Elisabeth Schwarzkopf and Goldsborough Orchestra in a concert at the RFH including decorated version of 'Voi che sapete' from *Figaro* (16 January)

1958 conducts *Anna Bolena* at Wexford Festival

1958 conducts premiere of *Noye's Fludde* at Aldeburgh Festival (18 June 1958)

1958–9 conducts a season of Cape Town SO (November to March), including his first performance of Janáček's *Sinfonietta*

1959 records Handel's *Fireworks Music* using forces deployed at the first performance (a wind band of 70 players, brought together at night, 13–14 April)

1959 conducts Goldsborough Orchestra in all-Handel concert at Festival Hall (15 April)

1959 makes first Janáček recording (*Sinfonietta* and four opera preludes)

1959 conducts at Aldeburgh Festival (*Rape of Lucretia, Noye's Fludde*)

1959 conducts *Turn of the Screw* for Associated-Rediffusion Television

1960 first return to Australia; tours for Australian Broadcasting Commission

1960 concerts in East Germany and Hungary

1960 first return to Czechoslovakia; visits Janáček Archive in Brno (3 September)

1961 first conducting engagement in Czechoslovakia (12 March)

1961 conducts *Káťa Kabanová* in Brno (21 March)

1961 gives series of broadcast talks, 'Style in Orchestration'

1962 conducts Melbourne SO, Sydney SO and four operas for the Australian Elizabethan Theatre Trust (*Ariadne auf Naxos, Don Giovanni, Traviata, Falstaff*) (March–July, with breaks to return to Europe)

1962 conducts for the first time at the Prague Spring Festival (19 May) and in Poland

1962 conducts Shostakovich's Symphony No. 9 with Polish Radio SO at Edinburgh International Festival, in the presence of the composer (27 August)

1962 conducts five operas at the Deutsche Staatsoper, East Berlin

1963 four-month tour of Australia (from February)

1963 publishes 'Sense about the Appoggiatura' in *Opera* (October)

1963 conducts BBC broadcast of *Messiah* in Basil Lam's edition (December)

1964 conducts British premiere of *The Makropulos Affair* at SWO (12 February)

1964 concerts in Sweden, Leningrad, Riga and Moscow

1964 opera debut at ROH conducting Shostakovich's *Katerina Izmailova* (8 December)

1965 publishes 'What Mozart Really Meant' in *Opera* (April)

1965 conducts *The Marriage of Figaro* at Sadler's Wells, the first historically informed version, including appoggiaturas and ornamentation (9 April)

1965 Erster Kapellmeister at the Hamburg Staatsoper (to 1969); family moves to Hamburg and Essex House is let

1965 conducts London premiere of *From the House of the Dead* at SWO (28 October) in Kubelík version, omitting changes made by Chlubna

1966 conducts televised *Billy Budd*, with cast led by Peter Pears and Peter Glossop, supervised by the composer (broadcast 11 December)

1966 records *Messiah* in Basil Lam's edition

1966–67 CM and JM build holiday home on island of Elba

1968 has appendicitis and is unable to conduct opening night of SWO at the Coliseum

1969 family moves back to England; buys 10 Hamilton Terrace, St John's Wood

1970 Musical Director of SWO at the Coliseum (later ENO) (1 January; to 1977)

1970 US debut in Cincinnati and Dallas, and with Chicago SO in all-Janáček programme (14 May: *Vixen* Suite, *Sinfonietta, Glagolitic Mass*)

1972 Stephen Arlen, Managing Director of ENO, dies; replaced by Lord Harewood

1972 debut at Metropolitan Opera, conducting Gluck's *Orfeo ed Euridice*

1973 death of Alan Patrick Mackerras (father) (20 August)

1973 conducts Sydney SO and Birgit Nilsson in the opening concert of the Concert Hall of the Sydney Opera House (29 September)

1974 conducts Janáček for the first time in Prague (*Taras Bulba*, 1 June)

1974 created CBE in New Year Honours

1976 records *Káťa Kabanová* (first of a series of five Janáček operas for Decca)

1977 death of Catherine Mackerras (mother) (7 February)

1977 Principal Guest Conductor of the BBC SO (to 1979)

1978 Janáček Medal awarded by the Czechoslovak Government (presented to CM on stage at the Coliseum, 28 December 1978)

1979 knighted in New Year Honours

1980 records authentic version of *From the House of the Dead* for Decca (March)

1980 conducts BBC SO at the Last Night of the Proms

1980 debut at Vienna Staatsoper (29 February, *Jenůfa*)

1981 records *The Greek Passion* in Brno with WNO soloists and Brno State Orchestra (1–6 June)

1982 records authentic version of *Jenůfa* for Decca (April)

1982 Chief Conductor of Sydney SO (to 1985)

1985 in Handel centenary year conducts five Handel operas

1985 ill for six weeks with hepatitis

1986 conducts Julian Lloyd Webber and LSO in premiere of CM's and David Mackie's reconstruction of Sullivan's Cello Concerto (April)

1987 debut with the OAE (2 June; made Emeritus Conductor in 2007)

1987 grand-daughter Alice dies of leukaemia (19 June)

1987 publication of Nancy Phelan's *Charles Mackerras: A Musician's Musician*

1987 Music Director of WNO (to 1992; thereafter Conductor Emeritus)

1989 conducts *Má vlast* at Prague Spring Festival (12 May)

1990 debut at Glyndebourne Festival Opera conducting *Falstaff* (29 July)

1991 conducts Met premiere of *Káťa Kabanová* (25 February)

1991 conducts Mozart's *Don Giovanni* for the reopening of the Estates Theatre in Prague (1 December)

1992 Principal Guest Conductor of SCO (to 1995); thereafter Conductor Laureate

1993 first concert with SCO (24 February)

1993 Principal Guest Conductor of San Francisco Opera (to 1996)

1993 Principal Guest Conductor of RPO (to 1996)

1994 awarded honorary doctorate by Masaryk University, Brno (27 May)

1996 awarded Medal of Merit by the Czech Republic

1996 crisis with right shoulder during performance of *Die Meistersinger* in Munich (22 May); a number of concerts and opera performances cancelled over the next year while CM had surgery on both shoulders

1996 with John Tyrrell publishes the 'Brno 1908' version of *Jenůfa*, an authentic edition excluding Kovařovic's reorchestrations and cuts

1997 made a Companion of the Order of Australia (AC) (26 January)
1998 Music Director of Orchestra of St Luke's, New York (to 2001)
1999 awarded honorary doctorate by Prague Academy of Performing Arts (14 May)
1999 Principal Guest Conductor of Czech PO (to 2003)
2000 makes first commercial recording of Janáček's Šárka (August)
2002 Principal Guest Conductor of Philharmonia Orchestra (December)
2003 made a Companion of Honour (CH) in the Queen's Birthday Honours
2004 debut with the Berlin Philharmonic (22 January)
2004 awarded honorary doctorate by Janáček Academy of Performing Arts, Brno (30 January)
2005 awarded Royal Philharmonic Society Gold Medal
2005 first recipient of the Queen's Medal for Music
2006 daughter Fiona dies of cancer (1 September)
2008 Honorary President of Edinburgh International Festival Society
2008 final concerts with Czech PO, including premiere of *Three Fragments from Juliette* (11 and 12 December)
2008 debuts with Leipzig Gewandhaus and Dresden Staatskapelle
2008 conducts Alfred Brendel's final concert with Vienna PO (18 December)
2009 final recording with Czech PO (*The Wood Dove*, 9–10 September)
2009 conducts *The Turn of the Screw* at ENO (22 October–7 November)
2009 final concert with Philharmonia (13 December)
2010 final concert with SCO (15 January)
2010 conducts *The Cunning Little Vixen* at ROH in Jiří Zahrádka's new edition (19 March–1 April)
2010 awarded Artis Bohemia Amicis by Czech Ministry of Culture in Prague (27 April)
2010 conducts *Così fan tutte* (with OAE) at Glyndebourne (22 May–12 June)
2010 dies of multiple myeloma in London (14 July)
2010 funeral at St Paul's, Covent Garden (23 July)

At his death Mackerras was scheduled to conduct two BBC Proms, the SCO in *Idomeneo* at the Edinburgh Festival and in *Messiah* in November, concerts with the Berlin Philharmonic, the Philharmonia and the RLPO, and at the ROH *Don Pasquale* (September) and *Hansel and Gretel* (December–January); a new ROH production of *A Village Romeo and Juliet* was planned for 2011.

Prologue: A Eulogy for Charles[1]

Janet Baker

It is always a touching thing, when we lose someone, to see how we gather together, close ranks and share our grief; so, this morning, we are here to support Judy and the family and each other.

A human being is a mystery; none of us knows another person completely but, when they leave us, we have the opportunity to celebrate the life they have lived and to remember. When we lose someone we also lose a part of ourselves; the link we form with another is unique; when it is broken, that particular relationship is irreplaceable.

Some of us are born under a lucky star, born with a singular purpose, special gifts, the means to express them and the opportunity to do so. Charles was one of those people. During our work in re-creative groups, performers develop a bond that is difficult to describe; it grows out of a common purpose, to serve the composer as best we can, and is, I believe, our first duty.

I have never known a musician who fulfilled that duty more faithfully than Charles did; the burning intention that shaped and drove him had one purpose: to put his gifts at the composer's service before anything else. He demanded the same dedication from his singers: he drove us very hard because he wanted us to match his vision, his search for perfection, and we responded to it. Our reward was the sense of total security we felt with him, coming up to us from the pit of the opera house, in a concert hall or recording studio; he was always impeccably prepared and the support he gave was like standing on solid rock.

That standard of preparation didn't mean rigidity or a lack of spontaneity; I remember during rehearsals for *Julius Caesar* how he would present us with bars of complicated ornamentation and cadenzas, which we duly got into our heads, to be met the next day by an excited conductor who had had more interesting thoughts overnight that he wanted us to memorise instead. This happened with alarming regularity and, as the first night approached, we would look at him in despair, as the new pieces of paper appeared, and say 'Not again, Charles'. He didn't take the slightest notice, of course, and expected us to get on with it, which we duly did.

In performance, there were always treasured moments of utter magic with him. These special moments are never guaranteed: they arise as they please and are out of human control; our contribution is to be as perfectly prepared as we can by hard work. Because of the discipline Charles brought

[1] This tribute by Janet Baker was read at Charles Mackerras's funeral at St Paul's, Covent Garden, on 23 July 2010.

to everything he did and inspired in his singers and orchestral players, there were many of these.

The last one I experienced was at the memorial service for Richard Hickox. The vast congregation in St Paul's Cathedral was waiting in silence for the service to begin and I was sitting directly in front of Judy, since I had been asked to read. We could see Charles standing in the north transept with his orchestra, waiting to begin; he raised his baton and in that one simple action the sound he drew from the players in Delius's *Walk to the Paradise Garden* set the atmosphere and we were swept up into something I can only describe as sublime.

That kind of power is the mark of the great musician and must be a heavy burden to carry if it is wielded with humility and integrity. Charles had in Judy a partner who supported him magnificently in every way; he was rooted firmly in the sanity of family life. His down-to-earth Australian qualities of common sense, directness, the courage to speak his mind, together with his immense practicality (much needed by the Director of an opera house) – all these gave him the stability necessary to operate for so long at such a level; they made his unbelievable workload possible.

He lived deeply and enjoyed the good things of life with the same enthusiasm that he brought to his work.

Charles as a world-famous conductor had a calling; he obeyed it with his whole being, dedicating his entire life to it, putting the gifts he was born with and acquired through sheer hard work completely at its service. He believed in something more important than himself; he was an inspiration to all his colleagues, encouraging and helping them, not least financially.

He reached out to countless numbers of people, bringing them beauty, hope and healing through his music, and in doing so has left the world a better place. A life described in such terms is meaningful beyond description and it is why we are privileged to be here this morning with Judy and the family to celebrate that life and rejoice in him as our friend and colleague.

1

An Immense Stylist Evolves: 1947–87[1]

Nigel Simeone

CHARLES Mackerras was was born on 17 November 1925 at Schenactady, New York, where his father Alan, an electrical engineer, was doing postgraduate work with General Electric. The family returned to Sydney – via London – in 1927, and Charles grew up under the benevolent eye of his immensely cultured mother, Catherine, joined in time by six siblings: Alastair (1928–99), Neil (1930–87), Joan (b. 1934), Elizabeth (b. 1937), Malcolm and Colin (twins, b. 1939). The young Charles grew up in a very musical family, and it was at home that he got to know Gilbert and Sullivan: 'I was sort of brought up with it. Everyone in our family knew Gilbert and Sullivan off by heart – all the operas, all the dialogues and all the jokes. [...] Also, when I was a kid I acted in the Gilbert and Sullivan operas because in those days little boys used to sing the girls' parts as well.'[2] Mackerras learned the piano and also had a natural talent for woodwind instruments: 'My first non-keyboard instrument was actually the flute, but then I read that there was a great shortage of oboists, bassoonists and horn players, and that there were scholarships going at the Sydney Conservatorium to study those three wind instruments. So I thought it would be nice to play the oboe.'[3] During his studies at the Sydney Conservatorium he also worked as a professional oboist in the Sydney Symphony Orchestra, and as a composer and arranger of film scores which already demonstrate a brilliant understanding of the orchestra (within a few years, that gift led to his first popular success, with the ballet *Pineapple Poll*). He left Sydney aboard the *RMS Rangitiki* on 6 February 1947, bound for London on a voyage via Panama and Curaçao that took over six weeks to reach Tilbury Docks. The most intriguing stop en route was at Pitcairn Island, a visit described by Charles in a letter sent to his mother after his arrival in London:

> We only stopped [at Pitcairn Island] for the Duchess [of Gloucester] to see it and she entertained certain islanders of note in her suite. It was considered such an event for the Duchess to visit their island that their first official public holiday was made for the occasion. To them it was the greatest & final olive branch extended by England for their

[1] 'An immense stylist' was a phrase used by Sir Mark Elder in a broadcast tribute to Mackerras on BBC Radio 3, 15 July 2010.

[2] Interview for the Prom performance of *Patience*, BBC Radio 3, 11 August 2009.

[3] Filmed interview with Paul Edmund-Davies for the Philharmonia Orchestra, published on the orchestra's website (www.philharmonia.co.uk) in October 2008.

> mutiny against King & Country! [...] As the islanders left, they sang. Seventh-day Adventist hymns in 3 parts & finally *God Save the King* in a funny old version in honour of the Duchess. Altogether it was a most charming day & effectively broke the monotony of the voyage.[4]

The 'funny old version' of the National Anthem was one of Mackerras's first experiences of hearing a familiar tune in an unfamiliar way – he later recalled that it included ornamentation.

London in 1947

CHARLES had been in England for just a few weeks when, on 2 April 1947, he played an audition for the BBC Symphony Orchestra. A report on this audition was written by the orchestra's principal conductor, Sir Adrian Boult. It suggests a young musician of considerable talent. Mackerras played Mozart's Oboe Quartet and his tone was described as 'rather monotonous – but pleasant. Has plenty of dynamic variety'. His sight reading was 'very good indeed', while his technique was 'up to the Mozart which is saying a good deal'. Under 'style and bearing', Sir Adrian wrote: 'Rhythmically attractive. A most promising oboist.'[5] Though Boult was unable to offer him a position in the orchestra, he gave him some valuable advice and wrote letters of introduction on his behalf over the next few years. In 1978, after hearing a broadcast of a BBC Symphony Orchestra concert on tour in Budapest, he wrote a short note which Mackerras kept filed in his box of 'Important Documents':

> Dear Charles,
>
> Just to say that my wife and I *much* enjoyed the *Falstaff* from Budapest the other night – the more you conduct that orchestra, the more we shall enjoy it. But don't bother to answer this!
>
> Yours ever,
>
> Adrian C. Boult[6]

Aware of Mackerras's conducting ambitions, after the 1947 audition Boult advised him not to take a post as an oboist with the Liverpool Philharmonic, as it would keep him away from London and from opportunities to work in opera. A few days later, Mackerras heard of a vacancy for a second oboe in the Sadler's Wells Opera, which was soon to embark on a three-month tour. He was given the job and was also taken on as a repetiteur for the company. On Monday 12 May he joined the orchestra in Southsea, and he was quickly drawn to the young principal clarinet, Judy Wilkins (b. 1922), who had recently finished her studies at the Royal College of Music with Frederick

[4] This letter is in the Mackerras family archives in London, as are all subsequent letters to Catherine Mackerras from Charles and Judy.

[5] Copy of this report in the Mackerras family archives.

[6] Mackerras family archives.

Thurston. They went dancing on the Wednesday, and the following Sunday she took him to the Isle of Wight (noting in her diary that 'I fell in a bog near Cowes!'). She wrote to her parents about 'Charlie, Second oboe. Actually he's very nice. Australian, young, just arrived over here and wants to become a conductor.'

A chance encounter during Mackerras's first weeks in London was to have a decisive impact on his career, as he later recalled:

> I had just bought a score of the Dvořák D minor Symphony in a shop in Kensington and I was studying this while drinking a cup of coffee in a café. This man opposite me said: 'Ah! I see you are studying the music of my country.' So we got into a conversation and I tried to tell him of my ambitions to become a conductor and all that, and he said, 'Well you should go to Prague and study with Václav Talich.'[7]

The gentleman in question was Josef Weisslitzer, an amateur cellist and member of the Anglo-Czechoslovak Friendship League. He was involved in the selection of likely candidates to study in Prague, and encouraged Mackerras to apply at once. At the end of May Mackerras was invited to London for an interview and took Judy with him. According to Nancy Phelan, he was nervous and 'appeared bumptious and over-confident',[8] but despite making a rather mixed impression on the panel he was awarded a scholarship. He heard the good news in June, while Sadler's Wells was in Leicester, and immediately asked Judy if she'd come with him to Prague – something she assumed, rightly, to be a kind of marriage proposal. Judy wrote on 27 June to her college friend Winnie Roberts (later Mrs Geraint Jones):

> My dear Winnie,
>
> You must think me awful not to have written ere this – I certainly am, I don't seem able to catch up with my correspondence at all. [...] It's a shattering thing but I'm really falling badly – seriously – in love! [...]
>
> A terribly young, yet amazingly mature young man who is determined to be a conductor, who is an excellent oboe player & who is just surviving 2nd oboe in this racket because he has jobs on the musical staff too & might possibly be allowed to conduct something, sometime. At the moment he only rises to choruses behind scenes, off stage etc.!
>
> This is hardly the *interesting* part. He has an excellent brain & knows a lot about most things (& unfortunately is a little inclined to let you know it, which takes a form of rather over-enthusiasm more than conceit – if you can *possibly* understand a word of that!), apart from which he is very attract*ive* & attract*ed* to me & altogether it is

[7] Interview with Paul Edmund-Davies in October 2008 (see note 3).

[8] Phelan 1987, p. 61.

developing into quite a big thing. But forget all that & I will explain everything when I see you. And don't tell *anybody* please. [...][9]

The first known photograph of Charles and Judy was taken on this tour, in the garden of Miss Kelly's house – presumably a guesthouse used by members of the company – in Liverpool (see Plate 4). News of the scholarship necessitated a rapid change of plans. Judy noted in her diary[10] that the final decision to get married was made on 19 August: 'Made up our minds to get married next Friday!', adding the next day: 'Flap. Ringing Winnie, Susan etc. etc.' and, on 21 August, one word: 'Panic.' Charles and Judy married at 12 noon on 22 August 1947 at Bishop's Cleeve Church, near Cheltenham. Given the short timescale, it had been impossible to invite Charles's parents, and on 24 August Judy wrote to Catherine, her new mother-in-law:

Dear Mrs Mackerras,

I wish we could have corresponded with you more about the decision to get married last week. When we arrived home after the tour & discussed it with my parents, it seemed that last week was the *only* chance & there was no time for exchanging letters with you. I do wish you could have been there.

We were married in a country church about 2 miles from my home. We particularly wanted to avoid a London wedding as there would have to have been so many people. As it was we gave everyone so little notice & chose such an out of the way spot that there were only 17 in all. [...]

We don't know yet whether I shall be able to go to Prague at first or not. The news should come any day. I do *hope* I can as I feel Charlie needs someone to look after him, apart from anything else. By the way, I persuaded him to go to the dentist when we were in Belfast!

We are spending this weekend in a lovely old country house near Broadway in the Cotswolds. It is about 700 feet up with magnificent view & surroundings. Next week we return to Whistling Down (the family are away on holiday, except my father who never moves if he can possibly help it!) to get down to some serious study of Czech. It is a pretty dreadful language, I must say.

Soon I hope we can send you some wedding photos. I've nothing of me alone I can send you at the moment except a most revolting passport photo which might give you a very bad impression! I'm so very glad that from what you know you have advocated this marriage. We are marvellously happy & both very sure we have done the right thing. [...]

[9] Mackerras family archives.

[10] Mackerras family archives.

Prague and Talich

PREPARATIONS for the trip to Prague began at once. Judy noted a 'Czech lesson' (one of several) on 5 September, and the couple set off for Prague from Victoria Station at 9:20 a.m. on Wednesday 24 September, arriving two days later, at 11:30 on 26 September. By 3 October it was confirmed that Charles was to join Talich's class and that Judy was to study with Vladimír Říha (1905–78), principal clarinet in the Czech Philharmonic, whose recordings included Mozart's Clarinet Concerto with Talich and the orchestra. Lasting musical experiences within the first few weeks of their arrival included Mackerras's first experience of Janáček's *Káťa Kabanová* (Prague National Theatre, 15 October) and Smetana's *Má vlast* (18 November), both conducted by Talich. A few days later, on 22 November, they visited the Villa Bertramka and looked at its Mozart treasures (Charles played Mozart's harpsichord, but it was out of tune). His first encounter with the British Council's amateur orchestra in Prague was less inspiring. Judy noted in her diary on 5 December: 'C. conducts first rehearsal of B.C. Orch. Five turned up! Played viola part.'

A bureaucratic muddle meant that Charles was not immediately able to study with Talich, and others were teaching the great man's classes because he was too busy as conductor of the National Theatre. But, after going to see Talich, Charles was invited to his rehearsals and subsequently to some private lessons. When the Communists seized power in the coup of February 1948, one of the first artistic casualties was Talich, who was sacked from his post at the National Theatre. Thereafter, Mackerras went at least once a week to visit the conductor – forced into inactivity and delighted to talk at length to such an enthusiastic young musician – at Talich's country villa in Beroun.

On 21 June 1948, Mackerras wrote a letter to his mother which revealed how absorbed he had become in Janáček's music – and it is also clear from this letter that Catherine had been doing some homework of her own on the composer:

> My Dear,
>
> I am writing this the day before we go off to the Šumava forest for a week or so, because from then on we will be rather uncontactable for a week until we come back to Prague for our last week in this country.
>
> Your last letter was very interesting indeed. I must say that it would surpass my wildest dreams if they formed a chamber orchestra & also wanted me to be Goossens' assistant! However this seems too good to possibly *really* come off, so I shall just dream about it at night! Still I hope something turns up for me out there for next year.
>
> How do you have so much information on Janáček? I must say I had hardly heard of him till I came here & realised how great he is. I am surprised that he should have had a Catholic upbringing, because in later life he seems to have expressed very Communistic

sentiments. However one can never tell now, because everything is twisted round till it's unrecognisable. Janáček spent most of his life collecting Moravian folk music & studying the accent of the Czech language & it was not until he was in the late 50's that he started serious composition of his 6 or 7 great operas & his religious works & his few good orchestral compositions.

The *Glagolskaja Mša* is certainly the most magnificent work & is quite unlike any other religious work you can think of. It is almost as barbarous as *Belshazzar's Feast* or Stravinsky's *Psalm Symphony*, but it is however a more 'folky' barbarousness & one has the impression that it is tremendously sincere. There are also some most beautiful parts, notably the passionate Gospodi pomiluj (Kyrie).

By the way, you say that I ought to hear a mass in Sub-Carpathian Ruthenia! That part was ceded to Russia [*recte* Ukraine] after the war as a reward of 'gratitude'. [...] That Sub-Carpathian Ruthenia could well have been where Janáček conceived his religious works. It is very primitive & wild, with great forests, and bears & wild animals, and the people are all very religious in a primitive sort of way. Very superstitious & gipsy like along with everything else. From what I have heard from people who had holidays there before the war, it is quite a unique place, quite uncanny & unreal.

I shall send you a letter or so from Šumava forest. It is in the South of Bohemia, along the Western border of the country.

Love,
Charlie.

The political situation in Prague was deteriorating, though Talich suggested that Mackerras should come back for some further study after getting more practical experience at Sadler's Wells. Back in London, Mackerras was equipped with a testimonial from Talich that made the same point:

> I have been working with Mr Charles Mackerras during this year, and I would like to state that in my opinion he has shown me that he possesses great talents for the art of conducting. He needs only the opportunity of plenty of practical experience with an orchestra, and I am glad to recommend him to any post which could give him that opportunity.
>
> Václav Talich
> Prague, 20.5.1948[11]

[11] Mackerras family archives.

Earliest opera conducting

MICHAEL Mudie at Sadler's Wells was happy to take him on as an assistant conductor with the company, and to offer him some opportunities to conduct. The first came on 20 October 1948, when Mackerras conducted *Die Fledermaus*. Judy's diary noted that it was '*Marvellous*. Everyone delighted' and Charles wrote to his mother to describe his debut and how he was taken through the score the next day by Michael Mudie: 'today he took me through the opera showing me all the mistakes I had made and how to rectify them. [...] He was very nice, saying that he had expected it to be good but was quite astounded at my performance. He said that he was only sorry that they couldn't give me more conducting.' Judy – who had been playing in the orchestra for the performance – wrote to Catherine on 6 November:

> Charlie was really marvellous in his first performance of *Fledermaus* & I was thrilled. I *wish* you could have been there. My mother & sister & one or two friends were. Everyone was most impressed & all the orchestra told me nice things about him. Certainly his stick technique is extraordinarily good & he has very much the right sort of mind for opera I think. Alert & sensitive. I fear the Wells are not going to give him as much conducting as he deserves though. C. has told you what Michael Mudie said, I think.

Mudie (1914–62) was a valued mentor to Mackerras, but he was also a sick man. As a result of disseminated sclerosis (usually known now as multiple sclerosis) he started to lose his sight in 1950 and by 1953 his physical condition meant that he had to abandon conducting altogether. His obituary in *The Times* (4 May 1962) was subtitled 'A gifted operatic conductor'. It described him as a musician who could have 'become our finest interpreter of opera' and 'a Verdi conductor of exceptional style and sensibility'. He was generous in sharing his experience and insight with Mackerras, and left a lasting impression on his young assistant. When Mackerras was asked in 2009 about where he learned his distinctive conducting style, he attributed it to Mudie:

> There was a wonderful conductor at Sadler's Wells when I first joined the orchestra [...] Michael Mudie. He had a superb technique and a wonderful way of conducting these Puccini operas and getting them beautifully together. I don't know if you realise this but *La Bohème* and *Tosca* – but especially *La Bohème* – the beginning of Act 1 and Act 4 are terribly difficult to conduct and to get really together. Also another couple of terribly well known operas that are difficult to get together are *Cavalleria rusticana* and *Pagliacci*. During our tour I learnt a lot from Michael Mudie[12]

[12] Interview with Igor Toronyi-Lalic, published online, www.theartsdesk.com, 22 October 2009.

Mudie's illness was responsible for Mackerras's first major success at Sadler's Wells. Enthusiastically prompted by Mackerras – who had been so moved by the work when he saw it in Prague – Mudie had been due to conduct the British premiere of *Káťa Kabanová* in April 1951, but as his illness progressed it was quite apparent that he would be unable to do it. Despite Mudie's protests (he wanted to carry on), Mackerras took over, with consequences that were career-changing for the 25-year-old conductor (see Chapter 3).

Thanks to an invitation from Bill Smith in Cardiff, Mackerras found additional work with the fledgling Welsh National Opera company. In 1950, he conducted several operas in Cardiff, writing to his mother about his experiences with amusing frankness on 14 May 1950:

> My dear Mother,
>
> After the most hectic few weeks I've ever been through, I now have a day off so I can now tell you some of my news. In the last few weeks I have not only been doing my work at the Wells, but rushing back & forth from Cardiff for singing rehearsals & marking all the orchestra parts for the Cardiff season (cuts etc.) It's just as well I took a lot of trouble over the parts, because it's an atrocious orchestra up here. They can't count their bars & play shockingly out of tune. We started with *Hoffmann* which is a fiendishly difficult opera for singers, orchestra *and* conductor & we got through reasonably well. It has been the most marvellous experience for me doing operas under these terrible conditions. The singers are mainly amateur & most unreliable & the orchestra, as I said, is very sticky. So *I* had to really know what I was doing. It makes one realise how comparatively easy it is conducting for the Wells where most people can be relied upon to come in right!

At the end of the same letter, Mackerras mentioned that he was already planning what became *Pineapple Poll*: 'My Ballet has been postponed till November as the musical rights to G & S operas do not run out till then!'

With such a broad range of interests – the first nights of *Pineapple Poll* (13 March 1951) and *Káťa Kabanová* (10 April) were given at Sadler's Wells Theatre less than a month apart – it is no surprise that Mackerras wanted to avoid being labelled as a specialist. After four years at the Wells, he was also starting to get regular work with the BBC, the repertoire ranging from eighteenth-century rarities to Verdi and light orchestral music. Judy wrote to Catherine on 18 March 1953 to tell her about his success on the radio: 'in three months he will have eight broadcasts which is quite a record, even for better known conductors than him'. Charles wrote to his sister Joan on 31 May 1953: 'One good thing about me and the BBC so far is that they haven't yet pigeon-holed me into any particular type of music. This is the fate that usually overtakes conductors for the BBC. You are either a "light" conductor, or a symphony conductor, or an operatic conductor, or a chamber orchestra conductor, or a ballet conductor, or a variety conductor, or some sort of specialist. Up to now I have not been put into any particular category and I have conducted all types of music for the BBC even including variety stuff (i.e. tap dancing numbers etc.).'[13] This versatility led to his appointment in 1954 as Principal Conductor of the BBC Concert Orchestra, a post he held until 1956, when he was succeeded by Vilém Tauský (another musician of wide-ranging sympathies who had been a Janáček pupil). In 1954 he also created another ballet with John Cranko, his collaborator on *Pineapple Poll*. This was *The Lady and the Fool*, based on little-known music by Verdi. It was first performed on 31 March 1954 and then reworked by Cranko for a performance at the Royal Opera House on 9 June 1955 which was Mackerras's conducting debut at Covent Garden. He wrote to his mother on 29 June:

> *The Lady and the Fool* was a great success at the Garden. To me it was ten times better than at the Wells. The whole thing looked more spacious, like a ballet in the grand manner, and of course the music sounded incomparably better played by the larger and better orchestra. Beryl Grey was wonderful in the part of the Lady and the whole thing has been quite a sensation.[14]

The same month, Mackerras recorded the complete *Lady and the Fool* with the Philharmonia – his first appearance with an orchestra which was to play such an important part in his later career but which also provided him, in the 1950s, with regular opportunities to record shorter orchestral works for EMI. In 1956, he became Principal Conductor of the English Opera Group, working closely with Britten for the next few years.

Contact with Britten

> I became associated with Britten during a season of *Let's Make an Opera*, which was an opera by him in which the audience participated. [...] The conductor had to address the audience and help them to sing these songs. There were four lovely songs. I [...] then became the musical director of the English Opera Group, in succession to Norman Del Mar – and I happened to hit the time when *The Turn of the Screw* was new. And I was able to conduct a few performances in London. Britten had done the world premiere in Venice. [...] When it came back to the Scala Theatre in London – not Milan – I did some performances [in September 1956]. [...] Then [in 1957] we went to Canada, to Stratford, Ontario, where Tyrone Guthrie was running

[13] Original in Joan Hall's files.

[14] Copy provided by Joan Hall.

> a Shakespeare Festival. I went with the original cast but I had to rehearse the orchestra, who didn't know it.[15]

THE visit to Stratford, Ontario, saw the first production of *The Turn of the Screw* in North America, and Mackerras conducted the performances on 3 and 4 September 1957. With the English Opera Group in 1956 he had also conducted the first performance of Lennox Berkeley's opera *Ruth* as well as Blow's *Venus and Adonis* and Holst's *Savitri*. But his most important Britten premiere was *Noye's Fludde* in 1958. Britten was pleased to have Mackerras as the conductor, since it was a challenge to keep everything together – especially the processions of animals. Britten wrote to his friend James Bernard: 'Thank God I have not got to control them myself.'[16] It was during the final rehearsals that Mackerras joked with friends about seeing Aldeburgh flooded with children and how for Britten being surrounded by so many boys was 'Ben's paradise'.[17] John Cranko – the choreographer of *Noye's Fludde* as well as Mackerras's erstwhile collaborator on *Pineapple Poll* and *The Lady and the Fool* – reported this careless talk to Britten, who was deeply offended. Mackerras was summoned by Peter Pears to see Britten at the Red House. He described the subsequent interview to John Bridcut:

> They told me what it was about and how upset Ben was, and he said, 'Am I a lecher just because I enjoy the company of children?' He was extremely calm – but in an icy kind of way. He was obviously furious. And Peter gave vent to his fury a great deal more than Ben. [...] So I became terribly nervous and I tried to explain. But, I mean, how *can* you explain that although we all revered Ben's musicianship and loved him as a man in many ways, we were slightly amused by the homosexuality. [...] I was terribly upset myself then. And I couldn't really explain it clearly to him.[18]

Mackerras knew that this had been a stupid lapse, and a parting of the ways seemed inevitable. But it didn't happen immediately, and he conducted the first performances of *Noye's Fludde* on 18 June 1958. In *Opera* (August 1958), Andrew Porter wrote that 'Charles Mackerras directed his wide-flung forces with uncommon command'. In the *Guardian* (19 June 1958), Philip Hope-Wallace described how Mackerras was seen 'actually moving around a pillar to be able to control all the sections in turn. It was a very happy and often strangely touching occasion.' Despite the seemingly irreversible turn his relationship with Britten had taken, Mackerras remembered *Noye's Fludde* as 'yet another manifestation of the diversity of Ben's genius. It's an

15 Interview with Igor Toronyi-Lalic, published online, www.theartsdesk.com, 22 October 2009.

16 Bridcut 2006, p. 234.

17 Bridcut 2006, p. 236.

18 Bridcut 2006, p. 237.

absolute masterpiece.'[19] He wrote to his mother about the work in a long letter postmarked 10 May 1959:

> *Noye's Fludde* (correct spelling) is a magnificent affair. Apart from doing it at Aldeburgh last year at its first performance and on TV, I just did several more performances in Lowestoft. It is starting to be performed very often now. It is an old miracle play from Chester which Ben has set in the Miracle play manner. It is performed in a church and the congregation joins in with hymns at various times. The whole show, apart from a very small orchestra and conductor and two professional singers, is entirely amateur. There is a large amateur orchestra of easy string parts, percussion parts, hand bells, bugles and recorders, as well as a colossal chorus of animals, which are performed by children. Noah's sons and their wives are also played by children. The whole thing is most ingenious and in many places very moving. During the storm, the entrance of the congregation singing 'O God our help in ages past' is extraordinarily effective and almost tear-jerking in its context.

At the 1958 Aldeburgh Festival, Mackerras also conducted Poulenc's *Les Mamelles de Tirésias* (with Jennifer Vyvyan as Thérèse and Peter Pears as her husband; the orchestral part was played on two pianos by Britten and Viola Tunnard) and a concert of wind music including Mozart's Gran Partita K361, Stravinsky's Octet and Handel's *Fireworks Music* (according to Donald Mitchell's programme note, this performance included flutes and clarinets doubling the oboe parts!).

Though the rupture with Britten was serious, Mackerras was invited back to Aldeburgh in 1959 to conduct *The Rape of Lucretia* and, as he mentioned in the letter to his mother, he also conducted further performances of *Noye's Fludde*. At the end of the year he conducted *The Turn of the Screw* for Associated-Rediffusion Television – a performance that greatly pleased Britten (Philip Reed has written that it was 'an interpretation the composer much admired'[20]). A few years later, in May 1963, he conducted *Noye's Fludde* at the Caerphilly Festival, with a cast led by Raimund Herincx as Noah and Margaret Price as Noah's wife.

Mackerras was in charge of a revival *Peter Grimes* at Sadler's Wells on 22 April 1965 – two weeks after triumphing with *Figaro* in the same theatre. Harold Rosenthal wrote in *Opera* (June 1965):

> The great feature of this performance was Charles Mackerras's outstanding handling of Britten's miraculous score. This was operatic conducting on the very highest level [...] Mr Mackerras not only created tension and excitement, but drew some first-rate playing from his orchestra.

[19] Bridcut 2006, p. 238.

[20] Philip Reed: 'Billy Budd', booklet note for Decca DVD 074 3256 (2008).

An undated letter from Britten written at the time of these *Grimes* performances suggests that, whatever damage Mackerras had done to their friendship during the *Noye's Fludde* rehearsals, Britten remained very cordial:

> My dear Charles,
>
> I am so very sorry that I couldn't come to P.G. at the Wells on Thursday, & after *Billy Budd* tomorrow I have to go abroad for some weeks. Maybe I shall 'catch' you at it before long. I hope so, because I hear on all sides how wonderfully you do the work. Thank you so much for the time & trouble you have taken over it.
>
> I am sorry about the postponement of the TV B. Budd, but I think it was wise (I am *not*, alas, impressed by the young Canadian baritone at Cov. Garden[21]) – & I look forward to being in on it with you next year.
>
> Yours ever,
> Ben[22]

Following the announcement of Mackerras's appointment as Erster Kapellmeister at the Hamburg State Opera (reported in *Opera* in November 1965), Britten sent his congratulations in an undated letter:

> My dear Charles,
>
> I was very glad indeed to read about your Hamburg appointment, glad – for them, very sad – for us! Can nothing be done to shake up our own opera houses? I hope you are pleased. It is a nice city, & although Liebermann is a bit prickly, I should think he'll be interesting to work with.
>
> I hope *Bohème* has gone (and is going) well. I look forward to B. Budd.
>
> Yours ever,
> Ben

The televised *Billy Budd* conducted by Mackerras – and supervised by Britten – was recorded in September 1966 and first broadcast by the BBC on 11 December. The cast was led by Peter Pears as Captain Vere (the role he had created in 1951, and in the premiere of the revised two-act version), Peter Glossop as Billy Budd and Michael Langdon as Claggart. The circumstances of this recording were described by Philip Reed in his notes for the DVD release:

> The production was filmed in London using a two-studio system, where the orchestra and conductor were placed in a studio quite

[21] Possibly a reference to the American baritone Robert Kerns (not 'Canadian' as Britten suggests), who made his Covent Garden debut as Billy Budd in 1964.

[22] Mackerras family archives, as are the other letters from Britten to Mackerras quoted in this chapter.

> separate from that containing the set and the singers, with the performers linked by audio-visual monitors. The conductor's task was made easier by an assistant[23] in the singers' studio who duplicated the principal conductor's beat and gestures. Although Britten was puzzled by this method – he felt it was inartistic and the presence of so many technicians distracting – he nevertheless attended several rehearsals, as well as the crucial studio recording, to offer advice and support. [...] He was very impressed by the end product.[24]

On 10 December 1966 (the day before the broadcast of *Billy Budd*) Britten thanked Mackerras for coming to a concert (probably the Olive Zorian Memorial Concert on 26 November, in which Britten, Pears, Julian Bream, Manoug Parikian, Helen Watts and Norman Del Mar all took part):

> Dear Charles,
>
> [...] It was very nice to see you all after the concert, and we both much appreciated your coming to it, knowing how busy you are. I am glad our little talk over *A Midsummer Night's Dream* helped a bit, and I hope your performance on Monday did not go as badly as you feared.
>
> With love to you all, and a special little bit for Catherine.
>
> Yours ever,
>
> Ben

Britten's letter referred to a revival of *A Midsummer Night's Dream* that Mackerras conducted in Hamburg at the end of 1966. The conductor's anxiety centred mainly on the role of Oberon, which was sung by a character tenor rather than Britten's specified counter-tenor. Mackerras was much happier with the new Hamburg production of *Albert Herring* that he conducted in June 1966, just before starting his first season with the company. The cast included Tatiana Troyanos and the great Wagnerian singer Martha Mödl.

In the early 1970s, Mackerras conducted several performances of *Gloriana* with Sadler's Wells Opera – at the Munich Olympic Games in 1972 and at the Proms for Britten's sixtieth birthday in 1973. Then, as on his 1992 recording with WNO, the fire and flexibility of Mackerras's conducting revealed the quality of a score that had been undervalued since its premiere. In 1971 he conducted *Billy Budd* at the Royal Opera House, returning there in 1974 for *A Midsummer Night's Dream* (with James Bowman as Oberon). Notable later Britten performances included *Billy Budd* at the Metropolitan Opera in 1992 (see Chapter 6) and *The Turn of the Screw* – which he considered Britten's 'ultimate masterpiece' – at ENO in 2009 (see Chapter 8).

[23] David Lloyd-Jones, who had worked with Mackerras as Associate Conductor for a BBC TV recording of *La Bohème* in 1965 (see Chapter 2).

[24] Philip Reed: 'Billy Budd', booklet note for Decca DVD 074 3256 (2008).

Mozart and Handel: *Figaro* and *Fireworks*

Mackerras's growing interest during the 1950s in historically informed performance was encouraged by friends such as the conductor and repetiteur Maurits Sillem (1929–2002; Sillem went on to be Head of the Music Staff at the Royal Opera House) and the musicologist H. C. Robbins Landon. One work fascinated him above all: Mozart's *Marriage of Figaro*. Mackerras had first conducted *Figaro* when he was entrusted with a new production at Sadler's Wells in 1951 – a quiet beginning to what quickly burgeoned into a lifelong quest. Mackerras became interested in Mozartian style, particularly vocal ornamentation and, above all, the correct realisation of appoggiaturas – and also in the evolution of the *Figaro* score and the revisions made during Mozart's lifetime. A letter sent by Maurits Sillem from Paris on 25 April 1956 reveals how serious their *Figaro* quest had already become:

> Dear Charles,
>
> 'Al desio' was written for Ferrarese del Bene, and sung by her as *the Countess* in Vienna (Summer 1789) replacing 'Deh vieni', but retaining the recit. 'Guinse alfin' immediately before it, *ignoring* the change of characters! (Source for this information: Peters full sc., note to p. 330).
>
> 'Un moto di gioia' replaced 'Venite inginocchiatevi' (not 'Deh vieni'), according to Paumgartner (*Mozart*, p. 499) in 1792.
>
> That, alas, is all I can tell you from here, handicapped as I am by lack of reference books (e.g. I know Paumgartner goes into some detail about the question – surely Köchel cat. too?) As regards the dramatic nonsense made of Act IV by the change, I think they simply let that go hang, and that Ferrarese's claims proved stronger! [...]
>
> To sum up, provided 'Ginse alfin' is sung by the *Countess* (not Susanna) *together* with 'Al desio' the order which you quote from Köchel is, *historically*, correct.
>
> The Donaueschingen score (probably the oldest existing copy) has notable divergences. It seems to be an early version before the first Prague version became crystallised.
>
> A. There is no E maj. duet (No. 5); instead a short (C maj. 2/4) song for Marcellina.
>
> B. There is no 'Non so più' (No. 6). (Recitatives around both numbers naturally different.)
>
> C. The C maj. trio (No. 13) lacks bars 53–61 and 118–133 (both repeats, or developments, of the same music).
>
> D. The version of Ctess's and Sus's lines in the above is quite different from 1. the usual, 2. the version proposed by Abert (Min. Eulenb. score) and Schünemann (war-time Peters score).

> The Donaueschingen parts (which were used for performances there in 1785 [?? according to the local register] 1787, 8, 1789, 91, 42 [i.e. 92?] show (by the presence of slips) that the opera was eventually performed there as we know it, and the Marcellina C major Aria 'No. 4' soon abandoned. […]
>
> I am in London 9–13 May, so do let us meet. Write and tell me when you are free […]
>
> Kindest r.
> Maurits[25]

That summer, Mackerras visited Donaueschingen – taking the family on the first of several summer holidays strategically based near interesting library collections – to look at the famous *Figaro* score housed in the Fürstliches Museum. This is a manuscript full score of the first two acts (the others are missing) dating from no later than 1787 that had long been known about as one of the opera's most interesting early sources, but which few conductors had ever troubled to examine. For Mackerras it was the first of several important discoveries, as he recalled in conversation with H. C. Robbins Landon in 1995: 'Not only was the version of the whole score quite different from any other, but it was also full of ornamentation of the various arias.' As well as consulting manuscript sources, Mackerras was delighted when Fritz Spiegl produced a copy of Domenico Corri's ornamented version of 'Voi che sapete'. On 12 March 1957, Jennifer Vyvyan and Mackerras recorded this and other decorated arias from *Figaro* for the BBC, broadcast ten days later in a programme called 'Vocal Embellishments in Mozart'.[26] He subsequently included it in a concert with the Goldsborough Orchestra at the Royal Festival Hall on 16 January 1958, this time with Elisabeth Schwarzkopf as the soloist. *The Times* (17 January 1958) praised Schwarzkopf's

> brilliant demonstration of eighteenth-century gracing in Mozart: the aria was Cherubino's *Voi che sapete*, whose melodic line must have been familiar to almost everyone in the audience. One can imagine that many ambitious singers of Mozart's day blurred and distorted such a line, and it would be difficult to imagine other modern sopranos who would give as clean, flexible and sympathetic an exposition of the little runs and rhythmic variations in this version as did Mme Schwarzkopf here. The favourite aria took on new life (or was it only rejuvenation?) because it was being treated as Mozart intended. Simplicity of line in Mozart is a myth; the audience recognised as much, and cheered until Mme Schwarzkopf and her colleagues repeated their delightful performance.

It took Mackerras several more years of research – whenever time permitted – examining dozens of variant versions (including *Harmoniemusik*

[25] Mackerras family archives.

[26] Information from Jonathan Crown, Jennifer Vyvyan's son.

Figure 1 Mackerras's piano-vocal score of *The Marriage of Figaro*, with his handwritten embellishments and corrections at the end of 'Dove sono'

arrangements that often had written-out ornamentation) before he was ready to perform the whole opera in a similar style. He published what proved to be an influential article in *Opera* (October 1963) called 'Sense about the Appoggiatura'. Cogently argued, quoting numerous eighteenth-century sources and extensively illustrated with musical examples, it made a compelling case for following the practices of the time in the performance of unwritten vocal appoggiaturas, rather than singing what appears to be the exact notation in the score. He quoted a telling remark by Saint-Saëns: 'Nowadays music is written pretty nearly as it should be executed; in the old days it was otherwise, and conventional signs were used which had to be translated. Performing old music as it is written is comparable to speaking a foreign language one does not know how to pronounce. The greatest difficulty, apparently, is the appoggiatura which is no longer in use in our time.'

Despite the evidence presented, not everyone was persuaded by Mackerras's arguments. Erik Smith (the record-producer son of Hans Schmidt-Isserstedt) was unconvinced, and argued his case for more restrained use of appoggiaturas in *Records and Recording* (January 1965). The following month, Mackerras responded with a vigorous article entitled 'Appoggiaturas Unlimited?' in which he restated and amplified the case he had made in *Opera*. Cathy Mackerras tells a charming story about Smith coming round to dinner one evening at the time of this appoggiatura dispute: 'We decided that we were going to make a trifle and that we would make Erik Smith *eat* an appoggiatura. So Fiona and I decorated the top of the trifle with musical notation, including the word "Amore" with a written-out appoggiatura [E–*D*–C] in edible silver balls, and made sure he got to eat that piece, with the appoggiatura on it. It was all very good-natured.'[27]

In April 1965, *Opera* published a long article by Mackerras entitled 'What Mozart Really Meant'. Having tackled performance-practice issues in his articles on appoggiaturas and embellishments, Mackerras here considered Mozart's revisions to the score: the new arias composed for Adriana Ferrarese del Bene when she sang Susanna in the 1789 Vienna revival; the changes made in ensembles, where the Countess originally always had the higher line but which Mozart later switched, putting Susanna on the top (Mackerras makes a strong case for reverting to the original version when the right singers are available); the problem of the order in Act 3 (he favoured the ingenious solution proposed by Robert Moberly and Christopher Raeburn); and variant versions of the Countess's 'Dove sono' and the Count's 'Vedrò, mentr'io sospiro' found in the early *Figaro* manuscript at the Istituto musicale in Florence. Decisions about these numbers – and about appoggiaturas and vocal embellishments – were all made on the basis of Mackerras's researches over the previous decade, and the result

[27] This anecdote and many of the subsequent ones come from a series of conversations with Cathy Mackerras during the preparation of this book. See Chapter 2 for further comments on Mackerras and appoggiaturas.

was a revelatory *Figaro* that opened at Sadler's Wells on 9 April 1965. It was an inspired example of practical musicology, even if Mackerras later decided that he had been a little carried away with the ornamentation in this production. A few critics had qualms, but for the most part this *Figaro* was recognised as an exceptional achievement. Arthur Jacobs in *Opera* (June 1965) considered the matter of the vocal decorations in detail:

> Mr Mackerras's [*Figaro*] was what it would be convenient to sum up as a 'decorated' performance. Convenient, but misleading. In reality, his additions to the text fall into two distinct categories. There are appoggiaturas, which are a matter of musical grammar and the form of which is historically authenticated within fairly narrow limits. (If we dislike them, we dislike Mozart's ideas of Mozart.) And there are cadenzas and other embellishments, the placing and the precise form of which are matters not of grammar but of taste (again, within historical limits). The appoggiaturas in this performance we have no rational grounds to question, unless we can fault Mr Mackerras's deductions from history; but the embellishments he used – including the final cadenza which he borrowed from Sir Henry Bishop's edition of the Letter Duet, as reproduced in his April article – we may reject if we wish, even though he can prove each of them to be paralleled in a contemporary or near-contemporary source. A certain shock-effect aroused by Mackerras's versions originates in the very fact that we are habituated to the 'plain' vocal lines. This effect, I venture to prophesy, we shall feel not half so much in a few years' time. But even now I can declare that, personally, I was never offended, generally pleased, and often ravished. Particularly valuable is the effect of enhancement lent to musical phrases when they return embellished later. The Countess's 'Dove sono' is a case in point: the opening four notes were slightly ornamented at the immediate repetition (bars 9–10) and then further ornamented at the later reprise of the section. The effect was to add cumulatively to the genuine feeling of the piece.

Winton Dean (with whom Mackerras was later to clash over matters of style and ornamentation in Handel) was not completely won over, but his review in the *Musical Times* (June 1965) recognised the importance of trying out musical solutions reflecting the practice of Mozart's time:

> One would expect a Mackerras *Figaro* to be lively, and it was (Sadler's Wells, April 13). The whole opera had undergone a thorough musical and dramatic spring-clean, which threw light in a number of dusty corners. Most conspicuous was the treatment of vocal ornament, on which a good deal of controversial ink has recently been expended. There are three issues here: appoggiaturas (chiefly but not exclusively in recitatives), cadenzas, and the adornment of a returning melody, a survival of the *da capo* aria. Mackerras is unquestionably right in treating appoggiaturas as obligatory, but the other two are matters

> of taste – though there are places where a cadenza is imperatively demanded. While recognising the practice of Mozart's day, we are not compelled to approve all Mackerras's solutions. Many (notably 'Deh vieni') were convincing, but the variations in 'Voi che sapete' and 'Dove sono' (not the cadenza in the latter) did seem an intolerable interference with melodies too beautiful to be confined to one hearing. Even so, it is right that these things should be put to the test. They were not the only musical innovations. The restoration of the top line in the Act 2 trio to the Countess was abundantly justified. Welcome too was the chance to hear the arias of Marcellina and Basilio in Act 4, which explained why they are cut. They are not bad Mozart, but they hold up the action without telling us anything new about the characters.

The Times reviewed the revival at the end of the year, and its headline on 31 December 1965 was unequivocal: 'A Figaro that Beats all Others':

> What chiefly makes this *Figaro* so enjoyable is the vital character of the music as a decent home cast sings it under Mr Charles Mackerras, with something like inspired support from the resident orchestra. [...] Miss Ava June and Mr Raimund Herincx, Miss Elizabeth Harwood and Mr Donald McIntyre and their colleagues [...] all sing their music as they act their parts, as if they really were the Almavivas and the Figaros, and as if their natural way of expressing their reactions to real events was to sing. [...] There are dozens, scores of moments in this performance which bring sudden accesses of enlightenment and joy into the heart of everyone who adores *Figaro*. Mr Mackerras is responsible for most of them.

This spirit of innovation informed by scholarship did not last when Mackerras was not conducting in the house. Writing in the November 1966 issue of *Opera*, Harold Rosenthal clearly regretted the change:

> Alas, no sooner has Charles Mackerras departed for Hamburg than, snip-snip, out come the pruning scissors, and into limbo go some of the appoggiaturas, cadenzas and other embellishments which we first heard 18 months ago and which were the result of months of work and preparation on the part of all concerned. A member of the theatre's music staff sitting behind me was rash enough to tell his companion: 'I think it'll sound better now ... of course we've only removed a few of the appoggiaturas'.

Fortunately, Mackerras was back in the pit for a revival in 1967, and Alan Blyth reviewed it in *Opera* (October 1967):

> This *Figaro* – taken all-round – is one of the most stylish and best integrated to be seen or heard in Europe today. Of course, elsewhere there are finer individual portrayals than some of those at the Wells, but surely no production where all the musical and dramatic points have been so carefully thought out. For this we must largely thank

> Charles Mackerras, whose authority in the pit on this occasion immediately restored to the company a confidence and enthusiasm so obviously lacking on many other nights.
>
> The overture was bubbling and brilliant, filling one with an anticipatory relish for what was to come, and throughout the evening the singers were given a lead in how to shape and phrase their music. One or two moments of faulty ensemble, specially in Act 2, indicated that another rehearsal or two would not have come amiss, but otherwise this was Mozartian conducting of wit, polish and warmth.
>
> Mackerras also restored the embellishments that were apparently left out of the revival a year ago. I find the cadenzas rather too 19th-century in style, and the Countess's 'Dove sono' too ornate, but these are matters of opinion. What cannot be disputed, and cannot be said too often, is how much the recitatives and arias gain in character by the inclusion of appoggiaturas.

Questions about performance practice in Handel had intrigued Mackerras even before he left Australia: the seeds were planted when Dr Robert Dalley-Scarlett, conductor of the Brisbane Handel Society, showed him a facsimile of Handel's autograph score of *Messiah*. After giving a wind-only version of the *Fireworks Music* at Aldeburgh in 1958 (using the modest and inauthentic forces available, including flutes and clarinets), he turned in 1959 – the 200th anniversary of Handel's birth – to a much more radical plan: to record the *Fireworks Music* using the forces deployed at the first performance, an enormous ensemble of wind instruments that could only be assembled in the middle of the night, once concerts and opera performances were over. The musicians gathered for this recording included many of the finest wind and brass players in London. The session took place on the night of 13–14 April 1959, between 11:00 p.m. and 2:30 a.m., at St Gabriel's Church, Cricklewood, and Mackerras wrote about it to his mother in his long letter of 10 May:

> Regarding my researches into old music, there is a lot of interest at present in 18th century performance practice, and it has been found that a great deal of the traditions built up in the 19th and 20th centuries as to old music performance is quite wrong. The kind of performance typified by Sargent is undoubtedly nothing to do with Handel or Mozart and there are many people who are working to try and find a way of performing this music which is more in tune with how the composers thought of their music. [...] It is obvious that one cannot ever retrieve the 18th century 'Geist' but at least one can get nearer to it than the Sargents and Klemperers do. Apart from my work on vocal and pianistic embellishments in Mozart and Haydn (which I think you know about), I have in the case of Handel merely edited the *Fireworks* and other music in accordance with the rhythms and practices of the 18th century. I told you in Cape

Town[28] about trills and also about the *double*-dotting of dotted passages, and in my Handel record I have merely followed this. It naturally makes the beginning of the *Fireworks*, for instance, sound like a different piece. The same as for instance the overture to the *Messiah* should be played in this manner, which gives it rather more life. People have been interested in this subject for years, but they have been chiefly scholars and musicologists. I, and certain others, try to show that music is more lively, interesting and beautiful when performed in this way.

For the Handel record, I simply reproduced some performance practice methods and played the *Fireworks* on exactly the combination Handel used, which was an extraordinary wind-band of about 70 players, including 26 oboes, 14 bassoons and lots of horns, trumpets, serpents, contra bassoons and drums. The other side of the record is a lovely concerto for two wind bands and strings which quotes a lot of Handel's other music, notably the *Messiah*. There is some fabulous horn playing on this disc, some of which is done by Barry Tuckwell, who is now probably the finest horn player in the world. In order to assemble the extraordinary orchestra for the *Fireworks*, we had to record it in the middle of the night, when no other orchestras were working. The session finished at 2.30 a.m. on the anniversary of Handel's death.

The concert with Schwarzkopf, by the way, was very interesting because this very great singer sang embellished versions of famous Mozart arias, which caused a bit of a stir in musical circles. [...] By the way, I hope to do that version of the *Water Music* which I played in Cape Town also in Australia. After the initial shock, I don't think anybody in his right mind can prefer Harty's version. Or don't you agree? However, I think the *Fireworks* recording should convince anybody. It is one of the most marvellous noises I have ever heard in my life, and most moving. [...]

Love, Charlie

The *Fireworks* record was very warmly received: Malcolm Macdonald in the *Gramophone* (June 1959) praised the splendid sound obtained by a 'strong-nerved recording staff', the 'judicious editing as to Handelian rhythms and ornamentation' and the performance as whole, concluding that it was 'an extravaganza which can scarcely fail to become a collectors' piece'. Such was its success that Pye invited Mackerras to make a recording (in September 1959) of another work with unusual forces: Janáček's *Sinfonietta*, along with four operatic preludes. Andrew Porter in the *Gramophone* (January 1960)

[28] Mackerras's mother visited Cape Town during the orchestral season he conducted there between November 1958 and March 1959. It gave him invaluable experience, and allowed him to conduct Mahler's First Symphony and Janáček's *Sinfonietta* for the first time (see Phelan 1987, pp. 113–14).

Figure 2 Mackerras's annotated score of 'La Réjouissance' from Handel's *Fireworks Music*

HMV 1. Tr etc with rep 3. TUTTI
2. Hn etc with repeats NO REP.
45
Ob. I
Ob. II
Tr. I
Tr. II
Tr. III
3RD oboe
Va
Timp.
Bassi
C#OB.2
f (p 2nd Time)
Ob. I
Ob. II
Tr. I
Tr. II
Tr. III
Timp.
Bassi
10
B. & H. 8812
OBOE 3

wrote that Mackerras's readings 'convey a sense of burning belief in and love of Janáček's music; they are well prepared; yet on each occasion it is as if the strangeness and beauty of the music were being revealed for the first time'.

Mackerras's next major Handel project was *Messiah*. He conducted a BBC broadcast of Basil Lam's edition in December 1963 and eventually persuaded EMI to record this version, with its extensive vocal and instrumental ornamentation. In *Gramophone* (March 1967), Christopher Bishop, producer of the recording, explained the reasons for 'Another *Messiah*' performed 'in the style of Handel's day':

> It is odd that it is necessary to attempt to justify the principle of ornamenting an eighteenth-century score [...] The practice of ornamentation was so much part of eighteenth-century music that no one at the time thought to produce editions of *Messiah* with all the embellishments written down. So to reconstruct a performance today, we need an editor and a conductor who are closely in sympathy with the style of the eighteenth century, and who are willing to see that the ornaments flow naturally from the music and do not appear to be 'added'. [...] Mackerras is a tremendous enthusiast, not only as an inspirer of his performers (this can be judged from the recording) but for the interpretation of old music. The now famous *Marriage of Figaro* performances he directed at Sadler's Wells, with their embellishments and cadenzas, did much to enhance his reputation in this field. It is rare to find a gifted conductor who is also prepared to be so thorough in the preparation of his work from the musicological point of view.

This recording stirred up some controversy. The Handel scholar Anthony Hicks attacked the Lam–Mackerras version in *Musical Times* (October 1966), six months before the recording was even released (but following a performance at the English Bach Festival). He found some of the editorial decisions 'rather disturbing' and objected to much of the ornamentation, both vocal and instrumental. But Mackerras's *Messiah* attempted the practical application of what was known at the time about Baroque performing style; while it was easy for academics to carp about the details, he was taking the risk of trying to put into practice ideas many of which had lain buried in treatises dating from Handel's time. So much has developed since 1966 in terms of performing styles that some of his *Messiah* may sound rather old-fashioned half a century on, but it still has tremendous verve and it was an important landmark. It had the bad luck to come out a few months after a rival small-forces version conducted by Colin Davis. This did not attempt anything as far-reaching in terms of embellishments, but several critics preferred Davis's lively but far more conventional approach. Roger Fiske in the *Gramophone* (March 1967) found it impossible to choose one over the other: 'I feel a great deal of admiration for what [Lam] has contributed to this performance, as also for the spirit and integrity of Charles Mackerras's conducting. This really is a most alive and fascinating performance, with splendid orchestral playing, soloists who all seem at the very top of their form, and excellent recording quality. Whether this is a better performance than Colin Davis's I am not prepared to say.'

It was not only *Messiah* that invited comparisons between Mackerras and Davis. Arthur Jacobs had previous written about their differing approaches to *Figaro* (*Guardian*, 11 November 1965):

> Colin Davis, who is shortly to relinquish the musical directorship of Sadler's Wells Opera, made his operatic début at the 'rival' theatre of Covent Garden last night. [...] Last April, Sadler's Wells unveiled its own excellent production, in which Charles Mackerras's sensitive conducting was backed by a scrupulous care not only for Mozart's original intentions but for the unwritten musical conventions of the time. Mr Davis takes a curiously inconsistent, not to say wilful, approach to ornamentation and other historical points of style. But it was tempting to surrender, for long stretches at least, to the sheer beauty and elegance of the well balanced sound.

Developing an operatic career

MACKERRAS was hurt and angry not to be asked to conduct the London premiere of Janáček's *Cunning Little Vixen* (22 March 1961), especially after successful revivals of *Káťa Kabanová* in 1959 (with Marie Collier in the title role – *Opera* in January 1960 described it as 'a triumphant success, and confirmation that the work is one of the masterpieces of 20th century opera') and February 1961 (with Amy Shuard as Káť'a). In an extremely candid letter to his mother dated 14 June 1961, Mackerras revealed how envious he was of the newly appointed Music Director of Sadler's Wells Opera, Colin Davis – a colleague with whom his relationships were destined to remain prickly:

> My dear Mum,
>
> [...] Colin Davis has been getting some bad reviews, but still these are a mere handful compared with the raving adulation he gets from most of the critics [...] It looks as if he is made for life. Never has any conductor had such success as he, and yet he is quite ordinarily competent really, nothing out of the box at all. It's almost enough to make one believe in pre-destination! [...] The Janáček opera *The Cunning Little Vixen* was an awful flop at the Wells, and I can't say I was very sorry, because I was absolutely furious that they didn't ask *me* to conduct it! I must confess to a great deal of jealousy over this whole Davis business. In a big place like London, one is used to other people having as much success as oneself, but it seems to me that he gets a disproportionate amount of success and engagements.

But, with a decade of experience at Sadler's Wells and several successful Italian operas at Wexford and Dublin in the late 1950s, Mackerras was starting to get invitations abroad, particularly to conduct opera. In 1962 he conducted *Ariadne auf Naxos*, *Don Giovanni*, *Falstaff* and *La Traviata* with the Australian Elizabethan Theatre Trust (precursor of Australian Opera), and at the State Opera (Deutsche Staatsoper) in East Berlin he conducted *Figaro* and *Fidelio*, *Don Carlos*, *Tosca* and *Der Rosenkavalier*, returning for more the following year, including a new production of *Carmen*. As reported in *Opera* (January 1963), he was offered a permanent post in East Berlin but declined it. He was paid in the non-convertible Ostmark, so Mackerras put this to good use by spending his fees on amassing a large library of orchestral parts – an invaluable resource in the years to come. In February 1964 Mackerras was back at Sadler's Wells for the first London production of Janáček's *Makropulos Affair*, with a cast led by Marie Collier as Emilia Marty. On 8 December 1964 he made his operatic debut at the Royal Opera House, conducting Shostakovich's *Katerina Ismailova*, with Marie Collier as Katerina. Georg Solti had been the Music Director there since 1961 and after the success of *Katerina Ismailova* he became an enthusiastic supporter of Mackerras, who greatly admired Solti's conducting and got on very well with him personally. Mackerras had first met Shostakovich in 1962, when he conducted a performance of the Ninth Symphony at the 1962 Edinburgh Festival at which the composer was present. On a subsequent visit to the Soviet Union, he was able to ask him about some points in *Katerina Ismailova*. Writing on 17 December 1964, Judy described the success of the Covent Garden performances to Charles's mother:

> Dearest Catherine & all,
>
> Somehow the pressure of living has become so great recently that neither Charles nor I can find time to write the long letter we *want* to write! This is a last minute attempt on my part to get something through before Christmas. I am just posting you a photo of F[iona] and C[atherine] taken only this month. [...] They are so full of enthusiasm for life generally & the theatre in particular (including opera) that we find them a rewarding pair after all these years! [...]
>
> I think our best news is that Charles has had an *enormous* success with his operatic début at Covent Garden. *Katerina Ismailova* (Shostakovich) has had three performances Dec. 8th, 14th & 16th. On each occasion Charles has received an ovation (before the 4th Act & at the end) which is unknown ever to have been given an English conductor & indeed rarely granted to anyone except Karajan, Giulini or Klemperer! The press has been unanimously excellent & has commented on his reception (will send you copies). We are very pleased, of course, & also a little surprised & mystified! Sadler's Wells are now coming up with a huge offer (already in the next season C. is contracted to do at the Wells, *Peter Grimes*, *Makropulos Case* & new productions of *Figaro*, *Don Giovanni* & *Carmen*). We are, as I say, a little mystified that after all this time he is *suddenly*, apparently, being acclaimed as an outstanding opera conductor. I've always been sure

> this was his strongest bent, so let us hope others continue to feel the same!
>
> Russia was musically very rewarding but in all other ways pretty grim & sinister. This will need a letter on its own. We met Shostakovich while we were there. [...]

Several engagements at Covent Garden followed during Mackerras's time in Hamburg and in his earliest seasons at ENO: *Turandot* in 1966, and again in 1967 and 1971 (with Birgit Nilsson), *Carmen* with Josephine Veasey (1967 and 1968), *Tosca* with Sena Jurinac (1968), *Così fan tutte* with a cast including Elisabeth Söderström and Lucia Popp, *Simon Boccanegra* with Peter Glossop and Rimsky-Korsakov's *Golden Cockerel* (all 1969), and Gluck's *Orfeo* with Yvonne Minton (1971). After Solti's departure from the Royal Opera in 1971, he continued to support Mackerras. Perhaps his most important intervention was with Decca Records: Solti was fascinated by *The Makropulos Affair* when he saw it at Sadler's Wells and contemplated making a recording for Decca. The idea was dropped, but Solti's enthusiasm for Janáček and for Mackerras's conducting was crucial in persuading the company to embark on Mackerras's Janáček series, starting with *Káťa Kabanová* in 1976.[29]

In 1968, Mackerras was sounded out about becoming Music Director of Sadler's Wells Opera (later English National Opera). Stephen Arlen, the Managing Director of Sadler's Wells, wrote to Mackerras in Hamburg on 9 October:

> What I wanted to discuss quietly and privately was whether you would be interested in the musical direction of Sadler's Wells Opera and if you were I could then discuss it formally with the Trust. Now we are established in the Coliseum I think we could provide someone like yourself with an instrument worth having and I think the opera could do with having a more experienced person in charge. You realise that this letter must be regarded as very very confidential in view of the arrangements we have here at the present time[30] and I would not like anyone to be hurt before I have had an opportunity of telling them what we have in mind.[31]

Mackerras replied on 12 October 1968:

> I am most interested in your suggestion about coming to the Wells as Musical Director. I have in fact a get-out clause in my Hamburg contract, although if you wanted me to start next season I would have to still do quite a lot in Hamburg for the first season. In other words

29 See James Mallinson's recollections in Phelan 1987, pp. 208–9.

30 Mario Bernardi (who was leaving to become founding conductor of the National Arts Centre Orchestra in his native Canada) and Bryan Balkwill were joint Music Directors.

31 Mackerras family archives, as is all other correspondence with Stephen Arlen.

> the change over might be a gradual rather than sudden one. At any rate, we can see how Liebermann reacts. [...] I take it of course that you would mean *sole* Musical Director, answerable only to you? If so, it sounds most promising.

He wrote again on 30 October to say that he had 'now spoken to Liebermann, who was a bit shattered, but none the less seemed willing to play ball. [...] I am sure that it can be worked OK, especially as I would do very little except the Wells and Hamburg if the idea comes off.' He then turned to practical matters:

> I would urgently like to see you, because I have literally hundreds of questions to ask you, and almost as many ideas and proposals for you! Could you slip over here for a few days? Apart from anything else, it might be a good idea if we talk to Liebermann together, as he is being really rather unexpectedly decent about it all. Also I want to make sure that he doesn't get Pauline Tinsley for an unlimited amount of time, so that she still has time for the Wells! If you come over, even for one day, you can stay with us and we can talk far into the night!

The next day he wrote again, alarmed that 'news of this proposed appointment has apparently already been leaked in England [...] Therefore, it is extremely urgent that we talk before Bryan Balkwill finds out about the whole thing in the wrong way.' Arlen duly went to Hamburg, and on 8 November 1968 Mackerras wrote to his accountant to say that he had 'just been offered the post of Musical Director of Sadler's Wells' and that 'Arlen would like to make the announcement of the new appointment as soon as possible'. On 13 November he wrote to Arlen about when and how the announcement should be made, adding: 'I hope you have been able already to talk to Bryan Balkwill, so my continuous presence around the Coliseum in December will not arouse the wrong kind of reaction!'

Some of the 'hundreds of questions' Mackerras had for Arlen are to be found on a closely typed four-page document in the conductor's files. The points included:

> *Duties of MD.* To choose repertoire? To choose which singers shall be members of the Company? To choose producers and designers for all operas, whether conducted by me or not? To have complete control over all artistic matters, in fact everything not directly related to money?
>
> *Singers.* How many of the singers who appear at the Wells are under full contract? Why do so many of the best singers leave Sadler's Wells as soon as they can? Is it that the Wells has *much* less money than Covent Garden. [...] This seems to me to be a very serious barrier to any great improvement in the Wells' singing standard. [...] I think this must be stopped. Can it be done by paying them more, or alternatively, by putting them on part-time contracts? This part-time or evening contract – Abend-Vertrag – works very well in Germany.

Coliseum. What do you think of the accusation that the size of the Coliseum is so great that it excludes the operas in which the Wells most excels? What are the acoustics really like? [...] With the acquisition of such a large theatre, will not the repertoire have to be different from before and larger [...] *Aida, Boris, Rosenkavalier* etc.? [...] If the repertoire is broadened, singers with larger voices will be needed to make this repertoire suitable for the Coli possible. Again, can the Wells afford singers like Charles Craig, Janet Baker, Stuart Burrows, Teresa Stratas, even Peter Glossop, Marie Collier, even for a small number of performances yearly so that all the British singers actually sing mainly in Britain?! How does Scottish Opera manage to afford so many international, ex-Wells singers which the Wells cannot?

Productions and Producers. Does the Wells Charter of employing only British artists also include producers and conductors and designers? In other words, can any of their three functions be done by foreigners if required? How much alteration does the scenery of most of your operas require to be made suitable for the Coli? Can many of the old and successful productions of the Wells be more or less thrown into the Coli without too much trouble and expense? I feel that the successful productions of an opera house should not be allowed to die so soon. [...] In Germany, many theatres share productions, so that the same production can be seen in say, Berlin, Hamburg, Munich etc. If this makes the productions *cheaper* for each theatre, would it be a good idea to occasionally adapt this system for the Wells?

Conductors. What is your plan for Bryan Balkwill, so that this very competent conductor does not leave, but still has no power to veto what I put in motion?

What is the nature of the contracts of the other conductors on the staff? I would like to see more experienced conductors used at the Wells. Why are, for instance, John Matheson, Alec [Alexander] Gibson, [...] Maurits Sillem [...] Edward Downes, David Lloyd-Jones, Rafael Kubelík [...] rarely if ever employed by the Wells. Money again?

New Productions. The following operas strike me as being suitable for the Wells at the Coli. They have also the advantage that they are either not done at Covent Garden, or the Covent Garden production is generally known to be bad. They could also be well cast two or three times over:

Rosenkavalier, Salome, Lohengrin, Boris, Otello, Falstaff, Sicilian Vespers, Nabucco, Wozzeck, Manon (Massenet), *Arden must Die,*[32] *The Nose*

[32] By Alexander Goehr. Mackerras had conducted the world premiere in Hamburg on 5 March 1967.

> Revivals urgently needed. Which of these have been bad box office at the Wells? *Fidelio, Peter Grimes, House of the Dead, Katya Kabanova, Rake's Progress, Queen of Spades, Eugene Onegin, Bartered Bride, Idomeneo, Andrea Chénier, Cav* and *Pag, Tosca, Bohème, Butterfly*.
>
> Why are the following singers not often employed at the Wells? [...] The names are mentioned at random rather than in alphabetical order or order of preference:
>
> Heather Harper, Elizabeth Harwood, Anna Reynolds, Marie Collier, April Cantelo, Elizabeth Bainbridge, Teresa Stratas, Margaret Price, Sheila Armstrong, Anne Howells, Monica Sinclair.
>
> Ryland Davies, Stuart Burrows, Charles Craig, Michael Rippon, Geoffrey Chard, John Mitchinson, Thomas Hemsley, Peter Glossop, David Ward.

The appointment was announced in the March 1969 issue of *Opera*:

> Sadler's Wells Opera: Mackerras in command. Charles Mackerras, 43, is to be musical director of Sadler's Wells Opera from next January. He will be solely responsible to Stephen Arlen, managing director. Although the two-company system is expected to be preserved (one company usually in London, one on tour), their artistic direction is now to be unified. There will no longer be two musical directors – hitherto, Mario Bernardi and Bryan Balkwill. Mr Bernardi's appointment to a new conducting post in Ottawa has already been announced; Mr Balkwill will conduct 'numerous guest performances' at the Coliseum from next season, including, once again, *The Force of Destiny*. At the Hamburg State Opera, where Charles Mackerras has been First Conductor since 1965, he will now be permanent guest conductor.

Almost as soon as he was appointed, Mackerras found that several of his cherished projects were threatened by financial woes: the cancellation of planned productions of Meyerbeer's *Le Prophète*, Prokofiev's *War and Peace* and Henze's *The Bassarids* (to be conducted by the composer) was announced on 9 February 1970 in the diary pages of *The Times*. Mackerras had written to Edmund Tracey, the company's dramaturg, from Dallas on 23 January, concerning the 'shattering news about cancelling *War and Peace* and *Prophète*', explaining that the changes would mean a season 'terribly short of more modern works'[33] and worried that the suggested replacements duplicated the Covent Garden repertoire. On his return from America, he wrote in the strongest terms to Arlen on 12 February (enclosing twenty copies, for members of the Trust): he was willing to concede that, given the financial crisis, repertoire changes would have to be made, but argued

[33] Mackerras family archives.

that the company's most desperate failing was its last-minute planning. This needed to change, 'otherwise none of us can proceed with any confidence at all'. Then came his most serious threat – and an offer to reduce his own salary in the interests of the company:

> I will now go so far as to say that unless plans for the 1970/71 season are complete by mid-March, and those for the season after that by the end of May 1970, i.e. repertoire agreed by the Trust and all singers, conductors, producers, etc. contracted, I cannot pursue my duties as Musical Director with any confidence, and shall be forced to resign at the end of this season.
>
> In view of the acute financial embarrassment in which the company finds itself, I state now that I would be willing to accept a reduction of £1500 in my salary during this first year of my contract as Musical Director, provided some concrete proposal is made for the use of this money as a contribution to the forward planning which I consider to be so absolutely vital, and upon which depends my being able to continue.

Ultimately, *War and Peace* and *The Bassarids* were rescued, the former a hugely successful production that opened on 11 October 1972 (conducted by David Lloyd-Jones). In December 1970, Mackerras wrote privately to David McKenna, chairman of the Sadler's Wells Trust, to explain that 'the General Manager [Arlen] and I will never agree on matters of planning [...] in fact we totally disagree on almost every subject with regard to the running of the Company and its artistic policy'.[34] He enclosed a copy of his letter of 12 February 'which I asked [Arlen] to distribute to the Trust meeting. He did not do so'. Again, it was doubtful whether Mackerras could remain much longer at the Coliseum, since his dealings with Arlen had reached an impasse. Circumstances changed with Arlen's sudden death from cancer in January 1972. Before this unexpected tragedy, Mackerras had approached Lord Harewood, asking if he would be prepared to take over at Sadler's Wells, but Harewood said he would not depose Arlen. Meanwhile – according to Harewood – Arlen had been trying to remove Mackerras: 'Jack [Lord] Donaldson, who was close to Arlen, had said to Harewood: "You know if Stephen had lived we would probably have had to get rid of Charlie." This would, Harewood said, "have been wrong – not a matter of opinion – wrong".'[35] So traumatised was Reginald Goodall by Arlen's death that he withdrew from conducting the forthcoming ENO production of *Rhinegold*; Mackerras took over, and the first night was a great success. With the arrival of Lord Harewood as General Manager of the company in 1972 (announced on 17 April), Mackerras felt that he was working alongside a kindred spirit. Just how much happier this relationship would be is evident from a letter

[34] Mackerras family archives.

[35] Gilbert 2009, pp. 241–2.

Mackerras sent to Harewood (then in Australia) on 3 March 1972, six weeks before the announcement of his appointment:

> Dear George,
>
> First let me thank you most warmly for your cable of good wishes for the *Rhinegold*. Despite a few criticisms of the staging and designs, some of which are true, the production has been a tremendous success and has received universally good notices, especially for me, even from the most dedicated Goodall fans [...]. Some of the lighting and scenery need seeing to, and I found that the original Valhalla concept was cut out for financial reasons. An extra £1500 will have to go into the budget for next season, to make an actual concrete Valhalla, not merely a projection, so that the projection of the rainbow and the shadows of the various singers and the GOLD are not continually thrown on to the rather dark Valhalla. Also, because of this rather silly projection of Valhalla, it means that the final scene, which should take place in the evening light actually is a dark scene, and the Sword and the Spear and the Rainbow Bridge all go for nothing. Two very interesting things emerged from the performance singing-wise. Emile Belcourt's simply marvellous Loge and Derek Hammond-Stroud's Alberich, both great performances in their way, and new to our *Ring*.
>
> I am now in the throes of *Bluebeard*[*'s Castle*] and Odious [*Oedipus Rex*]. I think you will be impressed by the productions of these. [Ronald] Dowd went into retirement by walking out on us without explanation and flying from America to Australia instead of to London to do Odious!! Thank God we managed to get John Mitchinson for most of the performances. [...]
>
> McKenna told me that he is working hard on the Arts Council about the change of name of the Company [to English National Opera] so that it should be announced in April or May, along with your appointment and the repertoire for the next season. All these things together will make a tremendous impact on the opera world, I think.
>
> I hope you are both enjoying sunny Aussie and the operas and the lovely new voices that must be coming out and wanting to rush over to England to make careers in the big metropolis!
>
> I will try and write again next Sunday, if there is any startling turn of events. Meantime both Judy and I both send you both our love. That is an involved clumsy sentence. The Germans do it more concisely: Viele Grüsse von Haus zu Haus.
>
> At any rate, LOVE![36]

When Mackerras left his post as Music Director in December 1977, Rodney Milnes summarised his achievements in the January 1978 issue of *Opera*:

[36] Mackerras family archives.

The eight years [...] are framed by Mozart and Janáček, and it would be with those composers that most would associate Mackerras's name. He is surely the foremost Janáček conductor of the day [...] Two years ago, after the Coliseum's new *Don Giovanni*, the Editor wrote: 'I can think of no present-day musician whom I would rather hear conducting a Mozart opera, and that includes the much-praised Karl Böhm'. Now whether or not you (or indeed the Editor) would agree in the light of last month's *Figaro* [a revival at Covent Garden conducted by Böhm], that is just the sort of enthusiastic reaction that a good Mackerras performance can elicit. But it would be unjust to stop there. Mackerras's Verdi performances at both London opera houses have been extravagantly and justly praised. They have been quite masterly, especially the *Aida* in 1973. His Massenet is also outstanding; it takes a musician of his vision to see the essential toughness lurking just beneath the sugary surface of a piece like *Werther*. For me no other conductor since Leibowitz has caught the dry, elegant wit of Offenbach; it was typical that even in so large a house he should have used the original orchestration of *La belle Hélène* and, what is more, made it work. It is sad that so fine a Handel conductor should have given only one of his works at the Coliseum; musically it was remarkable – and again, text played as important a part as it does in all his readings – and the production was not perhaps quite as dire as everyone thought it was at the time. His *Carmen*, in a good clean text, after much previous experimentation had critics reaching for their 'not-since-Beecham' superlatives. His Strauss is of so clean a quality – Mackerras the musician can sort out what is actually going on in the scores – that one regrets all the more that for reasons beyond his control he did not conduct *Salome* as planned. He revealed Donizetti to me, no mean feat since it took three performances of *Mary Stuart* to do it. Szymanowski, Stravinsky, Sullivan, Berlioz, Beethoven, Johann Strauss, Bartók, Puccini, Britten, Smetana, Wagner – he has conducted them all with virtually unqualified success in the eight years. The versatility of the man is truly bewildering. A repertory of 110 operas may have been commonplace in Germany earlier in the century, but there can surely be no conductor of comparable stature today with so catholic a repertory.

[...] There have been qualifications, often with reference to his Wagner (though his *Lohengrin* was, I thought, greatly underestimated). The fact that, as newly appointed Musical Director, he stood aside while the Goodall Ring was forged, yet cancelled foreign engagements to step in for the master when he fell ill before the first night of *Rhinegold*, speaks highly of him. He has since conducted six cycles within a year – April 1975 (tour) to February 1976 (London) – and others thereafter. In his most recent cycle he made the music sound more beautiful simply as music than any other conductor I have heard in the theatre.

It would perhaps be impertinent to suggest that he has changed in these eight years, yet it would also be unrealistic to claim that he has not. A colleague has described him as a conductor who prefers performance to rehearsal, a characteristic shared with Knappertsbusch. It seemed in those early days as though he were determined to get the best possible playing and singing by sheer dynamism. Many was the review in the early 70s that mentioned a fast overture, a driven first act and a noticeable settling down later on. This was certainly true of first nights. I remember a *Madam Butterfly* in which during the fastest-ever prelude I seemed to see 70 or so orchestral jaws dropping open in sheer amazement (and he kept it up through most of the performance, too). *C'etait magnifique, mais ce n'etait pas Puccini.* But recently, even the Editor complained that the first part of a Mozart evening was a little on the leisurely side, and in the last series of *Katya* performances I thought – and fervently hoped – that the first dozen bars of the prelude were going to last for an eternity. A Mackerras reading is never dull, is always imbued with powerful theatrical thrust. Perhaps he sometimes gets carried away by music, but is that not preferable to ever-calculating, ever-careful conducting? Either way, I believe that now the necessity to spur on his players has receded, so he has mellowed musically. What will we remember from the Mackerras years? Not just the Janáček, Mozart, Verdi and Strauss (do not forget his *Ariadne*). As Musical Director he has been involved in shaping a repertory balanced between bread-and-butter and caviare, in pushing even those pieces with which he was not personally concerned (*Euryanthe* was one). In his time we have had *War and Peace*, two Massenet operas (though with Lord Harewood and Edmund Tracey as colleagues he will not have had to push too hard for those), Donizetti, *Dalibor*, both versions of *Fidelio*, that extraordinary *Damnation of Faust*, and *The Bassarids*. He has shown a consistently constructive attitude to text: his articles on *Makropoulos* and Gluck's *Orfeo* in *Opera* are required reading on both pieces. He has built the orchestra into a remarkable instrument, one that has stood comparison with that at Covent Garden. He has nurtured company singers – draw up your own lists. He has proudly shown this company off at the Proms and in Vienna (the Viennese notices make fascinating and heart-warming reading).

Despite foreign engagements in Europe, Australia and America, he has not been an absentee Musical Director. 338 performances of 42 operas is a staggering record [...] But the proof is in the pudding, and our eating of it: a steadily rising standard of musical performance since he took over.

Is there anything we have not had? It is sad that *Brouček* has had to be postponed, that the rumoured *Prophète* and *Guillaume Tell* did not materialise, that he has not been able to conduct a Gluck opera in his own house as he has so memorably at Covent Garden and for

> the BBC, that he has not been able to try a Dvořák opera out on us, thus completing his Czech trilogy, and that there has been no new production of a Britten opera. But at only 52 Mackerras is still a young man. We are promised one new production and two major revivals a season for the time being. Anything could happen, and while we wait for it to happen let us be grateful for all that this most distinguished musician has already given us.

To this article, *Opera* added a list of all the new productions and revivals that Charles Mackerras conducted at the Coliseum during his time as Music Director of Sadler's Wells Opera/ENO, from 1 January 1970 until 31 December 1977 (see Appendix 1). On top of the forty-two operas he conducted with SWO/ENO in 1970–77, there were a further eleven that he had done with the company before his tenure: *Ariadne on Naxos, The Bartered Bride, Cavalleria rusticana, Don Pasquale, Hansel and Gretel, Luisa Miller, Pagliacci, The Rake's Progress, Rigoletto, Tosca* and *Peter Grimes*. By the end of 1977, his operatic repertoire was already vast: including overseas performances and broadcasts, it amounted to 110 works, and plenty more were to follow.

The next decade included periods as Principal Guest Conductor of the BBC Symphony and Chief Conductor of the Sydney Symphony Orchestra, and more operas in the Janáček series for Decca. He conducted eight performances of Meyerbeer's *Le Prophète* at the Metropolitan Opera in September and October 1979, with a cast including Marilyn Horne. During this visit he was also asked to substitute for an indisposed Rafael Kubelík at the New York Philharmonic. One consequence was that on 29 September he conducted the Saturday matinée of *Prophète* before conducting an evening concert with the Philharmonic. Mackerras admitted to Raymond Ericson in the *New York Times* (7 October) that 'I thought it was going to be nice to sit here, relax, enjoy the city and study some of the scores I'll have to conduct'. Things did not quite work out that way, and he described that Saturday as 'very exhausting, but when I thought about it, the two events were only slightly longer in playing time than *Götterdämmerung*'. For *Der Rosenkavalier* in December 1982 at the Vienna State Opera, the cast included Gundula Janowitz, Agnes Baltsa and Manfred Jungwirth. Since very limited rehearsal time was available, Mackerras talked to friends in the orchestra and decided it would be better to do the performances on no rehearsals at all – a decision that made for a notably good-natured and exhilarating evening. At Covent Garden, Mackerras conducted Gluck's *Alceste* for Janet Baker's farewell performances in 1981, while at the Coliseum his repertoire included Martinů's *Julietta*, Janáček's *Brouček*, Massenet's *Werther*, Wagner's *Mastersingers* and Bizet's *Pearl Fishers*. The decade following his departure from ENO had been highly successful, but it involved extensive travel. As Charles turned 60 in 1985, Judy felt strongly that he should think about taking up an appointment at home. Though he was reluctant to take on another music directorship, he certainly hoped he might be asked to succeed Colin Davis at Covent Garden. Alan Blyth (among others) was forthright in his support: his article in the *Daily Telegraph*, headed 'The Right Man', declared that 'Nobody, and I mean nobody, conducting opera today has such a wide range of works in his repertoire, or such a catholicity of taste, nor such a great experience of exercising his talents in the opera house. [...] Can anyone show just cause why such a comprehensively equipped musician should be passed over?'[37] But passed over he was, and Covent Garden's loss was quickly turned to advantage in Cardiff: in 1987, as Bernard Haitink began his tenure at the Royal Opera House, Mackerras became the new Music Director of Welsh National Opera.

[37] Quoted in Phelan 1987, p. 205.

2

A Personal Portrait of Charles Mackerras

David Lloyd-Jones

No other colleagues worked more closely with Charles for over forty years than I did, so much so that we also became great family friends. It was thanks to him that at least three important steps in my career took place. I first remember him when I was a schoolboy in London, regularly attending opera performances at Sadler's Wells in the early 1950s: after a performance, this strikingly gaunt, pale, hollow-eyed and red-haired young maestro would come on for the curtain calls. I met him next at auditions for Cedric Messina's 1965 BBC studio production of *La Bohème*, for which I was the associate conductor.[1] We hit it off immediately, and I performed the same task for him on three other occasions. It was Charles who got me my first job conducting for Sadler's Wells Opera and who, soon after, appointed me his Associate Conductor at ENO. Among other things, this involved my sitting behind him at orchestral and stage rehearsals and eventually taking over from him (with no rehearsal). He was partly influential in my being asked to found English National Opera North in 1978. Inevitably, the distance between London and Leeds made our meetings less frequent, but we still remained in close contact, and I attended his performances as often as I could. Coincidentally, we were fellow Scorpios: Charles's birthday was on 17 November, mine on the 19th, with the result that we and our wives used to meet up whenever possible for a meal on the 18th.

Opera was Charles's first love, and I very much doubt if there has ever been a person who has conducted such an enormous number of them over so wide a range of nationalities, periods and styles. It was virtually impossible to name an opera that he had not conducted, often in a variety of productions in countries all over the world. This vast experience, allied to his astonishing memory for detail, resulted in his total command over this complex medium in which first-hand experience is all-important. I wonder how many of the young concert conductors (often Eastern European) who eventually try their hand at opera would know about the traditional downward transposition of 'Di quella pira' (*Trovatore*) and where to begin it. In this connection I remember a singer of the Queen of the Night requesting that her B flat aria be put down a tone. Charles flatly refused, largely on the grounds that Mozart's sole operatic use of the key of A flat was in the Act 2 finale of *Così*. He had an encyclopaedic knowledge of cuts, both traditional and rare. I was lucky enough to be taken by Charles through certain standard operas, such

[1] This was a very exacting job, as Charles was with the orchestra in one studio, while I, relaying his beat from monitors to the singers and running around with them, was in another. Charles had performed the same task when younger.

as *Carmen* and *Butterfly*, before first conducting them. He knew every trick in the book (including how to deal with the Guiraud recitatives in *Carmen*) and could immediately remember important misprints still lurking in the standard orchestral parts. His understanding of singers' requirements, such as traditional pauses and high notes, was complete, as was his appreciation of fine singing, although, curiously, he rarely worked with singers at the piano. Having cut his teeth at Sadler's Wells, where there was no prompter, he was very good at giving left-hand cues to singers (who were performing from memory), with the result that he earned their affectionate nickname 'Chuck-'em-up-Charlie'.

Charles was no lover of attending the extensive production rehearsals (getting more numerous each decade) that opera ideally requires. At the first stage rehearsals he would occasionally say 'Why can't the chorus enter from stage left?', leaving the producer to remonstrate: 'Charles, we have been rehearsing this for a month. If you had put in such a request earlier I might have done something about it, but now it is far too late.' Critics and others often used to state that Charles was a very theatrical opera conductor, and this cannot be denied. However, in my opinion, this did not spring from a special interest in the dramatic side of opera so much as from his theatrical temperament, which had an intense, occasionally impatient quality, resulting more often than not in tempos that were on the fast (read 'theatrical') side. Like all true opera conductors, Charles was always concerned with balance between pit and stage. In this he was helped by his wide experience: he usually knew in advance where the danger spots were and how to deal with them. It also helped that he was a fine linguist, French, German, Italian and Czech (and therefore, to some extent, Russian) being effortlessly at his command. Only Charles could have been overjoyed at finding on the library shelves of a posh health farm that he and Judy attended a complete Italian edition of the works of Metastasio!

Opera, then, was a kingdom of which Charles had complete command and understanding. His concert repertoire, both symphonic and choral, was also extensive, though nobody, I think, could come close to that of Gennadi Rozhdestvensky. Charles's time with the BBC Concert Orchestra (the only non-operatic British orchestra of which he was principal conductor) meant that the lighter side of the repertoire was also very familiar to him. When I made in Australia a new recording of songs popularised by Peter Dawson, Charles knew them all, texts included. As a result he was very much at home with light music (hence *Pineapple Poll* et al.), but it has to be said that, thanks to his intense concentration on the finer details of execution, his appearance and attitude did not always convey the spirit of relaxation that is also a desirable quality in such works.[2] Charles was a very good concerto accompanist (just as Sir Malcolm Sargent was) and here again his

[2] Witness the varying effectiveness in this respect of the conductors of Vienna's New Year's Day concerts – events that Charles much enjoyed.

enormous experience with a variety of soloists and orchestras paid dividends. Altogether, his repertoire was very wide-ranging. He was prepared to take on any style, from the pre-Classical Europeans to Elliott Carter (not his personal choice), and spent much time researching the backgrounds and textual problems of each work that he had to deliver.

Charles's catalogue of commercial recordings is enormous. It started with his HMV 1951 account of *Pineapple Poll* with the Sadler's Wells Orchestra (still sounding well), following the highly successful premiere. After this he never looked back, and went on to make recordings for over a dozen different companies, ranging from Cavalieri (1600) to Bartók and Britten.[3] His extensive repertoire included the complete symphonies of Mozart, Beethoven and Brahms, all but the most youthful operas of Mozart and, of course, the operas of Janáček. He was always completely at home in the recording studio, where his fine ear for detail and exacting standards regularly produced excellent results, though at the sessions these qualities were not always appreciated by the recording teams, who, as ever, had their eyes firmly trained on the clock.

No account of Charles's musicianship can be given without mentioning the word 'appoggiatura' and the concept of vocal decoration. His interest in authentic performance practice went back to his wartime student days at the Sydney Conservatorium and eventually became ground-breaking. He met heavy resistance to any such practices during his time as Erster Kapellmeister at the Hamburg State Opera. After an unrehearsed trial performance of *Così* there in 1965, the head of the music staff congratulated him the next day on a fine performance. 'Yes, but not one damn appoggiatura the whole evening,' exclaimed Charles. 'Herr Mackerras,' was the reply, 'it is rumoured that you may soon be joining us as number two to GMD General Music Director] Leopold Ludwig. I should warn you that here in North Germany we do not make appoggiaturas.' 'That's nothing to be proud of,' said Charles; 'you might as well say that in North Germany you sing out of tune.' During his time at Hamburg he managed to bribe the largely American cast of *Die Zauberflöte* by offering them an American cigarette (he bought many duty-free packets during his regular journeys to England) for every new appoggiatura he required. 'I've got only two to go, David,' he told me triumphantly.[4] Charles was not the first conductor in Britain to urge the use of appoggiaturas; surprisingly, Sir Henry Wood had espoused the cause some fifty years earlier, but even he did not equal the crusading zeal that Charles brought to a practice that is now universally adopted, occasionally to excess. As far as vocal decoration in Mozart (and later Handel) is concerned, he managed to enthuse the influential record producer Walter Legge and

[3] In the Cavalieri recording, Herbert von Karajan's brother Wolfgang played the portative organ. Charles much enjoyed having to say 'Herr von Karajan you are dragging, Herr von Karajan please watch my beat', and so on.

[4] During his time in Hamburg Charles regularly stayed with us.

his wife Elisabeth Schwarzkopf on the subject.[5] Despite Charles's untiring research in contemporary treatises on the subject, especially during his days off during operatic engagements in Europe, not everybody agreed that his decorations were stylish, in particular in his beloved Handel.[6]

Let me now attempt an overview of Charles's qualities as a conductor. The first thing to say is that he was a musician through and through, indeed to some extent only a musician. Other conductors have side interests or hobbies, or are great general readers, but not Charles. One had the impression that, however delightful and amusing he could be as a social companion, his waking hours were devoted almost exclusively to thinking and reading about music. This led to another quality he possessed, an exceptional ability to focus on the work he was performing and to act as the composer's earthly advocate. I can remember a series of performances that we shared at ENO of *Káťa Kabanová*. I had done virtually all the preparatory rehearsals and tried my best to get the new Káťa to perform in the way that I knew Charles wanted. Before he took over – I think at the stage and orchestra rehearsals – I told him that I had been able to get so far with her but no further and warned him that he might have to adapt his performance to accommodate some of her limitations. I need not have worried. Charles completely mesmerised the singer and, deploying what the orchestra used to call his 'death-ray' look of alarm ('we can't let the composer down!'), licked her into shape. There was no feeling of 'this is how I want it', only of 'this is how I interpret Janáček's wishes as laid down in his score'. It was a perfect example of the quality that Charles always admired most in conductors, that of *Ausstrahlung*, a term usually translated as 'charisma'.

One of the most surprising aspects of Charles's technical grasp of the orchestra was that this former wind player had an uncanny knowledge and understanding of the endless intricacies of string bowing. He frequently challenged section leaders over what he considered to be the most appropriate bowing and, more often than not, was proved to be right. From Emanuel Hurwitz he also learned the value of 'prophylactic bowing', that is to say bowing which, if properly adhered to, prevented such things as unwanted crescendos. All this was to cut across string players' customary

[5] Schwarzkopf told her friend Christa Ludwig about it, and I was astonished to attend a 1960 performance of *Figaro* at the Vienna State Opera which General Music Director Karajan had decided on the day that he would like to conduct, in which Ludwig sang an impromptu decorated second verse of 'Voi che sapete'.

[6] Charles's devotion to authenticity occasionally had its bizarre side. At a symposium organised by the Friends of ENO following the new production in 1974 of *Don Carlos*, he challenged the fairly conservative designer over some relatively small detail which he considered to be not in keeping with the period. The designer defended himself and ultimately challenged Charles by saying 'you don't want to see Shakespeare's Cleopatra "authentically" acted by a teenage boy, do you?' 'Of course I do,' replied Charles, to everybody's astonishment and amusement.

use of 'bowings of convenience'. This did not necessarily endear him to string players, but it undoubtedly earned their respect.

Charles was a meticulous rehearser and a past master at spotting wrong notes in the parts. When he took over the famous Sadler's Wells/ENO *Mastersingers* that Reginald Goodall had regularly performed to general admiration, he discovered a wrong note in bar 26 of the Prelude to Act 1. Again, when he was obliged to conduct a ballet triple bill that had been in the repertoire of the Hamburg State Opera for a number of years, he spent most of his meagre rehearsal time correcting wrong notes, to the utter amazement of the orchestra. Charles did not waste rehearsal time and spoke only to the point. He became known to British orchestral players, even to those who did not fully go along with his manner, as an outstandingly efficient, hyper-professional rehearser. If time was short, Charles was the man who could sort things out to maximum effect. Ally this quality with his understanding of a whole range of styles, plus a clear and expressive stick technique, and you have a blueprint for the conductor par excellence. If he did not possess the unique personal magnetism of a Beecham or even a Barbirolli, he was in all other respects the genuine article.

What, if any, were Charles's limitations? Well, whatever the conductor's equivalent of a doctor's bedside manner is, it has to be said that in the early years of his career, Charles possessed it to a rather limited degree. By his own admission to me, and by common agreement within the profession, Charles as a young man could seem blunt to the point of rudeness. But it was not rudeness – it was simply stating things as he found (heard) them in the most straightforward and efficient way. With singers he could be equally direct. Instead of using, when they were flat, some euphemistic phrase such as 'I find that a little under the note' or 'that sounds a bit southern', Charles would say, to even the most distinguished singer, 'that's flat', and this in front of an orchestra and chorus. Some resented this treatment, but on the whole singers, being the lovely people they generally are and anxious to perform at their best, took it all in good part and thought 'it's just Charlie being Charlie again'. Orchestras were often amazed at their good nature. In this respect he mellowed greatly, and, in addition to his recent more diplomatic treatment of performers, I have in my memory bank a fund of his memorable jokes and quips.

It always surprised me that Charles, who, as I have said, had such a phenomenal memory for music as written, never in my experience conducted from memory even the pieces that he must have performed over a hundred times, such as the *Fledermaus* Overture. This, of course, is not a criticism, merely an observation. More to the point is a comment made to me by an admiring colleague: 'I sometimes wish that Charles would not let his head rule his heart so much.' It has to be conceded that there is some truth in this remark. Such was his profound interest in performance practice that the results were sometimes tinged with a cerebral quality. I think of his recordings of the two Elgar symphonies where, having listened to Elgar's own recordings, Charles insisted on inserting all the string slides heard on them into the orchestral parts. What was intuitive, even stylish, with the orchestras of Elgar's day sounds somewhat contrived in Charles's performances.

I have given as rounded a portrait as I can of a man and friend whom I admired almost unreservedly, who influenced me greatly, and whose myriad recorded performances will certainly withstand the test of time. He ended up a knight of the realm, an honorary Doctor of Music (Oxon), a Companion of Honour and a recipient of the Gold Medal of the Royal Philharmonic Society, no mean achievement for an ambitious young oboist from Down Under who slowly (fortunately) but surely reached the very top of his profession in Europe and the New World, and who is still remembered with enormous admiration and affection by a whole range of musicians, especially singers and fellow conductors.

3

Mackerras and Janáček

John Tyrrell

'If I'll be remembered for anything,' Charles Mackerras once said, 'it will be for Janáček.' Readers of this book will be aware that Mackerras is remembered for much more, but in a sense he was right: other composers on which he particularly left his imprint, such as Handel, Mozart, Beethoven and Brahms, were well known long before Charles Mackerras came along. He simply found new ways of presenting them, making them sound different and thus contributing to a new perception of how music from the Baroque to the late Romantic period might be played to contemporary audiences. But for Janáček he was there from the beginning, at least outside the Czech and German lands. He conducted the first Janáček opera to be performed in Britain in 1951. Almost sixty years later he conducted a Janáček opera (*The Cunning Little Vixen*) just months before he died. In between he conducted Janáček all over the world and made many recordings. And during these sixty years Janáček turned from a unknown, cult composer making little impact on British opera audiences in early productions to one of the most frequently performed twentieth-century opera composers. This was largely the doing of Charles Mackerras and his well informed, passionate and persistent advocacy.

Discovery

Mackerras discovered Janáček in Prague in the autumn of 1947. With the war over, he had moved from his native Australia to work in London, where from May 1947 he had taken up a thirteen-week appointment as second oboe and repetiteur at the Sadler's Wells Opera Company. But his heart was set on conducting and he believed that he would get quicker and greater experience of opera conducting in particular if he spent a year abroad. Germany and Austria seemed the obvious places, but they were devastated by the war. A chance encounter with a Czech expatriate musician who observed Mackerras reading a Dvořák score (the Seventh Symphony, as it happened)[1] suggested an alternative: Prague. Czechoslovakia, recently freed of Nazi rule and not yet having succumbed to Soviet rule, was comparatively unscathed by the Second World War and had managed to maintain concert and operatic activity, presided over by one of the great conductors of the twentieth century, Václav Talich. Mackerras applied for and obtained a British Council scholarship in Czechoslovakia for a year, and he arrived in

[1] Phelan 1987, p. 60.

Prague on 26 September 1947 with Judy Wilkins, whom he had married a month earlier.[2] 'On no account bring wife,' ordered the British Council, but Judy came anyway at her own expense. After various complications (the Prague Academy of Performing Arts had not been informed of his arrival), both Charles and Judy were eventually registered: she to further her clarinet studies, he to study conducting. Both began learning Czech and absorbing the atmosphere; in time, Charles began to take private conducting lessons with Václav Talich in addition to his studies at the Academy.[3]

'Saw *Káťa Kabanová* at Národní Theatre. Superb performance. Talich,' Judy wrote in her diary for 15 October 1947.[4] The Mackerrases had gone to the Prague National Theatre on spec that evening, since Talich was conducting and two of the leading Czech singers (Beno Blachut and Marta Krásová) were performing. Apart from playing oboe in Janáček's wind sextet *Mládí*, this was Mackerras's first encounter with Janáček,[5] an event which left a huge and lasting impression. 'During my year as a student in Prague,' Mackerras later recalled,

> it was a constant exciting experience to discover more and more works both operatic and symphonic by this great composer, and my wife and I used to travel to other cities, notably Brno, so as to be able to hear as many of Janáček's works as possible. By the end of that year, I had seen nearly all Janáček's operas, some in two or three different productions. I also had an opportunity of experiencing the different styles of Janáček performances which obtained in Czechoslovakia; the 'Prague Style', led by Talich, who brought out the smooth lyricism of Janáček, sometimes even 'beautifying' Janáček's often rough orchestration to give the music more luscious, even Straussian colours, and the 'Brno Style', which kept rigorously to Janáček's orchestration as he wrote it, 'warts and all'.[6]

It is now impossible to say exactly what they saw, since Judy's diary for 1948 has disappeared. At Prague's National Theatre, the only other production they could have seen was *Jenůfa* (and there were new, post-war productions of *Jenůfa* available in seven other Czechoslovak cities).[7] However the highly enterprising Grand Opera of the Fifth of May (which briefly operated

[2] Phelan 1987, pp. 70–1.

[3] Phelan 1987, pp. 70–1.

[4] Mackerras family archives.

[5] Phelan 1987, p. 75.

[6] Charles Mackerras: 'Introduction' [to *Káťa Kabanová*], disc notes to Decca recording of *Káťa Kabanová*, D51D 2 (1977), p. 3.

[7] Svatava Přibáňová: 'Přehled inscenací jevištního díla Leoše Janáčka z let 1894–1998/Overview of Stage Productions of Leoš Janáček's Work between 1884 and 1998', *Svět Janáčkových oper/The World of Janáček's Operas* (Brno: Moravské Muzeum, Nadace Leoše Janáčka and Město Brno, 1998).

independently in the old German Theatre in Prague before being taken over by the National Theatre) already had in its repertoire a rival production of *Káťa Kabanová*, memorable for its sets by the great stage designer Josef Svoboda, and, during the Mackerras's time in Prague, presented one of Janáček's rarest operas, *The Excursions of Mr Brouček*, in the first staged production in Prague (premiere: 6 February 1948) since its 1920 premiere.[8] Brno, however, offered three more Janáček operas: *The Cunning Little Vixen*, *The Makropulos Affair* and *From the House of the Dead*, all unavailable elsewhere in the world at the time and all on display, together with *Jenůfa* and *Káťa Kabanová*, in a special cycle of five Janáček operas which ran from 5 May 1948.[9] In his 1973 interview with Lord Harewood (see note 20) Mackerras remembers that while he was in Prague there was a 'Gastspiel from the Brno theatre in which they did all the well-known Janáček operas in one week, and then they repeated them the next week'. This was part of the 1948 Prague Spring Festival, in which from 22 May the Brno company presented *Jenůfa*, *From the House of the Dead*, *The Cunning Little Vixen*, *Káťa Kabanová* and *The Makropulos Affair* at the Grand Opera (*Lidové noviny*, 13 May 1948). Whether in Prague or in Brno (three hours away by train), or even in both, Mackerras would have been able to see all the Janáček operas that Brno had on offer and would thus have been in the enviable position, as one of few non-Czechs at the time, of having seen Janáček's six major operas in stage productions. 'It is a terrible pity,' Mackerras wrote to his mother in May 1948, 'that these works [Janáček operas] are quite unknown outside this country. They are certainly in the front rank of modern opera and in my opinion the best works ever produced by a Czech. When I get back I shall do my utmost to persuade Sadler's Wells to perform one of them, though I don't suppose they will.'[10] He was wrong, however: within a couple of years Janáček's opera *Káťa Kabanová* was staged by Sadler's Wells.

An apostle for Janáček in London

MACKERRAS returned to a modest appointment at Sadler's Wells from September 1948 as repetiteur with some conducting; within a year he was conducting *Fledermaus*, *Rigoletto* and other operas in the standard repertoire, more and more so as the health of the chief conductor, Michael Mudie (suffering from disseminated sclerosis), deteriorated.[11] While in Czechoslovakia, Mackerras had acquired a piano-vocal score of *Káťa Kabanová*. Armed with this and a tape of a broadcast Brno performance from the BBC, he managed to persuade Norman Tucker (from 1948 managerial

[8] Ibid.

[9] *Soupis repertoáru Českého divadla v Brně 1884–1974* [List of the repertoire of the Czech Theatre in Brno 1884–1974] (Brno: Státní divadlo v Brně, 1974), p. 149.

[10] Phelan 1987, p. 93.

[11] Phelan 1987, pp. 81, 85–6.

head of Sadler's Wells) and the music critic Desmond Shawe-Taylor of the merits of the piece.[12] Not only did Tucker sanction a production in the 1950/1 season, but he himself produced a singing translation (and would continue to do so for three more Janáček operas), while Shawe-Taylor became one of Janáček's strongest advocates in the press.

Káťa Kabanová thus became the first Janáček opera to be staged in Britain. While Mackerras's experience with Janáček in Czechoslovakia equipped him ideally to teach and rehearse the singers, Mudie, as chief conductor, was due to conduct. His condition, however, affected his eyesight, and with such unfamiliar music it became clear a week before the show opened that he could not go on.[13] So, at the age of twenty-five, Mackerras conducted the premiere and the six repeat performances that season.[14] Critical reaction to the opera was generally negative. A typical comment appeared in *The Stage* (12 April 1951): 'So short-winded and the phrasing so abrupt and broken up that one is never conscious of a continuous flow. It is a kind of perpetual recitative, and one waits in vain for a release into the clear waters of pure song.'[15] The doyen of British music critics, Ernest Newman (who had encountered *Jenůfa* in New York in 1924 and had made his feelings about it very clear at the time), dismissed Janáček as 'rather a scrap-by-scrap composer, finding it difficult to think consecutively for more than two or three numbers at a time' (*Sunday Times*, 15 April 1951). The *Glasgow Herald* summarised the general reaction: 'It is doubtful, however, whether [Sadler's Wells's] latest operatic venture has been worth all the time, energy and youthful talent expended on it.' In trying to work out why *Káťa* failed in 1951, Adrienne Simpson concluded that the performances were 'certainly ill at ease. Despite thirty orchestral rehearsals singers and players probably found Janáček's unusual idiom as difficult as the critics did. Audiences had not been prepared for the style of writing they were to hear'.[16]

There were two further performances in the autumn, with scarcely more box-office interest. By 1954, when the opera was revived for four performances to celebrate the hundredth anniversary of Janáček's birth, Mackerras was no longer on the Sadler's Wells music staff and instead the Czech conductor Rafael Kubelík took over. He had greater success in filling the theatre, partly due to the fact that, unlike the young Mackerras, Kubelík was internationally famous; by 1955, when there were three more

[12] Phelan 1987, p. 93.

[13] Phelan 1987, p. 94.

[14] See 'Janáček opera performances' in Appendix 1 for details of this and subsequent opera performances.

[15] This and other quotations from reviews printed in Adrienne Simpson: '*Káťa Kabanová* in the United Kingdom', *Leoš Janáček: Káťa Kabanová*, ed. J. Tyrrell (Cambridge: Cambridge University Press, 1982), pp. 121–2.

[16] Ibid., p. 122.

performances, opera-goers were keen to see in action the Music Director elect of Covent Garden.[17]

It was Kubelík, at Covent Garden, who introduced the next Janáček opera to British audiences, with *Jenůfa* in 1956. But neither *Jenůfa* nor *The Cunning Little Vixen*, at Sadler's Wells under Colin Davis in 1961, did noticeably better than *Káťa Kabanová*. Janáček's orchestral works, such as the *Sinfonietta* and *Taras Bulba*, had been presented to British audiences by Sir Henry Wood in the 1920s with some success, but his operas failed to find a receptive British audience in the 1950s. Keeping *Káťa Kabanová* in the Sadler's Wells repertoire was an act of faith on Tucker's part, and even by 1959 and 1961, when Mackerras conducted a few more performances at Sadler's Wells, it cannot be said that Janáček's operas appeared to have a future in Britain.

The turning point came in February 1964, when Mackerras introduced *The Makropulos Affair* to London audiences at Sadler's Wells, again with Tucker's support and his translation of the libretto. It was a fine production with a superlative cast of singing actors, including the wonderful Marie Collier as Marty, and somehow this strange opera caught the public imagination in England in a way that no Janáček opera had done in Britain before. Its success was such that Mackerras felt able to take Janáček's most demanding opera, *From the House of the Dead*, into the Sadler's Wells repertoire in October 1965. By then British audiences had had the opportunity of seeing both *Káťa Kabanová* and *From the House of the Dead* at the Edinburgh Festival, which in 1964 was daringly devoted to Janáček. The Prague National Theatre production of *From the House of the Dead* had certainly made its impact – how could such an extraordinary opera fail to? – but when Mackerras conducted it the next year it was in a version that, unlike the Prague production, had begun to move back to Janáček's original orchestration, cutting out many of the additions imposed upon the work by Osvald Chlubna and his associates. It was leaner, rawer and much less 'comfortable' than the version given in Edinburgh, and this was an important moment for Mackerras: from now on he would seek to get back as far as possible to Janáček's intentions – 'warts and all' – even if this meant adapting the performance materials himself.

Mackerras's reputation with Janáček operas had begun to win him engagements beyond Sadler's Wells. In 1972 and 1977 he took over revivals of the Kubelík *Jenůfa* at Covent Garden. In the 1980s he conducted *Jenůfa* in San Francisco and in Vienna, and *From the House of the Dead* in Paris. In the 1990s he returned to San Francisco for *Makropulos* and to Paris for *The Cunning Little Vixen*, and he conducted *Káťa Kabanová* in Sydney, Prague and the New York Met, where he also conducted *Makropulos*. Mackerras was not content to confine himself to the standard five Janáček operas. *The Excursions of Mr Brouček* was a particular favourite of his and he conducted

[17] Ibid., p. 123.

two surprisingly popular productions at English National Opera in 1978/9 (revived in 1983 and in 1992/3) as well as a series of performances at the Prague National Theatre, based on Jiří Zahrádka's new edition. Mackerras continued to conduct Janáček operas well into his eighties, with *Makropulos* (at ENO in 2006), *Káťa Kabanová* (Royal Opera House, 2007), and *The Cunning Little Vixen* (Royal Opera House, 2010).

Although Mackerras introduced only two Janáček operas to British audiences (both *From the House of the Dead* and *Brouček* were brought to the Edinburgh Festival by the Prague National Theatre before the London stage productions) and three others were first given in the UK by other conductors (*Jenůfa* by Kubelík, *The Cunning Little Vixen* by Colin Davis and *Fate* by Simon Rattle), he nevertheless dominated the scene from the outset. No other non-Czech conductor became so closely associated with Janáček's operas, a link that was tied even closer by his cycle of recordings for Decca (see 'Recordings' below). Mackerras thus set the stage for a new generation of non-Czech Janáček conductors to continue his legacy, and several of them, including John Eliot Gardiner and Simon Rattle, went to Mackerras for so-called 'driving lessons' in the scores.

Mackerras's Janáček was in line with his approach to other works. His were energetic performances that, although they gave lyrical passages their head, did not allow them to wallow, and as a whole the performances were pressed along urgently and excitingly: dramatic pacing was one of Mackerras's great gifts as a conductor. The sort of colours that Janáček loved – high strings, high woodwind, low prominent brass even more prominent percussion – were features that Mackerras thoroughly enjoyed and emphasised in his performances. Above all, there was a passion for getting things right. No detail was too small to be dismissed. The seemingly impractical parts for solo viola d'amore that Janáček wrote into several of his operas (*Makropulos*, for instance) were always included in the recordings, amplified if necessary. Whereas Czech conductors were content to present and continue a 'tradition', however far it departed from what Janáček wrote, Mackerras was always keen, through his own studies and those of others, to discover exactly what Janáček wrote and to see how far this could be put into practice in performance. The result is a Janáček conception that is as accurate as possible but – like his performances of 'authentic' Mozart – never a museum piece and always vividly brought to life. Mackerras was a true man of the theatre, and even his non-operatic performances are dramatic and thrilling in a way that often eludes other Janáček conductors.

Mackerras's view of Janáček

> What drew me to him is the wonderful, dramatic, earthy human, personal, passionate quality in his attitude, not only to his music but towards everything; his pantheistic feeling for nature, for life itself; the extraordinary subjects he chose for his operas, his unique way of setting words, his different interpretations of commonplace everyday speech; in fact, his tremendous creativity, his absolutely original mind.[18]

NANCY Phelan's biography of Mackerras includes an eighty-page Appendix reprinting his thoughts on his major preoccupations: conducting, Mozart, Handel, the appoggiatura and Janáček. As a highly intelligent, thoughtful and articulate musician, Mackerras was keen to back up his often controversial performance decisions through newspaper articles and interviews. For earlier music, the chief area of discussion was justifying new stylistic interpretations, such as his approach to ornamentation; for Janáček, there was a more basic problem of attracting potential audiences and explaining what they might find in the works.

Elated by his discovery of the *Káťa* interludes in Brno (see 'Authenticity and editions' below), Mackerras began writing about Janáček in a somewhat sensationalist article for *Music and Musicians* ('Long-lost music for a Janáček opera') published in February 1961. Here he reproduced four pages from Janáček's autograph, including parts of the two later-composed interludes, and sheets from the opera showing 'first thoughts' and 'second thoughts' of the same passage. It is clear from his commentary that by then he was well versed in Janáček's method of writing and revising, and that his researches had extended beyond *Káťa Kabanová* to the *Glagolitic Mass* and the *Sinfonietta*. Thereafter he confidently wrote about all aspects of Janáček. In 1964 he launched *Makropulos* before its stage premiere in Britain with an extensive article in *Opera* (February 1964) that included not only a general introduction to all aspects of the opera, but also a detailed thematic analysis, with a double page of motifs and their transformations during the opera. In 1965 he contributed to a conference in Brno on Janáček's opera with thoughtful comments on Janáček's orchestration (for instance identifying problems of balance) and the extent to which it was permissible for conductors to make changes.[19] As his services as a Janáček conductor were more and more in demand, his time for writing became limited and most of his thoughts on the composer were channelled into interviews. A long discussion with another Janáček enthusiast, Lord

[18] Phelan 1987, p. 309 (Appendix on Janáček).

[19] 'On the problems of interpretations of Janáček's orchestration', *Acta Janáčkiana*, i: *Operní dílo Leoše Janáčka, Sborník příspěvků z mezinárodního symposia, Brno, říjen 1965* [Leoš Janáček's operatic work: proceedings of the international symposium, Brno, October 1965] (Brno: Moravské museum, 1968), pp. 102–4.

Harewood (then Managing Director of Sadler's Wells Opera),[20] took up most of the programme for the new production of *Káťa Kabanová* in 1973. Here he commented on Janáček's style of opera:

> It has a different kind of dramatic quality to any kind of opera that had been written before. He was a composer I'd hardly even heard of and yet there was this absolutely personal, quite original language, which was not based particularly on folk music like, say, the originality of Bartók is to some extent based on Hungarian folk music. But he also was the only composer I'd ever heard of who used the whole tone scale constantly and yet was not in the least like Debussy [...] He got it from Debussy, but he used it in an entirely original way. In a way more than Bartók, who is a much more intellectual composer of about the same generation, which is why I compare them. Bartók was a knowledgeable musician, and he knew exactly about the effect of every orchestral instrument and where they were playing, whereas of course Janáček did a lot of it by feel.

'Was Puccini an influence on Janáček?' Harewood asked:

> Yes, I imagine so. But it seems to me that Janáček did not particularly study anybody's operas, that he did all these things by instinct, and that's why he's so original. He just started a new style of opera, of orchestration, of music, of musical language, or dramatic language, of everything. Simply because he had instinct but not a great deal of knowledge, nor a great deal of experience.

Another topic dwelt on was Janáček's method of transforming motifs, for instance in the double love scene in *Káťa Kabanová* in Act 2 for the 'serious' couple, Káťa and Boris, and the more light-hearted couple, Varvara and Kudrjáš:

> Well, it's wonderful the way he manages to contrast the two kinds of love. The passionate one that's partly going on off stage, and the other one where they're just having a roll in the hay, or not even that. The way that is expressed in the music and the way he transforms that marvellous love theme into the other kind of character, when it comes for the second time, is marvellous. Mind you, there are many other composers who are equally adept at transforming the characters of themes. [Wagner, for instance, as Harewood observed.] But Janáček does it so quickly [...] Where Wagner does take a long time to do it, Janáček manages to do it in one stroke. [...]
>
> In *The Makropulos Case* and *From the House of the Dead*, particularly, he will start off with one motif, and will change it into

[20] 'Janáček and Katya Kabanova – a conversation between Lord Harewood and Charles Mackerras', programme book for *Katya Kabanova* (Sadler's Wells Opera, 1973), unpaginated.

> another one. And then he will change that one into yet another one, and he will go on developing them until they are really unrecognisable. Whereas *Katya* has actual leitmotifs, and those motifs do appear in the same recognisable form throughout, unchanged. They all, except for the four note theme, appear and then never come back again, whereas the four note theme, which represents fate or impending doom in its slow form with the tympani and trombones, and represents the husband going away and coming back in its fast form, is used as a Wagnerian leitmotif throughout the whole thing.

And finally there was the problem of how to play it. Did Mackerras get the impression that the style, the natural, easy playing and singing style of Janáček, was really better in Brno than in Prague?

> I think that is a fair comment both about the singers and the orchestra. The orchestra does seem to be more at home playing that extremely awkward music. It is after all awkwardly written for the singers and awkwardly written for the instruments in the orchestra. I once conducted *Katya* in Brno, as a kind of celebration of the fact that I had 'discovered' two *intermezzi* which Janáček had composed later in order to bridge a change of scene that couldn't be done quickly enough. I had one rehearsal with the orchestra and singers, and I was really amazed at how that orchestra played so naturally. You see they'd found a way of getting over the awkwardness of Janáček. A way of faking it. The same as there are some parts of Wagner which are unplayable, but you learn a way of making it sound good. Well, that's the same with Janáček. And the Brno people played much more Janáček than anybody else, except I should think possibly that we in Sadler's Wells Orchestra run them a very good second. [...] It was our enthusiasm, and the fact the Sadler's Wells Orchestra learnt to play it and the singers all developed a kind of English Janáček style, that made the success possible.

Thirty years later, when Martina Sperling interviewed Mackerras, about to conduct a revival of *Jenůfa* at Welsh National Opera, he was able to look back on how the situation had changed:

> Conductors who were used to Puccini, Strauss, and Wagner found Janáček's orchestration very eccentric. A lot of it seemed virtually unplayable. However, that is one thing that has changed in the last few years. The fact that Janáček is now so popular and familiar means that younger players can overcome the difficulties much more easily than players of the twenties or thirties. As technique improved it became easier. When I recorded the Janáček operas 20 years ago with the Vienna Philharmonic they didn't find it difficult. The eccentricity of the orchestration is part of its originality. It's a pity to take away those eccentricities. Making Janáček sound more 'normal' can make

> it sound like Strauss or Dvořák. That's why I prefer to go back to Janáček's original even though it's so awkward to play and to balance.[21]

When, in 1995, I interviewed Mackerras in connection with the French premiere of *The Vixen*, which he was conducting at the Paris Châtelet, I was lucky to be given a fair amount of space and thus able to draw Sir Charles out on Janáček topics that he had not addressed elsewhere.[22] Naturally these included the difficulty of singing Janáček in French and working with French orchestras, but also how well orchestrated he considered *The Vixen* and *Brouček* were (he was unaware at the time that the latter was not entirely Janáček's doing; see Chapter 10), the huge difficulties he found in performing *Makropulos*, Janáček in the context of Mozart and Wagner, the choice of voices in *The Vixen* (and the view that the Dog could be played by a countertenor) and how he thought, forty years after he began conducting Janáček, that he knew better how to pace the operas, for instance the opening of *Káťa Kabanová* up to the heroine's entrance (which he had previously found 'boring').

Recordings

Mackerras's recording career as a Janáček conductor began in 1959, when he made a long-playing record comprising the *Sinfonietta*, the overtures to *Makropulos*, *Káťa Kabanová* and *From the House of the Dead* and the original overture *Jealousy* to *Jenůfa*. It was a prophetic record in many ways. *Jealousy* had been largely overlooked by Czech conductors and Mackerras would win acclaim in Czechoslovakia by championing it. While *Káťa* was where it all began with Mackerras, *Makropulos* and *From the House of the Dead* (he had conducted neither opera by this point) would become in a few years' time his greatest Janáček successes at Sadler's Wells. As for the *Sinfonietta*, he had conducted it publicly only once: away from the British press in the seclusion of his 1958 concert season in Cape Town, with extra brass from the army band at Simonstown Naval Base[23] (bringing in a military band was exactly in accordance with Janáček's wishes for his 'military' symphony). The *Sinfonietta*, *Taras Bulba* and the *Glagolitic Mass* would go on to be Mackerras's most performed and recorded Janáček works.

Despite a growing reputation as a Janáček conductor through numerous live and broadcast performances, it would be another seventeen years before the next Janáček recording, but it was one that cemented Mackerras's

[21] 'A perfect balance of sound: Sir Charles Mackerras on Janáček's *Jenůfa*; interview by Martina Sperling', programme book for *Jenůfa* (Cardiff: Welsh National Opera, 2003).

[22] '*La Petite Renarde rusée* à Paris: Un entretien de John Tyrrell avec Sir Charles Mackerras', programme book for Janáček: *La Petite Renarde rusée* (Paris Châtelet, 1995), pp. 38–42.

[23] Phelan 1987, p. 113.

reputation as a Janáček conductor internationally and promoted the composer's operas more effectively than anything else he did. In the final months of 1976 Mackerras recorded a performance of *Káťa Kabanová* for Decca and therewith initiated the cycle of five Janáček opera recordings that he conducted to great critical and popular acclaim. With Mackerras regarded as 'rough' and energetic, Decca decided the ideal orchestra would be the legendary 'smooth' Vienna Philharmonic. It was an inspired pairing and also very practical, since it meant that Czech singers would be over the border and not too far away for recording sessions. Most of Janáček's operas existed on decent Czech long-playing records, but foreign distribution was never Supraphon's strong point, so that these Czech records were only fitfully available in shops abroad. The Decca records, on the other hand, were well distributed and promoted, and in the decades since they were issued they have never been out of the catalogue. This practical reason, as well as the quality of the Mackerras performances, meant that there was now a consistent standard to aspire to when the various opera companies in Britain and elsewhere began to present Janáček operas.

The Decca series was only the beginning. He would later add to it recordings of two lesser-known operas not included in the series: *Fate*, in English (for EMI in 1989), and *Šárka* (for Supraphon in 2000). He also made second recordings of three of the operas: *Káťa Kabanová* (for Supraphon in 1997) and English versions of *Jenůfa* (Chandos, 2003) and *Makropulos* (Chandos, 2006). Apart from Janáček's folk-based second opera *The Beginning of a Romance*, Mackerras conducted all of Janáček's operas and made commercial recordings of all except *Brouček*. Non-commercial recordings of this opera, however, are able to demonstrate Mackerras's growing mastery of the work over thirty years, from a BBC studio recording in 1970 and a live broadcast in 1979 of the ENO production (both made available by Oriel Records) to his Prague National Theatre performance in 2003 (available on a promotional disc).

Of Janáček's choral works with orchestra, Mackerras frequently performed the *Glagolitic Mass* in both the 'classic' version and the Wingfield version and made recordings of both. His interpretation of the early cantata *Amarus* was captured on a recording, but sadly not Janáček's visionary *Eternal Gospel*, scheduled for performance and a recording in Brno in 2009 but thwarted by ill health. Mackerras gave a wide berth to Janáček's early folk-based *Lachian Dances* (assembled in 1924 but going back to 1889). Apart from that, Mackerras conducted all of Janáček's major orchestral works, including the posthumously completed works: *Danube*, the Violin Concerto and the incidental music for *Schluck und Jau*. However, the two works that became his calling cards throughout the world were his much-honed interpretations of *Taras Bulba* and the *Sinfonietta*.

Authenticity and editions

WHAT has always distinguished Mackerras from other conductors is his passionate interest in the authenticity of what is performed. For many years Janáček's orchestration was considered to be eccentric, if not downright perverse, amateurish and unplayable. This was a view especially prevalent in Prague, from the first opera performed there (*Jenůfa* in 1916), which was given in a version much revised by the conductor Karel Kovařovic, a version that not only reorchestrated the work but also made a series of cuts. This tradition persisted in Prague, with, for instance, Václav Talich conducting two mature operas, *Káťa Kabanová* and *The Cunning Little Vixen*, in 'retouched' versions. When it came to Janáček's final opera, *From the House of the Dead*, which the composer did not live to see staged, in its Brno premiere in 1930 it was given in a version that filled out the orchestration of Janáček's exceptionally spare score, made many changes to the verbal text and added a cathartic 'happy-ending' chorus in the wrong key. Janáček's Viennese publisher, Universal Edition, published both *Jenůfa* and *From the House of the Dead* in forms revised by others, and until recently these were the only versions available.

Mackerras, who had already begun to show an interest in the early performance materials of composers such as Mozart and Handel, was equally curious to see Janáček's autograph scores and in 1961 made his first research trip to the Moravian Museum in Brno, which houses the Janáček Archive. Examining Janáček's score of the *Sinfonietta*, he came across a few pages that seemed not to belong. He soon identified the music as extensions to the interludes for *Káťa Kabanová* that Janáček had written to facilitate the scene changes in Acts 1 and 2. With characteristic promptness he set about having the parts copied and introduced them in 1961, first when he was granted a guest performance of *Káťa* at the Brno opera and then at Sadler's Wells. His discovery caused quite a stir, and some embarrassment at the Brno archive, but in fact when Mackerras proudly presented the new parts to the Brno orchestra he found that they had them there already, only crossed out. Janáček's interludes, composed in 1926, had first been given in Prague in the German Theatre's production of *Káťa Kabanová* in February 1928, and soon after Janáček demanded that the interludes be performed everywhere.[24] This indeed happened in Brno in May 1928, but not thereafter: improvements in stagecraft had made the extensions unnecessary, at least in terms of setting the new scene.

If the interludes turned out to be something of a damp squib, they nevertheless whetted Mackerras's interest. A notorious case in point was the elaborate over-orchestration of *From the House of the Dead*. Mackerras acquired a microfilm of Janáček's complete autograph from the Moravian

[24] John Tyrrell, ed.: *Janáček's Operas: a Documentary Account* (London: Faber, 1992), pp. 279–80.

Museum and set about making a version that corresponded to this by removing many of the extra instruments from the printed score. He was not quite the first to do so, since Rafael Kubelík had given a concert performance in Munich (17 November 1961) which did much the same. What neither conductor realised at the time was that Janáček's autograph was not the final version of the opera by the composer, since the score had then been copied under Janáček's supervision by his two faithful amanuenses. Not only was this a copy in which Janáček had been able to clarify illegible and problematic passages, but, at least in the first two acts, he had made small corrections in his own hand in terms of doublings, tempo and metronome marks. Nevertheless, what Mackerras played in concert performance on BBC radio (26 September 1965) and in the stage production a month later was much nearer to the original than anything that was given in Czechoslovakia at the time. By the time of the Decca recording we were able (I was involved by this point) to introduce Janáček's own corrections to the copyists' score into the performing materials.

In 1971 Sadler's Wells (soon to be rebranded as 'English National Opera') revived the ever-successful *Makropulos*, now at the London Coliseum in central London, where the company had moved in 1968. This was the moment where I took my courage in my hands and wrote to Charles Mackerras to wish him well for the premiere on 19 February and to express a cautious hope that it might be possible to meet him: in 1966–67 I had studied the autographs of Janáček's operas in the Moravian Museum and I felt that some of this work could be helpful to him. In wondering whether my letter would get any response I had not reckoned on Mackerras's efficiency in dealing with correspondence. No sooner was the letter received than I was startled by a phone call from the great man, suggesting I drop in and see him at the theatre when I next attended *Makropulos*. Nor had I reckoned on the friendliness and warmth with which he greeted me. He expressed keen interest in my work at the Janáček Archive and asked my opinion about the new score of *Jenůfa* that Universal Edition had issued (I had published a review in the *Musical Times* praising the appearance of the score but regretting that it simply presented the Kovařovic version rather than attempting to go back to what Janáček actually wrote).[25] This immediately sparked off Mackerras's interest in the score. By now he had little time for sitting in archives, but good relations with the Moravian Museum meant that he was able to commission one of its employees at the time, Petr Oliva, to go through the materials in the museum and annotate the printed Universal Edition full score, showing what had been added and what it replaced. This was a rather more complicated task than discarding Osvald Chlubna's extra instrumentation in *From the House of the Dead* (which had been simply added in pencil to the copyists' scores) and much

[25] John Tyrrell: 'Revised Jenufa' [review of study score of *Jenůfa*, ed. Joannes Martin Dürr, Vienna: Universal Edition, 1969], *Musical Times*, March 1971, p. 268.

further work on the original parts was needed for the edition that Universal Edition subsequently issued. Nevertheless, by the time of the Decca recording (1981) Mackerras was able to present a version that approximated to Janáček's original, the first time for over seventy years that this had been possible (apart from a few excerpts broadcast on Brno radio during the war).

Mackerras's enterprise in such matters was noted by Janáček's publisher, Universal Edition, which invited him to make a new edition of *Káťa Kabanová* (1971, though not published as a commercially available study score until 1992). From this followed new, authentic scores of all of Janáček's operas whose copyright was owned by Universal, usually in conjunction with other scholars. I worked with Mackerras on the new score of *Jenůfa* (the 'Brno version 1908', published in 1996) and *From the House of the Dead* (due to be published in 2015–16); Jiří Zahrádka worked with Mackerras on new scores of *Šárka* (2002), *The Cunning Little Vixen* (2010) and *The Excursions of Mr Brouček* (not yet issued). Mackerras's version of *Makropulos* (1970) was made available as a hire score by Universal Edition; a final version edited by Jiří Zahrádka is in progress.

In his reminiscences, printed in this volume, Jiří Zahrádka describes his experience of working on editions with Mackerras. I can report much the same experience: the feeling of working as an equal rather than a subordinate, Mackerras's intense interest in trying to discover what Janáček actually wrote, and his concern that the published scores should reflect this as a critical edition – to which of course were added the immense practical experience of a lifetime of conducting these works and the ability to find fixes for what seemed to me impossible problems. For our work on *From the House of the Dead*, I would generally list problems and send sheets of questions to Mackerras, which he would then annotate with solutions and suggestions (a typical sheet appears in Figure 3).

There was always give and take. For instance, in the orchestral epilogue to Act 1 of *From the House of the Dead*, built oddly on the 'Skuratov theme', Janáček had included a reference in his autograph to the orchestral theme which accompanies the Prison Governor's entrance, now set contrapuntally on a high trumpet against the Skuratov theme. This appears on the Mackerras recording and was a particular favourite of his. However, as I had to point out, Janáček seems to have had second thoughts about it and it did not appear in the fair copy made by Václav Sedláček of this act, which Janáček carefully corrected. So in the end we compromised in the printed score by including it, but in square brackets and with a note explaining its origin. By the time we made a final pass through the material, Mackerras was seriously ill, and so I simply came with my sheets of problems and we went through them together, with me jotting down what he suggested. The last time this happened (12 August 2009) I took sheets for all three acts, assuming however that we would simply do Act 1. But, despite being very tired, he insisted on going through the lot: he knew by then that his time was limited.

Mackerras also edited the orchestral suite that his mentor Václav Talich

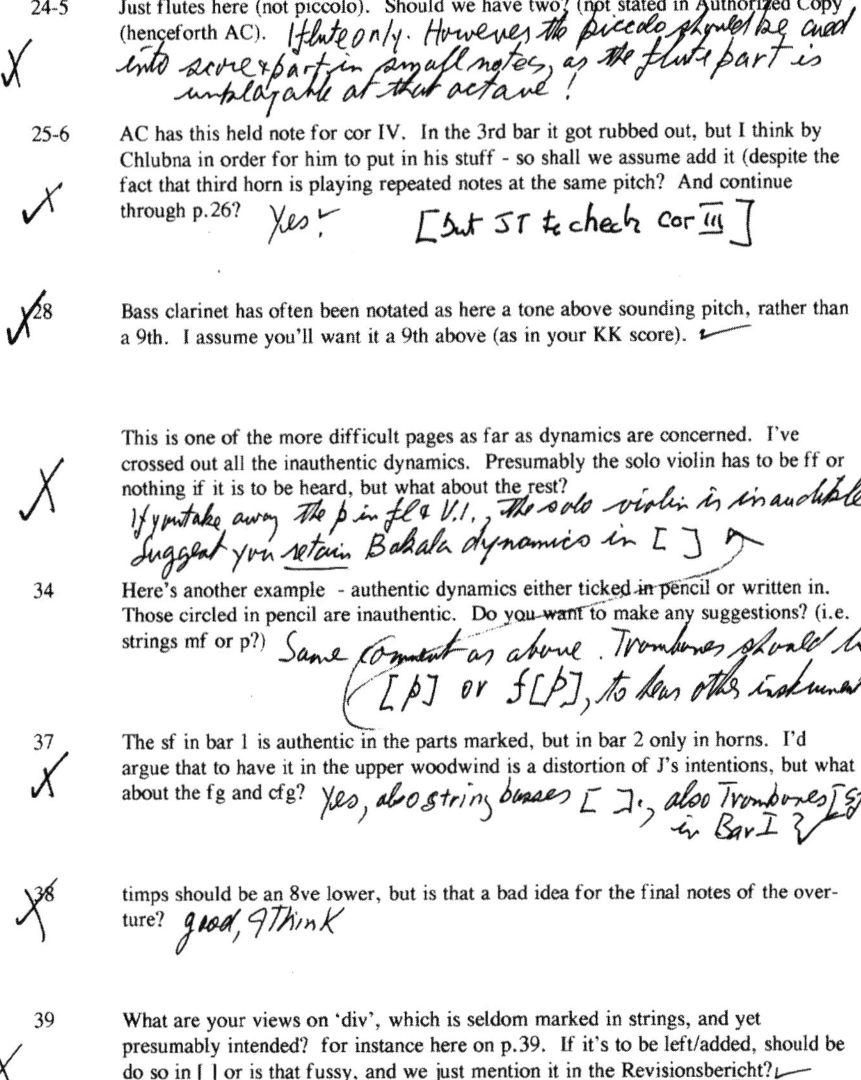
janed\zmdqs at 7 May 1993 FROM THE HOUSE OF THE DEAD ACT 1, |

24-5 Just flutes here (not piccolo). Should we have two? (not stated in Authorized Copy (henceforth AC). 1 flute only. However the piccolo should be cued into score & part in small notes, as the flute part is unplayable at that octave!

25-6 AC has this held note for cor IV. In the 3rd bar it got rubbed out, but I think by Chlubna in order for him to put in his stuff - so shall we assume add it (despite the fact that third horn is playing repeated notes at the same pitch? And continue through p.26? Yes! [But JT to check cor III]

28 Bass clarinet has often been notated as here a tone above sounding pitch, rather than a 9th. I assume you'll want it a 9th above (as in your KK score).

This is one of the more difficult pages as far as dynamics are concerned. I've crossed out all the inauthentic dynamics. Presumably the solo violin has to be ff or nothing if it is to be heard, but what about the rest? If you take away the p in fl & V.I., the solo violin is inaudible. Suggest you retain Bakala dynamics in [ ]

34 Here's another example - authentic dynamics either ticked in pencil or written in. Those circled in pencil are inauthentic. Do you want to make any suggestions? (i.e. strings mf or p?) Same comment as above. Trombones should be [p] or f[p], to hear other instruments.

37 The sf in bar 1 is authentic in the parts marked, but in bar 2 only in horns. I'd argue that to have it in the upper woodwind is a distortion of J's intentions, but what about the fg and cfg? Yes, also string basses [ ], also Trombones [sf] in Bar I?

38 timps should be an 8ve lower, but is that a bad idea for the final notes of the overture? good, I think

39 What are your views on 'div', which is seldom marked in strings, and yet presumably intended? for instance here on p.39. If it's to be left/added, should be do so in [ ] or is that fussy, and we just mention it in the Revisionsbericht?

Figure 3 Editing Janáček: comments by Mackerras in response to questions from John Tyrrell about *From the House of the Dead*

had made from *The Cunning Little Vixen*. In the same way as he restored Janáček's original orchestration to his operas, he stripped away all the additional orchestration and let Janáček's original orchestra speak for itself. He also extended the second movement by including more music from the end of the Prelude to make a neater and more logical join to the 'liberation' music (altogether only about six minutes of music from Act 1 is omitted in the Mackerras version). The revision process continued, and at Mackerras's memorial concert, given in London by the Philharmonia on 4 November 2010, the suite was performed, conducted by Alex Briger, with further minor revisions by Mackerras, not yet performed publicly and which he had been hoping to introduce himself.

At the same memorial concert Alex Briger conducted the final scene of *The Cunning Little Vixen*. This is the monologue by the Gamekeeper, who steps out of his normal character to present a vision of the beauty of nature and is finally joined by the animals and insects from the beginning of the opera, but now a new generation: an encapsulation of the cycle of life that the opera represents. Janáček enthusiastically attended rehearsals and was said to have wept during this final scene, telling the producer, Ota Zítek, standing next to him: 'You must play this when I die.' His wishes were respected and this scene became a centrepiece of Janáček's elaborate farewell ceremony at the Brno theatre.

Charles Mackerras came late to conducting *The Cunning Little Vixen*, and at the time of his Janáček cycle for Decca he had in fact not conducted the opera in the theatre.[26] It would be the last Janáček opera that he conducted, at the Royal Opera House revival in 2010. He was then in great pain, having fractured several ribs in a fall shortly before rehearsals began, but with indomitable will he conducted all seven performances, and he must have found comfort in the magical sounds that he drew from the orchestra in what is Janáček's most luminous and radiant score. According to his nephew Alex, the end of the opera was his 'most favourite passage in all music', and it was Mackerras's special request, as it had been Janáček's before, that this scene be played at any memorial concert for him.[27]

[26] Mackerras was disappointed not to be asked to conduct the British premiere at Sadler's Wells in 1961 (see Chapter 1). He had hoped to have the experience of conducting some performances of the Welsh National Opera production in 1980, but it was only in 1987 that he took over the revival of this production.

[27] Interview with Alex Briger, Paris, 26 May 2013.

4

Goat's Milk in Vienna
Three Memorable Meetings

Heinz Stolba

ONCE upon a time, in the early 1990s, a young music editor was asked by his employer, Universal Edition Vienna, the most important publishing house for twentieth-century music and the original publisher of the works of Leoš Janáček, to go to London at short notice to meet Sir Charles Mackerras. It was said that the world-renowned conductor was keen to discuss two Janáček topics: the finalisation of new performance material for the opera *Káťa Kabanová* (which he had edited) and the preparation of the 'Brno 1908' edition of the opera *Jenůfa*. For a young music editor to be sent to London for a meeting with the great Charles Mackerras may seem at first to be a great honour, but in fact none of my colleagues were queuing up for the job. Universal Edition had not yet started making new critical editions of the works of Leoš Janáček and so there was no editor at hand reasonably familiar with this composer's music. Nobody wanted to expose their weaknesses in a conversation with this leading Janáček conductor on a topic about which they had little idea. And so it was that the honour fell to the youngest member of the editorial team, without arousing any envy at all on the part of his colleagues.

The meeting was arranged without my involvement and was to take place at Universal Edition's London offices. I had never met Sir Charles previously, nor had I ever had contact with him by letter or by telephone. Moreover, as to the two projects that were the purpose of my visit, my employers in Vienna had not given me much to go on; it was my task to find out all further details during the trip itself. In the short time before my departure I tried to discover the basics about Leoš Janáček and his works, but it was obvious that the rudimentary scope of this research would in no way be up to the occasion. On top of this it was becoming clear to me that my schoolboy English was woefully inadequate for my first business trip to London; while it might be just about enough for simple social interactions, in serious negotiations it would quickly reach its limits. I was feeling more than a little nervous as I waited in a meeting room for the celebrated conductor.

Sir Charles's arrival was unmistakable; I could hear his confident voice as he greeted my London colleagues in the adjacent rooms. Then at last he was standing before me. Although I was in fact taller than him by a good hand's breadth, his commanding figure and urbane gestures overwhelmed me to such an extent that it seemed to me that he was the taller by the same amount. The man cast an immediate spell over me – and yet, at that moment, I would rather have been at the dentist or on the moon than in that room in London.

Once we had exchanged the usual formalities, the two of us took our places at a table on which lay full scores and piano-vocal scores of Janáček works, Sir Charles taking his ease in an armchair while I perched on the edge of the upright chair opposite like a schoolboy in an examination. Even if I'd so far managed to conceal my nervousness to some extent, what residue I still had of English deserted me as we began to talk. Given a certain cunning, it is sometimes possible to keep one's interlocutor unaware for a quite a while that one has no idea about the subject in hand, as is strikingly demonstrated by the media on a daily basis. I, on the other hand, stammered about in such a way that Mackerras must have realised in a matter of minutes that the person sent by Vienna to conduct these important negotiations was intellectually feeble and had not the slightest idea about the works of Leoš Janáček.

Sir Charles now straightened himself up in his armchair and asked, showing no sign of impatience, whether it might be better if we switched to German, apologising at the same time for the fact that he had not spoken that language for a long time. In something like a mental blackout, however, I took it that this would make the extent of my incompetence even more evident and further intensify the awkwardness of the situation. And so, rather than gratefully accepting his offer of rescue, I persisted in making a laughing stock of myself in English. Sir Charles was visibly amused by my pretensions, but then took the initiative without further ado and changed to German. His German was scarcely better than my English, but he simply launched into it, telling me about this and that in a humorous and compelling manner; he recounted anecdotes as well as he could and also demonstrated, laughing, his knowledge of Czech – and lo and behold, after a few minutes the grey cells of my brain seemed to release the barrier they had earlier raised. Sir Charles switched between languages without concern whenever he couldn't find a word or phrase, and assured me that it was not his aim to subject me to some painful on-the-spot examination of my Janáček knowledge.

Now that I'd relaxed a little, he began to tell me more and more about Janáček's life and music, about his habits and idiosyncrasies, and about the two specific projects for which I'd been brought to London. And now our hour and a half of conversation settled into something in which we were no longer sitting opposite one another but rather side by side, leafing through scores and scribbling notes and sketches on bits of paper. By the end, everything was as clear to me as it could possibly be, and Charles Mackerras said goodbye to me with such warmth as though we had always known one other. This made me realise the magnanimity of the man I'd just met in person. Moreover, I had just had my first 'proper' lesson on Janáček, the intensity and detail of which would have required an entire university semester. Through his generous and deeply human manner, Sir Charles had taken away all my shyness and from that moment had gained in me an ally in Janáček affairs.

Subsequently our collaboration deepened and extended to practically all of the works by Janáček that were published by Universal Edition. A number of years passed during which we didn't meet in person but were in continual contact, now and again by telephone but above all by Sir Charles's favourite mode of communication: fax. His arguments for this method, already dated by the turn of the twenty-first century, were disarming: you got everything in writing, just like in a letter, but without having to wait for the post, and – blissfully – no computer was needed!

Around the start of the new millennium, Sir Charles came to Vienna again to conduct. He informed me of this and we arranged to meet at his hotel, on a particular day and at a precisely specified time, as the schedule for his stay in Vienna had been choreographed down to the last detail. I was there on time and called him in his room from the hotel reception desk. Thrilled at the thought of our coming meeting, I no longer had reason to be nervous. Over the last ten years I had occupied myself intensively with Janáček's works and had risen to the post of chief editor at Universal Edition. The familiar voice on the telephone seemed pleased to hear me and asked me to be patient for a while: would I please wait in the lobby? A few minutes later a man came towards me – older, slimmer and not particularly tall – and only when he addressed me in his familiar voice did I realise that this was Sir Charles. I could not believe my eyes; in my memory he had been taller than me by half a head. He had certainly also lost an immense amount of weight, and I was unable to conceal my surprise at seeing him so thin. He explained that his earlier corpulence had interfered so much with his conducting that he had modified significant parts of his diet, and in particular had long given up dairy products.

We agreed to hold our discussion in the hotel's café and to celebrate this typical Viennese ambience with coffee and apple strudel. I confessed to Sir Charles that I'd remembered him as being much taller, and gradually I recapitulated my experiences of our first meeting in London, which greatly amused him. In view of the limited time at our disposal, however, I then moved quickly to a matter that, given my responsibilities as chief editor, lay close to my heart: Universal Edition was planning a new edition of Leoš Janáček's opera *The Cunning Little Vixen*. After the many Janáček projects on which we had collaborated, this was the first in which Charles Mackerras would not be directly involved. It would be sufficient for us merely to gain his patronage to ensure that, with his strong reputation as a Janáček expert and interpreter, no doubts would ever arise about the quality of the new edition. Sir Charles countered that he had not conducted the opera for quite some time,[1] and in any case there were no difficulties concerning the historical sources and the music itself was also generally 'unproblematic', so there was no particular need for his expertise here.

[1] At the time Mackerras had last conducted a run of performances in Paris in 1995 (JT).

I maintained that it was almost an obligation on his part to involve himself in this Janáček project, having done so in so many others, but he insisted that there was nothing he could contribute on this occasion. As my arguments were failing to move him from his position, we spent the little remaining time exchanging our current states of knowledge about *The Cunning Little Vixen*. Once again, of course, he had an immense body of information available that I couldn't begin to match, despite my now good preparation. As we talked, his enthusiasm for the subject seemed to grow, and he began to cite numerous passages from the opera to me – making conductor's gestures and singing loudly from memory, oblivious to the other customers in the café. He told me about the suite he had compiled from the material of the first act for concert performance,[2] and explained the way in which the tempos of particular sections should be understood in terms of the time signatures and how certain rhythmic proportions related to one another in the transitions between passages written in different time signatures, and so on. At the very start of the opera, which begins in 4/8 and should be conducted in quavers, a significant motif appears in demisemiquavers. Then the metre changes to 6/4, in which the equivalent note values must be taken four times faster to ensure a seamless musical transition. At the same time, however, in the first two bars of the new section the music overlaps with that of the previous bars, and Janáček continued to notate the initial demisemiquaver motif in these same short notes, which is now completely unplayable. There was, he said, no doubt concerning Janáček's musical intentions, but as a conductor one had to have the motif played in quavers, which in turn made it necessary to shorten and in some cases omit the rests in the first two 6/4 bars in a particular way, and so on. Sir Charles noticed that I'd been listening reverently to his comments. He apologised for his outpouring and, glancing at his watch, said that it was time for him to hurry off to an orchestral rehearsal.

Seizing the moment, I responded that in my view the *Vixen* situation had just fundamentally changed. Without intending it, he had just trumped my feeble arguments for his co-operation with his own irrefutable proof that a new edition without his involvement was wholly unthinkable! I had just heard a mass of information that demonstrated beyond doubt how valuable his advice on the interpretation of the opera would be for the new edition. Charles Mackerras thought for a moment and then asked whether I could meet him again the following day and bring a score of *The Cunning Little Vixen* with me. He said he would like to think the matter over again. I thanked him for the coffee and strudel and jokingly remarked as we parted that he had scarcely managed to drink half of his black coffee, for which his enthusiasm for *The Cunning Little Vixen* was surely to blame. He replied with equal jocularity that, despite the great Viennese café tradition, the

[2] A revision of the suite made by Václav Talich in 1937, slightly extended and with the orchestration reverting to Janáček's original (JT).

coffee here was generally nothing special, particularly when abstinence from dairy products forced one to drink it black. At home, he said, he drank goat's milk, but even a hotel as good as the one in which he was now staying could not extend to anything so exotic.

Next afternoon, duly armed with a *Vixen* score and some goat's milk, I reported again punctually at the hotel's café. Or, perhaps more accurately, out of breath and almost punctually. Back then, when food intolerances were little talked about, obtaining goat's milk was something of an adventure for the uninitiated, even in a major city like Vienna. I had just completed an odyssey of the city's alternative food shops and apologised for being late. Sir Charles seemed touched by my efforts for his welfare and told me that 'attempts at bribery' of this kind were unnecessary, since he had already decided to collaborate on the new *Cunning Little Vixen* edition anyway. He told me that – despite his many other important appointments – he had cancelled all other duties for that day so that we could discuss the project undisturbed.

Once again we took up our quarters in the café and again availed ourselves of coffee and apple strudel – this time accompanied by goat's milk, though I politely declined this. As the afternoon progressed and the café gradually emptied, our deliberations about the new edition grew more relaxed: we leafed back and forth through the score, the waiter cleared away the coffee things, we made notes on various matters and the waiter asked whether we would like anything else before the café closed, as it was used as a restaurant in the evenings. At this point we ordered an aperitif and sketched out the correct notation of duplets and quadruplets in triple time signatures, whereupon the café/restaurant began to fill up again, and while we were discussing the problem of Max Brod's German translation the waiter brought the menu and we ordered dinner and wine. We analysed Janáček's notation conventions with regard to the range of the xylophone, in due course the waiter brought us our dishes and enquired whether he should bring us another bottle of wine (which, naturally, we authorised him to do), and we clarified the issue of the doubling of certain roles with only one singer. As dessert was served, with which after brief consultation between us we requested some sweet wine, we addressed the topic of when Janáček used repeat signs merely by way of abbreviation and when these were in fact of formal significance, and the waiter brought coffee and remembered the goat's milk (from which I again abstained). We examined the passages in which the composer had notated the music without a time signature, and while the other customers in the restaurant gradually began to disappear again we agreed that the Janáček expert Jiří Zahrádka was undoubtedly the best academic editor for the planned new edition, and our waiter asked us whether there was anything else we wanted, as the restaurant would shortly be closing. At which point Sir Charles felt compelled to quickly order another bottle of their fine red wine, since it would not do to finish a good meal with goat's milk, and we speculated philosophically about the composer's penchant for flat (rather than sharp) accidentals and the associated question of notating passages enharmonically for greater readability, while our faithful waiter bore us stalwart company in the now empty restaurant, dutifully refilling our glasses. We agreed that it was necessary to define more precisely the type of playing technique and the use of mutes in the strings in certain places, and finally, by the time activities in the hotel and indeed in the streets had ground to a halt, our stalwart attendant, struggling to keep his eyes open, asked us whether we wanted anything more, as the bottle was again empty …

We were both in thoroughly good spirits by this advanced hour, and Sir Charles bade me goodbye expressing every confidence that the planned new edition of *The Cunning Little Vixen* would be a sure success. I was overwhelmed by the sheer volume of information he had given and thanked him euphorically for the offer he held out of collaboration. He brushed my words aside and indicated with a twinkle that he'd also learned something from me in Janáček matters – namely the insight that, from an editorial point of view, none of this composer's works can be considered 'unproblematic'.

The new edition[3] was indeed a success and, happily, the three meetings with Sir Charles Mackerras described here were followed by others that were again imbued equally with his devotion to music and his many human qualities. He was one of the best and most influential conductors of his time, with an unbelievable depth of experience; the most important orchestras played under his baton. His musical wisdom was incredible, his special devotion to and knowledge of Janáček's music legendary. His many wonderful performances captured on disc will remain a yardstick and reference point for future generations of conductors. But, for all these 'professional' qualities, I shall always remember Sir Charles as a wonderful and great man, friendly and generous even to a nervous, underbriefed and overparted fledgling editor.

Translated by Robin Thomson

[3] Published by Universal Edition in 2010 with the following words on the title page: 'edited by Jiří Zahrádka with performance suggestions by Sir Charles Mackerras' (JT).

5
The Lion: Charles Mackerras

Patrick Summers

> The one excellent thing that can be learned from a lion is that whatever a man intends doing should be done by him with a whole-hearted and strenuous effort.
>
> (Chanakya, 370–283 BC)

THAT Sir Charles Mackerras was one of the great renaissance men of classical music is now, thankfully, well known. Charles had a rare gift in an art that tends towards narcissism: one inevitably left a Mackerras performance feeling 'what a great opera or symphony', rather than 'what a great conductor'. This was how he purposefully and precisely lived his life and tirelessly shaped his career. *Music* and everything that moulded it was his total focus. His curiosity and industry never diminished, even when age forced him to conserve his physical resources. He was a lion whose winter was uniquely rich: that his career reached its apogee after the age of 60 was at odds with the youth-obsession of the era, but it was perfectly logical to him for an art that demands a lifetime of knowledge, experience and confidence.

I'd like to record some impressions of him that might reveal his character. He was proudly and fully a musician, and as a man he was, more than anyone I have ever known, inseparable from music. It was his greatest passion and deepest interest. Much as he loved his family and his small circle of close friends, music was what came first in his life, and everyone who knew him accepted the fact. These reflections will be – as memory so often is – brief glimpses of a person. He was a complex man, a fact somewhat belied by his professorial exterior. He was inevitably dressed in a colourful Coogi sweater accessorized only with various toolboxes of batons, pencils, erasers and Post-it notes.

His wide range of interests and tastes form a great part of his story, since his active repertoire and knowledge were the broadest of nearly any conductor in history. There were the two great Czech composers who brought him renown: his championing of Janáček was strongly documented, and he enjoyed the association, but Antonín Dvořák's music was the most central to his daily life, and he was the composer whose music you'd most likely have heard him unconsciously humming.

But his interests ran much deeper. A list that is by no means exhaustive would include Beethoven, Berlioz, Brahms, Delius, Donizetti, Elgar, Gilbert and Sullivan, Gounod, Haydn, Holst, Martinů, Puccini, Schubert, Schumann, Shostakovich, Stravinsky, Suk, Richard Strauss, Verdi, Wagner, and his most beloved Mozart and Handel. Many conductors have performed the works of these composers, but Charles's depth of knowledge, as well as his talent for making each sound authentic, was unsurpassed.

There was much more: he was proud to be one of the few conductors in history to have performed several operas by Johann Christian Bach, a composer highly influential both on Mozart and on Charles's Mozartian style. His first performance of the Haydn C Major Cello Concerto in 1962 was a source of great pride, as was his reconstruction of Sullivan's Cello Concerto with David Mackie. Among the many projects he didn't live long enough to bring to fruition, I know a complete recording of the Haydn symphonies was near the top of his list. Even in his final months he talked to me about his dream of recording Rossini's comedies in a 'historically informed' manner, and also Donizetti's *L'elisir d'amore*, 'a great opera filled with lazy traditions'. He cherished his relationship with Benjamin Britten, a man he consistently called 'the greatest musician I ever knew'.

I first met Charles at the San Francisco Opera in 1986, when he conducted Janáček's *Jenůfa* in a production, by Wolfgang Weber, that had all the qualities Charles valued: it was evocative, realistic and focused on the composer's intent. It was an extraordinary cast: Gabriela Beňačková in the title role, Leonie Rysanek (Kostelnička), Wieslaw Ochman (Laca), Neil Rosenshein (Števa) and even a young Deborah Voigt in the small role of an 'old shepherdess'. As a curious young conductor at the time, I attended as many of the rehearsals as I could, and Charles and I had an immediate rapport. I assisted him on a number of operas in San Francisco, *Lohengrin*, *Der Rosenkavalier*, *Semele* and *Rusalka* among them. Eventually, as my own career reached a stride and I stopped officially assisting, I often met up with Charles around the world and helped him as best I could, mostly because we enjoyed each other's company and both relished musical challenges. I spent a few memorable Christmases in the Mackerras home in St John's Wood, and these were always very interesting times, as Charles was more relaxed and reflective then than when he was working. We spoke on the phone nearly every week until his death, and Charles was a hearty purveyor of the only advanced communicative device he ever embraced, the fax. He was my mentor and friend, and I admired his clear, humorous and sensible approach to his life and work, which were inseparable elements to him. Though he was a deeply serious musician and scholar, humour was an important part of his personality. He loathed arrogance of any kind and had a laser-like ability to detect it, particularly in the classical music industry, where it is never in short supply.

Charles and I discussed a book project many times during the last ten years of his life, an idea that his wife, Judy, suggested one afternoon when she brought us tea amidst a particularly lively conversation about Mozart's *Idomeneo*. Judy spoke with the cultivated accent of a bygone era, sonically very different from Charles's voice, which was a melodious mixture of Australian and British. She set the tray down and said something about it being a shame none of this was written down, 'what with Charles's career going on a jolly long time, too long, really, for his health, but you are both too busy as it is,' and she left us to it, as she always did.

A book about music interested him a great deal, far more than a book about his career and personality. I had hoped to help him write essays on the many ideas that occupied him, but we never found the time, and once he was ill he had to conserve his remaining energy for performances. He considered his personal story to be largely told through his recorded legacy, and he was well aware that he was likely to be among the last conductors to have such a vast discography. Conductors young and old were constantly approaching him about solutions to musical issues, particularly in the quixotic Janáček operas, and he would inevitably respond because he liked the engagement with the music, though he would sometimes say to me: 'why don't they just listen to my recording?'

Perhaps his most important surface trait was that he was seemingly without a trace of sentiment, which was one of the qualities that made him such a great conductor. Much of the repertoire is vulnerable to interpretive sentiment, and his instincts on this were acute; he felt the last thing music needed was an added layer of its inherent qualities. Rehearsing the Welsh National Opera Orchestra in 2001 for *The Cunning Little Vixen*, he implored them not to romanticize the great arching tune that ends the first scene, tempting as it is: 'it is not a pretty little Schubert song; don't sentimentalize it, please!'

He had what he called an 'Australian gruffness' that made even him laugh. This isn't to say that he was emotionally cool; quite the opposite, but he distrusted overt displays of emotion, in life and, particularly, on the podium, even though they were an increasing trend in the conducting profession over the course of his career. He was a firebrand on the podium, to be sure, but his energy was solely on the music; he did not use it to draw attention to *his* performance. Only in his final decade did he relinquish some of this reserve, as his musical longevity and multi-layered legacies began to coalesce in his reflections. To many professional musicians, and certainly to me, he was the finest conductor of his generation. That he was not necessarily the most famous says considerably more about the zeitgeist than it does about his gifts. His career saw the dawning of the age of 'specialization' in the classical music industry and, though commentators always tried to pin Charles down to being a 'Czech' specialist, the whole concept was anathema to him. To Charles, all music of all eras was related, and he used techniques he garnered from years of studying Handel in his conducting of Donizetti; he brought to Richard Strauss a delicacy learned from his Mozartian preoccupations. This was, to him, the heart of the conductor's art. To specialize would have been to minimize and restrict an art he felt should be broad.

Conducting is a difficult art to articulate, because even practitioners don't agree on what it is. Charles did not admire conductors who expressed private emotional catharses in public, nor did he emulate those who used the profession to acquire and wield power. He felt it the conductor's task to illuminate as closely as possible the vision of a composer, and he accomplished this in hundreds of very practical and pragmatic ways. He believed that, if music was played with care and an awareness of scholarship, with a balance of intellect and emotion, its inherent qualities could be discerned; he did not agree with the imposition of a performer's personality on music, even as he acknowledged that conducting is a performance art and thus dependent on some level of charisma. He felt artists should serve composers, and the art of conducting, to him, was one of illuminating one's discoveries; the performance was always a means to an end, and the end was to reveal the music.

Many people hold that conducting can't be taught, and essentially Charles was among them. Yet he also recognized that conducting, like any art, involves technique and can thus be learned if one has a propensity, and he believed that the gift for conducting lay largely in the ear and the brain. For Charles, the gesture of the arm was just the physical representation of the more complicated process of a musician's knowledge and ideas. He greatly respected knowledge in all forms and was wary of words such as 'instinct' or 'opinion', as they implied something shallow to him. He felt one's instincts and opinions should be grounded in years of study and technique. He admired theory, but he was also highly temperate in character: he never put theory ahead of practice.

It surprised some that he worked tirelessly with a metronome, something many professional musicians would consider a little pedantic for an omniscient old conductor. He had an infallible memory for tempo: many times I saw him illustrate a tempo, tapping it out on a table – 'this is 120 beats to the minute' – and he was incredibly accurate. He could also illustrate tiny calibrations; for example, the almost imperceptible difference between 58 and 60 beats to the minute. In recording sessions he would often consult a metronome, having tried out many different tempos for months beforehand, knowing that in the heat of the moment something can feel fast or slow owing to various random influences. His thorough study with a metronome actually allowed him to achieve complete rhythmic freedom, and his performances never sounded metronomic. His Mozart scores were not highly marked: a few bowings and dynamic clarifications, and each movement of each symphony had a single metronome marking. He came to these choices from years of disciplined and intricate study. There was a brief vogue for a metronome that had a rubber pad you could strike and it would tell you what tempo you were conducting. We spent a hilarious afternoon at a restaurant in San Francisco trying to get it to work, but neither of us could get a steady reading from it, no matter how hard we hit the thing. The idea that two professional conductors couldn't do the one thing we were supposed to be able to do was a huge source of amusement for him.

He acquired many of the characteristics of his Czech conducting teacher, Václav Talich, whom he considered a perfect 'old school' type of conductor. When I pressed him about what exactly this meant, he had various replies: Talich was an erudite, broadly educated musician, someone who saw the world and its cultural history through the medium of music. He had little time for publicity or promotion, and was distrustful of conductors who were handed opportunities he had been forced to earn by talent. All of these qualities were present and amplified in Charles.

Charles's conducting technique, his beat, was unusual. He rolled his shoulders in a wave, as though an invisible tempo travelled through him from right to left. It allowed for perfect clarity from a distance, something quite necessary in operatic performance. Years of this deteriorated his rotator cuffs, which were eventually repaired in 1996–97, after which his technique simplified somewhat. He then stopped conducting large choral operas or very long works, because of the amount of 'vertical' conducting one had to do in opera, as a result of distance and the large number of people performing from memory. The 'ictus' of his beat, a word Charles always pronounced through laughter, was unmistakably clear: a slight little click of the wrist.

He loved and understood great singing. He could be an extraordinary accompanist and felt accompanying to be an essential part of the job, particularly in operas, believing that one's ego must be able to follow instead of lead – something often difficult for the type of personality drawn to the conducting profession. Singers he admired he would accompany wonderfully, and in truth he could sometimes be cantankerous with those who didn't impress him. As the pianist Alfred Brendel – a musician who was, for Charles, without peer – wrote me, what appealed to him about Charles's conducting was that it had 'a freshness that propelled the music forward, a special quality that was particularly pronounced in live performances, and didn't seem to diminish in old age – a fact that, in my experience, is virtually unique. Charles seemed incapable of dragging'. Charles's recordings of Mozart piano concertos with Brendel and the Scottish Chamber Orchestra were among his happiest times in the recording studio.

Apart from investing in every new metronome and tuner that came along, and recreating several historical ones, Charles was too driven and focused on music to be very susceptible to fads. But every once in a while he would surprise me. A few years before he died there was a craze for 'Six-Word Memoirs', inspired by an old Ernest Hemingway challenge and taken up with gusto by the online *Smith Magazine*. I shared a few with Charles over the phone, and he favored the humorous. Many were maudlin. His unsurprising favorite was, 'Palindromatically, Eros saw I was sore', because, as literature, it shared several qualities with Charles: slightly bawdy humor, intellect, several meanings, order, balance, and a nod to the famous palindrome about the Italian island of Elba ('Able was I ere I saw Elba'), where he and Judy had a modest holiday home that they loved. 'I know what my six-word obituary will be!', he cackled over the phone one day: 'He forced Janáček on the world!'

His obituaries were indeed filled with references to Janáček and Czech music in general, and, though he was always profoundly grateful for the association, he had a childlike wonder in recounting the utterly random nature of how it came about. It was very much in his character to delight in happenstance. Shortly after arriving in London from Australia, he sat down in a café and a man at an adjacent table looked at the Dvořák score he was studying and said: 'I see you are studying the music of my country'; the man told him of British Council grants to study in Czechoslovakia.[1] Charles applied, received the grant and headed for Prague, where he discovered the music of Janáček from his friend and fellow oboist Jiří Tancibudek. Charles became a fluent speaker of Czech and had an affinity for Eastern European culture in general. I believe the things he admired most about Janáček were the diversity of subject matter of his operas and the visionary voice of his orchestration. He sought to make performing editions of the operas that answered as many of the questions as possible and were practical for orchestras. This turned out to be a decades-long task.

In the post-war era there was much to figure out about Janáček, mostly because of the originality of the composer's mind and the sloppy way he wrote music down, which left a huge amount to decipher. It took Charles many decades to sort out, which he did with his usual stealthy scholarship and practicality. At the time when Charles went to Czechoslovakia, in the late 1940s, there was little known about Janáček beyond the accepted view at the time that he was a poor orchestrator, and several conductors had altered his scoring to make it more conventional. That Janáček tried to use the orchestra like a pipe organ fascinated Charles: those great blocks of sound and highly unusual combinations of instruments were so revolutionary that many tried to smooth the edges, but it was precisely the more brittle, angular sound of this music that intrigued Charles.

The fact that it seems incredible now that a conductor or editor would alter a composer's orchestration owes a great deal to Charles's career and sense of practical scholarship in trying to decipher Janáček's intentions. But the scholarship would have seemed dry and academic had it not worked in tandem with Charles's pragmatism and musicianship. He was a rare combination of a highly artistic scholar and a supremely intellectual artist.

Though most of our long friendship was conveyed by phone and fax, when we were working in the same place Charles delighted in taking road trips. One of his favourite ways to spend a day off was to travel somewhere to a nice restaurant, go record shopping and talk about music. In San Francisco we would often trek around the Bay Area. I recall a day at the old Tower Records in Berkeley, when LPs still occupied the bulk of the floor space. They had a huge inventory and he delighted in flipping through bins and finding old recordings, both his own and those of others. Over the store's sound system came Mozart's 'Haffner' Symphony. 'Not bad,' he muttered, 'good orchestra, but too much bow, too thick a sound.' As the recording progressed into the minuet movement, he got more and more agitated: 'the horn attacks are weak, and it's just too bloody slow'.

The recording in question was Charles's own, from the 1970s. When one

[1] For Mackerras's own recollection of this meeting, see Chapter 1.

hears his subsequent recordings of the 'Haffner', from the early 1990s with the Prague Chamber Orchestra and finally with his beloved Scottish Chamber Orchestra, one hears his probing musical mind at work. If they sound like the work of three different conductors, they are: Charles's incredibly fertile mind kept rethinking and exploring, and his Mozart interpretations seemed to get fresher and more buoyant as he aged. He always strived for an ideal, not necessarily perfection, as that would have implied stasis to him, but for a moment's ideal.

One of the rewards for him of the period instrument movement he helped pioneer was that many orchestras became increasingly skilled and were increasingly willing to use the techniques he had worked so hard to implement from his early days. It is telling that he never referred to the period instrument movement as 'authentic', because he found the word pompous and inaccurate; he preferred 'historically informed'. Still, it was especially gratifying to him that he managed to get even tradition-bound ensembles to articulate Mozart in the way he loved, and without a doubt the proudest moments of his final years were his appearances with the Berlin Philharmonic, an orchestra whose skill and tradition he deeply respected. He was wary, though, of any group that coveted their sound over an ability to acquire an appropriate sound for different eras; he admired virtuosity, flexibility and a sense of style, and it was achieving this with such a renowned ensemble that he most relished. We spoke the day after his Berlin appearance and his excitement was palpable. True to form, the conversation was all about the texture of the playing, the new colours the orchestra brought to music he'd conducted his whole life. He said not one word about himself.

He was adamant about the preparation of orchestral parts, sometimes to the distress of music librarians around the world. Charles didn't want to spend time in rehearsal worrying about misprints, dynamics, bowings, or what he considered 'clerical' details. In the garden of his London home there was a building designed to house gardening equipment where Charles stored hundreds of sets of orchestral parts. When he conducted Mozart's *Figaro* at the Salzburg Festival, he insisted that the Vienna Philharmonic play from *his* orchestral materials, even though many in the orchestra prided themselves on playing *Figaro* from memory.

But the orchestral materials he prepared were not pedantically over-marked. They were practical and useful, and left ample room for spontaneity. Laure Cambell, the veteran music librarian of the San Francisco Opera, worked on operas with Charles for more than 30 years and, while he did indeed want the parts marked well, she also noted: 'even as a younger man, Charles knew exactly what he wanted, and could communicate it either verbally or with the stick. This meant that markings for us to put in were spare and well considered. We always winced when a conductor showed up with 25 pages of stuff – 99.9% of the time it meant he was a poor communicator and a lousy conductor and no amount of marking would save him.'

Much of Charles's correspondence was about aspects of performance that many conductors either left to others or didn't bother with at all: the seating plan of the orchestra, the placement of the continuo in a Handel opera, the numbers of players, the acoustic of the hall, the number of rehearsals and the personnel required for them. He didn't automatically want more rehearsal: when offered a single *Rosenkavalier* rehearsal in Vienna, he opted for none, calculating that he needed three rehearsals to make a difference; one rehearsal would be felt as an annoyance. Given the fullness of his annual calendar, the advanced care he took over various details, none of which was ever seen by the public or often realized even by the musicians who played under him, demanded a large amount of his time. Add to this his own preparation, and it's clear that Charles was industrious by any measure.

Charles generally approved of the advent of supertitles, but he was also a proud proponent of opera in the vernacular, as this was very much the tradition in which he first worked. His views changed depending on the composer: he didn't like translated Handel operas, yet he thought Mozart could work well. He very much admired Andrew Porter's translations of the Wagner *Ring*, but felt Puccini almost never worked in translation. Surprisingly, perhaps, even after supertitles had a firm foothold with the public, his preference was overwhelmingly to perform the operas of Janáček in the dominant language of the audience, despite the exacting speech rhythms of the original vocal writing. He was always highly critical of singers who didn't make words clearly understood, and he also found it illogical for an entire cast to be singing in a language not their own.

Having performed a great many English translations, he loved recounting the awkward and unintentionally humorous prosody of some translated opera texts: such as this couplet from *Lucia di Lammermoor*:

> Lucy stood the weapon grasping.
> Arthur, stunned, just lay there gasping

Or this, from *Il Trovatore*:

> Fierce flaming faggots, licking my Mother
> one way or other; he'll have to die.

I heard him sing these hundreds of times, and they never failed to make him convulse in laughter. Since his background was grounded in translated opera, Charles often said the titles of operas in English: *The Mastersingers*; the *Twilight of the Gods*; sometimes even, though rarely, *The Rose Bearer.* He got a lifetime of amusement that a disgruntled Sadler's Wells board member had managed to misname two of Charles's favourite operas by complaining: 'I don't see why we have to present these modern operas like *Odious Rex* and *The Mackerras Case*.'

He accepted the basic idea of collaboration, and favored moderate producers. He was critical of productions that didn't follow the intentions of the composer, and he believed the conductor, not the director, should be the final arbiter of a work's dramatic intentions. The alchemy of the director–conductor relationship is a palpable one, and Charles sometimes did alter his musical performance in reaction to what he claimed to have disliked. When he conducted a production of Mozart's *Don Giovanni* at the Welsh National Opera, he and director Ruth Berghaus were not remotely in tune over the way the opera should be performed. Charles, in reaction to a production he openly disdained, delivered a particularly ferocious performance of the opera, and I think he actually enjoyed the experience, though he always grumbled about it.

Though he rarely said so, he was happy to have lived when he did. He disagreed with several trends in classical music: he disliked the current vogue of the conductor addressing the audience to talk about the music, feeling that the performance, not the performers, should be the focus of an orchestral concert. Though his own recording career continued to flourish, the decline of the recording industry was a source of frustration to him, as he loved the access recordings gave to so many centuries of music. And the kind of cultural defences of music and live performance in which any cultural leader must now engage were anathema to him; he simply couldn't conceive of having to defend something so basic to life as music was to him. Any time spent doing so was time not immersed in creating the art.

It amused him when later commentators said he didn't garner the top music directorships, and much was written about his being passed over for the Covent Garden position. The permanent directorships he held appealed to him because they gave him access to the music he wanted to conduct. He had absolutely no interest in administration or corporate events – he wanted above all to conduct and to immerse himself in the creations of composers. The high quality of London orchestras always thrilled him, and he loved being amidst that. He had huge admiration for James Levine and the ensemble he built at the Metropolitan Opera, but every time he praised them he always added how glad he was that the Met orchestra had been built by someone else. In contrast to many of his colleagues, he had little interest in conducting new productions. He far preferred to know what he was 'getting', as he put it, before agreeing to invest the time in conducting an opera. He had a view of opera production which would now be termed conservative, though in actuality he loved visionary new ways of looking at operatic works, as long as the music and the composer's intent stayed the focus. The moment a director's ideas took precedence, as when a production was referred to by its director rather its composer, he railed against it.

The subject of a permanent post was on everyone's mind when he conducted Verdi's *Un ballo in maschera* at the Royal Opera House, Covent Garden, on his eightieth birthday. He gave a quick curtain-call speech in which he alluded to his fifty years of conducting at Covent Garden, but 'always as a guest', at which the audience erupted in laughter. Only then did he realize how it must have sounded. 'I really didn't mean it to be funny,' he said, to even more laughter.

The great flowering of his career in later life was attributable to more than his considerable gifts; he owed some of it to technology. As opera houses slowly brought themselves into the technological age and were capable of regularly recording performances, he would spend several hours the day after a performance reviewing the tapes, taking copious notes which he would scribble out and give to the players. The notes were usually detailed and helpful, though sometimes they were hilarious: a note went to a bassoonist in San Francisco that said 'this passage should be more piquant', which sent the player in search of a dictionary. One legendary note, to a continuo player for *Semele*, was classic Charles: 'No! I did *not* say to *not* play the passages which are clearly marked *Tacet*!' ('*Tacet*' is an instruction not to play a particular passage that is played by others.) Detailed notes on Baroque trills were constantly dispatched: he liked trills to begin with a slow upper note, for which ensembles he worked with regularly had a shorthand: they called the trills 'Charlies'.

His notes were voluminous, right up to the last performance; they were playful but disciplined, and laced with a deep sense of responsibility and care for improvement. But beyond the notes to players, Charles was studiously attentive to himself. He made thousands of small adjustments based on what he heard in the tapes, and he solidified his already formidable sense of tempo as well as his tempo memory. It would be facile to say he was never satisfied. In fact, he was often quite happy with what he heard, but he was just so interested in the performance that the listening was not hard work to him. During the 1993 *Rosenkavalier* in San Francisco, I listened with him each day and marvelled that he never tired. For years afterwards, he asked me to send him tapes of my own performances, which I did, and he would send me detailed notes about those, too. These conversations were many times more constructive and instructive than reading even the few high-level music critics left in the world, because one always learned so much. He was never polemic; he was honest but positive; he had no cynicism about the *art* of music, though inevitably he had some about the *industry* of music.

Charles did read reviews, but was much more interested in the future than in what had already occurred. He had great respect for the few music critics who were knowledgeable and articulate. The moment he sensed intemperance or nastiness, though, he would never read them again. He admired critics who championed their passions, such as Desmond Shawe-Taylor, who helped Charles promote the Janáček operas in the early 1950s. He revered musicologists, and he was drawn to anyone from whom he could learn something. H. C. Robbins Landon was particularly important to him because Landon, a brilliant writer, also had a practical streak that appealed to Charles. They had both been to Donaueschingen in the mid-1950s to research Mozart, a connection that Charles always remembered, and they shared a great deal of knowledge with each other. Throughout his life, Charles read musicological material of all kinds in several languages.

He loved the company of musicians more than the company of anyone else. Retirement was unthinkable to him, as a life without daily music-making, at least in study, would not have been 'living' to him. When he was in recovery from rotator cuff surgery and was looking for a project to occupy him, I tried to persuade him to orchestrate Janáček's *Diary of One Who Vanished,* a work he loved. Instead he completed an orchestration of Sir Arthur Sullivan's Cello Concerto, and forever teased himself about choosing the more 'lowbrow' project (see Chapter 12).

Charles was not always a warm presence in rehearsals. Indeed, he could be ruthless when faced with what he perceived as a lack of energy. Rehearsing Dvořák's 'Song to the Moon' during the 1995 San Francisco *Rusalka*, Renée Fleming, as the title character, was perched high in a tree. Mid-aria, Charles stopped and said, angrily, 'Is this by Puccini?' Renée was startled and didn't know what to say. Charles kept going: 'I mean, it just gets slower and slower, stopping on every high note, like a bloody Italian aria.' 'It feels fast to me, maestro. I just need a little room.' 'Well, I'm not going to turn this into some schmaltzy Romantic aria.' They tussled around on the issue for many minutes, and the room was very tense. I couldn't think of a way to lighten the moment so I suggested we move past the aria into the next scene and deal with the issue privately.

'No, let's settle it now,' Charles snapped back, and he raised his baton. He began with a much slower tempo than they had done up to that time, and Renée sang the first phrase. Charles stopped, exasperated: 'I give you a slower tempo and you slow *that* down. What is it going to be?' Renée, highly intelligent and intuitive, knew she had to give in to relieve the tension. 'I'm sorry, Maestro, I will stay right with you.' Charles grumbled and started the aria again at a fairly rapid pace. The rehearsal proceeded and during the remaining days the aria was rehearsed at Charles's fairly quick tempo, albeit with a lovely folk-like quality, but I could tell Renée was frustrated. She came to me after the dress rehearsal asking if there was any way I could get Charles to give her a little room in the tempo of the opera's most famous aria. I told her I would bring it up with him if I had the opportunity, but I felt it best to avoid the subject.

When the opening night arrived and the aria started, I couldn't believe my ears: Charles started it at a tempo he knew Renée would love, and much slower than he had allowed in rehearsal. It was a gorgeous performance, and he kept it that way for the entire run. Renée thanked *me* afterwards, and I had to confess to her that I never mentioned a thing to Charles. Charles's *Rusalka* performances at San Francisco Opera that season remain the most beautifully conducted set of operas I ever heard in my many decades there. What could have been seen as a simple temper tantrum had a long-term benefit: Charles knew what Renée wanted, but over many days he slowly moulded it more towards what he wanted, then did what he considered to be his job; they met in the middle when it was most important – in performance.

Charles had a pointed sense of humor. I once attended a morning orchestral rehearsal with him, and the oboist gave the tuning note for the orchestra, a rather tenuous A. Charles, a former oboist, interrupted the poor guy with 'you must be joking'. In an elevator in Cardiff we found ourselves with his compatriot Dame Joan Sutherland, whom he'd known for many decades, from their early days in Sydney. We made a bit of polite small talk and the famous soprano began humming a tune. 'Hmmmm,' Charles grunted, 'you call *that* singing?' and we all dissolved in laughter. There is an oft-told story about Charles which, even if it is apocryphal, *could* be true (I could never get him either to confirm or deny it). At the scheduled end of an orchestral rehearsal in Paris, but with five more minutes needed, a manager cut the rehearsal with the clock. Charles understood the need for a union and for rules; he was not against any of those things, but when something tipped over into illogic he would react strongly. The story is that he had intended to rehearse for five more minutes and then release the orchestra from the next morning's rehearsal, which was on the day of the concert. But not being allowed an opportunity to communicate this, because the union steward cut him off, he came to the next morning's rehearsal only to announce that he didn't need them that day, and walked away.

Charles was fascinating on the subject of the mid-century conductors whose rehearsals and performances he had witnessed. As a young oboist in Sydney he was highly influenced by Eugene Ormandy, particularly by the force of his personality and the ease with which he drew a different sound out of the orchestra. He often noted that Ormandy's musical skills were made evident by the force of his personality, but Charles was wary of conductors he felt had this alchemy of skill and personality reversed. He reflected often about various aspects of Giulini and Klemperer, conductors whom the famous producer Walter Legge hired Charles to assist and, essentially, 'cover' in recordings with the Philharmonia in the 1950s. It was because of this association with Walter Legge that Charles recorded so much light music. The big-name conductors would have scheduled recording sessions for Beethoven or Brahms and, if they cancelled, the sessions would be used to record lighter music, which was when Charles would get his opportunity. While others were worried how it 'looked' for him to record light music, Charles was content to just keep growing, and he enjoyed the music a great deal because of what it taught him: in his 80s he could still sit at the piano and play most of Offenbach's *Gaîté Parisienne* from memory, though he'd not looked at a score of it in decades.

He believed deeply in an opera-house training for a conductor, having worked as a repetiteur at Sadler's Wells when he returned from Czechoslovakia, and all of the mid-century conductors he admired came up through that path. During those austere post-war London years, two other conductors came to London who would most profoundly influence Charles, and he often talked of them: Arturo Toscanini and Wilhelm Furtwängler. They perfectly illustrated to him the Dionysian and Apollonian approaches to art, concepts Charles often illustrated in a musical way by comparing Brahms and Mendelssohn. What Charles called the 'Brahmsian' way of conducting was to give music a rhythmic flexibility that brought out certain emotional qualities of it: if a passage had a beautiful soaring melody, to let it rhythmically expand, if a passage was more urgent, to allow it to surge forward, and so on. He called the antithesis of this approach the

'Mendelssohnian' approach, which had more rigid rhythms and assumed that the emotive qualities of music would be felt if a constant tempo was kept.

These different concepts interested Charles throughout his career. Toscanini he saw as the Apollonian, the more rigid type, and Furtwängler was the ultimate Dionysian, the supreme example of the 'Brahmsian' flexible conductor. He greatly admired both, and I believe, perhaps subconsciously, he was always seeking to combine the two qualities. I witnessed this particularly whenever Charles conducted late Romantic repertoire, anything written between 1850 and 1920. He longed to moderate the more extreme interpretations, to combine the best qualities of the 'philosophical' conductor (a concept he rather admired) with the more rhythmically strict 'intellectual' approach. Balance in all things was important to him, and he possessed the talents to moderate his own performance. Charles was also a master of one of opera's biggest challenges: balancing the performance from pit to stage. He worked tirelessly to be sure the stage was heard, especially in operas with very large orchestras, such as *Tristan* and *Rosenkavalier.*

In Benjamin Britten's opera *The Turn of the Screw*, the composer was having trouble conducting a 3/8 passage in the Act 1 finale. Charles and Norman Del Mar, who both assisted Britten, were convinced the passage should be conducted in one, but Britten was adamant it be executed in three. Del Mar placed himself in the firing line by opening a discussion with Britten, offending the famously touchy composer. Charles saw first-hand that 'Ben was indeed quite ruthless in getting rid of people who suddenly didn't appeal to him anymore'. To avoid the same fate, Charles explained that he 'used to actually start it off in three in order not to offend Ben, and then I used to go quietly into one in order to keep the tempo going properly, as Norman did'.

Charles loved Gilbert and Sullivan. Their operas took him back to his earliest memories as an oboist in Sydney, and to his childhood, when he would sing all the parts at family gatherings. 'Sullivan was quite an intellectual composer,' he would say. And so, too, was *Pineapple Poll*, Charles's ballet on a scenario inspired by the *Bab Ballads.* Anyone looking for a demonstration of Mackerras's abilities as an arranger and orchestrator should spend time studying this enthralling ballet. It always delighted him that G & S fans kept writing him after discovering new themes and musical juxtapositions in *Pineapple Poll.* And as much painstaking care and scholarship went into his recordings of the Gilbert and Sullivan operas with the Welsh National Opera as into any of the more 'serious' works he recorded. When he retired as Musical Director from the Welsh National Opera, members of the company wrote a parody song for him, based on the Sorcerer's Song from *The Sorcerer.* The original text – 'Oh, my name is John Wellington Wells, I'm a dealer in magic and spells' – was altered to 'Oh, my name is Sir Charles Mackerras, I live at 10 Hamilton Terrace'. He recounted it with hilarity for the rest of his life, particularly the revelation by one of the authors that, 'once we figured out your name rhymed with where you live, the thing wrote itself!'

He also created a wonderful ballet on Verdi themes, *The Lady and the Fool*, and his renown in other areas of the repertoire always overshadowed what a fine conductor of Verdi he was. His 1992 performances of *I vespri siciliani* in San Francisco were among the finest Verdi I ever heard, and he worked harder at delivering that opera than any other I recall. Perhaps because it was rarer, he felt it needed more of his advocacy. One of the issues surrounding *I vespri siciliani* was musical nationalism, and it was much on Charles's mind at the time. The quintessential Italian composer, Verdi, wrote this very French opera, and here it was being conducted by an Australian who lived in London and who was supposedly a Czech music specialist.

He conducted almost no American music, but not from a lack of interest; it was something he simply didn't get asked to do. Musical nationalism – like over-specialization – was one of his pet peeves. The industry's penchant for hiring an Italian to conduct Italian music, a German for German music, and so on, seemed very shallow to him. He knew he became an honorary Czech because of his advocacy of Janáček and his great love of Dvořák, Suk and Martinů, but he was also very aware that this kind of recognition had taken decades of hard work. Charles had an ability to make every composer sound 'right', but he knew it wasn't geographic; it was diligent creative work.

The symmetrical balance of Handel's music greatly attracted Charles. It was he, after all, who first recorded the *Music for the Royal Fireworks* with the 26 oboes of the original performance (see Chapter 1). Charles conducted many Handel operas, and he worked very hard at preparing the various companies for their demands. Communications between Charles and San Francisco Opera in preparation for his three Handel operas there show a rare sense of detail:

> The recorders appear in only two numbers and need only one orchestra reading and the final two rehearsals. The same with the horns, who appear only in one number in Act 1. There is only one bassoon part and one bassoon would actually be sufficient, although I would be quite happy to use two if it doesn't cost any more. In the Carnegie Hall performance, the second bassoon played one of the recorders and, indeed, if either of your oboes or bassoon players play the recorder, it might be better if they did in this performance.[2]

In another letter he wrote:

> The difficulty about Handel operas is that they exist entirely of arias with orchestra and recitatives *without* orchestra. *Julius Caesar*, even in the very cut form in which we did it at the Coliseum, is very long, over 3½ hours ... I would recommend the following rehearsal schedule:

2 Letter to Kip Cranna, 5 March 1985, regarding *Orlando* (San Francisco Opera Archives).

> 3 Orchestra readings, No. 1 with full orchestra, No. 2 with flutes, bassoons, and strings, No. 3 with bassoons and strings.
>
> 2 Sitzproben (Italiennes), 1 with full orchestra, and 1 with reduced orchestra.
>
> 2 stage and orchestra, one with chorus and one without.
> 1 general rehearsal possibly without chorus, assuming that the purely acting silent roles in [John] Copley's production are done by supers and not by chorus members.[3]

There is also some interesting correspondence about a production of *Salome* in San Francisco that he did not eventually conduct. This was a production planned for the season in which the opera company was outside of its home for repairs to the building from the 1989 earthquake. When he found out that the orchestra was to be behind the stage, in the cavernous Civic Auditorium, he withdrew. I was with Charles when he wrote this letter to Kip Cranna in March 1996, and was astounded that this information was at his command; he did not consult a score.

> I am interested that it is proposed to use the reduced orchestral version of *Salome*. I believe that the San Francisco Opera has never used this version before because there are quite a number of snags attached to it.
>
> First of all, the version is for 3 flutes, 4 oboes (including Heckelphone), 4 clarinets (including E flat and bass), 3 bassoons (including contra).
>
> The 5th horn is essential to act as a 'bumper' as the 1st horn part in the reduced version becomes impossibly exhausting for the 1st and 2nd horns. Likewise, the tuba part is a mixture of 4th trombone and tuba, consequently the player has to play both tuba and cimbasso. Please note that at least four percussion players are required for the *Dance of the Seven Veils*; in fact I would say that there is so much arranging and faking to be done in using the reduced version that it is hardly worth doing. Surely it would be better to cut out a couple of extra violins and keep to the original wind section.
>
> I see the necessity for saving money, but really the whole question of the reduction of both *Salome* and *Elektra* creates more problems than it solves.

Plans for Charles to conduct a *Ring* cycle in San Francisco in 1999 did not materialize: the length of the cycle was too taxing for him after his shoulder surgery. He tried very hard to make it work, as did San Francisco. It is intriguing that Charles was a great Wagnerian conductor, but his interest was solely in Wagner the musician and dramatist. He was wary of the various

[3] Letter to Terrence A. McEwen, 7 December 1980, regarding *Julius Caesar*, which was performed in 1982 (San Francisco Opera Archives).

assumptions of power and privilege that were associated with performances of Wagner. Charles disliked projection of any kind, and the forced profundity of Wagnerian performance, the reverence for the performance over the creation, even though he deeply admired the composer, was always an uneasy place for him. That said, he conducted a great deal of Wagner and loved doing so: *Die Meistersinger von Nürnberg* was his favourite Wagner opera, followed closely by *Tristan und Isolde*, *Lohengrin* and the *Ring* operas. He had respect but not affection for *Parsifal*, which he never conducted.

Charles was fascinated that many critics labelled his recordings of the Edinburgh Festival Beethoven symphonies as 'radical'. He was delighted, of course, by the praise, but to him he was simply using a lifetime's scholarship and knowledge to illuminate what Beethoven wrote. He certainly did not set out for radicalism. He knew, though, that the recorded Beethoven market was glutted, so he was delighted to find some critics declaring that it was one of the finest Beethoven cycles since Toscanini.

The conductor Fritz Steinbach's notes informed every measure of Charles's recordings of the Brahms symphonies, and they were the sort of musical legacy that particularly interested him, since they were practical suggestions rather than theorizing. The instructions on exactly where to linger on the upbeats, or where the tempo should be flexible, stimulated his imagination, though he was never pedantic about it; it simply sent him into a quest. The opening theme of the Second Symphony fascinated him: the phrasing of pairs of notes, rather than the endless smoothing of the line so common in modern performances. The younger Charles rather enjoyed trying to convince orchestras of the truth of his concepts; later in life he preferred orchestras that needed less persuasion – and he found willing collaborators for his Brahms recordings in the Scottish Chamber Orchestra. As his health deteriorated and he began to stay closer to home, he deepened his relationships with a smaller number of ensembles: in his last decade he greatly enjoyed his work with the Scottish Chamber Orchestra, the Philharmonia, the Czech Philharmonic, the Orchestra of the Age of Enlightenment, the Royal Opera House, English National Opera and Glyndebourne Festival Opera – as well as his guest appearances with the Berlin Philharmonic and Vienna Philharmonic.

Arthur Fleischmann (1896–1990), born in Bratislava but raised in Australia, became a renowned sculptor and was a pioneer in the use of Perspex. Fleischmann and Charles first met during the late 1930s in Australia and both subsequently settled in London. Fleischmann was also a connection to the Central European cultural tradition that would so occupy Charles's artistic life. He was proud that an artist of Fleischmann's distinction wanted to make a bust of him.[4] Charles's inner circle was small and included only a few male friends, who were mostly musical colleagues. He sincerely

[4] Charles sat for this bust in 1983. Made in bronze on a mosaic panel, it is now in the Australian National Portrait Gallery in Canberra (NS).

loved the company of women, and many of his favourite colleagues were female singers whom he admired. In the final months of his life, he spoke to me often about Joyce DiDonato, the great American mezzo-soprano, whom he greatly revered. He was busily planning all sorts of projects around her even a month before he died; knowing that I knew her well from her early days in Houston, he asked me if I thought Joyce would record a set of Rossini operas with him. He was energized and inspired by great talent, even when his body betrayed him. That said, the star status of a singer, even if they were friends, did not sway him in the face of artistic matters. Take this letter of 17 March 1986 to San Francisco Opera about the version of *Jenůfa* he was scheduled to conduct later that year:

> Regarding *Jenůfa*, I am horrified that Miss Rysanek is still making a fuss about the extra aria for the Kostelnička. As I presume she knew that we were doing the original version, I don't think she has any right to refuse to sing the principal addition to the original. I would have thought that this was a contractual matter, and that you could be entitled to cancel the contract if she refused to sing the version we wanted. We cannot claim to be doing the original version if she doesn't sing the aria and, as I have told you before, in any new production of *Jenůfa* I only do the original version. Thus, if she continues to refuse to sing the aria, we are going to land ourselves with a very great problem as to whether she or I have to withdraw from the project.[5]

Charles loved Leonie Rysanek, admired her tremendously and considered her a friend, but none of those facts would deter him from what he considered his duty: to perform the score as closely as possibly to what Janáček envisioned. Happily, Leonie Rysanek performed the aria.

Charles gave me a lot of good advice, but one conversation was particularly memorable. When I was initially approached by David Gockley, then General Director of Houston Grand Opera, in the mid-1990s, to be their Music Director, I made an exploratory trip to the city. I was struck by the open and kind nature of the place, belying every stereotype of Texas, even though the company was in the midst of a potential political storm: the Houston Symphony, which had been the orchestra for the company since its inception in 1955, had decided to stop playing opera, meaning that the company would have to create its own orchestra. The opportunity was daunting and rare: to build an orchestra nearly from scratch (some players were under contract when I got there) and to be involved in operatic commissioning and the training of young artists, two particular passions of mine. I was wary, though, of a small group of people connected with the company who were particularly prone to negative views of virtually everything. Any large organization, no matter how successful, foments a type of bitterness on its margins, but this group trafficked in a level of

[5] San Francisco Opera Archives.

cynicism and pettiness for which I was ill-prepared. It also became apparent that they had the ear of a local music critic whose opinions were obviously influenced by them (sometimes repeated verbatim). Charles and I talked over the experience, and I asked his advice on whether I should take the job, which was one of three I was offered at the time. My experience overall in Houston had been very positive, though I'd not yet conducted there, but I had these lingering doubts based on this rather poisonous little group, which the company took great pains to have me meet. Charles demonstrated his wisdom. '*If* you have analysed the situation accurately,' he said, 'they will have isolated themselves and are just background noise.' This was just the right advice: rather than telling me what to do, he reminded me that I needed to think more clearly about all of the positive things that could happen in Houston if I took the position, and not to over-react to surface distractions. In the end, the bitter little group had no effect on my work at all.

He was pragmatic and genuinely unemotional about many issues that others might have allowed to alter their lives: when he was once booed in Germany, he didn't stop conducting there – he simply stopped taking solo bows for the rest of the run. He understood that there was a contrarian for everything, and that the firmer a point of view the more possibility there was for opposition. As he aged, Charles tended to laugh off this sort of thing, and he encountered less of it as he acquired elder-statesman status. He certainly never altered his ideas about music simply because someone disagreed with him, and I never knew him to make a musical decision he couldn't defend with both passion and scholarship.

He loved a great play or musical. He often recalled seeing Rodgers and Hammerstein's *South Pacific* in its original London production[6] and spoke in superlatives about Ethel Merman – as had Toscanini. He was so fascinated by Alan Bennett's *The History Boys* that he asked me to buy a copy of the play for him the next time I saw it in a shop. He recounted details of seeing Laurence Olivier, Ralph Richardson and Maggie Smith in a variety of repertoire at the Old Vic. I took him to see Peter Schaffer's *Lettice and Lovage* in New York, which he absolutely loved, quoting several of Maggie Smith's best lines for months afterwards. And he enjoyed Mickey Rooney and Ann Miller in *Sugar Babies* (a 1980s homage to the bygone burlesque era), probably because the two Hollywood stars were his peers and shared a similar work ethic in a very different genre.

Though he was very proud of his many official honours, Charles rarely expressed a political thought. He was not an outspoken monarchist, though

[6] As an intriguing aside, in July 1958 Teddy Holmes of Chappell's in London wrote to Leonard Bernstein about possible conductors for the London premiere of *West Side Story.* It was conducted by Lawrence Leonard, who was 'strongly recommended by Charles Mackerras (a brilliant young conductor who I would have suggested, but unfortunately he is contracted to conduct in South Africa this winter). By the way, Mackerras has seen *West Side Story*' (NS).

he could not have imagined England without the Queen. He took a lot of pleasure in being addressed as Sir Charles. He was neither Theist nor Atheist, but went so far as Deism: he could acknowledge a possible higher power without accepting the prevailing view of what it might be. He was put off by overt religious display and uneasy about the presence of religion in public policy. He was utterly without prejudice about anyone, though the imposition of one group's beliefs on others filled him with incredulity. He was, despite his moderately gruff exterior, very gentle, a pacifist and a moderate. He liked balance, and almost everything in his life had an opposing counterweight.

The last time I saw him was the day after *The Cunning Little Vixen* opened at Covent Garden, in 2010, almost exactly 59 years after he first conducted Janáček in London. We had lunch on Marylebone High Street, near his home in St John's Wood. We had our usual lively conversation, but he tired quickly. I hailed a cab to take him home, and the cabbie misunderstood our directions and headed east towards Regent's Park instead of north and west. Charles, uncharacteristically, absolutely screamed at the poor driver, and it frightened me, as I knew it was not him but the poisonous medicine talking. He calmed a bit as we drove along Regent's Park, and he recalled the Christmas Day twenty years before when we had taken an afternoon walk there together. 'We talked about Dvořák, didn't we?' he asked, and I replied that we had indeed, and how wonderful it was that he remembered that. He began humming the opening of the Sixth Symphony as we arrived at Hamilton Terrace. He was physically very frail, and I had the cab wait while I helped him into the house. For the first time in our long friendship, he leaned on me; his arm was heavy. As he opened the door he quietly said, 'goodbye my boy,' and he turned and weakly hugged me – not a typical Charles gesture. He knew. I knew. Neither of us said anything else as he disappeared into the house.

When I returned to the taxi and explained Charles's outburst, the driver said, in his best Cockney accent: 'It's so nice to see a son take care of his Dad, with so many people being so uncaring these days.' I explained that Charles was my mentor, teacher and friend, but not my father. 'Funny,' he said to himself.

Charles would fulfill only one more engagement: *Così fan tutte* at Glyndebourne. I was in his native Australia when I received word that he had just died. When the call came I was in a rented apartment a few feet from Sydney Grammar School, where Charles had been a student as a boy. A few hours later I conducted a sitzprobe of Charles's favourite opera, Mozart's *Le Nozze di Figaro*, at Opera Australia, where he had enjoyed a long relationship. There was no time for grief, as there was work to do. I spent the remainder of the day along the shoreline of Sydney Harbour, a place Charles loved so much and where he had spent so many days of his youth before the war, before Czechoslovakia, before Janáček, before his career. I once thanked him for all he taught me and he said, typically, 'Oh, come on; I know all that, but we were having such a good time.'

Knowing Charles would far prefer his story told by the music he left behind, I find I now think of his last quarter-century symbolized by the final movement of one of the great Mozart symphonies he loved – the 'Haffner', 'Linz' or 'Jupiter' – because they share qualities with his personality: they begin quietly with great energy before they burst forth with a crackling and infectious glee. They are full of surprises and of laughter. They have an unexpected penultimate outburst before ending with a joy that balances emotion, intellect and impeccable taste. They leave us grateful.

6

'The Musical Values of Opera' WNO, 1987–92

Nigel Simeone

Remembering Charles in Wales

John Stein[1]

I first got to know Charles well when he came to Welsh National Opera to do Martinů's *Greek Passion* in 1981, though I'd played for him before when I was in the orchestra at Covent Garden – I remember playing *Tosca* with him there. Once we knew Richard Armstrong was going to resign, Brian McMaster came to the orchestra with various suggestions for his successor, and with *The Greek Passion* I had immediately been impressed by the chemistry Charles had with the orchestra, right from the start. We had lunch together during *Don Giovanni* rehearsals in 1984. Brian McMaster had asked me to sound out Charles if the opportunity came up, though Brian was very keen on modern productions and wasn't sure how Charles would be with those. Well, that lunch lasted five hours – we probably all had a bit too much to drink – but it clinched it. Afterwards we went back to the office in John Street and found McMaster. Charles announced: 'I'm coming here!' In a way, he didn't *need* to come to WNO – he had plenty of work all over the world – but just as we benefited so much from having him, it gave him the opportunity to perform operas he hadn't done in Britain before and to work with a new generation of singers.

On a personal level, too, Judy was becoming concerned about his nomadic lifestyle and was delighted at the idea of a more settled existence for them, without such extensive and exhausting travelling. They found a lovely flat in Kymin Terrace, Penarth (just south of Cardiff Bay), and liked it very much – it was a place where they could relax and be comfortable when they weren't in London. It was frustrating for him when the New Theatre in Cardiff was closed for renovations, making it necessary to travel to Swansea, forty-five miles away. He was always in great demand from other companies and I remember one dinner at Kymin Terrace that was interrupted by a phone call from Paris. Would Charles like to become music director of the Paris Opéra? Understandably, Judy was dead against it, having just persuaded Charles to settle down at WNO! The idea didn't go any further.

[1] This memoir by John Stein is the first of nine short contributions by different authors that appear at various points in chapters 6, 7, 8 and 13; they are distinguished from the main text by being printed in a different typeface.

The great thing about being Music Director of WNO was that Charles could conduct repertoire he wanted to conduct but might not be asked to do elsewhere. *The Trojans* and *Tristan* are good examples – two of the greatest things he did with us – and some of the Strauss operas. And, no matter what Charles did, he was the master of it. His knowledge was deep, and he was always searching for another way of doing a piece, however well he knew it. That searching never stopped. The real benefactors of his time at WNO were the chorus and the orchestra – as well as the young singers he nurtured, including Bryn Terfel and Rebecca Evans.

People often talk about the gruff, Aussie side of Charles, but there's a word I'd use to describe his conducting gestures that might come as a surprise: he could be a wonderfully elegant conductor on the rostrum, as well as an exciting one. He had an extraordinary ability to take on the character of the music – if you watched a film of him conducting without sound, you could almost work out what the piece was. With his left hand, even small gestures would change the sound in very subtle ways.

Charles's rhythm was amazing. There was always a pulse, but also a feeling of the music going from bar to bar – so his beat never felt perpendicular, but flowed forward. His Janáček is a good example. When he did *The Cunning Little Vixen* with us, he managed something in Janáček that no other conductor I've known has achieved: as well as bringing out all that frenetic detail and the sudden changes, he also felt the music in *long* paragraphs, rather than chopping it up. He was a wonderful judge of tempo, too, adjusting it according to the venue and the acoustics.

As an instrumentalist, when I had a solo, I would always feel that he was giving me all the time in the world: he had that gift of giving you a sense of freedom, even though we were, of course, doing the piece his way. All the players in the orchestra felt the same way about this sense of space he would give us – and woodwind players loved him because he spoke their language.

Partly because I had co-founded the WNO Orchestra (in 1970), I saw my role very much as the representative of the whole orchestra as well as the leader of the strings. A vital part of that job was protecting the relationship between conductor and orchestra – and resolving any differences. If things broke down, I felt I'd failed – but that was never an issue with Charles. He made my job as leader of the orchestra easy: there was such an immediate chemistry, and with just a smile or a glance he could bring out the shape of a phrase and it worked.

He knew that a Music Director had to know about any issues that might affect a player's performance, and he quickly found the best ways of working with particular players: with some breathing with them so that they felt secure, with others deliberately not looking at them in case it made them nervous. Naturally, all of this was based on a deep knowledge of how each instrument worked, but it was more than that, because he also made sure he understood what individual players needed from him to give of their best. He was exacting, of course, but he could be very considerate of individuals too.

It was the same with singers. If they were willing to *try* things such as embellishments and appoggiaturas, he was very tolerant, as long as they worked at it with him. Most of them did, but occasionally he'd get annoyed with a singer who wouldn't even consider what he had to say about style. He tended to think singers like that were lazy, and he was frustrated when he worked with them. On one occasion he finished with the orchestra an hour early so that he could work at the piano with a singer and show her exactly what he wanted. It was to no avail, and he grumbled that she'd 'got it all wrong'. But this was a rare exception. Among members of the company there was great loyalty to Charles, and the singers were not only interested in his discoveries about Mozartian style, but were also willing to make the effort to get it right.

Charles was a very practical man when it came to rehearsals. If there were multiple *divisi* strings, as there are in some parts of Strauss's *Salome*, he'd instantly find a solution to covering all the parts, reassigning a line from the second violins to the violas or whatever was needed. Nobody could hear the difference, and it always worked: that was his skill as an arranger coming out, obvious so early in *Pineapple Poll*, and now being applied to difficult passages in operas. He made it look easy.

With his vast knowledge and experience, Charles knew exactly what to rehearse with the orchestra: what to leave, what to do first so that the brass could go early, and – whenever possible – to bring singers into orchestral rehearsals earlier than usual so that they could get used to the tempos. It was all choreographed with great skill. If it was a repertoire piece the orchestra already knew well, he'd work on some important moments (in *Traviata* it was the prelude to Act 1, prelude to Act 2 and the 'Zingarelle') and trust the players to follow him for the rest. This meant that when he wanted to rehearse something in minute detail the orchestra understood that it was time well spent. And he would come up with some brilliant solutions. The opening phrase of the *Tristan* Prelude is very difficult for the cellos, so when we did it at WNO he had some of them slur the first two notes while the others changed the bow. That preserved the sense of line and made sure the tone was warm and not tentative. When he first came, I asked if he wanted sectionals. He was fascinated by the idea as he'd never done them with an opera orchestra before – he said he was 'used to hearing the whole thing' – but with *The Trojans* he found it very useful to have sectional rehearsals. Working with the orchestra, he came across as a natural teacher, wanting to share his knowledge but always open to new ideas.

One thing annoyed him above all, and that was extra players being changed without his knowledge between performances. I soon learned that if he was told in advance – if I gave him a ring on the morning of a performance and told him that so-and-so was ill, but that we'd been lucky enough to get such-and-such as a substitute – then he'd be fine about it, as long as he could spend time with the new player going over details. Being warned about this ahead of time was something he greatly appreciated: before he came to WNO he had often had problems with last-minute deputies. During his time at WNO he would sometimes ask for the same players to be engaged for every performance: that was the way he preferred to work, and I did everything to try to fix it that way.

Charles's searching nature, and his extreme thoroughness, meant that he knew the libretto of an opera as well as the score – and it mattered to him deeply in terms of what it revealed about a character's motivation and the development of the plot. So the text was really important, and that's one reason why he objected to productions which went *against* the composer or the librettist: he felt the work was being violated. He certainly wasn't against all new productions – he loved the ENO *Xerxes*, for instance, because it was faithful to the spirit of the score and the libretto.

When he came to WNO, the company had a reputation for using quite a lot of directors from Eastern Europe, and of course he'd had the experience of working with Ruth Berghaus on the WNO *Don Giovanni* in 1984. Though he hated that production, at least with Berghaus he could have a serious discussion: she was musical, directed the stage using a full orchestral score, and could talk intelligently about the music. So even if they saw the opera from a diametrically different point of view – and there were certainly arguments – at least he felt he was dealing with a serious person. He didn't always feel that way with some producers, who seemed not to know the music at all.

My wife Sheila and I got to know Charles very well during his time as Music Director at WNO: I saw him almost every day when he was down here, and he became like my musical father. At the end of a performance, Charles would always want to hear a recording, which was usually made by Judy or by my wife, Sheila, using a Sony Walkman under the seat. When we did *Salome* in Swansea, Sheila and I arranged a party after the show on the night it was broadcast on the radio. Sheila and Judy went back to our house to arrange things, and as I was leaving with Charles the BBC engineer came up with a copy of the tape. We started listening to it in the car and became so involved in it – listening and commenting – that I completely missed a turning and somehow we ended up in Newport, 20 miles further on. We kept on listening, I finally managed to turn round, and we arrived home just at that wonderful dissonant chord near the end – we probably woke all the neighbours. Charles's time at WNO was a very happy one not just for me and for the orchestra, but above all for Charles and Judy: they spent more time together and were able to get the relaxation she knew he needed.

His sense of curiosity, his searching nature, was apparent in so much of what he did with WNO. With *Lucia di Lammermoor*, not only did he go back to Donizetti's original – without all the later additions and transpositions that had become 'traditional' – but he also reseated the orchestra on the basis of an engraving he'd found of the layout used in Donizetti's time: with the conductor in the middle. He had the woodwind section behind him, blowing towards the stage, with the strings facing out to the audience in front of him. This made it easier for the singers to hear their cues, which are often played by the wind, and it changed the balance in a fascinating way.

Listening to recordings was important for Charles. When we were recording Delius with the orchestra, he'd listen to our performance after a session but then he'd listen to Beecham, because he knew there was something to learn from the way he did Delius. Beecham's editing often provided the solution to a problematic passage – but Charles also liked to look at early editions, and to hear early recordings, particularly listening out for portamento in the strings. Portamento fascinated him, and I'd often show him different fingerings so that it didn't sound like a caricature. He would always ask about different bowings, too, even in music he knew very well, and he'd like to try them out, hoping to finding new solutions to technical problems. Charles never made a secret of the fact that he often found Reginald Goodall's tempos too slow for his own taste but found other things to admire. After Reggie had conducted at a Gala Concert, Charles said to me: 'I don't know why, but things happen when Reggie conducts. What a *sound* that man has!'

The acoustics in the New Theatre were horrendous. We'd rehearse in a place with a good acoustic and suddenly we'd come into the New Theatre and the sound would be awful: it really was rather traumatic at times. But Charles always tried to make things work. Sometimes he'd say just before a performance that he'd take a passage quicker that night – to overcome the problems in a particular theatre, especially in the New Theatre.

Early on, Charles wanted to give concerts with the orchestra in St David's Hall, and the more we did these the more confident everyone became about playing on a concert platform rather than in a pit – it's a very different experience. Playing big ambitious works suited an orchestra that was used to performing Strauss and Janáček in the theatre. There was quite a battle with management over these: we were told the Arts Council was funding WNO for opera and that's what the company should stick to doing, and the BBC resisted too. But, because Charles had quite a lot of clout, we were able to go ahead. One of the first really big pieces was Mahler's Sixth Symphony, and I particularly remember doing the whole of Smetana's *Má vlast*, which was a wonderful experience.

Charles really appreciated what a leader does. He set up a scholarship for me to teach at the Royal Welsh College of Music and Drama: he understood what a leader needed to learn and how they should work, and he was delighted with the results of 'our' scholarship.

Charles was one of the two greatest conductors I've worked closely with; the other was Pierre Boulez. Both of them had the ability to make an orchestra play better than it thought possible. Several of my most memorable musical experiences were with Charles. The moment he stepped into the pit there was a sense of excitement; then he'd fling his arms wide and we'd be off – on many nights that would be the start of something unforgettable.

In May 1985, *Opera* magazine reported: 'Sir Charles Mackerras has been appointed Music Director of Welsh National Opera from 1 January 1987'. It was to be a fruitful and friendly partnership. WNO had given its first public performances in 1946, and when the local businessman Bill Smith became a partner he immediately invited the young Charles Mackerras – not yet 25 years old – to come and conduct Offenbach's *Tales of Hoffmann* in 1950 (see Chapter 1). The same year Mackerras also conducted *The Bartered Bride* and *Die Fledermaus* with the company. It was a baptism of fire: many of the singers were enthusiastic amateurs, and the orchestra was a very long way from the standard later achieved by WNO's own permanent orchestra, founded by John Stein and James Lockhart in 1970.

Within a few years, WNO had developed into a company that was able to attract rave reviews on its first visits to London, and it quickly became the most important touring opera company not only in Wales but also across west and central England. Mackerras returned to WNO in 1961 for Rimsky-Korsakov's *May Night*, including a London performance at Sadler's Wells. Twenty years later, in April 1981, he conducted the British premiere of Martinů's *Greek Passion*. On 27 October 1984 he conducted *Don Giovanni* in the controversial production by Ruth Berghaus that confirmed Mackerras's worst fears about 'concept' productions. Tom Sutcliffe in the *Guardian* (29 October 1984) described Berghaus's staging as 'a tedious and repetitive misrepresentation' (though Sutcliffe himself later changed his tune). Still, the prospect of working with a fine company of singers and an excellent orchestra clearly outweighed Mackerras's grim memories of the Berghaus experience, and he began his tenure with four operas in his first season: Berlioz's *The Trojans*, Puccini's *La Bohème*, Mozart's *Marriage of Figaro* and Janáček's *Cunning Little Vixen* – the first time he had conducted this work in the theatre. *The Trojans* opened on 28 February 1987 at the New Theatre, Cardiff. Mackerras believed it was a good choice, telling Hugh Canning in an interview for the *Guardian* published on the morning of the premiere: 'It is one of the greatest and grandest of all operas, a huge epic to challenge this ambitious and resourceful company. [...] Although I have already conducted the opera in Australia, you don't get the chance very often because it is done so rarely. The rehearsals have been going very well.'

In the same interview he was also candid about his reasons for taking the job: 'Now you may think it an extraordinary move to accept the job of Music Director immediately after I'd had the most monumental row with Ruth Berghaus over her production concept [of *Don Giovanni*]. But the orchestra is so hard-working, so interested in new ideas, so involved in the whole process – you don't find that in many operatic institutions. And the chorus, so alive and vivacious. I also find it very refreshing not to have to kow-tow to stars.'

The gamble of mounting an opera as gigantic as *The Trojans* for his first production paid off handsomely: it was hailed by Tom Sutcliffe as 'magnificent' (*Guardian*, 2 March 1987), and he had particularly warm words for the conducting: '*The Trojans* marks Sir Charles Mackerras's advent at WNO as Music Director. The orchestra play marvellously. And though some of the subtler aspects of the orchestra are submerged in the torrent of noise, this is a truly wonderful interpretation of the score that fully relishes the extraordinary originality of Berlioz's ideas. Mackerras takes a spacious approach that would be even more beguiling and moving in a larger theatre, though the focused impact of the Cardiff theatre is an absolute knockout. As the best sung production I can recall by WNO, this *Trojans* is a remarkable conclusion to a brilliant 12 months.' *La Bohème* quickly followed (it opened in Cardiff on 13 March), with Anne Williams-King as Mimi and Dennis O'Neill as Rodolfo. Curiously, the production of *Figaro* that opened on 19 May was not greeted so warmly: though Tom Sutcliffe described it as 'fun', he questioned the use of Mozart's 1789 revisions ('detrimental') and described Mackerras's conducting as 'robust, if not downright noisy [...] which is certainly not historical'.

The New Theatre closed for renovation before the start of the 1987/8 season, so *The Cunning Little Vixen* opened at the Grand Theatre, Swansea, in David Pountney's enchanting production (seen at Scottish Opera, WNO and subsequently ENO), with Anne Dawson as the Vixen, Rita Cullis as the Fox and Barry Mora as the Forester. Though he had already recorded the work for Decca, this first stage performance was an important landmark in Mackerras's career: he went on to conduct *Vixen* on many occasions and it became one of his particular favourites. The same season saw the first of Mackerras's Strauss productions with WNO: a new staging of *Salome* by André Engel, with Stephanie Sundine in the title role. After his disappointment with the *Figaro*, Tom Sutcliffe (*Guardian*, 29 March 1988) clearly felt that the company, and especially its conductor, were back on top form:

> A large part of the excitement of the Welsh National Opera's remarkable new *Salome* comes from the contained intensity and seriousness of Sir Charles Mackerras's conducting. Too often with this opera the temperature never falls. But Mackerras plays the prophet Jokanaan's music with frankness and purity of heart. The orchestra is cool and beautiful, registering the rich colour. Mackerras finds a sombre pace when apt, and invites attention to the revealing of a parable.
>
> This does not at all reduce the glamour. Strauss's miraculous score unfolds with lavish attention to every tiniest detail. But there is profound purpose. The excess does not swamp or sicken. Mackerras is not showing off. As with his sublime Janáček, he is born again and filled with discovery. This is what he came to the Welsh National Opera for.

A new production of *La Traviata* opened on 4 June (with Susan Patterson as Violetta, Laurence Dale as Alfredo and Barry Mora as Germont senior). Max Loppert (*Opera*, August 1988) was cautious about Göran Järvefelt's direction and Carl Friedrich Oberle's sets, but he wrote a perceptive analysis of Mackerras's qualities as a Verdi conductor:

> What gave the performance its musical authenticity was the magnificent conducting of Charles Mackerras. I had heard several Mackerras *Traviatas* (including the EMI/ENO recording) before this one, but none more unarguably authoritative in scale, manner, and dramatic purpose. He is not afraid to 'think big' where situation and musical form require it – the rhythmic energy found in cabalettas (notably 'Sempre libera') threatened tidy ensemble – yet the flexible phrasing, with rubato and tenuto perfectly judged, and pacing of lyrical meditations showed ideal intimacy and idiomatic command. This was Verdi conducting of rare quality, and it made all the difference in the world.

With WNO in 1989, Mackerras conducted Mozart's *Die Entführung aus dem Serail*, Strauss's *Die Frau ohne Schatten* and *Ariadne auf Naxos*, two concert performances of Janáček's *Fate* (*Osud*), Donizetti's *Lucia di Lammermoor* and Smetana's *Bartered Bride*. Mackerras's continuing exploration of Strauss included what is perhaps the most demanding of all his operas, *Die Frau ohne Schatten*, with Anne Evans as the Dyer's Wife, Christine Teare as the Empress and Jeffrey Lawton as the Emperor. While Max Loppert in *Opera* (April 1989) admired much of the singing, and found the conducting 'undeniably exciting' and the orchestral playing 'astonishing', he was worried about the balance between the stage and the pit in the New Theatre, with 'too little dynamic variety' and an acoustic that felt 'somewhat airless'. There were no such complaints about the much more intimate *Ariadne auf Naxos*. This new production by Giles Havergal – set in 1916 – got a mixed press, but William Mann in *Opera* found that Mackerras's conducting of *Ariadne* 'confirmed my estimate of his uncommon empathy with the operatic Strauss'. Mann was similarly impressed (*Opera*, May 1989) by the musical aspects of the new production of Mozart's *Entführung*, believing it to be 'the most successful as a total representation' of the recent versions he'd seen. He most praised the cast – especially Peter Rose's Osmin – and the conducting:

> The programme included Sir Charles Mackerras's note on the Turkish percussion band as used by Mozart in this opera. The overture at once let us hear the result, for the piccolo was a sopranino recorder, and its opening top C sounded an octave higher than usual; the cymbals and bass drum were higher-pitched, lighter, as well, the triangle more tinkling. [...] The whole gave extra sparkle to the opera's first pages, and again later. Sir Charles's interpretation of the whole score, no cuts at all, was strong on lightness and brilliance, as well as touching the heart in Constanze's arias, in the quartet and the glorious final duet of the courtly lovers.

The two concert performances of Janáček's *Fate* (*Osud*) in Birmingham and Cardiff were important landmarks for Mackerras himself, as well as for the company: it was the first time he had conducted the opera, sung in the English translation by Rodney Blumer (the *nom de plume* of Rodney Milnes). The triumphant Birmingham performance was very strongly cast (with Philip Langridge, Helen Field and Kathryn Harries as the three principals) and superbly played, and (as I wrote in the *Musical Times*, October 1990): 'Charles Mackerras conducted the opera magnificently: his way with both the fire and majesty of Janáček's music is without peer.' The same performers recorded the work for EMI a few days later for the Peter Moores Foundation (later reissued by Chandos in its 'Opera in English' series). Reviewing the recording in the *Guardian* (21 June 1990), Edward Greenfield described the score as 'one of the richest and most underprized of all [Janáček's] operas' and greatly admired Mackerras's ability to capture 'the gutsiness, passion and impetus of Janáček's inspiration'.

As well as playing in WNO's usual venues, both *Lucia* (in the original 1835 version which Mackerras was later to use at the Met) and *The Bartered Bride* were included on the programme for WNO's visit to the Dominion Theatre in London in December 1989. In an *Observer* feature (3 December 1989), Rupert Christiansen interviewed Brian McMaster (WNO's Managing Director) and Mackerras:

> That compulsive innovator and archive digger Sir Charles Mackerras is in his third season as musical director. [...] He believes that even standard works present opportunities for 'complete musical re-thinking' – his *Lucia*, for instance, is notable for its return to original performing practices and its eschewal of inauthentic textual accretions. Such an approach represents a distinct aspect of WNO's current policy: 'I took the job,' Mackerras claims, 'with the intention of placing as much accent as possible on the musical values of opera, which had previously suffered from the prominence given to production.'

Those musical values were highlighted in Meirion Bowen's review of the Dominion season in the *Guardian* (12 December 1989). What impressed Bowen was that, as well as being 'immaculately conducted', 'the music was so well executed. The WNO orchestra was throughout not merely reliable, but attentive to niceties of phrasing and ensemble to an extent rare among pit bands.'

This concentration on musical aspects did not please all the critics. Tom Sutcliffe (*Guardian*, 28 December 1989) felt that WNO was taking fewer risks than it had in the past in terms of controversial productions. He felt that part of the responsibility lay with its 'conservative music director (Mackerras)' – and so it did, but that merely underlined Mackerras's deeply held belief in the idea of *prima la musica* and in fidelity to the creators' intentions.

Mackerras's views on all matters concerning opera had often been explored in *Opera* magazine, and in February 1990 it published 'Where we are now', an interview by Rodney Milnes which ranged from changes in singing styles and 'authentic' performance practice to 'produceritis'. Contrasting singers from immediately after the war with those of the 1980s, Mackerras felt that fewer of the younger generation understood their roles as fully as their predecessors:

> English and American singers [...] try to master all styles, and they're good at it – but the old singers used to sing in one style only, even those within my living experience. After the war, when I started, they were still singing all the Italian operas in German in Germany, and at Covent Garden everyone was singing in English. It didn't occur to anyone to do anything else. That meant that on the whole, as they were all singing in their own language, their diction tended to be very good and consequently they really could project the meaning of what

> they were singing. I find nowadays that however intelligent singers are, they sound to some extent as if they don't actually understand the words or, at least, don't manage to convey their understanding. It's the same with so many producers. They don't feel the genius of the language.

On changes in singers' understanding of different musical styles, Mackerras showed that his own approach valued what had gone before as well as trying to recover a lost style:

> An interest in what we call 'authenticity', in a return to sounds the composer might have known, was founded by my generation. It has been quite a battle, and in a way it's gone full circle: a lot of the younger authenticists have gone back to many of the practices done by the older people. I'm always amazed at how much like a modern 'authentic' singer Isobel Baillie sounds. If you listen to her singing 'I know that my Redeemer liveth', it's uncannily reminiscent of Emma Kirkby.

He also believed a plurality of approaches to be a good thing, with so many different schools of performing practice:

> Variety is a healthy thing. Of course a lot of people who don't like that sound at all will say 'well, that shows you, none of them can agree'. But in the 18th century musicians didn't agree on how to play things, even people with very similar birth and background [...] So why shouldn't Hogwood be different from Harnoncourt?

Mackerras was always a pragmatist when it came to historically informed performance, and his knowledge of great performers from the more recent past meant that he could always see the best in different approaches, including the conducting of Wilhelm Furtwängler, which he hugely admired:

> The trouble with 'authentic' people is that they say they're going back to an 18th-century style, but in fact they're playing in a late 20th-century style that is a reaction against the way all 18th-century composers were played in the period between the wars. Yet there's still something marvellous about the way Furtwängler did the *Matthew Passion*. It may not have had much to do with authentic practice, but it was a great spiritual experience. I'll never forget hearing *Der Freischütz* in Salzburg conducted by Furtwängler. It was the only time I heard him conduct opera, and the sound of that overture, and the Wolf's Glen scene – it was the most wonderful experience. The dramatic propulsion of that performance was overwhelming.

He had some fascinating things to say about how acting styles on the operatic stage had changed in the course of half a century:

> There used to be an 'operatic' style of acting which made sense of the fact that an aria consisted of the repetition of words, or an ensemble

> repeated the same idea over and over again, which play directors find quite difficult to cope with. They either have to make everybody rush about the stage, or else they make them stand still and not express anything. The older generation found a way of doing that. You find it today only among singers who haven't been exposed to Western 'progress', like the Russians. I was thinking that only the other day, conducting Sergey Leiferkus singing Telramund in San Francisco. He is an opera singer who acts, with a kind of acting, some would say old-fashioned, that projects the character to the audience, projects every emotion without overdoing it, without being hammy.

Unsurprisingly, he laid the blame for this squarely at the feet of producers who were unsympathetic to opera, or who wanted to subvert it. He traced the start of this trend back to the 1960s, when producers were brought in from the straight theatre:

> That was the beginning of the end. When they started to say 'opera productions are ham, let's bring in people to show us how it should be, with none of that nonsense of big gestures'. And from then on singers who had been doing wonderful operatic acting became second-rate play actors. And they still are. I know there are some modern singers who are such good actors, and so good at doing what the producers tell them to, that they could conceivably work in the straight theatre. Look at the success that Willard White has had as Othello. Very often, though [...] among singers the great actors are the less great singers.

Asked about changes in the standards of orchestral playing, Mackerras had this to say:

> The WNO and the newer regional opera companies are certainly much better than they used to be. I don't know that the Covent Garden Orchestra is. Just after the war, and when Solti first arrived, it was a marvellous orchestra. It's still marvellous, but it was just as good then.

As for the standard of singing, he was unequivocal: it had improved enormously:

> Yes, oh far better, because of the rising standards of teaching and the expansion of the music colleges. Also because of the fact that American and British singers have become international. First of all the Americans went to Europe, to Italy and mainly to Germany, where there were a whole lot of little theatres where they could learn their trade. In England they learned their trade at the Carl Rosa, and partly at Sadler's Wells. But the English singers very rarely went international – Eva Turner was one of the very few. Today there are dozens, which shows just how much standards have risen. One thing I have to say, though – it's extraordinary how singers are always ill nowadays. When I was at Sadler's Wells for all those years, it was very rare for anybody to be off. Now it's almost the rule. I have hardly

> done a performance in recent years in which everybody, including the orchestra and the chorus and the principals have all been there. Is that simply because there's so much more opera, and therefore the ratio of ill people to healthy people is different, or is it that there are so many more viruses attacking us all? [...] There was one young singer, who shall be nameless, who cancelled Angelotti [in *Tosca*] the other day because he wasn't feeling 100 per cent. I could hardly believe my ears! That really shows the difference in attitude between the old singers and the new.

One of the changes Mackerras welcomed most warmly was the expansion of the repertoire in opera houses – a trend that was just beginning when he introduced *Káťa Kabanová* to London audiences in 1951:

> That's the great thing that's happened in the 40 years. I mean, who could have imagined that we would have seen all the Janáček operas, all the early Verdi, those extraordinary Rossini operas, even Cherubini? To think that there have been two different productions of *Médée* at Covent Garden since the war! Incredible! [Johann] Christian Bach, and that endless supply of Donizetti operas. And the 20th century, Busoni's *Doktor Faust*, rare Strauss, and Hindemith. It's marvellous that there should be enough audiences for us to put these things on. [...] The success of something like [Janáček's] *Osud* at the Coliseum, that's marvellous, and *Doktor Faust* too, together with the fact that they took care over the performing version of it, and did the Beaumont completion [...] getting the text right. And that, being interested in the subject myself, I regard as a Good Thing!

Audiences may have welcomed the chance to see hitherto unfamiliar operas, but their behaviour was, Mackerras felt, becoming more extreme, and they seemed to be more ready to boo than they had been in post-war London:

> Booing – or rather whistling – only used to happen in Italy. Nobody booed in England, or the Met, or Germany. Now, it's like terrorism. By giving your boo, you, one person, can spoil a performance for everyone. It's incredibly disheartening to singers. I know myself on the rare occasions, luckily, I've been booed, it's terribly depressing and hurtful. People who boo know that, they know they have it in their power to depress that great person up there on the stage who earns £5,000 a performance, they know 'I have it in my power, I alone have the key of this savage parade'. It's horrible!

With a cast including experienced singers such as Valerie Masterson (Fiordiligi) and Donald Maxwell, the revival of *Così fan tutte* in February and March 1990 was likely to be a solid musical success, but also in the cast also was a young singer making his professional operatic debut: Bryn Terfel sang Guglielmo. Hugh Canning in *Opera* (May 1990) described it as 'one of the funniest and most moving *Così*s I have ever seen' and Terfel's singing as 'a godsend', with a 'fine, rich voice and a vivacious stage personality'. In terms of the musical text, this was no routine revival. To celebrate the 200th anniversary of the premiere, Mackerras chose to present the score as Mozart had conducted it in January 1790. Canning was fascinated by the version used, though he hoped it was a one-off, and was unstinting in his praise of the conducting and the whole company's grasp of musical style:

> What a joy it was to hear this conductor in Mozart again: the fleet but never breathless tempo of the overture (one oboe slip apart) announced the sparkling comedy which *Così fan tutte,* despite its serious undertones, is and always should be. It was a pleasure, too, to hear so many appoggiaturas, bridging cadenzas and stylish decoration, particularly in the grand formal arias of Fiordiligi. Sir Charles was giving us a rare (and, I hope, unique) opportunity to experience this most endlessly fascinating of Mozart's operas as the composer himself conducted it at the Vienna Burgtheater in January 1790. As an anniversary exercise, then, it was intriguing to discover that Mozart made a small cut in Ferrando's 'Un aura amorosa' (!) – both of his other arias were given intact – that he excised the 'Taci, ohime' section from the sublime Fiordiligi–Ferrando duet (not so long ago we used to chide Karl Böhm and other 'traditional' Mozartians for this act of butchery!) and, most grievous of all, he dispensed with the wonderful canon quartet 'E nel tuo, nel mio bicchiero', re-setting the words to the music of the previous section 'Tutto, tutto' but retaining Guglielmo's dissenting wish that these dishonourable vixens were drinking poison. As I say, all very intriguing, but I don't think we need to hear it again until 2090. Composers do not always know best.

The other new production of the spring 1990 season was Strauss's *Der Rosenkavalier*. Tom Sutcliffe used his review in the *Guardian* (3 March 1990) as an opportunity to make an intemperate attack on Mackerras's musical directorship of the company, claiming that it had 'coincided with a disastrous decline in standards' and grumbling about the conducting and playing, 'which sounded rhythmically unsteady, rushed and under-rehearsed'. Rodney Milnes in *Opera* was milder, but did note problems with the balance between stage and the orchestra:

> A conductor as experienced as Charles Mackerras, while pacing the piece expertly (some standard cuts opened – bravo!), might have paid more attention to internal and external balance. [...] It sounded not so much like a conversation piece as a shouting match. [...] Grateful as one was for Mackerras's refusal to linger over the more glutinous passages [...] there was a tendency to hustle the singers on elsewhere, and he let rip mercilessly in the last 20 minutes, giving us an orchestral tone poem with occasional vocal obbligato.

The situation seemed to have improved markedly by the time this production arrived in Oxford on 24 March. In the *Musical Times* (July 1990)

Matthew Rye noted that 'the WNO orchestra were on top form [...] and Sir Charles Mackerras was able to bring out every delectable detail of the score'. Still, though *Der Rosenkavalier* had been a Mackerras speciality since the memorable ENO production in 1975, for whatever reason, the WNO *Rosenkavalier* (the company's first) didn't quite come off. In later years, Mackerras was to conduct some unforgettable concert performances of extracts from the opera, as well as an acclaimed revival at the Royal Opera House (all discussed in Chapter 7).

Mackerras was increasingly in demand by major international houses. On 25 February 1991, he conducted *Káťa Kabanová* at the Metropolitan Opera, in a production by Jonathan Miller with a cast including Gabriela Beňačková as Káťa and Leonie Rysanek as Kabanicha. Mackerras was introducing this work to the Met as he had to London audiences forty years earlier. This time, however, the critical reaction was very different from the dour reaction of most London critics in 1951. Martin Mayer in *Opera* (May 1991) could scarcely contain his enthusiasm:

> February 25 saw the simultaneous debuts at the Metropolitan Opera of Gabriela Beňačková, one of the greatest practising sopranos, *Katya Kabanova*, save only *Wozzeck* perhaps the best opera written in the 1920s, Jonathan Miller, a most thoughtful producer, and Robert Israel, the most intelligent American scenic designer. For once, everybody lived up to her or his reputation. Add to that Leonie Rysanek on stage and Charles Mackerras in the pit, and our cup ranneth over. Critics who are normally up the aisle before the curtain hits the stage were still at their seats applauding as an overwhelmed audience, very few of whom had ever heard the work before, summoned the cast back for a sixth curtain call.

Mackerras conducted no operas for WNO between March 1990 and September 1991, when the company unveiled a new production of Mozart's *Idomeneo*. This was first given at the Proms on 13 September 1991 before opening in Cardiff on 18 September and then touring extensively. Tom Sutcliffe reviewed the Cardiff opening night for the *Guardian* (21 September 1991), describing it as 'brilliantly cast and superbly directed' and declaring it to be WNO's 'best work since *The Trojans* in 1987, with Charles Mackerras's robustly authoritative conducting and a feast of fine singing'. The cast included experienced WNO company members such as Suzanne Murphy ('an intriguing and persuasive Elettra') and Dennis O'Neill ('a stunning Idomeneo') alongside the 'beautifully lyrical tenor' of John Mark Ainsley's Idamante, which had 'power, feeling and [...] profoundly touching dignity'. The cast for *Idomeneo* included one singer who was to work extensively with Mackerras in the years to come: Sutcliffe hailed 'a brilliant newcomer, Rebecca Evans, as Ilia. Evans brings ideal ease and legato to a really lovely timbre.' Having grumbled about Mackerras's 'conservatism' a few months earlier, Sutcliffe was unhesitating in his praise of the conductor on this occasion: 'Mackerras, always a marvellous Mozartian conductor, needs a production of this sophistication to reveal his true musical worth.'

When this production was revived in October 1995, another young singer made his professional debut in the cast: Toby Spence sang the part of Idamante. To accommodate a young singer, and to maximize the theatrical impact of *Idomeneo*, Mackerras proposed some modifications. On 7 April 1995, he wrote to the director Howard Davies. The main change he proposed was to revert to Mozart's original (1781) scheme for the start of Act 2, rather than his 1786 revision, made when the part of Idamante was sung by a tenor (the version that WNO had used for its 1991 production). The letter is very characteristic of the trouble Mackerras took over an opera about which he cared deeply, especially one where Mozart had changed his mind:

> I suggested changing the production of the opening of the second Act of our *Idomeneo* for several reasons:
>
> 1. I have found that, even with John Mark Ainsley, the long aria 'Non temer, amato bene' became rather boring. This is a great pity as the rest of the Act is so marvellous.
>
> 2. Although I am convinced that the form we used for the beginning of Act II is in fact the correct version of the opera when Idamante is sung by a tenor, many people, including some critics, do not agree with me and indeed I can see why people object to it.
>
> The aria sung by Arbace is very brilliant and very showy. The singer of the role is a very promising young tenor [Peter Hoare], and I am sure he will sing the aria beautifully. I have performed the Act in this form before where there has been a really good singer as Arbace, and I assure you that it does make a very effective opening to the Act. To me the chief benefit is that it tightens up the whole action so that the audience's attention is not allowed to flag before the really great succession of arias and choruses starts.
>
> I realise you are in New York until mid-May; either during your stay there or on your return I hope you could listen once again to the opening of Act II in its original form (i.e. starting with Arbace's aria, then going into Ilia's aria followed by 'Fuor del Mar'.) Please note that I am not insisting that we alter it, merely recommending that it would be more effective, but we should give a definite ruling fairly soon as the young man doing Arbace will have to learn the aria.
>
> All good wishes,
> Yours sincerely,
> Charles M.[2]

His international recognition is well exemplified by the performance of *Don Giovanni* that Mackerras conducted in Prague on 1 December 1991 at

[2] Mackerras family archives.

the reopening of the Estates Theatre, where the work had been given its first performance in 1787. Mackerras was immensely proud to be the conductor of this performance, given to commemorate the 200th anniversary of Mozart's death. For him it was an almost magical combination of Mozart, Prague and his fascination with musical history: to recreate *Don Giovanni* in the theatre where it had been given its premiere was a special experience for a conductor with such a strong and well-informed sense of history. Much more recent historical events were reflected by the presence of President Václav Havel, the nation's leader since the Velvet Revolution in 1989. The performance was filmed and later issued on DVD. It is a thrilling account of the score, despite some imperfections. Limited rehearsal time meant that Mackerras could not work on embellishments and other refinements with the singers, as he was able to do in later productions at Covent Garden, but he coaxed playing of tremendous vitality from the Orchestra of the Prague National Theatre. David Cairns reviewed the event in the *Sunday Times* (8 December 1991):

> A Mozart event to cap all other bicentenary celebrations took place last week in Prague: the reopening, with a riveting production of *Don Giovanni*, of the very building for which Mozart wrote this 'opera of operas'. Sunday's gala opening, given before President Havel and his ministers [...] was exhilarating but tense. By Wednesday night the cast was on cracking form. By no means all the singing [...] was of the highest standard; but, with Charles Mackerras in charge, it was intensely committed. Orchestral playing was stylish, wind and strings nicely balanced; drums and trumpets blazed.

The year 1992 began and ended with Janáček: in January a revival of John Copley's production of *Jenůfa* at Sydney Opera House, with Eilene Hannan in the title role, and in December a brand-new production by David Pountney of *The Excursions of Mr Brouček* by ENO at the London Coliseum. This was notable for the superlative orchestral playing and for the combination of humour, urgency and searing nobility that Mackerras brought to the score.

In April he was back at the Met to conduct five performances of Britten's *Billy Budd* with a cast led by Thomas Hampson (Billy Budd), Graham Clark (Vere – he was also to sing Brouček for Mackerras at ENO at the end of the year) and James Morris (Claggart). Tim Page reviewed the production for *Newsday* (7 April 1992):

> The Metropolitan Opera's production of Benjamin Britten's *Billy Budd*, created by the late John Dexter, has long been acclaimed one of the company's most satisfying. On Saturday afternoon, it returned to the repertory with a superb cast [...] and a conductor, Sir Charles Mackerras, who understands Britten's esthetic with rare acuity. For those who are moved by the opera (or those who have not yet seen it), a visit to the Met should be a priority. [...] The Met orchestra plays very differently for Mackerras than for its music director,

> James Levine. Levine stresses an aggressive brilliance and virtuosity; Mackerras summons a united, unified reserve, entirely appropriate to the material at hand. Whatever one thinks of the opera itself, the Met surpasses itself with this *Billy Budd*.

The first performance on 4 April was broadcast, and listening to it confirms Page's positive impressions, particularly his comments about the orchestral sound, which has both darkness and richness – similar in many ways to Britten's own conducting of the work, and to Mackerras's 1966 BBC TV version, but with even greater nobility and dramatic power.

Mackerras was always passionate about Gluck, and he performed the operas whenever the chance arose (including Dame Janet Baker's famous farewell performances of *Alceste* at Covent Garden in 1981). On 18 May 1992 he conducted the first night of a new production of *Iphigénie en Tauride* at the New Theatre, Cardiff, with a cast including Diana Montague, Alwyn Mellor, Peter Bronder, Simon Keenlyside and Peter Sidhom. Max Loppert (*Opera*, July 1992) was deeply impressed by this production, which was the last that Mackerras conducted as WNO's Music Director:

> For Gluck lovers this was manna itself after a very long spell of desert hunger. It was WNO's first Gluck opera presentation in nearly half a century of existence; the choice of *Iphigénie en Tauride* was welcome in myriad ways [...] On the opening night it surged out into the New Theatre with unstoppable force and speed. In clock-time the performance lasted just over two hours; in psychological time it passed in a flash, and with a searing immediacy that can have left few in the audience in doubt they were encountering one of the essential masterpieces of music-drama.
>
> No theatre, said Gluck, can be too small for it; but the New, medium in size, 'close-up' in sound projection, seemed just about perfect as an *Iphigénie en Tauride* auditorium. This is an advantage which the conductor, Charles Mackerras, seized to the full. He remains one of the world's master Gluckians, fierce in his insistence on both 'period' musical values – orchestral textures distinct in colour-details and layering of phrases, never smooth and sumptuous in the manner of a Muti – and modern communicative passion. Every note was rendered with head-on vitality; every phrase reverberated with dramatic intensity precisely directed. The bareness of the score was made, as it must be, its supreme virtue: the silences spoke as eloquently as the sounds, and where a single effect (such as the grimly buzzing string tremolo in Thoas's aria) needs to set the tone, Mackerras worked it with fiery authority. It was not spacious Gluck conducting. Edges were hard. Rhythms had a kick. Marbled neo-Classical grandeur gave way to immediacy of impact.

For Mackerras, his years at WNO were a chance to explore operas he had not conducted before (such as *Osud*, *Salome* and *Die Frau ohne Schatten*, as well as his first staged performances of *The Cunning Little Vixen*) along with others that he believed in passionately but had done only rarely (notably his first and last productions as Music Director, *The Trojans* and *Iphigénie en Tauride*). He performed more Strauss with WNO than at any other time in his career, and his Mozart with the company included a triumphant *Idomeneo* as well as performances of *Figaro*, *Entführung* and *Così* in which he was constantly rethinking his interpretations of works he knew intimately. Just as important as the repertoire was a relationship with the company that endured long after he left as Music Director. In the years that followed he was to conduct several major productions, starting with Wagner's *Tristan und Isolde*.

Mackerras did a great deal to raise the profile of the WNO Orchestra. Before becoming Music Director, he had conducted several concerts with the company's chorus and orchestra at St David's Hall, Cardiff: Haydn's *Creation* in 1983 and 1985, Haydn's 'Nelson' Mass and Beethoven's Seventh Symphony in 1984, and Handel's *Messiah* in 1985. In 1983 he conducted the WNO Orchestra in a complete performance of Smetana's *Má vlast*. With the encouragement of John Stein, Mackerras did much to develop the orchestra's concert-giving during his time as Music Director. For example, he conducted Mahler's Sixth Symphony in St David's Hall on 9 January 1988, and a few days later, on 14 January, Mozart's 'Haffner' Symphony, Weber's *Andante and Hungarian Rondo* for viola and orchestra (with Csaba Erdélyi) and Strauss's *Don Quixote* (with Raphael Wallfisch playing the Don's cello solos). In 1990 (17 August) Mackerras brought the WNO Orchestra to the Proms in London with a programme including Mozart's 'Prague' Symphony, Martinů's Piano Concerto No. 4 (Radoslav Kvapil), Janáček's *Wandering of a Little Soul* (Tasmin Little) and Dvořák's *Symphonic Variations*.

As well as concerts, there were also recordings that went way beyond the normal repertoire of an opera orchestra. In August 1989 Mackerras and the WNO Orchestra made the first of a Delius series (including *Brigg Fair*) for Decca's Argo label, following this a year later with *Sea Drift* (with Thomas Hampson as the soloist) and the *Florida Suite*. The Violin Concerto (with Tasmin Little) was recorded in May 1991. Then, in April 1993, came *Appalachia*, *A Song of the High Hills* and *Over the hills and far away*, with the Orchestra and Chorus of WNO and soloists including Rebecca Evans and Peter Hoare. Reviewing a reissue of these performances, John Steane wrote in *Gramophone* (October 1999):

> Mackerras's Delius from Wales is arguably the most fascinating of our age. Rich in variety, it is always distinctively sung and shaped, memorably fresh, freely animated, and at times unexpectedly vital, with climactic moments powerfully and often brassily realized. The lean strings contribute to these impressions, as does Decca's relatively dry recording ('forward facing' horns in the best traditions of the house). So, a closer than usual look into the Delian mysteries, but a proper investigation, not an inspection.

An Elgar disc was recorded in December 1990, including the two *Wand of Youth* suites, *Dream Children* and a hauntingly beautiful version of the songs from *The Starlight Express* with Alison Hagley and Bryn Terfel (less than a year after his debut with WNO).

The first opera Mackerras recorded with WNO during his time as Music Director was Janáček's *Fate*, in July 1989. It was an outstanding critical success as well as an important addition to Mackerras's Janáček discography. He recorded two further complete operas in 1992. In June–July there was an English-language version of Tchaikovsky's *Eugene Onegin* with a cast led by Kiri Te Kanawa and Thomas Hampson. Then, in October and November, came the first ever complete recording of Britten's *Gloriana*, made for Argo. Mackerras had conducted this work a number of times at ENO in the early 1970s, and he returned to it twenty years later with Josephine Barstow as Queen Elizabeth, supported by a remarkable cast including Della Jones, Yvonne Kenny and Janice Watson among the female soloists and Philip Langridge, Alan Opie, Bryn Terfel, Willard White, John Shirley-Quirk and John Mark Ainsley among the male soloists. It was an exciting opportunity for Mackerras to come back to a composer whose music he loved, leading a performance that was acclaimed by Alan Blyth in *Gramophone* (July 1993):

> Sir Charles Mackerras has long been an admirer of the piece [...] He presents it here with the utmost conviction, drawing together the motivic strands of the score into a unified, coherent whole (not an altogether easy task), appreciating the contrast of the public and private scenes, exposing the raw sinews of the writing for the two principal characters, and drawing superb playing from his own WNO Orchestra [...] Above all, Mackerras is obviously convinced of the work's stature and – as a longtime interpreter of the composer's music – places it, as it were, in the context of his whole output.

In September 1991, Mackerras conducted the first in a Gilbert and Sullivan series with WNO for the American label Telarc. *The Mikado* featured a starry cast led by Anthony Rolfe Johnson, Richard Suart, Richard Van Allan, Felicity Palmer and Marie McLaughlin. It set a new standard in performances of the Savoy Operas, with outstanding orchestral playing and operatic singers demonstrating a fine understanding of the idiom. This was followed by *The Pirates of Penzance* (May 1993), *HMS Pinafore* (June 1994), *The Yeomen of the Guard* and *Trial by Jury* (both made in 1995).

The last recording Mackerras made with WNO was in July 2003 – his second version of Janáček's *Jenůfa*, sung in English with a cast led by Janice Watson and Josephine Barstow. This was a performance praised not only for the exciting singing, but also for the brilliant playing of the WNO Orchestra. On 23 April 2005, in St David's Hall, Mackerras conducted the WNO Orchestra in the all-Wagner programme for which Anne Evans was coaxed out of retirement to celebrate Mackerras's eightieth birthday. The programme consisted of the *Tannhäuser* Overture and Venusberg Music, the Prelude and Liebestod from *Tristan* and extracts from *Götterdämmerung*.

Charles Mackerras made his final appearances with the company on 27 May and 2 June 2009 for two concert performances of Mozart's *Mitridate, rè di Ponto*. Rian Evans reviewed the Cardiff performance for the *Guardian* (3 June 2009):

> Musically, the opera is complex and emotionally perceptive enough to command attention. The periodic moments of distraction were those of sheer amazement at the young genius's extraordinary achievement and, at the other end of the spectrum, the just-as-amazing fact of the 83-years-young Charles Mackerras's energy and musicological genius on the podium. Mackerras made it clear that *Mitridate* is a masterpiece, paving the way for *Idomeneo*, the greatest opera seria of all.

3

1 Charles aged eight months with his mother, Catherine, in Detroit, 1926. His letters to her are among the most detailed and revealing accounts of his early years in Europe (see Chapter 1).

2 Alastair, Charles (with flute) and Neil Mackerras in the 1930s. The flute was Charles's principal instrument until he changed to the oboe.

3 Neville Amadio (flute) and Charles (oboe) in the Sydney SO, c. 1945. It was as an oboist that Charles first worked as a professional musician.

4

5

6

7

4 The earliest photograph of Charles and Judy, on tour with Sadler's Wells in June 1947. According to Judy's note on the back it was taken in 'Miss Kelly's garden' in Liverpool. They married a few weeks later.

5 Judy and Charles on their wedding day at Bishop's Cleeve, Gloucestershire, 22 August 1947

6 Studying a score, London, November 1953

7 Charles and gargoyle at Notre-Dame, Paris, in May 1955

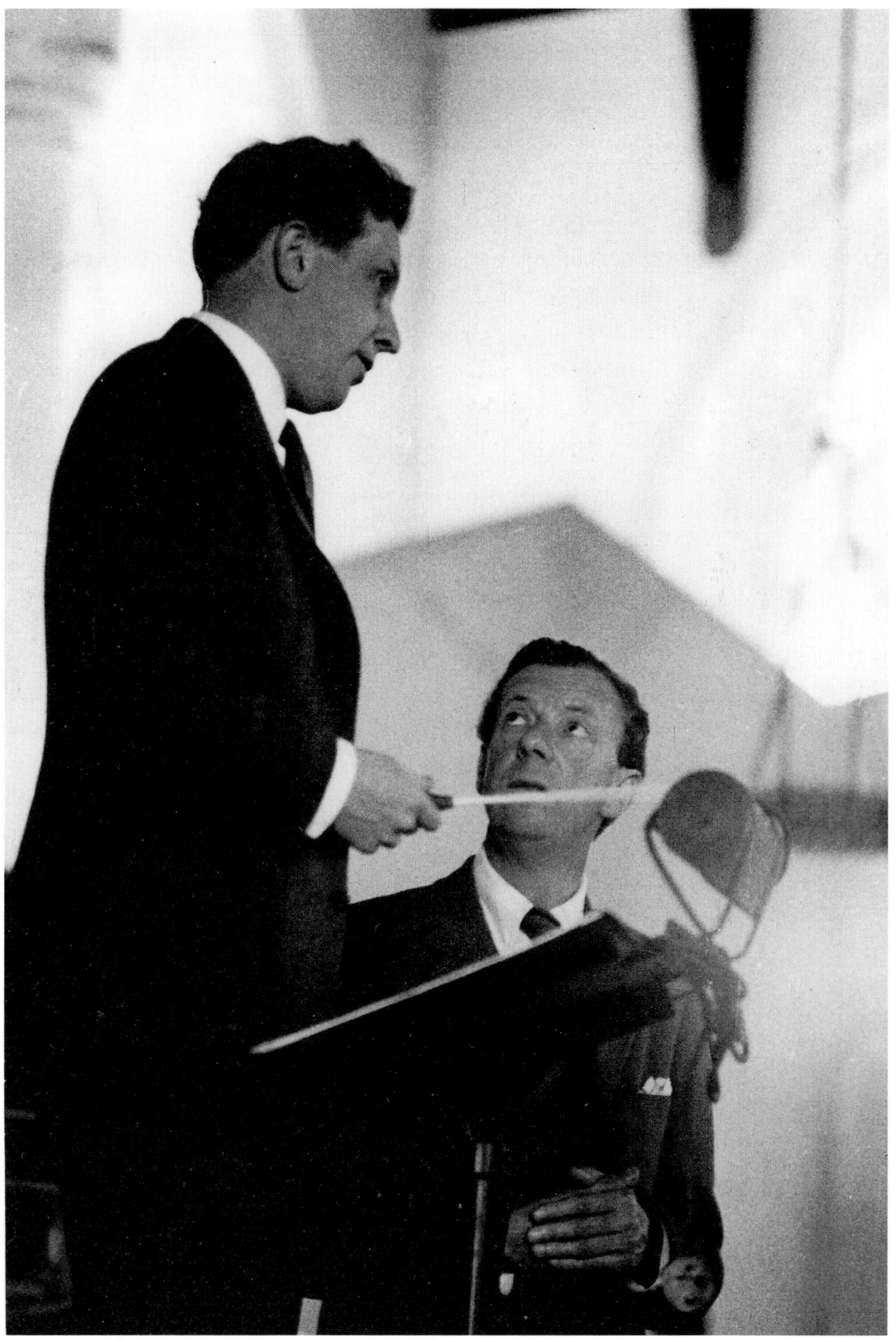

8 With Benjamin Britten rehearsing *Noye's Fludde* at Orford Church, June 1958. Mackerras's relationship with Britten is explored in Chapter 1.

9

10

11

9 At home in Essex House (where the family lived 1957–65) in autumn 1959

10 Rehearsing Janáček's *Káťa Kabanová* at Sadler's Wells in 1959 (see Chapter 3)

11 Conducting at the London Coliseum in 1973

12

13

12 Outside the Royal Opera House, Covent Garden, in March 1968. The poster includes *Tosca* conducted by Mackerras with Sena Jurinac in the title role. He began conducting regularly at Covent Garden in 1964.

13 With Birgit Nilsson for a televised performance of the final scene from *Salome* in December 1972. Mackerras was already a highly experienced conductor of televised opera. In 1973, Mackerras and Nilsson gave the opening concert at the Sydney Opera House.

14

15

16

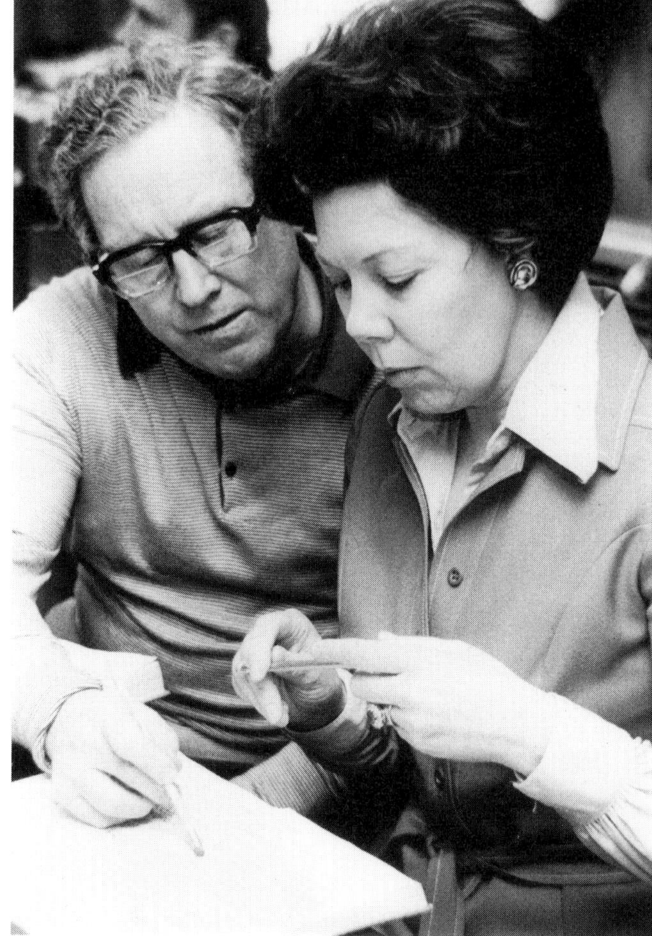

14 With Georg Solti – an important mentor and supporter – at Charles's fiftieth birthday party, November 1975

15 With Lord Harewood at Charles's fiftieth birthday party, November 1975. They were close friends, as well as colleagues at English National Opera (see Chapter 1).

16 With Janet Baker at recording sessions for Handel's *Judas Maccabeus* in April 1976. Dame Janet's reminiscences are published as the Prologue to this book.

17

18

19

17 Looking at the manuscript of a childhood composition at Rose Bay, Sydney, August 1978

18 In Vienna to record Janáček, autumn 1979. The ground-breaking Decca Janáček series was made there between 1976 and 1982.

19 Judy and Charles at Zdenka Podhajská's flat, 1 March 1980. Podhajská – who had served as the model for the illustrated cover of *Káťa Kabanová* in 1922 – was one of Mackerras's closest Czech friends. She gave him several Janáček treasures (see Plate 20).

20 

21 

22 

20 With his Kirckman harpsichord at Hamilton Terrace in 1981. A manuscript sketch by Janáček is on the wall behind him.

21 Rehearsing *Jenůfa* with Leonie Rysanek (who sang the Kostelnička) in San Francisco, September 1986. Mackerras considered Rysanek the finest Kostelnička he had ever conducted.

22 With Ann Murray and Yvonne Kenny on tour with ENO (*Xerxes*) in Kiev, 1990

23

24

23 With John Stein at a recording session in the Brangwyn Hall, Swansea, c. 1990. John Stein was co-founder of the WNO Orchestra and was influential in Mackerras's appointment as the company's Music Director. His reminiscences are printed in Chapter 6.

24 At Sydney Harbour in January 1992

25

26

25 Charles and Judy with their grandchildren (left to right: Nick, Daniel, Chloe, Fred, Ean and Pete), Swansea, 4 July 1992

26 Mackerras wrote the following caption: 'Outside the Usher Hall, Edinburgh, on 5th August 1995, the occasion of recording the Finale Act I of *Don Giovanni* with four natural horns'.

27

28

27 Stephanie Sundine, Anne Evans and Lotfi Mansouri with Charles on his seventieth birthday, San Francisco Opera, 17 November 1995. He formed close associations with Anne Evans and with SFO (for Dame Anne's reminiscences, see Chapter 7).

28 With Patrick Summers in San Francisco, November 1995. See Chapter 5 for Summers's evaluation of Mackerras's career and reminiscences of working with him.

29

30

29 Judy, Charles, Cathy and Fiona at Aldeburgh beach, 2002

30 With his sister Elizabeth Briger in Berlin, backstage at the Philharmonie in October 2005. Simon Rattle first invited Mackerras to conduct the Berlin Philharmonic in 2004 and he returned in 2005 and 2006. This photo was taken during his second visit, when the programme included Elgar's *Enigma Variations*.

31

32

31 After Handel's *Fireworks Music* at the 21st birthday concert for the Orchestra of the Age of Enlightenment in the Royal Festival Hall, 30 June 2007

32 Charles and Judy watching Haydn's *L'infedeltà delusa* on their Diamond Wedding anniversary at Buscot Park, Oxfordshire, 22 August 2007. David Lloyd-Jones is sitting directly behind Charles.

33

35

33 With Alex Briger in 2007, looking at the score of the first Australian opera, *Don John of Austria* by Isaac Nathan. Both Mackerras and Briger are direct descendants of Nathan. The opera was orchestrated by Mackerras and conducted by Briger during Mackerras's last visit to Australia.

34 At the Sydney Conservatorium in October 2007, during his last visit to Australia

35 In Dresden to conduct Schubert and Mozart in April 2008. Mackerras was very proud of the debuts in his later years with the great orchestras in Berlin, Leipzig and Dresden.

36

37

36 Rehearsing the Staatskapelle in Dresden, April 2008

37 With Alfred Brendel and Carol Høgel at the Edinburgh International Festival on 20 August 2008. Later that year, Mackerras conducted Brendel's final concerts in London and Vienna. (Brendel's reminiscences are printed in Chapter 13.)

38 After *Così fan tutte* at Glyndebourne on 12 June 2010, his last performance. Taken from the principal double bass desk, with Mackerras's personal copy of the bass part on the stand

39 In Elba, reading a newspaper on 5 July 2010, nine days before his death

38

39

7
Triumphs and Tribulations Opera, 1993–2001

Nigel Simeone

'Impeccable musicianship and enthusiasm for whatever he did'

Anne Evans

In the autumn of 1969 the Sadler's Wells Opera Company was on tour at the Empire Theatre, Liverpool. On arrival I took the lift up to the company's office to check in. A man with freckly eyes and red wavy hair slipped into the lift as the gate was closing. He looked me up and down. 'Who are you?' he asked. 'Cheeky chap,' I thought, summoning up all the *hauteur* of a junior principal who had joined the company only a year earlier, straight out of the Geneva Conservatoire, and was earning no less than £30 a week. 'I'm Anne Evans,' I said, 'and I'm singing Pamina tonight in *The Magic Flute*. Who are *you*?' 'I'm Charlie Mackerras,' he replied. 'I'm conducting it.' Collapse of junior principal. Charles Mackerras was the company's new music director and this was our first encounter.

After the *Flute* performance there was a party for the company at Liverpool's Bluecoat Chambers that was notable for the amount of alcohol consumed and the endless joke-telling. Charles always loved good jokes. Eventually my friend, the mezzo-soprano Katherine Pring, and I deposited him outside the Adelphi Hotel, where he was staying. I can see him now, tottering up the steps and disappearing into the foyer. Such was the start of a professional relationship that was to last thirty-six years.

I did some more Paminas with Charles and it soon became apparent that he could be ruthless in demanding the highest standards and that he was very ambitious for the company. Fun and frivolity were fine outside the rehearsal room, but his approach to work was deadly serious. He was determined that by the time the *Flute* reached the Coliseum the chorus members who had been singing the Three Ladies and the Three Boys would be replaced by young principals. Further, he told a Queen of the Night who was transposing one of her arias down that if she did not sing it in the higher key at the next performance she would be out. She managed to do so and she stayed.

In the following year it was my turn to be the target of Charles's wrath. He had cast me as Ilia in *Idomeneo* at the Coliseum. I worked hard on the role and he seemed pleased with the result, but every time I went for a music call with him I found he had thought up new decorations for the vocal line. I was still very green and by the first night was so confused about what I was supposed to sing that I took a wrong turning in my Act 2 aria.

Charles's hand shot up, telling me to stop until I had got myself together again. I turned to the prompter for help, but all he gave me were the words, when what I needed was an indication of whether the decoration went up or down. I wanted to rush off the stage in embarrassment. Charles gave me such a rocket in the interval that I burst into tears, but at the end of the performance he told me I had redeemed myself. He could be intolerant if he thought someone wasn't pulling his or her weight, but generous to anyone who he realised had made an honest mistake.

Charles was a master of many styles and it was my good fortune to sing a wide range of roles with him, seventeen in all. They ranged from Violetta in *Traviata* and Rosalinde in *Fledermaus* to the Marschallin in *Rosenkavalier* and Milada in Smetana's *Dalibor* at the Coliseum, and then more with the Welsh National Opera, starting with Donna Anna in Ruth Berghaus's enthralling but controversial production of *Don Giovanni* in 1984 and ending with Isolde in 1993.[1] What made working with Charles special was his impeccable musicianship and his enthusiasm for whatever he did.

His taste in productions was conservative, to say the least, and he had a terrific shouting match with Berghaus towards the end of the *Don Giovanni* rehearsals in Cardiff. Although we had had plenty of music calls with Charles, he had not been around for the stage rehearsals because of other commitments, and when eventually he did arrive he didn't like what he saw. Antony Peattie, acting as dramaturg, bravely stepped in, telling Charles that if only he had turned up much earlier he would have seen what the production was like. To our amazement, Charles recognised that Peattie had a point, and we all breathed a sigh of relief.

The highlight of my working relationship with Charles came with the WNO *Tristan und Isolde* in 1993. Charles had only conducted it in concert, and I had not performed it before. He was already starting to have trouble with his right shoulder, which was operated on in 1996, and was frustrated that he was unable to do any conducting for quite a long period before stage rehearsals were due to start. He used the time profitably, however, holding sessions in London with some of the cast, at both his house and mine. We spent hours probing the characters, finding the right colours and dynamics, and studying the music bar by bar. It was exhilarating, and by the time we got to Wales we were well prepared. Charles, however, was nervous about the sheer length of the opera and wondering if his shoulder would stand up to the relentless challenge of the rehearsals and performances. Miraculously it did. He had a triumph.

In 2003 I decided to retire. I had been singing professionally for thirty-six years or more and I wanted to go while I could still do it, rather than hang

[1] Anne Evans sang the following roles with Mackerras: SWO/ENO: Pamina in *The Magic Flute*, Ilia in *Idomeneo*, Countess in *The Marriage of Figaro*, Marzelline in *Fidelio*, Violetta in *La Traviata*, Lady Penelope Rich in *Gloriana*, Marschallin in *Der Rosenkavalier*, Rosalinde in *Die Fledermaus*, Helmwige in *Die Walküre*, Third Norn in *Götterdämmerung*, Milada in *Dalibor*; WNO: Donna Anna in *Don Giovanni*, Cassandra in *The Trojans*, Dyer's Wife in *Die Frau ohne Schatten*, Isolde in *Tristan und Isolde*; Edinburgh Festival: Leonore in *Fidelio*; BBC Radio 3: Rosanna in J. C. Bach's *Temistocle*.

around singing 'old bag' roles. I was due to sing the Marschallin at that year's Proms, in extended extracts from *Der Rosenkavalier* with Charles conducting, and it seemed the perfect occasion for a farewell appearance. And that, I thought, was that. But a year later I was having dinner with Charles and Judy when he said he would be eighty in 2005 and would be conducting some celebratory concerts. Would I take part in one? After all, he said, I had sung at his seventieth birthday concert in San Francisco. 'But I'm retired now,' I said. 'I can't do it.' Charles persisted and eventually, out of curiosity, I asked him what he expected me to sing, assuming it was a light song of some sort. 'Oh,' he said, 'the Liebestod from *Tristan* and the Immolation Scene from *Götterdämmerung*.' I practically fell off my chair: two years had passed since I had sung anything like that.

In the end I gave in, because he added a tempting carrot: the concert would be given with the orchestra of Welsh National Opera and would take place in Cardiff, where I had sung not only my first Isolde but also my first Brünnhilde. There was a splendid birthday party after the performance and Charles made a speech. He was so pleased with the concert, he said, that he thought he and I should return next year for a Strauss concert. This time I really did say no, but we didn't lose touch and remained great friends. Not long before he died, he asked me to have lunch with him in Covent Garden. He seemed frail, but the laughter flowed as happily as ever. I cannot say how much I still miss him.

THOUGH Mackerras relinquished his post as Music Director of Welsh National Opera in 1992, one of his greatest triumphs with the company came the following year (by which time he had been named WNO's Conductor Emeritus): Wagner's *Tristan und Isolde*. Mackerras had conducted concert performances in Australia in 1982 (Sydney on 5 and 7 August, Melbourne on 12 August) with Rita Hunter and Alberto Remedios. Maria Prerauer wrote about those Australian concerts in *Opera*: 'Paradoxically, the outstanding performance of the Australian's Opera's winter season was a concert: [...] As the first bars of the prelude floated out from the Sydney Symphony Orchestra, some alchemy seemed to occur, creating a potent theatrical illusion.'

The new WNO production (directed by Yannis Kokkos) was greeted with enthusiasm when it opened at the New Theatre, Cardiff, on 13 February 1993. In *Opera* (April 1993), Hugh Canning welcomed 'a proud Welsh Tristan' and an important milestone in the careers of both Charles Mackerras and Anne Evans:

> It was probably propitious that [Anne] Evans was able to make her first appearances as Isolde in the comparatively intimate surroundings of Cardiff's New Theatre under the eye of a conductor, Charles Mackerras, with whom she has had a long and fruitful professional relationship. [...]
>
> The dramatic momentum of Wagner's long paragraphs acquired

> tremendous, thrilling musical sweep, as Mackerras scrupulously observed Wagner's tempo markings. Indeed, although the orchestral playing was occasionally uncomfortably loud – as it will almost inevitably be in this smallish theatre – I don't think I have ever heard a *Tristan* in which the singers seemed at once so integrated into the orchestral sound and yet were never, well, hardly ever, overwhelmed by it. Mackerras's interest in the stylistic history of music in performance undoubtedly informed this highly individual and, for me, enthralling account of this wondrous score.

Tristan had not been seen in London since 1985 when WNO's *Tristan* arrived there for two performances at Covent Garden on 19 and 23 April 1993. Edward Greenfield (*Guardian*, 21 April 1993) hailed a 'great performance [...] under Sir Charles Mackerras with fine singing which vied with any rival in the world, and left most of them standing'.

Mackerras had first appeared with an American opera company when he conducted Mozart's *Magic Flute* at San Francisco Opera in 1969. In 1993 – at the request of the company's General Director, Lotfi Mansouri – he became Principal Guest Conductor in San Francisco. In his memoirs, Mansouri (1929–2013) wrote about the man he nominated as his favourite conductor:

> Sir Charles Mackerras brings just about everything to the table, even though his total lack of self-promotion may not have vouchsafed him the level of public acclaim lesser colleagues imagine they are entitled to. Nevertheless, I suspect that in years to come, as real quality rises to the surface, it will be generally acknowledged that Mackerras was a uniquely gifted conductor, incapable of giving a bad performance. He can do anything, from Handel to Strauss, and although he has one or two areas of expertise, particularly in the Czech repertoire, including a remarkable fluency in that complicated language, he has never fallen victim to overspecialization. His Mozart is as beautiful, idiomatic and downright stunning as his Janáček. He has a vast repertoire and an innate sense of tempi. [...] His years with us were among our very best. The orchestra adored him, the singers revered him, and he returned their affection without ever losing an ounce of his authority.[2]

The San Francisco *Rosenkavalier* in June 1993 had a cast led by Felicity Lott as the Marschallin, Frederica von Stade as Octavian and Eric Halfvarson as Ochs. Sophie was sung by Christine Schäfer, making her US operatic debut. After a return to Britain to conduct at the Edinburgh Festival (including a concert performance of *Così fan tutte*), Mackerras was back in San Francisco for three more operas in September and October: Verdi's *I vespri siciliani* (with Carol Vaness as the Duchess Elena), Puccini's *La Bohème* and Janáček's *Makropulos Affair* (with Stephanie Sundine as Emilia Marty; she had been Mackerras's Salome at WNO in 1988).

[2] Mansouri 2010, pp. 292–3.

In the spring of 1994, Mackerras went to conduct at the Bavarian State Opera in Munich at the invitation of Peter Jonas, the company's newly appointed Intendant, who had been Managing Director of ENO from 1985 to 1993. Plans for Mackerras to conduct a new production of Handel's *Giulio Cesare* came to nothing: he withdrew from the project before it went into rehearsal. But the affair was reported by Hugh Canning in the *Sunday Times* (27 March 1994):

> The trouble started with the dinosaur. Sir Charles Mackerras, Handelian extraordinaire, had been invited by Peter Jonas, in his first season as State Intendant of the Bavarian State Opera in Munich [...] to conduct a new production of Handel's masterpiece, *Giulio Cesare*, to be staged by the modish young British director, Richard Jones [...] Now, Sir Charles can be a bit of an old fogey when it comes to contemporary theatrical fashions. [...] The dinosaur, a huge model of a tyrannosaurus rex, was the limit, and Mackerras presented Jonas with an it's-me-or-it ultimatum, and the dinosaur won. At least until last Monday's first night in Munich's exquisitely elegant National Theatre, it did.

It is an amusing story, though it should be remembered that Mackerras had pulled out of *Giulio Cesare* before it actually came to a face-off between conductor and dinosaur. By the time this article appeared, Mackerras had already conducted three operas in Munich: *The Marriage of Figaro* (11 and 24 February), *Tosca* (19 and 21 February) and *Salome* (26 February and 1 March). Working with the bare minimum of rehearsal, Mozart, which Mackerras always wanted to prepare meticulously, was far more problematic than Strauss. As he told Alan Blyth (*Opera*, December 1995): 'in a city such as Munich, there's such a long tradition of performing Strauss that there's simply no need to rehearse the players. Provided they have confidence in you, they'll simply give you the benefit of their familiarity with the score. [...] You see, if you start questioning the performing style of such orchestras, you have to start from scratch.'

Mackerras's other opera in 1994 reflected his fondness for French repertoire. His feeling for its pacing and idiom was immediately apparent in the new production of Gounod's *Roméo et Juliette* at the Royal Opera House in October and November 1994, with Roberto Alagna and Leontina Vaduva. Reviews tended to be dismissive of the work itself (considering it sentimental and inconsequential), as they were at the revival in 2000 (with Alagna and Angela Gheorghiu), though Mackerras's conducting was admired by Tim Ashley for its 'tremendous electricity, disguising the fact that when Gounod isn't aspiring to be sexy, he can sometimes be distressingly cute' (*Guardian*, 19 February 2000).

At the start of 1995, Mackerras was in Sydney to conduct *Káťa Kabanová* for Australian Opera in a new production by Neil Armfield, with Eilene Hannan in the title role. Maria Prerauer (*Opera*, June 1985) wrote that Mackerras 'had the Australian Opera and Ballet Orchestra sounding as it seldom has before [...] the score came thrillingly alive'. He was back at the Royal Opera House in April with the visiting WNO for the first complete performance of any Gilbert and Sullivan operetta to be seen on the Covent Garden stage: *The Yeomen of the Guard* had been acclaimed by Tom Sutcliffe in his review of the first night in Cardiff as 'musically and dramatically crème de la crème' (*Guardian*, 15 December 1994). The premiere had been conducted by Gareth Jones, but Mackerras took over for the performances in Oxford (5 and 6 April 1994) and at Covent Garden (24, 25 and 26 April). This was a relatively rare opportunity to hear Mackerras conducting Gilbert and Sullivan in the theatre (as opposed to the 1989 BBC radio broadcasts, the Telarc recordings or the later semi-staged Proms of *Pinafore* and *Patience*), and it was a triumphant debut for a Savoy Opera at Covent Garden.

The following month, Mackerras stood in at short notice for four performances of *Peter Grimes* at the Teatro Politeama in Palermo, Sicily, given by the Royal Opera House on tour (4–7 May), with Anthony Rolfe Johnson and Jacques Trussel singing two performances each of the title role, Josephine Barstow as Ellen Orford and Bryn Terfel and Norman Bailey sharing the part of Balstrode. The reaction of the Italian press was ecstatic. The Rome paper *L'Unità* described the performance as 'amazing. In the production by Elijah Moshinsky that has now become a classic and on the podium, the fabulous Sir Charles Mackerras – a brilliant musician. Palermo is enjoying incendiary performances of *Peter Grimes*. [...] The fusion of orchestra, chorus and soloists (all superb actors) is unimaginable, as is the perfection of the production.'[3] *Grimes* was an opera Mackerras loved, but he conducted it only rarely after the 1960s.

At the end of May 1995, Mackerras was in Paris to conduct Janáček's *Cunning Little Vixen* at the Théâtre du Châtelet in a new production by Nicholas Hytner, with Thomas Allen as the Forester. Mackerras coaxed idiomatic Janáček playing from the Orchestre de Paris, and this enchanting production was filmed and subsequently released on DVD. In June, he travelled to Turkey with the SCO for three performances of Mozart's *Die Entführung aus dem Serail* in the Topkapı Palace in Istanbul, given as part of the 1995 Istanbul International Music Festival. A few days later he was back at the Bavarian State Opera in Munich for two performances of *Don Giovanni* (6 and 9 July), before travelling to Edinburgh to give a concert performance of the same opera (14 August). After more concerts in Edinburgh, Mahler's Second Symphony at the Proms (15 September) and a Janáček concert including the *Glagolitic Mass* in Brno, Mackerras arrived in Cardiff on 1 October for a WNO Gala to celebrate his forthcoming seventieth birthday, followed by a revival of *Idomeneo*. Between the second and third performances, Mackerras fitted in concert performances of *Die Entführung* in Edinburgh and Glasgow. He was back in Munich at the end

[3] Quoted in Giorgio Pugliaro ed.: *Opera '95: Annuario lirico dell'opera lirica in Italia* (Torino: EDT, 1995), p. 160.

of October for further performances of *Don Giovanni* (21 and 26 October), to which the Munich public reacted with hostility.[4] A single performance of Strauss's *Salome* on 28 October was more successful.

A return to San Francisco was a happier experience. On 17 November 1995 the company put on a seventieth birthday gala, with the likes of Renée Fleming, Anne Evans and Bryn Terfel celebrating the occasion (see Plate 27). The music, mostly conducted by Mackerras himself, ranged from Handel to Janáček, ending with 'Tutto nel mondo è burla' from Verdi's *Falstaff* – a work he conducted only rarely, apart from at his Glyndebourne debut in 1990.

A revival of *Madama Butterfly* was admired in the San Francisco press (Allan Ulrich in the *San Francisco Examiner* on 4 December 1995 praised the 'extraordinary sensitivity' of the conducting), but a more important event was Dvořák's *Rusalka*. Mackerras had studied this opera with Talich in Prague, but had never conducted it before. San Francisco provided him with a wonderful cast, led by Renée Fleming in the title role, Felicity Palmer as Ježibaba and Sergei Larin as the Prince. Describing the opera as a 'haunting romantic fantasy', Ulrich in the *San Francisco Examiner* (27 November 1995) was lukewarm about the staging, but praised 'a spectacularly satisfying musical adventure, boasting vocalism in the title role from Renée Fleming that secures her niche in the top rank of lyric sopranos [...] and conducting by Sir Charles Mackerras that makes as eloquent a case for this lovely, if dramatically wayward piece as this city is likely to hear'.

February and March 1996 saw a revival at Covent Garden of Handel's *Semele* (in John Copley's production, which Mackerras had conducted when it was new in November 1982), with a cast including Ruth Ann Swenson and Felicity Palmer. As Tom Sutcliffe noted in the *Guardian* (24 February 1996), 'the singing in the most important roles was superb. Ruth Ann Swenson [...] sings with astonishing purity and accuracy and best of all, her vocalising served a real comic instinct', while Felicity Palmer 'shot off a flurry of vocal fireworks, singing passagework at full tilt as if the fate of the world depended on her voice'. In April, there was a new production of Gounod's *Faust* for WNO, followed by a Gala Concert for the company's fiftieth anniversary (20 April), which was televised by S4C (it included – along with operatic items – what is probably the only performance Mackerras ever gave of Vaughan Williams's *Serenade to Music*, with sixteen soloists from the company). Writing to Anthony Freud (General Director of WNO), he was delighted to have been 'the only person still active who took part in all those performances of WNO in the early 1950s. As a matter of fact, the Brunch on Sunday after the concert was not only a wonderful affair but a

[4] Alex Briger was present at *Don Giovanni* and remembers that the Munich audience so disliked Mackerras's choice of speeds that this was one of the very rare occasions when he was booed (interview 26 May 2013). According to Tom Sutcliffe (personal communication), Margaret Price, who sang Donna Anna in these performances, was also unhappy about Mackerras's tempos.

chance to get together with some of the singers who actually took part in those performances in the 50s. I had no idea there were so many of them still around!' Later in the same letter, there was a hint of something more worrying: 'my arm is somewhat better through having had a bit of a rest this week; let's see how it is affected by the single performance [of *Faust*] on Friday.'[5]

Mackerras's right arm was becoming a matter of increasing concern, and disaster struck a month later. He was at the Bavarian State Opera to conduct Wagner at the Munich Opera Festival: *Der fliegende Holländer* on 14 and 18 May, and *Die Meistersinger von Nürnberg* on 22 May. During *Meistersinger* he tore a tendon in his right shoulder. He was given a cortisone injection during the second interval, enabling him to get to the end of the opera, with its huge final scene. It was courageous to keep going under these circumstances, but the result was severe damage to the rotator cuff (the muscles and tendons that stabilise the shoulder). For a conductor, this was a serious injury, since the symptoms include intense pain and weakness when lifting and lowering the arms. The only solution was surgery and rest – but there were longer-term consequences for Mackerras in terms of which operas would be physically possible, and several important engagements had to be cancelled at once. He was due to conduct *Aida* and *Billy Budd* at the Met in 1997 and wrote to Sally Billinghurst (the company's Assistant Manager) on 19 July 1996 explaining his plight:

> You can imagine how devastated I am that things have come to this pass, but I am assured that after the operation I shall be as right as rain. The operation is on 31st August and I will keep you posted, if I may, as to how things are progressing. The trouble is that it takes about 9 months before things are absolutely normal, and of course opera conducting is actually the worst for the shoulder because one has to raise the arms all the time, particularly when there is a large chorus participation, such as *Aida* and *Billy Budd*. As a matter of fact, I really think that if the operas had been *Figaro* or *Così* or a Handel, I might well have been O.K. by January or February, but as the operas concerned are actually two of the largest chorus operas ever written, I had no choice but to withdraw.[6]

In fact he was due to conduct *Figaro* with the ROH during its temporary move to the Shaftesbury Theatre – but it, too, became a casualty of Mackerras's physical condition. By the autumn of 1997 it was clear that he needed another operation, this time to repair the damage to his left shoulder. On 3 November 1997 he wrote to David Syrus, head of the music staff at the Royal Opera, full of regret at having to pull out – in a letter which

[5] Mackerras family archives.

[6] Mackerras family archives.

also reveals how delicate the matter of Mozartian performing style was at the ROH:

> My dear David,
>
> You can imagine how furious I was to have to give up the *Figaro* which we planned so carefully together. However, my Consultant tells me that if I postpone the operation to my left arm, it will result in my having to be off work for several months rather than several weeks. [...]
>
> It is possible that they will ask you to take over, which in my opinion would be the best solution! If that is the case, I would be most willing for you to retain the score which I lent you in case there might be any ideas in it which you would like to 'raid'. However, if they engage someone outside our circle who is not in sympathy with my kind of Mozart, then I would be grateful if you would return the score as soon as possible.
>
> With all best wishes,
>
> Charles[7]

A month earlier, on 7 October 1997, Mackerras had written to Peter Katona, Director of Casting at the ROH, giving fuller details about his troublesome shoulders:

> For a couple of months now my left shoulder has been giving me quite a lot of pain, especially when conducting, and Mr Bayley, the surgeon, was anxious to discover whether this was simply due to my using my left arm much more than usual, or whether there was some basic fault which needed an immediate operation. You may remember that I had already arranged to have the left shoulder done in October 1998. However, a test last Saturday showed that the tendon in the left arm is on the point of breaking and that therefore an operation, not later than December, is essential. Unfortunately I cannot have it immediately because my right arm is still not 100% cured, and the pain of the test on the left arm has meant that this and next week's performances [*La Clemenza di Tito* with WNO on 9 October and Schubert's 'Great' C major Symphony with the OAE on 15 October] are going to be very difficult for me, even though I am determined to go through with them.[8]

These continuing problems were immensely frustrating. Six months earlier, after the initial surgery on his right shoulder, Mackerras had been able to return to opera with a long run of fourteen performances of *Figaro* at Glyndebourne between 7 June and 28 July. Michael Tanner in the *Spectator*

[7] Mackerras family archives.

[8] Mackerras family archives.

(13 June 1997) wrote warmly about Mackerras's conducting, though he had qualms about the vocal embellishments:

> It is a long time since I responded so freshly to *Figaro*. Sir Charles Mackerras['s] presence made itself felt throughout, and nearly always beneficially. [...] Though he kept it spinning along at a rate which was appropriately breathless, at some key points he was prepared to relax the tempo indulgently, most strikingly at the Countess's entry on the scene after the Count's adamant refusal to hear a word on anyone's behalf. At that point, and at some others, he conducted with the warmth of a Bruno Walter, without creating a bizarre effect of conflicting styles. That is an achievement that few could bring off, and I can think of no conductor whom I would rather hear in this opera today. Once or twice I thought his ideas on embellishment got out of hand. For some reason, having kept them on a tight rein throughout most of the opera, when he got to Susanna's wonderfully sensual 'Deh vieni' – his last chance – he prescribed for Rosemary Joshua, who was already quite come-hither enough, a series of decorations so elaborate that the lilt of the line was lost, almost to the point of being unrecognisable.

Just as ornamentation had been a vexed issue at Sadler's Wells in 1965, so it was, apparently, at Glyndebourne in 1997. But on the evidence of the 14 June performance (broadcast on Radio 3) it is difficult to understand Tanner's reservations, since Rosemary Joshua's embellishments in 'Deh vieni' come across with such natural expressiveness.

The only other opera Mackerras conducted in 1997 was a new production of Mozart's *La Clemenza di Tito* for WNO, produced by Yannis Kokkos, who had previously staged the WNO *Tristan*. In the *Sunday Times* (28 September 1997) Hugh Canning began his review with a discussion of the conducting and the orchestral playing:

> I don't think I have heard a more thrilling account of its music than that currently conducted by Mackerras for WNO. From the portentous trumpets and kettledrum flourishes of the overture's opening bars to the grandiose final chorus, Mackerras delivers the music with a white-hot theatrical and emotional intensity that take the breath away. If the WNO orchestra does not yet match the grandeur of the conductor's vision, it surely will after a few repeats, and already there is much to enjoy in the crisp textures and lithe articulation of the strings, the wonderfully robust 'military' sounds of (natural?) brass and baroque timpani, the sweetly singing woodwinds (an especial bouquet to Peter Fielding for his clarinet and basset horn solos). Is there a finer Mozart conductor in the world than Mackerras? I certainly don't know of one.

With a cast that included Katarina Karnéus as Sesto, Isabelle Vernet as Vitellia and Lisa Milne as Servilia, this was a vocally lustrous account of the score, too, while Kokkos's production was straightforward and extremely effective (Canning summarised it as 'handsome, sombre, blissfully simple and serious').

Mackerras was never overtly political, though generous donations to Musicians Against Nuclear Arms, Friends of the Earth and environmental charities suggest a liberal outlook. (Judy was even more passionate about these matters and encouraged him to take an interest.) In a rare public outburst about a proposal to merge the Royal Opera with English National Opera, it is clear that he did not think much of either of the major political parties in Britain. When *Opera* magazine published responses (in January 1998) to the 'atmosphere of crisis' over opera funding at the Department of Culture, Mackerras did not hold back:

> The whole musical world [...] is amazed and upset by the notion that two great opera companies with such individual characteristics could be forced into one opera house. The Arts were systematically strangled by the Conservatives and now it seems that New Labour, for all its fine words about Culture and Education, is not even prepared to support our two diverse opera companies by keeping their subsidy in pace with inflation. And let's drop the cant about 'toffs" opera, 'people's' opera, 'elitism', 'accessibility', 'social relevance' and all the trendy jargon employed by the politically correct Press. Plenty of 'non-toffs' are prepared to queue for days and nights for a chance to hear the great singers who used to be heard regularly at the ROH. In my day at the Coliseum, there were always plenty of 'toffs' in the audience, in fact the 'people's opera', ENO, was run for years very successfully by a 'toff'. The trouble is that neither the glamorous 'canary fanciers' style nor the more controversial 'Opera-as-Theatre' style can exist without adequate funds. [...] Strapped for cash, the ROH employ more and more the promising, young singers normally associated with ENO, WNO or Glyndebourne instead of the world stars that the fans would have a right to expect. Added to that, the Royal Opera courts the opprobrium of its audiences by putting on operas in 'controversial' whacky productions more appropriate to the ENO.
>
> Unfortunately the ENO's policy of presenting controversial, 'relevant' productions, usually with first-class musical preparation, landed them in deep financial trouble in the form of a huge deficit when the 'Power House' regime retired. Thus, by force of financial circumstances, the two companies are becoming more alike. The State can seize on this and say 'why do we need two companies when they are indistinguishable except for the language they sing in?' Yes, we do need two companies and the differences between them should be widened not narrowed!
>
> But how to provide for them? New Labour is showing itself to be as philistine as the Conservatives (remember Tony Blair's *Desert*

> *Island Discs*?[9]), so it looks as if we cannot even expect to maintain the present status quo with provision for inflation.

Mackerras proposed a solution, which was to give the public exactly what it wanted – a programme of old favourites – until the economic situation improved:

> For a season or so the repertoire would have to be very popular in accessible and comprehensible productions, but a diet of Mozart, Verdi, Wagner, Puccini, Strauss, etc. never did any house any harm. I found as Musical Director of Sadler's Wells at the Coliseum that a couple of seasons of the most popular operas worked wonders in persuading the audiences to come to the (then) new venue. The implied elitism may offend some egalitarians, but the system works, as is proved all over the world where opera with great singing is revered. Could not the ENO then be given a larger, more realistic subsidy with which to do its special productions? If the Coliseum really is in such need of repair, couldn't it get money from the Lottery or even some altruistic sponsor? [...] Why couldn't the ENO run a season of operettas and musicals, to make a bit of profit to pay for their way-out opera productions? The National Theatre does wonders with its productions of well-loved musicals, why not ENO? But lavish and glamorous productions please, not drab backcloths or politically correct social comment on sleaze in the Balkans or the position of maid-servants in Johann Strauss's Vienna!
>
> When I started in opera, both the ROH and Sadler's Wells had a clear idea of their respective functions and of the money at their disposal. The Arts Council was run by people who loved the Arts and wanted them to prosper in Britain. Thatcherism ruined all that, but New Labour has a chance to redress the wrongs we have suffered in recent decades. Will it take up the challenge, or will Covent Garden really have to be privatised and handed to the 'toffs'?

The annual schedule sent to friends and colleagues for 1998 included a note at the top: '1997 was a very busy and successful year for Sir Charles in spite of the slow recovery following major surgery on his right shoulder in 1996. Now the over-used left shoulder must undergo some repair on 13th December to prevent further deterioration. Sir Charles hopes to continue with his schedule from the end of January 1998.' But in January 1998 a bad attack of sciatica forced Mackerras to spend in a week in hospital and necessitated more cancellations. By the end of February he was well enough to conduct a demanding Janáček programme in Manchester (including the *Glagolitic Mass*), before two performances of *La Clemenza di Tito* with

[9] This was broadcast on 24 November 1996. Blair chose only two pieces of classical music among his eight records: Barber's Adagio and Debussy's *Clair de lune*.

WNO at the Shaftesbury Theatre in London. Two weeks later, he set off for New York for *The Makropulos Affair* at the Met, with Catherine Malfitano as Emilia Marty (11, 13, 16 and 18 April). The fourth and last performance was broadcast and it revealed not only the dramatic intensity of Malfitano's Emilia (her voice back at its best after a couple of disappointing seasons) but also the virtuosity of the Met orchestra, whether in the most thunderous ostinato-driven passages or the many pages of ethereal strangeness.

A week later, Mackerras was in Prague to record *Rusalka* – a recording that went on to win the *Gramophone* Record of the Year in 1999. After a few days back in London, he flew to Sydney to start rehearsals for *Jenůfa* with Opera Australia, before taking a week's holiday at Port Douglas in Northern Queensland and taking the opportunity to explore the Great Barrier Reef. By 8 June, *Jenůfa* rehearsals had started, and he went on to conduct six performances. It is not surprising that when Mackerras saw Neil Armfield's new production – updated to concrete apartment blocks in 1950s Poland – he was reported to be 'rather shocked'. Musically it was a happier story, as Maria Prerauer (*Opera*, January 1999) reported: 'Mackerras, any staging objections notwithstanding, was in his musical element, bringing out all Janáček's pungent rhythms and drawing extraordinarily potent climaxes and great melodic sweeps of sound from the pit.'

Returning from Sydney on 19 July, Mackerras flew to Salzburg two days later to start rehearsals for *Figaro* – with which he made his debut at the Salzburg Festival. It was a production that he may well have found hair-raising – Michael Kennedy described it in *Opera* (November 1998) as 'silly' and 'odd' – but there was the pleasure of working with the Vienna Philharmonic Orchestra in the pit. He conducted seven performances between 15 and 29 August, and Kennedy praised the 'zest and finesse of the playing'.

September was dominated by concerts in Edinburgh and at the Proms with the Czech Philharmonic, but in November Mackerras travelled to New York for a two-month spell at the Met. This started with seven performances of *The Magic Flute* between 14 December and New Year's Day (a revival of John Cox's production with sets by David Hockney), before he conducted the first of six performances of *Káťa Kabanová* the very next day (2 January). The review of *The Magic Flute* in the *New York Times* (16 December), suggests a rather unsettled first night: 'Dawn Upshaw's [...] performance of the young woman's aria of quiet despair, "Ach, ich fühl's", seemed somewhat uneasy, but that may have been the result of mixed signals with the conductor, the well-respected Sir Charles Mackerras. On this occasion, he seemed overly intent on keeping the music moving. He began several arias and ensembles too quickly for his singers, and wound up having to pull back the tempos along the way.' By the time of the Met broadcast on 26 December, the cast had settled down – and one of the highlights of this revival was Matthias Goerne's house debut as Papageno. *Káťa Kabanová* reunited Mackerras with Catherine Malfitano (as Káťa), as well as with Katarina Karnéus, making her house debut as Varvara. The *New York Times* gave this revival an enthusiastic welcome but lamented that 'unfortunately, it may be all too easy to find a seat, since everyone seems on board for a fascinating adventure but the audience'.

There was no opera in 1999 until the summer, when Mackerras conducted Handel's *Rodelinda* at Glyndebourne with the OAE. The production was updated to the 1920s and included the somewhat improbable anachronism of the villainous Garibaldo being shot with a pistol. Lisa Milne was Rodelinda and the counter-tenor Andreas Scholl (indisposed on the first night) sang Bertarido. As for Mackerras and the period-instruments, Roger Parker in *Opera* (August 1999) noted that 'the band's sense of rhythmic energy and technical accomplishment could hardly be improved upon these days; each new musical world was set with precision, and the wind playing was often of extraordinary beauty'.

After two weeks' holiday on Elba and concerts at the Edinburgh Festival, Mackerras returned to the Met in September for *Lucia di Lammermoor* – the first time the original 1835 version had been performed in New York. He had long been sceptical about a spurious *Lucia* 'tradition' that was 'anachronistic, unstylish and generally to be deplored'. In a programme note, Mackerras explained his decision to return to Donizetti's original:

> There have been over 500 performances of *Lucia di Lammermoor* by the Metropolitan Opera since Marcella Sembrich made her American debut during the Met's first season in 1883. Many of the great divas have sung the role at the Met [...]
>
> Yet, I dare say that not one of these illustrious ladies sang *Lucia* as Donizetti wrote it. He could never have imagined that almost the whole role would have been transposed a step downwards in order to allow the singer to end her arias with a long high note. [...]
>
> This fall the Metropolitan Opera is performing *Lucia* for the first time in the original high keys in a style that its composer would have recognised. [...] The traditional cadenza with the flute in the Mad Scene is completely anachronistic, having probably been composed by Madame Marchesi or even Dame Nellie Melba herself. The simple vocal cadenza of the composer with its 'dying fall' and choral accompaniment is far more appropriate to the situation. [...]
>
> As the final top note began to take on more importance than the rest of the aria, so singers began to facilitate these notes by downward transpositions and cuts. However, the habit of actually leaving out several bars to give the singer a rest before pausing on the top note which the composer didn't write and didn't want, is actually a product of our present century. [...]
>
> If everything is cut out that does not include Lucia, and the rest transposed down, the opera loses much of its dramatic structure, and becomes nothing more than an evening for canary-fanciers. For instance, by cutting the scene for Lucia and Raimondo before the finale in Act II, merely because there is more for him than for her, a

> whole scene is lost which provides a contrast in feeling as the priest attempts to comfort Lucia with religion. [...]
>
> The flute obbligato in the Mad Scene was originally written for the glass harmonica. [...] Invented in 1761, by Benjamin Franklin, the instrument was said to produce mental instability and it is likely that Donizetti used it for that reason in *Lucia*, since there happened to be a member of the San Carlo [orchestra] who played it. [...] In the Met performances the obbligato for the Mad Scene will be played by both instruments together, thus justice will be done to both fast and slow passages – with the flute providing the virtuosity and the glass harmonica the eerie representation of Lucia's crazed mind.[10]

Lucia certainly upset some of the canary-fanciers among the Met's regulars (one horrified opera blogger condemned Mackerras for his 'killjoy actions'), and it is intriguing – and a little depressing – to find so much outrage about hearing what the composer had actually written. Mackerras conducted six performances between 29 September and 16 October, all with Andrea Rost in the title role. By the time *Lucia* next appeared on the Met schedule, two months later, the original version was forgotten and the *New York Times* welcomed 'a traditional *Lucia* with the frills fans love'.

In November 1999, Mackerras returned to ENO for the first time in several years to conduct a new production (by David McVicar) of Handel's *Alcina*, with Joan Rodgers in the title role. In January 2000, he was in Paris for *Così fan tutte* at the Palais Garnier: a revival of Ezio Toffolutti's 1996 production (originally conducted by Solti). Several members of the cast had sung Mozart with Mackerras before: Barbara Frittoli (Fiordiligi), Katarina Karnéus (Dorabella), Russell Braun (Guglielmo), Michael Schade (Ferrando), Nuccia Focile (Despina) and Rolando Panerai (Don Alfonso).

The Royal Opera House had been closed for renovation between July 1997 and December 1999, leading a peripatetic existence in other London theatres. Mackerras returned to the newly restored house in February 2000 for a revival of *Roméo et Juliette* with Roberto Alagna, now joined by Angela Gheorghiu. Mackerras got on well with them, but found all sorts of problems with the new building. He wrote to Patrick Summers on 18 February:

> The poor old ROH is still battling with many technical problems trying to cope with machinery that they do not properly understand. The place is like a fortress with all the swipe cards and combinations. It makes the Met look quite free and easy with regard to visitors! The chief difficulty with all modern buildings is how elevators are designed to work at a snail's pace (presumably against terrorism) but it does mean you can never calculate how long you have to leave to get anywhere for rehearsal.

[10] Typescript in Mackerras family archives.

> After *Roméo et Juliette* I have *The Greek Passion*, so I will certainly have had a lot of experience of the ROH by Easter![11]

These practical problems with the new house were something he was concerned about. In a long letter to Michael Kaiser, Executive Director of the ROH, he laid out some of the building's shortcomings:

> The dressing rooms are very cold. At the moment one switches on a small heater on arrival but it takes some time for the room to warm up. [...] Owing to the thickness of the doors, one cannot hear anybody knocking. The result is that those who know the general code simply barge in when they get no reply; those who do not know the code go away. [...] I am sure you know about the terrible problems with the lifts. These are so unreliable that no one has any possibility of arriving at an appointment on time. [...] Conductors have to walk through a long passageway on Level −1 to get to their entrance to the pit and I for one have to wear an overcoat and scarf to and from the pit in order not to freeze! Like many conductors I sweat a great deal during a performance. [...] As someone who has worked at Covent Garden for some 40 years, I felt I should write to let you know my feelings. [...] Having said all that, may I say how much I have enjoyed doing *Roméo et Juliette* and how excellent I find the orchestra, chorus and all the staff of the newly formed company.[12]

Mackerras was not much assuaged by Kaiser's reply. On 10 March 2000 he wrote again with more comments about the practical arrangements in the new building, as well as raising concerns about the absence of senior management at performances of *Roméo et Juliette*:

> The other day one of the artists failed to hear his call and was late on stage, and on the same evening, one of the Acts was delayed by 10 minutes because of the absence from the pit of many orchestra members. It transpired that apart from the snail-like elevators, there are no public address systems in the canteen or on the stairs leading to and from the stage. I have never heard of any opera house in which calls were not relayed to the canteen. [...]
>
> Many of us were very shocked that there seemed to be no members of the management staff at *Roméo et Juliette* performances (apart from the Opening Night, of course). On the occasion when Miss Vaduva took over at such incredibly short notice and did such a splendid job [...] there was no one at the end of the performance to say a grateful word to her for saving the show. In the next performance, when you yourself made an announcement that Angela would try her best, thereafter there was no member of the management on hand

[11] Mackerras family archives.

[12] Mackerras family archives.

> to decide what would have happened if Angela had indeed collapsed during the show. [...] We were not at all sure of her condition until about halfway through the opera. [...] Apart from the so-called 'feel good' effect on the artists, there is also the fact that management presence at all the performances does keep everyone on their toes and perhaps some of the less than ideal performances of some of the artists might have been noticed.[13]

Mackerras was back in April for a new production of Martinů's *Greek Passion*, directed by David Pountney. But between conducting *Roméo et Juliette* and *The Greek Passion* he was fitted with a pacemaker; on 12 April he wrote to Peter Katona: 'I have just returned from the Clinic [...] The left side is rather uncomfortable at the moment, but I am assured that it will get better very quickly and I am confident that I will be able to actually conduct the stage and orchestra rehearsals and be present at all other rehearsals. [...] I believe that you telephoned, thinking that I was already in hospital while I was in fact standing in front of the ROH orchestra in the Linbury Theatre!' Mackerras had recorded *The Greek Passion* two decades earlier, using Martinů's revised version. As is clear from his exchanges over the work with Aleš Březina (see Chapter 11), Mackerras was keen to conduct the newly reconstructed score of the opera as it had first been submitted to Covent Garden in 1957. In a thoughtful review (*Guardian*, 26 April 2000), Tim Ashley described Pountney's Covent Garden production as a 'triumph of great musicianship and compelling theatricality over uneven substance. [...] The performance, conducted with fiery nobility by Charles Mackerras, is fantastic too.'

It was fifty years since Mackerras had first conducted at WNO, and to celebrate this anniversary the company invited him to conduct *Carmen*, opening in Cardiff on 26 May. Bizet's masterpiece was a work he had often conducted at Covent Garden in the 1960s, as well as in a new ENO production in 1970, but he had not done it since. Rian Evans in *Opera* (August 2000) described it as 'an inspired form of celebration' and praised 'Mackerras's genius for pointing up the finer details at the same time as capturing the dramatic structure and breadth of the score'.

At the 2000 Salzburg Festival (3 and 6 August), Mackerras was reunited with the Vienna Philharmonic for two concert performances of Cherubini's *Médée* with Angela Denoke, Christine Schäfer and Michael Schade. In October he returned to San Francisco for two operas. The first was Handel's *Semele* with Ruth Ann Swenson as Semele. According to Joshua Kosman in the *San Francisco Chronicle* (3 November 2000), the first night did not go well: 'Wednesday's performance occasionally seemed like an assemblage of prime ingredients still waiting to gel. Charles Mackerras [...] struggled to keep control of the proceedings at key points, and much of the evening had a lumbering, overinflated feel' – hardly the usual description of Mackerras's

[13] Mackerras family archives.

Handel. *Der Rosenkavalier* opened on 17 November 2000, Mackerras's seventy-fifth birthday. Yvonne Kenny was the Marschallin, Susan Graham sang Octavian and Rebecca Evans was Sophie. Heather Hadlock, writing for the online *San Francisco Classical Voice*, described the production as 'a recreation of the 1911 world premiere, jaw-droppingly gorgeous. Every detail of color, light, sound, and gesture contributed to a series of stage pictures that delighted my senses. Led by Sir Charles Mackerras [...] the orchestra gave a brilliant account.' The Presentation of the Rose with Graham and Evans was 'almost scandalously beautiful' according to Hadlock. At the end of the performance, the company presented Mackerras with his own silver rose. For the last few performances, the Marschallin was taken over by Renée Fleming. Allan Ulrich reviewed the new cast in the *San Francisco Chronicle* (6 December 2000) and thought that this *Rosenkavalier* had got even better:

> The pacing has picked up in the past two weeks. Credit Sir Charles Mackerras, whose conducting has evolved from splendid to miraculous in the interim. The Opera Orchestra surpassed itself last night, illuminating the score with a robustness and elegance that only this conductor seems to inspire in them. Mostly what emanated from the pit had a weight and presence missing formerly. Moreover, the score is shaped with a masterful feeling for its emotional highs, but never at the expense of overwhelming the singers. After the first performance, Mackerras received from the company as a 75th birthday present a single silver rose. By now, he has earned the entire bouquet.

This turned out to be his last visit to San Francisco, and it was a fine farewell to a company with which he always had the friendliest relationship.

There was no opera in the first few months of 2001, but in April Mackerras travelled to the Met to conduct three performances of *The Makropulos Affair*, with Malfitano again singing Emilia Marty. Back in London, a Covent Garden revival of Elijah Moshinsky's production of *Die Entführung aus dem Serail* opened on 30 May. Roger Parker (*Opera*, August 2001) wrote:

> The ROH orchestra under Charles Mackerras played with tremendous verve, but also with an acute ear for detail: they repeatedly displayed new aspects of this ornate and extravagantly inventive score; tiny moments of orchestral combination emerged briefly, made their dramatic presence felt, and then merged with the background.

Die Entführung is an opera with some famously tricky corners, starting with the first aria, Belmonte's 'Hier soll ich dich denn sehen, Konstanze'. In an eightieth birthday interview with John Allison (*Opera*, November 2005), Mackerras recalled that 'my old boss in Hamburg, Rolf Liebermann, used to say he could judge whether a conductor had talent by that one aria. In fact, when I left Hamburg for ENO, he auditioned my prospective successors with children's matinee performances of *Entführung*. People may think of

Mozart as being a strict tempo man, but that aria requires so much nuance.' Just what this meant, Mackerras explained in detail in a chapter on 'Opera Conducting' in which he analyses the difficulties of this aria, which requires 'extremely sympathetic conducting'. He was not usually prone to giving technical explanations of the practical aspects of conducting, but does so here with a lucidity and wisdom born of experience, paying particular attention to the aria's difficult fermatas:

> Measures 18 and 19 are quite difficult. Here, the singer must take a final breath after the word 'zurück'. The conductor must wait not only for the breath, but also for the upbeat to the next phrase, 'gib mir'. By his or her gestures in measure 18 the conductor must arrange that between the first and second chords there is air and space, and by a cut-off gesture must ensure that the bass does not hang on longer than the upper parts, despite the apparent difference in note values. [...]
>
> Perhaps the most difficult phrase of all, for the singer and conductor, occurs in measures 53 to 55. The phrase is so long, high and difficult that it is virtually impossible to meet Mozart's requirement of not only a fermata but also a diminuendo. Most singers need measures 53 and 54 to be conducted *faster* than the main tempo. In measure 55, the wise conductor will allow the singer a long time to accomplish the triplet on the first beat, returning to the main tempo for the words 'mich ans Ziel'.[14]

That Mackerras put his own technical advice into practice is apparent from the broadcast of this Covent Garden production. Mackerras gives Kurt Streit (Belmonte) the requisite musical space and moves the music along almost imperceptibly to help the singer through the long and demanding high-lying phrases.

In November 2001, Mackerras conducted Smetana's *Bartered Bride* at Covent Garden, in a new English translation. Francesca Zambello's production (first seen in 1998) was not universally liked, but the diction of the singers was something that would have delighted Mackerras (as did the whole production). Nick Kimberley in *Opera* (January 2002) wrote that 'nobody could accuse the singers of needing surtitles. [Kit] Hesketh-Harvey's text rang out loud and clear.' Susan Gritton's Mařenka was singled out for praise, as was Mackerras's conducting. Edward Seckerson (*Independent*, 9 November 2001) described 'an exhilarating flourish from the strings and already you can't quite believe the tempo. Prestissimo doesn't quite do it justice. But it's not just fast, it's articulate, it dances, it sings. All Bohemian village life is here.'

[14] Mackerras: 'Opera Conducting' (2003), pp. 68–9.

8

Rethinking Old Favourites
Opera, 2002–10

Nigel Simeone

Viva Charlie!

Antonio Pappano

What's very interesting about Charlie is that there were two sides to his conducting. On the one hand, the philological side: his interest in authentic practices, the deep knowledge that he had of Handel and Mozart, and the specialised Janáček repertoire. But on the other hand, when you look at his entire repertoire, he conducted *everything* – from *Serse* to *Cavalleria* to *Lucia* to the *Ring* to *From House of the Dead* to *Katerina Ismailova*, and so on. This curiosity about different styles and about different types of theatre was always there. When he was a music director, he had the choice: he could conduct *Tristan* if he wanted to. But there was always something of the old-time greasepaint-considering musician that reminds me of a kind of Viennese Jewish *Musikant* – one of those guys who could do it all, do it right on the spot and put it all together; he was completely practical like that. So on the one hand he was living in an ivory tower of deep thought, contemplating how to make things sound, and on the other he was a real practising theatre musician. And I think the way he managed to mix all that was just fantastic.

This dramatic instinct applied to all sorts of music. I listened recently to him doing Mozart's 'Haffner' Symphony – and I happened to listen to a couple of other people doing it too, and his was by far the most *theatrical*. The problem is that the word 'theatrical' in some circles tends to be thought of as a put-down, but that's wrong, and it's especially wrong in Mozart. I'll never forget watching Charlie doing *Zauberflöte* here at Covent Garden with the orchestra. It was a sitzprobe and the music was just popping up out of the pit – I was sitting right behind him – and he was having a ball. There was absolute discipline, but at the same time he sounded like a kid having fun! It's interesting to think about his approach to conducting a work like *Zauberflöte*. He would always construct a box – a framework – and in that way his conducting was very structured. And yet within that framework he could play around, as long as the respect was there for the structure. So he was not a wild man; in fact, I would say that he was very classical in his approach to probably everything he conducted. And yet you got these performances of such immediacy, performances that are just jumping out at you, because – and this is the main thing – of his rhythm. He didn't spend a lot of time working on sound in rehearsals, but by calibrating the rhythmic precision – and this was never precision for its own sake, but a way of giving music rhythmic life – he would bring the score leaping off the page. And once he got that, people took care of the rest. It was quite amazing to see.

My wife, Pam Bullock, and I helped to coach *Lucia* for him at the Chicago Lyric Opera in 1986. I'll never forget it. He was having a rough time. The beginning of *Lucia* is extremely loud, and the poor tenor who sings Normanno comes on and the brass just wipes him out! Finally, Charlie tried to get the whole brass section to *tacet* – screamed Solti-like to try and get it down. But he was doing this because his consideration for the singers was always there. I make a joke of it, but there's a serious point: he knew that, if you couldn't hear the singer at the beginning of *Lucia*, you'd got no opera; the calling card of the piece is right there.

With singers in general, he was never unreasonable with the tempo. He had a natural sense of what the tempo should be: he didn't like wallowing, and he liked the accompaniments to bite at the heels of the singers, so to speak, and that means there's always this feeling that the action is being pushed forward. That's what you need – that conflict, that tension – and that's how you get real theatre. You certainly never get it if you follow. Charlie was by nature slightly impatient, but in the theatre that's good – believe me! I think, with orchestras, he mellowed a lot as he got older, and that's what I experienced with him here. He could sometimes be very cut and dried – after all, he grew up at a time when relationships between conductors and orchestras were different, it's just the way it was – but I learned a lot from him, in Mozart above all. I'll never forget *Zauberflöte* or *Don Giovanni* here – there wasn't one tempo that was wrong. As a conductor, when you give in a little bit to a singer, people always talk about rubato, but what you take you have to give back. It's hard to do, but actually he always did it – he would very much make up anything that had been taken. I think this was because for him there was an empirical law that a piece needed to have an internal rhythm. He'd come to that realisation through his rehearsal experience and through performances. He couldn't deal with it any other way, and so the singers – especially as he got older, and they respected him so much – the singers would just go with it.

In rehearsal he'd certainly say what was on his mind – at all times – and if he didn't understand a liberty that was being taken, or didn't like something a singer was doing, he could be pretty outspoken. But he'd be so disarming about it at the same time. He'd just explain that music has rules, that everything has to fit into a greater structure – he was all about that. He also cared deeply about diction. It was always very important for Charlie, as he saw it as part of the characterisation of a part.

One of the things I admired most about his Mozart is that you never stopped to think: Is this authentic, or is this big-band Mozart? It just never came up. Of course, you were listening to something that was always extremely alert and full of rhythmic energy, but you'd never even stop to think about things like vibrato – because there was such a *rightness* about the whole performance. There are words behind the music in operas, and he knew that this was the secret, the key. He knew exactly what every bar *meant* – and sometimes conductors don't really know this, certainly not with Charlie's level of detail. So the result was that the sense of characterisation, and the rhythm of the piece, and how to make the music jump out at you was all so focused – he could do it because he knew *why* he was doing it. It was the same with his Handel. You listen to his *Messiah* and whether it's on modern instruments or period instruments doesn't even come into question, because everything just works so well – I think that's a fantastic tribute to his musicianship. In the best sense, he just treated music as a human being, treated theatre as something to enliven our spirits, something that is never ordinary music-making: it needs something extra, because if you were a normal person you wouldn't sing about these things, but in opera they all do, so you're in a different world.

We did two runs of *Don Giovanni* at Covent Garden one year: Colin Davis did the first run and Charlie did the second. My God, the difference between the two! It was more than night and day. It so fascinates me that two musicians who were both real theatre men – both of whom adored Mozart – had such *completely* different approaches. Every *bar* was different; it was just extraordinary.

I think Charlie grew quite tired of radical productions, especially of Mozart or Handel. But he was fascinated by Richard Jones's production of Shostakovich's *Lady Macbeth of the Mtsenk District* because he'd conducted *Katerina Ismailova* here and didn't really know the original version. He was really curious about it – always hanging around the rehearsals. He was very taken with the production as well as the music, and I think he was probably much more open to modern stagings of those sorts of pieces, rather than somebody messing around with his beloved *Marriage of Figaro*. Opera stories are things to be respected, just as the score is – but that can be done imaginatively, as long as the director wants to bring out the theatrical truth, and Charlie certainly understood that. There was a kind of simplicity to him in a way: productions didn't have to be over the top, or twisted and turned, to make a deep sense to him; taken at face value, these pieces explained the universe to him and that's what mattered most to him. Before starting rehearsals, he always wanted to make sure he was getting sympathetic singers and asked quite a bit about the production. During my time he never did a new production here: he wanted to see it before conducting it, and he would come and check it out. He knew how important it was for a production to help singers to forget whatever vocal difficulties there are, and to be really involved in what they are doing – and understand exactly what their character is singing and thinking.

Charlie had carte blanche to conduct whatever operas he wanted to do here, and he was scheduled to conduct several at the time he died: *Don Pasquale*, *Hansel and Gretel* and *A Village Romeo and Juliet*. In his last years he suffered quite a lot because his shoulder gave him so much trouble – he stopped using a baton – and then he got very sick. But even so, that last *Vixen* was glorious, and he worked hard at it; his work ethic was amazing. I wish he'd done *Hansel* – it was an opera he adored, and I heard him conducting a scene from it with young singers at a reception for him at Australia House. It was really fantastic, because he knew his way around the opera so well and obviously loved it. He was also a fine Strauss conductor and did *Rosenkavalier* here. Mind you, he took Strauss at his word: in the first act Strauss says you can reduce the number of strings in the conversational passages, and Charlie reduced it so much that a lot of the strings played for about two-fifths of the time – but you heard everything!

I'm sure he had a huge influence on conductors such as Mark Elder and Paul Daniel, who started their careers under him at ENO. He certainly influenced me because of his chameleon-like quality: that ability to reinvent himself on a daily basis to suit whatever repertoire he was doing – and he did everything. That appeals to me a lot, because I live that kind of life. And surely that's the job of a true theatre musician. That may sound old-fashioned, but it isn't; he was someone who could do anything and everything, and it was all good.

As for his recordings, people should look at his symphony recordings, especially the Mozart and Beethoven: they are better than most – they really are – and it doesn't matter that some of them are on small labels. The Vienna Philharmonic Janáček recordings sound quite glossy – it's a different sound from the way his Janáček came across in the theatre – but you've got to understand what it must have taken for him to get that band to play this music at that kind of level. They just don't do stuff that's unfamiliar to them, and as a musician you have to marvel at that achievement.

There was nothing romantic about Charlie's gestures: on the podium he was unpretentious and very practical. But his eyes! Now *there* was something magical – you could see so much joy and intensity in those eyes.

A master of Mozart

Simon Keenlyside

Any singer working with Sir Charles Mackerras who was not more or less completely prepared could get short shrift from him. Charles was always fair, but he could be irascible with anyone who was not on top of their work. Even with the best will in the world, it must have been difficult at times for him to have acquiesced with the next generation of singers – some of them were young enough to be his grandchildren – especially when one remembers that he may already have conducted this or that Mozart opera hundreds of times, over more than half a century.

He was a great master. As with all the best conductors, the 'whole' was more than the sum of the parts. He did not suffer fools gladly. All musicians knew that there was not a single jot of artifice or veneer about his person. Frankly, I think that, for much of the greener parts of my working life, I was lucky to get away without any serious injury to my pride.

My experience with Charles was almost exclusively in the Mozart operas. His performances were grounded in a lifetime's research: musicological, historical and linguistic. In these respects his work was as remarkable as the live performances themselves, and his contribution to the bank of knowledge on authentic Mozart performance was significant.

There are still aspects of eighteenth-century music, of course, that are difficult to interpret. We know neither the precise pitch at which the music was played, nor, as often as not, the exact tempos. On one occasion at the Royal Opera House, Charles arrived at the outset of a rehearsal period for Mozart's *Zauberflöte* carrying with him a sheaf of papers. He had found an eighteenth-century letter, written by a patron of the opera and sometime acquaintance of Mozart shortly after the master's death. The writer bemoans the fact that 'No sooner was the Maestro dead, than the aria "Ach, ich fühl's" is halved in tempo'. This was already a strong indication in itself, but Mackerras subsequently found not only the pendulum marking for this aria, but also (at a later date) an intact pendulum by which to measure it. The new speed – Mozart's intended speed – is very much faster than anyone would normally sing it today. The musical pendulum, I hasten to add, was the forerunner of the metronome, which had not yet been invented.

Mackerras began by telling the soprano that she was welcome to sing the aria at the traditionally slower tempo. He told her that it would be easy to make him look a fool and to render his research dry and academic. Given the evidence lying on the piano in front of her, she realised that to sing it at the traditional tempo would be contrary to Mozart's express wishes. The soprano, Rebecca Evans, was keen to make the 'new' speed – actually Mozart's speed – work, and she achieved a most wonderful result.

What difference, then, could a faster tempo make to the scene or the character? I think a profound one. The aria 'Ach, ich fühl's' was no longer the dirge that it so often becomes. The character and her music still have a pulse. She reflects on the agonies of young love, but no longer in a way that can seem indulgently sentimental or even depressive. The little runs (now almost coloratura) are a good deal harder to execute, but they add a short-breathed and palpitating quality to the character. In short, the new speed makes a great deal of difference.

This small contribution by Mackerras to research ought to change the way any singer performs this famous aria in Mozart's *Zauberflöte*. I have my doubts, however, whether that will happen. Perception is everything, and a hundred years or more of performance practice, expectation, education and recordings will be hard to overturn. All the same, Sir Charles revealed yet another small seam of truth for anyone interested in mining it in the future.

A second arrow in Charles's quiver was the language itself. It is always a joy for any singer to perform with a conductor who knows what the text means. Understandably, especially during a performance, conductors may be reluctant to wait for a singer who is taking his or her time over a phrase – it's as if the singer has reneged on the 'deal' worked out in rehearsal. Unless a conductor understands the linguistic reasons for stretching the tempo in this way, he or she is unlikely to be sympathetic to what might otherwise be seen as a liberty. Charles not only knew what every single word of the libretto meant, but he also had an understanding of the distinctions between modern spoken Italian and the occasional anomalies in grammar and usage that crop up in the Da Ponte operas. In *Don Giovanni* I once witnessed him gently correcting one of my Italian colleagues on a finer point of grammar. Naturally she demurred: this was her mother tongue, after all. Charles asked her to go and look up the eighteenth-century construction. To her great credit, the following day she approached the front of stage and acknowledged that she had been wrong.

Third, and most important for the likes of me, there was the mastery of Charles's performances. They were very different. Even in his latter years, he did not fit expectation: the tendency that old age brings to many a wonderful old maestro to slow down all the tempos. With Charles it was quite the reverse: he was unsentimental and his music-making was vigorous and urgent. In the dramas, there was no time for reflection, and certainly no time to luxuriate in the gorgeous music. But though his Mozart conducting was quick, it was quite different from so many modern pacey performances which, to my mind, owe their present fashion of bland, unrelenting speed more to a reaction against so many of the lugubrious and reverential recordings of the 1950s and 60s than to any thought-through dramatic logic.

Mackerras was true to what Da Ponte and Mozart had written. *Le nozze di Figaro*, for example, has Beaumarchais's play *La folle journée* as its muse and foundation. Under the baton of Mackerras, it was as much of a romp – a riotous dance, a glorious tumble full of *all* life – as the play itself.

In *Don Giovanni*, I really felt a great life force under Charles's lead. His management of the growing hysteria in the drama was magnificent, as if one were a racing driver strapped into some high-performance car, driving full tilt. There was no time for remorse, nor space for regret or contemplation. The result was a gripping theatrical experience.

Charles was always clear about the relationship of one scene to another, and – just as Debussy had stressed in his letters – was adamant that the timing of the spaces between the notes and scenes was every bit as important as what we hear and sing. He drove these operas hard, but always with a sensitive ear to the relationship of the music to the dramatic predicament – and without any of the mawkish sentimentality that, to my mind, too often characterises performances of Mozart's music. The Mozart operas I was involved in with Charles were quite simply the best I've experienced.

It was in the opera house that Mackerras's career first flourished, and aptly enough it ended there too. In the last few months of his life Mackerras worked on two of his favourite operas: Janáček's *The Cunning Little Vixen* and Mozart's *Così fan tutte*, and he was due to conduct another – Mozart's *Idomeneo* – at the 2010 Edinburgh Festival. At the time of his operatic debut at Covent Garden in 1964 (conducting Shostakovich's *Katerina Ismailova*), Judy Mackerras had written to her mother-in-law: 'he is *suddenly*, apparently, being acclaimed as an outstanding opera conductor. I've always been sure this was his strongest bent, so let us hope others continue to feel the same!' Several decades later, Mackerras had become a revered figure, working at major international houses in Europe, the United States and his native Australia. But in his final decade, the house in which he appeared most often was Covent Garden.

Mackerras may have been getting older, but he was looking forward to new operatic challenges. On 22 November 2001 he wrote to Antonio Pappano – recently appointed Music Director of the Royal Opera House – to suggest some possible future projects:

My dear Tony,

I hear you are back at Covent Garden working on future plans next Monday, 26th November. This is unfortunately the very day I go to New York for a stint with the Orchestra of St Luke's and *Hansel and Gretel* at the Met.

Congratulations on just pipping us at the post with your *Manon* [in the *Gramophone* Awards]. I believe our Janáček *Šárka* virtually tied and they had to take a second vote!

My reason for writing to you is twofold. First, I understand that you are considering several Handel operas for a season in 2003 to be done with the Orchestra of the Age of Enlightenment, but that the singers are not decided on. Peter Katona mentioned to me that I might be asked to conduct this production and if I am to be involved in it I need to know very quickly, so that I can change some plans which have been made for the period in question.

Of the operas under discussion, I think that *Orlando* would be by far the best, assuming that David Daniels was going to play the title role. But I know that you also have as possibilities a revival of *Julius Caesar, Rinaldo* and *Admeto*. This is almost the only Handel opera I do not know and I only have the authority of Elaine Padmore who thinks it is a forgotten masterpiece.

As I am away from London for a couple of months, I would like to mention that I would be delighted to work with any one of the singers who have been mentioned or on any of the operas in question, except perhaps Angela Gheorghiu, who, in my view, is vocally and stylistically completely unsuitable for any role written before about 1820! Also, one would need close consultation regarding the Director as, I am sure you know, I have very strong views about 'concept' opera. Handel has been the greatest sufferer, perhaps even more than Wagner, from this kind of stage direction!

The other matter I wanted to mention to you is the fact that 2004 is both Dvořák and Janáček Years. The only viable Dvořák opera for Covent Garden will have been done by Renée Fleming and myself in 2003 in a semi-staged version and I want to ask if you would consider either *Káťa Kabanová* or *Jenůfa* for me, after which I might consider retiring from the operatic scene. Possibly the most suitable might be *Káťa* which is the first Janáček opera I ever conducted and was really the event which gave the impetus to raise Janáček from an eccentric unknown to the worldwide popularity which his operas enjoy at the moment.

I wish you every success in your new position. Someone like you is sorely needed here at the moment.

Yours ever,

Charles Mackerras[1]

[1] Mackerras family archives.

Mackerras and Pappano had the greatest mutual admiration, and they got on very well with each other at a personal level. During Pappano's tenure, Mackerras became a regular and cherished guest in the house, and – as Pappano has written above – he gave Mackerras pretty much carte blanche in terms of choosing the repertoire he wanted to conduct. Of the operas mentioned in Mackerras's letter, he conducted *Orlando* (with the OAE) and *Káťa Kabanová* at Covent Garden, both in 2007 rather than 2003/4. For 2003, the eventual Handel choice (which he also conducted) was *Semele*.

Christmas 2001 was spent in New York. After flying out on 26 November, Mackerras conducted Berlioz's *L'Enfance du Christ* at Carnegie Hall on 2 December with the Orchestra of St Luke's. At the Met he was rehearsing Humperdinck's *Hansel and Gretel*, which opened for a run of six performances on 19 December, with Jennifer Larmore as Hansel and Dawn Upshaw as Gretel. The production was venerable (1967) and traditional – much to the distress of some critics. But Mackerras himself was delighted by a staging where angels looked like angels and a finale where – as the *New York Times* (21 December 2001) put it – 'the witch is bested (and basted) and the stage suddenly fills with her revived victims, a beaming bevy of children in dapper folk-tale costume'. Whatever argument there may have been about this production, there was no doubt about the conducting: Martin Bernheimer in *Opera* (March 2002) wrote that 'Charles Mackerras revealed dauntless concern for subtle nuance at one extreme and for sweeping grandeur at the other'. This was an opera extremely close to Mackerras's heart (his daughter Cathy remembers him once telling her that it was his favourite opera of all – vying for that honour with *Figaro*) but it was not a work he had conducted much since Sadler's Wells in the 1950s. The broadcast of the Met performance of 29 December reveals just the qualities identified by Bernheimer: tenderness, affection and real nobility in the interpretation, supported by radiant playing from the Met orchestra.

These were to be Mackerras's last performances at the Met, as he found transatlantic travel too exhausting. Five years later, in November 2006, Mackerras recorded the opera for Chandos with Jennifer Larmore again singing Hansel, now partnered by Rebecca Evans as Gretel, and with miraculous playing from the Philharmonia. On 13 December 2009, at the Royal Festival Hall, a selection from *Hansel and Gretel* (with Caitlin Hulcup as Hansel and Rebecca Bottone as Gretel) formed part of the last concert he ever conducted with his beloved Philharmonia.

When Francesco Zambello's new production of *Don Giovanni* opened at Covent Garden in early 2002, it was double cast. The first cast had Bryn Terfel as Don Giovanni and was conducted by Colin Davis. Despite some good singing, Andrew Clements (*Guardian*, 24 January 2002) found it 'monumentally slow', while for Anna Picard 'Davis loses much of the rhythmic impetus through overly luxuriant, romanticised textures'. The second cast – conducted by Mackerras and with principals led by Simon Keenlyside's Don and Ildebrando d'Arcangelo's Leporello – took over on 18 February. The reaction was altogether more positive: here was a much fresher and more exciting *Don Giovanni*. For Edward Seckerson (*Independent*, 21 February 2002), the explanation for this lay, above all, in the pit:

> There's something else, something even more key to the success, the pace, the energy, and dynamism of the evening – and that's the conducting of Sir Charles Mackerras. Where Sir Colin Davis was grandly authoritative, Mackerras is lethally incisive. The opening gesture of the overture, cut to the bone, precipitous (no boomingly portentous overhang of string basses for Sir Charles) is shockingly abrupt, the ensuing allegro instantly conveying the reckless dash of the narrative. So many women, so little time.
>
> I honestly cannot remember when I last heard a better conducted *Don Giovanni* in the theatre. Rhythm, articulation, fluency and beauty of line – the playing was quite superb – but above all an acute sense of the score's earthy buffo elements.

Mackerras himself was delighted too. On 20 February 2002 he sent a letter 'to the Ladies and Gentlemen of "my" *Don Giovanni* Orchestra':

> Dear Friends,
>
> I want to thank you so much for the wonderful performance you did on Monday, which was virtually 100% of how I would like *Don Giovanni* to sound.
>
> Reviews that have already appeared seem to endorse my no doubt biased view of your performance on Monday.
>
> Many, many thanks and keep it up!
>
> Yours ever,
>
> Charles Mackerras[2]

But to get a performance as successful as this took a great deal of preparation. Especially with operas by Handel and Mozart, Mackerras took care to outline his approach to singers well in advance – especially those who had not worked with him before. His Donna Elvira for the 2002 *Don Giovanni* was Ana Maria Martinez, making her house debut. Mackerras wrote to her on 17 January 2001 – a year before the production opened – referring to a marked-up score and setting out his musical intentions:

> Dear Miss Martinez,
>
> May I say how glad we all are that you are taking part in this production of *Don Giovanni*. The general aim, in the interpretation of the opera, is to get as near to the known performance practice of Mozart's time, while retaining the dramatic life and vivacity which was also an important part of Mozart's own performances.
>
> You will see that there is a certain amount of ornamentation in some of the parts. These have been taken from authentic 18th century sources. There are also many more appoggiaturas than you will

[2] Mackerras family archives.

have been used to doing in the past. The downward appoggiaturas are marked with a cross (x), other appoggiaturas are written in real notes. These appoggiaturas, in both recitatives and ensembles, should be sung (spoken) naturally without any special accentuation, and certainly *not with any prolongation* of the appoggiatura notes. Please also notice that the recitatives are to be performed entirely freely, with little reference to the written rhythm or rests (pauses). The metronome marks which I have indicated show approximately the kind of tempo I would expect. Please note particularly that the aria 'Ah fuggi il traditor' is a quick bravura aria and not a slow, pompous piece as so often done by mainly German conductors. Note also that in the trio in the finale of Act I 'Protegga il giusto cielo' and 'Vendichi il giusto cielo', Donna Anna and Ottavio pray for God's help in a *legato* melody while Donna Elvira thinks only of vengeance and betrayal and should sing *non legato* and *forte*.

When you have had a chance to study this score, I look forward to working with you together on it when we have a day when we are both free at the same time.

With best wishes,
Yours sincerely,
Charles Mackerras[3]

In May and June, Mackerras returned to another favourite opera, a revival of *The Cunning Little Vixen*, with WNO. Rian Evans in *Opera* (August 2002) wrote that Mackerras 'brought to the music real humanity as well as his usual authority' and was particularly struck by the finale: 'Mackerras gave this ending a quality which combined nobility and serenity. It was indeed as life-affirming as Janáček intended.' There were no more staged operas in 2002, though Mackerras did conduct a concert performance of Donizetti's *Maria Stuarda* at the Edinburgh Festival (14 August) with Barbara Frittoli as Mary Queen of Scots and Anna Caterina Antonacci as Elizabeth.

Katie Mitchell's production of *Jenůfa* for WNO was first seen in 1999 (when it was conducted by Daniel Harding). For the 2002 revival (opening on 6 March in Cardiff), Mackerras was in charge. Rian Evans (*Opera*, May 2003) wrote that: 'His authority was stamped all over the proceedings. His influence was inspiring and, even if there were moments when there was too much sound coming from the pit [...] the passion and lucidity Mackerras brings to Janáček was undeniable. It was apparently his preference that conditioned the decision to sing this revival in English.' Jenůfa was sung at these performances by Susan Chilcott, her singing 'deeply expressive' and her portrayal marked by 'intelligence and generosity of spirit'. Chilcott gave an infinitely touching performance, but there is a poignant and tragic postscript: by the time the WNO forces were brought together to record the opera for Chandos in July, Chilcott was already mortally ill. She died of

[3] Mackerras family archives.

breast cancer two months later, in September 2003. (Her replacement on the recording was Janice Watson, another outstanding Jenůfa.)

There was more Janáček at the end of March: two performances of *The Cunning Little Vixen* with two different casts of students at the Royal Academy of Music (26 and 29 March). It was an impressive effort, and an indication of the extent to which Janáček's vocal and orchestral idiom was now understood by a new generation of musicians.

Semele returned to the Royal Opera in June–July 2003, with Ruth Ann Swenson again in the title role. The last *Semele* performance was on 11 July 2003, and three days later Mackerras was back in the house for another opera: on 14 and 17 July he conducted two performances of Dvořák's *Rusalka*. Mackerras had recorded the opera in 1998 with Renée Fleming in the title role, Franz Hawlata as the Water Goblin and Eva Urbanová as the Foreign Princess. All three reprised their roles in the Covent Garden performances, along with Sergei Larin as the Prince (a role he had sung with Mackerras in San Francisco) and Larissa Diadkova as Ježibaba. It was the first time *Rusalka* had been heard at Covent Garden. The results were exceptional – not surprisingly, since this was an opera Mackerras had studied in 1948 with Talich and had conducted at San Francisco Opera in 1995. Although these were billed as concert performances, the orchestra was placed in the pit (providing a realistic balance between stage and orchestra, apparent in the BBC broadcast of the second performance). Rodney Milnes was enchanted (*Opera*, October 2003):

> The Royal Opera's first encounter with Dvořák 's masterwork was so powerful musically that many overnight reviewers wondered why they had left it so long (over a century) and why they weren't staging it. Well, maybe they will, and this semi-staging (colour-changing backcloth, basic actions from soloists mostly off-book) certainly whetted the appetite.
>
> Charles Mackerras was in his element, drawing fat, lush yet sufficiently clear sound from an ROH Orchestra on absolutely top form. Such virtuoso orchestral passages as the transition from the Witch's spell to the sound of the off-stage hunt, or the evocation of a hot summer's night at the end of the second act, were toe-curlingly beautiful. Maybe he indulged his prima donna a little too freely, but with a soprano as commanding as Renée Fleming it must be hard not to.

The only major opera by Janáček that Mackerras had not recorded was *The Excursions of Mr Brouček*. It was not included in the Decca series, as the company believed that it would not be commercially viable, and plans to release a recording of the musically outstanding ENO production in 1992 also came to nothing. At the end of 2003, Mackerras embarked on his third new production of *Brouček*, this time at the Prague National Theatre – which had given the world premiere in 1920 (it was the only Janáček opera to be first performed in Prague rather than Brno) – and in the city where the opera is set. With a brand new edition of the score prepared by Jiří Zahrádka, Mackerras relished the opportunity to return to *Brouček*, despite its considerable physical demands in terms of the large chorus and orchestra. The opening night was on 20 December, followed by five more performances, ending on 11 January. For Mackerras, it turned out to be a frustrating and hugely disappointing experience. In a letter to Patrick Summers, sent on 7 January 2004, he revealed some of the problems:

> Dear Patrick,
>
> You must think me abominably rude that I have taken so long to answer your letter of over a month ago. However, we have had our problems commuting backwards and forwards from Prague over Christmas. As you know, I had looked forward immensely to doing Janáček's Prague opera, *Mr Brouček*, in Prague itself and indeed in the venue of the world premiere, the National Theatre. Although the cast of Czech singers is really first class, particularly the Brouček, Jan Vacík, and the other romantic tenor, Petr Straka, I am afraid the same cannot be said of the orchestra. I thought that by arranging to have 2 groups, *Besetzung* A and *Besetzung* B, the question of changing musicians might be solved, but apparently they are so badly paid that they have to continually work outside the theatre and the orchestral rehearsals really developed into a free-for-all, so that at a very late stage in the proceedings new players would come into the orchestra in important positions who had no idea of the difficulties of this complicated score. The exceptionally good English Horn player who was present at all 19 rehearsals suddenly disappeared at the Dress Rehearsal, leaving a young lad to flounder through the piece on the Opening Night. Thus, what I hoped was going to be one of the greatest pleasures of my career turned out to be one of the most arduous and stressful that I have ever done. The chorus was good though and the production, despite a squeaking revolve, excellent.[4]

The letter continued with much better news:

> Although I am terribly tired after the battle with the Prague Opera Orchestra, I am going to Berlin in a couple of weeks time to make my debut with the Berlin Philharmonic with my special composers, Dvořák, Janáček and Mozart (the latter with Mitsuko Uchida as soloist), so that is something to look forward to.

This debut, at the invitation of Simon Rattle (who had long been an admirer of Mackerras), turned out to be a spectacularly successful one: the review in the *Berliner Zeitung* on 24 January 2004 appeared under the headline 'Lob des Musikanten' ('In Praise of Musicians').

After this triumphant appearance in Berlin (followed by return visits in

[4] Mackerras family archives.

2005 and 2006), Mackerras went to Brno to conduct one more performance of *Brouček* and an all-Janáček programme including the *Glagolitic Mass.* In April 2004, he returned to Covent Garden for *Der Rosenkavalier*, in a revival of John Schlesinger's production. The cast was distinguished, led by Felicity Lott as the Marschallin, Angelika Kirchschlager as Octavian, Simone Nold as Sophie and Kurt Rydl as Ochs. Michael Kennedy, an authority on Richard Strauss as well as a vastly respected critic, began his review in the *Sunday Telegraph* (18 April 2004) with a question:

> How many opera composers are there whose music Sir Charles Mackerras doesn't conduct better than almost anyone else does? Not many. He was in the pit on Tuesday for the Royal Opera's revival of *Der Rosenkavalier* and Strauss's score was played with the panache it requires and at lively tempi which the composer would have approved, its opening prelude thrustingly erotic and that to Act III like a Queen Mab scherzo. The big luscious episodes were delivered generously, sentiment (with always a touch of irony) never strayed into sentimentality.

Reviewing the performance in the *Independent* (16 April 2004), Edward Seckerson was struck by the theatrical quality of the conducting:

> Mackerras's sense of pace and pulse is consistently invigorating. There are those who pore over this score as if the 18th century is wearing thin in real time, those for whom venerable is not vital. Mackerras will have none of that. His narrative drive is keen and eventful, fizzing with incidental detail. He reminds us that this is, indeed, a 'Viennese masquerade', as the Marschallin puts it, luxuriant but animated too. No point in waltz music if you can't dance to it. And the Royal Opera Orchestra certainly dances.

A concert performance of Weber's *Der Freischütz* at the Edinburgh Festival (17 August) was followed by a revival of *The Greek Passion* at Covent Garden (opening on 15 September). November and December were spent making recordings of *The Magic Flute* and *The Bartered Bride* for the Chandos/Peter Moores Opera in English series. Preparations for the first of these turned out to be a fraught affair: despite furious lobbying by Mackerras and Peter Moores, Chandos refused to use the Orchestra of the Age of Enlightenment for the recording. Mackerras wrote to Brian Couzens, Managing Director of Chandos, on 28 May 2003 in the strongest terms:

> Ever since the OAE was formed I have wanted to record a Mozart opera with them and the happy coincidence of their actually performing *The Magic Flute* 14 times in 2004 and then another 14 with me in 2005 seems to make an ideal opportunity to put their special type of musical expertise on to a recording. All the OAE's and my offers to help with extra rehearsals, which I was even willing to pay for myself, seem not to move you. [...] Apparently it does not matter to you that

> both the person paying for the recording and the person in charge of the music of the project want to use this superb period orchestra.[5]

It was to no avail. Instead, the LPO was engaged (and plays very well), but it is a shame that the opportunity was missed for Mackerras to record this opera with period instruments. The cast, however, is outstanding, including Simon Keenlyside as Papageno, Rebecca Evans as Pamina, John Graham-Hall as Monostatos, John Tomlinson as Sarastro and Elizabeth Vidal as the Queen of the Night. *The Bartered Bride*, with the Philharmonia and the Royal Opera Chorus, is just as successful, preserving Susan Gritton's delightful Mařenka on a recording.

Having just recorded *The Magic Flute*, Mackerras conducted two different productions of it during 2005. He began rehearsals for a revival of the opera at Covent Garden in January, and this opened 11 February with a schools' matinée performance. The cast included three of the principals from the Chandos recording (Keenlyside, Evans and Graham-Hall). In his review for *The Stage* (17 February 2005) George Hall wrote: 'You would have to go a long, long way to find a Papageno as expert and lovable as Simon Keenlyside: his performance is a classic of our time. Welsh soprano Rebecca Evans sings an impeccable Pamina, with not a note out of place.' As for the conducting, 'the achievement of conductor Charles Mackerras in the pit is a cause for celebration, as is his eightieth birthday later this year. He first conducted at this address back in 1955, and delivers yet another marvellous performance here.' Anthony Holden in the *Observer* (20 February 2005), had much the same view:

> Mackerras has as much spring in his musical step as ever, lifting the overture to new heights before setting such a cracking pace that the chorus, and some of the soloists, occasionally had trouble keeping up. [...] Rebecca Evans makes a very fetching Pamina and Anna-Kristina Kaappola a young-looking Queen of the Night who hits all those notes spot-on.
>
> Aside from Mackerras, the star of the show is Simon Keenlyside, as authentically Mozartian (or, more accurately, Schikanederian) a Papageno as you will ever see. It is not just Keenlyside's famed athletic prowess, which has him hurling himself around the stage in high style; his deadpan comic sense serves him as well as his effortlessly rich baritone in a part that might have been written for him.

In April, Mackerras went to Glyndebourne to start rehearsals for another *Magic Flute*, this time with the OAE in the pit. Though vocally not as strong as with the Covent Garden cast, one of the most exciting aspects of the Glyndebourne performances was the sound of the instruments, as Tim Ashley noted in his *Guardian* review (23 May 2005): 'Mackerras's interpretation of *Zauberflöte* has always combined serenity with great wit,

[5] Mackerras family archives.

and his deployment here of the Orchestra of the Age of Enlightenment adds an extra emotional dimension, with the darker sound of period instruments creating a mood of spiritual austerity that offsets the score's humour and humane warmth.'

At the 2005 Proms, Mackerras conducted Gilbert and Sullivan's *HMS Pinafore* (16 July) with a cast including Richard Suart as Sir Joseph Porter and Felicity Palmer as Little Buttercup. A couple of weeks later he was in Edinburgh to record Mozart's *Clemenza di Tito* for Deutsche Grammophon and to give a concert performance of it (16 August) with soloists including Hillevi Martinpelto as Vitellia and Magdalena Kožená as Sesto. Plans for DG to record a new *Figaro* with Mackerras at the same time fell through – an immense disappointment for him.

Sir Charles's eightieth birthday was fast approaching, and this was celebrated a few weeks early in Edinburgh and London with concert performances of Beethoven's *Fidelio* given by the SCO on 6 and 8 October. At the Royal Opera House, Mackerras conducted Verdi's *Un ballo in maschera*. The first night was actually on his birthday, 17 November, and was a celebration in just the way Mackerras would want: making music. Reviewing the opening night for the *Independent* (21 November 2005), Edward Seckerson tried to encapsulate what was so remarkable about the conducting:

> Sir Charles Mackerras [...] is 80, and he chose to spend the evening of the big day in his rightful place, on the podium of the Royal Opera House, conducting Verdi's *Un ballo in maschera* with an urgency that had nothing to do with the vanishing years and everything to do with dramatic imperative.
>
> It is easy to recognise and hard to explain what makes Mackerras such a great stylist. But it has to do with a scholar's instinct and understanding allied to real practical flair. That and his nose for pace, accent, colour and atmosphere bring the music off the page with tangy immediacy. This *Ballo* may on occasion have pressed the singers, but it gave them the context in which to seize their opportunities. Mackerras certainly seized his. At the close of the first scene, he sent Riccardo and his followers sprinting off in a riot of party-popping effervescence to meet with the notorious fortune-teller Ulrica. And because Verdi knew his business, we were then plunged, by way of thunderously fatalistic chords, into the prelude to scene two, where the hollowest of clarinets foreshadowed Ulrica's terrible predictions of Riccardo's murder.

Rupert Christiansen in the *Daily Telegraph* (21 November 2005), found some of Mackerras's speeds hectic, though the exhilaration was apparent too:

> There was a lack of emotional grandeur in the love duet, while the end of the opening scene found Oscar (Patrizia Biccire) rushed off her

> vocal feet by tempi seemingly intent on record-breaking rather than music-making.
>
> But there was no denying Mackerras's whiplash discipline over the orchestra, or his feeling for the clarity and bounce of this most classically graceful of Verdi's scores. How many other conductors could make the chords that herald Ulrica's appearance so electrifyingly precise? How many would bother to make the dance music in the last scene so, well, danceable?

For John Allison in the *Sunday Telegraph* (27 November 2005) it was the combination of detail and dramatic energy that made the performance memorable:

> Mackerras [...] invested details that too often pass unnoticed with new meaning. The biting chords that plunge us into the fortune-teller Ulrica's den had uncommon dramatic chill. And the operetta-ish moments, which make *Ballo* unique in Verdi's output, went with a rollicking swing only a true man of the theatre could summon up.

And what did Mackerras do when the run of *Ballo* performances ended on 13 December? With barely a day off to rest, he plunged straight back into rehearsals for his next opera at Covent Garden: a revival of *The Bartered Bride* that opened on 6 January 2006 and ran for six performances. His next opera was in May, back at the London Coliseum for a new ENO production of *The Makropulos Affair* which opened on 18 May. Despite being delighted with its musical aspects – led by Cheryl Barker's Emilia Marty and the very fine orchestral playing – he found little to enjoy in the visual aspect of the staging. He sent me a postcard about it on 26 May which summarised his view with typical candour:

> My dear Nigel,
>
> Thank you so much for your letter about *Makropulos*. I've enjoyed doing it at the ENO again after all these years & the orchestra is still damn good I think. However, of the 3 ENO productions I have done, this one is certainly the *least good*. Greetings & thanks again,
>
> Yours ever,
> Charles M.[6]

This production was recorded live (on the first four nights) for the Chandos Opera in English series, so its musical strengths have been preserved. It was the last time Mackerras conducted an opera that he had championed ever since giving the British premiere at Sadler's Wells in 1964.

The Edinburgh Festival in the summer of 2006 was the scene of his triumphant Beethoven symphony cycle with the Scottish Chamber Orchestra and Philharmonia (see Chapter 13), but also a time of personal

[6] Nigel Simeone archives.

tragedy, with the death of his daughter Fiona on 1 September 2006 – the very day he conducted the Ninth Symphony in the Usher Hall.

There was no more live opera in 2006, but on 22–27 November Mackerras made his sublime studio recording of *Hansel and Gretel*, mentioned earlier, in the Blackheath Hall. The new year began with another recording for the Opera in English series, made on 3–11 January 2007 in the Watford Colosseum. This was Mozart's *Così fan tutte*, in the English translation by Marmaduke Browne that had been used (revised by John Cox) for the ENO production in 1980. Though a few years earlier Mackerras had lost the battle over the choice of orchestra for the *Magic Flute*, he won it for *Così*, finally getting to record a Mozart opera with the Orchestra of the Age of Enlightenment. In the booklet for the CDs, Mackerras explained why he used Browne's translation, as well as describing some of the musical judgements regarding embellishments: 'In the case of this opera, we are lucky that a late eighteenth-century ornamented version is still preserved in the Fürstenberg Library at Donaueschingen. Several of these ornaments and cadenzas, particularly in Fiordiligi's arias, have been used in this recording.'[7]

Mackerras conducted just two operas in 2007, both at Covent Garden. The first was Handel's *Orlando*, an opera he had conducted at La Fenice in Venice in 1985 with Marilyn Horne. Rehearsals began in January and presumably it was during one of those that he went for lunch at Bertorelli's Italian restaurant in Floral Street (now closed) and was moved to write a letter of complaint to the General Manager, irritated by the constant presence of one of his pet-hates – piped music:

> Dear Sir,
>
> I am a regular Guest Conductor with the Royal Opera House, Covent Garden and have been a customer of Bertorelli's in Floral Street ever since it opened. When I am working at Covent Garden, I have been in the habit of eating lunch at Bertorelli's almost every day. I have always found the food and service excellent.
>
> I had lunch with a friend yesterday, 17th January, and imagine my horror on being assailed by loud pop music. This was so loud that conversation with my companion was virtually impossible. On my complaining to the Manager, he said [...] I was not the first person to complain about this new threat to the enjoyment of Bertorelli's excellent food.[8]

Mackerras conducted six performances of *Orlando*, with the opening night on 26 February. Anthony Holden reported in the *Observer* that this revival was 'primarily a vehicle for the rightly revered conductor Charles Mackerras, a veteran Handelian still bringing a spring to any orchestra's

[7] 'A note from the conductor', in booklet for *Così fan tutte*, Chandos CHAN 3152, pp. 20–21. Fiordiligi was sung on this recording by Janice Watson.

[8] Mackerras family archives.

step in his eighties. There is musicianship of an equally high order from the ear-popping American counter-tenor Bejun Mehta in the title role, joining winsome Swedish soprano Camilla Tilling (Dorinda).' Others in the cast included Rosemary Joshua (Angelica), Anna Bonitatibus (Medoro) and Kyle Ketelsen (Zoroastro), and in the pit Mackerras had the OAE.

Three months later he conducted *Káťa Kabanová* at Covent Garden. He had conducted it countless times since giving the British premiere in 1951, but never at the Royal Opera House. Tim Ashley wrote in the *Guardian* (23 June 2007):

> [Mackerras] brings a lifetime's experience and understanding to bear on the score, from which he extracts every shred of meaning and expressive potential. Throughout, you are struck as much by the lyrical beauty of Janáček's vocal and orchestral writing as by the work's neurotic undertow, which some conductors overemphasise in the mistaken belief that the opera is primarily an example of raw expressionism.

Charles and Judy's Diamond Wedding anniversary was on 22 August 2007. Their daughter Cathy organised a surprise party at Buscot Park in Oxfordshire. This celebration began with a picnic and a champagne toast, but the climax took place in the private theatre in Buscot's grounds: a performance of Haydn's *L'infedeltà delusa* given by Bampton Classical Opera (of which Mackerras was the patron). Cathy remembers it as an extremely happy occasion, and it was a wonderfully apt way to celebrate their anniversary: watching a performance of a rarely heard opera, surrounded by family and friends (see Plate 32).

In December 2007, Mackerras was at the Watford Colosseum to record Strauss's *Salome* for the Opera in English series, with the Philharmonia and a cast led by Susan Bullock (Salome), John Graham-Hall (Herod) and Sally Burgess (Herodias). Andrew Clements in the *Guardian* (6 November 2008) was particularly impressed by the conducting and playing:

> As this latest addition to Chandos's Opera in English series shows, [Mackerras] is an outstanding Straussian, and it's his account of a score that, [...] together with the Philharmonia's gorgeously vivid playing of it, [...] makes this so memorable. That's not to downgrade any of the singers, who all get Tom Hammond's no-nonsense English text across with enviable clarity.

Mackerras spent the autumn in Australia, but there was no opera on this visit apart from attending Alex Briger's performances of Isaac Nathan's *Don John of Austria* using Mackerras's orchestration. In 2008 he returned to Covent Garden for two Mozart operas. *The Marriage of Figaro* opened on 24 June and Mackerras was due to conduct the first eight performances. He missed the performance on 27 June, as he was suffering from a bad cold (David Syrus substituted capably), but he had recovered in time for the live BBC relay on 5 July. It was a performance of extraordinary energy and ebullience, but it also had moments of heart-stopping beauty, such as the ornamented reprise of 'Voi che sapete', sung pianissimo by Anna Bonitatibus. David McVicar's 2006 staging was stylish and intelligent, and the rest of the cast was strong, especially Ildebrando d'Arcangelo's Figaro and Aleksandra Kurzak's agile Susanna. Martin Kettle marvelled at the whole evening in his *Guardian* review (25 June 2008):

> Charles Mackerras first conducted *Figaro* in 1951. His 1965 performances at Sadler's Wells, in which he reintroduced 18th-century vocal ornamentations, sparked a performance revolution that continues to this day. Now 82, Mackerras understands *Figaro* better than anyone alive. On this evidence, he still conducts it better than anyone, too. From the scintillating overture, he was on top form, demanding the most attentive singing from an experienced cast who gave him their all. Perhaps the years told towards the end when the ensemble occasionally faltered, and Basilio's and Marcellina's final act arias were cut, but this was emphatically Mackerras's night. [...]
>
> It is hard to think of a more strongly cast *Figaro* in London since Karl Böhm's performances 31 years ago, with Hermann Prey in the title role. [...] In Mackerras's hands this is simply an unmissable Mozart masterclass.

The 2008/9 Covent Garden season opened with *Don Giovanni*, with a cast that included Simon Keenlyside's Don and Joyce DiDonato's Donna Elvira. Tickets for the first night had been offered at bargain prices to readers of the *Sun* newspaper and the performance was simultaneously relayed live to cinemas and subsequently released on DVD.

By 2009 Mackerras was starting to take longer and more regular breaks between performances, which were dominated by concerts with the Liverpool Philharmonic, the Philharmonia, the City of Birmingham Symphony Orchestra, the Scottish Chamber Orchestra and the BBC Philharmonic (at the Proms). There was less opera, but on 27 May and 2 June Mackerras conducted two concert performances of Mozart's *Mitridate* with WNO – his final appearance with the company.

In August 2009 Mackerras conducted a sparkling semi-staged performance of Gilbert and Sullivan's *Patience* at the Proms before going to Dartington to conduct Haydn's *Creation* at the Summer School (see Chapter 14). But he was forced to cancel a concert at the Edinburgh Festival (Haydn's *Seven Last Words* with the SCO) and a trip to Brno to record Janáček's *Glagolitic Mass* and *Eternal Gospel*.[9] He had been suffering from multiple myeloma[10] for more than a year, and as the disease progressed Mackerras was becoming frail, his health increasingly precarious. But he

[9] This was to have been a filmed concert. It is particularly sad that Mackerras never recorded Janáček's *Eternal Gospel* [*Věčné Evangelium*], composed in 1913.

[10] Multiple myeloma is a kind of bone cancer.

still seemed transformed every time he strode onto a concert platform or into an orchestra pit. In October he was back at ENO for some extraordinary performances of Britten's *Turn of the Screw*, a work he described as Britten's 'ultimate masterpiece', which he had conducted with the English Opera Group in the mid-1950s and recorded for television in 1959. Fifty years on, Mackerras returned to the work for six performances, opening on 22 October. There was chilling power and pace; a cast that included Rebecca Evans as the Governess, Cheryl Barker as Miss Jessel and Ann Murray as Mrs Grose – all three singers who had worked closely with Mackerras over the years; and an instrumental ensemble drawn from the ENO Orchestra that played with phenomenal precision and colour.

Despite his poor health, Mackerras conducted the students of the Royal Academy of Music in Handel's *Semele* in November 2009. He led the first two nights and then returned for the fourth, but was taken ill at the interval, and Jane Glover took over for the rest of the performance. It was a worrying sign, but a couple of weeks later he was well enough to conduct two concerts with the Philharmonia, both of them including opera (a Wagner programme with Christine Brewer and scenes from *Hansel and Gretel*). In January, Mackerras conducted a concert with the Scottish Chamber Orchestra but had to abandon plans for a recording of Strauss's *Ariadne*, fearing that he simply would not have the strength to complete the sessions (his place was taken by Richard Armstrong). Mackerras started to prepare *The Cunning Little Vixen* at Covent Garden in mid-February, with an opening night on 19 March. He had a fall at home on 21 February, breaking several ribs, but he was resolutely determined to conduct Janáček's opera at Covent Garden. At the performances, he was already seated in the pit before the start (I remember watching him leafing through the score while the audience took its place), and the orchestra produced a ravishing, radiant sound that pleased him more than anything else. It was an intensely moving experience to hear Mackerras conduct *Vixen* at a time when he was in such a frail condition. He adored this opera, and the final scene was one of the pieces he had chosen to have played at his funeral – as Janáček himself had.

Vixen left Mackerras exhausted, and he had to cancel two performances of Beethoven's Ninth Symphony (on 9 and 11 April) with the OAE in London and Valladolid. But the OAE was able to work with Mackerras again a few weeks later, for *Così fan tutte* at Glyndebourne. Mackerras conducted the first of seven performances on 22 May. During his stay at Glyndebourne he gave a filmed interview to James Whitbourn, who asked Sir Charles if he could explain the genius of Mozart's mature music:

> He has certain habits which occur in nearly every work of his, particularly in the late works. One is to repeat something in the minor key having just presented it in the major. Another thing is: having presented something in, say, four bar phrases, he then cuts it up and presents it again in three bar phrases or five bar phrases, or something

> unusual. The difference between a composer like Mozart and, let's say, Salieri or J. C. Bach [...] is that Mozart doesn't write in four-bar phrases all the time. [...] Even when you get to know the work, it's *still* unpredictable! On the dramatical side [...] it's so ingenious that one is still trying to work it out after fifty years.[11]

Fortunately, Mackerras was also enthusiastic about Nicholas Hytner's production:

> There are a few things that struck me as differently treated. So often, Dorabella is treated as a flibbertigibbet and Fiordiligi as a tremendously serious character, whereas I think Nicholas Hytner managed to just get a perfect balance between the characters of those two girls. The treatment also of the two male lovers was, I thought, ideal. In fact I thought it was an ideal production altogether. I've always been a great admirer of Nicholas Hytner.

Working on *Così* with the OAE was an enchanting experience for Mackerras. Some immensely poignant photographs taken in the pit by Chi-chi Nwanoku (principal double bass of the OAE) show Sir Charles beaming at the end of the performance on 12 June (see Plate 38). It was his last bow, his final appearance as a conductor.

Straight after *Così* he left with Judy for Elba, where they were soon joined by Ronnie Schneider, a regular guest at the house on Elba. By the time Cathy arrived, a week later, it was clear that Charles was seriously ill, and he was admitted to the local hospital for treatment. He was discharged on 9 July (and was in sufficiently high spirits as he left to sing Puccini – 'Sola, perduta, abbandonata' from *Manon Lescaut* – to his fellow patients). That night the whole family had a meal together. Charles and Judy flew home on 10 July and on Monday 12 July he was admitted to Parkside Hospital in Wimbledon, where he had been receiving treatment during the previous few years for multiple myeloma. He thought it was a routine stay, and on 13 July he phoned Jane Balmer at Askonas Holt to say that, although he would have to cancel the Prom on 25 July, he hoped to be well enough to do the late-night Prom of Dvořák and Mozart with the SCO wind ensemble four days later. But on the Wednesday, 14 July, he died peacefully at 8:45 p.m., with Judy holding his hand.

Among the first to pay tribute was Antonio Pappano:

> He was a force of nature, a true man of the theatre, who grappled with how to honour a composer's intentions with the utmost rhythmic flair, drama and enthusiasm. His performances were always so full of life it is almost impossible to imagine he is no longer. A true friend of the Royal Opera House, he is irreplaceable; we will miss him terribly.[12]

[11] 'Sir Charles Mackerras: The last interview', www.youtube.com/watch?v=OCTxPjilAWw.

[12] Antonio Pappano, press statement from the Royal Opera, 16 July 2010.

Three memorable collaborations

Nicholas Hytner

There are others who can speak more eloquently than I can about Charles Mackerras's pre-eminence as a musician – among them many of the greatest players and singers of the post-war era. I had the good fortune, however, to collaborate with Charles on three operas, and was able to see from the inside why and how he was infallibly the most theatrical of conductors.

His early career in the pit at Sadler's Wells embraced more or less everything from Gluck to Gilbert and Sullivan. He knew the entire operatic repertoire and and he knew how to make a proper show out of all of it. So that when he turned his attention to one of his great loves, Handel, he was able to erase the centuries-old conviction that Handel's operas contain marvellous music but are theatrically dead in the water. We worked together on the English National Opera production of Handel's *Xerxes*. He was suspicious, at first, of my attempt to create a stage world that embraced the pleasure gardens and coffee houses of Handel's London, and which acknowledged the ironic wit of Handel's literary contemporaries. But, although Charles was not sympathetic to the more voguish deconstructions of the current operatic stage, he knew what worked, and we quickly found common ground.

And how fortunate I was to be in his hands! There's a crucial moment in all Baroque and Classical operas where recitative gives way to aria – like the moment in a musical (and in a singspiel such as *Die Zauberflöte*) where speech gives way to song. It's astonishing how many conductors can't negotiate it – and astonishing, too, how electrifying it can be in the hands of a conductor who has the theatre running in his veins. Often, it's a matter of a millisecond's difference, but in a Handel opera, when aria follows recitative maybe thirty or forty times in the course of an evening, it's the difference between a thrilling show and a recital. Charles was a theatrical master.

I also noticed, awe-struck, how blissfully secure all his singers were when he was in the pit. It seems miraculous to me that an opera singer has any time to think about acting. Under normal circumstances, you might think they would give themselves over entirely to the physical and emotional effort they must put in to producing the right sound, to phrasing the music, to staying together with the orchestra. Charles gave them the confidence to fly on stage. They knew that he would always be with them, that they could respond spontaneously to each other and commit emotionally to the dramatic situation because he'd support them through it.

I saw a different kind of support when I went with him to Prague shortly after the Velvet Revolution. We were meeting singers for a production in Paris of *The Cunning Little Vixen*. Janáček's operas were, of course, his special preserve, and it was thrilling to learn from him about a composer whose music would not have come to the West without his advocacy. It became clear while we were in Prague that he had done more than bring Janáček to the West. During the Communist dictatorship, he had provided a lifeline for Czech musicians, and now, as we sat in a studio in the Conservatoire, I watched as a constant stream of musicians, of all ages, came to reintroduce themselves to him. They brought gifts for him – scores, flowers, bottles of wine, small tokens of their love and respect – and it was extraordinarily moving to see how important his friendship had been to them.

Our final collaboration was, I think, his last work in the theatre. He conducted *Così fan tutte* at Glyndebourne and, although his health was failing, he inspired the young cast and the Orchestra of the Age of Enlightenment (whose commitment to original practices he had anticipated by several decades) in a performance of amazing freshness and wit. And, of course, he gripped the audience throughout – there was never any diminution of his innate feel for theatrical ebb and flow, or of his determination that he could simultaneously deliver music-making of heart-rending profundity and a terrific show.

Charles Mackerras was not only a great musician; he was also one of the very greatest men of the theatre.

9
The Last Great 'Czech' Conductor

Jiří Zahrádka

SIR Charles Mackerras's warm relationship with the Czech lands and their musical culture began with his year of study in Prague (described in detail in Chapter 3). He had the great good luck to arrive in Czechoslovakia in September 1947, at a time when the country was still free, and to live only marginally through the period after the Communist coup of February 1948. He was still able to communicate with people whose activities were later proscribed, in particular the conductor Václav Talich, whose political problems began at the end of the war, when he was unjustly accused of collaboration. Paradoxically, this was another stroke of luck for Mackerras, since after February 1948, when Talich was dismissed from the National Theatre, he had more time for teaching. In this way Mackerras got to know the work of the most distinguished Czech conductor of his day, became better acquainted with Czech music and above all with the compositions of Leoš Janáček, whose idiosyncratic music bewitched him. After hearing Talich's version of *Káťa Kabanová* he sought out performances of other Janáček works throughout Czechoslovakia, in order to get to know as much as possible of this very individual composer.

Mackerras quickly understood that there were differences in the interpretation of Janáček's orchestral scores in Brno and Prague. The Brno interpretations still carried within them a thirty-year tradition moulded by the conductor Milan Sachs, whereas the Prague performances had a more powerful sound thanks to the revised instrumentation of Václav Talich. When, in the summer of 1948, he left Czechoslovakia (which, owing to the political situation, then became closed to him for many years), Mackerras took with him valuable experience gained from Talich, a detailed knowledge of Czech music and a good knowledge of Czech. Above all, however, he took with him a determination to introduce Janáček's works to the British public and to establish his music there. Through various projects over the next decade he managed to bring this about, becoming known as a promoter of Czech music. This may have been why he was invited to visit the Czechoslovak Socialist Republic in the summer of 1960.

First return

MACKERRAS'S first visit after his studies in the 1940s was initiated by the Czech Music Fund, which, among other things, received the performance royalties from Janáček's works. Mackerras visited Prague on the return journey from a conducting engagement in Hungary. After the brutal first half of the 1950s, the Communist Party of Czechoslovakia had, in the wake of the Eleventh Congress (1958), gradually begun to present a more ideologically relaxed image to the world. This was clearest on the cultural front, where, for the first time since the 'Victorious February of 1948', Czechoslovak artistic life began to reach beyond the border, to the cultural world in the West.

The Czech Music Fund was generous when hosting the young conductor from the West. According to Mackerras's reminiscences,[1] he stayed with his wife, Judy, in top hotels and was invited to formal dinners. Official organisations appeared in the very best light, and the invitation realised its goal so well that Mackerras took back a somewhat rose-tinted view of the political establishment of the day. As well as Prague, Mackerras visited the Janáček Archive of the Moravian Museum in Brno for the first time; there he became acquainted with its curator, Dr Theodora Straková, who showed him the Janáček collections. He began to study there for the first time on 3 September 1960,[2] looking through the composer's manuscripts and copies of the original performing scores. In particular he became acquainted with the markings of the conductor František Neumann, who gave most of the premieres of Janáček's later operas. In this way he got to the very roots of a Janáček interpretational tradition that differed significantly from the conception then current in Prague, but also from that on the Brno operatic stage.

This was probably the moment when Mackerras first completely understood Janáček's work and the unique journey he would need to undertake for its interpretation. With his own eyes he saw the original instrumentation of the operas, without the additions of the conductors, whether Václav Talich in Prague or Břetislav Bakala and Milan Sachs in Brno. Together with Theodora Straková and Janáček's pupil Osvald Chlubna, Mackerras also visited Janáček's native Hukvaldy. He did not conduct during this trip to Czechoslovakia, but it sowed the seeds of his later work with Czech orchestras, which would last for the next fifty years.

The following year the young conductor was invited to work with Prague Radio Orchestra, conducting Britten's *Sinfonia da Requiem* and Mahler's Symphony No. 6, a demanding programme. As the composer Václav Felix wrote in his review, 'The performance of the conductor completely satisfied us. With his temperament he knew how to galvanise the radio orchestra towards an intense expression right from the very first notes.'[3] He went on to make two recordings for radio with the same orchestra. Mackerras also visited Brno again that year. From 20 March 1961 he worked in the Janáček

[1] Phelan 1987, p. 126.

[2] Researchers' book, Music History Division, Moravian Museum, Brno, no shelfmark.

[3] Václav Felix: 'Mackerras – Britten – Mahler', *Hudební rozhledy*, xiv (1961), p. 303.

Archive[4] and a day later he conducted a performance of *Káťa Kabanová* at the Brno Opera.

This was a hugely important event for him, conducting a company which had given the premieres of most of Janáček's works, including *Káťa Kabanová* – the first foreigner to conduct a Janáček opera in Czech lands. Moreover, he included in his performance the recently found interludes (see Chapter 3). The reception was very warm: 'The performance of Janáček's musical drama under Mackerras's baton was a powerful experience. A fiery temperament and concentrated desire for an immediate impact eloquently distinguished his approach to Janáček's score, which he mastered securely to the smallest detail.'[5] Understandably, after only two rehearsals the conductor could hardly make much difference to the performance established by František Jílek over many years, but even so it was clear that a great Janáček interpreter was born, with a conception of the composer's work very different from that given in Czechoslovakia.

Pleasure in his success was tempered by news of the death of his beloved teacher Václav Talich on 16 March 1961. Mackerras had attempted to visit him on arrival, but Talich's poor state of health had prevented this. It is unclear whether Mackerras was fully aware at the time how impossible it had been made for Talich to work freely and to conduct the Czech Philharmonic or at the National Theatre.

In May 1962 Mackerras was not only invited to conduct concerts in Bratislava and Ostrava – the latter including a new piece by the Czech composer Jiří Jaroch, *The Old Man and the Sea* – but above all he appeared at the prestigious Prague Spring Festival. Although the festival was a relatively new one (dating from 1946), it had soon won international acclaim. Mackerras's concert at the 1962 Prague Spring Festival included pieces by Mozart, Haydn (the modern premiere of Haydn's C major Cello Concerto with the cellist Miloš Sádlo as soloist) and Stravinsky (Symphony in C).

Conducting Mozart meant, of course, a composer closely linked with Prague and a particular favourite and speciality of Mackerras. Critics, however, were nonplussed by Mackerras's approach, a reaction explained by the very conservative view in Czechoslovakia at the time of the interpretation of Classical and Baroque music (conductors took a more Romantic approach) and the poor standard of the orchestra, which had little experience with music of this period. The critics concentrated on the new piece by Jaroch and above all on the Stravinsky.[6]

Mackerras made further trips to Czechoslovakia in the following year (1963): a recording for the Bratislava Radio Orchestra (16 September),

[4] See note 2.

[5] 'VS' [Jiří Vysloužil]: 'Anglický dirigent L. Janáčkovi' [An English conductor for Janáček], *Lidová demokracie* (Brno), 23 March 1961.

[6] Petr Zapletal: 'Rozhlasový orchestr a jeho dirigent' [The Radio Orchestra and its conductor], *Hudební rozhledy*, xv (1962), p. 557.

more study of Janáček manuscripts and contemporary prints and copies of Mozart in the Brno museum (7–11 October)[7] and, above all, an appearance at the Brno Stadion, the hall in which Janáček's *Glagolitic Mass* had been heard for the first time. His concert included a novelty, a piece by a Czech emigrant working in Canada, Oskar Morawetz. As a friend of Czech music, Mackerras wanted to introduce a Czech artist whose work was unknown in his native country.[8]

While critics regarded Mackerras as an expert in and promoter of Czech music, he had conducted little of it in Czechoslovakia. Czech conductors kept their Smetana, Dvořák, Suk and Janáček for themselves. At the Prague Spring Festival in May 1966, he presented compositions by his favourite composers (Handel and Mozart), as well as pieces by Britten and Malcolm Arnold. But as an encore he gave the Polka from Dvořák's *Czech Suite*, thus smuggling in a taster for his interpretation of Czech music. The reviews turned out much better than four years earlier: 'The conductor Charles Mackerras took care to present a beautiful musicianly atmosphere in which there was no trace of striving for effect but was all the more pleasantly pervaded by an air of well-informed authority.'[9] Again, however, the critics were puzzled by his conception of Mozart and Handel and astonished that he conducted such works from the harpsichord. Most praise was given to the interpretation of Britten.

'Normalisation': the 1970s

MACKERRAS'S next appearance in the Czechoslovak Socialist Republic took place eight years later. The reason was partly the conductor's huge workload, but above all the cataclysmic turn of events in Czechoslovakia. The democratising attempts of the government of the time climaxed in the Prague Spring, after which came the occupation on 21 August 1968 by the 'fraternal' armies of the countries of the Eastern bloc, headed by the Soviet Union. After disturbances the following year, during which many people died, conditions changed considerably. This was the time of so-called 'normalisation', when those who had taken part in – or merely sympathised with – the changes before the occupation were persecuted, lost their jobs and in many cases were arrested. The new regime, supported by the secret service, remade society according to its own view and the wishes of the Soviet Union, and in many ways conditions returned to the situation in the 1950s. The world slowly forgot the stormy summer of

7 See note 2.

8 He was also a warmly supportive friend of Czech people. Cathy Mackerras recalls that, during the early 1960s, the family had numerous Czech house guests and one summer there were Czech visitors staying not only in every spare room, but also in tents in the garden at Essex House (NS).

9 Karel Mlejnek: 'Glosy o komorních souborech' [Glosses on chamber ensembles], *Hudební rozhledy*, xix (1969), p. 400.

1968 and the new leadership did all in its power to spread the news abroad of the 'normalisation of society'. Foreign artists were expected to give the impression that nothing had happened. No wonder that Mackerras, familiar with Czech society and its substance for a quarter of a century, did not fancy coming into this unhealthy climate.

It was only in 1974 that he returned to Czechoslovakia and the Prague Spring Festival, now as a much more established conductor, recognised throughout the world as an artist with great experience and a growing discography. And at the concert on 1 June 1974 he at last appeared to the Czech public as a conductor of Czech music, in a concert that included three Czech works, above all Janáček's *Taras Bulba*. This time the critics were unstinting in their praise. In his review, the Czech pianist and writer Václav Holzknecht drew attention to the interpretation of Janáček, which was quite different from local traditions, and made the point that Czech works were of global importance and could therefore be understood in different ways.[10]

For his autumn appearance in Brno, at the International Musical Festival, Mackerras also chose Czech repertoire, with another all-Czech programme (Dobiáš, Martinů and Janáček). The soloist in the Martinů Violin Concerto was Josef Suk, grandson of the composer Josef Suk and great-grandson of Dvořák. Once again, in the case of Janáček's *Taras Bulba* the critics were taken aback. It was clear that its sound-world, dramatic expression and tempos went against a long-standing way of playing Janáček. For Czechs this was an unknown Janáček, full of expression, emotion and sharp contrasts. According to the reminiscences of musicians, it was only under Mackerras's baton that they began to understand the beauty of Janáček's prelude *Žárlivost* [Jealousy], which until then they knew merely as a marginal work.[11]

Mackerras appeared again in the Czech lands only in 1979, at the Prague Spring Festival. This was the first time he conducted the most important Czech symphony orchestra, the Czech Philharmonic. The orchestra was fully employed at the festival and thus unable to provide an adequate number of rehearsals for individual concerts. Despite this, the reviews of Mackerras's performance praised above all his Janáček. Although some conservative musical circles still had reservations, these did not affect the overall view of him as a Janáček expert.[12] From that moment on he was invited by Czech orchestras especially as a conductor of Czech music. A factor in this was no doubt the outstanding recording of *Káťa Kabanová* he had made for Decca with the Vienna Philharmonic in 1977, with further Janáček operas added in subsequent years.

[10] Václav Holzknecht: 'Česká hudba a zahraniční dirigenti' [Czech music and foreign conductors], *Hudební rozhledy*, xxvii (1974), pp. 292–3.

[11] A comment by the violist Josef Přibáň, at the time a member of the Brno State Philharmonic Orchestra.

[12] Pavel Skála: 'Domácí orchestry festivalu' [Domestic orchestras of the festival], *Hudební rozhledy*, xxxii (1979), pp. 294–6.

Establishing a new approach to the interpretation of Czech music: the 1980s

Mackerras became a regular guest of Czech orchestras in the 1980s. On 6 October 1980 he performed and recorded Janáček's *Glagolitic Mass* with the Prague Radio Orchestra – the first time that he had studied this key work with a Czech orchestra. The line-up of soloists was exceptional, each a foremost Janáček interpreter of the time: Eva Děpoltová, Vilém Přibyl and Richard Novák.

Martinů had spent much of his life outside his native country, enjoying international success – while in Czechoslovakia there was a ban on his works. But after his death, in 1959, local attitudes changed and attempts were made to revive interest in his works, particularly in Brno, thanks to the conductor and dramaturg Václav Nosek. From the 1970s even official state circles began to take an interest in Martinů. A Bohuslav Martinů Society was founded, and in 1979, twenty years after the composer's death, his remains were brought from Switzerland to Czechoslovakia and placed in the family tomb in his native town of Polička.

The conductor who promoted Martinů abroad was again Charles Mackerras. When he conducted *The Greek Passion* at the Welsh National Opera, he suggested that Supraphon might make a recording of this opera. The firm agreed, in the hope that Mackerras's championship of Martinů abroad would create a boom similar to that in Janáček's works. And, to a lesser extent, this is what happened. The recording was made at the Brno Stadion with the Brno State Philharmonic and soloists from the Welsh National Opera. In many ways the recording has never been surpassed. Mackerras also conducted this opera at the Janáček Theatre in Brno, where it was currently in the repertoire. Mackerras went on to make several radio recordings, including Martinů's Double Concerto and an outstanding version of his *Les Fresques de Piero della Francesca.*

Mackerras's next appearance attracted much attention. In January 1984 he conducted the Czech Philharmonic in two large-scale vocal-instrumental pieces by Janáček: *Amarus* and the *Glagolitic Mass.* One of the performers was the Swedish soprano Elisabeth Söderström, who had featured in three of Mackerras's Decca recordings of Janáček operas. Mackerras had partially revised the score of the *Glagolitic Mass* on the basis of his study of sources in the Janáček Archive, adding a fourteen-bar section in 'Svet', cut at the premiere because of the high tessitura for the choir. The response was splendid, as is evident in Petr Vít's review: 'After the performance of the *Glagolitic Mass* Mackerras's conception reminded me of Janáček's irritated reply: "Not an old man, not a believer!" The conductor unleashed a thrilling drama of life and death, crushing us with the force of Janáček's genius.'[13]

[13] Petr Vít: 'Koncerty České filharmonie' [Concerts by the Czech Philharmonic Orchestra], *Hudební rozhledy*, xxxvii (1984), pp. 147–8.

The *Glagolitic Mass* was recorded in the following days by Supraphon, with the same performers – arguably the most impressive recording made by Mackerras of this work. Other recordings of this period include the wonderful series of all of Mozart's symphonies with the Prague Chamber Orchestra for Supraphon/Telarc (1986–90) and a programme for Czech Radio in 1986 in which Mackerras and his great friend and fellow-student Milan Munclinger recorded reminiscences of their teacher Václav Talich.

The year 1989 and its 'Velvet Revolution' arrived. Change was already in the air, and it seems symbolic that earlier that year the ceremonial opening of the Prague Spring Festival (12 May), always reserved for Smetana's *Má vlast*, had been conducted by Charles Mackerras. The 64-year-old conductor was performing it for the first time, but his study of the work went back forty years, under Talich. The reception was enthusiastic, with critics praising his feeling for drama, tempo contrasts and huge variety of expression.[14]

Mackerras the Czech conductor: the 1990s and beyond

In Czechoslovakia – free once again – Mackerras's work with Czech ensembles became even more intensive. His first return trip, within a year of the fall of the Communist regime, was to the Brno International Festival, where on 7 October 1990 he gave a concert which included Janáček's *Sinfonietta*, conducting it for the first time in the Czech lands. The response was glowing: the reviews described the conductor's interpretations as thrilling, especially in the *Sinfonietta*, where he 'used the composer's original instrumentation from the original draft, unavailable to us, and for instance extended the number of trumpets in the ceremonial fanfares'.[15] It is unclear which version this refers to: whether increasing the trumpets in the outer movements, as Talich did, or including the fanfare trumpets in the second movement. What is important, however, is that Czech audiences and musicians began to consider different versions. Mackerras started the trend of presenting Janáček's works with the maximum authenticity, thus bringing a breath of fresh air into Czech interpretational 'traditions'.

An extraordinary event in that same year was the reopening, after extensive reconstruction, of the Nostic Theatre (now the Estates Theatre), where Mozart's *Don Giovanni* had been heard for the first time; and this work was now chosen to reopen the theatre. Well known as a Mozart expert, Charles Mackerras conducted in this authentic venue a version linked with that of the premiere.

The Masaryk University of Brno, which had conferred its very first honorary doctorate on Janáček in 1925, awarded Mackerras an Honorary

[14] Petr Vít: 'Charles Mackerras řídil Mou vlast' [Charles Mackerras conducted *Má vlast*], *Hudební rozhledy*, xlii (1989), pp. 338–9.

[15] 'jd' [Jana Dvořáková]: 'Závěr s Mackerrasem' [Ending with Mackerras], *Brněnský večerník*, 8 October 1990.

Doctorate of Arts on 27 May 1994 for his exceptional services to Czech music. When, the next year, Mackerras opened the Brno 'Moravian Autumn' Festival with an exclusively Janáček programme, he included the *Glagolitic Mass* in Paul Wingfield's version, the first time it had been given in Czech lands. It provoked contradictory reactions: enthusiasm for something new and interesting as well as doubts about how far one should go in search of authenticity, a reaction that in many ways anticipated future discussion of this version of the work.

When this version of the *Glagolitic Mass* was given in Prague the following year, reviewers began to use the phrase 'Mackerras's Janáček'. Now used in a positive sense, the phrase expressed the view that this conductor had not only completely overturned the traditional view of how to interpret Janáček's works but also emphasised that they should be given with maximum authenticity. It was for this approach and his promotion of Czech music throughout the world that he was awarded a great honour by the Czech Republic, the medal 'Za zásluhy' (Medal of Merit).[16]

Working more and more with the Czech Philharmonic, Mackerras was appointed its Chief Guest Conductor from the 1996/7 season and served in this capacity for seven years. The result was a huge number of concerts with the orchestra in 1997 and the recording for Supraphon in March 1997 of Janáček's *Káťa Kabanová* using his own edition. The recording, which won a number of prizes (including the Cannes Classical Award 1999), was a particularly happy one and makes an interesting comparison with his recording of twenty years earlier with the Vienna Philharmonic. The following year, 1998, Mackerras made another opera recording with the Czech Philharmonic, this time for Decca, with three non-Czech soloists: Dvořák's *Rusalka*. This is another key recording, because once again Mackerras overturns the well-trodden path of Czech over-sentimentalised interpretation and over-rich sound, giving the work instead a sharper rhythmic structure and greater tempo contrasts. This was the view of critics, who awarded the record ten prestigious prizes, including the *Gramophone* Award of 1999. Mackerras also took the Czech Philharmonic on tour in Britain, appearing at concerts in Edinburgh (Usher Hall), London (Royal Albert Hall) and Birmingham (Symphony Hall), and gave five concerts with the orchestra in the Czech Republic. One of these was the opening of the Prague Spring Festival with the complete cycle of Smetana's *Má vlast*; Mackerras became the only foreign conductor to have been honoured twice in this way. A further honour was Mackerras's second Czech honorary doctorate, this time from the Prague Academy of Performing Arts, awarded on 14 May 1999.

[16] In 1978 Mackerras had been awarded the Janáček Medal by the Czechoslovak Government. It was presented to him by the Czechoslovak Ambassador, Zdeněk Černík, on stage at the London Coliseum after a performance of Janáček's *Excursions of Mr Brouček* on 28 December 1978, a few days before the award of his knighthood.

Mackerras made another opera recording with the Czech Philharmonic the next year: Janáček's first opera, *Šárka*, based on the new edition which he had supervised. Mackerras stepped down in 2002 from his position as Chief Guest Conductor of the Czech Philharmonic (his final concert was on 17 October), but his work with the orchestra hardly appeared to slacken.

An exceptional event at the end of 2003 was Mackerras's final appearance in a Czech opera house, when he presided over a new production of Janáček's *Excursions of Mr Brouček* in the new edition to which he had contributed and which returned the work to its original orchestration. The premiere took place at the Prague National Theatre on 20 December 2003. The low quality of the local orchestra and the ragged stage direction somewhat detracted from the event as a whole, although Mackerras's contribution was highly commended. The production was also taken to Brno as part of the big Janáček anniversary celebration in 2004, in which Mackerras also conducted the final concert of the festival. The festival formed the backdrop for Mackerras's third Czech honorary doctorate, awarded on 30 January, this time by the Janáček Academy of Performing Arts in Brno.

Mackerras's final recording in the Czech Republic and the last time he worked with the Czech Philharmonic took place on 9–10 September 2009, when he recorded Dvořák's symphonic poem *The Wood Dove*. After the recording had been completed, the microphone remained on, thus preserving Mackerras's farewell to the orchestra with which, over thirty years, he had given almost sixty concerts. He said, in Czech, 'This is perhaps the last time that I will have conducted you and I would like to say farewell and thank you for all the beautiful concerts that we have done together and the many records. And so I thank you very much for all these years.'[17] One of the players, Jaroslav Pondělíček, later remembered this occasion: 'With us Charles Mackerras was never a foreign conductor, we saw him as belonging to the Czech Philharmonic and his visits as a matter of course. When we saw him for the last time, he stood there after the concert and chatted with some of us, and suddenly said: 'I won't come again, I'm here for the last time.' We said that this can't be true and that we would wait for him. But he could not be persuaded. When he left the hall he turned round among the desks and said, half to himself, 'perhaps I will come again'.[18]

Sadly, this did not happen. Because of his failing health, Mackerras had to withdraw from the planned concert with the Brno Philharmonic in September 2009. The last time Mackerras visited the Czech Republic was on 27 April 2010, to receive the award Artis Bohemiae Amicis of the Ministry of Culture of the Czech Republic. When, a few months later, the news came of his death, the leader of the cellos in the Czech Philharmonic, František

[17] Transcribed from the programme *Charles Mackerras*, broadcast on Czech Radio on 17 November 2010.

[18] Transcribed from the Czech Television documentary *Sir Charles, thank you, děkujeme ...*, recorded in 2009.

Host, noted: 'The last great Czech conductor has died',[19] a statement that implied the greatest recognition of all. Following his death, many concerts, exhibitions, television and radio programmes were devoted to Mackerras; the Brno 2010 Janáček Festival was dedicated to his memory. Mackerras donated his royalties from his Czech recordings to the Leoš Janáček Foundation, which, every ten years, awards the Sir Charles Mackerras Prize to the conductor whose interpretation has most enriched Czech music.

Mackerras as a conductor of Czech music

How does Mackerras's conception of Czech music, especially that of Smetana, Dvořák, Suk, Janáček and Martinů, differ from that of Czech conductors? To answer this, one needs to go back almost seventy years, to when Mackerras studied with Václav Talich. There is no doubt that he gained his first opinions from his outstanding teacher. Although Talich was a very versatile conductor, his domain was Smetana, Dvořák and Suk. From Talich the young fledgling conductor would have taken on board his grand conception, the emphasis on the sound and colour of the orchestra, and also – and this is crucial – the need for a well-honed craft in mastering the work at hand. When, in 1986, Mackerras and Milan Munclinger reminisced about their studies with Talich, Munclinger remarked that when he observed Mackerras's work in rehearsal it greatly reminded him of Talich: above all his approach to the orchestra and communication with them, and the huge emphasis on technical perfection.[20] However, in his overall understanding of the works Mackerras is very different from Talich. This is particularly evident in their approach to Janáček, where Talich instinctively sought a big Romantic sound, which usually involved additional orchestral forces, for instance in *Káťa Kabanová* and *The Cunning Little Vixen*, or changes to the orchestration, for instance in *Taras Bulba* (the only Janáček work that survives in a Talich recording), where Talich replaced the violin solo with a group of violins, thus destroying the contrast with the full orchestra that Janáček intended. Talich's tempos were generally relaxed, emphasising accelerandos and ritardandos, often at the expense of the contrast created by blocks of different tempos.

Mackerras, on the other hand, studied the Janáček sources not in order to surprise the public continually with new versions but rather because he realised, perhaps the first of anyone, that the composer's version was the best, the most personal, and that later arrangements and reorchestrations denied Janáček his uniqueness and returned him to routine conceptions and earlier sound ideals. This goes especially for Mackerras's use of the

[19] Ibid.

[20] The radio documentary 'Vzpomínka na Václava Talicha' [A memoir of Václav Talich], recorded on 5 March 1986, is deposited in the archive of Czech Radio, shelfmark CR.HKV.2008.651.

composer's original orchestration. Mackerras was well aware of this and adapted himself to Janáček's individual world, which enabled him to make his mark as the most precise and best mediator and interpreter of Janáček's works. In Mackerras's interpretation, the music of this unique composer is extremely pungent and vivid, with a special timbre of unease – the result of the frequent absence of instrumental fillers and the use of extreme instrumental registers. Mackerras sharply breaks up the whole into contrasting sections by means of tempo and dynamics, emphasising rhythmic concision and Janáček's interestingly structured metrical sections. In his conception the bottom layers, played by brass and wind instruments, are well to the fore and the percussion particularly prominent. Mackerras's Janáček is powerful, emotionally exalted, rugged in sound, urgent in tempo and dynamic contrasts, but also capable of extreme tenderness – Janáček as he really is, without prettification and absolutely truthful. And one more general remark: Mackerras also conducted from the score, never from memory. This is because he continually strove for and found new connections and new details in the score. Mackerras's interpretations of the same piece are never the same, and over the years one can hear a clear development in his view of a particular composition and the polishing of its interpretation. This process continued right up to the end, astonishing for a conductor well into his eighties.

Translated by John Tyrrell

10

Reminiscences of a Friend and Colleague

Jiří Zahrádka

It was in 1995 that I first met Sir Charles Mackerras. As a new student of musicology at Masaryk University I attended rehearsals of the Brno State Philharmonic, where Sir Charles was rehearsing Janáček's *Glagolitic Mass*. I loved Janáček's music and admired Mackerras as a conductor; I had all his recordings of Janáček and Martinů. In the small space of the Besední dům, where once upon a time Janáček himself had also conducted concerts, I preferred to hide myself away on the balcony. I followed the very intense rehearsal when the organist had problems with the new Wingfield version of the score and Sir Charles wasn't able to explain his entries to him. Mackerras carried on even during the break, working with the organist, but all in vain. At what was clearly an inappropriate moment after this futile battle, I ventured to emerge and ask if I could bring my CDs of his recordings for him to sign. And something very surprising happened. Sir Charles smiled at me, spoke to me in his excellent Czech (after that we always spoke Czech) and enquired which recordings pleased me and why I liked Janáček. I no longer know what I said to him, but the result was that he told me to bring whatever I wanted for signing and that during the rehearsals I should sit on the chair behind him so that I could hear better. When I then brought a whole pile of CDs he was somewhat thrown, but he signed all of them for me. And I went on to ask him if he would also sign my 'klavírák' of *Jenůfa*. He didn't know the term, so I explained that it was an informal word for a piano-vocal score; it was a word he liked very much, repeating it several times. After that he often used this word in Czech. The *Glagolitic Mass* concert was fascinating, but at the time it didn't occur to either of us that within a short while we would start working together on preparing new Janáček editions.

Our next encounter was on a professional basis. Six years later I prepared the first (critical) edition of Janáček's opera *Šárka* for Universal Edition under Sir Charles's supervision. Once the score and all the performing material became available, Supraphon decided to record the opera with Sir Charles and the Czech Philharmonic. I came two days before the first rehearsal to make any necessary changes in the orchestral parts and on arrival shut myself away in the archive of the Rudolfinum, the home of the Czech Philharmonic, in whose Dvořák Hall the recording was being made. Ten minutes later Sir Charles came in, cheerful and in a good mood: 'I wanted to get to know you, young man. The first to publish *Šárka* – you must be a happy man!' It was a very nice meeting and all my fears evaporated (it was, after all, my first big edition, being played for the first time and also recorded).

The week of rehearsals with Sir Charles was very important for me. He had me there for all the rehearsals with the soloists, chorus and the orchestra.

At first the atmosphere wasn't too friendly: the Czech Philharmonic was going through a rough patch and work with them was not what one might have expected from such an august body. This and the limited time made rehearsals quite tense. Nevertheless, things began to pick up and *Šárka* shined in all her glory. At the end of the session Sir Charles said to me in the lift that he had thought he knew his Janáček but he was mistaken. For him, Janáček's first opera was a surprising discovery: it was unusual music, particularly in the orchestration, in which Janáček worked with tiny motifs; in its overall dramaturgical concision it approached his mature operas.

At the last moment, however, a problem suddenly blew up. The singer performing Lumír, who comes on only in the third act, had a car accident on the day of the recording and couldn't attend. They tried to find a substitute, but it soon became clear that no one would be able to take on such a demanding role on the spot. Things couldn't wait, as the rehearsals were due to finish. In the end they recorded the third act without Lumír, whose part was recorded six months later. The result was flawless: nothing untoward can be detected on the recording. It was a magnificent recording and the first of the version which the composer left us. It was even nominated for a Grammy award, which in the end it didn't win. (As Sir Charles wittily commented: 'We made a mistake in that not a single American took part.'). During the ten days of working on the recording I became very friendly with Sir Charles. His detailed knowledge of the score and uncompromising attitude to the participants' performance was evident: he demanded absolute discipline and concentration. He would cite Švejk: 'There must be discipline!'

Further work together – on the edition of *The Excursions of Mr Brouček* – was much more relaxed and direct. Preparing the edition had been demanding, since Janáček himself and many conductors – during his life and afterwards – made substantial changes, mainly in the orchestration but also dramaturgically. Some of the changes Janáček made under pressure, others of his own free will, but none were to the benefit of the work. Those sections later reorchestrated by the composer got mixed up with senseless cuts by conductors; in short, it was an editor's nightmare. I began to acquaint Sir Charles with these problems, telling him that the second half of the opera had been reorchestrated by his friend the conductor Vilém Tauský in 1936, and it was in this very luxuriant orchestration that the work was still being played today. He didn't believe me, and later he gleefully told me that he'd spoken to Tauský, who said he'd done nothing of the sort. Only when I showed Sir Charles the changes that Tauský had signed did he believe me. (When I was preparing the edition Tauský was already over 90 and no longer remembered his interventions in the score.)

As well as the editions of *Šárka* and *The Excursions of Mr Brouček* we worked together on *The Cunning Little Vixen*. Our work on these editions took the form mostly of consultation, with Sir Charles in his role as supervisor. Once I had completed the critical edition of the work on the basis of all relevant sources, I would hand the score over to Sir Charles. And then began a merry-go-round of mutual questions and suggestions for the practical solution of various passages. Some came about through rehearsals, in which occasional deficiencies were identified. In the end we decided that some of Sir Charles's practical suggestions should be reproduced as footnotes under the musical text. In this way the editions were strictly critical, corresponding to the composer's conception, while at the same time providing practical suggestions on how to solve problematic passages. This critical-practical model has proved successful. Our collaboration was excellent: Sir Charles was well versed in the problems, and had great practical experience and the necessary dose of tolerance. He always took account of the specialist position of the editor and was willing to correct his own view, however tried and tested over the years. In ten years of intensive work together there was not a single argument, and I believe that this editorial harmony is evident in the editions themselves.

By the time Sir Charles came to rehearse *The Excursions of Mr Brouček* with the Prague National Theatre, he was very well acquainted with the work's problems. I joined him at the beginning of December 2003 to sit in on the rehearsals, then in full swing. It was very interesting work, but any hope of a smooth rehearsal schedule was upset by the bad habits of Czech opera orchestras. Sir Charles began to get very angry when different players turned up every day, and he threatened to leave. In the end the situation was partly calmed down and the production went ahead more or less satisfactorily. His great dream was to bring out a recording of this opera on CD: it was the only Janáček opera (apart from the naive *The Beginning of a Romance*) that he had not recorded. Supraphon, however, withdrew from the recording on financial grounds, which very much upset Sir Charles. A live recording was issued by the Prague National Theatre (see Discography).

I particularly remember two moments from this period. The first was a lunch with Sir Charles at which he reminisced about his beginnings as a conductor, his friendship with Britten and so on. He asked me which Czech works and composers I liked. It surprised and delighted me that we agreed on almost everything. Today perhaps I can reveal, despite this being a private conversation, which works this great conductor of Czech music regarded particularly highly. Above all it was Janáček, whom he accepted without reservation as the most individual composer overall. He also loved Dvořák's symphonic works, especially Symphonies Nos 6–9. Of the operas he thought highly only of *Rusalka*. He respected Suk above all because of *Asrael*. From Smetana he loved *Má vlast* and the chamber works, particularly the string quartets. He had a more complicated relationship with Martinů. He thought well of only a few works: the Double Concerto, the Sixth Symphony ('*Fantaisies symphoniques*'), the Fourth Piano Concerto ('*Incantation*'), *Les Fresques de Piero della Francesca* and *Julietta*. It surprised me that he was less convinced by *The Greek Passion*, which he had recorded so magnificently. He regarded the original version reconstructed by Aleš Březina (see Chapter 11) more highly, and in that, too, we were as one.

A second memorable moment was when, for the first time, he introduced a small change into the score of *Brouček* against the original. This was at the end of the second Excursion, where the original instrumentation was conceived so that the work should sound comic. In the 1930s this passage was reinforced by trumpets added to the violins, making the ending more dramatic. And it was in this form that the conclusion of the opera was always played from the 1930s onwards. Mackerras rehearsed the original version but in the end called out: 'I can't do this, it's so undramatic,' and restored the trumpets. Although I explained to him that with the added trumpets the work came across as much more old-fashioned, I wasn't able to convince him.

The following January this production moved to the Janáček festival 'Brno 2004', where all of Janáček's operas were being staged. The organisation of the festival was in the hands of my wife, Šárka, and I was the dramaturg, in charge of the concept and planning. In addition to conducting the Prague production of *Brouček*, Sir Charles conducted the closing concert: the *Glagolitic Mass*, Janáček's incomplete 'Danube' Symphony and the Violin Concerto *The Wandering of a Little Soul*. Sir Charles spent a week in Brno, full of rehearsals, social meetings and also honours (an honorary doctorate from the Janáček Academy of Performing Arts). An interesting situation arose in connection with the performance of the *Glagolitic Mass*. He knew of my distrust of the so-called original version by Paul Wingfield but, apart from omitting the 'Intrády' at the beginning of the work, there was no time to make changes in his well-established reading. We also worked in the Janáček Archive, where we sorted out some unclear passages in *Taras Bulba*. These two months of continual contacts brought us still closer, and he also got on very well with Šárka.

Two years later, we attended Sir Charles's concert with the Vienna Philharmonic in Vienna on 15 September 2006 (Dvořák's overture *Amid Nature*, Mozart's Piano Concerto in C minor K491 with Alfred Brendel, Kodály's *Dances of Galánta* and Janáček's *Sinfonietta*). The concert was extraordinary; the performance of the *Sinfonietta* left an exceptionally powerful impression. After the concert Šárka and I went round to see Sir Charles and he told us the terrible news about the death of his daughter Fiona. He explained to us that he had to go on working, otherwise he would go mad, but for this brief moment he was able to forget everything. One couldn't help remembering Janáček's creative tension after the death of his daughter Olga. This grief and this strength to stand up creatively to the unhappy blows of fate were more than clear from Sir Charles's performance.

In 2009 Šárka and I spent several days in London, during which time we visited the house in Hamilton Terrace where the Mackerrases lived. It was a happy meeting. Judy made tea and Sir Charles, John Tyrrell (who came with us), Šárka and I talked about everything possible, but principally about Janáček. At the time, Sir Charles and I were working on the critical edition of *The Cunning Little Vixen*. Sir Charles showed me his archive and gave a demonstration of his rococo musical box during which he merrily conducted. These were pleasant and peaceful moments, untroubled by any fears about his health.

The last time I saw Sir Charles conduct was in March 2010, when he conducted *The Cunning Little Vixen* at the Royal Opera House. There was one funny moment associated with this visit. We had tickets for the Thursday performance, but Sir Charles thought that we were coming to the Monday performance and at the end waited for us in his dressing room. When we didn't turn up, Sir Charles phoned all round to find out if something had happened to us. When we eventually came to see him after the Thursday performance, he was glad to see us and took pleasure in the published score of *The Cunning Little Vixen* which I brought him. As always, he spoke nothing but Czech (ignoring another distinguished but non-Czech-speaking visitor), and he was witty and merry, but it was clear that he was extremely exhausted and I suspected then that we were seeing our friend for the last time. But it didn't turn out that way. The then Minister of Culture of the Czech Republic, Václav Riedlbauch, decided to award the prestigious prize Artis Bohemiae Amicis to Sir Charles, who came to Prague on 27 April 2010 to accept it personally. After the award Šárka and I saw him briefly. He told us that things were now very serious. Then we said goodbye, and it was now clear to us that this really was the last time. The news of Mackerras's death reached us that summer.

These are my memories of Sir Charles, of our working encounters which grew into a beautiful friendship. I feel his absence with every problem in a score that I'd like to consult him about. I miss his critical reading of my work, his cheerful and open character. And above all his art, which luckily survives on many recordings. Although he was a very strict and uncompromising conductor, he still remains in my memory as a man with a great sense of humour, friendly and benevolent. More than two generations older than me, he never behaved condescendingly towards me and always respected my views. He knew how to show that he valued someone's work. Working with him was a great education for me. Sir Charles remains for me one of the most distinctive conductors of the twentieth century and undoubtedly the greatest interpreter of Janáček's works.

Translated by John Tyrrell

11

Reconstructing a Better Version of *The Greek Passion*

Aleš Březina

NEXT to Dvořák and Janáček among Charles Mackerras's great passions for Czech music was Bohuslav Martinů. Knowledge of this fact gave me the courage in March 1995 to visit Sir Charles in the hotel Radisson Blu in Basle and present him with a copy of my recently published catalogue of the Martinů autographs in the Paul Sacher Foundation in Basle.[1] Astonishingly, he received me, though he didn't know me from Adam (and furthermore I had unwittingly awoken him from his afternoon rest before the concert). In the catalogue he was immediately taken by the fact that it contained several unknown sections of Martinů's *The Greek Passion*, from the discarded first version of this opera. Three months later he wrote to me:

> I have been asked to conduct a performance of *The Greek Passion* in a production by the young Australian director Baz Luhrman. The production will first be shown at the Bregenz Festival, then at the Edinburgh Festival, and finally at the Royal Opera House Covent Garden. As we discussed at the time, there are many faults in the dramaturgy of this opera and we are all keen to try and construct a version of the opera which will improve the dramatic flow. From what I understood from you at our meeting, you have found certain passages of music which Martinů discarded for one reason or another, and in the course of your researches you have also discovered several sheets of Martinů's autograph which might be of use to us in the reconstructing of a better version of *The Greek Passion*. Both Dr Alfred Wopmann of the Bregenz Festival and Mr Nicholas Payne of the Royal Opera House Covent Garden will shortly be in touch with you to see if you could possibly help us in this respect. [...] I look forward to hearing from you as to whether you would be willing to co-operate with us in what looks like being an extremely interesting venture.

Soon afterwards Dr Alfred Wopmann did indeed visit me in Basle, and at his request I began looking for the many tens of missing pages from the first version of *The Greek Passion*. In the next three years I gradually found them in a number of private and public libraries – in the home of Charlotte

[1] Aleš Březina: 'Die Martinů-Manuskripte in der Paul Sacher Stiftung Basel', *Schweizer Jahrbuch für Musikwissenschaft*, xiv (1994), pp. 157–274.

Reber[2] in Basle (thanks to the great help of Father Max Kellerhals), in the personal collection of the Martinů scholar Harry Halbreich in Brussels, in the Wienbibliothek im Rathaus and in the Universal Edition archive in Vienna, and also in a number of locations in the Czech Republic (the archive of the Bohuslav Martinů Institute, the Bohuslav Martinů Centre in Polička and the Czech Museum of Music in Prague). In 1998 I completed a complete reconstruction of the first version, and in May of that year Sir Charles carried out linguistic corrections to the composer's English libretto. Publication by Universal Edition in Vienna, however, needed another year of intensive work, so the premiere at the Bregenz Festival had to be postponed; because of other commitments, Sir Charles unfortunately had to pull out. He took charge, however, of the co-production at the Royal Opera House, Covent Garden, in 2000. Here he engaged strongly in the discussion about whether the first version of the work should be used unchanged for the production or whether individual passages from the second version should be inserted. In a letter of 22 May 1998 he wrote: 'my private view is that we may well end up with the pure London/Březina version at Covent Garden', adding in November 1998:

> I think it was a very good decision on all of our parts to do the complete First Version of the Greek Passion in Bregenz.[3] From that we can see how successful the version is and whether it would in fact be better to use any parts of the late versions of the opera for our performances in Covent Garden. I look forward very much to seeing the performance in Bregenz and hope that you will also be able to advise us on what you think about the respected merits of the first and later versions of the opera.

Mackerras's interpretation of David Pountney's thrilling staging at Covent Garden was a success with both the public and the critics, and *The Greek Passion* won the Laurence Olivier Award for the Best New Opera Production in 2001. In addition to the BBC3 broadcast of one of the subsequent performances, Sir Charles had recordings made at his own expense of two further performances of *The Greek Passion*, in the hope that it would be able to issue a recording of the opera. This has not happened so far, but could perhaps be done to commemorate his unrealised ninetieth birthday.

[2] The daughter of the Swiss manuscript collector Hans Conrad Bodmer, she married the Swiss surgeon Willy Reber, who himself also studied music privately with Martinů and conducting with Pierre Boulez. Thanks to the Rebers, part of Martinů's personal library survived, together with some of his manuscripts, including *The Greek Passion.*

[3] In the end, Bregenz settled on the first version but included the opening ten bars of the second version. Film commitments forced Baz Luhrman to withdraw; he was replaced by David Pountney.

Some years after the premiere of the first version of *The Greek Passion*, I managed to find and buy from a German collector the manuscript piano-vocal score of the two orchestral sections of *Three Fragments from the Opera Juliette*,[4] a unique work in Martinů's output by virtue of being the only suite that he made from his numerous stage works. At the time I was in the middle of preparing the international project 'Martinů Revisited', commemorating the fiftieth anniversary of the composer's death. I had included the world premiere of the *Three Fragments* in the opening concert, and in January 2006 I asked Sir Charles, a great lover of *Julietta* and some years previously the initiator of the English premiere of the opera, to conduct it. I told him also that I had managed to get Magdalena Kožená (whom he greatly admired) for the title role. He accepted the invitation with one reservation:

> In principle, I would be delighted to do this concert, although I must warn you that I may decide to retire during 2008 [...]. But assuming that I am not already retired by then, I would be delighted to conduct the Czech Philharmonic in *Scenes from Julietta* with Magdalena. [...] I would prefer if you would make the rest of the programme consisting of Janáček and/or Dvořák as it will almost certainly be the last time I ever conduct the Czech Philharmonic.

While preparing the edition we managed to find the autograph full score of the work, and so it was unnecessary to reconstruct the orchestration from the opera. Sir Charles flew to Prague and began rehearsing. The very next morning, however, he had an accident when leaving the Hotel International: making way for an older lady, he was caught in the back by the revolving doors. Despite his unpleasant injury, he rehearsed the programme and introduced the work at two concerts, at which the applause in the Rudolfinum rang to the rafters. These were indeed his last concerts with the Czech Philharmonic and were a fitting farewell for Sir Charles, not only to the Czech Philharmonic but also to the Czech public at large. A year later, the recording of the *Three Fragments from the Opera Juliette* gained a *Gramophone* Award.

The last communication I received from Sir Charles came from the realm of the spirits. In the summer holidays, in the middle of July 2010, the media brought the sad news that he had died. On returning to the Martinů Institute I found on my desk a posted envelope written in his characteristic manner, i.e. with Czech diacritics carefully added by hand, with a printed

[4] A year after the Paris premiere of *Julietta* (1938), Martinů chose some of the most significant music from the opera and arranged it as a suite for concert performance in order to promote his opera. No. 1 and No. 3 are with full orchestra; No. 2 is the famous scene 'Memories' with just a piano accompaniment, taken directly from the score in the original piano version. Intended for performance on French Radio, the work was not performed because of the worsening political situation and lay forgotten – seemingly even by the composer himself.

card inside announcing that he had moved. But by now no address could reach him. Never shall I forget his musical intelligence and liveliness, his graciousness, his humour and his willingness to listen to the opinions of others.

Translated by John Tyrrell

12

Reconstructing Sullivan's Cello Concerto

David Mackie

CHARLES Mackerras first came to prominence in 1951 with the ballet *Pineapple Poll*, which was based on a story by W. S. Gilbert; the music was arranged by Mackerras from the Gilbert and Sullivan operas, whose music copyright had expired at the end of 1950. Long an admirer of Sullivan's music, Mackerras then turned his attention to the virtually forgotten Cello Concerto. His 1953 performance, in a BBC Third Programme concert with William Pleeth as soloist and the Goldsborough Orchestra, was the first for over forty years. If little was known of Sullivan's non-G&S music in 1975 (D'Oyly Carte's centenary year), even less was known in 1953, and it is doubtful that many people would have tuned in to the Third Programme to hear this rarity. The BBC did not make a recording of the concert and it has been assumed that no recording was made by anyone: none has come to light. Unfortunately this turned out to be the concerto's last performance. Unpublished, the score and orchestral parts had been available for hire from Chappell and Co. but, along with much else, these were destroyed in a devastating fire that also caused loss of life at Chappell's premises on 6 May 1964.

In 1975, timed to commemorate the D'Oyly Carte centenary, there appeared a remarkable book: *Sir Arthur Sullivan, Composer & Personage* by Reginald Allen, Curator of the Gilbert and Sullivan collection at the Pierpont Morgan Library, essentially a life (but not a biography) of the composer compiled from the library's vast archive. I acquired a copy of the book in June 1976 and became aware of the extent and scope of the collection. Apart from the G&S material there was much, much more, including the manuscripts of several of the songs that I had studied at Birmingham as part of my MA on Sullivan's songs and, incredibly, a manuscript of the solo part of the Cello Concerto in a copyist's hand; dated '7/2/87', it appears to have been made for a performance that year by J. Edward Hambleton. Interesting as it was, this information was put to the back of my mind, as I was about to become Chorus Master and Associate Conductor of D'Oyly Carte and would soon be conducting the operas for the first time.

By the early 1980s there were signs that the D'Oyly Carte Opera Company might not last for another hundred years, as confidently predicted in 1975, and after a mere seven years it gave its last performance at the Adelphi Theatre, London, on 27 February 1982. I was now unemployed and I resolved to acquire a copy of the solo part of the Cello Concerto to see if a reconstruction would be possible: I had spent the better part of a decade immersed in Sullivan's music and I now had time on my hands. I wrote to the Pierpont Morgan and a photocopy of the manuscript duly arrived from New York, the envelope bearing the postmark 13 April 1982.

After his remarkable Op. 1 (*The Tempest*, 1861–2) Sullivan set out to establish his reputation with a series of works in many genres, both vocal and instrumental. The year 1866 produced three of his most substantial orchestral works: his 'Irish' symphony (eventually published in 1915), the concert overture *In Memoriam* (published in 1885) and the Concerto for Cello and Orchestra in D major. This was composed 'expressly for and dedicated to Signor Alfredo Piatti' (1822–1901), who gave the first performance at the Crystal Palace on 24 November 1866; he played it again in Edinburgh on 17 December. Further performances took place at a 'Sullivan Night' at Covent Garden on 18 October 1873; at the Town Hall, Westminster, (soloist J. Edward Hambleton) on 16 February 1887; and in the Winter Gardens, Bournemouth, (under the redoubtable Sir Dan Godfrey) on 12 May 1910 (soloist May Mukle). Its last known performance was that given by William Pleeth and Charles Mackerras on 7 July 1953.

The work was considered by some to be not wholly satisfactory (Sullivan's friend Rachel Scott Russell advised him to rewrite it) and this may be why it was never published. Perhaps its greatest weakness is the first movement, an Allegro moderato of just 75 bars, little more than a preamble to the second movement (an Andante espressivo of 147 bars). The third movement (457 bars) is an exhilarating Molto vivace, much of the solo part being in the nature of a 'moto perpetuo'. Halfway through this movement the opening material of the first movement makes a dramatic reappearance, and it could be argued that the work is thus cyclic in form. The striking opening of the work uses the notes of the tonic triad (D F♯ A) and these notes also form the opening of the second movement, which is in the dominant key of A. This is wholly characteristic, as much of Sullivan's writing is derived from triadic melodies.

I hoped eventually to produce a fully orchestrated reconstruction, but first an underlying harmonic structure had to be achieved. In a concerto the soloist does not play all the time (e.g. not in an orchestral tutti) and I was apprehensive as to how such gaps might be indicated. To my great relief, however, the copyist had indicated some thematic content for each bar – an Ariadne thread running throughout the entire 679 bars of the concerto and ensuring that, whatever I might arrive at by way of a reconstruction, there would be some genuine Sullivan (mainly melodic) in every bar.

The first task was to prepare the ground for a short score, i.e. to draw out 679 empty bars – a single stave for the solo part and a further two staves below for the realisation, effectively a basic harmonisation of the melodic line as a piano accompaniment, with indications as to the possible orchestration. Several indications are marked in the copyist's manuscript: an oboe solo in bars 26–8 of the opening movement; octave horns at bars 1–2 of the second movement (presumably soli) followed by violins (bars 3–4); clarinets and bassoons in the third movement at bars 194–6, presumably extending at least to bar 197, where the soloist enters with the movement's second subject. Other orchestral lines are simply marked 'tutti'.

I sat for hours at the piano, playing the single line over and over again, trying to decide what harmonies Sullivan would have used and how this might be translated into an orchestral texture. As so often with manuscripts, it was not always precisely clear what was intended, and occasionally decisions had to be made, both regarding certain notes and consequently regarding the harmonisation of certain passages. But eventually, as I became more familiar with the material and tried to relate it to the music of Sullivan that I already knew, an 'accompaniment' slowly began to emerge.

Some parts were easier to realise than others, particularly where there was a strong melodic line, as in the tutti sections. The opening theme of the first movement begins with a tonic triad which could be harmonised in a number of ways, although one did suggest itself almost immediately. With the entry of the solo cello at bar 31 things became more difficult. After an initial melodic phrase (which Sullivan may have taken from Mendelssohn's Cello Sonata in D, op. 58) the soloist plunges into rapid passagework, and finding the harmonic structure to support this took much longer. I eventually devised an accompaniment based on the triadic opening of the work.

The opening theme of the second movement is also based on the tonic triad, but it could not be harmonised in the same way, partly due to the fact that the first movement is in quadruple time while the second is in triple time; this illustrates how rhythm plays an important part in distinguishing melodies that may derive from the same material. Also, the opening triadic phrase is immediately followed by its retrograde, which simply suggested the tonic chord. This seemed a little bland, but I achieved some harmonic interest by setting the first four bars of the melody over a tonic pedal (a device much used by Sullivan) and adding a minor seventh to the tonic chord, effecting a brief modulation to the subdominant before returning to the tonic.

The third movement was perhaps the most difficult. Again there is much rapid passagework, where the soloist should not be swamped by too much accompaniment, and in some instances I thought it better to let the soloist be simply a solo instrument, with just an occasional chord every few bars. One sequence, repeated in the recapitulation, took some time to figure out. Coming in the middle of a long passage of unbroken quaver movement, this section seemed to be meandering aimlessly until I realised that it was essentially a decorated version of an underlying harmonic sequence which modulated through several keys; the problem was solved.

After the statements of the first and second subject material in the third movement, there is a passage where a development section would normally come in a sonata-form movement. At this point the soloist again seems to be indulging in 'figurations': some forty bars of chordal activation which also mask an underlying harmonic sequence. Having determined the sequence, I realised that an accompaniment to this could also be fashioned out of the initial triadic material, and was able to create a short 'development' from the opening phrase of both the first and second movements. I even discovered that a phrase from *Patience* (1881) fitted neatly against several bars of passagework in the solo part and used this in the realisation.

I began the first draft of the reconstruction on 21 May 1982 and completed it on 1 March 1983. The next step was to turn this short score into a full score, and this took much less time: begun on 23 March 1983, it was finished less than a month later, on 20 April, almost exactly a year to the day after I had received the manuscript from the Pierpont Morgan. As for scoring, I decided to use the same instrumentation as two famous nineteenth-century works: Mendelssohn's Violin Concerto and Schumann's Cello Concerto, the latter supposedly having been the inspiration for Sullivan's concerto.

Having reached this stage, I then wrote to Sir Charles Mackerras. He was in Australia at the time, but wrote back to say that he was very interested to hear that I had completed a reconstruction of the concerto and would very much like to see it when he returned. Shortly after I received his letter, and quite unexpectedly, I was contacted by the publisher Josef Weinberger to say that Sir Charles had passed on my letter and that they were interested in taking the project further, with a view to eventual publication. I then went to Weinberger and played over my reconstruction from the piano draft. They seemed pleased with what they heard, but said that they would like Sir Charles to put his seal of approval on whatever eventually appeared. Given his stature in the profession, his interest in Sullivan generally and the fact that he had conducted a performance of the original concerto, I had little choice but to acquiesce!

I met Sir Charles on his return to London and we went over my orchestral score together. He made a number of suggestions, one of them being that he seemed to remember that the string parts in the outer sections of the second movement (in ABA form) were marked pizzicato, rather like the accompaniment to Captain Corcoran's 'Fair moon, to thee I sing' from *HMS Pinafore* (1878) and Colonel Fairfax's 'Free from his fetters grim' from *The Yeomen of the Guard* (1888). He also thought that the original scoring lacked trumpets and timpani, although when finally published the score contained both. He told me that he had been asked several times if he might attempt a reconstruction himself but had never found the time to sit down and tackle it.

Having perused the score, Sir Charles then said, in so many words, 'take it away and thin it out a bit; I think it was more lightly scored'. Rather than simply alter the existing score, I started again and made a second full score, at the same time incorporating other changes to the realisation, including marking the string parts 'pizz' in the appropriate sections of the second movement; this was done between 27 November 1983 and 2 February 1984. I saw Sir Charles again and he said he thought it was a distinct improvement on the first version. Weinberger had decided to go ahead with the project and Sir Charles retained this second score to make further changes for publication. Some of his alterations were to my realisation of the harmonic underlay, although the majority were to the scoring itself. One major change, which I had not thought to attempt, was in the last movement. In the recapitulation of the second subject, he managed to introduce elements of the first subject material in a manner often used by Sullivan (indeed, he claimed to have invented it), where two seemingly disparate ideas, first heard separately, are then heard together.

At around this time Sir Charles was taken ill with hepatitis and had to stop conducting. He took advantage of this enforced idleness to revise and improve my second version into the score that was eventually published; he also added alternative cadenzas to the one at the end of the first movement. While Sir Charles was recovering from his illness and working on the concerto, to everyone's surprise yet another source turned up. This was a further copy of the solo part and had been made for May Mukle for the Bournemouth performance in 1910. The part had been handed down through her family and was unearthed by the conductor Tom Higgins. This version differs from the Pierpont Morgan copy in being incomplete in the third movement, there being no orchestral indications for a number of bars; also, where there are indications in movements 1 and 2 they are of bass rather than melody lines, and these were incorporated into the score.

With the reconstruction ready for publication, the next step was to prepare a piano reduction. My first version, finished by February 1986, was too complicated, as I had tried to include just about everything that was in the full score, making it virtually unplayable (clearly I hadn't learned from having had to reduce the scoring of my original conception). I therefore made a second, simpler version which I finished on 5 March 1986. I also recall Sir Charles (who had made his own piano reduction of *Pineapple Poll*) saying 'don't give too much away' (i.e. don't let the public see everything; make them buy a full score!). My revised reduction was accepted by Weinberger and published along with the full score.

The first performance of our reconstruction (at the Barbican, London) was on 20 April 1986 – three years to the day after I had completed the first orchestration of my original draft. The soloist was Julian Lloyd Webber, with the London Symphony Orchestra conducted by Sir Charles; later that year they recorded the work for EMI. A second performance took place in Manchester on 27 April. The soloist was again Julian Lloyd Webber, but this time with the Manchester Camerata conducted by Brian Wright. The critics were mostly unenthusiastic, one calling it 'merely a piece of juvenilia', another 'hardly a masterpiece'; perhaps the most positive comment came later, in a review of the recording, which said: 'cheerful, unpretentious, lopsided; the racy finale is best'. Whatever its shortcomings, the concerto has continued to receive performances and it is now possible to present a concert devoted entirely to Sullivan's music, on the traditional lines of an overture (several to choose from), a concerto and a symphony.

Reconstructing the concerto was a labour of love made easier by my absorption of Sullivan's music over the previous decade, but it was immensely fulfilling to produce a fully orchestrated work from a single line of music, without ever having heard the original. It was – to borrow a phrase from

W. S. Gilbert – a 'privilege and pleasure that we treasure beyond measure' to collaborate with Sir Charles, who had actually conducted it, enabling this 'lost' work to be performed again.

13
Three Orchestras

Nigel Simeone

In the later years of his career, Charles Mackerras formed particularly close associations with three orchestras: the Orchestra of the Age of Enlightenment, the Scottish Chamber Orchestra and the Philharmonia Orchestra. He continued to appear as a regular guest with other British orchestras, especially the Royal Liverpool Philharmonic, the BBC Philharmonic and the City of Birmingham Symphony Orchestra, and in the last few years of his life his career blossomed in Europe. As well as conducting regular concerts with the Czech Philharmonic (Principal Guest Conductor 1997–2003) and other leading orchestras in the Czech Republic (see Chapter 9), he made a hugely successful debut with the Berlin Philharmonic in 2004 at the instigation of Simon Rattle – in a programme of Dvořák, Mozart and Janáček – and this was followed by several return visits. He also made his first appearances with two other great German orchestras – the Gewandhaus Orchestra in Leipzig and the Staatskapelle in Dresden – and returned to the Vienna Philharmonic. Before he stopped travelling to the United States, Mackerras served as Music Director of the Orchestra of St Luke's in New York (1998–2001); and when he travelled to Australia – his last visit was in 2007 – he conducted the Sydney Symphony and Melbourne Symphony. The three orchestras at the core of this chapter were British ensembles with which he had particularly long and happy relationships. He was always fascinated by the possibilities of working with the period instruments of the OAE; he developed the SCO into one of the finest chamber orchestras in Europe; and he spent eight seasons as Principal Guest Conductor of the Philharmonia, an experience he described as 'among the most wonderful things to happen to me'.

The Orchestra of the Age of Enlightenment

'And there was light!' Sir Charles and the OAE

Chi-chi Nwanoku

It's an emotional experience remembering our performances with Sir Charles Mackerras. He worked with the Orchestra of the Age of Enlightenment from the end of its first season (June 1987) until *Così fan tutte* at Glyndebourne on 12 June 2010, the last performance he ever gave. He was a conductor I loved to work with – how could I not, when he always greeted me with such enthusiasm? As a musician, I was always able to trust myself completely in his hands – there was never any doubt. It was like one heart speaking to another through music, and often words weren't needed at all, because he showed everything with a look or a gesture. Sir Charles was not a glamorous figure in the current *celebrity* style; he was refreshingly, delightfully down-to-earth, and there was always such expressiveness and poetry in his gestures, with a fluidity that embodied the music. The Mozart operas we did with Sir Charles at Glyndebourne – *Magic Flute* and *Così fan tutte* – were memorable. Being a curious person, I want to know as much as possible about everything I play, so to learn about musical gems, especially from someone as wise as Sir Charles, was a privilege. And part of his wisdom was to understand that things could always change, or be tried in new ways: even in an opera he may have conducted hundreds of times, he never lost that desire to experiment. The last *Così* was very difficult for him – the cancer meant that he was in great pain – but once he was on the rostrum the energy and the sparkle were still there.

We did a lot of core repertoire with Sir Charles over the years in the OAE. One of the orchestra's first recordings was made with him, Schubert's 'Great' C major Symphony, and the symphony featured in later performances with him. I listened to the CD again recently and was riveted by its sheer compelling stature, rhythm and *life*! He was the embodiment of rhythmic energy. As an orchestral player, you always have to be open to what the person on the rostrum wants; you have to be ready to receive and replicate what they give (whether you agree with it or not!), but with Sir Charles there was always a convincing and inspiring interpretation that I felt compelled to go with. He breathed with the music, allowing it to say what it needed to, so as a player I always felt he gave me space and freedom to play it accordingly.

If I had to choose my Number One experience with the OAE, it was when Sir Charles conducted Haydn's *Creation* in 1989. I had played the piece several times before, but it was Sir Charles who made it come to life – to speak with an eloquence I'd never known before, to tell the story, making me hear it through his eyes and mind. I had the advantage of playing the double bass continuo for this performance, and Sir Charles put me in a place where bass players don't often find themselves: right at the front, under his nose, next to the fortepiano! When he talked to us during rehearsals, it was to find the best ways of bringing Haydn's musically explicit evocations of creatures, plants and mankind off the page, and to capture exactly the right mood. He split the tutti cellos and basses between the sides of the platform, which made for quite an effect when 'God created great whales' – they seemed to slither around the whole orchestra, with me swimming upstream in the middle! The most touching memory of Sir Charles's *Creation* was the depiction of Sunrise (No. 12, 'In splendour bright'). He talked to us about the moon and stars appearing for the first time in such a vivid way that I could almost *see* them! With every little dissonance, there appeared another star. And, when we played this movement, he made full use of Haydn's harmonies during the first few bars, creating so much expectation – until exactly the great moment when the entire orchestra at full tilt explodes as the sun bursts through. That really is an unforgettable moment in my musical life.

Sir Charles was extremely exacting in rehearsals and seemed to relish the collaboration with OAE, exploring what original instruments could (or couldn't!) do and never missing the opportunity to urge us to our limits. The results of this usually took us onto a different playing field that we were not expecting – to our benefit. His curiosity and excitement was palpable. He got frustrated occasionally – I remember once he asked a player 'Why can't you just get it … *right*?' – but an event like our *Creation* was a kind of magical adventure. With other repertoire and performances he did with us, including Handel, Mozart and Mendelssohn, it was unfailingly insightful. There were the operas, of course, and a lot else besides. The 'Haffner' Symphony and C minor Mass that we played at the Proms in 2006 – the concert Sir Charles dedicated to the memory of his daughter Fiona, who had died a few days earlier – are forever etched in my memory. Words could never give justice to the strength of music and emotion experienced that evening.

Few conductors I have worked with have come bearing such thorough knowledge of what ticks behind the notes on the page. That, coupled with his sheer joy in music-making, serving the orchestra and enabling us to better understand the whole – our responsibility in serving it – leaves me forever indebted.

When I played for Sir Charles, it felt as if the sky was the limit, and that I could lose myself completely in the music. I felt empowered in his hands.

FOUNDED in 1986, the Orchestra of the Age of Enlightenment had a policy from the start of inviting different conductors to work with it on period-instrument performances of a repertoire that stretched from Bach to the nineteenth century. It did not work exclusively with early music specialists, but also with modern orchestral conductors: in its first seasons the OAE engaged Sigiswald Kuijken, Gustav Leonhardt, Roger Norrington, Simon Rattle, Mark Elder and Charles Mackerras; later on, Vladimir Jurowski, Marin Alsop and Iván Fischer worked with the orchestra. This was an unusual practice for period-instrument groups, most of which were directed exclusively by one conductor, often its founder (as many still are today). Mackerras first conducted the Orchestra of the Age of Enlightenment on 2 June 1987 at the Barbican Hall in an all-Mozart programme. A few months later, he appeared with the OAE at the Queen Elizabeth Hall on two consecutive nights (9 and 10 October) in programmes that showed him exploring the possibilities of using period instruments in music of the early nineteenth century: Schubert, Weber and Mendelssohn. These concerts led to recordings: of Schubert's 'Great' C major Symphony and of Mendelssohn's 'Italian' Symphony and *Midsummer Night's Dream* incidental music. Both were made for the Virgin Classics label and were among the first recordings of these works on period instruments, in performances that stood out for their vitality and imagination as well as for the sound of the orchestra. The artistic success of this enterprise quickly led the self-governing OAE to invite Mackerras back for more concerts, including Haydn's *Creation* in 1989 – a work he repeated with the OAE at Glyndebourne in 2000 and at the Proms in 2002 (oddly, Mackerras never recorded the work; it remains one of the most surprising gaps in his discography).

In an interview to mark the twenty-first birthday of the OAE, Mackerras talked about the practical challenges facing the players – and he was clearly sympathetic to the difficulties:

> Playing a period instrument is like driving a car and having to double de-clutch. The handicaps that one suffers with those wind instruments are tremendous. Instruments were built so your fingers could go over the holes, but the holes were not necessarily in the best place for 'just' intonation. Playing the horn and making those chromatic notes with your fist, trying to get the tone consistent, is incredibly hard – the horn players have to work so much harder to get it in tune, although Andrew Clark and Roger Montgomery and all the other OAE horn players do it extremely well. And gut strings are unstable – they do go out of tune very quickly.[1]

Having discovered a group of players that was willing to make the effort to play these instruments, Mackerras was excited by the musical possibilities that opened up, and, as for overcoming the technical and mechanical difficulties, he had no doubts:

> I never wondered for a moment whether it was worth it: it was an inspiration. To be able to hear the phrasing, the sounds – the fact that the notes decay so much more rapidly, it opens up the texture. And it also answers a whole lot of questions, like the Overture to *Don Giovanni* – the minim in the bass and the crotchet at the top, they are really quite similar because of the way the sound decays. In modern times people mistakenly sustain it [the bass] through the bar. It's taught me a tremendous amount.[2]

[1] Wallace 2006, p. 18.

[2] Ibid.

In 1994 the repertoire Mackerras performed with the OAE moved forward to Wagner and Brahms. In terms of balance, the more transparent sound of old instruments made it possible to achieve a more natural balance between the orchestra and the soloist, Elizabeth Wallfisch. In May 1998 Mackerras conducted another programme of late Romantic repertoire with the OAE: Dvořák's *Czech Suite*, Chopin with Emanuel Ax (playing an early Erard piano) and the First Serenade by Brahms. The *Czech Suite* was a Mackerras speciality and he had recorded it in 1969 with the English Chamber Orchestra, but period-instrument Dvořák in 1998 was a real novelty. The first edition of the *Czech Suite* includes an endearingly eccentric footnote at the start of the fourth movement: 'In the absence of a Cor Anglais, a Basset horn may be used.' To replace an unusual instrument with one that was virtually obsolete in Dvořák's time was a curious suggestion – and the explanation was that Dvořák originally wrote the part for basset horn but changed it to cor anglais at the request of the publisher, Schlesinger. Mackerras liked to revert to the original basset horn whenever a player was available.

One of Mackerras's happiest experiences with the OAE was Mozart's *Magic Flute* at Glyndebourne in 2005. He had long wanted to perform this opera using period instruments and was delighted with the results. He was a great deal less delighted by the flat refusal of Chandos to employ the OAE for the recording he made about the same time for the Opera in English series (see Chapter 8). But he was able to use the orchestra for his Chandos recording of *Così fan tutte* (again in English), and at Glyndebourne in 2010 it was the OAE that was again in the pit for what turned out to be Mackerras's very last performances.

He always felt close to the musicians in this orchestra, and his work with the OAE coincided with three central events in his later life: when he first worked with the orchestra in 1987, he was also visiting his grand-daughter Alice in the Royal Free Hospital in the days before she died; it was with the OAE that he conducted the Mozart concert at the Proms in memory of his daughter Fiona in 2006; and it was with these players that he gave his own final performance.

The Scottish Chamber Orchestra

An electric entrance[3]

Rosenna East

From the front of the second violins in the Scottish Chamber Orchestra, we always had a straight line of sight to Sir Charles Mackerras waiting in the wings, minutes before a concert. Poised expectantly at the edge of our seats on stage, draped in long black evening dresses and surrounded by the auspicious red and gold of the Usher Hall, my desk partner and I cherished especially that private view of our maestro.

Receiving the nod from stage management that it was time to make his entrance, he was transformed. The brightness of his white tie and dress shirt were eclipsed by the beaming grin that would light up his no longer elderly face, as with a sharp backwards thrust of his shoulders he would shake off his years.

Pulled up like a cadet suddenly called to military attention, he would shoot out of the wings into the bright lights of the platform, heading for the podium like a boy to the sweetshop. His electric entrance, accompanied by rapturous applause before even a note had been played, never failed to inspire our orchestra to play at its best.

Performing or recording with Sir Charles, we only ever worked from his own personal orchestral parts. Nobody else's would do – no hire parts or modern editions. Sir Charles had collected his precious Breitkopf parts of the Beethoven and Mozart symphonies on trips to the former Communist bloc. Paid his fees from the Berlin Staatsoper in East German marks, unusable in Western Europe, he came up with the idea of spending the money on building his own library of orchestral repertoire. Any musician who worked with him will know how delicate those parts were. He would apologise for the lamentably poor quality of the East German paper, but we knew he was delighted to tell the story of their origins.

Revision after revision had been made to these treasured parts by Sir Charles. Corrections to historical misprints, as well as interpretative markings, were the result, first, of careful personal scholarship in the libraries and archives of the world, further honed by years of experience of what worked best in the concert hall. But his wealth of scholarly knowledge never closed down debate, as it might with some. He was always open to a new suggestion – from leader Chris George, with a new bowing that might just work better; or from David Watkin, principal cello, whose style of playing broken chords for cello continuo parts Sir Charles first adopted in our recording of Mozart's *Clemenza di Tito* and used from then onwards with such delight.

That continual striving for the highest standards of music-making gave Sir Charles a justifiable pride and pleasure in his work. The same enthusiasm

[3] This text is adapted from Rosenna East's tribute, first published in *The Herald* (Glasgow) on 17 July 2010. It is included here by kind permission of the publisher.

and delight which he brought with him to the stage was palpable in the recording studio. In the 'box' with the sound engineers and record producers, and with his principal players gathered around him to hear the recent takes, my memory is of him being meticulous with detail but, more often than not, delighted by what he heard. After our recordings of the Beethoven symphonies live from the Edinburgh International Festival in 2006, he was enormously proud to tell us that there would be no need for a 'patching' session – a recording session in which we would have expected to iron out the blemishes and mishaps of a live performance.

Days before he died, Sir Charles was still working on the score of *Idomeneo*, an opera that he adored and which he was due to conduct with us at the Edinburgh Festival 2010. To the end, his passion for his work, and for the music, remained undimmed – a lasting inspiration to all who knew him.

In July 1992, Charles Mackerras was appointed Chief Guest Conductor (later Conductor Laureate) of the Scottish Chamber Orchestra. The central focus of their work together was often at the Edinburgh International Festival, but there were also numerous recordings, including some of the finest of Mackerras's later years. He had worked extensively with chamber orchestras since the start of his career, beginning in the early 1950s with the Goldsborough Orchestra (which became the English Chamber Orchestra in 1960), and later with ensembles such as the Prague Chamber Orchestra, the Australian Chamber Orchestra and the Orchestra of St Luke's in New York. Some of his favourite repertoire was ideal for orchestras of this size: Haydn, Mozart, Schubert and much of Beethoven, as well as lesser-known composers that Mackerras championed, such as J. C. Bach, Arriaga and Voříšek.

One of his most productive relationships with any chamber orchestra was his long association with the Scottish Chamber Orchestra. This was an ensemble that was always happy to try out his ideas; not least the horn and trumpet players, who were willing and able to use natural instruments, and the strings, to use only sparing vibrato. In terms of orchestral sonority, this was an important development in Mackerras's musical thinking from the 1990s onwards: bringing elements of historically informed performance practice to what was essentially a modern chamber orchestra by using the likes of natural horns, narrow-bore trombones and period timpani. The results, particularly in the Mozart, Beethoven and Brahms recordings with the SCO, demonstrate how effective such an approach could be. Mackerras was never dogmatic about performance practice, but he always aimed for a stylish and idiomatic sound, whether he was working with old instruments or new ones. With the SCO, he often felt that he had the best of both worlds.

The lasting legacy of the work Mackerras did with the SCO includes an extensive discography. Several important recordings were made for the American label Telarc: complete recordings of five Mozart operas (including his only commercial recordings of *Figaro* and *Entführung*), Beethoven's *Fidelio*, symphonies by Schubert and a revelatory Brahms cycle. For other labels, the SCO and Mackerras recorded Mozart piano concertos with Brendel (Philips), *Idomeneo* (EMI), *La Clemenza di Tito* (DG), Beethoven's Symphonies Nos 1–8 and *Creatures of Prometheus*, Arriaga and Voříšek (Hyperion), and, finally, a remarkable series of late recordings for Linn, including Mozart's mature symphonies (Nos 29, 31, 32, 35, 36 and 38–41) and Requiem (edited by Robert Levin), three Beethoven piano concertos with Artur Pizarro, and a disc of Bartók and Kodály.

Numerous they may be, but Mackerras's recordings with the SCO reveal only some of the repertoire they performed live. One remarkable series given at the Edinburgh Festival in 1999 included all of Schumann's symphonies (with both versions of the Fourth), the *Overture, Scherzo and Finale* and the solo concertos. These were broadcast on BBC Radio 3 but no commercial recordings were made. Other repertoire that Mackerras performed with the SCO included concert performances of operas at the Edinburgh Festival: not only the Mozart series, which was recorded, but also Donizetti's *Maria Stuarda*, Verdi's *Macbeth* and Weber's *Der Freischütz*, along with oratorios such as Handel's *Saul* and *Jephtha* and Haydn's *Creation* and operatic rarities such as Benda's *Ariadne auf Naxos*. During the main concert season with the orchestra, he conducted large-scale works by Bach that he had performed rarely since the 1970s: the *St John Passion* and *Christmas Oratorio* (both in 1993) and the *St Matthew Passion* in 1995.

Working with the SCO was something Mackerras found increasingly congenial as he grew older: it gave him the opportunity to perform favourite repertoire with an ensemble that was the size he wanted and which played with astonishing finesse; it also allowed him to work on concertos with soloists he particularly admired, especially Alfred Brendel, with whom the orchestra collaborated not only in the studio but also in numerous live concerts in Scotland, at the Proms and on tour in Europe. But Mackerras's crowning achievements with the SCO are the Beethoven cycle from the 2006 Edinburgh Festival and the very late Mozart recordings, which are a joyous combination of stylishness, irrepressible energy and wisdom.

On Sir Charles Mackerras

Alfred Brendel

Philips, my former record company, and I were looking for the right conductor to do new recordings of some of Mozart's piano concertos. If you have ever tried to find a Mozart conductor, you know what a tall order this is. But after a performance of the D minor Concerto (K466) with the Scottish Chamber Orchestra at the Edinburgh Festival it was clear whom to aim at, and Sir Charles seemed to like the idea. Over the years, we recorded six of the concertos, with the G major K453 possibly the most vivid – the work was a Mackerras favourite. Ultimately, he conducted the very last performance of my career, K271 with the Vienna Philharmonic at the Musikverein in December 2008, which was taped by the Austrian Radio and issued by Decca.

When we embarked on our first recording venture in Edinburgh's Usher Hall, I was suffering from an appalling cold. I recall myself hanging over the keyboard trying to hear whether I was really playing Mozart's C minor Concerto (and I still rather like the recording).

Sitting at Edinburgh Airport one afternoon with Sir Charles, we were talking so intensely that we missed the plane which should have taken us to somewhere near Aldeburgh. I don't remember how we ever got there in the end.

Among orchestral musicians, the period-style trills he asked them to play were known as 'Charlies'. He was always equipped with a myriad of little stickers that he was able to place in the scores during playback in order to remind himself of what needed to improve.

Sir Charles was a unique combination of learnedness, practical professionalism and a temperament that imbued his live performances with a youthful drive right up to the end of his life. I greatly valued this freshness and radiance that, unlike the lingering of some of his ageing colleagues, always propelled the music forward.

At the end of the funeral at St Paul's, Covent Garden, the priest did something wonderful: he encouraged the mourners to give Sir Charles one last ovation. The applause was endless.

The Philharmonia Orchestra

Sir Charles at the Philharmonia

David Whelton

I first came to know Sir Charles when I was working at the Leeds Festival in the 1980s, with the big choral works he did there; I was very young and he was quite brusque. After I came to the Philharmonia in 1988, he had mellowed a great deal and I tried to get him then – I was always a big fan. So I went to see his agent at the time – Gorlinsky – and Gorlinsky threw me out! When Paul Findlay got Sir Charles to the RPO as his Principal Guest Conductor, I didn't want to tread all over Paul's plans, so I stood back. But after he left the RPO – and Gorlinsky had died – I tried again. I actually just jumped on the train and went up to see him in Edinburgh, and doorstepped him having lunch with Lord Harewood – that's all, and that was how it started. I chatted to him about the orchestra and the players we had, and then there was that magical moment when he took out his little handwritten diary and started rubbing things out, and he said: 'Well, I can do this, and this and this.'

The role of Sir Charles's agent, Robert Rattray, was crucial in all this. He was a marvellous colleague who did so much to structure the schedule in a way that made everything work for us. There were three things which I believe should have happened in Sir Charles's career. First, he should have been in charge of the Royal Opera House: it would have been transformed beyond belief at that point in the 1980s. Second, he should have gone to Robert Rattray earlier: they had known each other for years because of singers. And third, he should have had one of the big London orchestras.

Of course, by the time all this fell into place for us, we didn't have a vacancy, because Christoph von Dohnányi was our Principal Conductor, and very happy – and he was delighted for Sir Charles to become Principal Guest Conductor. But Mackerras should have had one of the big London orchestras: the imagination and character of his music-making was just breathtaking, and it was a great privilege for us to work with him. The orchestra suited him very, very well, because it's very quick and flexible, and very giving. It was an incredibly intimate relationship with everybody in the orchestra, because we all just sat round and discussed what he wanted to do. Sometimes he would ask for narrow-bore trombones or natural trumpets, and I'd say, 'Well, we can certainly do all that.' He'd want to know what to do next and I'd suggest that he just ring up the players. I knew they'd be thrilled to hear from him and get a direct contact like that. This had always been his way of working with singers, after all, and we were just translating that into the same kind of relationship with these wonderfully gifted players.

I must say that one of the best concerts of my life was his last Beethoven 'Pastoral' at the Royal Festival Hall in December 2009. In my job, you have a whole list of pieces where you search for the ideal performance as you go through life. And the 'Pastoral' is one of the *most* elusive pieces – it's almost impossible to capture it – but he did. On that one occasion it was just perfection itself. The earlier Tchaikovsky *Pathétique* was another unforgettable occasion: again, he seemed to capture that like nobody else. Of course, there were the pieces he wanted to do but never got round to: imagine what *Heldenleben* would have sounded like with the Philharmonia horn section – it would have been a real humdinger!

Another thing about the Philharmonia is that they had a complete understanding of what he wanted to achieve. I don't know how they did this, but the musicians told me they just looked at him and knew what he wanted. It was very strange – and when you talk to the players they don't understand how this happened either, but they *knew*. And, when you've got communication like that, everything becomes easy from that point on. My two regrets are that he died too early and that he didn't start earlier with us. But it was nearly ten glorious years, and fortunately we have quite a few live recordings made at concerts which serve as documents of what was achieved. Of course, it's part of a conductor's job to build relationships with an orchestra and try to get the best out of it, but in his case the concerts just took off: you had a sense of the orchestra always straining to give its best for him.

In a curious way, the Philharmonia has a tradition of working well with elderly conductors, such as Klemperer and then Kurt Sanderling. Sir Charles, though, had a life force, even when he was ill. One of the reasons the relationship was so good was because some of the players in the orchestra had worked with him before in different areas. They always sensed then that there was the potential for something very special, but the circumstances hadn't yet come together to make it happen. I think he'd always been tremendously good, and intellectually curious, with a superhuman appetite for hard work, but for a long time he felt he still had something to prove. And it wasn't until he finally convinced himself that he didn't have to do that any more, that he reduced the workload and created more space to be himself. Then the music-making went onto an even more extraordinary level, because within him there was a more relaxed sort of inner world. To an extent he got over the disappointment of not getting the job at Covent Garden – but only to an extent. I remember that when he was made a Companion of Honour in 2003 I went to represent the orchestra at Buckingham Palace. He was immensely pleased, like a kid in a toy shop. To be recognised by the Establishment in that way was a huge thrill for him.

Every time he chatted about orchestral repertoire, he was always talking about Mahler. But the conversations were driven partly by me, explaining that every orchestra needs this thorough grounding in the Classical repertoire – Mozart through to Schubert, Schumann and Brahms – because that's where you cultivate the sound of the string section, and the orchestra's character grows from that. So for me, given the vision he brought to those pieces and the freshness of his interpretations, it was very important for us that he did that repertoire. And of course he was very happy to do it. Then, from his side, he'd say: 'David, I want to do Sibelius this, Mahler that, Tchaikovsky the other,' and I said: 'Of course, that's all fine, it's all yours – just tell me when you want to do it and it'll be *done*.' Those were the sort of conversations we had, and it really was that easy – and very exciting too. It was very similar to dealing with Christoph von Dohnányi. You knew with him that when you went through a rehearsal schedule together it would work, and nothing would be changed. That's such a wonderful feeling for an orchestra – for all my colleagues here. Sir Charles was exactly like that: everything had been thought through; he came to every discussion completely prepared, with all his colossal experience, so it was all just terribly easy.

Above all, I think, for me, it was just a joy knowing that the programmes which came out of these conversations were going to be so wonderful. There was no hesitation – you just knew it would be marvellous. And, when it came to soloists, the Philharmonia can usually get the people a conductor wants; we're lucky in that it's easy for us to do.

It was a fantastic time, personally and professionally. And Sir Charles has left his mark on the orchestra: a conductor of that stature lives on in its DNA, and he also lives on as a benchmark against which other artists are measured and judged. With the Philharmonia, the orchestra has a very distinct sound – the character's there – and conductors come to the orchestra and enjoy that straight away. But the really great conductors like Sir Charles then mould and shape that sound in unforgettable ways. It was a special relationship, and I think we got the best from each other. But one reason for that was that he completely understood British musical life, and London in particular. It's the hardest thing for me and my colleagues to try and explain to conductors how London orchestras work – both the strengths and the weaknesses. As a musician, Sir Charles grew up with this orchestra – he knew it inside out – and that's why he knew how to get the best out of everybody. There was no mistaking that at all. When he came to us, there was never any doubt that it would work. They were some of the happiest years of my life, and very special.

An undated document among Charles Mackerras's papers was probably written around the time of his appointment as Principal Guest Conductor of the Philharmonia, in 2002. Headed 'Large works which I would like to conduct before I die!',[4] it gives a glimpse into the conductor's aspirations towards the end of his life (see Figure 4).

Some of the pieces on this list reflect Mackerras's love of French music (Debussy's *La Mer*, *Images* and *Nocturnes*, Ravel's *Daphnis et Chloé* and *La Valse*), and he clearly wanted to return to Stravinsky's *Sacre du Printemps* and *Petrushka*. As well as works by British composers (Delius and Elgar) and Russians (Shostakovich and Tchaikovsky), there are also large works by Sibelius and Strauss. He had done many of these with other orchestras, but some had not appeared in his programmes before: the prospect of Strauss's *Heldenleben* or Sibelius's First Symphony with the Philharmonia is a tantalising one. But Mackerras did go on to perform a number of the works from his wish list with the Philharmonia, including Elgar's First Symphony,

[4] Mackerras family archives.

Sebastian Ochsenkun.

Russian

Tchai Suite in G (or only Variations) or Overture Russlan Suite Coq d'Or

—

Shostakovitch 5th

?

Petroushka or Sacre de Printemps

—

Tchai. 5 or 6.

Large Works which I would like to conduct before I die!

Heldenleben — Till, Don Juan

Elgar I — Intro & Allegro

Shostakovitch 5 or 9

Brigg Fair, Paris, Appalachia, Irmelin, Fennimore

Village Romeo & J. (or parts)

La Mer — Images — Nocturnes

Tchaikovsky 5 or 6, Francesca da R., Romeo & Juliet

Daphnis & Chloe Suite No 2, La Valse

Sibelius 1, 2 or 5

Figure 4 Mackerras's list of 'Large works which I would like to conduct before I die!'

Tchaikovsky's *Pathétique* and Sibelius's Second (the Fifth was announced for a Philharmonia concert in the 2010–11 season, but Mackerras did not live to conduct it). The only operas on the list are by Delius; he was scheduled to conduct *A Village Romeo and Juliet* at Covent Garden in 2011. The absence of any Mahler from the list comes as a surprise, since he was a composer mentioned often in Mackerras's conversations with David Whelton, but he conducted only the Fourth Symphony with the Philharmonia.

The relationship between the Philharmonia and Mackerras as its Principal Guest Conductor was particularly warm and amicable, rooted in the tremendous admiration Mackerras had for the players. He had first worked with the orchestra in June 1955, when he recorded his Verdi ballet *The Lady and the Fool.* Throughout the rest of the 1950s he often stood in at sessions earmarked for Klemperer or Giulini when they were indisposed, recording overtures and other shorter orchestral pieces (see Discography). He first conducted the orchestra in a concert at the Royal Festival Hall on 5 March 1961: Prokofiev's 'Classical' Symphony, Mussorgsky's *Night on a Bare Mountain*, Khachaturian's Piano Concerto (with Mindru Katz as the soloist) and Rimsky-Korsakov's *Scheherazade.* He appeared with the orchestra from time to time in the 1960s and early 1970s, and again at a charity concert in the Royal Albert Hall, given on 16 January 1986 in aid of the Mexican Earthquake Fund: Verdi's Requiem with Ghena Dimitrova, Janet Baker, Ryland Davies and Robert Lloyd as the soloists.

David Whelton was appointed Managing Director of the Philharmonia in 1988 and, as he recalled, Mackerras was a conductor he wanted to engage for the orchestra. With Mackerras's existing commitments at WNO, in San Francisco and, especially, with the Royal Philharmonic Orchestra – of which Mackerras was Principal Guest Conductor from 1993 to 1996 – Whelton didn't feel he could poach him for the Philharmonia. But early in 2002 an ailing Wolfgang Sawallisch had to withdraw from a Beethoven cycle with the orchestra, and Mackerras was asked to take over the first two concerts, on 3 and 7 March. Though he had recorded a complete Beethoven cycle with the Liverpool Philharmonic in the 1990s, he had not conducted much orchestral Beethoven in London. Robert Maycock in *The Independent* (11 March 2002) congratulated the Philharmonia, which had 'managed a coup when it found Sir Charles Mackerras to take over for the first three symphonies':

> Everything was there at the outset in Beethoven's second *Leonore* overture. Rather than received tradition and best practice, the approach comes from acquired knowledge, personal practical experience and imaginative, lateral thinking. To the ear that means a mix of period-style influence and Romantic awareness: no original instruments but visible signs include a row of basses across the back, violins left and right, hard timpani sticks.
>
> The message was rhythmic vitality and definition, with a strong profile for the woodwind as well as the bass-line, coupled with lean

and vigorous string tone. Already in this [...] piece the playing had a sound of its own. Speeds were taut but never rigid, letting the music breathe without disrupting its momentum.

A magnificent *Eroica* in the second concert could have been the highlight of an entire season, but the real revelations came in the first two symphonies. Mackerras swapped their order in the programme, giving No. 1 the second half to itself as though to say this was the work of weight. Then he as near as contradicted himself by getting No. 2 played with brilliance, irresistible momentum and at times, as with the two moments in the Larghetto that anticipate the end of the *Pastoral*, an upsurge of intensity. Details were constantly alive and subtly ear-catching. Violins at one time played in a flurry rather than a fully articulated scale, the music of a young man in a rush, and at another enjoyed themselves in witty interplay between the sections. Repeats differed in tiny, cumulative ways such as the pattern of timpani attacks.

A few months later, on 25 June, Mackerras conducted a programme of Dvořák's *Amid Nature*, Mozart's Piano Concerto K488 (with Maria João Pires) and Berlioz's *Symphonie fantastique*. It was a concert that delighted both conductor and orchestra. Mackerras wrote to David Whelton the next day: 'I am still on quite a "high" after that performance in last night's concert,' asking him to display a thank-you letter on the orchestra's notice board:

To the Ladies and Gentlemen of the Philharmonia Orchestra

Before the euphoria wears off, I want to thank you from the bottom of my heart for your wonderful playing on Tuesday evening. I thought it was a really marvellous performance of the Berlioz, which became, in your hands, quite literally 'fantastique'!

I also thought that your performance of the unknown Dvořák piece on so little rehearsal was far better than any Czech orchestra who play these pieces every day.

I look forward eagerly to our next collaboration which is, from my point of view, not soon enough.

Many heartfelt thanks for an epoch-making concert.

Yours ever,

Charles Mackerras[5]

The euphoria was mutual, and on 28 June Whelton replied:

Congratulations on an absolutely stunning concert on Tuesday night. *Symphonie fantastique* was simply the best performance I have heard of this work – it was as if one was hearing it for the first time. I think the warmth and enthusiasm of the audience response said it all! [...] The Orchestra has a very special relationship with you, which is

[5] Mackerras family archives.

> manifest in the quality of music making. We are looking forward with great anticipation to all the plans we have discussed, and meanwhile would like to give you and Lady Mackerras all good wishes for a relaxing summer.[6]

At the time of this concert, Mackerras had close associations with the Orchestra of the Age of Enlightenment and the Scottish Chamber Orchestra but, though he conducted the RLPO, CBSO and BBC Philharmonic, he had no formal appointment with any symphony orchestra in London. The way was clear for him to work regularly with the Philharmonia, and both sides were eager to do more concerts together. David Whelton has written about how the relationship developed from there. By December, the budding association had been put on a formal footing. The concert on 8 December 2002, in which Mackerras conducted Beethoven's Ninth Symphony, preceded by the Second Piano Concerto with Murray Perahia, marked his appointment as Principal Guest Conductor of the Philharmonia. A few days later, Mackerras wrote to Whelton to say he was 'really delighted'. He was back with the orchestra in May 2003 with a pair of concerts (15 and 17 May). The first included his own suite from Janáček's *Cunning Little Vixen*, Bruch's Violin Concerto No. 1 (with Sarah Chang) and Elgar's First Symphony; the second opened with Dvořák's *Othello* Overture, Nikolai Lugansky was soloist in Tchaikovsky's First Piano Concerto and the programme ended with Brahms's Third Symphony.

The year 2004 was the 150th anniversary of Janáček's birth and the 100th of Dvořák's death. With the Philharmonia, Mackerras conducted Dvořák's Sixth Symphony, *Carnival* Overture and Cello Concerto in programmes alongside Janáček's *Taras Bulba* and *Glagolitic Mass*. In a series of concerts in March and April 2005, the orchestra performed all four Brahms symphonies with other orchestral works by Brahms (Piano Concerto No. 2 with Till Fellner, Serenade No. 2, *Tragic Overture*, *Academic Festival Overture*) and concertos by Mozart and Dvořák. Tom Service reviewed the first concert, given in the Festival Hall on 17 March, for the *Guardian* (19 March 2005):

> Hearing Charles Mackerras's performance of Brahms's First Symphony with the Philharmonia Orchestra was a revelatory experience, in which all of the hackneyed preconceptions about a composer and a piece were turned on their heads. Instead of sombre, self-conscious gloom, Mackerras made this piece thrillingly dynamic, energising every bar and every phrase. He gave the lie to the idea that Brahms orchestration is opaque and stodgy, making the orchestral textures lyrical and transparent whether in the radiant colours of the slow movement, with its seraphic solo violin line, or the dark visions in the opening of the finale. It was as if the piece were being imagined for the first time.

[6] Mackerras family archives.

Matthew Rye (*Daily Telegraph*, 24 March) reacted with similar enthusiasm to the second concert, given on 22 March, including the A major Serenade and the Third Symphony:

> Mackerras's approach to Brahms goes beyond simply being true to the instrumentation (he followed Brahmsian practice in dividing first and second violins across the front of the stage and placing the double basses centrally at the back). Here he was also led by the reported example of the composer's earliest interpreters, Hans von Bülow and Fritz Steinbach, in their use of flexible tempi. Rather than being completely metronomic, the speeds expand and contract with the meaning and expressiveness of the music, yet while this could suggest an exaggerated approach, the subtlety of Mackerras's conducting made the music sound truly organic, living and breathing before us. This was as true of the small-scale but often melancholy Serenade – the Philharmonia's woodwind and horns on shining form – as of the grander expanses of the Symphony, where the long-term dynamics of the music's course were as evident as its bar-to-bar detailing. And it is so refreshing to see a conductor still on a mission to change our perception of great music in his 80th year.

By the time Mackerras returned to the orchestra in June, he had become the most recent winner of the Gold Medal of the Royal Philharmonic Society (awarded to him on 11 May at the Dorchester Hotel). The two major works performed on 16 June were Mozart's Requiem in Robert Levin's edition and Elgar's Second Symphony. George Hall reviewed the Mozart in the *Guardian* (16 June 2005): 'Musically, this revision is as convincing as we are likely to get. This performance benefited from the Philharmonia Chorus's vigorous attack and a Philharmonia Orchestra playing with a strong sense of period style. But Mackerras's ability to energise music without coercing it paid special dividends, allowing him to inject genuine fear into the Dies irae and a solemn grandeur into the fugues.'

For a special gala concert (20 June 2006) to celebrate Mackerras's eightieth birthday year, the Philharmonia engaged Alfred Brendel as soloist in Mozart's final piano concerto, framed by the Overture and Venusberg Music from Wagner's *Tannhäuser* and Schubert's 'Great' C major Symphony. The orchestra was in Edinburgh on 1 September 2006 to play the Ninth Symphony at the end of a cycle that Mackerras had otherwise given with the Scottish Chamber Orchestra.

Mackerras stood in for an indisposed Christoph von Dohnányi in early 2007 for three further performances of Beethoven's Ninth Symphony (26, 30 January, 1 February) in Cardiff, Birmingham and Bristol (a live recording of the Birmingham performance was made available on the Philharmonia website as a download).

On 12 May 2007, Mackerras conducted the orchestra's last concert in the Queen Elizabeth Hall (used while the Royal Festival Hall was closed for refurbishment), including Beethoven's Violin Concerto with Viktoria

Mullova and Mozart's 'Jupiter' Symphony. The next day he sent a charming note to David Whelton:

> My dear David,
> [...] I am really overwhelmed that you, who are obviously a great wine connoisseur yourself, should have chosen such really *outstanding* vintages to present to me! I studied a chart of recent vintages & found that if I laid down some of the bottles as recommended, the wines would mature after my death, perhaps, or certainly after my retirement! However, whenever I do get a chance to drink them, I certainly want to thank you again most sincerely for your wonderful gift.
>
> One of the most wonderful things to happen to me in the twilight of my career is my association with the Philharmonia. I just love the musicians of this orchestra & I will certainly try & keep the association for as long as I can last out physically. With renewed thanks & good wishes,
>
> Yours ever,
> Charles M.[7]

Six weeks later, conductor and orchestra were back in the reopened Royal Festival Hall for a suitably triumphant programme: the Prelude to Act 1 of Wagner's *Meistersinger*, Mozart's grandest piano concerto (No. 25, K503) with Mitsuko Uchida and Janáček's *Sinfonietta* – the only time Mackerras conducted this favourite *cheval de bataille* with the Philharmonia. His fee for this concert was donated to Friends of the Earth to support its work on climate change: the conductor declared that it had 'influenced a colossal shift in the political debate and public perception of this issue'.

The concerts in 2008 were in two distinct groups. The first was a cleverly planned series of three concerts, each including a third symphony (by Schumann, Brahms and Beethoven) and a tone poem by Strauss (*Till Eulenspiegel*, *Also sprach Zarathustra* and *Don Juan*). Each programme also included a work involving a soloist: Beethoven's Fourth Piano Concerto with Lars Vogt, Mozart's Piano Concerto No. 18, K456, with Till Fellner, and Strauss's *Four Last Songs* sung by Solveig Kringelborn. Two Dvořák symphonies (Nos 7 and 8) were the major works in his programmes in October 2008, the second of which also marked Alfred Brendel's retirement from the London concert platform with Mozart's Piano Concerto K271.

Back with the orchestra in February 2009, Mackerras turned to Tchaikovsky's *Pathétique* and Elgar's First Symphony. Andrew Clements reviewed the Elgar in the *Guardian* (17 February 2009):

> One of the great delights of Charles Mackerras's burgeoning relationship with the Philharmonia has been the way in which it has enabled him to provide a reminder of the range of his sympathies.

[7] Mackerras family archives.

> His greatness as a Mozart interpreter, a pioneer in the period-instrument movement and a champion of the Czech repertoire (Janáček in particular) are only part of a much bigger story. [...]
>
> Elgar's First was the main work in Mackerras's second programme, and it was remarkable to hear the work presented with all the accretions of what passes for a 'performing tradition' stripped away. This was Elgar very much as a quintessentially European rather than indelibly English composer – as a contemporary and equal of Richard Strauss whose music needs no special pleading or allowances made.
>
> Yet this businesslike briskness never undervalued the symphony's poetry, or its power. With the violins divided to his left and right in authentic Elgar fashion, and the double basses and brass arrayed across the back of the platform, the orchestral sound had extraordinary depth and detail.
>
> The Philharmonia played superbly for Mackerras. They matched his breathtaking speed for the scurrying opening of the scherzo, kept the hymning of the great slow movement free of sentiment, and generated the power Mackerras kept in reserve until the climax of the finale. At that moment, the symphony's motto theme returned not only without any trace of triumphalism, but with a positive viciousness in the syncopated efforts of the percussion to knock it off course.

Two further concerts followed in December 2009: the first was an evening of Wagner extracts, with Christine Brewer in magnificent voice as Isolde and Brünnhilde; the second included Beethoven's *Pastoral* (a performance described by David Whelton as 'quite simply perfect, sublime'[8]) and scenes from Humperdinck's *Hansel and Gretel* – an opera that Mackerras adored and had recorded with the Philharmonia. It turned out to be his farewell to the orchestra. Plans were already announced for concerts in the following season – including Sibelius's Fifth Symphony – and Mackerras had plenty of ideas for future collaborations with an orchestra with whom he had developed an extraordinarily warm relationship. Writing the day Mackerras's death was announced, Alistair Mackie, the orchestra's Chairman and co-principal trumpet, wrote with feeling:

> Sir Charles has a very special place in the heart of every musician in the Philharmonia Orchestra. I can think of no other conductor with his unique blend of passion, integrity and musicianship. He was completely lacking in pomposity or self-regard: for him, the joy was all in the music and in making and communicating that music. Performing with him felt like an entirely shared experience, and a wholly joyous one. Our musical world is greatly reduced by today's sad news; we will all miss him terribly.[9]

[8] Interview with David Whelton on 11 November 2013.

[9] From a tribute published online.

14
Coda
Nigel Simeone

In his obituary in *Opera* (September 2010), Lord Harewood wrote that 'The word "polymath" might have been coined to describe Charles's activities as a musician. I think he was the best conductor of Mozart of my time in the theatre, and undoubtedly the best at Handel [whose] operas never sounded so good without him. I emphasise these virtues, but of course we all think of him as the man who unlocked the secrets of Janáček and his operas.' He ended by saying that he was 'probably the most complete opera conductor of his generation'. This was no exaggeration, and to it should be added his achievements – especially in the last two decades of his life – as a symphonic conductor whose performances of standard repertoire were almost always full of new insights, as well as an innate sense of musical drama. He did not know the meaning of complacency in his conducting – there was a duty to the composer that had to be honoured. Asked why he always used a score, he once remarked that there were always new things to discover, even as the performance was going along.

When Charles married Judy, they wanted to start a family, though Charles was worried that children might distract him from music – so the responsibility of their upbringing would rest firmly with Judy. He was not being selfish about this, but merely explaining just how central music was to his existence. To underline the point, he recalled his first trip to Prague for a Czech television documentary in 2009: 'I always say I had two honeymoons: one with my wife and the other one was with Janáček!'

Their first daughter, Fiona, was born on 8 August 1949 and their second, Catherine (Cathy), arrived the following year on 17 November – Charles's birthday. It was Judy who dealt with all the practicalities of bringing up two children. The girls saw their father as a kindly figure, but he was often away, and usually had his head in a score when he was at home. As they became teenagers, Fiona and Cathy started to develop a deep love of music that drew them closer to their father: as Judy told her mother-in-law in 1964, 'They are so full of enthusiasm for life generally & the theatre in particular (including opera) that we find them a rewarding pair after all these years!' According to Cathy, 'he worked extremely hard, but time was always made – usually thanks to Mum's careful planning of his schedule – for holidays, and for time with the family and some relaxation'. But, apart from his leisure interest in sailing (an enthusiasm he shared with his father), Charles's energies were almost entirely directed towards music. He was an Australian who lived for many years in Hamilton Terrace, just around the corner from Lord's Cricket Ground – but he had absolutely no interest in the game, and never went. Though he read the papers assiduously, he didn't much care for politics: for Charles, most politicians – regardless of party – were ambitious philistines who never understood the importance of the arts, let alone the need to fund them properly. But he was one of the earliest supporters of Amnesty International in the 1960s (Cathy recalls that, during her schooldays, he encouraged her and Fiona to write letters on behalf of Prisoners of Conscience, and he also wrote a number himself). And, thanks to Judy's enthusiasm, he later developed an interest in environmental matters and in preserving wildlife. A great enthusiast for David Attenborough's natural history programmes, he sent a card to congratulate Attenborough on his eightieth birthday in May 2006, six months after Charles's own. Attenborough – a fellow Companion of Honour and an enthusiastic music lover – sent a charming reply:

> I'm delighted to know the eighties aren't so bad. I spent my birthday filming in the Galapagos – not because I was trying to avoid celebration but simply because the schedules worked out that way. In the event it wasn't a bad place to have one's 80th. The giant tortoises look so ancient they make one feel quite young! [...]
>
> With best wishes and great admiration,
> David Attenborough.
>
> P.S. Perhaps if they ever have a gathering of all those Companions of Honour we may be able to meet & I can do more than simply applaud you from among your enthusiastic audiences.[1]

While music was at the heart of everything he did, as he grew older, his family became ever more important. But Judy always had been, and no account of Charles's career would be complete without recognising the decisive part she played in it: their marriage was as close as it was long, and his success owed a great deal to her support. She dealt with practicalities such as travel arrangements and managed all the finances (including establishing scholarships at several music colleges and assigning royalties to particular causes). Above all, she made sure that he could devote his energies to music. Cathy Mackerras has described them as 'a complete partnership, discussing everything together. When Dad was working away without her he would telephone several times a day – for advice on some domestic matter, but also to tell her how a rehearsal had gone and to share the ups and downs of each day.' Throughout their marriage she acted as a sounding board for Charles himself when it came to important career decisions. He never liked to turn down work, but she tried to manage his schedule so that it did not become unduly overloaded – Cathy remembers many occasions at home when her parents would plan future engagements together. Judy advised and encouraged him with the insight and understanding of someone who had herself been a professional musician. She also gave him the stability and the love he needed to overcome family tragedies and personal disappointments.

[1] Mackerras family archives.

Lotfi Mansouri surely got to the heart of their relationship when he wrote: 'If he has a secret weapon, it is his wife Judy. As Judy Wilkins, she was a first-rate clarinettist, having finally surrendered her career to his many years ago. She is both his kite and his anchor, always smoothing his path.'[2]

Charles's siblings were all extremely successful in their own ways, and he was very supportive of Fiona and Cathy in their studies and professional work (in teaching and in community arts). Once they had children of their own, Charles became a doting grandfather. Two of his nephews – Elizabeth's son Alexander (Alex) Briger and Joan's son Drostan Hall – became conductors. It was thanks to one of Charles's performances that Alex decided early on the direction his career should take:

> When I was a kid, I wanted to be a pilot, but then, when I was about 12, I saw Charles conducting Mahler's Fourth with the Sydney Symphony and that did it: from that moment on, I wanted to be a conductor like him. I wanted to control sounds like that, and right away I became very serious about music. I bought the Tennstedt recording of Mahler Four with the London Philharmonic, and then years later the LPO asked me to conduct it, which was wonderful – and Charlie came to that, which touched me very much. But when I was growing up, I never told him I wanted to be a conductor – nobody knew how he'd take it and he was always the patriarch of the family – the eldest, and the most successful. But it was quite obvious that I wanted to become a musician, and I studied the violin at the Sydney Conservatorium. I started conducting a small chamber orchestra and when we were doing the Bach Third Orchestral Suite and Handel's *Fireworks* I wrote to ask his advice about tempi and so on. Then I told him I wanted to study conducting at the Hochschule in Munich – and he was very encouraging, but he'd still never seen me conduct. I formed a youth orchestra in Germany because I needed conducting experience. It went well, and I invited Charles to become a patron, which he did. He told me to do Mahler's First with the orchestra – which was a great idea – and I invited my cousin Drostan – Joan's son, and a wonderful violinist – to come over and play the Bruch Violin Concerto for a concert in Munich at the Prinzregententheater. It was a family event, with these two cousins performing together, and Charles and Judy came over. That was the first time he saw me conduct – and the first time he heard Drostan playing a concerto, which he played beautifully – and straight away he said to me, 'I want you to come over and assist me'. Being family members, the whole thing could have gone horribly wrong, but he'd seen us both now and took us both seriously as musicians.[3]

[2] Mansouri 2010, p. 293.

[3] Interview with Alex Briger, Paris, 26 May 2013. All subsequent quotations from Briger are from the same interview.

As his assistant, Alex grew close to his uncle, though Charles was no less exacting with his nephew than with anyone else, as Alex recalls: 'The first proper opera I did was *Jenůfa* with him at Australian Opera. I conducted all the piano rehearsals and he'd let me make a mistake once, and forgive me once, but if you did it a second time he would get very impatient.' Alex witnessed some amusing moments in rehearsal and performance. Crisis management is a skill any opera conductor needs – probably one reason why Charles always used a score – and a typical instance of this happened during a rehearsal of *Káťa Kabanová* at Australian Opera:

> When Charles did *Káťa* in Australia, I remember a funny incident near the end of Act 1. The singers were going wrong – they were not watching the conductor, but following each other's cues as they do – and then there's this general pause [immediately before fig. 30] where Tikhon turns to Káťa and says: 'Are you angry with me?' Káťa's reply is 'No', but from the pit Charles's voice answered 'Yes!'

For the most part, Charles got on extremely well with singers – he understood them but never indulged them. The only times he would become impatient were if they hadn't learned their parts properly or if they refused to go along with his ideas about matters of style. Alex Briger was an assistant on the Telarc Mozart opera recordings:

> For *Figaro* he had a great cast, and Carol Vaness sang the Countess beautifully. But he argued with her about the decorations in 'Dove sono', which she thought were too much. The producer James Mallinson made peace between them by suggesting they record both versions – one with all the embellishments and one without – to see which worked best. Well, that's what they did, with the embellished one appearing in the supplement. It really mattered to Charles: this was *Figaro*, which meant everything to him and which he'd been thinking about for so many years.

The successful preparation of an opera recording depends on a number of musicians, and Charles had two favourite repetiteurs, whose job was to work with the singers in great detail, paying particular attention to matters of language as well as the musical text. Alex remembers that 'his two favourites were John Fisher for most of the Italian repertoire and Ronnie Schneider for German repertoire. Both of them are amazing musicians who could make a piano sound like an orchestra – Charles loved that about them, and the immense care they always took over the language, as well as their complete understanding of things like appoggiaturas.'

As for Mackerras himself, Briger was constantly amazed by the depth of his knowledge: 'I went through the *Sinfonietta* with him, note for note, and I remember him saying, "just give the third horn a cue here, because he's got a very difficult page turn in the part and could do with a bit of encouragement". What other conductor would even think about that?'

When Alex was studying in Munich in the 1990s, he witnessed the highs and the lows of his uncle's work in German and Austrian opera houses:

> He did a *Don Giovanni* in Munich and it wasn't good at all – and a horrible experience for him. I think it was the only time in his career that he got booed, and he was actually weeping afterwards. The production had been conducted first by Colin Davis, and you can't imagine two more different Mozart conductors. Anyhow, Charles asked for a rehearsal with the orchestra and that went badly because they didn't like the fast tempi. None of the singers were doing appoggiaturas. And because it was so much quicker than anyone was used to, it just wasn't together. When he came into the pit after the interval, he was booed – it was awful. Even worse, when the Commendatore appeared, there were no trombones. They were still in the bar, thinking they still had five minutes before they were needed. But at about the same time, in the same theatre, he did the best *Salome* I've ever heard – and with no rehearsal. He kept his beat as tiny as possible to make sure the orchestra didn't overwhelm the singers – he looked like one of those wonderful old German Kapellmeisters – and the concertmaster came up to him afterwards and told him it was the only time they'd ever been able to hear all the singing in *Salome*!
>
> Then there was *Figaro* at the Salzburg Festival. I don't know why he didn't get asked there more often. But of all the performances I've heard live, only two have stuck in my memory as being perfect in every way. There was a Mahler 9 with Abbado and the Berlin Philharmonic in Munich – and there was this performance of *Figaro* in Salzburg with Charles. The cast was superb, all the appoggiaturas were right, and the Vienna Philharmonic played beautifully for him. But at dinner afterwards, one of the oboists came over and asked why some bits were so fast – not at all how Karajan used to do it. And Charles explained it to him – he was like a walking Mozart encyclopedia, so he had a reason for *everything*. Anyway, this went on for about half an hour, with Charles telling him – in German, of course – exactly why he chose those tempi, and how they related to each other. And at the end of it, the oboist got up, saying, 'but it's still all far too fast!' Well, you can imagine. Charles turned to me and said: 'What can you do? It's their tradition and they will never change.' But what a fantastic performance it was.

Alex also witnessed the huge success Mackerras had late in his career with one of the great European orchestras:

> You have to thank Simon Rattle for inviting Charles to Berlin in 2004. Simon revered him, admired him so much, and really wanted to get him to Berlin. Well, they loved him – and asked him back several times afterwards. I think Charles was more excited about working

> with the Berlin Philharmonic than almost anything else in his career: I mean, for him there was no more prestigious orchestra on earth. He was quite strict with them, as always – he was just himself – and I remember Mitsuko Uchida played Mozart's Concerto K482, and that went so well – it was just fantastic. And to finish, they gave an incredible performance of the Janáček *Sinfonietta*. Judy was there to celebrate with him, which was lovely: he'd finally made it to the Berlin Philharmonic at the age of 79!

In the midst of these triumphs, Charles and his family had to come to terms with tragedy. The death in June 1987 of his beloved grand-daughter Alice – Cathy's first child – was a shattering blow: he had adored her, and been distraught when he learned that she was suffering from leukaemia. But the treatment had appeared to be working, and she helped cut the cake at the double birthday party in Australia House to celebrate Charles's sixtieth birthday and Cathy's thirty-fifth birthday. Charles's way of dealing with this awful loss was to immerse himself in music – to throw himself into it with even greater vigour, as a way of coping with his feelings, something he was able to express through music with a depth and passion that was far harder with words.

He was to be cruelly tested again twenty years later. Fiona, Charles and Judy's first daughter, fell ill with cancer, and by the summer of 2006 she was extremely sick. Before Charles went to the Edinburgh Festival to conduct all the Beethoven symphonies, they spent time together in London. She died on 1 September, the very day of the performance of the Ninth Symphony with the Philharmonia. Judy and Cathy decided that the news should be kept from him until after the concert. Cathy recalls that it was a heartbreaking decision, 'but we were talking about Dad here – he *had* to conduct that concert, and he just couldn't have done it if we'd told him beforehand'. Charles himself would certainly have approved: had he known, it would have been impossible to go on; as it was, he was able to conduct one of the most incandescent performances he ever gave of the Ninth (it is the version included in the Hyperion set). His niece, Christina Briger, was able to get a train to Edinburgh so that someone would be there to look after him afterwards. A report in *The Scotsman* (9 September 2006) noted that 'the audience for Beethoven's 9th Symphony at the Usher Hall last week knew nothing of the tragedy that preceded the performance' – but neither did its conductor until the concert was over. He wanted at once to do something in Fiona's memory, and on 8 September the Prom in which he conducted the Orchestra of the Age of Enlightenment in Mozart's 'Haffner' Symphony and Robert Levin's completion of the Mass in C minor was dedicated to her memory. It was an emotionally charged evening: the 'Haffner' an astonishingly joyous and spirited celebration, the C minor Mass a deeply felt threnody.

For the last few years of his life, Charles himself had multiple myeloma (discovered by chance following a blood test). As it became more debilitating, he dealt with it stoically, going obediently for treatment at the hospital in Wimbledon where his specialist was based. Inevitably this had an impact on his work, but he was determined not to let it frustrate projects that he believed in – not all of them glamorous international events. For instance, at St David's Hall, Cardiff, on 30 March 2009, he conducted the student orchestra of the Royal Welsh College of Music and Drama in Beethoven's Ninth Symphony (it turned out to be the last performance he ever gave of the work). By a happy chance, his daughter Cathy was in the Bristol Choral Society, which joined the student chorus for the occasion. She recalls that 'it was always wonderful singing for Dad – I was so proud of him on those occasions, and he was brilliant with amateur choirs. He was always fussy about clear diction – and gave us extremely clear cues. When I was in the CBSO Chorus, we did the *Glagolitic Mass* with him, and later on I sang in several performances of the Mozart Requiem and Beethoven Nine, including the one with the students of at the Royal Welsh College. He inspired everybody even though he really wasn't well. I have lovely memories of the way he always beamed at me in the alto section if we had an entry he particularly liked.'

A few months later, Charles was at the Dartington Summer School to conduct Haydn's *Creation*. Cathy joined the choir again, along with Charles's niece Judy (daughter of Neil Mackerras), who had gone to Dartington to look after her uncle and was driving him daily for radiotherapy in Plymouth. Richard Morrison wrote a memorable and moving account of this performance in an article for *The Times* (26 August 2009), 'An act of creation that had me in tears':

> Dartington is one of the oldest of all summer schools. The place is bewitching. It's a medieval estate on rolling hills above the River Dart, reconstructed in the 1920s [...] But I had a special reason to attend last week. For more than 60 years, Sir Charles Mackerras had been a tremendous, galvanising presence on the British musical scene: a no-nonsense Aussie whose pragmatism and passion, wit and warmth, scholarship and musical curiosity, have been the driving force behind many of the finest nights I've spent in any opera house or concert hall. But Mackerras is now 83 and in far from robust health. He has had to pull out of a concert tonight at the Edinburgh Festival. One engagement, however, he was determined to keep. Long ago he agreed to conduct Haydn's oratorio *The Creation* in Dartington. And because I had sung under his baton as a piping treble 45 years ago, I was equally determined to do so once again – though this time as a rather rusty baritone. So I signed on for the volunteer chorus.
>
> It turned out to be the most emotional musical occasion I have attended all year – and I've been to a few. For a start there was intense poignancy in the choice of work. *The Creation* is a faith-infused and blissfully optimistic piece that Haydn wrote in his own old age. It's

> also a work that Mackerras had conducted regularly throughout his long career. So you felt as if you were receiving the distilled wisdom of not one great musical veteran but two – communing across the centuries.
>
> This sense that priceless nuggets of experience were being passed down the generations was enhanced by the circumstances of the performance. Here, Mackerras was working not with top professionals but an orchestra mostly of students and an ad hoc chorus of us amateurs. He could have lowered his expectations, or been condescending, or opted for safety first and put the brakes on his famously sizzling speeds. He did none of that. He growled and grunted; cajoled and coaxed; insisted and inspired. Not on his own behalf, of course, but on Haydn's.
>
> The result was astonishing. People were lifted to a level far above what they had thought was possible. To take part was both draining and exhilarating. I think everyone sensed that we would never experience anything quite like it again.
>
> Afterwards, in the bar, over many a glass of red wine, Mackerras reminisced with mesmerising clarity – about working with Britten, about being a music student in 1940s Prague, about coming to Britain just after the war as a humble oboist and getting his first conducting break, and about the geniuses and giants, charlatans and ogres, encountered in six decades of music-making. Everybody, not least the maestro himself, seemed to want that night to go on and on.
>
> Nobody knows what the future holds – whether for Mackerras (twice each day he disappeared to hospital for treatment), or for this summer school, which will undergo big changes to its facilities and leadership in 2010 when Gavin Henderson leaves after 25 years. But the great thing about making music is that it reminds you – indeed forces you – to live for the moment. And that extended moment when Mackerras conducted *The Creation*, perhaps for the last time, will live forever in the memory of all who witnessed it.

There was certainly increasing frailty, and Charles often experienced excruciating pain, but the concerts and operas of his last year all had that sense of exhilaration described so acutely by Richard Morrison, whether in *The Turn of the Screw* at the Coliseum, or in *The Cunning Little Vixen* at Covent Garden – where occasional shortcomings in the cast were more than compensated for by orchestral playing that was utterly radiant, and by the sense of life-affirming joy in the conducting.

Charles's funeral at St Paul's, Covent Garden, on the morning of 23 July 2010 was a moving and tremendously sad occasion – but it was never a gloomy one: too many of those present had such vital and recent memories of his music-making at its best. As well as the eloquent remarks from Janet Baker printed at the start of this book, there were tributes from his brother Colin and from his daughter Cathy, whose affectionate comments included some touching thoughts on Charles as a father:

> I happened to be born on his 25th birthday, so he called me his 'twin', and birthdays were always very special. Our childhood was, of course, surrounded by music. *Pineapple Poll* being arranged while my sister and I were toddlers, everyday life being peppered with operatic quotes, being taken to historic occasions such as the first performance of Britten's *Noye's Fludde*. When we were older, we were roped in to mark orchestral parts, and were tutored in the relevant leitmotifs before being allowed to go to a performance of Wagner's *Ring*.
>
> We went to events in the 1960s which have proved to be turning points, such as the Sadler's Wells *Figaro* and the recording sessions of the *Messiah*. Discussions of ornamentation and appoggiaturas took place alongside more mundane topics at meal times. He was always a kind and generous Dad. Broadminded and understanding when we were teenagers, supportive of our studies and work, and then – as grandchildren came along – he became an equally generous grandfather, always concerned about their welfare and very proud of their achievements. [...]
>
> Dad believed that a divine spirit was most evident in nature. He described himself as a pantheist. He wanted the final scene of *The Cunning Little Vixen* to be played at his funeral, as it was at Janáček's own, expressing as it does a belief in the cyclic renewal of nature – of new life following death.[4]

Some of his favourite music was performed by musicians he had worked with closely: members of the Orchestra of the Age of Enlightenment played the slow movement from Mozart's Gran Partita, wind players from the Royal Opera House played the first movement of *Mládí* ('Youth') – the first work by Janáček that Mackerras ever knew, having played it as an oboist in Sydney – and Rosemary Joshua sang the 'Et incarnatus est' from Mozart's C minor Mass, as she had at the Prom Charles dedicated to Fiona's memory in 2006. With sunlight streaming through the windows of the church, it was an occasion for each person to reflect on what this man's music-making had meant to them, uplifted by the beauty of the music, not least Charles's recording of the last scene from *The Cunning Little Vixen*. Immediately after this, Rev. Simon Grigg, Rector of St Paul's, Covent Garden, addressed the congregation: 'I'd like, in the tradition of the opera, to give Sir Charles Mackerras a standing ovation.' For more than a minute, there was thunderous applause, and even some cheers: it seemed a marvellously appropriate farewell to a man for whom every performance was an opportunity to breathe new life into the music he loved.

[4] Transcription of remarks by Cathy Mackerras, spoken at her father's funeral.

Mark Elder knew Charles well. He was always grateful for the confidence Mackerras had shown in him when he first came to English National Opera. This is how Elder summed up his legacy for BBC Radio 3 on the day his death was announced:

> He was an immense *stylist* who could turn his hand to conducting music from an enormously wide variety of different countries and periods. He was as masterful conducting Baroque music as he was showing us all how we must keep an open mind when interpreting Mozart, to conducting the great repertoire operas of Verdi or Richard Strauss, and inspiring us to understand that the music of Janáček was some of the greatest music of the twentieth century.[5]

Interviewed by Czech television in 2009, Charles tried to explain how he approached the task of conducting and what he aimed to achieve in every performance:

> I always try to find something new in everything I do, no matter how many times I do it. I think that's really the main function of a conductor – to try and discover more things. That is one of the reasons that I don't ever conduct from memory. Because frequently – even at performances –I suddenly look at the score and I say to myself: 'Oh! I haven't noticed *that* before!' I always try to find – and frequently *do* find – something new in every performance that I do. When one is performing a piece of music – whatever it is – there is always in one's mind a mixture between the emotional and philosophical significance of the music, and technical questions: keeping it together or having it in tune, or whatever. I think one must just keep a balance between these things: the *spirit* of the music and the accuracy and technical correctness of the performance. Every musician has to do that. However carried away they might be by the excitement of the music, they have to make sure that it's in tune and together, with everything in the right place.[6]

This is all good practical advice, but there is far more to being a great conductor. On the *Today* programme, James Naughtie asked Charles to try and explain the mystery of the relationship between a conductor and an orchestra: what makes the difference?

> I've never quite worked it out, because some conductors have perfect knowledge of the music and are nice tactful people who work together very well – everything the orchestras would like them to be – and yet they don't quite click with the musicians. It's something to do with

[5] Mark Elder on *In Tune*, BBC Radio 3, 15 July 2010.

[6] Mackerras interviewed in 2009 for the Czech Television documentary *Sir Charles, thank you, děkujeme …*, first broadcast by ČT2 on the evening of 25 December 2010.

emanation, I'm convinced – I'm always talking about *Ausstrahlung* in German – but that's what it really is. The sort of personality that goes out to the orchestra and they get the impression that if you are really crazy about the music, that they will be too. In fact, conducting is *persuading* every musician in the orchestra to play it your way and with enthusiasm and willingness.[7]

[7] Mackerras interviewed by James Naughtie on *Today*, BBC Radio 4, 4 April 2009.

1	THU		17	SAT	
2	FRI		18	SUNDAY	
3	SAT		19	MON	Week 29
4	SUNDAY		20	TUE	
5	MON	Week 27	21	WED	
6	TUE		22	THU to Manchester	
7	WED		23	FRI rehearsal BBC Phil	
8	THU return from Elba		24	SAT	
9	FRI		25	SUNDAY Prom Schumann Strauss	
10	SAT		26	MON	Week 30
11	SUNDAY		27	TUE reh. SCO prom	
12	MON Bank Holiday (Northern Ireland)	Week 28	28	WED " " "	
13	TUE		29	THU LateNight Prom.	
14	WED		30	FRI	
15	THU		31	SAT	
16	FRI			SUNSETS: 4th, 21.20; 11th, 21.15; 18th, 21.08; 25th, 21.00. For complete Calendar see back of December sheet.	

Figure 5 Mackerras's calendar for July 2010, showing the two Proms that he was due to conduct on 25 and 29 July. He died in London on 14 July.

Appendix 1
Mackerras in Performance

A comprehensive documentation of the performances conducted by Charles Mackerras over more than sixty years is beyond the scope of this book. The following lists include performances that Mackerras conducted with some of the opera companies and orchestras with which he worked closely, and they also relate to specific chapters in the book. Mackerras was an astonishingly busy conductor, so these lists can only give a snapshot of his activity with a few selected organisations. Each list is as complete as we have been able to make it with the information available.

A SWO/ENO performances, 1970–77

B Janáček opera performances, 1951–2010

C San Francisco Opera performances, 1969–2000

D WNO performances, 1950–2009

E ROH performances, 1955–2010

F Performances in Czechoslovakia and the Czech Republic, and with Czech orchestras abroad, 1961–2008

G OAE performances, 1987–2010

H SCO performances, 1993–2010

I Philharmonia performances, 2002–09

A SWO/ENO performances, 1970–77

(See Chapter 1)

The following is a list of operas conducted by Mackerras with SWO/ENO during his time as the company's Music Director. Figures in brackets represent the number of performances of each work Mackerras conducted, including those on tour (at home and abroad) as well as concert performances at the BBC Proms. Performances with the company after 1 January 1978 are not included.

1970
New productions: Beethoven: Leonore, p. Basil Coleman, d. Tony Abbott, Joan and Ann Bloomfield (7); Bizet: Carmen, p. John Copley, d. Stefanos Lazaridis and David Walker (5).
revivals: Mozart: The Magic Flute (1); Mozart: Don Giovanni (4); Mozart: Idomeneo (2); Puccini: La Bohème (1); Wagner: The Flying Dutchman (2).
Total: 22

1970/1
New productions: Handel: Semele, p. and d. Filippo Sanjust (6); Beethoven: Fidelio, p. and d. as for Leonore in 1970 (5); Mozart: The Seraglio, p. Copley, d. Lazaridis (3).
revivals: Bizet: Carmen (4); Mozart: The Magic Flute (6); Puccini: Madam Butterfly (6); Rossini: The Barber of Seville (4); J. Strauss: Die Fledermaus (3); Janáček: The Makropulos Case (4); Wagner: The Valkyrie (2). Total: 43

1971/2
New productions: Wagner: Lohengrin, p. Colin Graham, d. Michael Knight (4); Wagner: The Rhinegold, p. Glen Byam Shaw and John Blatchley, d. Ralph Koltai (4); Bartók: Duke Bluebeard's Castle, p. Shaw, d. Koltai (8).
revivals: Mozart: The Seraglio (6); Mozart: The Marriage of Figaro (9); Berlioz: The Damnation of Faust (3); Janáček: The Makropulos Case (3); Stravinsky: Oedipus Rex (8); Bizet: Carmen (4). Total: 49

1972/3
New productions: Verdi: II trovatore, p. Copley, p. Lazaridis (12).
revivals: Britten: Gloriana (7); Bartók: Duke Bluebeard's Castle (4); Stravinsky: Oedipus Rex (4); Puccini: Madam Butterfly (2); Bizet: Carmen (6); Puccini: La Bohème (1); Mozart: Così fan tutte (2); Verdi: La Traviata (3); Wagner: The Rhinegold (2). Total: 43

1973/4
New productions: Janáček: Katya Kabanova, p. Blatchley, d. Lazaridis (8); Donizetti: Mary Stuart, p. Copley, d. Desmond Heeley (6); Massenet: Manon, p. Colin Graham, d. Alix Stone (8).
revivals: Wagner: The Valkyrie (1); Sullivan: Iolanthe (4); Verdi: La Traviata (6); Britten: Gloriana (1); Verdi: A Masked Ball (3); J. Strauss: Die Fledermaus (1). Total: 38

1974/5
New productions: Verdi: Don Carlos, p. Graham, d. Christopher Morley (5); Mozart: The Magic Flute, p. Anthony Besch, d. John Stoddart (1); Strauss: Der Rosenkavalier, p. Copley, d. David Walker (9).
revivals: Verdi: La Traviata (1); Janáček: Katya Kabanova (5); Donizetti: Mary Stuart (2); Wagner: The Mastersingers of Nuremberg (6); Bizet: Carmen (1); Wagner: The Rhinegold (3); Wagner: The Valkyrie (3); Wagner: Siegfried (3); Wagner: The Twilight of the Gods (3); Sullivan: Patience (4); Britten: Gloriana (3). Total: 49

1975/6
New productions: Offenbach: La Belle Hélène, p. Copley, d. Bruno Santini (5); Szymanowski: King Roger (New Opera Company prod.); p. Besch, d. Stoddart (2).
revivals: Mozart: The Magic Flute (6); J. Strauss: Die Fledermaus (1); Strauss: Der Rosenkavalier (5); Donizetti: Mary Stuart (2); Janáček: The Makropulos Case (3); Wagner: The Rhinegold (4); Wagner: The Valkyrie (4); Wagner: Siegfried (4); Wagner: The Twilight of the Gods (4); Mozart: Idomeneo (4). Total: 44

1976/7
New productions: Mozart: Don Giovanni, p. Besch, d. Stoddart (6); Smetana: Dalibor, p. Blatchley, d. Lazaridis (4); Massenet: Werther, p. Copley, d. Lazaridis (5).
revivals: Wagner: The Mastersingers of Nuremberg (4); Sullivan: Patience (1); Verdi: La Traviata (4); Janáček: Katya Kabanova (3). Total: 27

1977/8 (to 31 December 1977)
New production: Puccini: La Bohème, p. Jean-Claude Auvray, d. Hubert Monloup (8).
revivals: Wagner: The Rhinegold (1); Wagner: The Valkyrie (1); Wagner: Siegfried (1); Wagner: The Twilight of the Gods (1); Massenet: Werther (5); Smetana: Dalibor (5); Janáček: From the House of the Dead (1). Total: 23

Source: Opera (January 1978).

B Janáček opera performances, 1951–2010

(See Chapter 3)

Performances given in London unless otherwise stated. Those marked with an asterisk (*) were broadcast.

10 April 1951, SWO
Káťa Kabanová (in English), British premiere
p. Dennis Arundell; d. John Glass, L. W. Anson
further perfs: 14, 18, 20 April, 10, 19 May, 6 June, 19 September, 6 October 1951

18 November 1959, SWO
Káťa Kabanová (in English), revival of 1951
further perfs: 20, 24, 28 November, 2 December 1959

10 February 1961, SWO
Káťa Kabanová (in English), revival of 1951
further perfs: 15, 17, 25 February 1961

21 March 1961, Janáček Theatre, Brno
Káťa Kabanová (in Czech), revival of 1953
p. Oskar Linhart; d. Miloš Tomek

12 February 1964, SWO
The Makropulos Affair (in English), British premiere
p. John Blatchley; d. Motley
further perfs: 14, 18, 21, 25, 27 February 1964; Zagreb, 14 May; Paris, 18 May 1965

5 May 1965, SWO
The Makropulos Affair (in English), revival of 1964
further perf: 8 May 1965

26 September 1965, BBC broadcast, Manchester
From the House of the Dead (in English) (BBC Northern Singers and BBC Northern SO)

28 October 1965, SWO
From the House of the Dead (in English), London premiere
p. Colin Graham; d. Ralph Koltai
further perfs: 30 October, 2, 5 November, 9, 14 December 1965

1 March 1970, BBC broadcast, Manchester
The Excursions of Mr Brouček (in English) (BBC Northern Singers and BBC Northern SO)

19 February 1971, SWO, Coliseum
The Makropulos Affair (in English), revival of 1964
further perfs: 23, 26* February, 3 March; Bristol, 8 April; Oxford, 23 April; Manchester, 7 May; Leeds, 21 May; Newcastle, 4 June 1971 (not all conducted by Mackerras)

26 January 1972, SWO, Coliseum
The Makropulos Affair (in English), revival of 1964
further perfs: 7, 10 February 1972

13 April 1972, ROH
Jenůfa (in English), revival of 1956
p. Christopher West; d. Jan Brazda
further perfs: 20, 25, 29 April, 2 May; 8, 11, 14, 17 June 1977

12 September 1973, SWO, Coliseum
Káťa Kabanová (in English)
p. John Blatchley; d. Stefanos Lazaridis
further perfs: 14, 18, 21* September, 11, 16 October 1973 (some perfs conducted by David Lloyd-Jones)

22 March 1974, SWO, Coliseum
Káťa Kabanová (in English), revival of 1973
further perfs: Manchester, 16, 25 April; Leeds, 15, 21 May; Newcastle, 5 June 1974 (some perfs conducted by David Lloyd-Jones)

8 September 1974, BBC Proms
Káťa Kabanová (in English), concert perf

12 September 1974, SWO, Coliseum
Káťa Kabanová (in English), revival of 1973
further perfs: 14, 17, 19, 25, 28 September 1974 (some perfs conducted by David Lloyd-Jones)

9 November 1975, Deutsche Oper am Rhein, Düsseldorf
Káťa Kabanová (in German), revival of 1973
p. Bohumil Herlischka; d. Ruodi Barth, Liselotte Erler

13 November 1975, ENO
The Makropulos Affair (in English), revival of 1964
further perfs: 15, 21, 27 November 1975 (not all conducted by Mackerras)

17 February 1977, ENO
Káťa Kabanová (in English), revival of 1973
further perfs: 18, 19, 22, 25 February, 3 March 1977 (not all conducted by Mackerras)

30 December 1977, ENO
From the House of the Dead (in English), revival of 1965
further perfs: 4, 6, 10,* 13, 19 January 1978

28 December 1978, ENO
The Excursions of Mr Brouček (in English)
p. Colin Graham; d. Peter Docherty
further perfs: 2, 4, 16* January 1979

1 July 1979, Janáček Theatre, Brno
The Makropulos Affair (in Czech), revival of 1978
p. Václav Věžník; d. Ladislav Vychodil, Kateřina Asmusová

29 February 1980, Staatsoper, Vienna
Jenůfa (in German), revival of 1964
p. Richard Bletschacher after Otto Schenk; d. Günther Schneider-Siemssen, Hill Reihs-Gromes
further perfs: 4 March 1980; 21, 24 October, 2, 5 November 1982; 3, 6, 12 December 1984; 7, 11, 14 December 1987

14 November 1980, Opéra, Paris
Jenůfa (in French)
p. Götz Friedrich; d. Reinhard Zimmermann, Jan Skalický
further perfs: 17, 20, 25, 29 November, 3, 4, 10 December 1980

23 December 1983, ENO
The Excursions of Mr Brouček (in English), revival of 1978
further perfs: 29, 31 December 1983; 4, 6, 13 January 1984

14 September 1986, San Francisco Opera
Jenůfa (in Czech)
p. Wolfgang Weber; d. Leni Bauer-Ecsy
further perfs: 19, 23, 27 September, 2, 5 October 1986

26 September 1987, WNO, Swansea
The Cunning Little Vixen (in English), revival of 1980
p. David Pountney; d. Maria Björnson
further perfs: Swansea, 7 October; Oxford, 28 November; Southampton, 2 December; Plymouth, 9 December 1987

10 March 1988, Opéra-comique, Paris
From the House of the Dead (in Czech)
p. Volker Schlöndorf; d. Jennifer Bartlett.
further perfs: 12, 14, 26, 28 March, 1 April 1988

22 April 1989, ENO
The Makropulos Affair (in English), revival of WNO production
p. David Pountney; d. Maria Björnson
further perfs: 25, 28 April, 4, 11 May 1989

30 June 1989, WNO
Fate (in English), Birmingham, concert perf
further concert perf: Bristol, 8 July 1989

25 February 1991, Met
Káťa Kabanová (in Czech)
p. Jonathan Miller; d. Robert Israel
further perfs: 1, 7, 13, 16*, 19, 23, 28 March 1991

1 May 1991, ENO
The Cunning Little Vixen (in English), based on WNO 1980
further perfs: (matinée), 4 (evening), 10, 14, 18 May 1991

9 January 1992, AO, Sydney
Jenůfa (in English), revival of 1974
p. John Copley; d. Allan Lees
further perfs: 14, 17, 22, 25, 30 January 1992

16 December 1992, ENO
The Excursions of Mr Brouček (in English)
p. David Pountney; d. Stefanos Lazaridis, Marie-Jeanne Lecca
further perfs: 19, 22, 31 December 1992; 5, 8, 12*, 15 January 1993

14 October 1993, San Francisco Opera
The Makropulos Affair (in Czech)
p. Lotfi Mansouri, Elisabeth Söderström; d. Leni Bauer-Ecsy
further perfs: 17, 22, 27, 30 October 1993

12 January 1995, AO, Sydney
Káťa Kabanová (in English)
p. Neil Armfield; d. Brian Thomson, Jennie Tate
further perfs: 17, 20, 23, 28, 31 January, 4, 8 February 1995

29 May 1995, Châtelet, Paris
The Cunning Little Vixen (in Czech)
p. Nicholas Hytner; d. Bob Crowley, Jean-Claude Gallotta
further perfs: 4, 6, 8, 11, 14 June 1995

28 March 1997, Rudolfinum, Prague
Káťa Kabanová (in Czech), concert perf

11 April 1998, Met
The Makropulos Affair (in Czech), revival of 1996
p. Elijah Moshinsky; d. Anthony Ward, Dona Granata
further perfs: 13, 16, 18* April 1998

2 July 1998, OA, Sydney
Jenůfa (in English)
p. Neil Armfield; d. Dan Potra, Tess Schofield
further perfs: 4, 8, 11, 16, 18 July 1998

2 January 1999, Met
Káťa Kabanová (in Czech), revival of 1991
further perfs: 5, 9,* 13, 16, 21 January 1999

23 April 2001, Met
The Makropulos Affair (in Czech), revival of 1996
further perfs: 26, 28 April 2001

24 May 2002, WNO, Cardiff
The Cunning Little Vixen (in English), revival of 1980
further perfs: Bristol, 31 May; Birmingham, 6 June 2002; concert perf Oxford, 19 June 2002

6 March 2003, WNO, Cardiff
Jenůfa (in English), revival of 1998
p. Katie Mitchell; d. Vicki Mortimer
further perfs: Cardiff, 6, 8 March; Birmingham, 13 March; Southampton, 20 March 2003

26 March 2003, RAM, London
The Cunning Little Vixen (in English)
p. Anna Sweeny; d. Michael Holt
further perf: 29 March 2003

20 December 2003, NT, Prague
The Excursions of Mr Brouček (in Czech)
p. Jiří Nekvasil; d. Daniel Dvořák
further perfs: 26, 29 December, 2 January; Brno 29 January 2004

18 May 2006, ENO
The Makropulos Affair (in English)
p. Christopher Alden; d. Charles Edwards
further perfs: 20, 24, 26, 30 May, 2 June 2006

19 June 2007, ROH
Káťa Kabanová (in Czech), revival of 1994
p. Trevor Nunn; d. Maria Björnson
further perfs: 22, 25, 28 June, 2, 5 July 2007

19 March 2010, ROH
The Cunning Little Vixen (in English), revival of 1990
p. Bill Bryden; d. William Dudley
further perfs: 22, 25, 29 March, 1 April 2010

Sources: Charles Mackerras annual schedules (from 1992); official websites of Royal Opera House, Covent Garden, London; Staatsoper, Vienna; Metropolitan Opera, New York; San Francisco Opera; Isabel Murphy (Welsh National Opera), Joseph Colomb (Paris performances); Jiří Zahrádka (Czech performances); Sacha Wagner (Deutsche Oper am Rhein); Sigrid Arnold (Theatermuseum Düsseldorf/ Sammlungen); Michael Pedersen (Opera Australia); David Lloyd-Jones; Sadler's Wells and English National Opera Archives; http://opera.archive.netcopy.co.uk.

C San Francisco Opera performances, 1969–2000

(See Chapter 5)

22 October 1969
Mozart: Die Zauberflöte
p. Paul Hager; d. Toni Businger
further perfs: 25, 28, 31 October 1969; Berkeley, 2 November

5 November 1969
Rossini: La Cenerentola
p. and d. Jean-Pierre Ponnelle
further perfs: 8, 11, 16 November 1969

13 October 1971
Tchaikovsky: Eugene Onegin
p. Paul Hager; d. Paul Walter
further perfs: 16, 19, 22, 31 October 1971

27 October 1971
Verdi: Un ballo in maschera
p. Piero Faggioni; d. Lloyd Burlingame
further perfs: 30 October, 2, 5, 7 November 1971

28 May 1982
Handel: Giulio Cesare
p. John Copley; d. John Pascoe
further perfs: 2, 5, 8, 13 June 1982

14 September 1985
Handel: Orlando
p. John Copley; d. John Pascoe
further perfs: 18, 21, 24 September, 3, 6 October 1985

13 October 1985
San Francisco Arts for Life (benefit concert for San Francisco AIDS Foundation, the Shanti Project and the AIDS Program of Hospice of San Francisco). Mackerras conducted music by Sullivan, Verdi, Handel and Beethoven.

14 September 1986
Janáček: Jenůfa
p. Wolfgang Weber; d. Leni Bauer-Ecsy
further perfs: 19, 23, 27 September, 2, 5 October 1986

11 November 1989
Wagner: Lohengrin
p. Wolfgang Weber, d. Beni Montresor
further perfs: 17, 21, 26, 29 November, 2, 8 December 1989

5 June 1993
Strauss: Der Rosenkavalier
p. Lotfi Mansouri; d. Thierry Bosquet (after Alfred Roller)
further perfs: 8, 11, 18, 23, 27 June 1993

10 September 1993
Verdi: I vespri siciliani
p. Christopher Alden; d. Paul Steinberg
further perfs: 14, 17, 23 26, 29 September, 2 October 1993

19 September 1993
Puccini: La Bohème
p. Sandra Bernhard, d. David Mitchell
further perfs: 19, 22, 25, 28 September, 6, 16 October 1993 (perfs on 9, 13 October cond. Patrick Summers)

14 October 1993
Janáček: The Makropulos Affair
p. Lotfi Mansouri, Elisabeth Söderström; d. Leni Bauer-Ecsy
further perfs: 17, 22, 27, 30 October 1993

17 November 1995
Gala Concert to Celebrate the Seventieth Birthday of Sir Charles Mackerras
Music by Stravinsky, Handel, Mozart, Dvořák, Janáček, Wagner, Purcell, Sullivan, Strauss and Verdi, conducted by Mackerras, Patrick Summers and Donald Runnicles (soloists incl. John Mark Ainsley, Anne Evans, Rebecca Evans, Renée Fleming, Felicity Palmer, Susan Quittmeyer, Stephanie Sundine, Bryn Terfel)

26 November 1995
Dvořák: Rusalka
p. Laurie Feldman; d. Günther Schneider–Siemssen
further perfs: 30 November, 2, 6, 8, 10 December 1995

2 December 1995
Puccini: Madama Butterfly
p. Sandra Bernhard; d. Toni Businger
further perfs: 4, 9 (matinée), 9 (evening) December 1995

1 November 2000
Handel: Semele
p. John Copley; d. Henry Bardon
further perfs: 4, 7, 22 November 2000

17 November 2000
Strauss: Der Rosenkavalier (revival)
further perfs: 20, 24, 29 November, 2, 5, 7, 10 December 2000

Sources: Charles Mackerras annual schedules (from 1992); San Francisco Opera online performance archive (http://archive.sfopera.com).

D WNO performances, 1950–2009

(See Chapter 6)

1950
Offenbach: The Tales of Hoffmann
Smetana: The Bartered Bride
Strauss: Die Fledermaus

1961
Rimsky-Korsakov: May Night

29 April 1981, Cardiff
Martinů: The Greek Passion (in English)
p. Michael Geliot; d. John Gunter
further perfs: Cardiff, 6, 8 May; Bristol, 15 May; Coventry, 21 May 1981

13 October 1983, SDH, Cardiff
Smetana: Má vlast

15 December 1983, SDH, Cardiff
Haydn: The Creation

27 October 1984, Cardiff
Mozart: Don Giovanni (in Italian)
p. Ruth Berghaus; d. Marie-Luise Strandt
further perfs: Cardiff, 31 October, 2 November; Liverpool, 15 November; Bristol, 20, 23 November; Birmingham, 27, 29 November; London, 4, 8 December; Southampton, 13 December 1984

18 December 1984, SDH, Cardiff
Haydn: Nelson Mass
Beethoven: Symphony No. 7

17 March 1985, Brangwyn Hall, Swansea
Handel: Messiah

15 December 1985, SDH, Cardiff
Haydn: The Creation

28 February 1987, Cardiff
Berlioz: The Trojans (in English)
p. Tim Albery; d. Tom Cairns
further perfs: Cardiff, 7, 14 March; Liverpool, 21 March; Southampton, 11 April; Bristol, 18 April 1987

13 March 1987, Cardiff
Puccini: La Bohème (in Italian)
p. Göran Järvefelt; d. Michael Yeargan
further perfs: Liverpool, 17, 19 March; Birmingham, 24 March; Oxford, 1 April

20 May 1987, Cardiff
Mozart: The Marriage of Figaro (in Italian)
p. Giles Havergal; d. Sue Blane
further perfs: Cardiff, 23 May; Wiesbaden, 29, 30 May; Swansea, 10 June; Birmingham, 24 June 1987

26 September 1987, Swansea
Janáček: The Cunning Little Vixen (in English)
p. David Pountney; d. Maria Björnson
further perfs: Swansea, 7 October; Birmingham, 14 October [given in memory of Alice Templeton, Charles's grand-daughter]; Liverpool, 23 October 1987

9 January 1988, SDH, Cardiff
Mahler: Symphony No. 6

14 January 1988, SDH, Cardiff
Mozart: Symphony No. 35 'Haffner'
Weber: Andante and Hungarian Rondo (Csaba Erdélyi)
Strauss: Don Quixote (Csaba Erdélyi, Raphael Wallfisch)

25 March 1988, Swansea
Strauss: Salome (in German)
p. André Engel; d. Aidan Long
further perfs: Swansea, 29 March, 16 April; Southampton, 26 April; Oxford, 7 May; Birmingham, 12, 14 May; Bristol, 18 May 1988

4 June 1988, Cardiff
Verdi: La Traviata (in Italian)
p. Göran Järvefelt; d. Carl Friedrich Oberle
further perfs: Cardiff, 7, 10 June; Southampton, 18 June; Bristol, 22, 25 June; Birmingham, 29 June 1988

11 March 1989, Cardiff
Mozart: Die Entführung aus dem Serail (in English)
p. Giles Havergal; d. Peter Watson
further perfs: Cardiff, 21, 23 March; Oxford, 28 March; Liverpool, 7 April; Birmingham, 12 April; Southampton, 20 April; Bristol, 26 April 1989

25 February 1989, Cardiff
Strauss: Die Frau ohne Schatten (in English)
p. Gilbert Deflo, d. Carlo Tommasi
further perfs: Cardiff, 4, 25 March; Oxford, 1 April; Liverpool, 8 April; Bristol, 29 April 1989

5 June 1989, Cardiff
Strauss: Ariadne auf Naxos (in English)
p. Giles Havergal; d. Russell Craig
further perfs: Cardiff, 8 June; Southampton, 21, 24 June; Birmingham, 28 June, 1 July; Bristol, 5, 7 July; Swansea, 12 July 1989

30 June 1989, Birmingham
Janáček: Fate [Osud] (in English; concert perf)
further perf: Bristol 8 July 1989

23 September 1989, Cardiff
Donizetti: Lucia di Lammermoor (in Italian)
p. Rennie Wright; d. Ultz
further perfs: Cardiff, 30 September, 6 October; Liverpool, 13 October; London, 6, 8 December; Bristol, 12, 15 December 1989

5 October 1989, Cardiff
Smetana: The Bartered Bride (in English)
p. Rudolf Noelte; d. Jan Schlubach
further perfs: Cardiff, 7 October; Liverpool, 12 October; London, 7 December; Bristol, 13, 16 December 1989

14 February 1989, Cardiff
Mozart: Così fan tutte (in Italian)
p. Liviu Ciulei; d, Radu Boruzescu
further perfs: Cardiff, 24 February, 8 March; Birmingham, 15 March; Oxford, 22 March; Southampton, 30 March 1989

1 March 1990, Cardiff
Strauss: Der Rosenkavalier (in English)
p. Wolfgang Weber; d. Carl Friedrich Oberle
further perfs: Cardiff, 7, 10 March; Birmingham, 13, 17 March; Oxford, 21, 24 March 1990

9 May 1991, SDH, Cardiff
Delius: Dance Rhapsodies Nos 1 and 2
Delius: Violin Concerto (Tasmin Little)
Sibelius: Symphony No. 2

13 September 1991, BBC Proms, RAH, London
Mozart: Idomeneo (in Italian), concert performance
p. Howard Davies; d. William Dudley
further (staged) perfs: Cardiff, 18, 21, 25 September; Liverpool, 10 October; Birmingham, 15, 18 October; Oxford, 5, 8 November; Southampton, 12, 15 November; Bristol, 19 November 1991

18 May 1992, Cardiff
Gluck: Iphigénie en Tauride (in French)
p. Patrice Caurier; d. Christian Ratz
further perfs: Cardiff, 22, 28 May; Liverpool, 4 June; Southampton, 10 June; Birmingham 16, 18 June; Oxford 7, 9 July 1992

13 February 1993, Cardiff
Wagner: Tristan und Isolde (in German)
p. and d. Yannis Kokkos
further perfs: Cardiff, 20 February (broadcast), 6 March; Bristol, 13 March; Liverpool, 20 March; Birmingham, 15 April; London ROH, 19, 23 April 1993

13 December 1994, Cardiff
(conducted by Gareth Jones)
Sullivan: The Yeomen of the Guard (in English)
p. Tim Hopkins; d. Peter J. Davison
Perfs conducted by CM: Oxford, 5, 6 April; London ROH, 24, 25, 26 April 1995

1 October 1995, SDH, Cardiff
'Towards 70: A celebration in honour of Sir Charles Mackerras'
Music by Sullivan, Mozart, Verdi, Wagner, Mackerras, Janáček, Berlioz, Richard Strauss (Josephine Barstow, Anne Evans, Rebecca Evans, Katerina Karnéus, Antony Rolfe Johnson, Jonathan Summers)

5 October 1995, Cardiff
Mozart: Idomeneo (in Italian; revival)
further perfs: Bristol, 11, 18 October 1995

16 April 1996, Cardiff
Gounod: Faust (in English)
p. Christopher Alden; d. Bruno Schwengl
further perfs: 18, 26 April 1996

24 September 1997, Cardiff
Mozart: La clemenza di Tito (in Italian)
p. Yannis Kokkos; d. Yannis Kokkos
further perfs: Cardiff, 3 October 1997; Oxford, 9 October; Birmingham, 6 November; Liverpool, 13 November; Bristol, 20 November 1997; ROH, London, 5, 7 March 1998

26 May 2000, Cardiff
Bizet: Carmen (in French; revival)
p. Patrice Caurier, d. Christian Fenouillat
further perfs: Cardiff, 3, 9 June; Bristol, 13, 16 June 2000

24 May 2002, Cardiff
Janáček: The Cunning Little Vixen (in English; revival)
p. David Pountney; d. Maria Björnson
further perfs: Bristol, 31 May; Symphony Hall, Birmingham, 6 June; Oxford, 19 June 2002

6 March 2003, Cardiff
Janáček: Jenůfa (in English; revival)
p. Katie Mitchell; d. Vicki Mortimer
further perfs: Cardiff, 8 March; Birmingham, 13 March; Southampton, 20 March 2003

1 March 2005, Welsh Millennium Centre, Cardiff
St David's Day Gala

23 April 2005, SDH, Cardiff
Wagner: Tannhäuser: Overture and Venusberg Music
Wagner: Tristan und Isolde: Prelude and Liebestod (Anne Evans)
Wagner: Götterdämmerung extracts (Anne Evans)

27 May 2009, Birmingham
Mozart: Mitridate, rè di Ponto (in Italian, concert perf)
further perf: Cardiff, Welsh Millennium Centre, 2 June 2009

Sources: Charles Mackerras annual schedules (from 1992); WNO Archives; Isabel Murphy (WNO); *Opera*.

E ROH performances, 1955–2010

(See especially Chapter 8)

1954/5

9 June 1955
Verdi, arr. Mackerras: The Lady and the Fool
choreography by John Cranko;
d. Richard Beer

1964/5

8, 14, 16 December 1964
Shostakovich: Katerina Ismailova
p. Vlado Habunek; d. Božidar Rašica

1965/6

6, 11, 14, 19, 22, 24 January, 20, 24, 28 May 1966
Puccini: Turandot
p. Sandro Sequi; d. Cecil Beaton

1966/7

6, 9, 12, 14 January, 24 February, 6 March 1967
Puccini: Turandot
p. Sandro Sequi; d. Cecil Beaton

11, 16, 19, 24, 27 May, 1, 5, 9 June 1967
Bizet: Carmen
p. Anthony Asquith rev. John Copley;
d. Georges Wakhevitch

1967/8

3, 7, 15, 19, 23, 28 February, 5, 8 March 1968
Bizet: Carmen
p. Anthony Asquith rev. John Copley;
d. Georges Wakhevitch

22, 30 March, 2, 5, 11, 15 April 1968
Puccini: Tosca
p. Franco Zeffirelli; d. Renzo Mongiardino

8, 12, 16, 18 July 1968
Così fan tutte
p. John Copley; d. Henry Bardon

1968/9

4, 6, 9, 14, 17, 20 January 1969
Mozart: Così fan tutte
p. John Copley; d. Henry Bardon

30 April, 6, 10, 14, 20, 22, 26 May 1969
Verdi: Simon Boccanegra
p. Tito Gobbi; d. Giancarlo Bartolini Salimbeni

29 May, 4, 10, 14, 17, 20 June 1969

Verdi: Aida
p. Peter Potter; d. Nicholas Georgiadis

1969/70

12, 16, 22, 27, 30 December 1969, 2 January 1970
Rimsky-Korsakov: Le Coq d'or
p. Robert Helpmann rev. Ande Anderson; d. Loudon Sainthill

26, 28 May, 1, 4, 9, 16 June 1970
Puccini: Tosca
p. Franco Zeffirelli; d. Renzo Mongiardino

1970/1

6, 9, 12, 15 January, 3, 12, 18 February 1971
Puccini: Turandot
p. Sandro Sequi; d. Cecil Beaton

9, 13, 16, 19, 21 July 1971
Gluck: Orfeo ed Euridice
p. John Copley; d. Philip Prowse

1971/2

30 December 1971, 3, 5, 11, 17 January 1972
Britten: Billy Budd
p. Basil Coleman; d. John Piper

13, 20, 25, 29 April, 2 May 1972
Janáček: Jenůfa
p. Christopher West; d. Jan Brazda

24, 27, 30 May, 3, 6, 9 June 1972
Gluck: Orfeo ed Euridice
p. John Copley; d. Philip Prowse

1972/3

23, 27, 31 March, 3, 6, 9, 12, 17 April 1973
Verdi: Aida
p. Peter Potter; d. Nicholas Georgiadis

23, 26, 30 May, 2, 6, 11 June 1973
Verdi: Il trovatore
p. Luchino Visconti; d. Filippo Sanjust

1973/4

2, 4, 11, 15, 19 January 1974
Britten: A Midsummer Night's Dream
p. John Gielgud; d. John Piper

1, 4, 10, 13, 17, 20, 24 May 1974
Verdi: Otello
p. Peter Potter; d. Georges Wakhevitch

22, 25, 28 May, 7, 10 June 1974
Janáček: Jenůfa
p. Christopher West; d. Jan Brazda

1974/5

8, 12, 16, 18 November 1974
Puccini: Tosca
p. Franco Zeffirelli; d. Renzo Mongiardino

5, 7, 10, 13 December 1974
Gounod: Faust
p. John Copley; d. Desmond Heeley

1976/7

8, 11, 14, 17 June 1977
Janáček: Jenůfa
p. Christopher West; d. Jan Brazda

1978/9

21, 27, 29 December 1978, 3, 6 January 1980
Verdi: Un ballo in maschera
p. Otto Schenk; d. Jürgen Rose

1981/2

26 November, 1, 4, 9, 12, 15 December 1981
Gluck: Alceste
d. John Copley, p. Roger Butlin

1982/3

25, 29 November, 1, 4, 7, 11, 14 December 1982
Handel: Semele
p. John Copley; d. Henry Bardon

1984/5

18, 22, 26, 29 September 1984
Puccini: Tosca
p. Franco Zeffirelli; d. Renzo Mongiardino

1988/9

22, 28, 30 December 1988, 3, 7 January 1989
Handel: Semele
p. John Copley; d. Henry Bardon

1994/5

28 October, 1, 4, 9, 12, 15, 17 November 1994
Gounod: Roméo et Juliette
p. Nicolas Joël; d. Carlo Tommasi

1999/2000

18, 21, 26 February, 1, 6, 9 March 2000
Gounod: Roméo et Juliette
p. Nicolas Joël; d. Carlo Tommasi

25, 27, 29 April, 3, 5, 8 May 2000
Martinů: The Greek Passion
p. David Pountney; d. Stefanos Lazaridis

2001/2

30 May, 2, 4, 7, 9 June 2001
Mozart: Die Entführung aus dem Serail
p. Elijah Moshinsky; d. Sidney Nolan

7, 10, 12, 20 November 2001
Smetana: The Bartered Bride
p. Francesca Zambello; d. Alison Chitty

18, 20, 23, 28 February 2002
Don Giovanni
p. Francesca Zambello; d. Maria Björnson

2002/3

25, 28 June, 2, 5, 8, 11 July 2003
Handel: Semele
p. John Copley; d. Henry Bardon

14, 17 July 2003
Dvořák: Rusalka (concert perfs)

2003/4

13, 19, 22, 24, 27, 30 April 2004
Strauss: Der Rosenkavalier
p. John Schlesinger; d. William Dudley

2004/5

15, 19, 21, 23, 25 September, 1 October 2004
Martinů: The Greek Passion
p. David Pountney; d. Stefanos Lazaridis

11, 14, 16, 21, 23, 26, 28 February, 3, 4 March 2005
Mozart: Die Zauberflöte
p. David McVicar; d. John F. Macfarlane

2005/6

17, 21, 25, 29 November, 3, 7, 10, 13, 16 December 2005
Verdi: Un ballo in maschera
p. Mario Martone; d. Sergio Tramonti

6, 9, 12, 14, 17, 20 January 2006
Smetana: The Bartered Bride
p. Francesca Zambello; d. Alison Chitty

2006/7

26 February, 1, 3, 7, 9, 13 March 2007
Handel: Orlando
p. Franceso Negrin; d. Anthony Baker

19, 22, 15, 28 June, 2, 5 July 2007
Janáček: Kát'a Kabanová
p. Trevor Nunn; d. Maria Björnson

2007/8

24, 30 June, 2, 5, 10, 12, 16 July 2008
Mozart: Le nozze di Figaro
p. David McVicar; d. Tanya McCallin

2008/9

8, 10, 12, 15, 18 September 2008
Mozart: Don Giovanni
p. Francesca Zambello; d. Maria Björnson

2009/10

19, 22, 25, 29 March, 1 April 2010
Janáček: The Cunning Little Vixen
p. Bill Bryden; d. William Dudley

Sources: Charles Mackerras annual schedules (from 1992); Royal Opera House archives online (http://rohcollections.org.uk); *Opera*.

F Performances in Czechoslovakia and the Czech Republic, and with Czech orchestras abroad, 1961–2008

(See Chapter 9)

* concert recorded by Czech Radio

† concert recorded by Czechoslovak Television

12 & March 1961, Obecní dům, Prague, PRO
Britten: Sinfonia da Requiem
Mahler Symphony No. 6

13–16 March 1961, Prague, PRO
radio recordings
Britten: Young Person's Guide to the Orchestra *
Walton: Symphony No. 2

21 March 1961, Janáček Theatre (on the Ramparts), Brno
Janáček: Káťa Kabanová

10 May 1962, Reduta, Bratislava, Slovak PO
Britten: Variations on a Theme of Frank Bridge
Beethoven: Piano Concerto No. 5
Bartók: Concerto for Orchestra

14 May 1962, Společenský sál, Ostrava, Janáček PO
Jiří Jaroch: The Old Man and the Sea [Stařec a moře]
Debussy: La Mer
Schubert: Symphony in C ('Great')

19 May 1962, Obecní dům, Prague, PRO*
Mozart: Divertimento in D major
Haydn: Concerto in C major for Cello and Orchestra, Hob. VIIb/1 (modern premiere)
Stravinsky: Symphony in C
Jaroch: The Old Man and the Sea

16 September 1963, Radio Studio, Bratislava, PRO in Bratislava*
Walton: Variations on a Theme by Hindemith

10 & 11 October 1963, Stadion, Brno, Brno State PO
Prokofiev: Piano Concerto No. 2
Berlioz: Symphonie fantastique*
Oskar Morawetz: Overture to a Fairy Tale

16 May 1966, Rudolfinum, Prague, ECO
Handel: Concerto Grosso in G minor Op. 6 No. 6
Mozart: Sinfonia Concertante in E flat for violin and viola*
Britten: Variations on a Theme of Frank Bridge*
Arnold: Sinfonietta No. 2
Dvořák: Czech Suite, Polka [encore]*

1 June 1974, Obecní dům, Prague, PRO
Haydn: Trumpet Concerto
Voříšek: Symphony in D
Iša Krejčí: Twenty Variations on an Original Theme in the Style of Folk music [Dvacet variací na vlastní téma ve slohu národní písně]
Janáček: Taras Bulba

28 September 1974, Stadion, Brno, Brno State PO
Václav Dobiáš: Sonata for piano, wind quintet, timpani and strings* [not extant]
Martinů: Violin Concerto No. 1
Janáček: Žárlivost [Jealousy]; Taras Bulba

30 May 1979, Obecní dům, Prague, CPO
Janáček: The Cunning Little Vixen, Suite (arr. Talich)*
Prokofiev: Symphony-Concerto for cello and orchestra
Stravinsky: Petrushka

6 & 7 October 1980, Obecní dům, Prague, PRO*
Britten: Sinfonia da Requiem
Janáček: Glagolitic Mass

8 & 9 February 1982, Obecní dům, Prague, PRO*
Martinů: Double Concerto for two string orchestras
J. C. Bach: Symphony for two orchestras in E flat, Op. 18 No. 1
Shostakovich: Violin Concerto No. 2

15–16 February 1982, PRO*
radio recording
Martinů: Double Concerto for two string orchestras; Les Fresques de Piero della Francesca

20 & 21 January 1984, PRO*
radio recording
Martinů: Field Mass

26 & 27 January 1984, Rudolfinum, Prague, CPO*
Janáček: Amarus; Glagolitic Mass

3 February 1984, Janáček Theatre, Brno, Brno State PO
Martinů: Les Fresques de Piero della Francesca
Mysliveček: Cello Concerto in C major
Janáček: Amarus

25 & 26 May 1986, Obecní dům, Prague, CPO†
Dvořák: Amid Nature [V přírodě]
Beethoven: Piano Concerto No. 4
Janáček: The Cunning Little Vixen, Suite (arr. Talich)
Martinů: Symphony No. 6

12 & 13 May 1989, Palác kultury, Prague, CPO†
Smetana: Má vlast

7 October 1990, Janáček Theatre, Brno, Brno State PO†
Martinů: Špalíček, Suite (arr. Mackerras); Double Concerto for two string orchestras
Janáček: Sinfonietta

6 & 7 July 1991, Obecní dům, Prague, CPO
Strauss: Don Juan; Horn Concerto No. 1
Dvořák: Symphony No. 7

28 August 1991, Usher Hall, Edinburgh, CPO
Lukáš Matoušek: Fanfares for 17 November [Fanfáry pro 17. listopad]
Dvořák: Symphony No. 7
Janáček: Glagolitic Mass

1 December 1991, Estates Theatre, Prague
Re-opening of the Estates Theatre
Mozart: Don Giovanni

26 May 1994, Rudolfinum, Prague, BBC SO
Glinka: Overture to Ruslan and Ludmila
Tchaikovsky: Piano Concerto No. 1
Shostakovich: Symphony No. 10

21 September 1994, Rudolfinum, Prague, FOK
Dvořák: Cello Concerto
Suk: Asrael

25 September 1995, Janáček Theatre, Brno, Brno State PO†
Janáček: The Cunning Little Vixen, Suite (arr. Jílek); Taras Bulba; Glagolitic Mass (Wingfield version)

21 March 1996, Rudolfinum, Prague, CPO
Suk: Praga
Janáček: Glagolitic Mass (Wingfield version)

28 March 1997, Rudolfinum, Prague, CPO
Janáček: Káťa Kabanová (semi-staged)

3 & 4 April 1997, Rudolfinum, Prague, CPO
Suk: Fantastic Scherzo;* A Summer's Tale*
Dvořák: Violin Concerto

10 & 11 April 1997, Rudolfinum, Prague, CPO
Dvořák: Symphony No. 5
Martinů: Double Concerto for two string orchestras
Janáček: Sinfonietta

4* & 6 December 1997, Rudolfinum, Prague, CPO
Brahms: Tragic Overture [4 December only]
Suk: A Summer's Tale, movement No. 4 [6 December only]
Suk: Fantasy in G minor for Violin and Orchestra
Shostakovich: Symphony No. 10

18 & 19 December 1997, Rudolfinum, Prague, CPO
Martinů: Symphony No. 6; Kytice

4 September 1998, Usher Hall, Edinburgh, CPO
Smetana: Festival Overture in D; Wallenstein's Camp
Mahler Symphony No. 1

5 September 1998, Usher Hall, Edinburgh, CPO
Smetana: Má vlast

7 September 1998, RAH, London, CPO
Janáček: The Cunning Little Vixen, Suite (arr. Jílek); Taras Bulba
Mahler: Symphony No. 1

9 September 1998, Symphony Hall, Birmingham, CPO
Janáček: The Cunning Little Vixen, Suite (arr. Jílek)
Beethoven: Piano Concerto No. 5
Dvořák: Symphony No. 8

4, 5 & 6 February 1999, Rudolfinum, Prague, CPO
Smetana: Wallenstein's Camp
Bartók: Music for Strings, Percussion and Celesta
Schubert: Symphony in C ('Great')

11 & 12 February 1999, Rudolfinum, Prague, CPO
Beethoven: Missa solemnis

6 & 7 May 1999, Rudolfinum, Prague, CPO
Haydn: Symphony No. 100
Haydn: Trumpet Concerto
Debussy: Prélude à l'après-midi d'un faune
Hindemith: Symphony Mathis der Maler

12* & 13 May 1999, Rudolfinum, Prague, CPO
Smetana: Má vlast

21 & 22 December 1999, Rudolfinum, Prague, CPO*
Martinů: Špalíček Suite; Violin Concerto No. 1; Symphony No. 5

28 August 2000, Usher Hall, Edinburgh, CPO
Britten: Sinfonia da Requiem
Suk: Asrael

30 & 31 August 2000, Playhouse, Edinburgh, CPO
Ballet performances by Netherlands Dance Theatre, choreography by Jiří Kylián
Britten: Sinfonia da Requiem
Janáček: Sinfonietta

1 September 2000, Usher Hall, Edinburgh, CPO
Mahler: Das Lied von der Erde
Janáček: Sinfonietta

4 & 5 January 2001, Rudolfinum, Prague, CPO
Dvořák: The Golden Spinning Wheel
Franz Krommer (Kramář): Oboe Concerto in F major
Brahms: Symphony No. 1

22 & 23 March 2001, Rudolfinum, Prague, CPO
Dvořák: Scherzo capriccioso; Legends; Symphonic Variations

28 & 29 March 2002, Rudolfinum, Prague, CPO
Dvořák: The Water Goblin; The Noonday Witch; Symphony No. 7

4 & 5 April 2002, Rudolfinum, Prague, CPO
Dvořák: The Wood Dove
Bartók: Piano Concerto No. 3
Shostakovich: Symphony No. 5

17 & 18 October 2002, Rudolfinum, Prague, CPO
Janáček: The Cunning Little Vixen, Suite (arr. Talich with CM's arrangement of original instrumentation); Sinfonietta
Dvořák: Symphony No. 6

22 May 2003, Rudolfinum, Prague, CPO*
Janáček: Žárlivost; Taras Bulba
Martinů: Piano Concerto No. 4
Suk: Fantastic Scherzo

20 December 2003 (& further performances), National Theatre, Prague
Janáček: The Excursions of Mr Brouček

29 January 2004, Janáček Theatre, Brno
Prague National Theatre production of Janáček: The Excursions of Mr Brouček

5 February 2004, Janáček Theatre, Brno, Brno State PO*
Janáček: Glagolitic Mass (Wingfield version); Violin Concerto; Danube Symphony

22 March 2004, Musikverein, Vienna, CPO
Dvořák: Scherzo capriccioso; Piano Concerto
Janáček: Schluck und Jau; Sinfonietta

23 March 2004, Musikverein, Vienna, CPO
Janáček: Sinfonietta
Dvořák: Symphony No. 9 ('From the New World')

8 September 2004, RAH, London, CPO
Dvořák: Scherzo capriccioso, Violin Concerto; Symphony No. 9

13 March 2005, Obecní dům, Prague, FOK
Dvořák: Amid Nature; Symphony No. 8; Symphony No. 9

5 & 6 April 2007, Rudolfinum, Prague, CPO
Haydn: Symphony No. 49
Suk: Asrael

21 May 2007, Obecní dům, Prague, FOK
Elgar: Cockaigne Overture; Cello Concerto
Janáček: Glagolitic Mass

11 & 12 December 2008, Rudolfinum, Prague, CPO
Dvořák: The Water Goblin; The Noonday Witch
Martinů: Three Fragments from Juliette [world premiere]

Sources: Archiv České filharmonie; Archiv Národního divadla v Praze; Archiv Českého rozhlasu v Praze; Archiv festivalu Pražské jaro; Archiv Národního divadla Brno; Archiv Filharmonie Brno; Archiv Mezinárodního hudebního festivalu Brno; Archiv Janáčkovy filharmonie Ostrava; Archiv Slovenské filharmonie; Janáčkův archiv Moravského zemského muzea; Archiv orchestru hl. města Prahy FOK; daily newspapers, specialist journals – *Hudební rozhledy, Opus musicum, Slovenský hudobný život.*

G OAE performances, 1987–2010

(See Chapter 13)

2 June 1987, Barbican Hall, London
Mozart: Don Giovanni Overture
Mozart: Symphony No. 36 ('Linz')
Mozart: 'Haffner' Serenade
[CM's first concert with the OAE]

9 October 1987, QEH, London
Schubert: Rosamunde Overture and incidental music
Weber: Clarinet Concerto No. 2 (Antony Pay)
Mendelssohn: Symphony No. 4

10 October 1987, QEH, London
Mendelssohn: Midsummer Night's Dream Overture and incidental music
Schubert: Symphony in C ('Great')

11 October 1989, QEH, London
Haydn: The Creation (Lynne Dawson, Anthony Rolfe Johnson, David Wilson-Johnson, Choir of the Enlightenment)

18 November 1990, QEH, London
Mendelssohn: Hebrides Overture
Crusell: Clarinet Concerto Op. 11 (Antony Pay)
Schubert: Symphony in B minor ('Unfinished')

19 October 1992, QEH, London
Mozart: Symphony No. 32
Mendelssohn: Violin Concerto (Monica Huggett)
Schubert: Die vierjährige Posten Overture
Schubert: Symphony No. 4

9 May 1994, QEH, London
Wagner: Tannhäuser Overture
Wagner: Wesendonck Lieder
Wagner: Siegfried Idyll
Brahms: Violin Concerto (Elizabeth Wallfisch)

25 August 1994, Usher Hall, Edinburgh
Beethoven: Symphony No. 4
Beethoven: Symphony No. 7

26 August 1994, Usher Hall, Edinburgh
Beethoven: Symphony No. 9 (Amanda Roocroft, Fiona Janes, John Mark Ainsley, Neal Davies, The New Company)

15 October 1997, QEH, London
Mendelssohn: Trumpet Overture
Beethoven: Violin Concerto (Thomas Zehetmair)
Schubert: Symphony in C major ('Great')

19 May 1998, QEH, London
Dvořák: Czech Suite
Chopin: Piano Concerto No. 1 (Emanuel Ax)
Brahms: Serenade No. 1

13, 16, 19, 22, 25, 27 June, 2, 10, 12, 15 July 1999, Glyndebourne
Handel: Rodelinda (Lisa Milne, Kurt Streit, Umberto Chiummo, Jean Rigby, Gianluca Belfiori Doro)

25 November 1999, RFH, London
Beethoven: Symphony No. 4
Beethoven: Symphony No. 6

7 May 2000, Glyndebourne
Haydn: The Creation (Lisa Milne, Ian Bostridge, David Wilson-Johnson)

23 January 2001, QEH, London
'The Leipzig Gewandhaus, 8 December 1855'
Weber: Oberon Overture
Beethoven: Piano Concerto No. 5 (Robert Levin)
Schumann: Introduction and Allegro appassionato (Robert Levin)
Schumann: Symphony No. 2
Mozart: Le Nozze di Figaro, excerpts (Nuccia Focile, James Rutherford)

20 July 2002, BBC Proms, RAH, London
Haydn: The Creation (Christiane Oelze, Paul Groves, John Relyea, Choir of the Enlightenment)

14 October 2002, QEH, London
Schubert: Symphony in B minor ('Unfinished')
Beethoven: Symphony No. 3

11 October 2004, QEH, London
'The Prague Connection'
Mozart: Don Giovanni Overture
Mozart: Bella mia fiamma K528 (Hillevi Martinpelto)
Mozart: Concerto for basset clarinet (Antony Pay)
Mozart: Non più di fiori (Hillevi Martinpelto and Antony Pay)
Beethoven: Ah! Perfido (Hillevi Martinpelto)
Voříšek: Symphony in D

21, 25, 28, 31 May, 3, 5 June 2005, Glyndebourne
Mozart: Die Zauberflöte (Christopher Maltman, Lisa Milne, Eric Cutler, Aline Kutan, Alfred Reiter, Claire Ormshaw)

25 April 2006, QEH, London
Mozart: Le nozze di Figaro – Overture; Al desio di chi t'adora (Rebecca Evans)
Mozart: Don Giovanni – Batti, batti, o bel Masetto (Rebecca Evans)
Mozart: Rondo in A for Piano and Orchestra, K386 (Susan Tomes)
Mozart: Ch'io me scordi di te, K505 (Rebecca Evans, Susan Tomes)
Mozart: Il re pastore – L'amerò, sarò costante (Rebecca Evans)
Mozart: 'Posthorn' Serenade

8 September 2006, RAH, London
Mozart: Symphony No. 35 ('Haffner')
Mozart: Mass in C minor, ed. Levin (Rosemary Joshua, Sarah Fox, Eric Cutler, Nathan Berg, Choir of the Enlightenment)
[in memory of Fiona Mackerras]

26 February, 1, 3, 7, 9, 13 March 2007, ROH
Handel: Orlando (Rosemary Joshua, Camilla Tilling, Suzanne McNaughton, Bejun Mehta, Kyle Ketelsen, David Lucas)

30 June 2007, RFH, London
Handel: Music for the Royal Fireworks
[the final item in the OAE's 21st birthday gala concert; harpsichord continuo played by Vladimir Jurowski]

16 August 2008, RAH, London
Handel: Belshazzar (Rosemary Joshua, Bejun Mehta, Iestyn Davies, Paul Groves, Robert Gleadow, Choir of the Enlightenment)

13 November 2008, RFH, London
Mozart: Nozze di Figaro Overture
Mozart: Agnus Dei from Coronation Mass (Rebecca Evans)
Mozart: Dove sono (Rebecca Evans)
Mozart: Symphony No. 32
Mozart: Giunse alfin il momento – Al desio (Rebecca Evans)
Mozart: Giunse alfin il momento – Non tardar, amato bene (Rebecca Evans)
Beethoven: Symphony No. 6

22, 27, 30 May, 4, 6, 9, 12 June 2010, Glyndebourne
Mozart: Così fan tutte (Sally Matthews, Barbara Senator, Anna Maria Panzarella, Allan Clayton, Robert Gleadow, Pietro Spagnoli)

Sources: Charles Mackerras annual schedules; www.classicalsource.com.

H SCO performances, 1993–2010

(See Chapter 13)

All given at the Usher Hall, Edinburgh, unless otherwise stated

24 February 1993, Royal Concert Hall, Glasgow
Handel: Concerto a due cori No. 2
Handel: Concerto a due cori No. 3
Mozart: Piano Concerto No. 25 K503
Schubert: Symphony No. 4
repeated 25 February 1993, Queen's Hall, Edinburgh; 26 February 1993, Music Hall, Aberdeen

6 April 1993, QEH, London
Handel: Concerto a due cori No. 2
Handel: Concerto a due cori No. 3
Mozart: Concertone K190
Bartók: Music for Strings, Percussion and Celesta

7 April 1993, City Hall, Glasgow
Bach: St John Passion
repeated 8 April 1993, Usher Hall, Edinburgh; 9 April 1993, Music Hall, Aberdeen

16 August 1993
Mozart: Così fan tutte (Felicity Lott, Marie McLaughlin, Jerry Hadley, Alessandro Corbelli, Nuccia Focile, Gilles Cachemaille, Edinburgh Festival Chorus)

17 August 1993
Janáček: Říkadla (SCO Chorus)
Janáček: Capriccio (Peter Donohoe)
Schubert: Rosamunde, incidental music (SCO Chorus)

2 December 1993, Queen's Hall, Edinburgh
Haydn: Symphony No. 100
Field: Piano Concerto No. [?2]
Bartók: Music for Strings, Percussion and Celesta

3 December 1993, Music Hall, Aberdeen
Haydn: Symphony No. 100
['different concerto', unspecified]
Bartók: Music for Strings, Percussion and Celesta

9 December 1993, Queen's Hall, Edinburgh
Bach: Christmas Oratorio (Joan Rodgers, Diana Montague, Neill Archer and Michael George)
repeated 10 December 1993, City Hall, Glasgow

14 April 1994
Wagner: Siegfried Idyll
Weber: Piano Concerto No. 2 (Nikolai Demidenko)
Weber: Konzertstück (Nikolai Demidenko)
Beethoven: The Creatures of Prometheus

15 April 1994, Music Hall, Aberdeen
Wagner: Siegfried Idyll
Weber: Piano Concerto No. 1 (Nikolai Demidenko)
Weber: Konzertstück (Nikolai Demidenko)
Beethoven: The Creatures of Prometheus

22 April 1994, City Hall, Glasgow
Handel: Jephtha
repeated 23 April 1994, Usher Hall, Edinburgh

15 August 1994
Mozart: Le nozze di Figaro (Carol Vaness, Nuccia Focile, Alessandro Corbelli, Alastair Miles, Susanne Mentzer, Suzanne Murphy, Alfonso Antoniozzi, Ryland Davies, Rebecca Evans, SCO Chorus)

17 August 1994
Beethoven: Leonore (Janice Watson, William Kendall, Rebecca Evans, Paul Charles Clarke, Donald Maxwell, Franz Hawlata, Neal Davies, Ivor Klayman, William Durran, SCO Chorus)

28 March 1995
SCO 21st Anniversary Concert
Mozart: Vado, ma dove? K583
Mozart: Smanie implacabili from Così fan tutte
Mozart: Voi che sapete from Le nozze di Figaro
Handel: Music for the Royal Fireworks
[Other items were conducted by Ivor Bolton]

30 March 1995, Queen's Hall, Edinburgh
J. C. Bach: Symphony Op. 18 No. 1
Mozart: Piano Concerto No. 24 K491
Beethoven: Symphony No. 5

14 April 1995, City Hall, Glasgow
Bach: St Matthew Passion (John Mark Ainsley, Simon Keenlyside, Joan Rodgers, Patricia Bardon, Ian Bostridge, and David Wilson-Johnson, SCO Chorus, Choristers of St Mary's Cathedral, Edinburgh)
repeated 15 April 1995, St Mary's Cathedral, Edinburgh

22, 24 & 26 June 1995, Topkapı Palace, Istanbul
Mozart: Die Entführung aus dem Serail

25 June 1995, St Irene's Church, Istanbul
Handel: Suite from the Water Music in F and D
Mozart: Flute Concerto in G
Britten: Variations on a Theme of Frank Bridge
Beethoven: The Creatures of Prometheus

14 August 1995
Mozart: Don Giovanni (Bo Skovhus, Umberto Chiummo, Christine Brewer, Jerry Hadley, Felicity Lott, Alessandro Corbelli, Nuccia Focile, SCO Chorus)

21 August 1995
Dvořák: Piano Concerto (András Schiff)
Dvořák: Violin Concerto (Yuuko Shiokawa)
Dvořák: The Noonday Witch
Dvořák: Cello Concerto (Boris Pergamenschikow)

13 October 1995, Theatre Royal, Glasgow
Mozart: Die Entführung aus dem Serail
repeated 14 October 1995, Usher Hall, Edinburgh

25 February 1996, Barbican Hall, London
Mozart: Die Zauberflöte Overture
Mozart: Symphony No. 41
Bruckner: Requiem [Probably the only time Mackerras conducted a work by Bruckner.]

29 February 1996
Beethoven: Piano Concerto No. 3 (Alfred Brendel)
Mozart: Die Zauberflöte Overture
Mozart: Symphony No. 41

12 August 1996
Beethoven: Fidelio (Anne Evans, Ildikó Raimondi, John Mark Ainsley, Heinz Kruse, Franz-Josef Kapellmann, Siegfried Vogel, David Wilson-Johnson, Edinburgh Festival Chorus)

28 November 1996
Brahms: Academic Festival Overture
Brahms: Symphony No. 1
Brahms: Symphony No. 2
repeated 29 November 1996, City Hall, Glasgow

5 December 1996
Brahms: Variations on a Theme by Haydn
Brahms: Symphony No. 3
Brahms: Symphony No. 4
repeated 6 December 1996, City Hall, Glasgow

25 August 1997
Mozart: Symphony No. 39
Mozart: Piano Concerto No. 20 K466 (Alfred Brendel)
Mozart: Symphony No. 40
Mozart: Piano Concerto No. 24 K491 (Alfred Brendel)
Mozart: Symphony No. 41

27 August 1997, Queen's Hall, Edinburgh
'The Art of Embellishment' (Inge Dam-Jensen, Nuccia Focile, Mhairi Lawson)
J. C. Bach: Cara la dolce fiamma, from Adriano in Siria
Mozart: Non so d'onde viene
Handel: Dove sei, amato bene?
Gluck: Che faro senza Euridice
Anon: Auld Robin Gray
Anon: Queen Mary's Lamentation
Mozart: Voi che sapete (embellished by Domenico Corri)

1 September 1997, RAH, London
Handel: Jephtha (Joan Rodgers, Felicity Palmer, Deborah York, Michael Chance, Anthony Rolfe Johnson, Alastair Miles, The New Company)

30 October 1998, City Hall, Glasgow
Mozart: Symphony No. 31 ('Paris') [including both slow movements]
Bach: Ich habe genug (Olaf Bär)
Brahms: Serenade No. 1
repeated 31 October 1998, Usher Hall, Edinburgh

30 April 1999, City Hall, Glasgow
Strauss: Serenade Op. 7
Dvořák: Czech Suite
Dvořák: Nocturne Op. 40
Brahms: Violin Concerto (Antje Weithaas)
repeated 1 May 1999, Usher Hall, Edinburgh

15 August 1999
Handel: Saul (Lisa Milne, Joan Rodgers, David Daniels, Ian Bostridge, Toby Spence, Neil Jenkins, Neal Davies, Bryn Terfel, Thomas Trotter, Edinburgh Festival Chorus)

23 August 1999
Schumann: Symphony No. 1
Schumann: Violin Concerto (Christian Tetzlaff)
Schumann: Symphony No. 4, original version

28 August 1999
Schumann: Overture, Scherzo and Finale
Schumann: Piano Concerto (Alfred Brendel)
Schumann: Symphony No. 2

2 September 1999
Schumann: Symphony No. 3
Schumann: Cello Concerto (Clemens Hagen)
Schumann: Symphony No. 4, revised version

6 May 2000
Haydn: Symphony No. 83
Mozart: Piano Concerto No. 25 K503 (Ivan Moravec)
Schubert: Symphony No. 4
repeated 7 May 2000, City Hall, Glasgow

11 September 2000, Schubertiade Festival, Schwartzenberg, Austria
Mozart: Symphony No. 31 ('Paris') [with both slow movements]
Mozart: Piano Concerto No. 22 K482 (Alfred Brendel)
Mozart: Piano Concerto No. 27 K595 (Alfred Brendel)
repeated 13 September 2000, Lucerne Festival

15 February 2001
Janáček, arr. Tognetti: String Quartet No. 1
Mozart: Bella mia fiamma (Christine Brewer)
Beethoven: Ah! Perfido (Christine Brewer)
Dvořák: Symphony No. 9
repeated 16 February, City Hall, Glasgow

23 June 2001, Aldeburgh Festival, Maltings, Snape, Suffolk
Haydn: Symphony No. 67
Mozart: Piano Concerto No. 9 K271 (Alfred Brendel)
Mozart: Piano Concerto No. 25 K503 (Alfred Brendel)
repeated 25 June 2001, Concertgebouw, Amsterdam

13 August 2001
Mozart: Idomeneo (Ian Bostridge, Lisa Milne, Barbara Frittoli, Lorraine Hunt Lieberson, Anthony Rolfe Johnson, Paul Charles Clarke, John Relyea, Edinburgh Festival Chorus)

27 August 2001
Handel: Messiah (Lisa Milne, Catherine Wyn-Rogers, Robin Blaze, Paul Agnew, Neal Davies, SCO Chorus)
[Two Handel organ concertos were inserted into the performance, played by Silas Standage with the BT Scottish Ensemble]

5 September 2001, RAH, London
Mozart: Symphony No. 32
Mozart: Piano Concerto No. 25 K503 (Alfred Brendel)
Stravinsky: Concerto in D
Schubert: Symphony No. 4

14 March 2002
Schubert: Symphony No. 6
Mozart: Piano Concerto No. 17 K453 (Alfred Brendel)
Mozart: Piano Concerto No. 25 K503 (Alfred Brendel)
repeated City Hall, Glasgow, 15 March 2002; Konzerthaus, Vienna, 17 and 18 March 2002; Cultural Centre, Lucerne, 20 March 2002

9 May 2002
Brahms: Variations on a Theme by Haydn
Brahms: Alto Rhapsody (Marjana Lipovšek)
Brahms: Symphony No. 1
repeated 10 May 2002, City Hall, Glasgow

14 August 2002
Donizetti: Maria Stuarda (Barbara Frittoli, Anna Caterina Antonacci, Rachel Hynes, Jonathan Lemalu, Paul Charles Clarke, Christopher Purves)

19 August 2002
Mozart: Serenade K361, 'Gran Partita'

25 August 2002
Handel: Jephtha (Ian Bostridge, Sarah Fox, Jane Irwin, Bejun Mehta, Jonathan Lemalu, Thomas Henderson, Edinburgh Festival Chorus)

12 December 2002
Mozart: Die Zauberflöte Overture
Mozart: Symphony No. 41
Mozart: Requiem
repeated 13 December 2002, City Hall, Glasgow

29 January 2003, City Hall, Perth
Schubert: Symphony No. 4
Schubert: Symphony in C ('Great')
repeated 30 January 2003, Usher Hall, Edinburgh

2 February 2003, Barbican, London
Mozart: Symphony No. 31 [with both slow movements]
Mozart: Piano Concerto No. 17 K453 (Alfred Brendel)
Schubert: Symphony No. 4
repeated 4 February 2003, Philharmonie, Cologne; 6 February 2003, Palais des Beaux-Arts, Brussels

16 August 2003
Brahms: Symphony no. 4
Brahms: Piano Concerto No. 1 (Christian Zacharias)
Brahms: Symphony No. 1

18 August 2003
Brahms: Symphony No. 3
Brahms: Piano Concerto No. 2 (Christian Zacharias)
Brahms: Symphony No. 2

27 August 2003
Verdi: Macbeth (Violeta Urmana, Mark Delavan, Marius Brenciu, Alfredo Nigro, John Relyea, Tim Mirfin, Paul Anwyl, Thomas Henderson, Oliver Boyd, Edinburgh Festival Chorus)

26 February 2004, Queen's Hall, Edinburgh
Dvořák: Legends Op. 59 (selection)
Bartók: Divertimento
Bartók: Music for Strings, Percussion and Celesta
repeated 27 February 2004, Barony Hall, Glasgow

4 March 2004, Queen's Hall, Edinburgh
Kodály: Dances of Galánta
Dvořák: Biblical Songs
Beethoven: Symphony No. 7
repeated 5 March 2004, Glasgow

17 August 2004
Weber: Der Freischütz (Hillevi Martinpelto, Ailish Tynan, Jonas Kaufmann, Ronan Collett, Christopher Maltman, John Relyea, Matthew Rose, Siegfried Vogel, Carolyn Dobbin, Catriona Holt, Gail Johnston, Madeleine Shaw, Philharmonia Chorus)

20 August 2004
Mozart: Symphony No. 38
Mozart: Piano Concerto No. 12 K414 (Alfred Brendel)
Mozart: Piano Concerto No. 17 K453 (Alfred Brendel)

21 October 2004
Haydn: Symphony No. 104
Mozart: Mass in C minor
repeated 22 October 2004, Royal Concert Hall, Glasgow

16 August 2005
Mozart: La Clemenza di Tito (Hillevi Martinpelto, Lisa Milne, Magdalena Kožená, Christine Rice, John Relyea, SCO Chorus)

23 August 2005
G. Benda: Ariadne auf Naxos (Dagmar Menzel, Rainer Trost)
Mozart: Zaïde (Kate Royal, Kurt Streit, Rainer Trost, Christopher Purves)

6 October 2005
Sir Charles Mackerras 80th Birthday Party
Beethoven: Fidelio (Christine Brewer, Thomas Moser, Matthew Rose, Terje Stensvold, Lisa Milne, Timothy Robinson, Peter Rose, SCO Chorus)
repeated 8 October 2005, Barbican, London

15 March 2006, Concert Hall, Perth
Haydn: Symphony No. 96 ('Miracle')
Beethoven: Piano Concerto No. 4 (Artur Pizarro)
Mozart: 'Posthorn' Serenade
repeated 16 March 2006, Usher Hall, Edinburgh

15 August 2006
Beethoven: Symphony No. 3
[Each of the Beethoven symphonies was performed as a single work in nine early-evening concerts at the Edinburgh International Festival. Symphony No. 9 was performed on 1 September 2006 by the Philharmonia.]

17 August 2006
Beethoven: Symphony No. 2

19 August 2006
Beethoven: Symphony No. 5

22 August 2006
Beethoven: Symphony No. 6

24 August 2006
Beethoven: Symphony No. 4

26 August 2006
Beethoven: Symphony No. 7

27 August 2006
Beethoven: Symphony No. 8

30 August 2006
Beethoven: Symphony No. 1

5 October 2006
Haydn: The Creation (Susan Gritton, Timothy Robinson, Peter Rose, SCO Chorus)

6 October 2006, City Hall, Glasgow
Haydn: The Creation (Susan Gritton, Timothy Robinson, Peter Rose, SCO Chorus)

21 March 2007, Concert Hall, Perth
Mozart: Symphony No. 39
Mozart: Symphony No. 40
Mozart: Symphony No. 41 ('Jupiter')
repeated 22 March 2007, Usher Hall, Edinburgh

28 February 2008, Queen's Hall, Edinburgh
Mozart: Vesperae solennes de confessore K339 (Lucy Crowe, SCO Chorus)
Mozart: Exsultate jubilate (Lucy Crowe)
Mozart: Symphony No. 38 ('Prague')
repeated 29 February, City Hall, Glasgow

20 August 2008
Mozart: Symphony No. 40
Mozart: Piano Concerto No. 24 K491 (Alfred Brendel)
Dvořák: Nocturne Op. 40
Dvořák: Czech Suite

30 October 2008, Concert Hall, Perth
Programme included
Beethoven: Piano Concerto No. 3 (Artur Pizarro)

31 October 2008, City Hall, Glasgow
Mozart: Symphony No. 31 ('Paris')
Beethoven: Piano Concerto No. 4 (Artur Pizarro)
Mozart: Symphony No. 36 ('Linz')

14 January 2010, Queen's Hall, Edinburgh
Mozart: Symphony No. 35 ('Haffner')
Strauss: Horn Concerto No. 1 (Radovan Vlatković)
Strauss: Le Bourgeois Gentilhomme
repeated 15 January 2010, City Hall, Glasgow

Sources: Charles Mackerras annual schedules; www.heraldscotland.com; www.scottishmusiccentre.com.

I Philharmonia performances, 2002–09

(See Chapter 13)

All given at the Royal Festival Hall, London, unless otherwise stated

3 March 2002
(CM replacing Wolfgang Sawallisch)
Beethoven: Overture Leonore No. 2
Beethoven: Symphony No. 2
Beethoven: Symphony No. 1

7 March 2002
(CM replacing Wolfgang Sawallisch)
Beethoven: Egmont Overture
Beethoven: Piano Concerto No. 1 (Murray Perahia)
Beethoven: Symphony No. 3

25 June 2002
Dvořák: Amid Nature
Mozart: Piano Concerto K488 (Maria João Pires)
Berlioz: Symphonie fantastique

8 December 2002
Beethoven: Piano Concerto No. 2 (Murray Perahia)
Beethoven: Symphony No. 9 (Janice Watson, Cornelia Kallisch, Timothy Robinson, Alfred Reiter, Philharmonia Chorus)
[This concert marked CM's appointment as Principal Guest Conductor of the Philharmonia]

15 May 2003
Janáček, arr. Mackerras: The Cunning Little Vixen Suite
Bruch: Violin Concerto No. 1 (Sarah Chang)
Elgar: Symphony No. 1

17 May 2003
Dvořák: Othello Overture
Tchaikovsky: Piano Concerto No. 1 (Nikolai Lugansky)
Brahms: Symphony No. 3

8 November 2003
Dvořák: Symphonic Variations
Beethoven: Piano Concerto No. 3 (Maria João Pires)
Beethoven: Symphony No. 7

13 November 2003
Strauss: Till Eulenspiegel
Shostakovich: Cello Concerto No. 1 (David Cohen)
Sibelius: Symphony No. 2

20 June 2004, De Montfort Hall, Leicester
Janáček: Taras Bulba
Dvořák: Cello Concerto (Natalie Clein)
Dvořák: Symphony No. 6

23 June 2004, Corn Exchange, Bedford
Janáček: Taras Bulba
Brahms: Violin Concerto (Joshua Bell)
Dvořák: Symphony No. 6
repeated 24 June 2004, RFH, London

28 June 2004, Symphony Hall, Birmingham
Dvořák: Carnival Overture
Dvořák: Cello Concerto (Natalie Clein)
Janáček: Glagolitic Mass, ed. Wingfield (Christine Brewer, Louise Winter, John MacMaster, Neal Davies, London Philharmonic Choir, London Symphony Chorus, Thomas Trotter)
repeated 29 June 2004, RFH, London

15 March 2005, Corn Exchange, Bedford
Brahms: Symphony No. 1
Brahms: Piano Concerto No. 2 (Till Fellner)
repeated 17 March 2005, RFH, London

22 March 2005
Brahms: Serenade No. 2
Mozart: Piano Concerto K488 (Paul Lewis)
Brahms: Symphony No. 3
repeated 24 March 2004, De Montfort Hall, Leicester

3 April 2005, Anvil, Basingstoke
Brahms: Academic Festival Overture
Mozart: Violin Concerto K219 (James Ehnes)
Brahms: Symphony No. 4
repeated 5 April 2005, RFH, London

10 April 2005
Brahms: Tragic Overture
Dvořák: Cello Concerto (Truls Mørk)
Brahms: Symphony No. 2

12 June 2005
Mozart: Symphony No. 40
Mozart: Piano Concerto K491 (Mitsuko Uchida)
Mozart: Requiem, ed. Robert Levin (Susan Gritton, Catherine Wyn-Rogers, John Mark Ainsley, Peter Rose, Philharmonia Chorus)

14 June 2005, Symphony Hall, Birmingham
Mozart: Adagio and Fugue K456
Mozart: Piano Concerto K466 (Mitsuko Uchida)
Elgar: Symphony No. 2
repeated 16 June 2005, RFH, London

17 June 2005, Sheldonian, Oxford
Mozart: Adagio and Fugue K456
Mozart: Piano Concerto K466 (Mitsuko Uchida)
Mozart: Symphony No. 40

11 February 2006, QEH, London
Mozart: La Clemenza di Tito Overture
Mozart: Piano Concerto K466 (Emanuel Ax)
Mahler: Symphony No. 4 (Sarah Fox)

16 February 2006, QEH, London
Mozart: La Clemenza di Tito Overture
Mozart: Piano Concerto K453 (Piotr Anderszewksi)
Mahler: Symphony No. 4 (Sarah Fox)

10 June 2006, QEH, London
Wagner: Tannhäuser Overture and Venusberg Music
Mendelssohn: Violin Concerto (Alina Ibragimova) [originally announced as Mozart: Violin Concerto K216 with Janine Jansen, who withdrew from the concert with an eye infection]
Schubert: Symphony in C ('Great')

20 June 2006, QEH, London
Eightieth Birthday Gala Concert
Wagner: Tannhäuser Overture and Venusberg Music
Mozart: Piano Concerto K595 (Alfred Brendel)
Schubert: Symphony in C ('Great')

1 September 2006, Usher Hall, Edinburgh
Beethoven: Symphony No. 9 (Janice Watson, Catherine Wyn-Rogers, Stuart Skelton, Detlef Rolf, Edinburgh Festival Chorus)

26 January 2007, SDH, Cardiff
Beethoven: Symphony No. 9 (Elizabeth Atherton, Lilli Paasikivi, Toby Spence, Matthew Rose, Philharmonia Chorus, Members of Bristol Choral Society)
repeated 30 January 2007, Symphony Hall, Birmingham; 1 February 2007, Colston Hall, Bristol

9 May 2007, Anvil, Basingstoke
Mendelssohn: Hebrides Overture
Beethoven: Violin Concerto (Viktoria Mullova)
Mozart: Symphony No. 41
repeated 10 and 12 May 2007, QEH, London

24 June 2007
Wagner: Die Meistersinger Prelude to Act 1
Mozart: Piano Concerto K503 (Mitsuko Uchida)
Janáček: Sinfonietta

3 April 2008
Strauss: Till Eulenspiegel
Beethoven: Piano Concerto No. 4 (Lars Vogt)
Schumann: Symphony No. 3

6 April 2008
Strauss: Also sprach Zarathustra
Mozart: Piano Concerto K456 (Till Fellner)
Brahms: Symphony No. 3

10 April 2008
Strauss: Don Juan
Strauss: Four Last Songs (Solveig Kringelborn)
Beethoven: Symphony No. 3

9 October 2008
Mozart: Symphony No. 39
Bruch: Violin Concerto No. 1 (Sergey Khachaturyan)
Dvořák: Symphony No. 7

12 October 2008
Haydn: Symphony No. 104
Mozart: Piano Concerto K271 (Alfred Brendel)
Dvořák: Symphony No. 8
repeated 14 October 2008, Anvil, Basingstoke

5 February 2009
Mendelssohn: Midsummer Night's Dream Overture
Mozart: Piano Concerto K491 (Yefim Bronfman)
Tchaikovsky: Symphony No. 6

12 February 2009
Mozart: Symphony No. 32
Mozart: Piano Concerto K466 (Lise de la Salle)
Elgar: Symphony No. 1

10 December 2009
Wagner: Tannhäuser Overture and Venusberg Music
Wagner: Tristan und Isolde Prelude and Liebestod (Christine Brewer)
Wagner: Götterdämmerung, selections: Dawn and Sunrise – Siegfried's Rhine Journey – Siegfried's Funeral Music – Brünnhilde's Immolation (Christine Brewer)

13 December 2009
Beethoven: Symphony No. 6
Humperdinck: Hänsel und Gretel, selection: Overture – Opening Duet – Sandman's Song – Prayer – Dream Pantomime (Rebecca Bottone, Caitlin Hulcup

Sources: Charles Mackerras annual schedules; Philharmonia archives.

Appendix 2
Desert Island Lists

Nigel Simeone

Desert Island Discs

Few of the 'castaways' on the BBC Radio 4 programme *Desert Island Discs* have been invited three times, but Charles Mackerras appeared in 1959, 1975 and 1999. Each guest is asked to choose eight records, and on each occasion Charles chose different records. They reflect his love of old recordings – Furtwängler, Toscanini, Talich and Bruno Walter were all choices. The repertoire includes not only Handel, Mozart, Dvořák and Janáček, but also Wagner, Verdi, Bellini and Mahler. As well as the eight records, guests are to asked to choose a book (apart from The Bible and the complete works of Shakespeare, which are provided automatically) and a luxury item. All three books were chosen to improve his language skills, and on his first two appearances he chose the same luxury: wine. By the time of his second appearance in 1975, castaways were also asked to nominate one disc that they would keep if all the others were lost. It is difficult to argue with Charles's choices of Verdi's *Otello* (1975) and Mozart's *Figaro* (1999).

24 August 1959

1 Mozart: 'Riconosci in quest'amplesso' from The Marriage of Figaro
Glyndebourne Festival Opera, Vittorio Gui

2 Verdi: 'Va, pensiero' from Nabucco
Westminster Choir, NBC Symphony Orchestra, Arturo Toscanini

3 Mozart: Clarinet Concerto in A major
Vladimir Říha, Czech Philharmonic Orchestra, Václav Talich

4 Bellini: 'Mira, O Norma' from Norma
Maria Callas, Ebe Stignani, La Scala Orchestra, Tullio Serafin

5 Handel: Music for the Royal Fireworks – Overture
Wind ensemble, Charles Mackerras

6 Trad., arr. Mackerras: Vom Himmel hoch
Elisabeth Schwarzkopf, Philharmonia Orchestra, Charles Mackerras

7 Mahler: 'Der Abschied' from Das Lied von der Erde
Kathleen Ferrier, Vienna Philharmonic Orchestra, Bruno Walter

8 Janáček: Sinfonietta
Vienna Philharmonic Orchestra, Rafael Kubelík

Book: A foreign translation of a long English novel

Luxury item: Wine

18 January 1975

1 Mozart: Symphony No. 38 in D major 'Prague'
London Philharmonic Orchestra, Charles Mackerras

2 Mozart: Clarinet Quintet in A major
Thea King, Aeolian String Quartet

3 Dvořák: Cello Concerto in B minor
Mstislav Rostropovich, Czech Philharmonic Orchestra, Václav Talich

4 Verdi: Otello – Act 2 finale
Ramón Vinay, Giuseppe Valdengo, NBC Symphony Orchestra, Arturo Toscanini
(Castaway's favourite)

5 Janáček: The Makropulos Affair – Act 1 Prelude
Pro Arte Orchestra, Charles Mackerras

6 Wagner: Magic Fire Music from Die Walküre
Vienna Philharmonic Orchestra, Wilhelm Furtwängler

7 Mahler: Symphony No. 7 in E minor
Chicago Symphony Orchestra, Georg Solti

8 Handel: Hallelujah Chorus from Messiah
Ambrosian Singers, English Chamber Orchestra, Charles Mackerras

Book: The Bible in German

Luxury item: Wine

7 March 1999

1 Wagner: 'Selig wie die Sonne' from Die Meistersinger von Nürnberg
Elisabeth Schumann, Lauritz Melchior, Friedrich Schorr, Gladys Parr, Ben Williams, London Symphony Orchestra, John Barbirolli

2 Sullivan arr. Mackerras: Pineapple Poll – finale
Philharmonia Orchestra, Charles Mackerras

3 Janáček: Káťa Kabanová – Act 1 Prelude
Czech Philharmonic Orchestra, Charles Mackerras

4 Mozart: Clarinet Quintet in A major – 3rd movement
Thea King, Gabrieli String Quartet

5 Mozart: 'Riconosci in quest'amplesso' from The Marriage of Figaro
Scottish Chamber Orchestra, Charles Mackerras
(Castaway's favourite)

6 Dvořák: Symphony No. 7 in D minor – 3rd movement
Czech Philharmonic Orchestra, Václav Talich

7 Schubert: Symphony in B minor ('Unfinished') – 2nd movement
Berlin Philharmonic Orchestra, Wilhelm Furtwängler

8 Mahler: 'Der Abschied' from Das Lied von der Erde
Janet Baker, Royal Concertgebouw Orchestra, Bernard Haitink

Book: Translation of Shakespeare in German, Italian or Czech

Luxury item: If hot island, a big bottle of suntan lotion; if cold island, a comfortable pillow

Five Mackerras favourites among his own recordings

In 2006, I gave a talk about Charles Mackerras for a music society and wrote to him beforehand asking if he could nominate five favourites from his own records. It must have seemed a rather frivolous inquiry, but with characteristic diligence he replied by return of post. These are the five recordings Mackerras chose from his vast discography:

Beethoven: Symphony No. 9 (RLPO, EMI Eminence)

Brahms: Symphony No. 1 (SCO, Telarc)

Handel: Julius Caesar (Baker, ENO, EMI [now Chandos])

Janáček: Kát'a Kabanová (Söderström, VPO, Decca)

Mozart: 'Prague' Symphony (Prague CO, Telarc)

Mackerras's chosen menu for *Food of Love*

Charles Mackerras's great passions were music and his family. Aside from those, he much enjoyed sailing when on Elba, and he always enjoyed good food and wine. In 1971 the Bath Festival published *Food of Love*, edited by Adrian Bell (London: Pitman, 1971). Mackerras (pp. 74–5) chose the following as his ideal menu – one that clearly reflects his love of Italy:

Menu:
Spaghetti carbonara

Veal créole (veal escalopes and Gruyère cheese pan-fried in seasoned flour, with a sauce of onion, garlic, tomatoes, pimento, marjoram)

Framboises des bois with fresh cream and kirsch

Wines:
Appetiser: Vin Santo
Verdicchio
Château Batailley 1961

Music:
Preferably no music with food but, if necessary, a long Serenade or Divertimento by Mozart or Haydn played as softly as possible!

Discography

Malcolm Walker

This discography was begun in 1984, following a commission from the Mackerras family to contribute to Nancy Phelan's biography of the conductor, published in 1987. At the time, Sir Charles generously gave up a whole morning and went through his diaries to fill in a number of missing dates and facts, a gesture warmly appreciated by the compiler. In the intervening years the discography has been maintained and updated. Sir Charles's recording career spanned 58 years and was extremely varied in scope. During that time he was never exclusive to a single company. His services to Czech music, especially Dvořák, Janáček and Martinů, conveyed his passion for a country that he first visited not long after the end of the Second World War. His endeavours on behalf of Handel, Mozart, Beethoven and Brahms produced revelatory recordings – as did his devoted advocacy of Arthur Sullivan.

Note by NS

The format of the entries is as follows: Date (year, month, day), venue, soloists, chorus, orchestra, label; title of work; catalogue number of CD, DVD or other format. In the interests of space and clarity, only CD catalogue numbers are given unless the recording in question has not been released on CD (for details of LP releases, readers are referred to Malcolm Walker's earlier discography in Phelan 1987). It is a measure of the length of Mackerras's recording career that his earliest record – of *Pineapple Poll* – was first issued on twelve 78 r.p.m. sides, and his latest were quickly made available as downloads as well as compact discs. The present discography lists downloads in cases where no CD has been released, or where a commercially available download has superseded a previously issued CD.

There was no more assiduous home recordist than Mackerras: he arranged for hundreds of his performances to be taped by friends, relatives or willing sound engineers, and the enormous archive of his live performances recorded from broadcasts or in-house is now divided between the British Library and the Music Preserved collection at York University. It is to be hoped that some of these may be made available one day, but they are readily available for consultation by students of Mackerras's work.

Given Mackerras's own enthusiasm for off-air recordings, it was an easy decision to include CDs of broadcasts and live performances made available on non-commercial labels. The broadcasts released by the Oriel Music Trust are particularly valuable, including the Sadler's Wells *Marriage of Figaro*, English-language Janáček performances and the Sullivan series from 1989 (proceeds from the Oriel Music Trust discs benefit the Musicians' Benevolent Fund).

There are few major gaps in the Mackerras recorded repertoire, but among the most conspicuous is Haydn's *Creation*, one of his favourite works. Perhaps the most celebrated premiere he conducted was Britten's *Noye's Fludde*. Though the BBC recording of this is unpublished, it has been included here as an important surviving document of a landmark in Mackerras's career. As this discography demonstrates, Mackerras's recorded legacy is not only extensive but also reflects the broad range of his musical enthusiasms.

Abbreviations

AAI	American Academy and Institute of Arts and Letters, New York City
ACO	Australian Chamber Orchestra
AR	No. 1 Studio, Abbey Road, London
BBCCO	BBC Concert Orchestra
BBCGG	BBC Studios, Golders Green, London
BBCMV	BBC Studios, Maida Vale, London
BBCPO	BBC Philharmonic Orchestra
BBCSO	BBC Symphony Orchestra
BCH	Blackheath Concert Halls, London
BHS	Brangwyn Hall, Swansea
BTH	Barking Town Hall
CD	compact disc
CHD	Caird Hall, Dundee
CHG	City Halls, Glasgow
CPO	Czech Philharmonic Orchestra
DL	download
ECO	English Chamber Orchestra
ENO	English National Opera
HPO	Hamburg Philharmonic Orchestra
HWH	Henry Wood Hall, London
KH	Kingsway Hall, London
LD	laser disc
LP	long-playing record
LPO	London Philharmonic Orchestra
LSO	London Symphony Orchestra
LTH	Leeds Town Hall
[m]	monophonic recording
NBH	Studio 7, New Broadcasting House, Manchester
NPO	New Philharmonia Orchestra
OAE	Orchestra of the Age of Enlightenment
ODP	Obecní dům, Prague (Smetana Hall)
OSL	Orchestra of St, Luke's, New York
PAO	Pro Arte Orchestra
PCO	Prague Chamber Orchestra
PHL	Philharmonic Hall, Liverpool
PO	Philharmonia Orchestra
RAH	Royal Albert Hall, London
RFH	Royal Festival Hall, London
RLPO	Royal Liverpool Philharmonic Orchestra
ROHCG	Royal Opera House, Covent Garden
RP	Rudolfinum, Prague (Dvořák Hall)
RPO	Royal Philharmonic Orchestra
RTB	Radio-Télévision Belge
SAK	St Augustine's, Kilburn, London
SCO	Scottish Chamber Orchestra
SJH	St Jude on the Hill, Hampstead Garden Suburb, London
SO	Symphony Orchestra
SSO	Sydney Symphony Orchestra
SV	Sofiensaal, Vienna
SWO	Sadler's Wells Opera, London
UHE	Usher Hall, Edinburgh
VHS	VHS video cassette
WalAH	Walthamstow Assembly Hall
WalAR	Walthamstow Assembly Rooms
WemTH	Wembley (now Brent) Town Hall
WNO	Welsh National Operar
WP	Wiener Philharmoniker
WTH	Watford Town Hall
45	45 r.p.m. record

1951 June 7–8. AR. Sadler's Wells Orchestra. EMI/Columbia
Sullivan (arr. Mackerras): Pineapple Poll – ballet
CD: 344123-2. Originally released on six 78 r.p.m. discs with catalogue no. DX 1765/70.

1951 July 10–11. AR. Sadler's Wells Orchestra. EMI/Parlophone
Auber: Les Rendez-vous – ballet
Warlock: Capriol Suite
Toye: The Haunted Ballroom – ballet
Unpublished. All the recordings from these sessions were rejected. The standard of playing was not high enough to satisfy either conductor or producer.

1955 May 4. AR. Peter Dawson *bass-baritone*. LSO. EMI/HMV
A. Arlen: Clancy of the Overflow
CD: EMI Australia 837801-2
DL: Beulah 2PD53 (stereo)
Speaks/Hedgecock/Cobb/Willeby: Mandalay Scena – medley
45: [m] 7EG 8157 LP: [m] PD1
The 73-year-old Dawson's final session for EMI, and his only recording in stereo.

1955 June 21, 22 and 30. AR. PO. EMI/HMV
Verdi: The Lady and the Fool – ballet
CD: Testament [m] SBT 1326
Mackerras's first association with the Philharmonia Orchestra. These sessions were mostly recorded in stereo until the equipment broke down.

1956 April 4. AR. LSO. EMI/HMV
Handel: Berenice – Overture (minuet); Water Music Suite (arr. Harty): Allegro; Bourrée; Hornpipe; Allegro deciso
CD: Testament SBT 1253
Clarke: Suite in D for trumpet and Strings – The Prince of Denmark's March [Trumpet Voluntary] (George Eskdale *trumpet*, Brass Ensemble)
45: [m] 7EP7031
Jacob: Fanfare and British National Anthem (God save the Queen)
Unpublished.

1956 April 16. AR. Orchestra of ROHCG. EMI/HMV
Delibes: Lakmé – Act 2: ballet music
45: [m] 7EP 7069
Verdi: Otello – Act 3: ballet music
CD: Testament SBT 1327

1956 April 23. AR. Orchestra of ROHCG. EMI/HMV
Delibes: La Source – ballet music
CD: 344123-2

1956 April 25. AR. PO. EMI/HMV
Copland: Rodeo – Hoe Down
Unpublished.

1956 April 25 and 28. AR. PO. EMI/HMV
Messager: Les Deux Pigeons – ballet suite
CD: 575221-2

1956 April 30. AR. PO. EMI/HMV
Copland: Quiet City
Unpublished.

1956 May 23. AR. LSO. EMI/Columbia
Coates: The Merrymakers Overture; The Three Bears Fantasy; London Again Suite – Oxford Street: March
CD: Dutton CDVS 1964

1956 May 24. AR. LSO. EMI/Columbia
Coates: By the Sleepy Lagoon; Summer Days Suite – At the Dance; Three Men Suite – The Man from the Sea; The Three Elizabeths Suite – Queen Elizabeth: March
CD: Dutton CDVS 1964

1956 June 4. KH. RPO. EMI/HMV
Burkhard: Der Schuss von der Kanzel – Overture
Rezniček: Donna Diana – Overture
CD: 344123-2

1956 June 9. AR. PO. EMI/HMV
Sullivan: Iolanthe – Overture; The Mikado – Overture; Ruddigore – Overture; The Yeomen of the Guard – Overture
CD: CDM 566538-2; Dutton CDVS 1964

1956 June 15 or 18 (live; broadcast June 26). Jubilee Hall, Aldeburgh. Heather Harper *soprano* Venus; Thomas Hemsley *baritone* Adonis; Maria Zeri *soprano* Cupid. Chorus and Orchestra of the English Opera Group.
Blow: Venus and Adonis (ed. Imogen Holst)
DL: Music Preserved mpLive LM7410 (spoken introduction by Alec Robertson)
Arda Mandikian *soprano* Savitri; Peter Pears *tenor* Satyavan; Thomas Hemsley *baritone* Death; Chorus of the English Opera Group. Orchestra of the English Opera Group
Holst: Sāvitri
DL: Music Preserved mpLive LM7410 (spoken introduction by Imogen Holst)
Two performances of this double bill were given at the Aldeburgh Festival on 15 and 18 June.

1956 October 6 (live). Scala Theatre. Una Hale *soprano* Naomi; April Cantelo *soprano* Oprah; Anna Pollak *mezzo-soprano* Ruth; Peter Pears *tenor* Boaz; Thomas Hemsley *baritone* Head reaper; Chorus and Orchestra of the English Opera Group.
Berkeley: Ruth
DL: Music Preserved mpLive LM7418 (spoken introduction by Lord Harewood)

1956 October 22. AR. PO. EMI/HMV
Gounod: Faust – Act 5: ballet music
LP: [m] DLP 1177
Wolf-Ferrari: Il segreto di Susanna – Overture; I quattro rusteghi – Prelude; Intermezzo
CD: Testament SBT 1327

1956 October 23. AR. PO. EMI/HMV
Copland: El salón México
CD: 344123-2
Wolf-Ferrari: I gioielli della Madonna – Act 3: Intermezzo; Danza napolitana; Festa popolare
CD: Testament SBT 1327

1956 October 24. AR. PO. EMI/HMV
Wolf-Ferrari: I gioielli della Madonna – Act 2: Intermezzo
CD: Testament SBT 1327
Berlioz: La Damnation de Faust Op. 24 – Marche hongroise
LP: [m] DLP 1168
Berlioz: Les Troyens – Act 1: Marche troyenne; La Damnation de Faust Op. 24 – Menuet des follets; Ballet des sylphes
CD: 344123-2
Mussorgsky (orch. Lyadov): Sorochinski Fair – Gopak
Unpublished.

1956 October 25. AR. PO. EMI/HMV
Mussorgsky (orch. Lyadov): Sorochinski Fair – Gopak
Glière: The Red Poppy Op. 70 – Russian Sailors' Dance
CD: 344123-2
Glazunov: Concert Waltz No. 1 Op. 47
Glinka: Ruslan and Ludmilla – Overture
Rimsky-Korsakov: Tsar Sultan – The Flight of the Bumble Bee
LP: [m] DLP1170
Wirén: Serenade for Strings Op. 11 – 3. Scherzo; 4. March
Unpublished.

1956 October 26. AR. PO. EMI/HMV
Chabrier: Le Roi malgré lui – Fête polonaise
LP: [m] DLP 1177
Ippolitov-Ivanov: Caucasian Sketches Op. 10 – No. 4. Procession of the Sardar
Rimsky-Korsakov: The Snow Maiden – Dance of the Tumblers
LP: [m] DLP 1170

1956 October 27. AR. PO. EMI/HMV
Berlioz: Le Carnaval romain Overture Op. 9
Chabrier: España
LP: [m] DLP 1177

1956 November 2. KH. PO. EMI/HMV
Verdi: La forza del destino – Overture; Luisa Miller – Overture; Nabucco – Overture
CD: Testament SBT 1326

1956 November 3. KH. PO. EMI/HMV
Verdi: Alzira – Overture
CD: Testament SBT 1326

1956 November 30. AR. PO. EMI/HMV
Wirén: Serenade for Strings Op. 11 – 3. Scherzo; 4. March
Unpublished.

1956 December 17 (broadcast). BBC Third Programme. [a]Joan Sutherland *soprano*; [b]April Cantelo *soprano*; [bc]Raymond Nilsson *tenor*; [b]Dennis Brain *horn*; Goldsborough Orchestra
Haydn: Se ti perdo amata sposa; Pietà di me, Benigni[ab]; Armida – Cara, è vero, io son tiranno[c]
CD: Mondo Archives AAC 012–013

1957 May 25. AR. Elisabeth Schwarzkopf *soprano*. PO. EMI/Columbia
Franck (arr. Mackerras): Panis angelicus
Trad. (arr. Mackerras): O du fröhliche
CD: CDM 763574-2
Silcher (arr. Mackerras): Die Lorelei
Gruber: Stille Nacht
Unpublished

1957 May 26. AR. Elisabeth Schwarzkopf *soprano*. PO. EMI/Columbia
Humperdinck (arr. Mackerras): Weihnachten
Trad. (arr. Mackerras): Vom Himmel hoch; In dulci jubilo; Easter Alleluia; The First Nowell
CD: CDM 763574-2
Silcher (arr. Mackerras): Die Lorelei
Bach (arr. Gounod and Mackerras): Ave Maria
Unpublished.

1957 June 1. AR. Elisabeth Schwarzkopf *soprano*. PO. EMI/Columbia
Trad. (arr. Brahms): Volkskinderlieder – No. 4, Sandmännchen
Trad. (arr. Mackerras): Maria auf dem Berge
F. Gluck (arr. Mackerras): In einem kühlen Grunde
CD: CDM 763574-2
Trad. (arr. Fiske): O Tannenbaum
Unpublished.

1957 June 30. AR. Elisabeth Schwarzkopf *soprano*. PO. EMI/Columbia
Trad. (arr. Mackerras): O come all ye faithful
CD: CDM 763574-2
Silcher (arr. Mackerras): Die Lorelei
Unpublished.

1957 July 1. AR. Elisabeth Schwarzkopf *soprano*; Julian Bream *guitar*; PO. EMI/Columbia
Gruber: Stille Nacht
CD: CDM 763574-2 (includes duet version [mono] and solo version [stereo]).
Booklet notes by Mackerras.

1958 January 8. KH. Philharmonia (Promenade) Orchestra. EMI/Columbia
Verdi: I vespri siciliani: Act 3: ballet music (The Four Seasons), abridged
CD: Testament SBT 1327

1958 May 16. BBC Television Studios, Lime Grove. Tito Gobbi *baritone*; LSO
Verdi: Falstaff – Ehi Tavaniere; Otello – Credo in un Dio crudel
Puccini: Tosca – Va, Tosca!; Gianni Schicchi – Dite mi voi
DVD: EMI DVB 500687–9

1958 May 26, 27 and 30. WalAR. London Proms SO. Decca/RCA
Grieg: Two Elegiac Melodies Op. 34; 2 Norwegian Melodies Op. 63 – No. 2. Cowkeeper's Tune Country Dance; (orch. Huppertz): Lyric Pieces Op. 65, No. 6. Wedding Day at Troldhaugen
Sibelius: Finlandia Op. 26; King Christian II – incidental music Op. 27: No. 1. Elegie, No. 2. Musette; Kuolema Op. 44 – Valse triste; Pelleas and Melisande, incidental music Op. 46 – No. 8. Entr'acte
LP: LSC 2336 DL: ReDiscovery RD175

1958 June 18 (live). Orford Church, Suffolk. Owen Brannigan *bass* Noah; Gladys Parr *mezzo-soprano* Mrs Noye; Trevor Anthony *spoken* The Voice of God; Thomas Bevan *treble* Sem; Brian Weller *treble* Ham; Michael Crawford *treble* Jaffet; Chorus of Animals, an East

Suffolk Children's Orchestra; English Opera Group Players.
Britten: Noye's Fludde
Unpublished. A recording of this premiere made by the BBC Transcription Service is in the Britten–Pears Library, Aldeburgh.

1958 June 24–25. WalAR. PAO. Pye/PRT
Donizetti: La Fille du régiment – Overture; Don Pasquale – Overture
Falla: El sombrero de tres picos – Neighbour's Dance; Miller's Dance; Final Dance
LP: GSGC 14011
Mozart: Les Petits Riens K299b
LP: GSGC 14033
Smetana: The Bartered Bride – Overture
Weinberger: Schwanda the Bagpiper – Polka and Fugue
CD: EMI 234720-2

1958 June 26–27. WalAR. Joseph Cooper *piano*. PAO. Pye/PRT
Litolff: Concerto symphonique No. 4 in D Op. 102 – Scherzo
Tchaikovsky: Piano Concerto No. 3 in E flat Op. 75
Turina: Rapsodia sinfónica Op. 76
Weber: Konzertstück in F minor
LP: [m] CML 33006
Saint-Saëns: Wedding Cake Op. 76
45: [m] CEM 36015

1958 July 1. AR. PO. EMI/Columbia.
Tchaikovsky: Symphony No. 5 in E minor Op. 64 – 3. Waltz; Eugene Onegin Op. 24 – Act 2: Waltz; The Nutcracker Op. 71 – Waltz of the Flowers; Swan Lake Op. 20 – Act 1: Waltz; The Sleeping Beauty Op. 66 – Waltz
LP: [m] S-35752

1958 July 7. KH. Philharmonia (Promenade) Orchestra. EMI/Columbia
Verdi: Il trovatore – Act 3: ballet music
CD: Testament SBT 1327

1958 September 22–29. Herkulessaal, Munich. Rita Streich *soprano*. Bavarian Radio SO. DG
Mozart: Ah se in ciel, benigne stelle K538; Mia speranza adorata! ... Ah, non sai qual pena sia K416; Nehmt meinem Dank, ihr holden Gönner K383; Non, che sei capace K419; Popoli de Tessaglia! ... Io non chiedo, eterni Dei K316/K300b; Vado, ma dove? K583; Vorrei spiegarvi, oh Dio! K418
CD: 431 875-2

1958 November 12. KH. PO. EMI/Columbia
Meyerbeer (arr. Lambert): Les Patineurs, Nos 1, 3, 5, 6 8
CD: 344123-2
Ponchielli: La Gioconda – Dance of the Hours
LP: [m] 33SX 1207; SCX 3291

1959 March 25. St Gabriel's, Cricklewood. PAO. Pye/PRT
Handel (ed. Mackerras): Concerto a due cori No. 2 in F
CD: Testament SBT 1253

1959 April 13 (23:00)–14 (02:30). St Gabriel's, Cricklewood. Wind Ensemble. Pye/PRT
Handel (ed. Mackerras): Music for the Royal Fireworks
CD: Testament SBT 1253

1959 April 16. AR. Richard Lewis *tenor*. (Robert Masters) Chamber Orchestra. EMI/HMV
Trad.: Ar hyd y nos; Bingo; The briery bush; Buy broom buzzems; The foggy, foggy dew; King Arthur's servants; Leezie Lindsay; Mo nigheann, chruinn, donn; O waly waly; There's none to soothe
CD: Regis RRC1375
All songs arr. Arne Dørumsgaard.

1959 April 17. AR. Richard Lewis *tenor*. (Robert Masters) Chamber Orchestra. EMI/HMV
Trad.: Dafydd y garreg wen; Fine flow'rs in the valley; Grad geal mo chridh; She moved thro' the fair; The Helston Furry Dance; I will give my love an apple; The Maypole song; O love, it is a killing thing; The stuttering lovers
CD: Regis RRC1375
All songs arr. Arne Dørumsgaard.

1959 May 25. KH. PO. EMI/Columbia
Chopin (orch. Jacob): Les Sylphides – ballet
LP: [m] 33SX 1207; SCX 3291

1959 July 18. WalAR. PAO. Pye/PRT
Mozart: Divertimento in E flat K113; Six German Dances K600; March No. 1 in C K408; March No. 2 in D K408; Two Minuets K604
LP: GSGC 14033

1959 July 19–24. WalAR. PAO. Pye/PRT
Janáček: Sinfonietta; Věc Makropulos – Act 1: Prelude; Kát'a Kabanová – Prelude; From the House of the Dead – Prelude (Raymond Cohen *violin*); Žárlivost [Jealousy]
CD: EMI 234720-2; Testament SBT 1325

1959 October 29 (live). Wexford Festival. Nicola Nicolov *tenor* Aroldo; Mariella Angioletti *soprano* Mina; Aldo Protti *baritone* Egberto; Trevor Anthony *bass* Briano; John Dobson *tenor* Godvino; Griffith Lewis *tenor* Enrico; Elizabeth Bainbridge *mezzo-soprano* Elena; Wexford Festival Chorus; Radio Éireann Light Orchestra
Verdi: Aroldo
Omega Opera Archive 3249

1960 June 6. WemTH. Charles Mackerras *bass drum*; LSO; Antal Doráti *conductor*. Mercury
Liszt: Les Préludes
CD: 462 953-2
A change to the recording schedule found the orchestra without a percussion player. Mackerras, who was visiting the Mercury mobile recording van, offered to assist (information from Philip Stuart).

1960 September 28. KH. PO. EMI/Columbia
Dvořák: Slavonic Dance in C major Op. 46 No. 1; Slavonic Dance in A flat Op. 46 No. 3; Slavonic Dance in E minor Op. 72 No. 2
LP: [m] 33SX 1389; SCX 3427
Dvořák: Slavonic Dance in E minor Op. 46 No. 2
Unpublished.

1960 October 3 and 5. AR. RPO. EMI/HMV
Sullivan (arr. Mackerras): Pineapple Poll – ballet
CD: CDM 566538-2; (Arabesque) Z 8016

1960 October 31. AR. PO. EMI/Columbia
Bartók (orch. Székely): Romanian Folk Dances
Brahms (orch. Parlow): Hungarian Dance No. 5; Hungarian Dance No. 6
Dvořák: Slavonic Dance in E minor Op. 46 No. 2
Enesco: Romanian Rhapsody No. 1 Op. 11
CD: Testament SBT 1325
Smetana: The Bartered Bride – Polka; Furiant
LP: [m] 33SX 1389; SCX 3427

1961 April 17–18 and May 9. AR. PO. EMI/HMV
Johann Strauss II (arr. Doráti): Graduation Ball – ballet
CD: 344123-2

1961 May 8–9. AR. PO. EMI/HMV
Offenbach (arr. Rosenthal): Gaîté parisienne – ballet suite
LP: [m] CLP 1722; CSD 1533

1961 July 19[a] and 21[b], 22[c] and 23[d]. WalAR. LSO. Mercury
Brahms: Hungarian Dance No. 1 in G minor[d]
Glinka: Spanish Overture No. 1: Jota aragonesa[c]
Meyerbeer: Le Prophète – Coronation March[b]
Nicolai: Die Lustigen Weiber von Windsor – Overture[a]
Offenbach (arr. André): Orphée aux enfers – Overture[d;] Can-Can
Smetana: The Bartered Bride – Dance of the Comedians[d]
Johann Strauss I: Radetzky March Op. 228[b]
Suppé: Banditenstreiche – Overture[d]
Tchaikovsky: Mazeppa – Cossack Dance[c]
Thomas: Mignon – Overture[d]
Weber: Abu Hassan – Overture[d]

Weber (orch. Berlioz): Invitation to the Dance[b]
CD: 434 352-2
Brahms: Hungarian Dance No. 20 in E minor[d]; Hungarian Dance No. 21 in E[d]
LP: [m] GL 5698

1962 January 11. AR. Owen Brannigan *bass*; PAO. EMI/HMV
Binge: The Grand Old Duke of York; The story of Cock Robin
Hely-Hutchinson: The owl and the pussycat; The table and the chair
Liza Lehmann (arr. Mackerras): Henry King; Matilda
Trad.: The duck and the kangaroo
Trad (arr. Hely-Hutchinson): The jolly beggar
CD: ABC 442 9077

1962 January 12. AR. Owen Brannigan *bass*. PAO. EMI/HMV
Diack (arr. Mackerras): Jack and Jill; Little Jack Horner; Sing a Song of Sixpence
Hely-Hutchinson (re-arr. Mackerras): Old Mother Hubbard
Trad. (arr. Hughes): Doctor Foster
CD: ABC 442 9077

1963 August 14–23. St Vedast's, Foster Lane. Fernando Germani *organ*; PAO. EMI/HMV
Handel: Organ Concertos Op. 4 and Op. 7
According to notes made at the sessions by engineer Neville Boyling, very little was musically acceptable for commercial release.

1963. Sydney. SSO. ABC
Nathan (orch. Mackerras): Don John of Austria – Overture
CD: 480 1379

1964 April 26–27. AR. [a]Elizabeth Harwood *soprano;* [b]Owen Brannigan *bass*; [c]Hendon Grammar School Choir; [d]PAO. EMI/HMV
Arne: Where the bee sucks[ad]
Boyce (arr. Tomlinson): Hearts of Oak[bcd]
Davy (arr. Tomlinson): Bay of Biscay[b]
Horn (arr. Mackerras): Cherry Ripe[ad]
Morley (arr. Mackerras): It was a lover and his lass[abcd]
Trad. (arr. Mackerras): A-hunting we will go[bcd]; The ash grove[bcd]; The Miller of Dee[bd]; The Vicar of Bray[bcd]
Trad. (arr. Tomlinson): The bailiff's daughter of Islington[abcd]; Charlie is my darling[abcd]; Early one morning[acd]; John Peel[bcd]; The oak and the ash[ab]; Ye banks and braes[ad]
CD: CD-CFP 4556

1965 January 12–15. WemTH. LSO. Philips
Gluck: Orfeo ed Euridice – ballet music
Rameau: Castor et Pollux – ballet suite
LP: PHC9002
Cherubini: Anacréon – Overture
Unpublished.
Johann Strauss II: Die Fledermaus – Overture
LP: 6833 131
Johann Strauss II: Der Zigeuenerbaron – Overture
LP: 6599 829

1965 September 25 (broadcast date). BBC Studios, Manchester. Ronald Dowd *tenor* Filka Morozov; Gregory Dempsey *tenor* Skuratov; Michael Maurel *baritone* Shishkov; Michael Rippon *bass* Alexander Petrovich Goryanchikov; Robert Savoie *bass-baritone* Commandant; Margaret Neville *soprano* Alyeya; John Mitchinson *tenor* Tall Prisoner/Tcherevin; Frederick Westcott *bass* Short Prisoner; Stephen Manton *tenor* Old Prisoner; John Andrew *tenor* Shapkin; male voices of the BBC Northern Singers; BBC Northern Orchestra. Radio adaptation by Dennis Arundell (including spoken narrations)
Janáček: From the House of the Dead (in English)
CD: Oriel Music Trust OMT 851

1965 November 1–2. No. 3 Studio, Decca Studios, Broadhurst Gardens. Wilfred Brown *tenor* Boy/The first follower of Envy/First Aerial Spirit; April Cantelo *soprano* Girl/Zempoalla/Orazia; Robert Tear *tenor* Fame;

Christopher Keyte *bass* Envy/Ismeron; Ian Partridge *tenor* Second follower of Envy/God of Dreams/Second Serial Spirit; Bernard Richards *cello continuo*; Raymond Leppard *harpsichord continuo*; St Anthony Singers. ECO. Decca/L'Oiseau-Lyre
Purcell: The Indian Queen – incidental music
CD: 433 166-2; 476 1552

1966 January 8 (live). Sadler's Wells Theatre. Donald McIntyre *baritone* Figaro; Elizabeth Harwood *soprano* Susanna; Raimund Herincx *baritone* Count; Ava June *soprano* Countess; Anne Pashley *mezzo-soprano* Cherubino; Noel Mangin *bass* Doctor Bartolo; Rita Hunter *soprano* Marcellina; Chorus and Orchestra of SWO.
Mozart: The Marriage of Figaro (in English)
CD: Oriel Music Trust OMT 805

1966 May 6 (UK broadcast date). RTB Concert Studio, Brussels. Pauline Tinsley *soprano* Agrippina; Alexander Young *tenor* Nerone; April Cantelo *soprano* Poppea; Stafford Deam *bass* Claudio; Monica Sinclair *mezzo-soprano* Ottone; Raimund Herincx *baritone* Pallante; Patricia Kern *mezzo-soprano* Narciso. Chorus and Orchestra of RTB.
Handel (ed. Mackerras): Agrippina
Celestial Audio CA 581

1966 May 28 (live). Royal Opera House. Amy Shuard *soprano* Turandot; Franco Corelli *tenor* Calaf; Elizabeth Vaughan *soprano* Liù; John Bonhomme *tenor* Ping; John Dobson *tenor* Pang; Ronald Lewis *baritone* Pong; David Kelly *bass* Timur; Robert Bowman *tenor* L'Imperatore Altoum; Eric Garrett *bass* Un mandarino; Chorus and Orchestra of ROHCG
Puccini: Turandot
CD: Omega Opera Archive 2069

1966 June 19–22. Konzerthaus, Vienna. Maureen Forrester *mezzo-soprano* Orfeo. Teresa Stich-Randall *soprano* Euridice. Hanny Steffek *soprano* Amor. Wiener Akademiechor. Orchester des Wiener Staatsoper. Vanguard
Gluck: Orfeo ed Euridice
CD: OVC 4039/40

1966 June 29–30; July 13, 15–16 and August 5–9. KH. Elizabeth Harwood *soprano*. Janet Baker *mezzo-soprano*. Paul Esswood *counter-tenor*. Robert Tear *tenor*. Raimund Herincx *bass-baritone*. Ambrosian Singers. ECO. EMI/HMV
Handel (ed. Lam): Messiah
CD: 569449-2

1966 July 10. AR. Christa Ludwig *mezzo-soprano*. NPO. EMI
Reger: An die Hoffnung
Unpublished. Christa Ludwig fell ill during the session.

1966 September 6 and 8. BBC Television Studios. Peter Glossop *baritone* Billy Budd; Peter Pears *tenor* Edward Fairfax Vere; Michael Langdon *bass* John Claggart; John Shirley-Quirk *baritone* Mr Redburn; Bryan Drake *bass-baritone* Mr Flint; David Kelly *bass* Mr Ratcliffe; Kenneth MacDonald *tenor* Red Whiskers; David Bowman *baritone* Donald; Dennis Wicks *baritone* Dansker; Robert Tear *tenor* The Novice; Robert Bowman *tenor* Squeak; Delme Bryn-Jones *baritone* Bo'sun; Eric Garrett *baritone* First Mate; Norman Lumsden *bass* Second Mate; Nigel Rogers *tenor* Maintop; Keith Raggett *tenor* Arthur Jones; Benjamin Luxon *baritone* Novice's Friend; Ambrosian Opera Chorus; LSO. *Stage Director:* Basil Coleman. *TV Producer:* Cedric Messina. BBC, licenced to Decca
Britten: Billy Budd Op. 50
DVD: 074 3256

1967 May 14. Hamburg. HPO. Checkmate
Brahms: Symphony No. 1 in C minor Op. 68
LP: C 76001

1967 May 15 and 18. Hamburg. HPO. Checkmate
Tchaikovsky: Symphony No. 4 in F minor Op. 36
LP: C 76004

1967 May 16–17. Hamburg. HPO. Checkmate
Tchaikovsky: Symphony No. 6 in B minor Op. 74
LP: C 76009

1967 May 23. Hamburg. HPO. Checkmate
Dvořák: Symphony No. 8 in G Op. 88
LP: C 76006 DL: ReDiscovery RD087

1967 September 30–October 4. Eberthalle, Harburg (Hamburg). Tatiana Troyanos *mezzo-soprano* Dido; Barry McDaniel *baritone* Aeneas; Sheila Armstrong *soprano* Belinda; Patricia Johnson *mezzo-soprano* Sorceress; Margaret Baker *soprano* First Witch/ Second Woman; Margaret Lensky *contralto* Second Witch; Paul Esswood *counter-tenor* Spirit; Nigel Rogers *tenor* Sailor; Hamburg Monteverdi Choir; North German Radio Chamber Orchestra. DG/Archiv
Purcell: Dido and Aeneas
CD: 477 5350

1968 February 28 (live). Royal Opera House. Josephine Veasey *mezzo-soprano* Carmen; Jean Bonhomme *tenor* Don José; Robert Massard *baritone* Escamillo; Joan Carlyle *soprano* Micaela; George Macpherson *bass* Zuniga; Maria Pellegrini *soprano* Frasquita; Anne Howells *mezzo-soprano* Mercédès; John Dobson *baritone* Dancairo; Kenneth MacDonald *tenor* Remendado; Chorus and Orchestra of ROHCG.
Bizet: Carmen
CD: Oriel Music Trust OMT 941

1968 April 12 (broadcast date). BBC Television Studios. Stuart Burrows *tenor* The Duke of Mantua; Peter Glossop *baritone* Rigoletto; Colette Boky *soprano* Gilda; Stafford Dean *bass* Sparafucile; Elizabeth Bainbridge *mezzo-soprano* Maddalena; [unidentified orchestra]
Verdi: Rigoletto (in English)
CD: Oriel Music Trust OMT 898. Soundtrack of BBC1 TV broadcast.

1968 May 8. AR. Christa Ludwig *mezzo-soprano*. NPO. EMI/Columbia
Berg: Sieben frühe Lieder – Nos 1–3
Unpublished.

1968 May 8–9. AR. NPO. EMI/ Columbia
Rossini (arr. Charles Godfrey Jnr): Guillaume Tell – ballet music
Delibes: Sylvia – Les Chasseresses; Intermezzo; Valse lente; Pizzicati; Cortège de Bacchus
CD: 575221-2

1968 May 9 and **1969** April 1–2[a]. AR. NPO. EMI/Columbia
Gounod: Faust – Act 5: ballet Music
CD: 575221-2

1969 January 9–11. WemTH. Simon Wolff *treble*; Paul Esswood *counter-tenor*; Roland Tatnell *counter-tenor*; Alexander Young *tenor*; John Shirley-Quirk *baritone*; Michael Rippon *bass*; Tiffin School Choir; Ambrosian Singers; Maurits Sillem *harpsichord*; Alan Harverson *organ*; ECO. DG/Archiv
Purcell: Ode on St Cecilia's Day
CD: 447 149-2; 477 5350

1969 January 30–February 1. AR. Raymond Lewenthal *piano*. LSO. CBS
Henselt: Piano Concerto in F minor Op.16
Liszt (arr. Lewenthal): Totentanz S126
CD: Elan 82284

1969 February 1. AR. LSO. CBS
Haydn: Symphony No. 18
LP: 32160342
CD: Haydn House HH 28132

1969 February 8. WalAH. LSO. BBC Radio Classics
Busoni: Lustspiel-Ouvertüre
Cherubini: Symphony in D
Respighi: Trittico botticelliano
CD: 15656 91372

1969 April 1–2. AR. NPO. EMI
Delibes: Coppélia: Prélude; Mazurka; Valse; Czardas
CD: 575221-2

1969 April 27 and May 18. AR. Pinchas Zukerman *violin*. LSO. CBS
Saint-Saëns: Introduction and Rondo Capriccioso Op. 28
CD: Sony 48276
Vieuxtemps: Violin Concerto No. 5 in A minor Op. 37
CD: Sony 48274
Chausson: Poème Op. 25
Wieniawski: Concert Polonaise Op. 4
LP: 72828

1969 May 15 (live). Royal Opera House. Peter Glossop *baritone* Simon Boccanegra; David Ward *bass* Jacopo Fiesco; Elizabeth Vaughan *soprano* Amelia/Maria; Carlo Cossutta *tenor* Gabriele Adorno; Delme Bryn-Jones *baritone* Paolo Albani; Hugh Sheane *bass* Pietro; Chorus and Orchestra of ROHCG
Verdi: Simon Boccanegra
CD: Oriel Music Trust OMT 145

1969 May 19–20. WTH. ECO. Philips
Voříšek: Symphony in D
CD: 475 7061

1969 May 22–27. AR. Beverly Sills *soprano*; [b]Jean Knibbs *soprano*; [b]Margaret Cable *soprano*; [b]Gloria Jennings *contralto*; [c]Keith Erwen *tenor*; [a]Leslie Fyson *baritone*; [a]Ambrosian Opera Chorus; RPO. Westminster (now DG)
G. Charpentier: Louise – Depuis le jour
CD: EMI CDC-747332-2; DG 471 766-2
Massenet: Manon[a] –Voici les élégants (Chorus); Suis-je gentille ainsi (Air de Manon); Je marche sur tous les chemins; Oui, dans le bois (Fabliau)
LP: HMV ASD 2513; Westminster WST 17163
Meyerbeer: Les Huguenots – O beau pays de la Touraine[b]; Robert le Diable – Robert, toi que j'aime[c]
Thomas: Hamlet – A vos jeux ... Partagez-vous mes fleurs ...Pâle et blonde dort sous l'eau profonde; Mignon – Oui, pour ce soir ... Je suis Titania
CD: Decca 467 906-2

1969 June 1. WemTH. ECO. Philips
Dvořák: Czech Suite Op. 39
CD: 442 660-2; 475 7061

1969 June. AR. Beverly Sills *soprano* Queen Elizabeth I; Peter Glossop *baritone* Duke of Nottingham; Beverly Wolff mezzo-*soprano* Sarah, Duchess of Nottingham; Róbert Ilosfalvy *tenor* Robert Devereux, Earl of Essex; Kenneth Macdonald *tenor* Lord Cecil; Don Garrard bass Sir Walter Raleigh; Gwynne Howell *bass* Page; Richard Van Allan *bass* Cavalier; Ambrosian Opera Chorus; RPO. Westminster
Donizetti: Roberto Devereux
CD: DG 471 224-2

1969 August 25–31. WemTH. Rafael Puyana *harpsichord*; David Sandeman *flute*; Neil Black *oboe*; Thea King *clarinet*; Raymond Cohen *violin*; Terence Weil *cello*. Philips
Falla: Harpsichord Concerto
CD: 432 829-2

1969 November 16 (live). War Memorial Opera House, San Francisco. Teresa Berganza *mezzo-soprano* Cenerentola; Sheila Marks *soprano* Clorinda; Sona Cercená *mezzo-soprano* Tisbe; Pietro Bottazzo *tenor* Ramiro; Renato Capecchi *baritone* Dandini; Paolo Montarsolo *bass* Don Magnifico; Clifford Grant *bass* Alidoro; Chorus and Orchestra of San Francisco Opera
Rossini: La Cenerentola
CD: Mike Richter AE 201; The Opera Lovers CEN 196 901

1969 November 20 (live) London Coliseum. Margaret Neville *soprano* Ann Trulove; Gregory Dempsey *tenor* Tom Rakewell; Eric Stannard *bass* Trulove; Raimund Herincx *baritone* Nick Shadow; Edith Coates *mezzo-soprano* Mother Goose; John Fryatt *tenor* Sellem; Ann Howard *mezzo-soprano* Baba the Turk; Peter Tracey *baritone* Keeper; Chorus and Orchestra of SWO
Stravinsky: The Rake's Progress
CD: Oriel Music Society OMS 049/3

1969 Hamburg, unidentified television studio. Raymond Wolansky *baritone* Peter I; Peter Haage *tenor* Peter Ivanov; Hans Sotin *bass* Van Bett; Lucia Popp *soprano* Marie; Ursula Boese *mezzo-soprano* Witwe Browe; Herbert Fliether *baritone* Admiral Lefort; Noel Mangin *bass* Lord Syndham; Franz Grundheber *bass* Officer; Chorus of Hamburg State Opera; Hamburg State Philharmonic Orchestra; Joachim Hess *television director*; Rolf Liebermann *artistic director*
Lortzing: Zar und Zimmermann
DVD: Arthaus Musik 101 269

1970 February 17–24. Kleiner Redoutensaal der Hofburg, Vienna. Tatiana Troyanos *mezzo-soprano* Anima; Hermann Prey *baritone* Corpo; Kurt Equiluz *tenor* Intelleto; Herbert Lackner *bass* Consiglio; Theo Adam *bass* Tempo; Paul Esswood *counter-tenor* Piacere; Rudolf Resch *tenor* Compagne I; Leopold Spitzer *bass* Compagne II; Teresa Zylis-Gara *soprano* Angelo custode; Edda Moser *soprano* Vita mondana; Ernst Gutstein *bass* Mondo/Anima dannata; Sylvia Geszty *soprano* Anima beata; Arleen Augér *soprano* Eco; Vienna Chamber Choir; Vienna Capella Academica; DG/Archiv
Cavalieri: Rappresentatione di Anima, et di Corpo
CD: 453 165-2

1970 March 1 (broadcast date). BBC Studios, Manchester. John Winfield *tenor* Mr Brouček; Anne Pashley *soprano* Málinka/Etherea/Kunka; Jennifer Eddy *soprano* Pot-boy/Child Prodigy/Student; David Hillman *tenor* Mazal/Starry Eyes/Petřík; Elizabeth Bainbridge *contralto* Kedruta; Bryan Drake *baritone* Sacristan/Lunobor/Domšík; Thomas Hemsley *baritone* Würfl/Wonderglitter/Councillor; Kenneth MacDonald *tenor* A Composer/Harper/Miroslav; Neilson Taylor *baritone* Apparition; BBC Northern Singers; BBC Northern SO.
Janáček: The Excursions of Mr Brouček (in English)
CD: Oriel Music Trust OMT 004–005

1970 March 31[a] and April 3[b], 6[c], 7[d], 8[e] and 10[f]. KH. Monserrat Caballé *soprano*; [a]Bernabé Marti *tenor*; LSO. EMI
Puccini: La Bohème – Donde lieta uscì; La Bohème – Sì, mi chiamano Mimì; Gianni Schicchi – O mio babbino caro; Madama Butterfly – Un bel dì vedremo; Tu, tu, piccolo iddio!; Manon Lescaut – In quelle trine morbide; Sola, perduta, abbonata; La Rondine – Chi il bel sogno di Doretta; Tosca – Vissi d'arte; Turandot – Signore, ascolta; Tu che di gel sei cinta; Le Villi – Se come voi piccina
CD: CDC 747941-2
Donizetti: Poliuto – Ah! Fuggi da morte[a]
Giordano: Andrea Chénier – Vicino a te[a]
Meyerbeer: Les Huguenots – Oh ciel! ou courez-vous?[a]
Puccini: Manon Lescaut – Tu, tu, amore[a]
Verdi: Un ballo in maschera – Teco io sto[a]
LP: ASD 2723

1970 April 15–17. LTH. Heather Harper *soprano*; Patricia Clark *soprano*; Paul Esswood *counter-tenor*; Alexander Young *tenor*; Michael Rippon *bass*; Christopher Keyte *bass*; Leeds Festival Chorus; ECO. DG/Archiv
Handel: Israel in Egypt
CD: 429 530-2

1970 June 4 and 15. BTH. LPO; [a]Band of H.M. Welsh Guards; [a]Guns of the Royal Horse Artillery. EMI/CFP
Glinka: Ruslan and Ludmilla – Overture
Mussorgsky (arr. Rimsky-Korsakov): A Night on the Bare Mountain
Tchaikovsky: 1812 Overture Op. 49 [a]
Wagner: Lohengrin – Act 3: Prelude
CD: CD-CFP 9000

1970 October 25. London Coliseum. Itzhak Perlman *violin*, Orchestra of SWO. BBC
Saint-Saëns: Introduction and Rondo capriccioso Op. 28
DVD: Medici Arts 308 552 8

1970 December 28–29. Anvil Studios, Denham. ECO. DG/Archiv
M. Haydn: Symphony in D minor P27; Symphony in G P16 with **Mozart**'s Introduction K444; Symphony in D (Turkish Suite for Voltaire's Zaire)
LP: 2533 074
CD: Haydn House HH 10581

1971 February 26 (live). London Coliseum. Marie Collier *soprano* Emilia Marty; Gregory Dempsey *tenor* Albert Gregor; Francis Egerton *tenor* Vítek; Barbara Walker *soprano* Kristina; Raimund Herincx *bass-baritone* Baron Jaroslav Prus; David Hillman *tenor* Janek Prus; Eric Shilling *baritone* Dr. Kolenatý; Edith Coates *mezzo-soprano* Charlady; Emile Belcourt *tenor* Count Hauk-Šendorf; Donna-Faye Carr *soprano* Chamber-maid; Tom MacDonnell *baritone* Stage Carpenter; Chorus and Orchestra of SWO
Janáček: The Makropulos Affair (in English)
CD: Oriel Music Society OMS 015/2

1971 April 23. ABC Studios, Sydney. New Sydney Woodwind Quintet. SSO. ABC/World Record Club (Australia)
Sitsky: Concerto for Woodwind Quintet and Orchestra
LP: R 04694

1971 October 22 (live). War Memorial Opera House, San Francisco. Thomas Stewart *baritone* Evgeny Onegin; Stuart Burrows *tenor* Lenski; Evelyn Lear *soprano* Tatyana; Edna Garabedian *mezzo-soprano* Olga; Helen Vanni *mezzo-soprano* Larina; Donna Petersen *mezzo-soprano* Filipjewna; Ara Berberian *bass* Prince Gremin; John Walker *tenor* Triquet; Philip Booth *bass* Zaretzky; Daniel Sullivan *bass* Captain; Chorus and Orchestra of San Francisco Opera.
Tchaikovsky: Eugene Onegin Op. 24 (in English)
CD: John Wegner 2 SFO-02; Mike Richter CD-ROM

1971 November 11 (live). War Memorial Opera House, San Francisco. Martina Arroyo *soprano* Amelia; Helen Donath *soprano* Oscar; Irene Dalis *mezzo-soprano* Ulrica; Luciano Pavarotti *tenor* Riccardo; Franco Bordoni *baritone* Renato; Richard Mundt *bass* Samuel; Philip Booth *bass* Tom; Allan Monk *baritone* Silvano; Joe Pinedo *tenor* Judge; Daniel Sullivan *tenor* Servant; Chorus and Orchestra of San Francisco Opera
Verdi: Un ballo in maschera
CD: Butterfly BMCD 022

1971 December 12–14. AR. Andreas Röhn *violin*. John Constable *harpsichord continuo*. ECO. DG/Archiv
Viotti: Violin Concerto No. 16 in E minor (with Mozart's parts for trumpet and timpani K470a); Violin Concerto No. 24 in B minor
CD: 442 8654

1971 December 24 (broadcast date), BBC Television studios (?). Michele Molese *tenor* Hoffmann; Elizabeth Harwood *soprano* Olympia/Giulietta/Antonia; Geraint Evans *baritone* Dr. Coppélius/Dappertutto/Miracle/Lindorf; Gillian Ramsden *mezzo-soprano* Nicklausse; Derek Hammond-Stroud *baritone* Spalanzani/Nathanaël; Graham Allum *tenor* Frantz/Pitichinaccio; John Lawrenson *baritone* Schlémil/Crespil; Reginald Barrett *tenor* Cochenille; Margaret Lensky *contralto* Antonia's Mother; Ambrosian Opera Chorus; LSO
Offenbach: The Tales of Hoffmann (in English – abridged version)
CD: Celestial Opera CA 043. Soundtrack of BBC2 TV broadcast

1972 January 9–10. BTH. Rita Hunter *soprano* Brünnhilde. Alberto Remedios *tenor* Siegfried. LPO. EMI/CFP
Wagner: Götterdämmerung – Act 1: Dawn; Zu neuen Thaten; Act 2: Siegfried's Rhine Journey; Act 3: Siegfried's Funeral March; Immolation Scene
CD: CD-CFP 4670

1972 May 18–21. LTH. Donald McIntyre *bass* Saul; Ryland Davies *tenor* Jonathan; James Bowman *counter-tenor* David; John Winfield *tenor* Abner/Witch of Endor; Margaret Price *soprano* Merab; Sheila Armstrong *soprano* Michael; Stafford Dean *bass* Doeg/Apparition of Samuel; Gerald English *tenor* An Amalekite/High Priest; Leeds Festival Chorus; ECO. DG/Archiv
Handel: Saul
CD: 447 696-2

1972 July 23. WTH. LSO. Vanguard
Stravinsky: Petrushka (1911 version)
CD: 08406571

1972 July 25. RAH. [a]David Mason; [b]Felicity Palmer; [b]Maureen Lehane; [b]Alexander Young; [b]Benjamin Luxon; [b]BBC Chorus; [abc]NPO.
Haydn: Trumpet Concerto in E flat[a]; Mass in B flat[b]; Symphony No. 93 in D major[c]; Orfeo ed Euridice – Act 4[b]
CD: Mondo Archives AAC 012–13

1972 August or September (live). London Coliseum. Jon Sydney *tenor* Manrico; Gabrielle Lavigna *mezzo-soprano* Azucena; Rita Hunter *soprano* Leonora; Norman Bailey *baritone* Conte di Luna; David Gwynne *bass* Ferrando; Anne Collins *mezzo-soprano* Ines; Chorus and Orchestra of SWO
Verdi: Il trovatore (in English)
CD: Opera Depot 10609-2
Performances took place on 23 August and 7, 12, 15 and 21 September.

1973 January 15. BTH. LPO. EMI/CFP
R. Strauss: Till Eulenspiegels lustige Streiche Op. 26; Don Juan Op. 20
CD: CD-CFP 6043

1973 April 12 (live). Royal Opera House. Gilda Cruz-Romo *soprano* Aida; Carlo Bergonzi *tenor* Radames; Mignon Dunni *mezzo-soprano* Amneris; Gian-Piero Mastromei *baritone* Amonasro; Forbes Robinson *bass* Ramphis; Dennis Wicks *bass* Il Re; Kiri Te Kanawa *soprano* Una Sacerdotessa; William Elvin *baritone* Un Messaggero; Chorus and Orchestra of ROHCG
Verdi: Aida
CD: Premier Opera CDNO 472

1973 April 26 and 29. BTH. LPO. Maurits Sillem *harpsichord continuo*. EMI/CFP
Mozart: Symphony No. 36 in C K425; Symphony No. 38 in D K504
CD: CD-CFPSD 4781

1973 June 30 (live). Teatro La Fenice, Venice. Werner Hollweg *tenor* Tito; Beverly Wolff *mezzo-soprano* Sesto; Yasuki Hayashi *tenor* Servilia; Janet Coster *mezzo-soprano* Vitellia; Ilse Gramatzki *soprano* Annio; Harald Stamm *bass* Publio; Coro del Teatro La Fenice, Venice; Orchestra del Teatro La Fenice, Venice
Mozart: La Clemenza di Tito
CD: Mondo Musica MFOH 10820

1973 September 21 (live). London Coliseum. Dennis Wicks *bass* Dikoi; Kenneth Woollam *tenor* Boris Grigorievitch; Sylvia Fisher *soprano* Marfa Kabanova (Kabanicha); Robert Ferguson *tenor* Tichon Kabanov; Lorna Haywood *soprano* Katerina Kabanova (Katya); Paul Crook *tenor* Vanya Kudriash; Barbara Walker *soprano* Varvara; Christian Du Plessis *baritone* Kuligin; Sheila Rex contralto Glasha; Audrey Gunn *mezzo-soprano* Feklusha; Chorus and Orchestra of SWO.
Janáček: Katya Kabanova (in English)
CD: Oriel Music Society OMS 25/2

1973 September 29 (live). Opera House, Sydney. [a]Birgit Nilsson *soprano*; SSO. ABC
Wagner: Die Meistersinger von Nürnberg – Act 1: Prelude; Tannhäuser – Dich, teure Halle[a]; Tristan und Isolde –Prelude; Liebestod[a]
CD: 476 6440
Wagner: Götterdämmerung – Prologue: Siegfried's Rhine Journey; Act 3: Funeral March, Immolation Scene[a]
CD: 476 6440; 476 5957
DVD: 476 6440

1973 December 13 (live). London Coliseum. Janet Baker *mezzo-soprano* Mary Stuart; Pauline Tinsley *soprano* Elizabeth; Keith Erwen *tenor* Leicester; Don Garrard *bass* Talbot; Audrey Gunn *soprano* Anna; Christian Du Plessis *baritone* Cecil; Chorus and Orchestra of SWO
Donizetti: Mary Stuart (in English)
CD: Mitridate (Ponto) PO 1031

1974 January 31–February 4. Grosser Musikvereinsaal, Vienna. Edith Mathis *soprano*; Birgit Finnilä *contralto*; Peter Schreier *tenor*; Theo Adam *bass-baritone*; Austrian Radio Chorus and SO. DG/Archiv
Handel (orch. Mozart): Der Messias
CD: 427 173-2

1974 June 5 (live). Royal Opera House. Carlo Cossutta *tenor* Otello; Kiri Te Kanawa *soprano* Desdemona; Piero Cappuccilli *baritone* Iago; John Dobson *tenor* Cassio; Adrian de Peyer *tenor* Rodrigo; Gwynne Howell *bass* Lodovico; Paul Hudson *bass* Montano; Elizabeth Bainbridge *mezzo-soprano* Emilia; Chorus and Orchestra of ROHCG
Verdi: Otello
CD: House of Opera CDDB 877

1974 July 13. All Hallows', Gospel Oak, London. NPO. Vanguard
Mussorgsky: Khovanshchina – Prelude (Dawn over the Moscow River); (orch. Ravel): Pictures at an Exhibition
CD: 1504

1974 August 10 (live). RAH. BBCSO. BBC
Wagner: Rienzi – Overture
CD: BBCRD 9101

1974 November 21 (live). London Coliseum. Janet Baker *mezzo-soprano* Mary Stuart; Ava June *soprano* Elizabeth; Keith Erwen *tenor* Leicester; John Tomlinson *bass* Talbot; Audrey Gunn *soprano* Anna; Christian Du Plessis *baritone* Cecil; Chorus and Orchestra of ENO
Donizetti: Mary Stuart (in English)
CD: Oriel Music Society OMS 097

1974 December 8 (live). Royal Opera House. Stuart Burrows *tenor* Faust; Kiri Te Kanawa *soprano* Marguerite; Norman Treigle *bass-baritone* Mephistofélès; Thomas Allen *baritone* Valentin; Anne Howells *mezzo-soprano* Siébel; Heather Begg *mezzo-soprano* Marthe; Michael Maurel *baritone* Wagner; Chorus and Orchestra of ROHCG
Gounod: Faust
CD: Oriel Music Society OMS 313

1974 December 24 (broadcast date). Unidentified TV studio. Eric Shilling *baritone* The Learned Judge; Norma Burrowes *soprano* The Plaintiff; John Brecknock *tenor* The Defendant; Denis Dowling *baritone* Counsel for the Plaintiff; Harold Blackburn *bass* Usher; Peter Lehmann Bedford *bass* Foreman of the Jury; Ambrosian Opera Chorus; ECO. Peter Potter *television director*
Sullivan: Trial by Jury
DVD: House of Opera DVDCC 1391
A Granada TV production made as part of the 'Parade' arts series.

1974 December 29 (broadcast date). BBCGG. Janet Hughes *soprano* Phénice/Mélisse/Coryphée; Janet Price *soprano* Sidonie/Une amante heureuse; Geri Nrunin *soprano* Armide; Thomas Allen *baritone* Hidraot; Leslie Fyson *tenor* Aronte; Philip Langridge *tenor* Artémidore; Bruce Brewer *tenor* Renaud; Wendy Eathorne *soprano* Une naiade/Lucinde; Ann Howard *mezzo-soprano* La Haine; Gerald English *tenor* Le Chevalier Danois; BBC Singers; BBCCO
Gluck: Armide
CD: Celestial Audio CA 448

1975 February 1 (live). London Coliseum. Lois McDonall *soprano* Marschallin; Josephine Barstow *soprano* Octavian; Valerie Masterson *soprano* Sophie; Neil Warren-Smith *bass* Baron Ochs; Eric Shilling *baritone* Faninal; Paul Crook *tenor* Valzacchi; Sarah Walker *mezzo-soprano* Annina; Tom Swift *tenor* Italian Singer; Judith Turner *soprano* Marianne; Dennis Dowling *baritone* Police Inspector; Jon Sydney *tenor* Innkeeper;

Harry Coghill *bass* Notary; Terry Jenkins *tenor* Marschallin's Major-Domo; Kenneth Woollam *tenor* Faninal's Major-Domo; Chorus and Orchestra of ENO
R. Strauss: Der Rosenkavalier (in English)
CD: Celestial Audio CA170

1975 April 2 and 15. BTH. LPO. EMI/CFP
Mozart: Symphony No. 40 in G minor K550; Symphony No. 41 in C K551
CD: CD-CFP 4253

1975 April 16–17. BTH. Allan Schiller *piano*. LPO. EMI/CFP
Mozart: Piano Concerto No. 23 in A K488; Piano Concerto No. 20 in D minor K466
CD: CD-CFPSD 4781

1975 May 17 (live). London Coliseum. Peter Knapp *baritone* King Roger; Janet Gail *soprano* Roxana; Henry Howell *tenor* The Shepherd; John Winfield *tenor* Edrisi; Richard Angas *bass* The Archbishop; Amilia Dixey The Deaconess; Chorus of the New Opera Company; RPO
Szymanowski: King Roger (in English)
CD: Oriel Music Society OMS 036/2

1975 August 12–14. HWH. [a]Leslie Pearson *organ*; chorus[b], LPO. Reader's Digest
Bax: Coronation March (1953)[a]
LP: RDS 8024
Beethoven: Die Ruinen von Athen Op. 113 – Turkish March
Berlioz: La Damnation de Faust Op. 24 – Marche hongroise
Chabrier: Marche joyeuse
Elgar: Imperial March Op. 32
Gounod: Faust – Soldiers' Chorus[b]
Halvorsen: Entry of the Boyars
Meyerbeer: Le Prophète – Coronation March
Rimsky-Korsakov: Le Coq d'or – March
Sibelius: Karelia Suite Op. 11 – Alla Marcia
Tchaikovsky: Marche slave Op. 31
CD: Menuet 160029-2
DL: Reader's Digest Music 'Classics of the March'

1975 October 1–7
Notre Dame de Liban, Paris. Mirella Freni *soprano*; Teresa Berganza *mezzo-soprano*; Paul Kuentz Chamber Orchestra. DG/Archiv
A. Scarlatti: Stabat Mater
CD: 459 454-2

1976 March 13 (live). London Coliseum. John Mitchinson *tenor* Idomeneo; Anthony Roden *tenor* Idamante; Kenneth Woollam *tenor* Arbace; Lucia Popp *soprano* Ilia; Rita Hunter *soprano* Elettra; Ashton Smith *bass* Gran Sacerdote; Clifford Grant *bass* La Voce; Chorus and Orchestra of ENO
Mozart: Idomeneo
CD: Oriel Music Society OMS 030
Sung in English apart from Lucia Popp, who sings Ilia in Italian; she was a late replacement for an indisposed Lois McDonall.

1976 March 30. Palais Garnier, Paris. Nicolai Gedda *tenor* Faust; Roger Soyer *bass* Méphistofélès; Mirella Freni *soprano* Marguerite; Tom Krause *baritone* Valentin; Renée Auphan *soprano* Siébel; Jocelyne Taillon *mezzo-soprano* Marthe; Jean-Louis Soumagnas *baritone* Wagner; Choeurs et Orchestre du Théâtre National de l'Opéra.
Gounod: Faust
DVD: Dreamlife DLVC-1025

1976 April 4–9 and 11–12. WTH. Ryland Davies *tenor* Judas Maccabaeus; Felicity Palmer *soprano* Israelite Woman; Janet Baker *mezzo-soprano* Israelite Man; John Shirley-Quirk *baritone* Simon; Christopher Keyte *bass* Eupolemus; Paul Esswood *counter-tenor* Messenger; Wandsworth School Choir [choir-master: Russell Burgess]; ECO. DG/Archiv
Handel: Judas Maccabeus
CD: 447 692-2

1976 May 5–7. HWH. Heinrich Schiff *cello*; NPO. DG
Fauré: Elégie Op. 24
Lalo: Cello Concerto in D minor
Saint-Saëns: Cello Concerto No. 1 Op. 33
CD: 431 166-2

1976 May 20 and 22–23. HWH. Maurice André *trumpet*; Maurits Sillem *harpsichord continuo*; ECO. DG
Stölzel (ed. Thilde): Trumpet Concerto in D
Telemann: Concerto–Sonata in D
Torelli (attrib): Trumpet Concerto in D
Vivaldi: Double Trumpet Concerto in C RV537 (both parts played by Maurice André)
CD: 474 3312

1976 September (live). Staatsoper, Köln. Anja Silja *soprano* Minnie; Róbert Ilosfalvy *tenor* Dick Johnson; Wassili Janulako *baritone* Jack Rance; Cologne Opera Chorus; Gürzenich Symphoniker
Puccini: La Fanciulla del West
CD: Opera Depot OD 10167-2

1976 October 8 and December 19. AR. LSO. EMI
Handel (ed. Mackerras): Music for the Royal Fireworks; Concerto a due cori No. 2 in F
CD: HMV 572329-2
Handel (ed. Mackerras): Concerto No. 1 in F; Concerto No. 3 in D
CD: HMV 572329-2; Testament SBT 1253

1976 22 October (live). London Coliseum. Neil Howlett *baritone* Vladislav; John Mitchinson *tenor* Dalibor; Malcolm Rivers *baritone* Budivoj; Dennis Wicks *bass* Beneš; Ramon Remedios *tenor* Vítek; Anne Evans *soprano* Milada; Chorus and Orchestra of ENO
Smetana: Dalibor (in English)
CD: Oriel Music Society OMS 034/3

1976 December 1–4, 6–7, 13–14. SV. Dalibor Jedlička *bass* Savël Prokofjevič Dikoj; Peter Dvorský *tenor* Boris Grigorjevič; Naděžda Kniplová *soprano* Marfa Ignatěvna Kabanová (Kabanicha); Vladimír Krejčík *baritone* Tichon Ivanyč Kabanov; Elisabeth Söderström *soprano* Kateřina (Káťa); Zdeněk Švehla *tenor* Váňa Kudrjáš; Libuše Márová *mezzo-soprano* Varvara; Jaroslav Souček *baritone* Kuligin; Jitka Pavlová *soprano* Glaša; Gertrude Jahn *mezzo-soprano* Fekluša; Vienna State Opera Chorus; WP. Decca
Janáček: Kát'a Kabanová
CD: 421 852-2; 475 6872

1977 January 23–25. AR. Maurice André *trumpet*; ECO. EMI
Handel (arr. Jean Thilde): Sonata for flute and harpsichord Op. 1 No. 9
Albinoni (arr. Paumgartner): Trumpet Concerto in B flat Op. 7 No. 3; Trumpet Concerto in D Op. 7 No. 6
Telemann (ed. Töttcher and Grebe): Trumpet Concerto in D
Hertel: Trumpet Concerto in E flat
CD: CDM 763528-2

1977 March 26–27. HWH. LPO. EMI/CFP
Verdi (arr. Mackerras): The Lady and the Fool – ballet suite: Nos 4, 3, 5, 6, 10, 12 and 6
Sullivan (arr. Mackerras): Pineapple Poll – ballet suite: Nos 1, 2, 3, 4, 6, 7, 10 and 11
CD: CD-CFP 4618

1977 May 4 (live). RFH. Sheila Armstrong *soprano*; BBCSO. BBC
Mahler: Symphony No. 4
CD: BBCRD 9101

1977 November 28–30. HWH. Ingrid Dingfelder *flute*; ECO Enigma/ASV
C. P. E. Bach: Concerto in D minor for Flute and Orchestra Wq22
Hoffmeister: Concerto in D for Flute and Orchestra
CD: CDQS 6012

1977 December 13 (live). London Coliseum. John Brecknock *tenor* Werther; Janet Baker *mezzo-soprano* Charlotte; Joy Roberts *soprano* Sophie; Patrick Wheatley *baritone* Albert; Harold Blackburn *bass* Le Bailli; John Tomlinson *bass* Johann; Terry Jenkins *tenor* Schmidt; Chorus and Orchestra of ENO. EMI (now Chandos)
Massenet: Werther (in English)
CD: Chandos CHAN 3033

1978 January 10 (live). London Coliseum. Emile Belcourt *tenor* Filka Morozov; Gregory Dempsey *tenor* Skuratov; Geoffrey Chard *baritone* Shishkov; Patrick Wheatley *bass* Alexander Petrovich Goryanchikov; Denis Dowling *bass* Commandant; Sandra Dugdale *soprano* Alyeya; Kenneth Woollam *tenor* Tall Prisoner; John Tranter *bass* Short Prisoner; Chorus and Orchestra of ENO
Janáček: From the House of the Dead (in English)
CD: Oriel Music Trust OMT 392

1978 February 1–4. Dablice Studio, Prague. PCO. Supraphon/EMI
Handel: Water Music – Suites in F, D and G
CD: CDZ 762509-2

1978 February 18–19. Dablice Studio, Prague. PCO. Supraphon/EMI
Handel: Concerti grossi Op. 3
LP: ESD 7089; EMX 412086 1

1978 August (live). Aix-en-Provence Festival. Janet Baker *mezzo-soprano* Dido; Norma Burrowes *soprano* Belinda; Claire Livingstone *mezzo-soprano* Sorceress; Marie Slorach *soprano* First Witch; Linda Ormiston *contralto* Second Witch; Alan Titus *baritone* Aeneas; Dennis O'Neill *tenor* Sailor; Susanne Ross *soprano* Second Lady; Paul Esswood *counter-tenor* Attendant Spirit; Chorus of Scottish Opera; Orchestra of Scottish Opera
Purcell: Dido and Aeneas
DVD: Premiere Opera DVD 5934

1978 September 25–27, 30; October 2–4 and 9–11. Vienna Film Studios, Vienna. Elisabeth Söderström *soprano* Emilia Marty; Peter Dvorský *tenor* Albert Gregor; Vladimír Krejčík *tenor* Vítek; Anna Czaková *mezzo-soprano* Kristina; Václav Zítek *baritone* Jaroslav Prus; Zdeněk Švehla *tenor* Janek; Dalibor Jedlička *bass* Dr. Kolenatý; Jiří Joran *bass* Stage Hand; Ivana Mixová *contralto* Stage Dresser; Beno Blachut *tenor* Hauk-Šendorf; Blanka Vitková *contralto* Chambermaid; Chor der Wiener Staatsoper. WP. Decca
Janáček: Věc Makropulos
CD: 430 372-2; 475 6872

1979 January 9. HWH. Jennifer Smith *soprano*. PO. BBC Radio Classics
Berlioz: Le Jeune Pâtre breton Op. 13 No. 4; Les Nuits d'été Op. 7
CD: 15656 91532

1979 January 16 (live). London Coliseum. Gregory Dempsey *tenor* Mr Brouček; Lorna Haywood *soprano* Málinka/ Etherea/Kunka; Marilyn Hill Smith *soprano* Pot-boy/Child Prodigy/Student; Henry Howell *tenor* Mazal/Starry Eyes/Petřík; Dennis Wicks *baritone* Sacristan/Lunobor/Domšík; Geoffrey Chard *baritone* Würfl/Wonderglitter/ Councillor; Stuart Kale *tenor* A Composer/Harper/Miroslav; Niall Murray *baritone* Poet/Cloudy/Vacek; John Mitchinson *tenor* Apparition; Chorus and Orchestra of ENO.
Janáček: The Excursions of Mr Brouček (in English)
CD: Oriel Music Trust OMT 870

1979 July 24 (live). RAH. [a]Harold Lester *piano*. BBCSO. BBC Radio Classics
Janáček: The Ballad of Blaník
Martinů: Double Concerto for Two String Orchestras, Piano and Timpani[a]
CD: 15656 91352

1979 November 26–27. SV. WP. Decca
Janáček. Žárlivost
CD: 414 483-2; 475 6872

1979 November 27. SV. WP. Decca
Janáček (arr. Václav Talich): The Cunning Little Vixen – Suite
CD: 414 129-2; 475 6872

1979 (live). Opera House, Sydney. John Shaw *baritone* Simon Boccanegra; Donald Shanks *bass* Jacopo Fiesco; Isobel Buchanan *soprano* Amelia/Maria; Lamberto Furlan *tenor* Gabriele Adorno; Gregory Yurisich *baritone* Paolo Albani; Bruce Martin *bass* Pietro; Chorus and Orchestra of Australian Opera
Verdi: Simon Boccanegra
CD: Celestial Audio CA 433

1980 February 25–28 and March 3–5. SV. Jiří Zahrádniček *tenor* Filka Morozov; Ivo Židek *tenor* Skuratov; Václav Zítek *baritone* Šiškov; Dalibor Jedlička *bass* Alexandr Petrovič Goryančikov; Antonín Švorc *bass-baritone* Commandant; Jaroslava Janská *soprano* Aljeja; Vladimír Krejčík *tenor* Tall Prisoner; Richard Novák *bass* Short Prisoner; Beno Blachut *tenor* Old Prisoner; Zdeněk Švehla *tenor* Voice/Čerevin; Eva Zigmundová *mezzo-soprano* Wench; Zdeněk Soušek *tenor* Šapkin/Kedril; Jaroslav Soušek *baritone* Čekunov/Don Juan; Vienna State Opera Chorus; WP. Decca
Janáček: Z mrtvého domu [From the House of the Dead]
CD: 430 375-2; 475 6872

1980 March 24–25. SV. WP. Decca
Janáček: Sinfonietta; Taras Bulba
CD: 410 138-2; 475 6872

1980 April 20 (broadcast date). BBCMV. Emile Belcourt *tenor* Mercury; Kenneth Woollam *tenor* Midas; Rosalind Plowright *soprano* Xanthe; Norman Bailey *baritone* Jupiter; Arlene Saunders *soprano* Danae; John Dobson *tenor* Pollux; Bernard Dickerson *tenor* König I; Stuart Kale *tenor* König II; Alan Watt *baritone* König III; Geoffrey Moses *bass* König IV; Elizabeth Gale *soprano* Semele; Linda Finnie *mezzo-soprano* Leda; Alison Hargan *soprano* Europa; Patricia Price *mezzo-soprano* Alkmene; BBC Opera Chorus. BBCSO
R. Strauss: Der Liebe der Danae
CD: Oriel Music Trust OMT 871

1980 August 10. BBCMV. BBCSO. Redcliffe Recordings (under licence)
Whettam: Sinfonia intrepida
CD: RRCD 16

1980 August 16[a] and 18[b]. AR. LSO. Centaur
Debussy: La Mer[a]
Ravel: Daphnis et Chloé – Suite No. 2[b]
CD: CRC 2090

1980 August 18, 21, 23, 24 and September 6, 21–23. AR. Valerie Masterson *soprano* Violetta; John Brecknock *tenor* Alfredo Germont; Christian du Plessis *baritone* Giorgio Germont; Della Jones *mezzo-soprano* Flora Bervoix; John Gibbs *baritone* Baron Douphol; Roderick Earle *bass* Doctor Grenvil; Denis Dowling *baritone* Marquis d'Obigny; Geoffrey Pogson *tenor* Viscount Gaston de Letorieres; Shelagh Squires *mezzo-soprano* Annina; Edward Byles *tenor* Joseph; Chorus and Orchestra of ENO. EMI (now Chandos)/Peter Moores Foundation
Verdi: La Traviata (in English)
CD: CMS 763072-2; CHAN 3023

1980 November (live). Palais Garnier, Paris. Jane Berbié *mezzo-soprano* Grandmother Buryjovka; Guy Chauvet *tenor* Laca Klemeň; Jean Dupouy *tenor* Števa Buryjovka; Nadine Denize *mezzo-soprano* Kostelnička Buryjovka; Rachel Yakar *soprano* Jenůfa; Philippe Rouillon *baritone* Mill foreman; Fernand Dumont *baritone* Mayor; Anna Ringart *soprano* Mayor's Wife; Elaine Lublin *soprano* Karolka; Chorus and Orchestra of the Théâtre National de l'Opéra.
Janáček: Jenůfa (in French)
DVD: Opera Passion DVD 1061

1981 March 13, 14, 16–18, 23–26. SV. Dalibor Jedlička *bass* Forester; Lucia Popp *soprano* Vixen/Young Vixen; Libuše Márová *contralto* Dog; Eva Zigmundová *mezzo-soprano* Forester's Wife/Owl; Vladimír Krejčík *tenor* Schoolmaster/Gnat; Richard Novák *bass* Priest/Badger; Václav Zítek *baritone* Harašta; Beno Blachut *tenor* Pásek; Ivana Mixová *mezzo-soprano* Pásek's Wife/Woodpecker/Hen; Gertrude Jahn *mezzo-soprano* Cock/Jay; Peter Šaray *treble* Frog/Grasshopper; Miriam Ondrášková *soprano* Cricket; Eva Hříbková *soprano* Frantík; Zusana Hudečková *soprano* Pepík; Eva Randová *mezzo-soprano* Fox; Vienna State Opera Chorus; Bratislava Children's Choir; WP. Decca

Janáček: Příhody lišky Bystroušky [The Cunning Little Vixen]
CD: 417 129-2; 475 6872

1981 June 1–6. Stadion, Brno. John Mitchinson *tenor* Manolios; Helen Field *soprano* Katerina; John Tomlinson *bass* Grigoris; Phillip Joll *baritone* Kostis; Geoffrey Moses *bass* Fotis; Arthur Davies *tenor* Yannakos; Rita Cullis *soprano* Lenio; Catherine Savory *soprano* Nikolios/Old Woman; Jeffrey Lawton *tenor* Panais; John Harris *tenor* Michelis; David Gwynne *bass* Old Man/ Patriarcheas; Jana Jonášová *soprano* Despino; Michael Geliot *speaker* Ladas; Kühn Children's Chorus; Czech Philharmonic Chorus; Brno State Philharmonic Orchestra. Supraphon
Martinů: The Greek Passion (Revised version)
CD: 10 3611-2

1981 August 14 (live). Melbourne. Alberto Remedios *tenor* Tristan; Rita Hunter *soprano* Isolde; Margreta Elkins *mezzo-soprano* Brangaene; Bruce Martin *bass* Marke; John Shaw *baritone* Kurwenal; Ronald Stevens *tenor* Melot; Robert Gard *tenor* Hirt/Steuerman/ Stimme eines jungen Seemans; Melbourne SO
Wagner: Tristan und Isolde
CD: JDT Productions RHSC 119

1981 December 12 (live). Royal Opera House. Janet Baker *mezzo-soprano* Alceste; Robert Tear *tenor* Admète; John Shirley-Quirk *baritone* High Priest/ Thanatos; Maldwyn Davies *tenor* Évre; Jonathan Summers *baritone* Hercule; Philip Gelling *bass* Herald/Apollo; Matthew Best *bass* Oracle; Chorus and Orchestra of ROHCG. Royal Opera House Heritage Series
Gluck: Alceste (Paris version)
CD: ROHS 010

1982 February 8 or 9 (live). ODP. Jiří Tomášek *violin*; Prague Radio SO. Praga
Shostakovich: Violin Concerto No. 2 in C sharp minor Op. 129
CD: PR 250052

1982 February 15–16. RP. [a]Josef Ružička *piano*. [a]Jan Bouse *timpani*. Prague Radio SO. Supraphon
Martinů: Double Concerto for Two String Orchestras, Piano and Timpani[a]; Les Fresques de Piero della Francesca
CD: SU 3276-2; SU 4042-2

1982 March 28 (live). Barbican Hall. ECO. BBC Radio Classics
Walton: Siesta
Bach (arr. Walton): The Wise Virgins – ballet suite
Walton (arr. Mathieson): Henry V – Passacaglia: The Death of Falstaff; Touch her soft lips and part
CD: 15656 91612; BBCM 5021 2

1982 April 1, 10, 14 and 22 (live). London Coliseum. Janet Baker *mezzo-soprano* Mary Stuart; Rosalind Plowright *soprano* Elizabeth; David Rendall *tenor* Leicester; Alan Opie *baritone* Cecil; John Tomlinson *bass* Talbot; Angela Bostock *soprano* Anna; Chorus and Orchestra of ENO. EMI (now Chandos)/Peter Moores Foundation
Donizetti: Mary Stuart (in English)
CD: CMS 769372-2; Chandos CHAN 3017

1982 April 17, 19–21, 24–29. SV. Marie Mrazová *contralto* Grandmother Buryjovka; Wieslaw Ochman *tenor* Laca; Peter Dvorský *tenor* Števa; Eva Randová *mezzo-soprano* Kostelnička Buryjovka; Elisabeth Söderström *soprano* Jenůfa; Václav Zitek *baritone* Mill Foreman; Dalibor Jedlička *bass* Mayor; Ivana Mixová *soprano* Mayor's Wife; Lucia Popp *soprano* Karolka; Věra Soukopová *mezzo-soprano* Herdswoman/Old Woman; Jindra Pokorná *mezzo-soprano* Barena; Jana Jonášová *soprano* Jano; Vienna State Opera Chorus; WP. Decca
Janáček: Jenůfa (Brno 1908 version)
CD: 414 483-2; 475 6872
Peter Dvorský recorded his part in a tracking session at Kingsway Hall, London, on 5 March 1983. The Kovařovic version of the final scene is included as a supplement.

1982 November 26–27. KH. PO. Decca
Sullivan (arr. Mackerras): Pineapple Poll – ballet
CD: 436 810-2; 480 1284
Sullivan: Overture di Ballo
CD: 436 813-2; 480 1285

1983 February 13–14. St John's, Smith Square. ECO. EMI Eminence
Dvořák: Serenade for Strings Op. 22
CD: CD-CFP 4597

1983 August 11–12 and 15. Concert Hall, Opera House, Sydney. ACO. Conifer
Haydn: Symphony No. 80 in D minor; Symphony No. 81 in G minor
CD: CDCF 165

1983 September 21 (live). Staatsoper, Vienna. Nicola Martinucci *tenor* Manrico; Mariana Paunova *mezzo-soprano* Azucena; Ghena Dimitrova *soprano* Leonora; Giorgio Zancanaro *baritone* Conte di Luna; John-Paul Bogart *bass* Ferrando; Ewald Aichberger *tenor* Ruiz; Chorus and Orchestra of the Vienna State Opera.
Verdi: Il trovatore
CD: Cin Cin 1006–07

1984 January 20–21. RP. Václav Zítek *baritone*. Czech Philharmonic Chorus. CPO. Supraphon
Martinů. Field Mass
CD: C37 7735; SU 4042-2

1984 January 27–29. RP. Elisabeth Söderström *soprano*; Drahomíra Drobková *contralto;* František Livora *tenor*; Richard Novák *bass*; Jan Hora *organ*; Czech Philharmonic Chorus; CPO. Supraphon
Janáček: Glagolitic Mass
CD: C37–7448; SU 4042-2

1984 January 30. RP. Květoslava Němečková *soprano*; Leo Marian Vodička *tenor*; Václav Zítek *baritone*; Czech Philharmonic Chorus; CPO. Supraphon
Janáček: Amarus
CD: C37–7735; SU 4042-2

1984 July 22–23 and 27. AR. Elizabeth Harwood *soprano*; Emma Kirkby *soprano*; Valerie Masterson *soprano*; James Bowman *counter-tenor*; Anthony Rolfe Johnson *tenor*; John Shirley-Quirk *bass-baritone*; Wandsworth School Choir; ECO
Handel: Various works; Soundtrack for *God Rot Tunbridge Wells* (TV film, directed by Tony Palmer)
CD: TPCD 114 DVD: TPDVD 114

1984 August 1–7. AR. Janet Baker *mezzo-soprano* Julius Caesar; Valerie Masterson *soprano* Cleopatra; Sarah Walker *mezzo-soprano* Cornelia; Della Jones *mezzo-soprano* Sextus; James Bowman *counter-tenor* Ptolemy; John Tomlinson *bass* Achillas; Christopher Booth-Jones *baritone* Curio; David James *counter-tenor* Nirenus; Chorus and Orchestra of ENO. EMI (now Chandos)/Peter Moores Foundation
Handel (ed. Mackerras): Julius Caesar (in English)
CD: CMS 768760-2; CHAN 3019

1984 August 29 (live). RAH. Australian Youth Orchestra. ABC
Sculthorpe: Sun Music II
Hurst: Swagman's Promenade – Waltzing Matilda; Click go the shears
CD: 476 5919

1984 August (live). UHE. Australian Youth Orchestra. ABC
Holst: The Planets – Jupiter
CD: 476 5919; 476 6813

1984 October 3–7. RP. [a]Zdeněk Tylšar *posthorn*; PCO. Telarc
Mozart: Serenade in G K525 (Eine kleine Nachtmusik); Serenade in D K320 (Posthorn)[a]
CD: CD 80108

1985 January 26–27. St John's, Smith Square. ECO. ASV
Mozart: Symphony No. 32 in G K318; Symphony No. 35 in D K385; Symphony No. 39 in E flat K543
CD: ASV 6071

1985 March 11–12. SAK. LPO. EMI.
Elgar: Falstaff Op. 68
CD: CDC747416-2; CDR 572553-2

1985 March 13. AR. LPO. EMI
Elgar: Variations on an Original Theme Op. 36 (Enigma)
CD: CDC 747416-2

1985 April (live). Teatro La Fenice, Venice. Marilyn Horne *mezzo-soprano* Orlando; Lella Cuberli *soprano* Angelica; Jeffrey Gall Medoro; Adelina Scarabelli *soprano* Dorinda; Giorgio Surjan *bass* Zoroastro; Orchestra del Teatro La Fenice di Venezia
Handel: Orlando
CD: Mondo Musica MFOH 10502

1986 April 21–22, AR. Julian Lloyd Webber *cello*; LSO. EMI.
Sullivan (reconstructed by Mackerras and David Mackie): Cello Concerto in D
Herbert: Cello Concerto No. 2 Op. 30
Elgar: Romance for Cello and Orchestra Op. 62
CD: CDC 747622-2

1986 May 13, 14 and 16. WTH. [b]Cathryn Pope *soprano*; [b]Sarah Walker *mezzo-soprano*; [a]Choir of Tiffin Boys' School; LSO. Telarc
Tchaikovsky: The Nutcracker – ballet Op. 71[a]; Pique Dame – Duet of Daphnis and Chloë[b]
CD: CD 80137

1986 June 14–16. RP. PCO. Telarc
Mozart: Symphony No. 36 in C K425; Symphony No. 38 in D K504
CD: CD 80138
Mozart: Symphony No. 40 in G minor K550; Symphony No. 41 in C K551
CD: CD 80139

1987 March 30–31. WTH. RPO. Telarc
Tchaikovsky: The Sleeping Beauty Op. 66 – suite; Swan Lake Op. 20 – suite
CD: CD 80151

1987 May 3–4. PHL. RLPO. EMI
Brian: The Tinker's Wedding Overture; Symphony No. 7 in C; Symphony No. 31
CD: CDC 749558-2; CDM 764717-2

1987 July 1–7. RP. PCO. Telarc
Mozart: Symphony No 25 in G minor K185/K173d; Symphony No 28 in C K200/K189k; Symphony No 29 in A K201/K186a
CD: CD 80165; CD 80300
Mozart: Serenade in D K239 (Serenata notturna); Serenade in D K250/248b ('Haffner')
CD: CD 80161

1987 August 30–September 1. WTH. LPO. EMI Eminence
Stravinsky: The Rite of Spring (1947 version); Fireworks Op. 4; Circus Polka; Greeting Prelude
CD: CD-EMX 9517

1987 October 11–12. AR. OAE. Virgin
Schubert: Symphony No 9 in C ('Great')
CD: VC 790708-2; VC 759669-2; 561806-2

1987 October 13–15 and 22. AR. OAE. Virgin
Mendelssohn: Symphony No. 4 in A Op. 90; A Midsummer Night's Dream – incidental music Opp. 21 and 61: Overture; Scherzo; L'istesso tempo; Allegro vivace; Intermezzo; Nocturne; Clowns' Dance; Wedding March
CD: VC 790725-2; VC 759264-2

1987 Opera House, Sydney. Rosamund Illing *soprano*; Elizabeth Campbell *mezzo-soprano*; Christopher Doig *tenor*; Rodney Macann *baritone*; Sydney Philharmonia Choir; SSO. ABC
Beethoven: Missa solemnis Op. 123
CD: 476 3517

1988 January 1–5. HWH. Felicity Lott *soprano*; Felicity Palmer *mezzo-soprano*; Philip Langridge *tenor*; Robert Lloyd *bass*; Huddersfield Choral Society; RPO
Handel (arr. Mozart): Messiah
CD: CD RPD 001R; Signum SIGCD 074

1988 June 13 (live). London Coliseum. Ann Murray *mezzo-soprano* Serse; Christopher Robson *counter-tenor* Arsamene; Jean Rigby *mezzo-soprano* Amastre; Rodney McCann *baritone* Ariodante; Valerie Masterson *soprano* Romilda; Lesley Garrett *soprano*

Atalanta; Christopher Booth-Jones *baritone* Elviro; Chorus and Orchestra of ENO
Handel: Xerxes (in English)
DVD: Arthaus Musik 100 076
Christopher Robson confirms 'the last performance of the run' was filmed, i.e. 13 June.

1988 June 15–16. WTH. [a]Ben Kingsley *narrator*; LSO. Pickwick/IMP
Britten: The Young Persons' Guide to the Orchestra[a]
Prokofiev: Peter and the Wolf[a]
Dukas: L'Apprenti sorcier
CD: Cala CACD 1022
Kingsley's narration was recorded at CTS Studios, Wembley, on 21 September 1995.

1988 June 27–28. PHL. [a]Women's Voices of the Liverpool Philharmonic Choir; RLPO. Virgin
Holst: The Perfect Fool – ballet music; The Planets[a]
CD: VC 790825-2

1988 July 4–5. SJH. Raphael Wallfisch *cello*; LSO. Chandos
Dvořák: Cello Concerto in B minor Op. 104
Dohnányi: Konzertstück Op. 12
CD: CHAN 8662

1988 July 5–6. AR. [a]Christine Pendrill *cor anglais*; LSO. Pickwick/IMP
Sibelius: Symphony No. 2 in D Op. 43; Lemminkaïnen Legends Op. 22 – No. 2, The Swan of Tuonela[a]
CD: PCD 927

1988 July 10–17. RP. PCO. Telarc
Mozart: Symphony No. 24 in B flat K182/K173d; Symphony No. 26 in E flat K184/K161a; Symphony No. 27 in G K199/K161b; Symphony No. 30 in D K202/K186b
CD: CD 80186; CD 80300
Mozart: Symphony No. 31 in D K297 ('Paris'); Symphony No. 33 in B flat K319; Symphony No. 34 in C K338
CD: CD 80190; CD 80300
Mozart: Symphony No. 32 in G K318; Symphony No. 35 in D 385; Symphony No. 39 in E flat K543
CD: CD 80203; CD 80300

1988 October 14 (live). Opera House, Sydney. Donald McIntyre *bass-baritone* Hans Sachs; Donald Shanks *bass* Pogner; Gerald Sword *tenor* Vogelgesang; Neville Wilkie *bass* Nachtigall; John Pringle *baritone* Beckmesser; Robert Allman *bass* Kothner; Lawrence Allen *tenor* Zorn; John Miley *tenor* Eisslinger; Christopher Dawes *tenor* Moser; Stephen Bennett *bass* Ortel; Arend Baumann *bass* Schwarz; David Hibberd *bass* Foltz; Paul Frey *tenor* Walther; Christopher Doig *tenor* David; Helena Doese *soprano* Eva; Rosemary Gunn *mezzo-soprano* Magdalene; Chorus of Australian Opera; Elizabethan Philharmonic Orchestra; *Stage director*: Michael Hampe; *Video directors*: Peter Butler and Virginia Lumsden. RM Associates
Wagner: Die Meistersinger von Nürnberg
DVD: Arthaus Musik 101 122

1988 November 8–9. John Harms Center for the Arts, Engelwood, NJ. OSL. Telarc
Haydn: Symphony No. 31 in D; Symphony No. 45 in F sharp minor
CD: CD 80156

1988 December 29–30. Opera House, Sydney. [a]Dennis Hennig *piano*; ACO. Conifer
Martinů: Sinfonietta giocosa[a]
Suk: Serenade in E flat Op. 6
CD: CDCF 170

1988 Opera House, Sydney. ACO. Omega
Schubert: Symphony No. 5 D485; Symphony No. 6 D589
OCD 1005

1989 January 9–10. WTH. LPO. EMI Eminence
Walton: Symphony No. 1 in B flat minor
CD: EMX 2151; 575569-2
Walton: Siesta
CD: 575569-2

1989 January 11. WTH. LSO. EMI Eminence
Walton: Symphony No. 2
CD: EMX 2151; 575569-2

1989 January 31 and February 1–2, 5–6 and 8–13. Konzerthaus, Vienna; Samuel Linay *treble* Sali as a child; Arthur Davies *tenor* Sali; Pamela Mildenhall *girl soprano* Vrenchen as a child; Helen Field *soprano* Vrenchen; Thomas Hampson *baritone* The Dark Fiddler; Barry Mora *bass-baritone* Manz; Stafford Dean *bass* Marti; Arnold Schönberg Choir; Orchestra of ORF, Vienna. Argo
Delius: A Village Romeo and Juliet
CD: 430 275-2
DVD: 074 1779DH (as soundtrack of Petr Weigl's television production)

1989 April. PHL. RLPO. EMI Eminence
Rachmaninov: Symphony No. 3 in A minor Op. 44; Symphonic Dances Op. 45
CD: CD-EMX 2154

1989 May 21 and 23. HWH. Hideko Udagawa *violin*; LSO. Chandos (under licence)
Bruch: Violin Concerto No. 1 in G minor Op. 26
Brahms: Violin Concerto in D Op. 77
CD: CHAN 6695

1989 July 13–18. BHS. Helen Field *soprano* Míla Válková; Philip Langridge *tenor* Živný; Kathryn Harries *soprano* Míla's Mother; Peter Bronder *tenor* A Poet/A Student; Stuart Kale *tenor* Dr. Suda; Chorus and Orchestra of WNO EMI (now Chandos)/Peter Moores Foundation
Janáček: Fate [Osud] (in English)
CD: CDC 749993-2; CHAN 3029

1989 August 16–20. BHS. [a]Thomas Hampson *baritone*; [a]Chorus and Orchestra of WNO. Argo
Delius: Brigg Fair; North Country Sketches; A Village Romeo and Juliet – Walk to the Paradise Garden; In a Summer Garden
CD: 430 202-2
Delius: Sea Drift[a]; Florida Suite
CD: 430 206-2

1989 August 25–29. Dobříš Castle, Prague. PCO. Telarc
Mozart: Symphony No. 14 K114; Symphony No. 15 K124; Symphony No. 16 K128; Symphony No. 17 K129; Symphony No. 18 K130
CD: CD 80242; CD 80300
Mozart: Symphony No. 19 K132; Symphony No. 20 K133; Symphony No. 21 K134
CD: CD 80217; CD 80300

1989 September 4–5. CHG. John O'Conor *piano*; SCO. Telarc
Mozart: Piano Concerto No. 21 in C K467; Piano Concerto No. 27 in B flat K595
CD: CD 80219

1989 October 1 (broadcast date). BBCGG. Eric Shilling *baritone* The Learned Judge; Sandra Dugdale *soprano* The Plaintiff; Neil Jenkins *tenor* The Defendant; Derek-Hammond-Stroud *baritone* Counsel; Forbes Robinson *bass* Usher; Leslie Fyson *baritone* Foreman; Ambrosian Singers; BBCCO.
Sullivan: Trial by Jury
CD: Oriel Music Trust OMT 856

1989 October 8 (broadcast date). BBCGG. Derek Hammond-Stroud *baritone* Sir Joseph Porter; Brian Rayner Cook *baritone* Captain Corcoran; Neil Jenkins *tenor* Ralph Rackstraw; Valerie Masterson *soprano* Josephine; Gillian Knight *contralto* Little Buttercup; Forbes Robinson *bass* Dick Deadeye; Leslie Fyson *baritone* Bill Bobstay; Christopher Keyte *bass* Bob Becket; Glenys Groves *mezzo-soprano* Cousin Hebe; Ambrosian Singers; BBCCO
Sullivan: HMS Pinafore (including dialogue)
CD: Oriel Music Trust OMT 856

1989 October 15 (broadcast date). BBCGG. Derek Hammond-Stroud *baritone* Major-General Stanley; Eric Shilling *baritone* Pirate King; Leslie Fyson *baritone* Samuel; Neil Jenkins *tenor* Frederic; Forbes Robinson *bass* Sergeant of Police; Valerie Masterson *soprano* Mabel; Meriel Dickinson

mezzo-soprano Edith; Maureen Morelle *soprano* Kate; Joyce Mandre *soprano* Isabel; Della Jones *mezzo-soprano* Ruth; Ambrosian Singers; BBCCO.
Sullivan: Pirates of Penzance (including dialogue)
CD: Oriel Music Trust OMT 858

1989 November 5 (broadcast date). BBCGG. Raymund Herincx *baritone* Hildebrand; Philip Langridge *tenor* Hilarion; Derek Hammond-Stroud *baritone* Gama; Forbes Robinson *bass* Arac; Valerie Masterson *soprano* Princess Ida; Anne Collins *contralto* Lady Blanche; Jane Coster *mezzo-soprano* Melissa; Della Jones *mezzo-soprano* Psyche; Paul Hudson *bass* Scynthius; BBC Singers; BBCCO.
Sullivan: Princess Ida (including dialogue)
CD: Oriel Music Trust OMT 854

1989 November 12 (broadcast date). BBCGG. Richard Van Allen *baritone* The Mikado; Neil Jenkins *tenor* Nanki-Poo; Derek Hammond-Stroud *baritone* Ko-Ko; Forbes Robinson *bass* Pooh-Bah; Christopher Booth-Jones *baritone* Pish-Tush; Valerie Masterson *soprano* Yum-Yum; Sally Burgess *mezzo-soprano* Pitti-Sing; Glenys Groves *mezzo-soprano* Peep-Bo; Gillian Knight *contralto* Katisha; Ambrosian Singers, BBCCO.
Sullivan: The Mikado (including dialogue)
CD: Oriel Music Trust OMT 860

1989 November 26 (broadcast date). BBCGG. Valerie Masterson *soprano* Elsie Maynard; Philip Langridge *tenor* Colonel Fairfax; Derek Hammond-Stroud *baritone* Jack Point; Sally Burgess *mezzo-soprano* Phoebe Meryll; Anne Collins *mezzo-soprano* Dame Carruthers; Eric Shilling *bass* Sergeant Meryll; Forbes Robinson *baritone* Wilfrid Shadbolt; John Heddle Nash *baritone* Sir Richard Cholmondely; Sandra Dugdale *soprano* Kate; Neil Jenkins *tenor* Leonard Meryll; Ambrosian Singers, BBCCO.
Sullivan: The Yeomen of the Guard (including dialogue)
CD: Oriel Music Trust OMT 862

1989 December 3 (broadcast date). BBCGG. Eric Shilling *baritone* Duke of Plaza-Toro; Vernon Midgely *tenor* Luiz; Forbes Robinson *bass* Don Alhambra; Neil Jenkins *tenor* Marco; Anne Collins *contralto* Duchess of Plaza-Toro; Leslie Fyson *baritone* Antonio/Annibale; Sandra Dugdale *soprano* Gianetta; Della Jones *mezzo-soprano* Tessa; Marilyn Hill Smith *soprano* Casilda; BBC Singers; BBCCO.
Sullivan: The Gondoliers (including dialogue)
CD: Oriel Music Trust OMT 863

1989 December 19 (broadcast date). BBCGG. Derek Hammond-Stroud *baritone* Robin Oakapple; Neil Jenkins *tenor* Richard Dauntless; Eric Shilling *baritone* Sir Despard; Philip Summerscales, *baritone* Adam Goodheart; Sandra Dugdale *soprano* Rose Maybud; Della Jones *mezzo-soprano* Mad Margaret; Anne Collins *contralto* Dame Hannah; Forbes Robinson *bass* Sir Roderick; BBC Singers; BBCCO.
Sullivan: Ruddigore (including dialogue)
CD: Oriel Music Trust OMT 861

1990 January 4–5. PHL. [a]Liverpool Philharmonic Choir; RLPO. Virgin
Mussorgsky (orch. Ravel): Pictures at an Exhibition; Night on the Bare Mountain
Borodin: Prince Igor – Overture; Polovtsian Dances[a]; In the Steppes of Central Asia
CD: CUV 5 61135 2

1990 January 11–13. PHL. RLPO. EMI Eminence
Mahler: Symphony No. 5 in C sharp minor
CD: CD-EMX 2164

1990 February 19. WTH. Ofra Harnoy *cello*; LPO. RCA
Bloch: Schelomo
Bruch: Kol Nidrei Op. 47
CD: RD 60757

1990 March 12–14. WalAH. [a]Kees Hülsmann *violin*; LSO. Telarc
Rimsky-Korsakov: Scheherazade Op. 35[a]; Capriccio espagnol Op. 34
CD: CD 80208

1990 March 19 (live). St David's Hall, Cardiff. [a]Kiri Te Kanawa *soprano*; Orchestra of WNO. EMI
Mozart: La Clemenza di Tito – Overture; Se all' impero[a]; Chi sà, chi sa, qual sia K582[a]; Don Giovanni –Ah fuggi il traditor[a]; Exsultate, jubilate K165[a]; Nehmt meinem Dank, ihr holde Gönner K383[a]; Le nozze di Figaro – Overture; Porgi amor[a]; E Susanna non vien … Dove sono[a]; Vado ma dove? K583[a]; Die Zauberflöte – Ach, ich fühl's[a]
VHS: MVC 991 242 3
LD: 991 242 1

1990 April 2–3. WalAH. LSO. Argo
Elgar: Symphony No. 1 in A flat Op. 55; Cockaigne Op. 40
CD: 430 835-2

1990 September 4–5. UHE. John O'Conor *piano*; SCO. Telarc
Mozart. Piano Concerto No. 19 in F K459; Piano Concerto No. 23 in A K488; (ed. Paul Badura-Skoda and Mackerras): Concert Rondo in E flat K386
CD: CD 80285

1990 September 9–16. Dobříš Castle, Prague. PCO. Telarc
Mozart: Symphony No. 1 in E flat K16; Symphony in F K Anh223/K19a; Symphony No. 4 in D K19; Symphony No. 5 in B flat K22; Symphony No. 6 in F K43; Symphony in B flat K45b; Symphony No. 7 in D K45
CD: CD 80256; CD 80300
Mozart: Symphony No. 8 in D K4; Symphony No. 9 in C K73; Symphony K81/73l; Symphony in D K97/K73m; Symphony in D K95/K73n
CD: CD 80272; CD 80300
Mozart: Symphony No. 11 in D K84/K73q; Symphony No. 10 in F K74; Symphony in F K75; Symphony No. 12 in G K110; Symphony in C K96/K111b; Symphony No. 13 in F K112
CD: CD 80273; CD 80300

1990 October 4–10. Stadion, Brno. [a]Jirí Skonojska *piano*; Brno State Philharmonic Orchestra. Conifer
Martinů: Double Concerto for Two String Orchestras, Piano and Timpani[a]; Špalíček – suite (arr. Mackerras)
CD: CDCF 202

1990 October 16–18 and 21. AR. Ann Murray *mezzo-soprano*; Thomas Allen *baritone*; LPO. Virgin
Mahler: Des Knaben Wunderhorn
CD: VC791432-2; VBD 561507-2

1990 November 13[a], 14[ab], 15[b] and 16[b]. AR. OAE. Virgin
Schubert: Symphony No. 5 in B flat D485[ab]
CD: 561806-2
Schubert (completed Brian Newbould): Symphony No. 8 in B minor D759[b]
CD: 561806-2

1990 November 20. SAK. Jonathan Snowden *flute*; LPO. EMI Eminence
Mozart: Flute Concerto No. 1 in G K313
CD: CD-EMX 2181
Mozart: Andante in C K315
Unpublished.

1990 November 23–24. HWH. Ofra Harnoy cello; LPO. RCA
Tchaikovsky: Andante cantabile Op. 11
Tchaikovsky (arr. Jacob Harnoy): Valse sentimentale Op. 51 No. 6; Sérénade mélancolique Op. 26; Eugene Onegin Op. 24 – Lensky's aria
Bruch: Canzone Op. 55; Adagio on a Celtic Theme Op. 56; Ave Maria Op. 61
CD: RD 60757

1990 November 25. AR. Ofra Harnoy *cello*; LPO. RCA
Tchaikovsky: Pezzo capriccioso in B minor Op. 62
CD: RD 60757

1990 November (live). London Coliseum. Benjamin Luxon *baritone* Gianni Schicchi; Alison Hagley *soprano* Lauretta; Anne Collins *mezzo-soprano* Zita; David Maxwell Anderson *tenor* Rinuccio; Dennis Wicks *bass* Simone; Chorus and Orchestra of ENO.

Puccini: Gianni Schicchi (in English)
CD: Oriel Music Trust OMT 812

1990 December 18–20. BHS. [a]Alison Hagley *soprano*; [a]Bryn Terfel *baritone*; Orchestra of the WNO. Argo
Elgar: The Wand of Youth – Suite No. 1 Op. 1a, Suite No. 2 Op. 1b; Dream Children Op. 43; The Starlight Express – incidental music Op. 78[a]
CD: 433 214-2

1990 December 20. BHS. Orchestra of WNO. Argo
Delius: On hearing the first cuckoo in Spring; Irmelin Prelude; Fennimore and Gerda – Intermezzo
CD: 433 704-2

1990 December 31. HWH. Ofra Harnoy *cello*; LPO. RCA
Tchaikovsky: Variations on a Rococo Theme Op. 33; Nocturne in C sharp minor Op. 19 No. 4; (arr. Jacob Harnoy): The Seasons Op. 37b – 10. October
CD: RD 60757

1991 January 3–5. PHL. Joan Rodgers *soprano*; Della Jones *mezzo-soprano*; Peter Bronder *tenor;* Bryn Terfel *baritone*; Liverpool Philharmonic Choir; RLPO. EMI Eminence
Beethoven: Symphony No. 9 in D minor Op. 125
CD: CD-EMX 2186; 575751-2

1991 March 12–14. AAI. OSL. Telarc
Haydn: Symphony No. 100 in G; Symphony No. 103 in E flat
CD: CD 80282

1991 March 14–15. AAI. OSL. Telarc
Handel: Water Music – Suites in F, D and G
CD: CD 80279

1991 March 16 (live) Metropolitan Opera House, New York City. Aage Haugland *bass* Savël Prokofjevič Dikoj; Wieslaw Ochman *tenor* Boris Grigorjevič; Leonie Rysanek *soprano* Marfa Ignatěvna Kabanová (Kabanicha); Allan Glassman *tenor* Tichon Ivanyč Kabanov; Gabriela Beňačková *soprano* Kateřina (Káťa); Peter Straka *tenor* Váňa Kudrjáš; Susan Quittmeyer *mezzo-soprano* Varvara; Vernon Hartman *baritone* Kuligin; Sondra Kelly *contralto* Glaša; Loretta Di Franco *mezzo-soprano* Fekluša; Metropolitan Opera Chorus and Orchestra.
Janáček: Káťa Kabanová
CD: The Opera Lovers KAT 199101; WH 178-2

1991 May 11–12. BHS. [a]Tasmin Little *violin*; Orchestra of WNO. Argo
Delius: Violin Concerto[a]; Two Aquarelles; Dance Rhapsody No. 1; Dance Rhapsody No. 2
CD: 433 704-2

1991 May 21–23. SAK. LPO. EMI Eminence
Dvořák: Symphony No. 7 in D minor Op. 70; Symphony No. 9 in E minor Op. 95
CD: CD-EMX 2202

1991 May 23–24. SAK. David Theodore *oboe*; Robert Hill clarinet; John Price *bassoon*; Nicholas Busch *horn*; LPO. EMI Eminence
Mozart: Sinfonia Concertante in E flat K297b
CD: CD-EMX 2181

1991 June 1–3. PHL. [a]Tasmin Little *violin*; [b]Rafael Wallfisch *cello*; RLPO. EMI Eminence
Delius: Concerto for Cello and Orchestra[a]; Concerto for Violin, Cello and Orchestra[ab]; Paris
CD: CD-EMX 2185

1991 June 13–22. UHE. Barbara Hendricks *soprano* Pamina; Jerry Hadley *tenor* Tamino; June Anderson *soprano* Queen of Night; Thomas Allen *baritone* Papageno; Ulrike Steinsky *soprano* Papagena; Gottfried Hornik *baritone* Speaker/Second Priest; Helmut Wildhaber *tenor* Monostatos; Petra Maria Schnitzer *soprano* First Lady; Gabriele Sima *mezzo-soprano* Second Lady; Julia Bernheimer *contralto* Third Lady; Peter Svensson *tenor* First Priest/ Second Armed Man; Alastair Miles *bass* Second Armed Man; Daniel Ison *treble*

First Boy; Nathan Watts *treble* Second Boy; John Dawson *treble* Third Boy; Anthony Negus *glockenspiel*; Scottish Chamber Chorus; SCO. Telarc
Mozart: Die Zauberflöte
CD: CD 80302

1991 July 1–2. PHL. RLPO. EMI Eminence
Mahler: Symphony No. 1
CD: CD-EMX 2197; 573510-2

1991 September 2–4. BHS. Donald Adams *bass* The Mikado; Anthony Rolfe Johnson *tenor* Nanki-Poo; Richard Suart *baritone* Ko-Ko; Richard Van Allan *bass* Pooh-Bah; Nicholas Folwell *baritone* Pish-Tush; Marie McLaughlin *soprano* Yum-Yum; Anne Howells *mezzo-soprano* Pitti-Sing; Janice Watson *soprano* Peep-Bo; Felicity Palmer *mezzo-soprano* Katisha; Chorus and Orchestra of WNO. Telarc
Sullivan: The Mikado (omits Overture and dialogue)
CD: CD 80204

1991 September 13 (live). RAH. Dennis O'Neill *tenor* Idomeneo; John Mark Ainsley *tenor* Idamante; Anthony Roden *tenor* Arbace; Rebecca Evans *soprano* Ilia; Suzanna Murphy *soprano* Elettra; Paul Charles Clarke *tenor* Gran Sacerdote; Ashley Thorburn *bass* La Voce; Chorus and Orchestra of WNO
Mozart: Idomeneo
DVD: Celestial Audio CV 050 (Audio DVD)

1991 October 28–29. CHG. John O'Conor *piano*; SCO. Telarc
Mozart: Piano Concerto No. 17 in G K453; Piano Concerto No. 24 in C minor K491
CD: CD 80306

1991 December 1 (live). Estates Theatre, Prague. Andrei Bechasný *baritone* Don Giovanni; Nadezdha Petrenko *soprano* Donna Anna; Vladimír Doležal *tenor* Don Ottavio; Jiřína Marková *soprano* Donna Elvira; Luděk Vele *baritone* Leporello; Dalibor Jedlička *bass* Commendatore; Zdeněk Havránek *baritone* Masetto; Alice Randová *soprano* Zerlina; Chorus and Orchestra of the Prague National Theatre. Supraphon
Mozart: Don Giovanni
DVD: SU 7012

1992 February 24[a]–25[b]. WalAH. [a]Robert Cohen *cello*; RPO. Argo
Elgar: Froissart Op. 19[b]; Cello Concerto in E minor Op. 85[a]; Variations on an Original Theme Op. 36 (Enigma)[b]
CD: 436 545-2

1992 March 7–9. AAI. OSL. Telarc
Haydn: Symphony No. 101 in D; Symphony No. 104 in D
CD: CD 80311

1992 April 24 (live). RFH. LPO.
Dvořák: Symphony No. 8 in G Op. 88; Symphonic Variations Op. 79
CD: LPO 0055

1992 April 26–27 and 29. HWH. LPO. EMI Eminence
Dvořák: Symphony No. 8 in G Op. 88; Symphonic Variations Op. 79
CD: CD-EMX 2216

1992 June 25–26. PHL. RLPO. EMI Eminence
Beethoven: Symphony No. 5 in C minor Op. 67; Symphony No. 7 in A Op. 92
CD: CD-EMX 2212; 575751-2

1992 June 27–July 6, **1993** February 17–18. BHS. Kiri Te Kanawa *soprano* Tatyana; Neil Rosenshein *tenor* Lensky; Patricia Bardon *mezzo-soprano* Olga; Linda Finnie *mezzo-soprano* Larina; Nicolai Gedda *tenor* Triquet; Thomas Hampson *baritone* Evgeny Onegin; John Connell *bass* Prince Gremin; Richard Van Allan *bass* Zaretsky/Captain; Chorus and Orchestra of WNO. EMI (now Chandos)/Peter Moores Foundation
Tchaikovsky: Eugene Onegin (in English)
CD: CDS 555004-2

1992 October 20–21. HWH. Monica Huggett *violin*; OAE. EMI Eminence
Beethoven: Violin Concerto in D Op. 61
CD: CD-EMX 2217

1992 October 26–30 and November 2–6. BHS. Josephine Barstow *soprano* Queen Elizabeth; Philip Langridge *tenor* Earl of Essex; Della Jones *mezzo-soprano* Lady Essex; Jonathan Summers *baritone* Lord Mountjoy; Yvonne Kenny *soprano* Penelope Rich; Alan Opie *baritone* Sir Robert Cecil; Richard Van Allan *bass* Sir Walter Raleigh; Bryn Terfel *bass-baritone* Henry Cuffe; Willard White *baritone* Blind Ballad Singer; John Shirley-Quirk *baritone* Recorder of Norfolk; John Mark Ainsley *tenor* Spirit of the Masque; Chorus and Orchestra of WNO. Argo
Britten: Gloriana
CD: 440 213-2

1992 November 14–15. HWH. Monica Huggett *violin*; OAE. EMI Eminence
Mendelssohn: Violin Concerto in E minor Op. 64
CD: CD-EMX 2217

1993 January 3–4 and 6–7. WalAH. June Anderson *soprano*; ECO. Decca
Mozart: [operatic arias]
Unpublished

1993 February 27–March 1. UHE. John O'Conor *piano*; SCO. Telarc
Field: Piano Concerto No. 2 in A flat H31; Piano Concerto No. 3 in E flat H32
CD: CD 80370

1993 March 15[a]–16[b]. WalAH. [b]Della Jones *mezzo-soprano*; RPO. Argo
Elgar: Symphony No. 2 in E flat Op. 63[ab]; Sea Pictures Op. 37[b]
CD: 443 321-2

1993 April 26–28. BHS, Wales. [a]Rebecca Evans *soprano*; [a]Peter Hoare *tenor*; [b]Daniel Washington *baritone*; [ab]Chorus and Orchestra of WNO. Argo
Delius: A Song of the High Hills[a]; Appalachia[b]; Over the Hills and Far away
CD: 443 171-2

1993 May 4–6. BHS. John Mark Ainsley *tenor* Frederic; Rebecca Evans *soprano* Mabel; Richard Van Allan *bass* Sergeant of Police; Donald Adams *bass* Pirate King; Richard Suart *baritone* Major-General Stanley; Gillian Knight *contralto* Ruth; Julie Gossage *soprano* Edith; Jenevora Williams *soprano* Kate; Nicholas Folwell *baritone* Samuel; Chorus and Orchestra of WNO. Telarc
Sullivan: The Pirates of Penzance (omits Overture and dialogue)
CD: CD 80353

1993 July 1–2. Performing Arts Center, Purchase, NY. OSL. Telarc
Mozart: Serenade in B flat K361
CD: CD 80359

1993 August 2–13. UHE. Felicity Lott *soprano* Fiordiligi; Marie McLaughlin *soprano* Dorabella; Nuccia Focile *soprano* Despina; Jerry Hadley *tenor* Ferrando; Alessandro Corbelli *baritone* Guglielmo; Gilles Cachemaille *baritone* Don Alfonso; Edinburgh Festival Chorus; SCO. Telarc
Mozart: Così fan tutte
CD: CD 80360

1993 November 26–27 and 29. All Saints' Church, Petersham. Mikhail Kazakevich *piano*; ECO. Conifer
Beethoven (ed. Barry Cooper): Piano Concerto No. 2 in B flat Op. 19, Piano Concerto No. 4 in G Op. 58
CD: CDCF 237

1993 December 4–5. UHE. [a]Eric Ruske *horn*; [b]Richard Suart *baritone*; SCO. Telarc
Mozart: Horn Concerto No. 1 in D K412/K386b[a]; Horn Concerto No. 2 in E flat K417[a]; Horn Concerto No. 3 in E flat K447[a]; Horn Concerto No. 4 in E flat K495[a]; (completed by John Humphries): Fragment in E for horn and orchestra K494a[a]; Rondo in E flat K371[a]
Flanders and Swann (after Mozart): Ill wind[b]
CD: CD 80367

1993 December 12–14. SJH. ECO. Novalis
Handel: Music for the Royal Fireworks; 3 Concerti a due cori HWV 332–334
CD: 150 102-2

1994 January 6[a]–7[b]. CTS Studio, Wembley. RPO. Tring
Sibelius: Symphony No. 2 in D Op. 43[ab];

Lemminkaïnen Legends Op. 22 – 2, The Swan of Tuonela[b]; Finlandia Op. 26[b]
CD: TRPO 13

1994 January 9– 10. CTS Studios, Wembley. RPO. Tring
Berlioz: Symphonie fantastique Op. 14; Le Carnaval romain Op. 9
CD: TRPO 12

1994 January 21–22 and 24. Danish Radio Concert Hall, Copenhagen. [a]Tina Kiberg *soprano*; [a]Randi Stene (contralto); [ab]Peter Svensson *tenor*; [a]Ulrik Cold *bass*; [a]Per Salo *organ*; [ab]Copenhagen Boys' Choir; Danish National Radio Chorus; Danish National Radio SO. Chandos
Janáček: Glagolitic Mass (ed. Wingfield)[a]
Kodály: Psalmus Hungaricus[b]
CD: CHAN 9310

1994 April 16–17. UHE. Nikolai Demidenko *piano*; SCO. Hyperion
Weber: Piano Concerto No. 1 in C; Piano Concerto No. 2 in E flat; Konzertstück in F minor
CD: CDA 66729

1994 April 18–19. CHG. SCO. Hyperion
Beethoven: Die Geschöpfe des Prometheus – ballet Op. 43
CD: CDA 66748; CDH 55196

1994 May 20–21. HWH. [a]Stephanie Gonley *violin*; ECO. EMI Eminence
Dvořák: Legends Op. 59; Nocturne in B Op. 40; Romance in F minor Op. 11[a]
CD: CD-EMX 2232

1994 June 5–8. BHS. Richard Suart *baritone* Sir Joseph Porter; Thomas Allen *baritone* Captain Corcoran; Michael Schade *tenor* Ralph Rackstraw; Rebecca Evans *soprano* Josephine; Felicity Palmer *mezzo-soprano* Little Buttercup; Donald Adams *bass* Dick Deadeye; Richard Van Allan *bass* Bob Bobstay; Valerie Seymour *soprano* Cousin Hebe; John King *baritone* (Trio No. 9) Bob Becket; Philip Lloyd Evans *baritone* (Trio No. 10) Bob Becket; Chorus and Orchestra of WNO. Telarc
Sullivan: HMS Pinafore (omits Overture and dialogue)
CD: CD 80374

1994 July 10[a] and 17[b]. CTS Studios, Wembley. RPO. Tring
Shostakovich: Symphony No. 5 in D minor Op. 47[ab]; Festive Overture in A Op. 96[b]
CD: TRPO 32

1994 July 31–August 12. UHE. Alastair Miles *bass* Figaro; Nuccia Focile *soprano* Susanna; Alessandro Corbelli *baritone* Count Almaviva; Carol Vaness *soprano* Countess Almaviva; Susanne Mentzer *mezzo-soprano* Cherubino; Suzanne Murphy *soprano* Marcellina; Alfonso Antoniozzi *baritone* Bartolo/Antonio; Ryland Davies *tenor* Don Basilio/Don Curzio; Scottish Chamber Chorus; SCO. Telarc
Mozart: Le nozze di Figaro
CD: CD 80388

1994 September 9–10. NBH. RLPO. EMI Eminence
Beethoven: Symphony No. 1 in C Op. 21; Symphony No. 3 in E flat Op. 55
CD: CD-EMX 2246; 575751-2

1994 September 24–25. ODP. Ofra Harnoy *cello*; CPO. RCA
Dvořák: Cello Concerto in B minor Op. 104; Silent Woods B182; Rondo in G minor Op. 94
CD: 09026 68186 2

1994 September 26–27. NBH. RLPO. EMI Eminence
Beethoven: Symphony No. 4 in B flat Op. 60; Symphony No. 6 in F Op. 68
CD: CD-EMX 2245; 575751-2

1994 November 10–11. BHS.
1995 February 13–15. Music Hall, Cincinnati, Ohio (vocal over-dubbing). Fernando de la Mora *tenor*; Orchestra of WNO; Telarc
Gounod: Roméo et Juliette – Ah lève-toi, soleil; Faust – Salut! Demeure chaste et pure
Verdi: La Traviata – De' miei bollenti spiriti; O mio rimorso; Rigoletto – Ella mi fu rapita ... Parmi veder le lagrime; La donna è mobile
Puccini: La Bohème – Che gelida manina; Tosca – Recondita armonia; E lucevan le stele

Cilea: L'arlesiana –E la solita storia
Bizet: Carmen –La fleur que tu m'avais jetée; Les Pêcheurs des perles – Je crois entendre encore
Donizetti: La Fille du régiment – Ah! mes amis
Ponchielli: La Gioconda – Cielo e mar
Massenet: Werther – Pourquoi me réveiller
Giordano: Fedora – Amor ti vieta

1994 November 13–14 and 18. SJH. ECO. Novalis
Handel. Concerto HWV 335a; Concerto HWV 335b; Concerto grosso Op. 3 No. 1; Rinaldo – Overture; Solomon – Arrival of the Queen of Sheba; Alcina – Dream Music; Messiah – Overture; Pifa (versions for Oboe and strings, and strings alone); Serse – Ombra mai fù (instrumental version); Acis and Galatea – Overture; Saul – Dead March; Giulio Cesare – Sinfonia for four horns; Scipio – March

1994 November. SJH. Ann Murray *mezzo-soprano*; OAE. Forlane
Handel. Alcina – Mi lusinga il dolce affetto; Verdi prati, selve amene; Stà nell'Incana; Ariodante – E vivo ancora? ... Scherza infida; Dopa notte; Giulio Cesare – Va tacito e nascosto; Se in fiorito ameno prato; Piangerò, la sorte mia; Dal ondoso periglio ... Aure, deh, per pieta; Serse – Frendere tenere e belle ... Ombra mai fù; Se bramata d'amar, chi vi sdegna; Crude furie degl'orrido abissi

1994 November (live). Royal Opera House. Roberto Alagna *tenor* Roméo; Leontina Vaduva *soprano* Juliette; Robert Lloyd *bass* Frère Laurent; Sarah Walker *mezzo-soprano* Gertrude; Peter Sidhom *baritone* Capulet; Paul Charles Clarke *tenor* Tybalt; Jeremy White *bass* Grégorio; François Le Roux *baritone* Mercutio; Anna Maria Panzarella *soprano* Stéphano; Chorus and Orchestra of ROHCG; *Video Director*: Brian Large
Gounod: Roméo et Juliette
DVD: Opus Arte OAR 3106 D

1995 March 8[a] and 11[b]. AR. RPO. Tring
R. Strauss: Also sprach Zarathustra Op. 30[b]; Don Juan Op. 20[a]; Till Eulenspiegels lustige Streiche Op. 28[a]
CD: TRPO 71

1995 March. Stadtcasino, Basel. Basler Sinfonie-Orchester. Novalis
Hindemith: Amor und Psyche; Symphonie: Mathis der Maler

1995 March. Reformierte Kirche, Arlesheim, Switzerland. Bruno Canino *piano*; Basler Sinfonie-Orchester. Novalis
Hindemith: Die vier Temperamente
CD: 150 118-2

1995 April 8–10. UHE. SCO. Hyperion
Arriaga: Symphony in D; Los esclavos felices – Overture
Voříšek: Symphony in D Op. 24
CD: CDA 66800

1995 April 18–May 1. BHS. Alwyn Mellor *soprano* Elsie Maynard; Neill Archer *tenor* Colonel Fairfax; Richard Suart *baritone* Jack Point; Pamela Helen Stephen *mezzo-soprano* Phoebe Meryll; Felicity Palmer *mezzo-soprano* Dame Carruthers; Donald Adams *bass* Sergeant Meryll; Donald Maxwell *baritone* Wilfrid Shadbolt; Peter Savidge *baritone* Sir Richard Cholmondely; Clare O'Neill *soprano* Kate; Peter Hoare *tenor* Leonard Meryll; Ralph Mason *tenor* First Yeoman; Peter Lloyd Evans *baritone* Second Yeoman; Chorus and Orchestra of WNO. Telarc
Sullivan: The Yeomen of the Guard (omits dialogue)
Richard Suart *baritone* The Learned Judge; Rebecca Evans *soprano* The Plaintiff; Barry Banks *tenor* The Defendant; Eric Garrett *bass* The Usher; Peter Savidge *baritone* Counsel for the Plaintiff; Gareth Rhys-Davies *baritone* Foreman of the Jury; Chorus and Orchestra of WNO. Telarc
Sullivan: Trial by Jury
CD: 2CD 80404

1995 April 26 (live). Royal Opera House. Alwyn Mellor *soprano* Elsie Maynard; Neill Archer *tenor* Colonel Fairfax; Richard Suart *baritone* Jack Point; Pamela Helen Stephen *mezzo-soprano* Phoebe Meryll; Felicity Palmer *mezzo-soprano* Dame Carruthers; Donald Adams *bass* Sergeant Meryll; Donald Maxwell *baritone* Wilfrid Shadbolt; Peter Savidge *baritone* Sir Richard Cholmondely; Clare O'Neill *soprano* Kate; Peter Hoare *tenor* Leonard Meryll; Ralph Mason *tenor* First Yeoman; Peter Lloyd Evans *baritone* Second Yeoman; Chorus and Orchestra of WNO.
Sullivan: The Yeomen of the Guard
CD: Oriel Music Trust OMT 393
The WNO production (24, 25 and 26 April) was the first time any Gilbert and Sullivan opera had been staged at the Royal Opera House.

1995 June 11–13. Salle Ravel, Opéra-Bastille, Paris. Mikhail Rudy *piano*; Solistes de l'Orchestre de l'Opéra National de Paris. EMI
Janáček: Capriccio; Concertino
CD: CDC 555585-2

1995 June (live). Théâtre du Châtelet, Paris. Eva Jenis *soprano* Vixen; Hana Minutillo *mezzo-soprano* Fox; Thomas Allen *baritone* Forester; Josef Hajna *tenor* Schoolmaster/Mosquito; Richard Novák *bass* Priest/Badger; Jean-Philippe Marlière *bass* Lapák/Innkeeper; Libuše Márová *mezzo-soprano* Forester's Wife/Owl; Sarah Connolly *mezzo-soprano* Innkeeper's Wife/Cock/Jay; Florence Bonafous *soprano* Hen; Ivan Kusnjer *baritone* Harašta; Françoise Martinaud *soprano* Woodpecker; Maîtrise des Hauts-de-Seine; Choeur du Châtelet; Orchestre de Paris. Nicholas Hytner *stage director*; Brian Large *video director*.
Janáček: Příhody lišky Bystroušky [The Cunning Little Vixen]
DVD: Arthaus Musik 100 240

1995 July 31–August 11. UHE. Bo Skovhus *baritone* Don Giovanni; Christine Brewer *soprano* Donna Anna; Jerry Hadley *tenor* Don Ottavio; Felicity Lott *soprano* Don Elvira; Alessandro Corbelli *bass* Leporello; Umberto Chiummo *bass* Il Commendatore/Masetto; Nuccia Focile *soprano* Zerlina; Scottish Chamber Chorus; SCO. Telarc
Mozart: Don Giovanni
CD: CD 80420

1995 December 15, 17–18 and 20–21. Lefak Auditorium, Queen's College, New York City. Renée Fleming *soprano*; [a]Krista Bennion Feeney *violin*; OSL. Decca
Mozart. Il sogno di Scipione – Lieve son al par del vento; La finta giardiniera – Geme la tortorella; Crudel, Oh Dio! Fermate; Ah, dal pianto, dal singhiozzo; Il re pastore – L'amerò, sarò costante[a]; Zaide – Ruhe sanft, mein holdes Leben; Nehmt meinem Dank, ihr holden Gönner K383; Die Entführung aus dem Serail – Ach, ich liebe; Le nozze di Figaro – Giunse alfin il momento ... Deh vieni non tardar; Giunse alfin il momento ... Al desio di chi t'adora K577a; Don Giovanni – In quali eccessi ... Mi tradì; Die Zauberflöte – Ach, ich fühl's
CD: 452 602-2

1996 March 4 (live). Royal Opera House. Ruth Ann Swenson *soprano* Semele; Felicity Palmer *mezzo-soprano* Juno/Ino; Philip Langridge *tenor* Jupiter; Michael Chance *counter-tenor* Athamus; Peter Rose *bass* Cadmus/Somnus; Robin Leggate *tenor* Apollo; Judith Howarth *soprano* Iris; Chorus and Orchestra of ROHCG
Handel: Semele
CD: House of Opera CD 610

1996 March 21 (live) RP. Eva Urbanová *soprano;* Bernarda Fink *contralto*; Leo Marian Vodička *tenor*; Peter Mikuláš *bass*; Jan Hora *organ*; Prague Philharmonic Choir. CPO. Supraphon
Janáček: Glagolitic Mass (ed. Wingfield)
DVD: SU 7009–9

1996 August 2–8. UHE. Gabriela Beňačková *soprano* Leonore; Anthony Rolfe Johnson *tenor* Florestan;

Franz-Joseph Kapellmann *bass* Don Pizarro; Siegfried Vogel *bass* Rocco; Ildikó Raimondi *soprano* Marzelline; John Mark Ainsley *tenor* Jacquino/First Prisoner; David Wilson-Johnson *baritone* Don Fernando/Second Prisoner; Edinburgh Festival Chorus; SCO. Telarc
Beethoven: Fidelio; Leonore Overture No. 3 Op. 72b
CD: CD 80439

1997 January 6–30. UHE. SCO. Telarc
Brahms: Symphony No. 1 in C minor Op. 68; Symphony No. 1 – original version of 2. Andante sostenuto (completed by Robert Pascall); Symphony No. 2 in D Op. 73; Symphony No. 3 in F Op. 90; Symphony No. 4 in E minor Op. 98; Variations on a Theme by Haydn Op. 56*a*; Academic Festival Overture Op. 80
CD: CD 80450

1997 February 11–19. Air Studios, Lyndhurst Gardens. Andrea Rost *soprano*; [a]Aquiles Machado *tenor*; RPO. Sony
Verdi: Rigoletto – Gualtier Maldè ... Caro nome; La Traviata – E strano! E strano! ... Ah fors'e lui ... Follie, follie ... Sempre libera[a]; Teneste la promessa ... Addio del passato
Puccini: La Bohème – Sì, mi chiamano Mimì; Quo m'en vo' soletta; Gianni Schicchi – O mio babbino caro
Donizetti: Don Pasquale – Quel guard il cavaliere ... So anch'io la virtù magica; L'elisir d'amore – Prendi, prendi, per me sei libero; Lucia di Lammermoor – Regnava nel silenzio ... Quo rapito in estasi; Il dolce suono ... Ardon gl'incensi ... Alfon son tua ... Spargi d'amaro pianto
CD: SK 62789

1997 February 25–27. UHE. SCO. Hyperion
Schubert (ed. Brian Newbould): Symphony in D D615; Symphony in D D708a; Symphony in D D936a
CD: CDA 67000

1997 March 21–27. RP. Luděk Vele *bass* Savël Prokofjevič Dikoj; Peter Straka *tenor* Boris Grigorjevič; Eva Randová *mezzo-soprano* Marfa Ignatěvna Kabanová *soprano* (Kabanicha); Miroslav Kopp *tenor* Tichon Ivanyč Kabanov; Gabriela Beňačková *soprano* Kateřina (Káťa); Joszef Kundlák *tenor* Váňa Kudrjáš; Dagmar Pecková *mezzo-soprano* Varvara; Zdeněk Havránek *baritone* Kuligin; Martina Bauerová *contralto* Gláša; Dana Burešová *mezzo-soprano* Fekluša; Chorus of the Prague National Theatre; CPO. Supraphon
Janáček: Kát'a Kabanová
CD: Supraphon SU 3291-2

1997 April 4, 6 and 8. RP. CPO. Decca
Suk: Fantastic Scherzo Op. 25
CD: 466 443-2

1997 April 5–6. RP. Pamela Frank *violin*; CPO. Decca
Dvořák: Violin Concerto in A minor Op. 53; Romance in F minor Op. 11
CD: 460 316-2

1997 June 25–26. HWH. Emanuel Ax *piano*; OAE. Sony
Chopin: Piano Concerto No. 2 in F minor Op. 21; Andante spianato and Grande Polonaise Op. 22
CD: SK 63371

1997 July. UHE. Bryn Terfel *bass-baritone*; John Fisher *harpsichord continuo*; SCO. DG
Handel. Judas Maccabaeus – I feel, I feel the Deity within ... Arm, arm ye brave!; Dettingen Te Deum – Vouchsafe, O Lord; Samson – Honour and arms scorn such a foe; Berenice – Si, tra I ceppi e le ritorte; Alcina – Verdi prati, selve amene; Orlando – O voi, del mio poter ... Sorge infausta una procella; Acis and Galatea – I rage, I melt, I burn ... O ruddier than the cherry; Semele – Where'er you walk; Alexander's Feast – Revenge, Timotheus cries ... Behold, a ghastly band; Giulio Cesare – Va tacito e nascosto; Serse – Frondi tenere e belle ... Ombra mai fu; Messiah – Thus saith the Lord of Hosts ... But who may abide; Why do the nations; Behold, I tell you a

mystery ... The trumpet shall sound
CD: 453 480-2
All with ornamentation by Mackerras.

1997 August 2–13. AR. Andrea Rost *soprano* Lucia; Louise Winter *mezzo-soprano* Alisa; Bruce Ford *tenor* Edgardo; Anthony Michaels-Moore *baritone* Enrico; Alastair Miles *bass* Raimondo; Paul Charles Clarke *tenor* Arturo; Ryland Davies *tenor* Arturo; London Voices; The Hanover Band. Sony
Donizetti (ed. Mackerras): Lucia di Lammermoor
CD: SK2 63174

1997 November 25–26 and 28. PHL. RLPO. EMI Eminence
Beethoven: Symphony No. 2 in D Op. 36; Symphony No. 8 in F Op. 93
CD: CFP 6068; 575751-2

1997 December 5–6[a] and 7–8[b]. RP. [a]Pamela Frank *violin*; CPO. Decca
Suk: Fantasy for violin and orchestra Op. 24a; Summer's Tale Op. 24b
CD: 466 443-2

1998 February 13–20. AR. Ruth Ann Swenson *soprano*; Orchestra of the Age of the Enlightenment. EMI/Angel
Handel (ed. Mackerras): Semele – Endless pleasure, endless love; O sleep, why dost thou leave me?; Myself I shall adore; Giulio Cesare – V'adoro, pupille; Se pietà di me non senti; Da tempeste il legno infranto
Mozart: Die Entführung aus dem Serail – Welcher Weschsel ... Traurigkeit; Martern aller Arten; Misera! dove son ... Ah! non so io che partò K369; Lucio Silla – In un istante ... Parto m'affretto
CD: CDC 556672-2

1998 March 10–12. CHD. SCO. Telarc
Schubert: Symphony No. 8 in B minor D759; Symphony No. 9 in C ('Great')
CD: CD 80502

1998 March 14–17. UHE. Alfred Brendel *piano*; SCO. Philips
Mozart: Piano Concerto No. 20 in D minor K466; Piano Concerto No. 24 in C minor K491
CD: 462 622-2

1998 April 28–May 9. RP. Renée Fleming *soprano* Rusalka; Ben Heppner *tenor* Prince; Franz Hawlata *bass* Water Goblin; Dolora Zajick *mezzo-soprano* Witch; Eva Urbanová *soprano* Foreign Princess; Ivan Kusnjer Hunter/Gamekeeper; Zdena Kloubová *soprano* Turnspit; Kühn Mixed Choir; CPO. Decca
Dvořák: Rusalka
CD: 460 568-2

1998 May 20–21. HWH. Emanuel Ax *piano*; OAE. Sony
Chopin: Piano Concerto No. 1 in E minor Op. 11; Variations on 'Là ci darem la mano' Op. 2
CD: SK 60771

1998 November 10–13. CHG. SCO. Telarc
Brahms: Serenade No. 1 in D Op. 11; Serenade No. 2 in A Op. 16
CD: CD 80522

1999 March 15–18 and May 24–26. CHD. Yelda Kodalli *soprano* Konstanze; Paul Groves *tenor* Belmonte; Désirée Rancatore *soprano* Blondchen; Lynton Atkinson *tenor* Pedrillo; Peter Rose *bass* Osmin; Oliver Tobias *speaker* Bassa Selim; Scottish Chamber Chorus; SCO. Telarc
Mozart: Die Entführung aus dem Serail
CD: CD 80544

1999 April 8–11. RP. Czech Phiharmonic Orchestra. Supraphon
Dvořák: Slavonic Dances Op. 46 and Op. 72
CD: SU 3422-2

1999 May 12 (live). RP. CPO. Supraphon
Smetana: Má vlast
CD: SU 3465-2

1999 July 3, 5–6, 8–9. Watford Colosseum. Renée Fleming *soprano*; London Voices; LPO. Decca
Bellini: Norma – Casta diva
Verdi: Les Vêpres siciliennes – Merci, jeunes amies; Simon Boccanegra – Come in quest'ora bruna
Puccini: Gianni Schicchi – O mio babbino caro; Madama Butterfly – Un

bel dì vedremo; La Bohème –Quando m'en vò; Turandot – Signore, ascolta!
Leoncavallo: Pagliacci – Qual fiamma
Cilea: Adriana Lecouvreur –Io son l'umile ancella
Catalani: La Wally – Ebben? ne andrò lontana
Massenet: Manon – Je suis encore tout étourdie; Adieu, notre petite table
Bizet: Carmen – Je dis que rien
Gounod: Roméo et Juliette – Ah! Je veux vivre
CD: 467 049-2
Verdi: La Traviata – Ah fors'e lui
Unpublished.

2000 February 26 (live). Royal Opera House; Robert Alagna *tenor* Roméo; Angela Gheorghiu *soprano* Juliette; Gillian Knight *mezzo-soprano* Gertrude; Alastair Miles *bass* Frère Laurent; Sorin Colibran *bass* Capulet; Tito Beltran *tenor* Tybalt; Roderick Earle *bass* Le Prince; Jeremy White *bass* Grégorio; William Dazeley *baritone* Mercutio; Jenny Grahn *soprano* Stéphano; Graeme Broadbent *baritone* Pâris; Chorus and Orchestra of ROHCG
Gounod: Roméo et Juliette
CD: House of Opera CD 633

2000 April 29 (live). Royal Opera House. Jorma Silvasti *tenor* Manolios; Marie McLaughlin *soprano* Katerina; Gregory Yurisich *bass* Grigoris; Roderick Earle *bass* Kostandis; Gwynne Howell *bass* Fotis; Timothy Robinson *tenor* Yannokos; Jenny Grahn *soprano* Leonio; Peter Wedd *tenor* Nikolios; Robin Leggate *tenor* Panait; Alasdair Elliot *tenor* Adonis; Peter Auty *tenor* Michelis; Elizabeth Sikora *mezzo-soprano* Old Woman; Hilary Taylor *soprano* Despino; Jeremy White *bass* Archon; James Bobby *baritone* Dmitri; Grant Dickson *bass* Old Man; Chorus and Orchestra of ROHCG
Martinů: The Greek Passion (original London version)
CD: Mondo Archives AAC 020–021

2000 May 15. BBCMV. Paul Watkins *cello*; BBCSO
Sullivan (reconstructed by Mackerras and David Mackie): Cello Concerto in D
CD: BBC MM203

2000 July 24 (live). RAH. BBCSO. BBC
Sullivan: Macbeth Overture
CD: BBC MM203

2000 August 16–20. Rudolfinum Studio, Prague. Eva Urbanová *soprano* Šárka; Peter Straka *tenor* Ctirad; Ivan Kusnjer *baritone* Přemysl; Jaroslav Březina *tenor* Lumír; Prague Chamber Choir; CPO. Supraphon
Janáček: Šárka
CD: SU 3485-2
Lumír's part was recorded six months later.

2000 September 4–8. UHE. Barbara Frittoli *soprano*; SCO. Erato
Mozart: Così fan tutte – Temerari, sortite ... Come scoglio; Ei parte ... Per pieta; Le nozze di Figaro – Porgi, amor; E Susanna non vien! ... Dove sono; Idomeneo – O smania! Oh furie! ... D'Oreste, d'Aiace; Don Giovanni – In quali, o Numi ... Mi tradi quell'alma ingrate; Crudele! ... Non mi dir; Bella mia fiamma, addio! K528
CD: 8573–86207-2

2000 September 17–20. CHD. Alfred Brendel *piano*; SCO. Philips
Mozart: Piano Concerto No. 22 in E flat K482; Piano Concerto No. 27 in B flat K595
CD: 468 367-2

2001 March 17–25. RP. Czech Phiharmonic Orchestra. Supraphon
Dvořák: Scherzo capriccioso Op. 66; Legends Op. 59
CD: SU 3533-2

2001 June 14. RP. CPO. Supraphon
Dvořák: The Golden Spinning Wheel Op. 109
CD: SU 4012-2

2001 July 3–6. UHE. Alfred Brendel *piano*; SCO. Philips
Mozart: Piano Concerto No. 9 in E flat K271; Piano Concerto No. 25 in C K503
CD: 470 287-2

2001 July 27–August 8. UHE. Ian Bostridge *tenor* Idomeneo; Lorraine Hunt Lieberson *mezzo-soprano* Idamante; Anthony Rolfe Johnson

tenor Arbace; Lisa Milne *soprano* Ilia; Barbara Frittoli *soprano* Elettra; Paul Charles Clarke *tenor* Gran Sacerdote; John Relyea *bass* La Voce; Ian Page *harpsichord continuo*; Ursula Smith *cello continuo*; Edinburgh Festival Chorus; SCO. EMI
Mozart: Idomeneo
CD: 557260-2

2001 October 7–8. Rudolfinum Studio, Prague. Czech Phiharmonic Orchestra. Supraphon
Dvořák: Symphonic Variations Op. 78
CD: SU 3533-2

2002 January 21–23. WTH. Ingrid Jacoby *piano*. RPO. Dutton
Shostakovich: Concerto No. 1 in C minor for Piano, Trumpet and Orchestra Op. 35; Concerto No. 2 in F Op. 102
Ustvolskaya: Concerto for Piano and Orchestra
CD: CDLX 4804

2002 August 14 (live). UHE. Barbara Frittoli *soprano* Maria Stuarda; Anna Caterina Antonacci *soprano* Elisabeta; Paul Charles Clarke *tenor* Leicester; Jonathan Lemalu *bass-baritone* Talbot; Rachel Hynes *soprano* Anna; Christopher Purves *baritone* Cecil; Chorus of Scottish Opera; SCO
Donizetti: Maria Stuarda
CD: Premiere Opera CDNO 2164 2

2002 October 17–18 (live). RP, Prague. CPO. Supraphon
Janáček: Sinfonietta; (arr. Mackerras): The Cunning Little Vixen – Suite
CD: SU 3739-2032

2002 October 20. RP, Prague. CPO. Supraphon
Janáček: Schluck und Jau
CD: SU 3739-2032

2002 November 16 (live). Bridgewater Hall, Manchester. BBCPO. BBC Music Magazine
Mahler: Symphony No. 6 in A minor
CD: BBC MM251

2002 December 14–16. CHD. [a]Susan Gritton *soprano*; [a]Catherine Wyn-Rogers *contralto*; [a]Timothy Robinson *tenor*; [a]Peter Rose *bass*; [a]Scottish Chamber Chorus; SCO. Linn
Mozart (ed. Robert Levin): Requiem K626[a]; Adagio and Fugue in C minor K546
CD: CKD2002

2003 March 26 (live). Royal Academy of Music. Jenny Ohlson *soprano* Vixen; Rodney Clarke *baritone* Forester; Andrew Clarke *tenor* Schoolmaster; Matilda Paulsson *contralto* Forester's Wife; Joakim Schuster *bass* Priest/ Badger; Delphine Gillot *soprano* Fox; Elizabeth Claxton *contralto* Owl/Hen; Anna Dennis *soprano* Rooster/Jay; Seung-Wook Seong *bass* Harašta; Kevin Kyle *tenor* Pásek; Louise Reitberger *soprano* Pásek's Wife; Royal Academy Sinfonia
Janáček: The Cunning Little Vixen (in English)
CD: RAM 022

2003 May 22 (live). RP. CPO. Supraphon
Janáček: Žárlivost; Taras Bulba
CD: SU 3739-2032
DVD: SU 7009–9

2003 July 20–26. BHS. Elizabeth Vaughan *soprano* Grandmother Buryjovka; Nigel Robson *tenor* Laca; Peter Wedd *tenor* Števa; Josephine Barstow *soprano* Kostelnička Buryjovka; Janice Watson *soprano* Jenůfa; Neal Davies *bass* Mill Foreman; Alan Fairs *bass-baritone* Mayor; Charlotte Ellett *soprano* Mayor's Wife; Chorus and Orchestra of WNO. Chandos/Peter Moores Foundation
Janáček: Jenůfa (Brno 1908 version) (in English)
CD: CHAN 3106

2003 December 30 and **2004** January 3 (live). Prague National Theatre. Jan Vacík *tenor* Mr Brouček; Jitka Svobodová *soprano* Málinka/Etherea/Kunka; Jana Sibera *soprano* Pot-boy/Child Prodigy/ Student; Peter Straka *tenor* Mazal/ Starry Eyes/Petřík; Yvona Škvárová *contralto* Kedruta; Roman Vocel *baritone* Sacristan/Lunobor/Domšík; Jiří

Sulženko *baritone* Würfl/Wonderglitter/ Councillor; Vladimír Doležal *tenor* A Composer/Harper/Miroslav; Ivan Kusnjer *baritone* Apparition; Chorus and Orchestra of the National Theatre, Prague.
Janáček: Výlety pane Broučkovy [The Excursions of Mr Brouček]
CD: Národní divadlo, 2 CDs, no catalogue number.

2004 January 22 (live). Philharmonie, Berlin. Berliner Philharmoniker.
Dvořák: Symphonic Variations Op. 78
Janáček: Žárlivost; Sinfonietta
Disclosure DS 00552

2004 February 5. Janáček Theatre, Brno. [a]Helena Kaupová *soprano*; [c]Dagmar Vaňkátová *soprano*; [a]Eva Garajová *contralto*; [a]Peter Straka *tenor*; [a]Richard Novák *bass*; [a]Aleš Bárta *organ*; [b]Roman Patočka *violin*; [a]Czech Philharmonic Choir of Brno; [abc]Brno State Philharmonic Orchestra
Janáček: Glagolitic Mass (ed. Wingfield)[a]; Putování dušičky [Violin Concerto][b]; Dunaj [Symphony][c]
CD: Státní filharmonie Brno, no catalogue number.

2004 February 29 and March 1. UHE. SCO. Linn
Bartók: Music for strings, percussion and celesta Sz106; Divertimento for strings Sz113
CD: CKD 234

2004 March 7. Greyfriars Church, Edinburgh. SCO. Linn
Kodály: Dances of Galánta
CD: CKD 234

2004 March. Jerwood Hall, LSO St Luke's. [a]Majella Cullagh *soprano*; [b]Elizabeth Futral *soprano*; [c]Diana Montague *mezzo-soprano*; The Hanover Band. Opera Rara
J. C. Bach (decorations by Mozart): Adriano in Siria – Cara, la dolce fiamma[ab]; La clemenza di Scipione – Infelice in van m'affanno (aria of Arsinda)[a]; Deh, quel pianto omai tergete (duet of Arsinda and Luceio)[ab]
Mozart (decorations by Mozart): Non so d'onde viene K294[ab]; Lucio Silla – Ah se a morir mi chiamo[ac]; Le nozze di Figaro – Voi che sapete[c]; Die Entführung aus dem Serail – Marten aller Arten[a]; La clemenza di Tito – Ah perdona al primo affetto (duet of Servilia and Annio)[bc]
CD: ORR232

2004 May 15 (live). Royal Opera House. Felicity Lott *soprano* Feldmarschallin; Angelika Kirchschlager *mezzo-soprano* Octavian; Simone Nold *soprano* Sophie; Kurt Rydl *bass* Baron Ochs; Eike Wilm Schulte *baritone* Faninal; Adrian Thompson *tenor* Valzacchi; Kari Hamncy *mezzo-soprano* Annina; Piotr Beczala *tenor* Ein Sänger; Elizabeth Gale *soprano* Marianne Leitmetzerin; Jeremy White *bass* Polizeikommisar; Chorus and Orchestra of ROHCG
R. Strauss: Der Rosenkavalier
CD: Premiere Opera CDNO 1449–3

2004 August 5–11. UHE. Alfred Brendel *piano*; SCO. Philips
Mozart: Piano Concerto No. 12 in A K414; Piano Concerto No. 17 in G K453
CD: 475 6930

2004 August 17 (live). UHE. Jonas Kaufmann *tenor* Max; Hillevi Martinpelto *soprano* Agathe; John Relyea *bass* Kaspar; Christopher Maltman *baritone* Ottokar; Siegfried Vogel *baritone/speaker* Kuno/Samiel; Ronan Collett *baritone* Kilian; Matthew Rose *bass* Hermit; Alish Tynan *soprano* Ännchen; Scottish Chamber Chorus, PO
Weber: Der Freischütz
CD: The Opera Lovers FREI 200401

2004 November 4–11. BCH. John Tomlinson *bass* Sarastro; Barry Banks *tenor* Tamino; Peter Bronder *tenor* First Priest/First Armed Man; Christopher Purves *bass-baritone* Speaker/Second Priest/Second Armed Man; Elizabeth Vidal *soprano* Queen of Night; Rebecca Evans *soprano* Pamina; Majella Cullagh *soprano* First Lady; Sarah Fox *soprano* Second Lady; Diana Montague *mezzo-soprano* Third Lady; Simon Keenlyside *baritone* Papageno; Lesley Garrett

soprano Papagena; John Graham-Hall *tenor* Monostatos; Geoffrey Mitchell Choir; LPO. Chandos/Peter Moores Foundation
Mozart: The Magic Flute (in English)
CD: CHAN 3121

2004 December 15–21 and 23. BCH. Susan Gritton *soprano* Mařenka; Paul Charles Clarke *tenor* Jeník; Timothy Robinson *tenor* Vašek; Peter Rose *bass* Kecal; Neal Davies *bass-baritone* Krušina; Diana Montague *mezzo-soprano* Háta; Geoffrey Moses *bass* Toby Mícha; Yvonne Howard *mezzo-soprano* Ludmila; Yvette Bonner *soprano* Esmeralda; Robin Leggate *tenor* Circus Master; Kit Hesketh-Harvey *speaker* Indian; Chorus of the ROHCG; PO. Chandos/Peter Moores Foundation
Smetana: The Bartered Bride (in English)
CD: CHAN 3128

2005 August. UHE. Rainer Trost *tenor* Tito; Hillevi Martinpelto *soprano* Vitellia; Magdalena Kožená *mezzo-soprano* Sesto; Christine Rice *soprano* Annio; Lisa Milne *soprano* Servilia; John Relyea *bass* Publio; Ronald Schneider *harpsichord continuo*; David Watkin *cello continuo*; Scottish Chamber Chorus. SCO. DG
Mozart: La Clemenza di Tito
CD: 477 5792

2005 September 10–13 (live). ODP. Prague SO. Supraphon
Dvořák: Symphony No. 8 in G Op. 88; Symphony No. 9 in E minor Op. 95
CD: SU 3848-2

2006 February 16. RFH. Sarah Fox *soprano*; PO. Signum
Mahler: Symphony No. 4 in G
CD: SIGCD 219

2006 April. CHG. Bryn Terfel *bass-baritone*; [a]Miah Persson *soprano*; [b]Christine Rice *mezzo-soprano*; David Watkin *cello continuo*; Duncan Williams *harpsichord continuo*, [c]*keyed glockenspiel*; [d]Greg Lawson *mandolin*; SCO. DG.
Mozart: Le nozze di Figaro – Non più andrai; Io to lascio, o cara, addio KAnh216/K621a; Così fan tutte – Soave sia il vento[ab]; Männer suchen stets zu naschen K433/K416c; Così dunque tradisci ... Aspri rimorsi atroci K432/K421a; Così fan tutte – V'adoro ... Il core vi dono[b]; Un bacio di mano K541; Don Giovanni – Quel casinetto è mio ... Là ci darem[a]; Die Zauberflöte – Ein Mädchen oder Weibchen; Le nozze di Figaro – Hai già vinta la causa! ... Vedrò, mentr'io sospiro; Nun, liebes Weibchen, ziehst mit mir K625/K592a[a]; Die Zauberflöte – Der Vogelfänger bin ich ja; Le nozze di Figaro – Crudel! Perchè finora; Don Giovanni – Deh, vieni alla finestra; Bastien und Bastienne – Diggi, daggi; Die Zauberflöte – Pa-Pa-Pa-Pa-Papageno![a]; Don Giovanni – Guardate! Questo non picciol libro ... Madamina!; Die Zauberflöte – Bei Männern[a]; Le nozze di Figaro – Tutto è disposto ... Aprite un po' quegli occhi
CD: 477 5886

2006 May 18, 20, 24 and 26 (live). London Coliseum. Cheryl Barker *soprano* Emilia Marty; Robert Brubaker *tenor* Albert Gregor; John Graham Hall *tenor* Vítek; Elena Xanthoudakis *soprano* Kristina; John Wegner *baritone* Baron Jaroslav Prus; Thomas Walker *tenor* Janek Prus; Neal Davies *bass-baritone* Dr. Kolenatý; Graham Clark *tenor* Count Hauk-Šendorf; Graeme Danby *bass* Stage Hand; Kathleen Kuhlmann *mezzo-soprano* Cleaner. Susanna Tudor-Thomas *mezzo-soprano* Chambermaid; Chorus and Orchestra of ENO. Chandos/Peter Moores Foundation
Janáček: The Makropulos Affair (in English)
CD: CHAN 3138
Includes an interview with Sir Charles Mackerras by Rodney Milnes.

2006 June 10 (live). Queen Elizabeth Hall. [a]Alina Ibragimova *violin*, PO.
Wagner: Tannhäuser – Overture and Venusberg Music
Mendelssohn: Violin Concerto in E minor Op. 64[a]

DL: available briefly for download from philharmonia.co.uk
Schubert: Symphony No. 9 in C ('Great')
CD: SIGCD 133

2006 August 15[c], 17[b], 19[e], 22[f], 24[d], 26[g], 27[h], 30[a], September 1[i] (live). UHE. [abcdefgh]SCO; [i]Janice Watson *soprano*; [i]Catherine Wyn-Jones *mezzo-soprano*; [i]Stuart Skelton *tenor*; [i]Detlef Roth *bass*; [i]Edinburgh Festival Chorus; [i]PO. Hyperion/BBC
Beethoven: Symphony No. 1 in C Op. 21[a]; Symphony No. 2 in Op. 36[b]; Symphony No. 3 in E flat Op. 55[c]; Symphony No. 4 in B flat Op. 60[d]; Symphony No. 5 in C minor Op. 67[e]; Symphony No. 6 in F Op. 68[f]; Symphony No. 7 in A Op. 92[g]; Symphony No. 8 in F Op. 93[h]; Symphony No. 9 in D minor Op. 125[i]
CD: CDS44301–05

2006 November 22–27. BCH. Jennifer Larmore *mezzo-soprano* Hansel; Rebecca Evans *soprano* Gretel; Rosalind Plowright *mezzo-soprano* Gertrude; Robert Hayward *baritone* Peter; Jane Henschel *mezzo-soprano* Witch; Sarah Tynan *soprano* Dew Fairy; Diana Montague *mezzo-soprano* Sandman; New London Children's Choir; PO. Chandos/Peter Moores Foundation
Humperdinck: Hansel and Gretel (in English)
CD: CHAN 3143

2007 January 30. Symphony Hall, Birmingham. Elizabeth Atherton *soprano*; Lilli Paasikivi *contralto*; Toby Spence *tenor*; Matthew Rose *bass*; Philharmonia Chorus, members of Bristol Choral Society, PO.
Beethoven: Symphony No. 9 in D minor Op. 125
DL: available briefly for download from philharmonia.co.uk

2007 April 5–6 (live). RP. CPO. Supraphon
Suk: Asrael Op. 27
CD: SU 4043-2

2007 July 3–6, 8–11 and August 15, 17–18, 20. Watford Colosseum. Janice Watson *soprano* Fiordiligi; Diana Montague *mezzo-soprano* Dorabella; Lesley Garrett *soprano* Despina; Toby Spence *tenor* Ferrando; Christopher Maltman *baritone* Guglielmo; Thomas Allen *baritone* Don Alfonso; Geoffrey Mitchell Choir; OAE. Chandos/Peter Moores Foundation
Mozart: Così fan tutte (in English)
CD: CHAN 3152

2007 July 28 (live). RAH. BBCPO. BBC
Schumann: Konzertstück for Four Horns in F Op. 86 (David Pyatt, Michael Thompson, Martin Owen, Cormac ÓhAodáin *horns*)
CD: BBC MM314
Janáček: Sinfonietta
CD: BBC MM302

2007 August 3–9. CHG. SCO. Linn
Mozart: Symphony No. 38 in D K504 ('Paris'); Symphony No. 39 in E flat K543; Symphony No. 40 in G minor K550; Symphony No. 41 in C K551
CD: CKD308

2007 October 11–13 (live). Opera House, Sydney. SSO
Dvořák: Symphony No. 7 in D minor Op. 70
Smetana: Má vlast – 2. Vltava
Janáček: Sinfonietta
CD: SSO 200705

2007 October 18 and 20 (live). City Recital Hall, Sydney. Cheryl Barker *soprano* Donna Agnes; Sally-Anne Russell *mezzo-soprano* Dorothy; Steve Davislim *tenor* Don John; Grant Doyle *baritone* Philip II of Spain; Paul Whelan *bass-baritone* Don Quexada; Sydney Philharmonia Chamber Singers; SSO; Alexander Briger *conductor*. ABC
Nathan (arr. and orch. Mackerras): Don John of Austria
CD: ABC 476 4114
Recorded in the presence of Mackerras.

2007 October 24 and 26–27 (live). Opera House, Sydney. SSO.
R. Strauss: Also sprach Zarathustra Op. 30
CD: SSO 200705

2007 November 24 (live). Hamer Hall, Melbourne. Melbourne SO. ABC
Wagner: Tannhäuser – Overture and Venusberg Music
Delius: A Village Romeo and Juliet – The Walk to the Paradise Garden
Elgar: Variations on an Original Theme Op. 36 (Enigma)
CD: ABC 476 3224

2007 December 16–18 and 20–22. Watford Colosseum. Susan Bullock *soprano* Salome; John Wegner *bass-baritone* Jokanaan; John Graham-Hall *tenor* Herod; Sally Burgess *mezzo-soprano* Herodias; Andrew Rees *tenor* Narraboth; Rebecca de Pont Davies *mezzo-soprano* Page; Michael Driett *baritone* First Nazarene; Robert Parry *tenor* Second Nazarene; Graeme Broadbent *bass* First Soldier; Alan Ewing *bass* Second Soldier; Roger Begley *bass* Cappadocian; Gerald Strainer *tenor* Slave; Anton Rich *tenor* First Jew; Wynne Edwards *tenor* Second Jew; Colin Jusdon *tenor* Third Jew; Alasdair Elliott *tenor* Fourth Jew; Jeremy White *bass* Fifth Jew; PO. Chandos/Peter Moores Foundation
R. Strauss: Salome (in English)
CD: CHAN 3157

2008 April 26 (live). Frauenkirche, Dresden. Genia Kümeier *soprano*; Christa Meyer *mezzo-soprano*; Timothy Robinson *tenor*; Oliver Ringelheim *tenor*[a]; Matthew Rose *bass*; Staatsopernchor Dresden. Staatskapelle Dresden. Carus
Schubert: Mass No. 6 in E flat D950[a]
Mozart: Vesperae solennes de confessore in C K339
CD: 83 249

2008 September 8 and 12 (live). Royal Opera House. Simon Keenlyside *baritone* Don Giovanni; Marina Poplavskaya *soprano* Donna Anna; Joyce DiDonato *mezzo-soprano* Donna Elvira; Ramón Vargas *tenor* Don Ottavio; Kyle Ketelsen *bass* Leporello; Miah Persson *soprano* Zerlina; Robert Gleadow *bass* Masetto; Eric Halfvarson *bass* Commendatore; Chorus and Orchestra of ROHCG. *Stage Director:* Francesca Zambello. Opus Arte
Mozart: Don Giovanni
DVD: OA 1009 D; OABD 7028 D (Blu-ray)
Includes Antonio Pappano in conversation with Mackerras and Zambello.

2008 October 9[a] and 12[b] (live), RFH. PO. Signum
Dvořák: Symphony No. 7 in D minor Op. 70[a]; Symphony No. 8 in G major Op. 88[b]
CD: SIGCD 183

2008 November 2–5. Perth Concert Hall, Perth. Artur Pizarro *piano*; SCO. Linn
Beethoven: Piano Concerto No. 3 in C minor Op. 37; Piano Concerto No. 4 in G Op 58; Piano Concerto No. 5 in E flat Op. 73
CD: CKD336

2008 November 24–30 and **2009** April 1. AR. Daniele De Niese *soprano*; [a]Bryn Terfel *baritone*; [b]Apollo Voices; OAE. Decca.
Mozart: Exsultate, jubilate K165; Bella mia fiamma, addio! ... Resta, oh cara K528; Le nozze di Figaro – Giunse alfin il momento ... Al desio di chi t'adora; Così fan tutte – Una donna a quindici anni; Idomeneo – Quando avran fine omai ... Padre, germani, addio!; Don Giovanni – Ah! fuggi il traditor; Idomeneo – Oh, temerio Arbace! ... Per quel paterno amplesso; Il re pastore – L'amerò, sarò costante; Don Giovanni – Là ci darem la mano[a]; Vesperae solennes de confessore in C K339 – Laudate Dominum[b]
CD: 478 1511

2008 December 5–6. RP. CPO. Supraphon
Martinů (arr. Zbyněk Vostřák): Juliette – Suite H253b
CD: SU 3994-2; SU 4042-2

2008 December 11–12 (live). RP. [a]Magdalena Kožená *mezzo-soprano* Juliette; [a]Steve Davislim *tenor* Michel; [a]Frédéric Goncalves *baritone* Seller of Memories/Old Man Youth; [a]Michèle Lagrange *mezzo-soprano* Old Woman/Young Arab; [a]Nicolas Testé *bass* Old Man/Old Arab/Night Watchman; CPO. Supraphon
Martinů: Juliette – Three Fragments H253a[a] – Scene in the Forest; Scene of Memories; Finale
CD: SU 3994-2
Dvořák: The Water Goblin Op. 107; The Noon Witch Op. 108
CD: SU 4012-2

2008 December 18 (live). Grosser Saal, Musikverein, Vienna. Alfred Brendel *piano*. WP. Decca
Mozart: Piano Concerto No. 9 in E flat K271
CD: 478 2116

2009 February 8 (live). RFH. PO. Signum
Mendelssohn: A Midsummer Night's Dream Overture Op. 21
Tchaikovsky: Symphony No. 6 in B minor Op. 74
CD: SIGCD 253

2009 July 11–17. CHG. SCO. Linn
Mozart: Symphony No. 29 in A K201/186a; Symphony No. 31 in D K297/300a; Symphony No. 32 in G K318; Symphony No. 35 in D K385; Symphony No. 36 in C K425
CD: CKD 350

2009 September 9–10. RP. CPO. Supraphon
Dvořák: The Wild Dove Op. 110
CD: SU 4012-2

Bibliography

This selective bibliography includes books and articles to which frequent reference is made in the main text, and others that are of particular interest.

A Works by Charles Mackerras, including interviews
(in chronological order)

'What Records have Taught Me', *Records and Recording*, October 1959, pp. 11 and 50.

'Music for Frustrated Conductors' [review], *Records and Recording*, December 1959, p. 25.

'Television Opera and the Musician', *Musical Events*, January 1961, pp. 6–8.

'Long-lost Music for a Janáček Opera', *Music and Musicians*, February 1961, pp. 16–17, 38.

'Sense about the Appoggiatura', *Opera*, October 1963, pp. 669–78.

'Janáček's *Makropulos*', *Opera*, February 1964, pp. 79–86.

'Appoggiaturas Unlimited', *Records and Recording*, February 1965, pp. 14–17.

'What Mozart Really Meant', *Opera*, April 1965, pp. 240–6.

with Basil Lam: '*Messiah* – Editions and Performances', *Musical Times*, December 1966, pp. 1056–7.

'Is the Conductor the Boss?' [interview by Arthur Jacobs], *Opera*, October 1967, pp. 790–7.

with Stanley Sadie: 'Editing Mozart's Operas', *Musical Times*, August 1968, pp. 722–3.

'Mozart's Minims', *Musical Times*, April 1969, p. 374.

'Which *Orfeo?*', *Opera*, May 1972, pp. 393–7.

'Janáček and Katya Kabanova – a conversation between Lord Harewood and Charles Mackerras', programme book for *Katya Kabanova* (Sadler's Wells Opera, 1973), unpaginated.

'Charles Mackerras talks to Alan Blyth', *Gramophone*, March 1975, p. 1626.

'*Káťa Kabanová*: some observations on recording Janáček's opera', *Gramophone*, October 1977, p. 596.

Appendices ['The Appoggiatura', 'Mozart', 'Handel', 'Janáček', 'Aspects of Conducting'] in Nancy Phelan: *Charles Mackerras: A Musician's Musician* (London: Gollancz, 1987), pp. 253–335.

'Janissary Music', programme book for *Die Entführung aus dem Serail* (Welsh National Opera, 1989), pp. 10–11.

'Where we are now' [interview by Rodney Milnes], *Opera*, February 1990, pp. 169–74.

'*La Petite Renarde rusée* à Paris: Un entretien de John Tyrrell avec Sir Charles Mackerras', programme book for Janáček: *La Petite Renarde rusée* (Paris Châtelet, 1995), pp. 38–42.

'Mackerras at 70 – straight from the shoulder' [interview by Alan Blyth], *Opera*, December 1995, pp. 1408–14.

'From where I sit' [interview by Michael Quinn], *Gramophone*, December 1999, p. 29.

'Opera Conducting', *The Cambridge Companion to Conducting*, ed. José Antonio Bowen (Cambridge: Cambridge University Press, 2003), pp. 65–78.

'A perfect balance of sound: Sir Charles Mackerras on Janáček's *Jenůfa*' [interview by Martina Sperling], programme book for *Jenůfa* (Welsh National Opera, 2003).

'My Life with Janáček's Music' [interview by John Tyrrell], booklet notes for Supraphon CD SU3739-2032 (2004), pp. 7–16.

'A Life in Music' [interview by John Allison], *Opera*, November 2005, pp. 1299–1305.

'A Mozartian Journey' [interview by Richard Fairman], *Opera*, January 2006, pp. 20–7.

B Works by others

(arranged by author)

Bishop, Christopher: 'Another *Messiah*?', *Gramophone*, March 1967, pp. 464–5.

Blyth, Alan: 'Charles Mackerras on opera in Hamburg and London', *Times*, 26 June 1968.

Bridcut, John: *Britten's Children* (London: Faber and Faber, 2006), esp. pp. 234–40.

Cole, Hugo: 'The case of the missing concerto', *Guardian*, 18 April 1986.

Gilbert, Susie: *Opera for Everybody: The Story of English National Opera* (London: Faber and Faber, 2009).

H[arewood, George, Earl of]: 'Sadler's Wells: *Katya Kabanova* (Janáček)', *Opera*, June 1951, pp. 368–71.

Harewood [George, Earl of], Janet Baker, Anne Evans and Rodney Milnes: 'Le grand Charles' [tributes], *Opera*, September 2010, pp. 1060–5.

Hendershott, Judith: 'The Long Road Home', *Independent*, 5 April 1996.

Kennedy, Michael: 'Maestro with a Message', *Sunday Telegraph*, 18 September 2005.

Langley, Lee: 'Covent Garden Conjurer', *Guardian*, 31 December 1971 [interview].

Mackerras, Catherine: *The Hebrew Melodist: A Life of Isaac Nathan, 'Father of Australian Music'* (Sydney: Currawong Publishing, 1962) [dedicated 'To my son Charles Mackerras, a great-great-great grandson of Isaac Nathan'].

Mansouri, Lotfi: *An Operatic Journey* (Lebanon, NH: Northeastern University Press, 2010), esp. pp. 292–3.

Milnes, Rodney: 'The Mackerras Years', *Opera*, January 1978, pp. 13–19.

Morrison, Richard: 'An act of creation that had me in tears', *Times*, 26 August 2009.

Moss, Stephen: 'The Modest Maestro: Charles Mackerras', *Guardian*, 20 August 2005.

—— 'Handel in Performance' [interview with Charles Mackerras and Janet Baker], *Opera*, February 1985, pp. 142–53.

Phelan, Nancy; with appendices by Charles Mackerras: *Charles Mackerras: A Musician's Musician* (London: Gollancz, 1987).

Priest, Joan: *Scholars and Gentlemen: A Biography of the Mackerras Family* (Brisbane: Boolarong, 1986).

Rosenthal, Harold: 'People: 82 Charles Mackerras', *Opera*, April 1970, pp. 291–6.

Simeone, Nigel: 'Charles Mackerras 1925–2010: A tribute to a great conductor', *International Record Review*, September 2010, pp. 16–18.

Wallace, Helen: *Spirit of the Orchestra* (London: Orchestra of the Age of Enlightenment, 2006), esp. pp. 15–18.

Editions and Arrangements by Charles Mackerras

(in chronological order)

Sullivan, Arthur: *Pineapple Poll: Ballet.* Based on the music of Arthur Sullivan, arr. for piano solo by Charles Mackerras (London: Chappell & Co., 1951). [Full score for hire only]

Mozart, Wolfgang Amadeus: *Sleigh Ride*, arr. for orchestra by Charles Mackerras. Piano-conductor and parts (London: Josef Weinberger, 1955).

Dvořák, Antonín: *Songs my mother taught me*, arr. for orchestra by Charles Mackerras. Piano-conductor and parts (London: Josef Weinberger, 1955).

Verdi, Giuseppe: *The Lady and the Fool*: suite from the ballet selected and arr. for piano solo by Charles Mackerras (London: G. Ricordi & Co, 1955).

Puccini, Giacomo: *The Witches' Dance*, arr. Charles Mackerras. Piano conductor and orchestral parts (London: G. Ricordi & Co., 1956).

Sibelius, Jean: *Berceuse*, arr. Charles Mackerras. Piano-conductor and orchestral parts (London: Josef Weinberger, 1956).

Cadenzas to Mozart's Violin Concerto in G K216 (London: Elkin & Co., 1956).

Cooper, Peter: *Tango-Caprice*, orchestration by Charles Mackerras (London: Elkin & Co., 1958).

Wolf-Ferrari, Ermanno: *Overture: The Inquisitive Women (Le donne curiose)*, ed. Charles Mackerras. Piano-conductor (London: Josef Weinberger, 1959).

Handel, George Frideric: *The Music for the Royal Fireworks.* For wind instruments or wind and strings, ed. Anthony Baines and Charles Mackerras. Full score (London: Oxford University Press, 1960).

Mozart, Wolfgang Amadeus: Konzert-Rondo A-dur [K386]. Reconstructed and ed. Paul Badura-Skoda and Charles Mackerras. Study score (Mainz: B. Schott's Söhne, 1962). [Two-piano reduction also published]

Nathan, Isaac: *Don John of Austria*, orchestrated by Charles Mackerras. Full score (unpublished; registered with the Australian Performing Rights Association, 21 May 1963). [Copy in the Australian Broadcasting Corporation Music Library, Sydney]

Ireland, John: *The Overlanders*: suite for orchestra, arr. Charles Mackerras. Study score (London: Boosey & Hawkes, 1971).

Handel, George Frideric: *Semele*, ed. Anthony Lewis and Charles Mackerras. Piano-vocal score (London: Oxford University Press, 1971).

Sullivan, Arthur: *The Yeomen of the Guard: Overture*, ed. David Lloyd-Jones and Charles Mackerras. Miniature score (London: Eulenburg, 1979).

Sullivan, Arthur: Concerto for violoncello and orchestra, reconstructed by David Mackie and Charles Mackerras. Study score (London: Josef Weinberger, 1986). [Cello and piano reduction also published]

George Frideric Handel: *Xerxes*, ed. Charles Mackerras and Noel Davies. English version by Nicholas Hytner. Piano-vocal score (London: Chester Music, 1987).

Janáček, Leoš: *Káťa Kabanová*, ed. Charles Mackerras. Study score (Vienna: Universal Edition, 1992). [Piano-vocal score also published]

Janáček, Leoš: *Jenůfa – Její pastorkyňa*. Brno version (1908), ed. Charles Mackerras and John Tyrrell. Study score (Vienna: Universal Edition, 1996). [Piano-vocal score also published]

Janáček, Leoš: *Šárka*, ed. Jiří Zahrádka, supervised by Charles Mackerras. Piano-vocal score (Vienna: Universal Edition; Brno: Editio Moravia, 2002).

Janáček, Leoš: *Příhody lišky Bystroušky – The Cunning Little Vixen*, ed. Jiří Zahrádka, with performance suggestions by Charles Mackerras. Study score (Vienna: Universal Edition, 2009). [Piano-vocal score also published]

Index

Note: Buildings (e.g. Royal Albert Hall) are indexed under the cities in which they are found, while Companies (e.g. Royal Opera House) are indexed alphabetically. Works (e.g. *Don Giovanni*) are listed under their respective composers. Titles in Italian, German and French are given in the original language; those in other languages (e.g. Czech) are given in standard English translations. The Discography is not indexed.